MIDDLE EAST
past and present

Muhammad, by an anonymous Iranian painter, probably of the late nineteenth century. The panels around the painting identify the Prophet: "Muhammad ibn-Abdullah, may the blessing and peace of God be upon him."

Yahya Armajani
JAMES WALLACE PROFESSOR OF HISTORY, EMERITUS
MACALESTER COLLEGE

Thomas M. Ricks
BIRZEIT UNIVERSITY

MIDDLE EAST
past and present

Second Edition

PRENTICE-HALL, INC., Englewood Cliffs, N.J. 07632

Library of Congress Cataloging in Publication Data

ARMAJANI, YAHYA.
  Middle East : past and present.

  Bibliography: p.
  Includes index.
  1. Near East—History. I. Ricks, Thomas M.
  II. Title.
  DS62.A73 1986   956   85-6515
  ISBN 0-13-581554-1

Editorial/production supervision: *Edith Riker*
Cover design: *Lundgren Graphics, Ltd.*
Manufacturing buyer: *Barbara Kittle*

Printed in the United States of America

10 9 8 7 6 5 4 3 2 1

ISBN 0-13-581554-1   01

Prentice-Hall International (UK) Limited, *London*
Prentice-Hall of Australia Pty. Limited, *Sydney*
Prentice-Hall Canada Inc., *Toronto*
Prentice-Hall Hispanoamericana, S.A., *Mexico*
Prentice-Hall of India Private Limited, *New Delhi*
Prentice-Hall of Japan, Inc., *Tokyo*
Prentice-Hall of Southeast Asia Pte. Ltd., *Singapore*
Editora Prentice-Hall do Brasil, Ltda., *Rio de Janeiro*
Whitehall Books Limited, *Wellington, New Zealand*

FOR RUTH AND JANICE

محبت نه برولیت که اذر برشف
مدت ینمارضی است که جان دل شف

List of Maps

Contents

Preface

A few years ago I accepted the invitation of the publishers to prepare a second edition of this book. Unfortunately the project was postponed twice because of an illness and a long convalescence. When I was ready to start, it became advisable to seek the assistance of another historian in order to relieve the pressure on me and, at the same time, ensure the continuity of later editions. The only person I had in mind was Professor Thomas Ricks, formerly of the history departments of Macalester College and Georgetown University and presently of Birzeit University. He very kindly accepted.

Inasmuch as the publishers did not want the second edition to be larger than the first, it became necessary to cut certain parts and to rearrange others. This has resulted in more revision than is usual in a second edition. In addition to updating, we have added a new chapter on the Arabian Peninsula and the Persian Gulf states. We have also increased the number of maps, replaced the chronology with a glossary, and have updated the bibliography.

Professor Ricks has provided me with information on social and economic history and has done most of the research on the updates. For the sake of a uniform style, I have written the book. Both of us have gone over the entire book and accept responsibility for all mistakes of commission and omission. Thanks are due to the many colleagues who, through the years, have informed me of mistakes and made suggestions for improvement. Thanks are also due to the editors at Prentice-Hall for their careful scrutiny and many useful suggestions. I hope that they will see the result in this volume.

YAHYA ARMAJANI
San Diego, California

Preface to the First Edition

This book is a result of twenty years of teaching Middle East history in a liberal arts college. It is written for students and general readers who have no knowledge of the history and culture of the area, and for teachers who may or may not be experts in the field themselves. The materials found in this book have been discussed and sifted in the classroom year after year and only those appear which have helped students to appreciate the past and present problems, accomplishments, and contributions of the peoples of the Middle East.

The Middle East is presented in four parts. Part One deals with the advent and spread of Islam; Part Two with the Ottoman and Safavid empires; Part Three with Western imperialism and the Middle East; and Part Four with the modern period, during which the Middle East was divided into many nation-states. Those who are teaching a year-long course on the Middle East may profitably use the first two parts for the first semester and the last two for the second.

Many peoples have helped form the culture described in this volume, but no adequate understanding of Middle East history is possible without a discussion of at least three groups: the Arabic-speaking peoples, the Iranians, and the Turks. Any survey that neglects any one of the above is bound to present a distorted picture of the area. Without counting lines or words, I have tried to give each group its proper place in the history of the region as a whole.

This history, like any other history, has a point of view. Its viewpoint is that of a native. I hope that my Iranian birth and upbringing has not prevented me from presenting, insofar as the main issues are concerned, the Arab and Turkish points of view. My aim has been to write it in such a way that those who read it will be looking from the inside out and not from the outside in. This is not to say that foreign appraisal of a culture is not valuable or necessary. But it helps us gain that quality of human perception that we call "understanding" if we study the Middle East not because its oil is essential to the United States, but because the virtues and vices, wisdom and follies of its people have influenced the destiny of the world and might do so again.

In preparing this volume I have used the works of Arab, Iranian, Turkish, and Western scholars. I wish it were possible for me to mention them all, but their number, scattered over the years, is so large that listing them would fill pages. Without their scholarship I could not have written this book and my gratitude to them is deep and sincere.

For the past fifteen years the Louis W. and Maud Hill Family Foundation of St. Paul, Minnesota, has helped four colleges in the city to carry on area study programs cooperatively. As coordinator of the Middle East area, I have received grants from the foundation to travel in the countries of the Middle East for study and research. In a real sense this volume is a result of its faith in our program and is offered as a token of my gratitude for its interest.

My thanks are due to Mr. Kenneth Holmes, Emeritus Professor of History at Macalester College, who read most of the manuscript and offered useful suggestions. I do not know what I would have done without the aid of Boyd C. Shafer, James Wallace Professor of History at Macalester, who read the whole manuscript. His knowledge of history and his ten years' experience as editor of the *American Historical Review* made his numerous suggestions invaluable. I am grateful to Professor Nikki Keddie of the University of California at Los Angeles, who also read the whole manuscript. This volume has been enhanced by her keen and penetrating criticism and suggestions. My thanks go also to my students, Allen Gibas and James Polzin, who read half and all of the manuscript, respectively, and offered suggestions. If, despite the efforts of these people, there are still mistakes and shortcomings, I assume full responsibility for them and for interpretations and conclusions.

Finally, I want to thank my patient and long-suffering secretaries, Katherine Cross and Nancy Nielsen, who typed the manuscript again and again, enough to have gained them each full credit for a course on Middle East history. My wife and family, who have lived with the preparation of the manuscript for at least three years, do not need to be told that I am grateful—they know it.

YAHYA ARMAJANI
St. Paul, Minnesota

Introduction

The area that we are about to study has been in the forefront of the news since before the turn of the twentieth century. It has been the meeting place, often violent, of diverse ethnic, religious, and national groups. It has threatened the peace of the world more than once. The name of the area under consideration is nearly as controversial as the many issues and problems besetting the region. We are using the term "Middle East" instead of "Near East," "West Asia," or "Southwest Asia," because it has become the most familiar. Even Arabs, Iranians, and Turks are beginning to use it.

Unfortunately the majority of those who use the term Middle East do not agree about the area it covers. At one extreme are those who use the term to denote the whole Islamic world from Morocco to Indonesia and from Sudan to Uzbekistan. At the other extreme are those who use it to refer only to the Fertile Crescent[1] and Egypt.

From A.D. 635 to roughly the year 1000, Egypt, Arabia, the Fertile Crescent, and Iran[2] had a common history. From about 1300 to 1920, Turkey and the above areas minus Iran shared a common history. Consequently, the choice in this volume of a limited area—namely Egypt, Turkey, Iran, Arabia, and the Fertile Crescent—is not as arbitrary as it might seem. For over 1,300

[1]"Fertile Crescent" is used to define a territory covered by Iraq, Syria, Lebanon, Jordan, Israel, the West Bank, and Gaza.
[2]"Iran" is used throughout the text in place of "Persia."

1

years the above area was the main arena for cultural, political, and economic activities which in turn influenced the outlying regions. An understanding of the movements in this area will serve as an important means towards understanding the life and culture of the surrounding regions.

The whole territory is as large as the United States and is roughly a square surrounded by intruding bodies of water: the Persian Gulf, the Red Sea, the Mediterranean Sea, the Black Sea, and, in a way, the Caspian Sea. Except for southern Egypt and Arabia, the area lies north of the tropics.

THE LAND

Geographically, the Middle East is divided into three zones.

The Southern Zone comprises all of Egypt, stretches northward on the lower curve of the Fertile Crescent, and includes all of the Arabian Peninsula. It is an extension of the African Sahara, including the Arabian plateau, and has an average elevation of from 2,000 to 3,000 feet. The highlands of this plateau lie on the eastern coast of the Red Sea. They have an elevation of 9,000 feet, and go higher in a southeasterly direction towards Yaman, where they reach 14,000 feet. This range prevents the scant moisture of few clouds from reaching the land in central Arabia, thus creating one of the most awesome deserts in the world, the "Empty Quarter" in the southeastern part of the peninsula.

The Northern Zone comprises the northern tier of the Middle East. Geological disturbances have created three extensive mountain ranges: the Taurus in Turkey, the Zagros in western Iran, and the Alborz in northern Iran. In these rugged ranges Mount Ararat (17,000 feet) in eastern Turkey is well known to westerners as the landing place of Noah's Ark and to the Armenians as the center of the Armenian homeland. Another well-known mountain, Mount Damavand (19,200 feet), is situated in northern Iran and is snowclad all year round. It is the highest peak west of the Himalayas and is mentioned in Iranian legends.

Most of Turkey lies on the Anatolian plateau. The average elevation is between 3,000 and 5,000 feet, with the upland ranges reaching 6,000 to 8,000 feet above sea level. The average rainfall is between 10 and 17 inches, and the temperature ranges from 30°F. in January to 86°F. in July.

Over half of modern Iran lies on the Iranian plateau, which extends beyond the borders of the country into Pakistan and Afghanistan. Its elevation is between 200 and 8,000 feet above sea level. Unlike the Anatolian plateau, the Iranian plateau is surrounded by mountains and has no outward drainage of any sort. Consequently, the inner region of the Iranian plateau is almost rainless and contains two deserts. To the north lies the Dasht-e Kavir, which is made up of salt wastes; to the south lies the Dasht-e Lut, which consists of sand dunes like a normal desert. The average rainfall on the outer rim of the plateau is 9.2 inches and the temperature ranges from 35°F. in January to 85°F. in July.

The Intermediate Zone is situated between the northern and southern zones. This area curves upward from southern Palestine to the southern

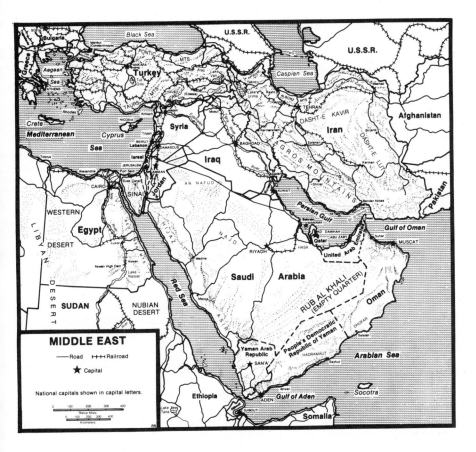

foothills of the Taurus and then down to the Tigris-Euphrates Valley through the Persian Gulf to Oman. In the west are two small mountain ranges that run parallel to the Mediterranean. These are the Lebanon and the Anti-Lebanon mountains. The elevation ranges from 5,000 feet in the south to 16,000 feet in the north. This zone between the mountains of the north and east and the rifted region of Egypt and Arabia to the south and west sheltered the deposits of marine life which, through tectonic disturbances, resulted in the great oil fields on both sides of the Persian Gulf.

By far the most important geographical phenomenon common to all of the Middle East is aridity: it is estimated that 90 percent of the Middle East is arid. Water is the most important human and economic factor, for where there is no water there is no life. Five to six percent of the Middle East area is cultivated, and of this one-fifth needs water. To preserve water, the ancient Assyrians, Babylonians, and Romans built cisterns and viaducts. The ancient Iranians built *qanats*, or underground conduits, that brought water over scores of miles from the mountains to the plains. To this day Bedouin women in Arabia and the Sahara wash their hair with camel urine in order to save water for human and animal consumption. Standing at the foot of the Sphinx outside Cairo and looking down the Nile River, one can observe that where water comes there is vegetation; one inch beyond the reach of water nothing grows.

Consequently, geographers describe the Middle East in at least six different categories.

1. The desert, in which nothing grows, such as the land east and west of the Nile, the Empty Quarter in Arabia, and the Kavir and the Lut in Iran.
2. The arid steppe south of the Fertile Crescent, where in spring camels feed on scrub and thorn and Bedouins go from one temporary water hole to another.
3. The less arid steppe of southern Turkey, western Iraq and eastern Iran, where land is uncultivable but good enough for grazing sheep and goats.
4. Oases, which have a permanent water supply and can therefore support dwellings and, in places, major towns.
5. The mountain region of Turkey and Iran, which contains cultivated green valleys, terraced hillsides, and numerous villages.
6. The coastal areas of the Black Sea, Caspian Sea, Red Sea, Mediterranean Sea, and the Persian Gulf; the abundance of these waterways has made it possible for every Middle Eastern country to have a sea outlet.

The Middle East is fed by only two river systems: the Nile and the Shatt al-Arab. The Nile River is fed by the Blue Nile, rising from the highlands of Ethiopia, and by the White Nile, flowing from the highlands of Central Africa. They join at Khartoum and flow north to the Mediterranean Sea, thus completing a journey of 4,145 miles. The Nile River has divided the Libyan Desert by the creation of Egypt, the cultivated portion of which is an oasis of about ten miles on both sides of the river. Egypt then is truly the "gift of the Nile." The Nile is doubly life-giving, for not only does it bring water, but also in its annual flooding it deposits some 100 million tons of extremely rich sediment to replenish the soil.

The other river system in the Middle East is the Shatt al-Arab, which serves as part of the boundary between Iraq and Iran. It is formed by the junction of the twin rivers, the Euphrates and the Tigris, some sixty miles north of the Persian Gulf. Both rivers rise in the highlands of Turkey and take a circuitous journey southward until they join. Shatt al-Arab is in turn joined by the Karun, a river in Iran that comes down from the Zagros Mountains and is navigable as far north as Ahvaz. Worthy of mention in this parched area are Kizel Irmak (Red River) in northern Turkey, and Sefid Rud (White River) and Karkheh in north and south Iran respectively. Of less significance geographically but explosive politically are the Jordan, Litani, and Orantes rivers, which irrigate portions of Syria, Lebanon, Jordan, Israel, and the West Bank.

With the exception of the Caspian littoral in northern Iran and parts of northeastern Turkey, the rainfall is inadequate; furthermore, what little there is falls only during the spring and winter. Drought in the summer is the general rule. Usually one can expect hot summers and warm winters in Arabia, the Fertile Crescent, Egypt, and parts of Iran, and cold winters and cool summers in the mountainous regions of Turkey, Iran, and Lebanon.

There is ample evidence that perhaps millennia ago there were large forests in the area; but due to war, neglect, and goats, with very few exceptions the Middle East is now a deforested region. On the southern shores of the Caspian and Black seas, and in the mountains of Lebanon and the Zagros region, there is an abundance of pine, oak, and juniper. In the rest of the area the only tree present everywhere is the poplar.

Wheat, barley, rye, beans, lentils, onions, pomegranates, pears, and plums are harvested in most countries of the Middle East. Citrus fruits grow in Lebanon, Israel, and Iran; apples in Lebanon; figs and nuts in Turkey and Iran; olives in Israel, Jordan, and Iran; and grapes in most parts of the area. Persian peaches and melons are world famous and so are the dates of Iraq. Dates are a staple food for the majority of peoples in the Persian Gulf area. Date pits are used as animal fodder, the fiber of the tree is woven into rope, and the wood is used for fuel.

Chief among the cash crops are cotton in Egypt, flax and hemp in the Fertile Crescent, coffee in Yaman, and tea, opium, and tobacco in Iran and Turkey.

It is quite likely that many animals, such as the dog, sheep, goat, pig, and ass, were first domesticated in this area. Owing to the scarcity of grazing lands, the number of cattle is insignificant and the milk yield is quite low. Horses and camels, it is believed, were brought from the East. Notwithstanding the fame of Persian cats and Arabian horses, the most distinctive animal in the area is still the camel. As a beast of burden, it has not yet been fully replaced by modern means of transportation. The camel is so essential a part of the Bedouin life that Arabic contains scores of words to denote the various stages of its growth. The camel provides milk and meat for the nomad, its hair is turned into tents and cloaks, its dung into fuel, and its urine into hair wash. In addition to being the "ship of the desert," it turns the waterwheel and pulls the plow.

Seafood abounds in the area, even though its use by the inhabitants is limited because of the dietary laws of Islam and Judaism. The sardines of the Persian Gulf, the caviar of the Caspian Sea, and the tuna of the Black Sea are world famous.

Not only is the Middle East limited in its agricultural production, but it also has scant mineral resources other than oil. Indeed, the vast resources of oil have made the area one of the richest in the world and marked it as a prime center of international intrigue and power politics. It is estimated that by A.D. 2000 the world oil demand, except for the Soviet Union and China, will be one and a half billion tons annually. It is quite likely that half this amount will be coming from the Middle East. Moreover, the supply of oil there is so extensive that it will not be exhausted for a long time. Practically all of the oil lies in Iran, Iraq, Saudi Arabia, and Kuwait. The oil resources of the other Middle Eastern countries are negligible.

Another factor contributing to the importance of the area is its strategic location. It connects the three continents of Africa, Asia, and Europe. Located at the eastern end of the Mediterranean, the Middle East touches the three major oceans of the world. It has often been referred to as the "Bridge to the East," or the "Crossroads of Asia," and from the earliest times it has served as the land route to China and India from Europe.

The three narrows, or straits, of the Middle East make it an important maritime route connecting different parts of the world. The sixteen-mile-long Bosporus and the twenty-five-mile-long Dardanelles, or Hellespont, are joined together by the Sea of Marmora and link the Black Sea with the Mediterranean. These straits have witnessed untold numbers of conquerors. Long before Xerxes flogged it in anger and particularly from the nineteenth century to the present, it has been a center of political and economic controversy in the history of the world. The second famous waterway is the Strait of Bab al-Mandab at the southern end of the Red Sea. It links the Mediterranean Sea, via the Suez Canal, with the Arabian Sea and the Indian Ocean. The third is the Strait of Hormoz, which links the region drained by the Tigris and Euphrates to the Indian Ocean by way of the Persian Gulf.

In more modern times, the advent of railroads has made a deep impression on the Middle East. As evidence of this, one might mention the Berlin-Baghdad Railway, which became the *cause célèbre* of the nineteenth-century "Eastern Question." More recently, by way of air travel, one cannot go very far without landing at one or more of the modern airports of the Middle East.

In addition to its economic and strategic importance the Middle East is the birthplace of some of the earliest human civilizations and the cradle of three of the most important religions of the world—namely, Judaism, Christianity, and Islam. Consequently, the historian and the theologian, as well as the economist and the political scientist, find the area a fertile ground for study and investigation.

The Middle East as a whole may be likened to the early architectural pattern of houses in the region: four wings and a central patio. One wing is Turkey to the northwest, the second Iran to the east, the third Saudi Arabia to the south, and the fourth Egypt to the southwest. The central "courtyard" is the Fertile Crescent, which at present contains Lebanon, Syria, Israel, the West Bank and Gaza, Jordan, and Iraq. Each of these wings has an entrance to the central courtyard. Turkey and Iran, in addition to their front doors, both have back doors. Turkey's opens toward Europe and Iran's toward Asia. In history, whenever the front entrance of either of these countries to the central courtyard has been closed, the country involved has been concerned, though it has not necessarily believed itself to be threatened. Hence, throughout history the peoples of Asia Minor—first the Byzantines and then the Turks—have afforded a liaison between Europe and the Middle East, while the Iranians have performed the same role between the peoples of China and India and the West.

On the other hand, the other two wings—Saudi Arabia and Egypt—have not had back doors to other areas, or at least they have not used them. Traditionally, the flow of the economic, cultural, and manpower movements from Arabia and Egypt has been toward the Fertile Crescent. Consequently, each time the front door of either of these two countries to the central courtyard has been closed, the country has felt itself threatened. Furthermore, throughout history, the many powers that gained control of the Fertile Crescent were usually able to conquer Egypt and the Arabian Peninsula, but not necessarily Turkey and Iran. Hence, this factor, in addition to the modern phenomenon of "Arabism," accounts for the extreme interest of Saudi Arabia and Egypt in the twentieth century in the affairs of the Fertile Crescent as opposed to the relative indifference of both Turkey and Iran.

THE PEOPLE

Most of the inhabitants of the Middle East, such as Egyptians, Lebanese, Turks, and Iranians are Caucasian people of the same general type as the Greeks, Italians, Spanish, and Irish. There are Negroid people scattered in the area, particularly in the Sudan, Saudi Arabia, and the Persian Gulf region. There are also some Mongoloid people, especially the Turkmans of northeast Iran and central Iraq. With the exception of a few isolated pockets, however, the Middle East has been a crossroads for so long that racial mixing has made it literally impossible to separate the people according to physical differences.

What differentiates the peoples of the Middle East more than any other factor is language. The four major languages are (in order of population size): Arabic, Turkish, Persian, and Kurdish.

The Semites.   Those who speak Semitic languages live in a relatively contiguous area and are not as scattered as the Indo-Europeans or as separated as the Turkic peoples. The dominant Semitic-language group in the Middle East is the Arabic-speaking peoples. These do not comprise a nation-state for there are regional, nationalistic, and religious differences among them. There are linguistic and cultural ties between the Arabic-speaking peoples of the Middle East and those of the Sudan and North Africa as far west as the Atlantic Ocean. Linguistically related to the Arabs are the Israelis, who speak Hebrew and who comprise a separate state in the Middle East. Another related group are the Assyrians, also called Chaldeans, who speak Syriac. The Assyrians are Christians and live mostly in Iran and Iraq with small numbers in Syria and Lebanon, and much larger numbers in the United States.

The Turkic Peoples.   The dominant group in the Middle East in this category is the Turks. They have linguistic ties with the Turkmans and Uzbeks in the east and the Hungarians and Finns in the west. As we shall see in this study, the Turks are relative newcomers to the Middle East.

The Indo-Europeans.   The dominant group in this category are the Iranians, who have linguistic and cultural ties with the peoples of Afghanistan, Tajikistan, and parts of Turkmanistan and Uzbekistan as well as Pakistan. There is a linguistic affinity between Persian[3] and most of the languages of India and Europe. In the Middle East, the Armenians and the Kurds are related linguistically to the Persians. Religiously, however, they are separate

---

[3]The term "Persian" instead of "Farsi" is used throughout the text for the major Indo-European language of Iran; the latter term, made popular in the United States in the 1950s, is simply the Persian word for "Persian."

both from the Persians and from each other. The Armenians are scattered throughout most of the countries of the Middle East as well as of the world. Their major concentration is, of course, in the Soviet Republic of Armenia. The Kurds, on the other hand, are predominantly rural people, and most of them live in a region comprising parts of Turkey, Iran, and Iraq. Both groups are minorities and have nationalistic aspirations.

RELIGIOUS GROUPS

The diversity of linguistic groups is confounded by religious differences; and the latter are, at times, more serious. The majority of the people of the Middle East are Muslims, who are divided into Sunni and Shi'i communities. Most of the Muslims of the world belong to the Sunni group. They consider themselves the adherents of the *Sunna*, or "practices," of the Prophet. They believe themselves to be orthodox Muslims, but their orthodoxy is questioned by Wahhabism, which is the state religion of Saudi Arabia. The four main divisions of the Shi'is are: (1) Ja'fari, or Twelvers; theirs is the state religion of Iran and they are scattered in other countries of the Middle East; (2) Ismaili, or Seveners, are scattered throughout the world of Islam; (3) Zaydis, whose faith is the state religion of Yaman; and (4) Alawis, who live in northern Syria, Yaman, and Morocco. Within the Islamic community are the Sufis, who have not separated themselves to form a sect, but whose mysticism is suspect by the *ulama*, the "clergy" of Islam. More will be said about these groups in the discussion of the development of Islam.

No introduction to the Middle East would be complete without some discussion of the non-Muslim religions of the area. As these will not be discussed in the following pages, each receives a brief description here. The largest religious minority in the Middle East is the Christians. They are divided into four communions.

The Eastern Orthodox Church. Historically, this church grew out of the four original Eastern patriarchates—Constantinople (now Istanbul), Alexandria, Antioch, and Jerusalem—which separated from the Western Church in 1054. Later the church became divided along national lines such as Greek Orthodox, Russian Orthodox, and so forth. Each group is independent, autocephalous, and has its own patriarch. The patriarch of Constantinople is, however, first among equals. The adherents of the patriarchate of Constantinople are mostly Greek, while those of Alexandria, with their headquarters in Cairo, are Arab and Greek. The majority of Christians in the patriarchates of Antioch and Jerusalem are Arab. Damascus is the center for the patriarchate of Antioch.

Oriental churches. This communion has several branches.

1. *The Coptic Church of Egypt.* This church, whose patriarch resides in Cairo, rejected the decision of the Council of Chalcedon and became monophysite—that is, it emphasized the single nature of Christ. It is similar to the Ethiopian Church, except that in Egypt the liturgy is in Coptic and Arabic. It must be

noted that the language of the Copts is Arabic. Coptic is used in parts of the liturgy only.

2. *The Syrian Church,* sometimes called "Jacobite." This church is also monophysite and was organized under the patriarch of Antioch with residence in Homs, Syria. Its liturgy is conducted in Syriac.

3. *The Armenian Church.* Usually referred to as "Gregorian," this church is within the Eastern Orthodox tradition. Its most important patriarch is the Catholicos of Etchmidzin in the Soviet Republic of Armenia. It has been a national church since the Armenians had a national existence in the Caucasus. During their long history the Armenians were caught between the Byzantine-Persian wars and later between the Ottoman-Persian wars. Consequently, in recent centuries they have been vassals to both the Ottomans and the Persians and later to the Russians. One of the results of the Bolshevik Revolution was the formation of the Armenian Soviet Republic with Erivan as its capital. Outside the republic there are Armenian communities in most of the countries of the Middle East.

4. *The Nestorians.* The Nestorians believe in the dual nature of Christ. Before the advent of Islam they were the main propagators of Christianity throughout Asia. From their bishoprics in Iran they sent missionaries as far as China. As a "nation" they are called Assyrians and speak Syriac, which belongs to the Semitic family of languages. Their patriarch, the Mar Shimmun, is a temporal as well as religious ruler. For centuries the agricultural Syrians lived under the suzerainty of Iran, while the highlanders, known as the Jeeloo, lived under the domination of the Turks. During World War I both groups became pawns in international rivalry. In the Middle East the largest Assyrian settlements are in Iran and Iraq.

Roman Catholics. Roman Catholics are divided into two groups. One group follows the Latin rite and is composed of Roman Catholic Europeans who have settled in the Middle East and individual converts from the various Orthodox and Oriental churches. The other and by far the larger group is the Uniate Church. This term refers to the Orthodox who accept the supremacy of the pope but who are allowed to use the Oriental rite in worship and whose clergy have permission to marry. On the whole, the Uniates have held to their original national traditions and have their own patriarchs. The Uniate Church is composed of Greek Catholics, Syrian Catholics, Armenian Catholics, Chaldean Catholics (Nestorians), Coptic Catholics, and Maronite Catholics. The Maronites represent the largest subdivision and reside mainly in Lebanon.

Anglican and other Protestant Churches. The Anglican church serves the British communities in the Middle East as well as the converts from the Oriental churches and a few from Islam and Judaism. The Protestant churches have evolved principally from the missionary activities of American churches in the nineteenth and twentieth centuries. Their members are converts from the Oriental churches as well as from Islam, Judaism, and Zoroastrianism.

Judaism is the second non-Islamic religion of the Middle East and is the raison d'être for the establishment of the state of Israel as well as the state religion. All of the original Jewish inhabitants of the Middle East are Sephardim, while the Ashkenazim, who all reside in Israel, are newcomers from Europe and the United States. Most of the countries of the Middle

East, with the exception of Saudi Arabia, Jordan, and Yaman, still claim small Jewish communities.

A third non-Islamic religion native to the Middle East was Zoroastrianism, the religion of the Iranians until the Arab conquest. As a religion, it profoundly influenced Judaism, and, more especially, Christianity and Islam. Two of its offshoots, Mithraism and Manicheanism, rivaled Christianity for the allegiance of the people of the Roman Empire. After the Arab conquest, a large number of those who were not killed or converted fled to India to form the present Parsee communities of India and Pakistan. A small number of Zoroastrians still live in Iran.

Among the other non-Islamic religions in the Middle East, the following must be mentioned:

The Druzes. This religion, whose adherents live in the mountains of Lebanon, Syria, and Israel, is an offshoot of the Ismaili subdivision of the Shi'a, who accepted the Fatimid caliph Hakim (996–1021) as the incarnation of deity. The name is perhaps derived from its first missionary who was called Darazi (1019). Theologically, they drew from many other religions and beliefs, and in time became a distinct people who refuse to accept any converts.

The Yazidis. Even though they deny the existence of the devil in their religion, their neighbors refer to them as "devil worshippers." Yazidism is also a radical offshoot of Shi'a Islam and is a mixture of Muslim, Jewish, Christian, Manichean, and Shamanistic beliefs. There are some 25,000 believers and they live in northern Syria and Iraq.

The Sabians. Not to be confused with Sabaeans of pre-Islamic Arabia, the Sabians (or Mandeans) are more popularly but perhaps erroneously called the "Christians of St. John the Baptist." Their religion is of Judeo-Christian orientation and is mentioned three times in the Koran. Perhaps because of this the Muslims gave them the status of "people of the Book." The Arabs, impressed by the fact that these people washed themselves frequently as a religious ritual, referred to them as *mughtasilah* ("those who wash themselves")—hence their possible connection to the disciples of John the Baptist. Today they live mostly in Iraq and are recognized for specialization as silversmiths.

The Bahais. This religion is an offshoot of the Shaykhi sect of Shi'i Islam. Begun in Iran in 1844 as the Babi movement, the Bahais later split from the Babis in 1863, organizing a religion of their own. During its century and a quarter of turbulent existence, Bahaism has veered away from the major original tenets and has become syncretistic, embracing all religions of the world. The majority of Bahais live in Iran, though unrecognized; but their headquarters is in Haifa, Israel, and they have "assemblies" in many parts of the world.

DIVERSITY AND UNITY

Superimposed over these religious communities, which have also enjoyed varying degrees of communal and political autonomy for centuries, are eleven modern states and some seven shaykhdoms, each with varying degrees of independence and development. Since no state, with the possible exception of Saudi Arabia, is made up of one religious community, the transcendent religious and communal loyalties often clash with the more limited national loyalties. Consequently, in all of the states of the Middle East it has become customary to identify each person according to his religion; and more often than not, members of the minority religions feel that they are second-class citizens. To avoid this, Lebanon has devised a formula in which religious communities have been given political power commensurate with their numbers. A Maronite Catholic is always president, a Sunni Muslim the prime minister, a Shi'a Muslim the speaker of the parliament, an Orthodox Christian in one ministry, a Druze in another, and so on. This is precarious, to say the least, but is more conducive to peaceful coexistence than the situation in Iraq, where the Shi'a majority are more or less governed by a Sunni minority. Also, in their midst they have the Kurds, whose religion is Sunni but whose language is Iranian and is related to Persian; and the Armenians and the Assyrians who neither speak the same language nor profess the same religion as the rest of the Iraqis.

It is evident that there is much cultural diversity in the Middle East, and the danger of overgeneralization about the peoples and cultures of the area is great. Throughout the Middle East, group identifications are still strong. Individuals find themselves with conflicting loyalties sometimes on linguistic grounds such as Arabic, Armenian, Hebrew, Kurdish, Persian, Syriac, or Turkish; sometimes on religious levels such as Bahai, Druze, Jew, Orthodox, Protestant, Roman Catholic, Sabian, Shi'a, Sunni, Yazidi, or Zoroastrian; and sometimes on national grounds when loyalty is expressed in terms of nation-states. This last form of loyalty is strongest among the Israelis, Iranians, Egyptians, and Turks, and, to a lesser degree, among the citizens of the various Arab states. It is this diversity that has led anthropologist Carleton Coon to suggest that the Middle East is a mosaic of peoples, a kind of patchwork quilt of different cultural groups.

Nevertheless, in this patchwork quilt there are threads that run through the whole so that one can discern similar patterns and observe a unity. One of these patterns is the community life of the people. It is safe to say that all over the Middle East there are three types of community life: the nomad, the village, and the town.

Nomads.   Probably fewer than 5 percent of all the peoples of the Middle East are now *nomadic.* There are almost no nomads in Lebanon, while in Saudi Arabia perhaps they number as high as 25 to 30 percent. The main concern of the nomads is to search for grassland, and therefore water; but depending on the locale, their main acitvity is the herding of sheep, goats, or camels. The nomads of the Fertile Crescent and Arabian Peninsula who look for water on a virtually flat landscape are called "horizontal," while the nomads of mountainous Iran and Turkey who live higher in search of grass during the summer are called "vertical." But whether horizontal or vertical, their communities are organized along similar lines; and they are governed by a leader, usually hereditary, who is called "shaykh" or "khan." The nomads are practically self-sufficient; and to acquire the few necessities that they cannot produce, they sell sheep, milk, butter, cheese, and wool to the townsmen. They live in tents and can move at a moment's notice with their meager possessions. Their loyalty lies with the tribe rather than with the central government. They do not understand, or find them unacceptable if they do understand, such modern notions as the income tax, parliaments, military service, or national frontiers. In earlier centuries the nomadic tribes were considered to be the backbone of a kingdom. They were given autonomy in their region, and in turn they supplied the king or caliph with troops in time of war. The regularity of their paying tribute varied directly with the power of the ruler. In these days of national budgets, national armies, and national education, plus the fact that the settled communities have less need of the products of the nomads, the tribes are fighting a losing battle; they and their nomadic ways of life will someday disappear.

Villages.   Estimates are that between 75 and 80 percent of the people of the Middle East live in the second type of community, the agricultural *village.* Farming is the main economic activity, supplemented by crafts. The village, the center of community life, is a cluster of houses built close together. In most of the Middle East these houses are built of sun-dried brick. With the exception of northern Syria and some parts of Arabia, where the homes are built like inverted cones, village homes throughout the area are usually one- or two-story rectangles. In the mountainous regions, the villages cling to the hillside and, as nearly all of them are away from the main highways, they go almost unnoticed. Many of the farmers use methods that have not changed in thousands of years. Others have adopted somewhat improved practices, while still others have begun to use modern farm machinery. Plagued by unscientific farming, illiteracy, disease, and absentee landlordism, the farmers of the area accumulate little economic surplus. With few exceptions, they lead lives of grinding poverty.

The villagers' clothing is quite simple and ranges from the "nightgown" of the Egyptian to the long shirt and trousers of the Iranians. Bread, supplemented by vegetables, is the staff of life. The village women do not suffer the general seclusion of their sisters in the towns nor enjoy the freedom of the tribal women. The villager, on the whole, appears as docile and content as the tribesman appears proud and restless. Most of the modern states of the Middle East have inaugurated long-range and far-reaching programs to improve the life of the peasant. These range from division of land to the introduction of education and the establishment of cooperatives. One of the most advanced programs was in Iran, where thousands of educated young men were enlisted in "literacy corps," or "health corps," or the like, and worked for two years in villages throughout the country in lieu of their military service obligation. These programs were ended in 1979.

Towns.   Urban community life has always existed in the Middle East. Indeed, Damascus boasts of being the oldest continuously inhabited city in the world; and other cities such as Baghdad, Beirut, Cairo, Esfahan, Istanbul, Jerusalem, and Mecca are old by any standards. It is difficult to generalize about the cities and towns of the Middle East except to say that they contain the most extreme contrasts. Modern apartment buildings stand next to thousand-year-old mosques or homes built of sun-dried bricks. The richest men in the country live in cities and so do the poorest. In the streets illiterates rub shoulders with the most educated. A few women wear the latest fashions from Paris and dance to the most recent tunes, while only blocks away their less fortunate but more numerous sisters live the secluded life of old.

The governments of the Middle East have been city governments for centuries, and to this day they usually operate in the interests of the city dwellers. The rising middle class of the Middle East lives in cities, and it is here that political parties are formed, new constitutions are drafted, and political demonstrations are staged to make or break governments. At the same time, farmers are increasingly attracted to the cities because of jobs in commerce and industry. Hence, the population explosion is everywhere apparent in the cities as dislocated villagers crowd into slum dwellings. City dwellers of the Middle East are in transition between the established patterns of the past and the unaccomplished hopes of the future. They are caught between the placid villagers who do not want to go any place and satisfied Europeans who feel that they have already arrived. At best, city dwellers carry the burden of the whole country on their shoulders. At worst, they are shrewd opportunists who profit from the confusion of their fellow countrymen.

Family life. In the villages as well as the urban centers the family has always been the most important social, political, and economic unit. The traditional Middle Eastern family gives status and self-respect to the individual. City life and institutions have not, as yet, disrupted this. Without a family the average Middle Easterner is nothing. The kinship group provides economic and political security. Even if one leaves the village or the nomadic tribe, one retains an identity with one's family.

The smallest unit in the social structure and production process of the Middle East is the household. In many cases this is an *extended family* household, in which the senior male is the patriarch and represents the family in all matters. In modern times political loyalties are often based on family ties.

The *nuclear family* is now widespread in the Middle East, especially in the city. Whether the family will be extended or nuclear depends upon such factors as economic productivity, patterns of land tenure, and urbanization. While it is true that the family provides security, contact with Western culture has created many tensions within families; occasionally, conflicts within households or larger groups become extremely serious.

Women. With the exception of the nomads, the sexes have been traditionally segregated; and women have been markedly subordinate to men. The veil, covering the faces of women, became the prime symbol of Muslim conservatism with regard to the status of women. Even though the veil has been lifted in many parts of the Middle East, there is much resistance to the changing status of women, and the Middle East is still a man's world.

Social classes. There are many evidences of class awareness in the Middle East, and usually three class levels are identified in the cities and villages. These are the elite, the small middle class, and the vast mass of poor people. There is relatively little stratification among the nomads except for hereditary nobility. Social status influences speech habits, gestures, and other aspects of daily behavior, and one can readily discern class levels in a community if one spends a little time there. Some of the major factors in the determination of social status are loyalty to family, size of family, age, land holdings, wealth, political power, religion, education, and artistic knowledge.

For many centuries the economic differences between the ruling elite and the masses have been great. Socially they were not entirely separated and ideologically they shared similar goals and values. Both landlords and peasants slept on the floor, sat on the floor, ate similar food, wore a similar style of clothing, and kept themselves warm during the winter in the same way. They were both practicing Muslims, believed in Islamic institutions, and had similar ideas of right and wrong. To be sure, the economic differences were apparent in that the landlord's food was more plentiful and his clothing and bedding were of better material. Westernization, however, has radically changed this situation. Not only has it widened the economic gap, but it has also created other gaps where the illiterate poor man does not feel as comfortable in the presence of his wealthy master as his father once did. The ruling elite, whose education has given them knowledge of the West and whose wealth has enabled them to adopt Western ways, have separated themselves from their poorer compatriots. They do not live in the same type of house as their fathers did, nor do they sleep and sit on the floor, nor eat similar food. They have all of the gadgets of comfort enjoyed in the West, whereas the villagers' lives have changed very little. More often than not a member of the new elite is not a practicing Muslim and does not hold to the values of the past. Even his daily speech has so many Western words in it that an illiterate poor man has difficulty understanding his language.

Today, the social structure of the Middle East is undergoing vast change. There has been land reform and there will be much more. Even where there has been little reform, the all-powerful position of the landlord is giving way. A man can improve his social class position if he has sufficient education. A certain amount of wealth is always helpful; but some observers believe that a military career, coupled with education, is an excellent means of acquiring influence and power. With the improved means of communication and the increase in the number of schools, the illiterate masses of today will provide the skilled workers of the society of the future and will grasp a good share of the political power in the process.

NATIONALISM

Nationalism is another sentiment common to practically all the people of the Middle East. Nationalism in itself is divisive. Even though it sets the Egyptians against the Syrians and the Iraqis against the Iranians, nevertheless, the ingredients of this nationalism are common to all.

Pride in the past.   One of these ingredients is pride in the glory of the past. The Middle Easterner, whether he be Arab, Iranian, Turk, or Kurd, wants everyone to know about his past and appreciate it. The past gives him reason for his boastful pride. If the greatness of any nation lies in the power of its armies and its ability, by brute force, to impose its will upon others, then the people of the Middle East can claim this greatness. There were times when Middle Eastern nations such as the Egyptians, Babylonians, Assyrians, Iranians, Arabs, Turks, and Kurds had the "atomic" weapons of their day. By brute force they built great empires and imposed their will on more people than some of the great empires in the West. In the following chapters we shall encounter great generals such as Khalid ibn-al-Walid, Sa'd ibn-Waqqas, Mahmud of Ghazna, some of the Ottoman sultans, Chengiz Khan, Tamerlane, Nader Shah, and a host of others, any of whose military exploits and shrewd imperial strategy overshadow many a famous counterpart in Europe. The "Pax Romana" imposed by the Roman Empire was quite insignificant when compared to the peace imposed by the descendants of Chengiz Khan in Asia. In the latter part of the thirteenth century, Marco Polo could travel from either western Russia or the eastern Mediterranean over the length of north and central Asia to the capital of Kublai Khan in Peking on well-established roads without fear of molestation.

There are those who believe that greatness is not measured in terms of brute force alone, but in terms of qualities of intellect, which make lasting contributions towards the betterment of civilization. In this too the peoples of the Middle East can take pride. A typical day in the life of a Western man is enriched by many contributions from the Middle East. His year is determined by the birth of a Palestinian; and the month, the week, the day, and the hour are based on a system of reckoning and calendar started by the Egyptians and Babylonians and perfected by the Persians. He washes himself in a "bath" introduced into Europe by the Turks and dries himself with a "Turkish" towel.

At breakfast he may drink coffee (*qahwa*—Arabic). He drives to his work on wheels, a discovery by someone in the ancient Middle East. During the day he may use scientific and business words such as algebra (*al-jabr*— Arabic), alcohol (*al-kohl*—Arabic), or tariff (*ta'rifa*—Arabic). His books are named after Biblos—hence "Bible" and "bibliography"—a town in Lebanon where the idea of a book was first conceived. His post office is an institution of the Iranians reported by Herodotus; he writes on paper brought to the West by Muslims; and he uses "Arabic numerals," devised in India and brought to Europe by the Arabs.

At home he may relax on his divan (*deevan*—Persian) or sofa (*suffa*— Arabic) and read a magazine (*makhzan*—Arabic). Later he puts on his pajamas (*pa-jameh*—Persian) and lies down on the mattress (*matrah*—Arabic). Indeed, more and more Western historians acknowledge the great debt which the Renaissance owes the Muslims of the Middle Ages who preserved and built upon all the important learning of the Greeks and the Romans and passed it on to Europe.

Long before the Renaissance, Muslims of diverse nationalities in the Middle East collected books on all subjects in Latin, Greek, Syriac, Persian,

Sanskrit, Chinese, and any other language they could find and brought them to Baghdad. The caliph, Ma'mun, established a "Bureau of Translations" under the leadership of the Christian Hunayn ibn-Ishaq (809–873) and had these manuscripts, mostly Greek, translated into Arabic, which was considered a holy language just as Latin was considered holy in Europe. Later Muslims studied these and built upon them and produced philosophers such as Averröes (ibn-Rushd) to whom St. Thomas Aquinas was indebted; and mathematicians such as Omar Khayyam who devised the Jalali calendar still used in Iran today, which is more accurate than its Gregorian counterpart in use in the West. In medicine Muslims produced a host of famous physicians, among them Razi and Avicenna, whose writings were the standard textbooks of medicine in Europe until the eighteenth century and whose portraits adorn the great hall of the school of medicine at the University of Paris. In the following chapters appear scientists, philosophers, geographers, historians, men of letters, and artists whose contributions to civilization are unquestioned.

There are still others who believe that true greatness requires a spiritual basis to make it humane and constructive. In this also the people of the Middle East have contributed much. The three great monotheistic religions of the world have their origins in the Middle East. There is Judaism, given form by Moses, who was born in Egypt; Christianity, founded by Jesus, born in Palestine; and Islam, founded by Muhammad, born in Arabia. Every one of these religions is in turn indebted to the less-known Zoroastrianism, founded in Iran. To these religions of the Middle East, Western civilization owes its most cherished values and goals and its concepts of God and man, and of life and afterlife. Pride in the past is the mainstay of every nationalist.

Frustration.   Indeed, the memory of former physical strength, intellectual attainment, and spiritual contribution is so vivid in the mind of the Middle Easterner that he is often in danger of living in the past without any thought of the present or the future. Whenever, on the other hand, he is conscious of the present, he is overwhelmed by a feeling of frustration. This sense of frustration is the second ingredient in his present-day nationalism. He is dependent not only upon the technology of the West, but he also, sometimes reluctantly, wears Western-style clothes, eats Western food, enjoys Western music, lives under Western law, reads Western philosophy, and likes Western institutions.

Whenever Middle Easterners are together they talk about the long distance they have to go to catch up with the West and their frustration with a society that is not moving fast enough. Whenever they face a Westerner, their pride intervenes and they become defensive and, sometimes, belligerent. On the one hand, they feel that they have to borrow from the West in order to survive; and on the other hand, they resent having to do so. Yet there is no precedent for this guilt feeling about borrowing in the Islamic Middle East. When Islam emerged from the Arabian desert, it was a new, vigorous faith without a set of traditions and within the context of a pastoral culture. In general, it delighted in satisfying an insatiable curiosity and widening its horizons without hesitation. Islam became fascinated with Hellenistic thought, adopted the Iranian method of administration, and did not hesitate to borrow heavily from any culture within reach. The question arises, then, why this hesitation to borrow now?

For one thing, there is the pride of a religious society that replaced Christianity in many areas and is now hesitant to learn from a civilization that goes by the name of Christian. Perhaps the more important reason is that the countries and cultures from which Islam borrowed were either decadent or had just been defeated. Consequently, a victorious Muslim army took over ideas just as it confiscated war booty. The situation is radically different now. In the modern encounter with the West, the Muslims are not confident of their own position, and any borrowing arises from weakness rather than strength. Furthermore, the leaders of Islam are afraid that those of their coreligionists who adopt Western ways do not do so with the idea of enriching their heritage, but with the idea of replacing it with the superior institutions of the West.

Zealots versus Herodeans.   A third ingredient of modern nationalism is *secularism.* The influence of modern scientific civilization is uniformly great in all the countries of the Middle East, although it is more advanced in some countries than in others. Islam is going through the same kind of struggle that Christianity did during the eighteenth and nineteenth centuries. Like Christianity, Islam has to react one way or the other to modern science, ideas, and institutions. There are at least two types of reactions. In his *Civilization on Trial,* Arnold Toynbee says that "whenever one civilized society finds itself in this dangerous situation *vis-à-vis* another, there are two alternative ways open to it of responding to the challenge." One is "zealotism," which "takes refuge from the unknown in the familiar," and in a struggle against superior tactics and new weapons the society "responds by practicing its own traditional art of war." The other he names "Herodeanism," which "acts on the principle that the most effective way to guard against the danger of the known is to master its secret," and in the struggle against superior tactics and new weapons "responds by discarding its traditional art of war and learning to fight the enemy with the enemy's own tactics and weapons."

In the Middle East the zealots are, for the most part, headed by religious leaders who are fearful of Western institutions and the encroachment of Western ideas. They want to go back to the purity of Islam, "when it was pure and unadulterated with foreign ideas." Precisely, they mean the time of the first four caliphs when the Koran was the only book and the Sunna the only law. Some of the more "progressive" in this group, to minimize any idea of borrowing, have gone so far as to claim that the Koran was the first to predict most of the modern scientific and technological advances from electricity and telephones to jets and spaceships. Recently the zealots have captured the imagination of the youth and the loyalty of the dispossessed, partly because of the failure of the westernizers and partly because of the neocolonial policies of the West. Zealots have already captured the entire apparatus of government in Iran and are powers to be reckoned with in every other country of the Middle East.

The Herodeans, on the other hand, react differently. They are, for the most part, headed by the young progressives who see salvation in total modernization. These modernizers are, in turn, divided into three groups. One is still oriented toward the western European form of political democracy. They are imbued with ideas of the Enlightenment and those forces that brought about the American and French revolutions. A second group of modernizers follows the ideas of democracy that have been "purified" and "fulfilled" by the communist revolutions in the Soviet Union and China. They are attracted by the dialectics of Karl Marx and the meteoric rise of communist power. A third group of modernizers, while favoring the West over the communist world, calls itself neutral and tries to supplement the political democracy of the West with social reform, while at the same time being attracted by the "one-party democracy of the communist world." With the exception of those who are doctrinaire communists and, therefore, anti-religious, the majority of the modernizers are secularists who, while they do not oppose religion, do not find Islam or any other religion relevant to the problems of the day.

Islam is going through the same inner struggle in adjusting to modern conditions that Christianity experienced in the nineteenth century. Since Islam does not distinguish between the "secular" and the "religious," the laws of Islam drawn up in the seventh and eighth centuries are religiously binding in the twentieth century and make the problem of adjustment more difficult. On the other hand, the student of modern movements in the Middle East must always bear in mind that the identification of culture and religion has always been looked upon with favor by Islam, even though such identification has been generally decried by Christianity.

Xenophobia.   A fourth ingredient in nationalism is suspicion. A modern nationalist, whether he be Arab, Iranian, or Turk, is suspicious of Europe. At best he will be considered "gullible" and at worst "communist" or "imperialist," depending upon his circle of friends. The Middle East may be compared to a campfire. There was a time when its flames went high and illuminated the surrounding areas. Its light and warmth attracted many people and, in that fellowship, much was learned and shared. However, as will be seen in these pages, the people went into a deep slumber and the ashes of time covered their huge fire. Now they have awakened and want to push away the ashes and, with the use of embers, start a new fire. In this attempt they are confronted with two problems. The first problem is that every time, especially in the past century and a half, they have attempted to push the ashes away, they have been prevented by outside hands. These hands have been British, Russian, French, German, and American. Consequently, Middle Eastern nationalists are suspicious of the policies of Europe, and have come to believe that the countries of the West, communist and noncommunist, do not approve of their awakening. The simple remark of a tourist expressing sorrow over the disappearance of the camel or the covered bazaar is not taken as an innocent comment but rather as an ominous design to discourage progress. This xenophobia, often based on reality and sometimes on imagination, is an important element in the thought processes of the people of the Middle East.

Confusion. The second problem caused by the attempt to build a new fire is that of choice. It is difficult to know which log to use. This causes confusion, which is a fifth ingredient of nationalism. As heirs to an ancient culture, Middle Easterners have a problem about what to keep and what to discard. As a people facing the aggressive culture of the West yet desiring change, their problem is what to accept and what to reject. These decisions are not easy, and as a result there is sharp disagreement between mother and daughter, father and son, friend and friend. Take, for example, the question of music. There are those who reject Western music and there are those who despise their own traditional Eastern music. Among those who love Western music there is a sharp disagreement between those who love classical Western music and those who admire jazz. In this conflict one should not overlook those who want to combine the two! This confusion is typical of every aspect of life, be it food, dress, education, politics, or even religion.

ISLAM

The vivid general pattern that unifies the patchwork quilt known as the Middle East is, of course, Islam. Even though there are many sects and schools of thought in Islam, reputedly some seventy-two of them, it is still the strongest common experience of the peoples of the area. Many writers are in the habit of saying that Islam is not only a religion, but a way of life. Of course, in a sense, every religion is a way of life. By this statement they mean that Islam attempts to regulate the whole of life. Hence, it not only sets up spiritual goals, but also provides the institutions, laws, and the general environment in which those goals should be attained. It leaves little to the individual. Islam tells its adherents when and how to pray, how many times and in what direction; it has laws about marriage and divorce, property, and inheritance; it has rules for the art of war and the maintenance of peace. These are practically the same in all Islamic countries. For over 1,300 years Muslims have fought others and each other, built institutions, written books, organized revolts, and erected edifices, all in reference to Islam— either for it or against it or under its aegis. Consequently, Middle Eastern history cannot be understood without a thorough knowledge of Islam and its leaders.

Before we begin, a word of explanation is necessary. The civilization now under study was triggered by an initial Arab conquest and hence is sometimes called "Arab" civilization. Unfortunately, the modern states that go by the name of "Arab" consider themselves the sole heirs of that culture and boast of "Arab" contributions to the civilization of the world. This is as confusing as it is untrue. Originally, the bedouins of Arabia, when they conquered Syria, Mesopotamia, Egypt, and Iran, were conquering non-Arab countries. In the process these sons of the desert brought with them not only Islam, but also the Arabic language which they believed to be the "language of angels." Furthermore, they imposed this language upon the conquered people, to the extent that it became the medium of instruction as well as that of official communication. Consequently, all of the scholars within a certain period wrote in Arabic, irrespective of their national origin. A vast majority of these scholars were not Arabs. Indeed, a number of them, such as the celebrated Ibn Khaldun of North Africa, did not even think very highly of the Arabs.

Later, some of the people who had been conquered by the Arabs in the seventh and eighth centuries, such as the Syrians, Egyptians, and North Africans, adopted Arabic as their language. Others, however, such as the Iranians, Turks, Kurds, and Indians, who had never adopted Arabic as their spoken language, discontinued the use of it in their writing in the same way that many Europeans gave up the use of Latin.

Indeed, until the emergence of Arab nationalism in the twentieth century, the term "Arab" was applied almost solely to the inhabitants of the peninsula of Arabia. Even after World War I, the Egyptians would not accept the idea advanced by some of the leaders in the Fertile Crescent that "everyone who speaks Arabic is an Arab." This pan-Arab formula failed to attract many followers until after World War II.

The desire to unite all who speak Arabic in one "Arab" nation is understandable and may be quite legitimate, even though it has many opponents within the Arabic-speaking community. But this is hardly justification for calling everyone in the Middle Ages who wrote in Arabic an Arab. To add further confusion, some scholars in the United States, in an attempt to reserve the now-coveted word "Arab" for those who wrote in Arabic in the Middle Ages, have applied the word "Arabian" to the early conquerors from the desert. This is not only arbitrary, but it has even resulted in such absurd claims as that the Persian Gulf should be called "Arabian Gulf."

The map of the Middle East has been revised so many times since the conquest of Islam that these problems plague other peoples as well. Today the people of Soviet Uzbekistan claim Avicenna, the great physician and philosopher of the eleventh century, as Uzbek because he was born in Bokhara, which is now located in Uzbekistan. Iranians claim him as their own because his mother tongue was Persian and he lived and died in Iran. The office of information of the League of Arab States considers Avicenna as the "contribution of the Arabs" to the world simply because he wrote his scientific works in Arabic. To whom does Avicenna belong?

To avoid confusion we will not consider the period under consideration either Arab or Iranian and will admit that it had a character of its own. Perhaps the best name for it is "Islamic," despite its limitations, because Islam was the principal common denominator of the whole area and because Islam made Arabic a holy language, such that all learned works were written in it. Even though some of the contributors to this civilization were not Muslims themselves, there is no question that they did their work under the aegis of Islam.

Chapter One
The Middle East Before Islam

Muhammad was born in what is now Saudi Arabia in A.D. 570. He formed the first Islamic government when he was fifty-two years old. By 633, the year of his death, Islam was poised for conquest and nearly ready to launch its aggressive campaigns—campaigns that, even in their initial stages, reached all the way to Iran in the northeast and to Egypt in the northwest.

The Arabian Peninsula is a desert country with an inhospitable climate. In the pre-Islamic period, a small percentage of the population lived in the few towns located on trade routes. The bulk of the population was made up of nomadic tribes. The land was so barren and uninviting that the two superpowers who were contesting the territory north of the peninsula did not bother to venture into the interior. They were satisfied with maintaining garrisons to defend themselves against periodic raids by the nomadic tribes. Consequently, they did not know much about Arabia.

The interest of Muslim historians in pre-Islamic Arabia centered on the correct interpretation of certain historical allusions in the Koran, as well as in the pre-Islamic literature. They were also interested in genealogy because it was an important factor in determining the amount of stipend a Muslim Arab was to receive. This was about the extent of their interest. They summed up the history of pre-Islamic Arabia by a single term: "The Period of Ignorance." They meant, of course, ignorance of the Koran and the blessings of Islam, but they used the term to refer to all aspects of the pre-Islamic period. Even the celebrated historian Ibn Khaldun (1332–1406) considered the bedouin dwellers of this vast wilderness as illiterates who did not care for craft industries and who were destructive to civilization. He states that "The Arabs [bedouin] use stones . . . to support their cooking pots. So they take them from buildings which they tear down for that purpose. . . . They tear down roofs to get wood for burning." This description of the nomads was generally true; but Arabia had many cities, and the dwellers of these cities were far more sophisticated than the above description implies. Although our present knowledge of ancient and medieval Arabia is still fragmentary, we know more now than we did before, thanks to archaeological discoveries and scholarship.

THE SABAEANS AND THE NABATAEANS

Because of its more favorable climate, the southern coast of Arabia developed several trading and cultural centers. Regions in the south such as Oman, Hadramut, Yaman, and others were centers of kingdoms that traded with peoples outside the peninsula. Their caravans traveled north to what is now Jordan and Syria by way of the western route along the Red Sea, and to what is now Iraq by way of the eastern route along the Persian Gulf. They had commercial agents in the eastern Mediterranean and Egypt. Perhaps the most enterprising among them were the Sabaeans, whose home base was the southwest corner of the peninsula. The Sabaeans traded extensively with Ethiopia, Egypt, and Syria. In addition to spices from India, they dealt in gold and slaves from Ethiopia, silk from China, and pearls from the Persian Gulf.

Gradually the power of the southern kingdoms spread over the whole peninsula. North Arabia was mainly nomadic, but the centers that the south Arabians had established along their caravan routes attracted the more enterprising among the bedouins. Perhaps because of their proximity to Syria and Egypt in the north and the influence of south Arabian traders, petty kingdoms had arisen in the north by the third century B.C. The most important of these were the Nabataeans, who wrested commercial control from the south and established themselves at Petra, north of the Gulf of Aqaba. Their merchants traded to the north as far as the Aegean and Italy.

By the first century A.D., the Greeks had pushed the Nabataeans south into to central Arabia. We do not have much information about the centuries immediately preceding the advent of Islam. All we know is that trade flourished and that tensions arose between the city dwellers and the nomads, who were a menace to the flow of commerce. On the whole, the cities were at the mercy of the bedouins. City merchants protected their caravans by making alliances with the bedouin tribes. Sometimes more than one city would join an alliance, and sometimes rival alliances were formed. The bedouins, for their part, would go wherever there was booty to be had. In part, the message of Islam can be understood in the light of this tension and Muhammad's attempt to resolve it.

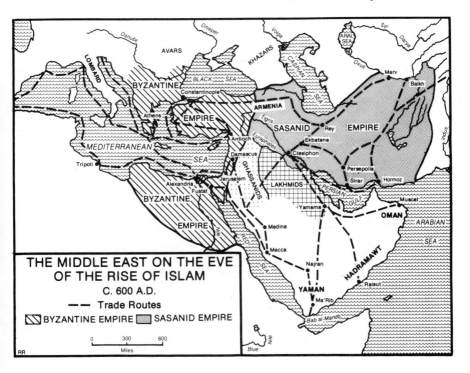

THE MIDDLE EAST ON THE EVE
OF THE RISE OF ISLAM
C. 600 A.D.
— — Trade Routes
BYZANTINE EMPIRE ▨ SASANID EMPIRE

0   300   600
Miles

THE BYZANTINES AND THE SASANIDS

The two superpowers in the north were neither interested nor able to bring
stability to Arabia, even though both claimed suzerainity over parts of the
peninsula. To the west was the Byzantine Empire, which controlled all of the
Balkans and Asia Minor, the eastern shores of the Mediterranean, Egypt,
and parts of North Africa. It was the heir of the Roman Empire, and its
capital was at Byzantium, or Constantinople. The official religion of the
empire was Eastern Orthodox Christianity, and its language was Greek. To
the east were the Iranians, ruled by the Sasanids, heirs of the ancient Achae-
manean Empire. The Sasanids controlled both sides of the Caspian Sea, the
eastern part of the Fertile Crescent, and the whole territory between the
Tigris and Indus rivers. Their winter capital was at Ctesiphon on the banks
of the Tigris, and their summer capital at Ekbatana, the modern Hamadan.
Their religion was Zoroastrianism and their language was called Pahlavi, or
middle Persian. Both the Sasanian and Byzantine empires were autocratic,
and both used religion as a tool of the state. Linguistically and culturally,
however, the Iranians were the more homogeneous and therefore were
much more proud of their heritage. These two empires were constantly at
war, neither side being strong enough to subdue the other for any length of
time.

A few years before the birth of Muhammad, the two empires were
ruled by two great contemporaries. In Byzantium the emperor was Justinian

(527–565), and in Sasanian Iran the Shahanshah was Khosrow Anushiravan (531–571). Both rulers were active, ambitious, and believers in absolute power. Both were reformers and law givers. The two "brothers," as they called one another, concluded an "eternal peace." Justinian paid 11,000 pounds of gold for it because he wanted to be free to attack Italy. However, the peace did not last even a decade. By A.D. 540 the armies of Anushiravan were poised outside Antioch. Justinian was desperate. He bought a five-year truce in 545 for a reputed 2,000 pounds. Finally, in 562 Justinian agreed to pay an annual tribute of 30,000 pieces of gold for a fifty-year peace, but hostilities were resumed almost as soon as he died. War between the two empires had become a habit.

One must not assume, however, that the Sasanians and the Byzantines spent all of their time in warfare. In peacetime there were diplomatic and commercial as well as cultural exchanges. Brisk trade went on in spices, stones, ivory, and silk. The Byzantines had time to develop art, illuminate manuscripts, build magnificent churches, and immerse themselves in deep theological questions. The Sasanians, in their territories, were enlightened patrons of letters, carried on trade with India and China, built beautiful edifices, developed a complete administrative organization, and established the educational institution of Gundi Shapur, which became the greatest intellectual center of the time. Interchange in trade, art, and thought continued in spite of war.

But war also continued. The empires produced two other giants: Khosrow Parviz (583–628) in Iran and Heraclius (610–641) in Byzantium. Khosrow Parviz, who, ironically enough, was reinstated in 589 by the Byzantine emperor Maurice, declared war on Phocas, the centurion who had revolted against Maurice and had killed him in 603. For nineteen years the Sasanians swept everything before them. By 613 the Sasanians had captured Dara, Antioch, Aleppo, and Damascus. In 614, Khosrow Parviz sacked Jerusalem and carried away to Iran the "True Cross," a most cherished Christian possession, believed to be the actual cross on which Jesus was crucified. In 616, Khosrow marched into Alexandria. By 619, Sasanian troops once again, for the first time since Darius II, occupied Egypt. In the meantime, another Sasanian army had overrun all of Asia Minor and, after capturing Chalcedon in 617, was poised across the Bosporus from Constantinople.

In 610, the same year that Muhammad received the call from God to be His Messenger, Heraclius became emperor of Byzantium. For twelve years he suffered defeat at the hands of the Sasanians and spent his time preparing for war. In 622, the same year that Muhammad assumed the role of prophet-king in Medina, Heraclius struck back at the Sasanians. He won victory after victory against the vain and tired Sasanian army. In 628 he stood at the gates of Ctesiphon. Khosrow Parviz was killed by one of his own sons, and Heraclius got back all that he had lost, including the "True Cross." But it was an empty victory, for Iran and Byzantium had bled each other to exhaustion. Death was not long in coming. The blow was dealt by the Arabs, the inhabitants of the Arabian Peninsula to the south, who were vassals of both.

The wars between Sasanian Iran and Byzantium did not reach Arabia. It was considered an inhospitable territory by the civilized empires to the north. Moreover, the roaming bedouins, who comprised five-sixths of the population, proved uncontrollable. To protect themselves from periodic raids from the desert, the two empires had given autonomy to two strong tribes, who were supposed to keep the raiders in check. Thus, the Sasanians had allowed the Ghassanid tribe to be under the "protection" of the Byzantines, while the Byzantines, in turn, had accepted the same relationship between the Lakhmids of Hira and the Sasanians. South Arabia, however, especially Yaman, because of its milder climate, settled culture, and proximity, was under the suzerainty of Iran most of the time. In Sasanian inscriptions one finds the names of Hamir, Aiden, Yaman, and other places in south Arabia as tribute-paying regions. However, the Byzantines also had contact with them through Ethiopia and the Red Sea.

MECCA AND THE KA'BA

The most important city in Arabia along the trade route was Mecca, about fifty miles east of the Red Sea. Mecca owed its continuous existence to a well, *Zamzam;* its economic prosperity to the fact that it was on the spice route from south Arabia to the Mediterranean ports in the north; and its prominence to the existence of the *Ka'ba,* an ancient shrine that was the major religious center for most of the inhabitants of the peninsula.

Mecca's commerce flourished and was protected from Bedouin raids partly because of religion and partly because of alliances with the tribes. Its trade was international. The merchants of Mecca had secured safe-conduct for their caravans from Byzantium, Ethiopia, and Iran. They acted as agents for the different tribes and took their goods for sale in return for safe-conduct along the routes. They had established months of truce during which there would be no raids. This agreement was meticulously kept because it enabled the tribes to perform their pilgrimage to the holy city of Mecca.

The shrine called the Ka'ba is what makes Mecca a holy city. This cubic structure was considered holy because of a black stone embedded in one of its corners. Probably more than a thousand years before Christ, the Arabs of the area saw a meteor fall from the heavens and, because of this, regarded it as holy. They took this black stone and built it into the Ka'ba. Neighboring tribes began to come every year to worship the Ka'ba. In the course of centuries a pantheon grew around the Ka'ba; its worship became universal among the pagan Arabs of the peninsula, and an annual pilgrimage was established. By an unwritten law, all raiding was forbidden at this time and also during two other months, and tribes could come and go unmolested. The pilgrim changed his clothing for two pieces of white cloth without seams. Then he went to the great square in the center of which was the Ka'ba. He kissed the black stone and circled around the Ka'ba seven times, three times running and four times walking, each time kissing the black stone. He then recited a prayer in a location that in Islamic times came to be known as the "Place of Abraham," based on the tradition that it was Abraham who had built the Ka'ba in the first place. Then he went outside the city gate and approached two hills, Safa and Marwa. After climbing to the summit of each hill and reciting prayers seven times, the pilgrim returned to Mecca and walked around the Ka'ba again, kissing the Black Stone.

Then followed about six days of rest during which the pilgrim might engage in business transactions, games, and contests, and listen to poetry. On the eighth day, he walked to the nearby village of Mina and spent the night there. The next morning he walked to Mount 'Arafat and from there to Muzdafila to spend the night.

The tenth day was the high point of the pilgrimage, for it was the day of sacrifice followed by the great feast. On this day the pilgrim went to Mina and approached a temple with three huge pillars. This temple was probably the place of sacrifice for the appeasing of evil spirits and represented the great devil. Then he acquired an animal commensurate with his wealth and sacrificed it on the spot. This done, he put on his regular clothes and went back to Mecca for another round of barter before returning home.

Except for raiding and searching for water, this was the sum total of the Arab's religious, economic, and cultural life. The religious ritual at the Ka'ba is performed to this day by Muslims without much change.

Mecca grew as a metropolis. Arabs who made the annual pilgrimage brought their tribal gods and placed them in the enclosure around the Ka'ba. After the rituals of pilgrimage, the Arabs bartered goods, took part in athletic contests, including camel and horse racing, and exhibited their prowess in reciting poetry. The poet was at once a bard, an oracle, an historian, a moralist, and a man of mysterious power. He vilified rival tribes in satire and malediction and moved his own clansmen to courage, honor, and bravery. Only a few examples of pre-Islamic poetry have survived. Legend says that they were prize-winning poems that had been hung on the entrance to the Ka'ba—hence, they are called *mu'alliqat*, "the suspended ones." From the content of these surviving poems we may assume that at least three things were dear to the heart of the Arab—dark wine, a rushing charger, and a long day spent with a lovely damsel in a black tent in the desert.

The poet Imru' al-Qays boasts about his amorous exploits:

. . . Many's the fair veiled lady, whose tent few would think of seeking,
I've enjoyed sporting with, and not in a hurry either,
slipping past packs of watchmen to reach her, with a whole tribe
hankering after my blood, eager every man-jack to slay me,
what time the Pleiades showed themselves broadly in heaven
glittering like the folds of a woman's bejewelled scarf . . .

The poet Tarafa explains his philosophy of life:

. . . But for three things, that are the joy of a young fellow,
I assure you I wouldn't care when my deathbed visitors arrive—
first, to forestall my charming critics with a good swig
of crimson wine that foams when the water is mingled in;
second, to wheel at the call of the beleaguered a curved-shanked steed
streaking like the wolf of the thicket you've startled lapping the water;

and third, to curtail the day of showers, such an admirable season,
dallying with a ripe wench under the pole-propped tent,
her anklets and her bracelets seemingly hung on the boughs
of a pliant, unriven gum-tree or a castor-shrub.
So permit me to drench my head while there's still life in it,
for I tremble at the thought of the scant draught I'll get when I'm dead.

And the poet Zuhayr describes his despair:

Weary am I of the burdens of life; whoever lives
fourscore years, believe me you, grows very weary.
I have seen the Fates trample like a purblind camel; those they strike
they slay, those they miss are left to live on into dotage. . . .
I know what is happening today, and what passed before that yesterday,
but as for knowing what tomorrow will bring, there I'm utterly blind.[1]

Mecca therefore became the economic and cultural center of central and north Arabia. The political control of the city was in the hands of the Quraysh tribe. Indications are that at the time of Muhammad the Quraysh tribe had passed the zenith of its power and was losing its prestige and control. The disunity among the clans invited rival tribes from neighboring settlements to challenge their prestige. Nevertheless, the Quraysh were still in a position of power and influence. When the pilgrimage season was over, the tribes on the one hand scattered over the peninsula and engaged in the time-honored custom of raiding for water, wealth, and women. On the other hand, the leaders of the Quraysh tribe sent well-protected caravans north to Syria, Egypt, and Iran to sell their goods and replenish their stock for the business of the next season. Consequently, the curious among the Quraysh were not ignorant of the outside world. No doubt they were affected by the frequent wars between Byzantium and Iran and had learned how to play one against the other. As there were Jewish and Christian tribes and settlements in Arabia, the pagan Arabs no doubt knew something about their beliefs. Among the gods, the Arabs knew the name of Allah (the same as El-loh and Elohim of the Old Testament); and in Mecca a small group of people, known by the name of *Hanif,* seem to have had monotheistic beliefs.

---

[1]From A. J. Arberry, trans., in *Aspects of Islamic Civilization,* (Ann Arbor, 1967), pp. 20ff.

Chapter Two
Muhammad: The Messenger of Allah

In the setting briefly described above, and probably in the year A.D. 570, Muhammad was born in the neighborhood of Mecca. He belonged to the Quraysh tribe, and was a member of the minor and apparently less prosperous clan of Hashim. Before he was born, his father, Abdullah, died, and his mother, Amina, died when he was a child of six. He was cared for by his granduncle, Abdal-Muttalib, and after the latter's death by his uncle, Abu Talib.

The life of Muhammad, like the lives of other prophets, has probably been fictionalized by his adoring followers, who attempted to write a biography a century or so after his death. There is no record of the life of Muhammad until he reached the age of twenty-four, and even then the information is meager. Sifting and putting together the many stories about his early life, one may safely assume that he got a job with one of the business enterprises in which the Quraysh tribe was engaged. He probably travelled as a caravan boy to the Fertile Crescent, Egypt, and perhaps to Iran. Many a night he must have listened to the conversation between his masters and Christian and Jewish merchants. He must have had a feeling of frustration as he heard the Jews and Christians back their arguments by referring to a book while his own people had no book to quote. Early in life he must have wished his people also had a book. More than once we read in the Koran, "Now you have a book in Arabic," as though this were a most important thing.

In any case, whatever Muhammad did, it is fairly certain that it must have been in the field of business, for he became familiar with all aspects of trade. In the year 594, when Muhammad was twenty-four years old, a rich widow by the name of Khadija was looking for a man who knew enough about business to be employed as "manager." Khadija had lost her second husband and had decided to personally supervise his commercial activities. The fact that she could do so shows that in pre-Islamic Arabia women did not have such a lowly position as is often claimed. To be sure, for economic reasons some of the tribes practiced female infanticide, but nevertheless, women could not only hold property but could also be self-supporting if they so chose. A friend of the family recommended Muhammad for the job. He was honest, experienced, and also of the Quraysh tribe. Khadija employed him and a year later they were married—she being forty years of age and he only twenty-five. Since she was wealthy, had a superior social position, and was his employer, perhaps the tradition is correct in stating that it was she who proposed marriage.

Overnight, as it were, Muhammad was catapulted from a caravan boy to head of a prosperous business concern and became a man of influence in the Quraysh tribe. For twenty-five years he enjoyed a blissful life with Khadija. Two sons and four daughters were born, but unfortunately the sons died in infancy. He had a happy life at home and a prosperous business. Like other rich men of Mecca, he had also acquired and furnished one of the volcanic caves at Hira on the outskirts of Mecca and would go there to escape the heat and noise of the city in order to meditate.

THE CALL AND THE NIGHT OF POWER

In the year 610, toward the end of the month of Ramadan, while Muhammad was resting in the cave, it seemed to him that he heard a voice, which he later described as the "ringing of the bells." Ramadan was a month of fasting in pre-Islamic Arabia, as it is now in the world of Islam; and Muhammad, being a religiously inclined person, was very likely fasting. This voice said to him, "Recite in the name of the Lord who created, created man of a blood clot. . . ." He was frightened. According to tradition, Muhammad thought he had become "possessed" just like the poets he despised, so much so that he even thought of committing suicide. He must have been puzzled. In the name of which lord should he speak? After all, there were over 300 of them around the Ka'ba. He told his wife about this experience, and Khadija thereupon went to her cousin Waraqa, who was a Christian, and related Muhammad's experience. Waraqa is supposed to have exclaimed, ". . . and lo, he will be a prophet to this people. Bid him to be of good heart." Muhammad had received his call. The night of this momentous day was to be celebrated as "The Night of Power."

When, after a brief interval, Muhammad heard the voice again bidding him to "arise and warn," there was no question in his mind that he had been chosen by Allah to be His messenger. Khadija was the first to believe in him as the Prophet of Allah. From then on the revelations came to him at more frequent intervals, and the "voice" was identified by him as the voice of the angel Gabriel, who dictated the words of Allah to him.

For nearly ten years Muhammad preached the unity of God as opposed to the polytheism of the city of Mecca.

> Say: He is Allah, the One!
> Allah, the eternally Besought of All!
> He begetteth not nor was begotten.
> And there is none comparable unto Him (Koran, sura 112).

Muhammad's concept of Allah and the latter's habit of revealing Himself to prophets had come from the Jews and Christians. It was quite natural, therefore, for Muhammad to consider himself a prophet in the Judeo-Christian tradition and to speak about Adam, Noah, Abraham, Moses, Jonah, the Children of Israel, Mary, and Jesus. Like the prophets of old, he spoke against idolatry and preached the one living Allah who had power over all life. Allah was interested not only in the Jews and Christians, but also in the Arabs. It was He who had saved the Ka'ba from destruction at the hand of Abraha, the Abyssinian ruler of Yaman who had used elephants in his attack on Mecca. Since this had taken place around the last decade of the sixth century, it was still vivid to his hearers.

> Hast thou not seen how the Lord dealt with the owners of the elephant? Did he not bring their stratagem to nought, and send against them swarms of flying creatures, which pelted them with stones of baked clay, and made them like green crops devoured [by cattle]? (Koran, sura 105).

Muhammad took advantage of the months of pilgrimage when thousands came to Mecca. He preached on Allah the Compassionate and the Merciful, Allah who had sent Muhammad to dissuade them from idolatry and to warn them about the Day of Judgment and the resultant punishment or reward awaiting them in the afterlife. It was in these warnings that he waxed eloquent. He warned them about the time

> When the sun is overthrown,
> And when the stars fall,
> And when the hills are moved,
> And when the camels big with young are abandoned,
> And when the seas rise,
> And when souls are reunited . . .(Koran, sura 81).

He assured them that ". . . When the trumpet shall sound one blast and the earth with the mountains shall be lifted up and crushed with one crash. Then, on that day will the Event befall. . . . On that day ye will be exposed; not a secret of you will be hidden. . ." (Koran, sura 69).

Not many followed him. His wife, his cousin Ali, and his servant Zayd were among the first. There were a number of slaves who heeded his warning, but they did not have any influence. About the only man of consequence who accepted his message was Abu Bakr, a man of great stature among the Quraysh. The rest either ignored him or, worse, ridiculed him and said he was mad and possessed, as the following passages indicate.

> By the Star when it setteth,
> Your comrade erreth not, nor is deceived;
> Nor doth he speak of his own desire . . . (Koran, sura 53).

And, ". . . Thou art not, for thy Lord's favor unto thee, a madman." And again, "By the morning hours and by the night when it is stillest, thy Lord hath not forsaken thee nor doth he hate thee . . ." (Koran, sura 53).

However, the Quraysh did not look with pride at having a prophet in their midst. Muhammad's fellow businessmen saw in his preaching their own economic ruin. The spread of the new faith would destroy the pantheon around the Ka'ba and, indeed, the Ka'ba itself. Consequently, pilgrimage would be abandoned; and without pilgrimage, Mecca would cease to exist and the Quraysh would lose their economic prominence. As a matter of fact, until the discovery of oil in the third decade of the twentieth century, Arabia's greatest source of income had been from pilgrimage. Thus the old struggle between prophetic demands and business profits manifested itself. No doubt Muhammad understood that the prosperity of the Quraysh was at stake, but there was nothing he could do about it. He continued to preach his message with conviction and simplicity.

To escape persecution, a number of Muhammad's followers decided to migrate to Ethiopia, but this did not prove very successful. The temptation for Muhammad to gain success by compromise must have been great. At one time he agreed that perhaps three of the deities in the pantheon, Lot, Manat, and Uzza, all female, were genuine even though inferior to Allah. Later, however, he renounced this statement and proclaimed only Allah.

In this struggle, the life of Muhammad was not in danger. He belonged to the clan of Hashim and its leader, Abu Talib, was his uncle. Even though the old man never accepted the claim of his nephew, he nevertheless protected him. Instead, the brunt of the persecution was borne by the slaves who accepted Muhammad. According to the laws of pre-Islamic Arabia, slaves did not enjoy any protection. Perhaps it was to persuade the opposition to leave these slaves alone that the following revelation was received by Muhammad:

> Say: O disbelievers! I worship not that which ye worship; nor worship ye that which I worship; and I shall not worship that which ye worship, nor will ye worship that which I worship. Unto you your religion, and unto me my religion (Koran, sura 109).

The darkest year in the life of Muhammad was 619. In that year Abu Talib, his foster father, uncle, and protector, died. His place was taken by Abu Lahab, a fanatical foe of Muhammad's message, a person about whom Muhammad had received a revelation:

The power of Abu Lahab will perish, and he will perish. His wealth and gains will not exempt him. He will be plunged in flaming fire, and his wife, the wood carrier, will have upon her neck a halter of palm-fibre (Koran, sura 111).

To make matters worse, his beloved Khadija also died in that year. The loss of Khadija to Muhammad was like the loss of an anchor to a ship. From then on the tide of life tossed him to and fro. He had not taken a second wife during the twenty-five years Khadija was alive. During the ten years after her death, he married about as many wives. He married some of the women in order to protect and support them, for their husbands had given their lives for his cause, and custom demanded that he should marry them. Others he married for political reasons, to cement relations with other tribes. One gleans from the Koran and from tradition that he was never again as happy in his home life after Khadija's death.

THE MOVE TO MEDINA

For the first time, Muhammad thought of leaving Mecca and seeking his fortune elsewhere. He tried to explore the possibilities in the neighboring settlement of Taif, but the anger of the inhabitants of Taif towards him was much greater than he had imagined. He was nearly stoned to death and had to go into hiding. Only the intercession of some of the tolerant leaders of the Quraysh assured Muhammad enough protection for him to return to Mecca.

Fortunately for Muhammad, the city of Yathrib, some 200 miles to the north of Mecca, had developed problems that, in the end, proved beneficial to his cause. Yathrib had been originally settled by three Jewish tribes of Banu Nadir, Banu Qurayza, and Banu Qaynuqa. Later the city had been invaded by two heathen tribes of Aws and Khazraj, who claimed to have come from south Arabia. They usurped land from some of the Jews, reduced others to slavery, and made alliances with the rest. Later, differences arose between Aws and Khazraj over leadership and they fought each other. The insecurity resulting from this internecine struggle became so intense that no one felt safe to go about his business. No doubt the more level-headed among the two tribes felt that the dissension should be ended, but no one had enough prestige to do this. Clearly this was work for an arbiter who would have to come from outside. Muhammad became the much-needed arbiter. The choice of Muhammad was not entirely accidental. In the first place, the Yathribites were familiar with the message of Muhammad. Their fellow townsmen, the Jews, had told them about Moses and their prophets and had assured them of the coming of a Messiah. Consequently, Muhammad's words did not fall on unfamiliar ears. Furthermore, it must be recalled that Yathrib was located on the trade route between Yaman and Damascus, and that the city was the economic rival of Mecca. The Yathribites knew about the feud between Muhammad and the other leaders of the Quraysh. They saw in Muhammad not only a new prophet, but also a man of ability who was familiar with the inner councils of the Quraysh, and who could lead them in their rivalry against the city of Mecca.

In 620, six Khazrajites met Muhammad and held a preliminary conversation. The next year they appeared with more converts to the new faith. By 622, a substantial number from Yathrib, both Aws and Khazraj, invited Muhammad to come to their city. Under the circumstances, Muhammad had no real choice, reluctant as he must have been to leave the city of his birth. He sent a number of his followers in small groups, among whom were such wealthy Quraysh men as Umar and Uthman. He himself, together with Abu Bakr, his father-in-law, Ali, his cousin and son-in-law, and his two wives, slipped out of Mecca unnoticed and arrived in Yathrib about September 24, 622. This was called *Hijra*, or the emigration. Some seventeen years later Umar, as the caliph of Islam, designated this year as the year one in the Muslim calendar. Even though Muhammad had concluded a treaty with the Yathribites, known as the Treaty of Al-Akaba, it took courage for the Meccans to take their wealth, women, and children and settle among strange and enemy tribes. Henceforth, these people were called *Muhajirun*, or emigrés, while the members of the Aws and Khazraj tribes who had welcomed Muhammad became known as *Ansar*, or helpers. In time the city was no longer called Yathrib, but *Madinat al-Nabi*, the City of the Prophet, or simply Medina.

THE MERGING OF GOVERNMENT AND RELIGION

Three major problems faced Muhammad in the new city. The first was that in Medina he was not only a prophet of Allah, but also the head of a state. He had to see to the welfare of the community, act as judge, legislate, and organize his followers. It has been suggested that in Medina his role as prophet was overshadowed by his duties as a political leader. Perhaps it is nearer the truth to say that in his mind and in the opinion of his followers, the two offices were combined. According to the Old Testament, when Moses spoke, regardless of the subject, it was not Moses but rather Yahweh who was actually speaking. In the same way, the legislation of Muhammad as the political leader, and his various judgments and declarations, were considered not merely the declarations of the man Muhammad, but also the solemn commands of Allah. In his person, as prophet-king, government and religion merged; and the spiritual and the temporal became one and inseparable. Islam became a theocratic institution and has remained so, at least in theory, to this day.

Consequently, the revelations of Muhammad in Medina do not have the simplicity nor the poetical beauty of those in Mecca. They tend to be repetitious and verbose. Whereas the revelations in Mecca warned and beseeched, those in Medina have a tendency to command and threaten. Going through an index of legislation in the Koran, one finds such subjects as ablutions, adultery, almsgiving, arbitration, booty, contracts, divorce, drink, fighting, forgiving, general conduct, good, idolatry, justice, marriage, orphans, parents, war, women, worship, and a host of other rules, spiritual, moral, and temporal. All of these are commandments of Allah for the regulation of life in the Islamic community. Throughout the centuries, believers from diverse nationalities have had to struggle with these laws by interpreting them time and again, but change them they could not. In a theocracy, the religion and the state are inseparable. The modern Muslim is caught on the horns of a dilemma. On the one hand, as a Muslim he has identified his nationality with his religion. On the other hand, as a modern, he wants a society in which religion and state are separate. The choice is a difficult and a revolutionary one. Even in Turkey, where the choice has been made and a "secular" state has been established, it has been difficult for the people to adjust themselves to the new concept. The modern claim is that a "Turk" may be a Muslim, a Christian, a Jew, an agnostic, or even an atheist; but in the consciousness of the people a "Turk" is still synonymous with a Muslim. All the non-Muslim citizens of Turkey are in a class by themselves and are not really Turks. Consequently, a modern-day young man who calls himself a Muslim may or may not be a religious man. In his mind, religion and nationality are so intermingled in the concept of Islam that he may be loyal to Islam as a political institution without having any purely religious loyalties.

THE JEWISH QUESTION

The second problem that confronted Muhammad in Medina was what might be termed the "Jewish Question." It has been mentioned that the city of Medina had a large Jewish population. It has also been mentioned that Muhammad considered himself a prophet in the Judeo-Christian tradition. Historians agree that Muhammad had every expectation of being welcomed among the Jews and the Christians. He felt somewhat closer to Judaism than to Christianity; and in Mecca he had already adopted many of the Jewish practices, such as observance of fast days, prayer toward Jerusalem, and so forth. When he arrived in Medina he expected the Jews to accept him as a prophet and help him root out paganism. In this he was sorely disappointed. Not only did the Jews of Medina refuse to accept him as a prophet, but they mocked him as pretentious and ridiculed his lack of knowledge of the Old Testament. They accused him of garbling the Scriptures and refused to accept an Arab as the Messiah. Muhammad, nevertheless, persisted in his hope.

> Oh ye who believe, Be mindful of your duty
> to Allah and put faith in His Messenger.
> He will give you twofold of His mercy . . . (Koran, sura 57).

He also reminded the Jews that they did not have a monopoly on the blessings of God. "That the People of Scripture [i.e., Jews and Christians] may know that they control naught of the bounty of Allah, but that the bounty is in Allah's hand to give to whom He will" (Koran, sura 57).

When these and similar pleas were met with stubborn resistance, Muhammad retaliated by accusing the Jews of perverting the word of God and later resorted to massacre and banishment. It is difficult to determine from this distance in time whether the Jews of Medina and its environs remained neutral in the struggle that was going on between Muhammad and the Meccans (to be discussed below) or resorted to fifth column activities. It is certain, however, that Muhammad accused them of "siding with the confederates" (that is, Meccans and bedouin tribes). In about 625, Muhammad banished the Jewish tribe of Banu Nadir from Medina. Two years later some 600 of the Banu Qurayza were slaughtered and the rest sent into exile. In 629, the Jews of Khaybar, an oasis north of Medina, were expelled. In each case their lands were given to the increasing number of outsiders who had flocked to Medina to join Muhammad.

It was perhaps because of his experience with the Jews that Muhammad decided to chart an independent course and organize an Arab religious community. He did not reject the Judeo-Christian tradition, but instead claimed that the Jews and the Christians had disobeyed the commandments of God, and, in some instances, had garbled the Scriptures. He who, according to Jewish custom, used to pray facing north toward Jerusalem one day abruptly turned south toward Mecca. Since that time all Muslims pray facing Mecca with the conviction that the Ka'ba was built by Abraham at the behest of Allah. As the Ka'ba had been defiled by the presence of pagan gods and goddesses, the mission of Muhammad was to destroy the idols and restore the worship of Allah. Saturday and Sunday being Jewish and Christian holy days, Muhammad chose Friday. The Jews used to call the people to the synagogue for prayer by the blowing of a horn, and the Christians by the ringing of a bell. Muhammad instituted the use of the human voice. He introduced enough changes in prayer, fasting, dietary laws, and other rituals to constitute a separate and distinct religious community.

THE WARS WITH MECCA

The third and the most important problem that Muhammad had to solve was his dealing with the Meccans. Perhaps the thought had occurred to him in Mecca, but certainly very early in Medina he had decided that he was not going to be like Jesus and some of the other prophets who had preached but left the fate of the message to their followers and God. Like Moses, he decided to establish the rule of Allah on earth in the form of an independent state with laws handed down by Allah Himself. This could be done only through diplomacy, war, and conquest. During the ten years in Medina, from 622 until his death in 632, Muhammad engaged in war practically every year. He personally participated in most of them. These wars were explicitly for the purpose of imposing the rule of Islam on the Arabs. Since the most powerful antagonist was the city of Mecca, Muhammad gave this city his special attention.

Almost immediately after his arrival in Medina, Muhammad had to provide for the welfare of his followers from Mecca as well as for his supporters in Medina. For this he had ordered sorties against Meccan caravans. In 624, the second year of the Hijra, in Ramadan, the month of truce, he learned about a rich caravan led by Abu Sufyan headed for Mecca, and decided to attack it. Abu Sufyan, the head of an important clan of Quraysh, had heard about the plan and had sent to Mecca for aid. Some 900 Meccans and 300 Muslims met at Badr, about twenty miles southwest of Medina.

The battle was brief, small, and desperate, but Muhammad won. Some European historians have emphasized the fact that, as battles go, this was quite insignificant, with a total of only some sixty casualties on both sides. But Muslim historians have called it "the battle of battles." It was indeed one of the most important engagements in the history of Islam. If Muhammad had lost, very likely Islam would have been nipped in the bud. The victory, however, confirmed Muhammad's leadership, and "proved" that he was fighting for Allah. "Allah had already given you the victory at Badr," says the Koran. The victory was believed to be a miracle and the news traveled across the desert from tent to tent. Muslims in subsequent battles were convinced that they were fighting for Allah. They believed that if they died they had "witnessed" and would go to paradise; if they lived they could partake of the booty. This first battle became the pattern for the future in which the soldiers of Allah would repeat the "witness" and go into battle with contempt for death.

The Meccans, however, could not let the defeat go unavenged. The next year Abu Sufyan marched at the head of 3,000 men. In most of the desert battles, the women would come along to encourage their men in battle. Muhammad, it is reported, would choose one of his wives by lot to accompany him in each campaign. When the two sides met at Uhud, Muhammad got a sound beating and was wounded. Apparently the defeat was caused by a disobedient Medinese tribe. In any case, the Meccans, for reasons that are not clear, did not pursue their victory; and Muhammad recovered from both the wound and the defeat.

Muhammad could not succeed in unifying the Arabs under Islam without Mecca, and the Meccans could not afford to have Muhammad's soldiers raiding their caravans. Once more, in 627, Abu Sufyan came toward Medina with a large army. Muhammad decided to stay in the city and defend the one access to it. Even this would have been most difficult had it not been for the advice of Salman the "Persian," probably an Arab orderly of a Persian officer, to dig a trench. This Muhammad did, to the disgust of his followers. The Meccans, who had had no experience with this type of warfare, were equally disgusted with such a cowardly method. Cowardly or not, it was effective; and after a week of reciting poetry derogatory of Muhammad, the Meccans lifted the siege and went home. This battle has been called "the Battle of the Trench."

The war was costing the Meccans a great deal of money, not to mention the disruption and loss of trade. Muhammad, on the other hand, did not have much to lose and felt that time was on his side. Furthermore, his shift of the direction of prayer from Jerusalem to Mecca and his respect for the Ka'ba had made it evident that Muhammad regarded Mecca as holy and had incorporated pilgrimage to Mecca into his new religion. Thus, Mecca continued to retain its economic predominance as a place of pilgrimage; and with this assurance, the Meccans did not have any reason to continue the warfare. Muhammad, for his part, used good judgment and allowed diplomacy to replace the sword. In 628, he concluded the peace of Hudaybiyah, which put the Muslims and the Meccans on an equal footing and won permission for the Muslims to make the pilgrimage to Mecca.

This treaty ended the war between the two cities. A number of important people from the Quraysh, among them Khalid ibn-al-Walid and Amr ibn-al-As, who were destined to become two of the famous generals of Islam, submitted to Muhammad's leadership. Two years after the treaty of Hudaybiyah, which was to have lasted for ten years, Muhammad found an excuse to approach Mecca with his army. He probably had assurance that the Meccans would not oppose him. The new religion, with its veneration for the Ka'ba, enhanced the economic position of the Quraysh. Abu Sufyan himself came and offered his allegiance. Others followed and Muhammad entered his native city as a victor. He ordered the destruction of all the idols around the Ka'ba and proclaimed it forbidden to pagans. He was magnanimous to his defeated fellow tribesmen. Much to the relief of the Medinese, he decided to go back to Medina and continue using it as his political capital. Mecca, however, remained the religious capital of Islam.

Muhammad's work was not finished. It was his purpose to unify Arabia. He continued his wars of conquest. Soon delegations from all parts of Arabia—Oman, Hadramut, and even Yaman—came to accept Islam. The ceremony was simple—a verbal confession and the payment of *Zakah*, a religious tax, were sufficient to initiate a whole tribe into the new religion. Whether they came out of conviction or expediency is difficult to judge.

In 632, the tenth year of the Hijra, Muhammad made what became his last pilgrimage to Mecca. He was the acknowledged Messenger of Allah and the Lord of Arabia. It is said that he made a speech so moving that it remained in the memory of his hearers and has come to be known as his "Farewell Address."

In this speech he told his followers that every Muslim is a brother unto every other Muslim. Thus he abolished tribal loyalty and substituted loyalty to Islam. He also admonished his followers to consider ties of faith more binding than ties of blood. He virtually abolished raiding, by forbidding his followers to appropriate anything that belonged to their brothers unless willingly given to them. Three months later (June 8, 632) he died in the arms of his favorite wife, Ayisha, and was buried where he died, under the floor of her room.

Muhammad left behind a religious community that was at the same time an armed encampment. Its house of worship was also a court of law as well as a military command headquarters. He established a religion without a hierarchy or clergy; where every believer was also a military conscript; and where the leader in worship was also the commander in battle. Tradition says that he wrote letters to the potentates of his time and invited them to embrace Islam. There is no evidence, however, that Muhammad intended his message to go beyond Arabia. He did what he set out to do: now the Arabs also had a prophet and a Book. He tried to establish a brotherhood of Muslims; but he was not interested in the brotherhood of all peoples of the world, unless the whole world would accept Islam. He said, "I am a man like you," and as a man he had his strengths and weaknesses. He had such an inspiring personality that, years later, his followers studied every detail of his conduct and every word that he had uttered. His life served as a model for personal piety and governmental policy for all generations.

Chapter Three
Islam: The Message of Allah

The chief designation for Muhammad is the "Messenger of Allah." The Muslims have always considered the message to be of greater significance than Muhammad the Messenger. Muhammad is not central to Islam as Jesus is to Christianity. Strictly speaking, Muslims are not the people of Muhammad in the way that Christians are the people of Christ. Rather, they are the people of the Book—the Koran, which is the message of Allah.

This message is called *Islam* and those who accept it are called *Muslims.* The word "Islam" is derived from the three-consonant root *slm,* which means "submission." Another meaning of the word is *peace,* because peace follows the surrender (submission) of an enemy in war. Hence the Arabic greeting in Islamic countries, *salam alaykum,* means "Peace be unto you." Some ultramodern Muslims of the twentieth century claim that the meaning of Islam is "the religion of peace." Historically, however, the meaning of Islam has been "the religion of submission"—submission to the will of Allah. The grammatical construction *Islam,* based on the root *slm,* means "the submitting." *Muslim* means "he who has submitted," *muslima* means "she who has submitted." In non-Arab Islamic countries the term *mosalman* is used instead of *muslim.*

By this definition, anyone who has submitted to the will of God is a Muslim, for the word simply means that he has submitted. According to Islamic tradition, the first person who submitted was Abraham. In one sense, for example, a Jew is a "muslim" and so is a Christian. This broad definition of Islam is perfectly legitimate and may, someday, become an instrument of ecumenicity. Up to now, however, only a small number of individuals throughout the history of Islam have thought in such inclusive terms. The narrower definition of Islam is the more historically accurate one. Islam, therefore, is surrender to the will of Allah as revealed to Muhammad, the Messenger of Allah, and the head of the state.

The religion that goes by the name of Islam contains the terms of the surrender of the individual to the will of Allah. Man agrees to live under the jurisdiction of Allah as revealed through His Messenger, which means that all his actions are regulated by the laws promulgated by Allah. Before Islam became involved in theology and philosophy, it dealt with law. As a theocracy, Islam has always considered law as the most important factor in religion. The study of the laws of Allah, *Shari'a*, is the most important discipline in the world of Islam. In the beginning, a simple theology provided a background for the law. The outlines of the simple theology and rules of conduct had taken shape before the death of Muhammad and may be found in the pages of the Koran.

The terms of the "submission" contain at least ten articles. Five of these are articles of belief, and five are articles of practice or religious duties.

ARTICLES OF BELIEF

1. Doctrine of the Unity of God. The first and the greatest dogma of Islam is: There is (absolutely) no god save Allah. The unity of God is the cornerstone of Islamic faith. Without this, everything falls apart and is devoid of meaning. The Koran rejects the Christian Trinity as blasphemy. Indeed, the idea that God might have a partner is considered to be an unforgivable sin. Allah is the supreme creator, lawgiver, judge, sustainer, provider, and ordainer. Allah has many attributes. He is compassionate and merciful, but these seem to be overshadowed by his majesty, might, and power. Allah is best known through His names, which seem to be synonymous with His attributes. The Muslim rosary has ninety-nine beads, which represent as many names of Allah. Some of these names are "victor," "opener," "subduer," and "bestower." There is no doubt that this uncompromising belief in one powerful and transcendent God is the main source of the strength of Islam. The Koran, like the scriptures of other religions, contains its share of contradictions about God. Later Muslim theologians wrestled with these problems and they still do. In Islam, however, such discussions have been considered as intellectual pastimes and are not vital to everyday life. The believer, no matter how intellectually alert, has a sense of resignation (Islam) and is content with things as they are, or appear to be.

2. The Doctrine of Prophethood. This is the belief that of all the prophets that God sent for the guidance of the people, Muhammad is the last. After Him there will be no other. He is sometimes considered the "finisher of the prophets." Furthermore, all the prophets sent by God are within the Judeo-Christian tradition, beginning with Adam, continuing on to Noah, Abraham,

Moses, David, Jesus, and ending with Muhammad. The founders of other religions are not mentioned in the Koran and are therefore ignored by Muslim theologians and historians. Assuming that God sent so many prophets at short intervals for the guidance of Man, it seems rather odd that He would not send another one for nearly 1,400 years. Perhaps the early Muslims, like the early Christians, did not expect the world to last so long.

The Koran mentions four major prophets with special titles. It speaks for the personal humility of Muhammad in that his title is the most modest. In the Koran Abraham is called "the friend of God"; Moses is called "the spokesman of God"; Jesus is called "the spirit of God" and "the word of God"; Muhammad is called "the messenger of God."

3. The Doctrine of the Book.   Next to the doctrine of the unity of God, this is by far the most important doctrine in Islam. In Christianity, the New Testament is important mainly because it contains the biography of Jesus Christ, who is at the center of the faith. On the other hand, in Islam Muhammad is important mainly because he is the bearer of the Book (Koran), which is at the center of the faith.

When God sent prophets He gave each one a Book. Each Book contained practically all that man needed to know for his guidance in that age. Sometimes God had one of His angels dictate the Book to the prophet. It is believed that the angel Gabriel dictated the last Book of God, the Koran, to the last prophet, Muhammad. The Koran, according to orthodox Muslims, is the uncreated word of God and existed with God when He created the universe. Being the incarnate Word of God, the Koran cannot be duplicated, either in the perfection of its contents or in the excellence of its language. Indeed, about the only miracle attributed to Muhammad is the miracle of the Koran.

All ideas and institutions, beliefs, and practices, must conform to the Koran. The Muslims speak of the Koran as having "descended" to Muhammad from time to time. Muhammad, therefore, is not the author of the Koran. God is the author and Muhammad, as it were, is the recorder. The Muslims are followers of the Koran, the Book, in which the terms of Islam, the submission, are inscribed. They are not followers of Muhammad and, in that sense, do not like to be called Muhammadans. Since the Koran was dictated to Muhammad in the Arabic language, the orthodox have always frowned at the idea of translating it. The vast majority of the Muslims of the world do not understand Arabic. But since almost all Muslims have adopted the Arabic alphabet for their language, they are at least able to read the Koran even though they don't understand most of it. It is believed that there is merit in repeating the actual words of Allah.

According to Muslims, the Old and New Testaments also have "descended" from Heaven and were given to Moses, the prophets, and Jesus. Inasmuch as the Koran is the last and the latest Word of God, it supersedes all others and is more relevant to the problems of modern man.

The Doctrine of the Book has contributed to both tolerance and rigidity in Islam. It made the Muslims tolerant of Jews and Christians and, later, of other religions. According to this doctrine, Islam has divided all humanity into two categories: people with a Book and people without a Book. Jews and Christians are "people of the Book." These people are not to be forced to accept Islam. If persuasion does not avail, they should be allowed to remain in their own faiths under the protection of Islam. As a result of this doctrine, Jews and Christians have lived among Muslims with a good deal of religious freedom. In fact, whenever Jews were persecuted in Christian Europe, they went to the Muslim countries and there lived in peace. The Doctrine of the Book is the basis for what became known as the "millet" system, or a system of autonomous communities in the Ottoman Empire. It must be noted that "millet" is a term applied to religious groups, although it is sometimes used to denote political nationality.

For the modern Muslim, however, the millet system has been vexing as well as a source of embarrassment. It is evident that the idea of nationality, imported from the West, is political in nature and makes it possible for people of different religions to belong to the same nation; but it also clashes with the Islamic idea of religion as the basis of nationality. Muslim countries of the twentieth century that, on the one hand, want to be democratic and extend equality to all citizens and at the same time be Muslims, have found themselves tangled in inconsistencies. For example, in a number of Muslim countries the millet system is preserved side by side with a modern constitution that declares equality for all. Indeed, in some countries non-Muslims cannot aspire to high positions; and even with all the good intentions of the modern Muslim, non-Muslims are second-class citizens.

It was stated above that the Doctrine of the Book has also contributed to the rigidity of Islam. The Koran, being the uncreated Word of God, has become a closed book. No one may question its authority or study it critically. Any attempt to try to trace the development of religious and legal ideas in the Koran is considered sacrilegious. Nevertheless, it is doubtful that all of the Koran was written during Muhammad's lifetime. Moreover, there is no certainty that all of the Koran was originally contained in one volume. In 651, there were enough variations of the different sections of the Koran to induce Caliph Uthman to appoint a commission to produce an authorized version. The result was that Uthman canonized one version and reputedly destroyed all others. Apparently he was not successful in destroying all, for by 933, which is the date of the last canonization, there were admittedly seven different readings.

4. The Doctrine of the Final Judgment. The most eloquent verses of the Koran deal with eschatological topics such as Heaven, Hell, Day of Judgment, Resurrection, and also a faint idea of Purgatory and Limbo. In these concepts Muslims have practically the same views as Christians. However, Muhammad is not considered to be an intercessor. Only "those who repent and believe and are righteous in act" and those who are martyrs for the faith will go to Paradise.

5. The Doctrine of Angels and Jinns. These are mentioned in the Koran as populating heaven and earth. Angels are creatures of God who continuously worship Him and do His bidding. Their duties are to record men's actions, be witnesses on the Day of Judgment, hold God's throne, and generally be useful to those whom God favors. Jinns are also created by God and some of them are believers. There are some jinns who have rebelled and have turned into *shaytans*, "satan." In this form they try to lead people astray and to oppose the Prophet. Their leader is Iblis, who was an angel but fell from grace by refusing to pay homage to Adam.

ARTICLES OF PRACTICE

To the Muslim, these are more important than the articles of faith. Islamic disputation is centered more on practice and observance than on theological or philosophical speculation. Although the above articles, especially the unity of God and the Book, set the tone, the articles of practice are considered the pillars of Islam.

1. The Witness. Every Muslim must make a profession of faith or bear witness to his beliefs. This, in fact, is the creed of Islam in one sentence: "There is no God except Allah; Muhammad is the Messenger of Allah." This states the unity of God and is a reminder of the terms of submission brought by the Messenger of Allah. This is the most oft-repeated sentence in the world of Islam. It is whispered in the ear of the newborn child, it is repeated by him throughout his life, and it is the last sentence uttered when he is laid in the grave. It is used to call the faithful to prayer, and it has served as the battle cry of Muslim soldiers in all the wars of Islam. The utterance of this sentence will admit a nonbeliever into the fold of Islam.

2. Prayer. A Muslim, male or female, must pray five times a day—morning, noon, midafternoon, sunset, and night. The prayer must be in Arabic and it must be performed toward Mecca. There are certain postures that one assumes during prayer, such as standing erect, bowing with hands on knees, sitting on haunches, and prostrating oneself. It is preferable to pray in a mosque, but it is not mandatory. One has to pray wherever convenient, at home, place of work, or mosque. There is very little corporate worship in Islam. There is no such thing as "membership" in a mosque. Islam does not have a priesthood, there is no ordination rite, nor is there a well-defined hierarchy. The religious leaders who perform marriage, conduct funerals, and sometimes preach are called *imam* in Arabic-speaking countries, *mulla* in Iran, and *hojja* in Turkey. The more educated ones are called *ulama*, "learned." They usually teach in schools and theological seminaries. In the Muslim world seminaries train not only preachers but also lawyers and teachers of Arabic, the language of the Koran.

3. Giving. "Giving," not specifically almsgiving, is the third pillar of Islam. There are two types of giving in Islam. The first is the voluntary almsgiving that is common to all religions. The other is *Zakah*, an obligatory offering tantamount to a tax levy. During the time when the Islamic supranational state was in power, this tax was collected from all Muslims. It was used by the government both for war and peace. Customarily, $2\frac{1}{2}$ percent of a person's income was expected, though this was never uniformly enforced.

Zakah was an obligation imposed only on Muslims. The "people of the Book" paid a different type of tax called *jizya*, or head tax. This was paid for protection. Since all wars in Islam were theoretically for the expansion and propagation of Islam, non-Muslims would not be recruited for the army. In place of military service, non-Muslims had to pay this special tax. In the absence of any mosque organization or community, all voluntary giving was collected by the government. These offerings, which were collected in the form of real estate as well as cash, were, and still are, kept in a special account called *waqf* ("religious endowment") by the government. All modern Muslim states have a bureau or a ministry of religious endowments.

4. Fasting. This is carried out during the month of Ramadan (or Ramazan), the ninth of the Muslim calendar, which was holy for the Arabs before Islam and continued as such perhaps because Muhammad received his call in this month. The fasting begins at dawn usually after a meal and ends at dusk every day when the fast is broken. The nights should be spent in keeping vigil and in reading the Koran. In most Muslim countries all offices are closed in the morning during this month, and sometimes no restaurants are permitted to remain open.

5. Pilgrimage. Every Muslim is enjoined, if he can afford it, to go to Mecca at least once in his lifetime. The person who has made the pilgrimage, or *hajj*, is given the title of *al-hajj* and in non-Arab countries, *haji*. The rituals of pilgrimage in and around Mecca are the same as they were long before Islam.[1] Hundreds of thousands of Muslims from all parts of the world make this pilgrimage every year. There is no question that the experience is very uplifting for the faithful and the spectacle very impressive. Furthermore, the *hajj* has given, and continues to give, a sense of solidarity to the Muslims of the world.

6. Holy War. Some Muslims have elevated holy war, *jihad*, as the sixth pillar of Islam. This concept has caused a great deal of misunderstanding among non-Muslims and even among Muslims. The meaning of the word is "struggle"—namely, struggle against the forces of ungodliness in one's soul or in the community. Since all wars in early Islam were considered to be struggles against the enemies of God, jihad has been identified with war. There are numerous references in the Koran to war and the Muslim's duty to fight. "Warfare is ordained for you, though it is hateful to you; but it may happen that ye hate what is good for you" (Koran, sura 2:216). "Then when the sacred months have passed, slay the idolaters wherever ye find them, and take them [captive], and besiege them, and prepare for them each ambush. But if they repent and establish worship and pay the poor-due, then leave their way free. Lo! Allah is forgiving, merciful" (Koran, sura 9:5). To these and other verses like them Islam owes its great expansion. Indeed,

[1]See p. 25–26.

all land not within the domain of Islam was considered the domain of war. In more recent years, however, the faithful have not responded to the call. Many a modern nationalist uses "jihad" in the sense of struggle against poverty, disease, ignorance, as well as colonialism and imperialism.

7. *Good Works.*   In addition to the above articles on faith and practice, there is a general category in Islam called "good works." There are laws against gambling, usury, using alcohol, and eating pork. Muslims are enjoined to take care of orphans, to be kind, to deal honestly, and to forgive. In general, a Muslim is encouraged, wherever he is, to do that which is permitted, and to refrain from that which is forbidden, and leave the rest to "Allah the Compassionate and the Merciful."

Chapter Four
The Advent of the Islamic State

THE FIRST FOUR CALIPHS

Abu Bakr (632–634)
Umar (634–644)
Uthman (644–656)
Ali (656–661)

THE PROBLEM OF SUCCESSION

The problem of succession after the death of Muhammad, coupled with the sudden expansion that produced enormous intercultural conflicts and administrative difficulties, caused great havoc in the newly created Islamic state. The rivalry among the claimants for the position of caliph was so strong that it resulted in a bitter civil war only twenty-five years after the Prophet's death. The conflict was so intense that three of the first four caliphs were assassinated. It is no exaggeration to say that the struggle has continued, in one form or another, to this day. According to an eminent Muslim historian of the twelfth century, "No other issue in Islam has caused more bloodshed than the caliphate."

The death of Muhammad on June 8, 632, was actually the passing of two persons: the Prophet of Allah and the head of state. Since Muhammad was the last of the prophets, he could not have a successor. The head of state, however, had to have a successor or caliph. Even before Muhammad's body had been interred, a bitter struggle arose over the succession. Because Muhammad had not designated anyone, there was more than one claimant for the position. The Medinese, who had supported the Prophet all along, felt that they deserved the honor of providing the caliph. The Meccans, on the other hand, who, with the Prophet, were members of the influential Quraysh tribe, believed that the Arabs would "recognize authority only in the Quraysh."

Umar, who eventually became the second caliph, was present at a crucial meeting of the two groups and told the story a few years later. Many ideas had been proposed, among them a confederation of the tribal leaders. Gradually the discussion turned into heated argument, and the parties were about to come to blows. At this point, according to a prearranged plan, Umar nominated Abu Bakr and swore allegiance to him; the other Meccans followed. Then the not-too-solid ranks of the Medinese broke, and they did the same. Umar ends his narrative by saying, "We jumped on Sa'd ibn-Ubada [the man whom the Medinese wanted for the office] and someone said that we had killed him. I said, 'God killed him!' "

There was a third group that was almost forgotten in the struggle for leadership. This was the immediate family of the Prophet: Fatima, the Prophet's only surviving daughter, her husband Ali, and a number of their followers. They believed that Ali, the cousin and son-in-law of the Prophet and the consort of the daughter of Muhammad, was the natural and rightful successor. Later it was claimed that Muhammad had indeed made a Will appointing Ali but that the Will had been destroyed. It is reported that Fatima made a moving speech on behalf of her husband but it was of no avail and Ali paid allegiance to Abu Bakr.

ABU BAKR

Among the Quraysh, Abu Bakr was one of the oldest Muslims both in age and in faith to Islam. He was both a close friend and the father-in-law of Muhammad. His short rule of a little over two years was spent in reunifying Arabia under Islam. It will be remembered that Muhammad was a trader and was familiar with the difficulties that merchants were having among themselves and with the bedouin tribes. For these problems he had solutions that he put in motion in Medina. One was the principle of economic egalitarianism forbidding the exploitation of the poor and the weak by the rich and the strong. He preached a more equitable distribution of wealth. Secondly, he tried to replace the allegiance of the Arabs to their particular tribes by an allegiance to Islam. He preached the brotherhood of Muslims and established the community, or *ummah*, of Islam. This is a very important concept, and the word appears in every discussion of Islam both past and present. It should not be confused with the concept of "nation." Ummah is the brotherhood of Muslims rather than the brotherhood of humanity.

The allegiance of the Arab tribes to Islam proved to be superficial.

With the Prophet gone, the tribes began to follow their old ways. They severed the strongest bond that tied them to Islam, which was the obligatory paying of the Zakah tax. For a people who were not used to paying taxes, Zakah was an economic burden that hampered their freedom. Some tribes chose to forget what little they had accepted of Islam. Other tribes, not to be outdone by the Quraysh, claimed prophets of their own. To Abu Bakr and his advisors this was intolerable, and they decided to meet the challenge with force.

The Meccans who, under the canopy of Islam, had virtual control of Medina, waged war on the rest of Arabia. Khalid ibn-Walid was the commander in these wars. His brilliant generalship was such that one by one the tribes were subdued. By the time Abu Bakr lay on his deathbed in 634, the victorious army of Khalid had followed some of the belligerent tribes into Syria and had defeated a detachment of the Byzantine army.

UMAR

To make sure that no struggle would arise over the succession, Abu Bakr, before his death, named Umar as his successor. This ambitious and energetic man, who had reached the top position at the age of forty-three, was not only one of the early believers but was also a father-in-law of the Prophet. His full name was Umar ibn-al-Khattab. Under his inspired leadership, the Arabs of the desert erupted like a volcano and consumed everything before them. In the course of a decade they defeated the Byzantine Empire and spread westward to the Mediterranean and southward to Egypt. At the same time, another branch of their armies conquered the Sasanid Empire and advanced to central Iran. This spectacular and speedy victory by a subject people over two of the largest empires of the time has baffled historians and has, therefore, been the subject of much speculation. And yet, Rome was destroyed by the Huns, and the Chinese were conquered by the Mongols. The reasons are not difficult to find.

Muhammad's vision of community, so far as can be determined, did not extend beyond the Arabs. Abu Bakr had his hands full most of the time he was caliph, so that actually he was quite reluctant to order Khalid to go into Iraq and Syria. But Khalid had already penetrated into Syria, and Abu Bakr acquiesced to what had already been accomplished. Umar, however, consciously planned and led the eruption.

Umar, who did so much to spread the new faith, was the St. Paul of Islam. But unlike St. Paul, who appealed to Rome for protection, Umar challenged and defeated the Byzantines and Sasanids. Umar was an Arab, a devout follower of Islam, and a confirmed believer in the theocracy for which he was Commander of the Believers. As such he wanted to establish an Arab empire with Arabia as the center of power. To implement this purpose, Umar banished all non-Muslims, even Christians and Jews, from Arabia so that Arabia would be completely Muslim land.

Fortunately for Islam, Umar was not alone. Khalid ibn-Walid and Amr ibn-al-As, two of the most talented generals in the history of warfare, were as young as Umar and equally enthusiastic. Aside from their personal faith in Islam, they saw in it the means for a great adventure. Furthermore, Umar and his lieutenants were impelled to lead a campaign outside of Arabia. The restless bedouins who had followed the banner of Muhammad had shown their fickleness by abandoning the new religion after the Prophet's death. Abu Bakr had to subdue them again, but they were still restless. As Muslims, they were not allowed to fight each other nor raid each others' tents. Raiding had been the habit of generations and could not be given up so easily. So Umar encouraged them to fight non-Muslims outside Arabia, thereby ridding himself of bedouin intransigence at home and affording the new government the prospects of victory abroad. Moreover, it was not difficult to induce the tribesmen to fight outside Arabia, for the wealth of Iran and Byzantium was proverbial. The prospects of such rich economic rewards strengthened by the faith that he was fighting for the cause of Allah, made the Arab soldier a formidable foe. The Muslim bedouins believed that if they were killed, they would go to Paradise; and if not, they would share in the booty. Few soldiers went to war expecting to be killed. One Muslim historian writes that Abu Bakr called the people to jihad and reminded them of the booty they could capture from the Greeks!

In addition to the individual desire for booty, the desire of the insolvent government of Medina for tribute must not be overlooked. "Fight against such of those who have been given the Scripture . . ." says the Koran, "until they pay tribute. . . ." Experience had shown the first two caliphs that they could not collect the Zakah from the tribes in Arabia without the use of force. So they tried to use the tribes to collect tribute from the "people of the Book" outside Arabia. They must have been surprised by their own success. Shortly afterward, they had simplified their demands into three words, "Islam, tribute, or sword."

Most Muslim historians emphasize the religious motivation in the advancement of Islam. Most modern interpreters of Islamic history have tried to minimize it. If the former exaggerated, as they did, the latter have read history poorly. It is impossible to conclude that Islam did not play an important role. It was the battle cry of every soldier and the rallying point of every tribe. Without Islam there could not have been a cohesion of the various tribes, and without this unity they would not have been much more than raiding parties. In the mind of every Arab from Umar down to the lowliest soldier, Allah, Muhammad, war booty, tribute, martyrdom, and Paradise were all part of the same indivisible package.

The reasons for victory, like everything else, are not all based on the initiative and ability of the aggressor. The two giants in the north, Byzantium and Iran, had been fighting each other for centuries. Tired and bleeding, they expected a few years of peace. After all, they were the only real adversaries. They did not expect anyone to attack them, and least of all the bedraggled bedouins of the desert. Wars cost money and money comes from taxing the people. The peoples of Byzantium and Iran were burdened with heavy taxes to defray the great expenses of the war and to provide the high standard of living to which the leaders of both countries were accustomed. Moreover, the early vigor of both Christianity and Zoroastrianism had given way to endless theological divisions in Byzantium and priestly oppression in Iran. To these people, the simple and theologically uncomplicated belief in Allah must have been like a breath of fresh air.

It must be remembered, too, that there were many Arab tribes in the Fertile Crescent, north of the Arabian Peninsula. Some of them were kinsmen of the tribes to the south. They must have welcomed the opportunity to be rid of their Greek and Iranian overlords.

By 634, Khalid ibn-Walid, after a series of forced marches, attacked eastern Syria. He could not have done this had it not been for the assistance of the Ghassanids, who were Arabs and had treaty agreements with the Byzantines. By February 635, Khalid laid seige to the city of Damascus. He gave the inhabitants three choices which became standard in subsequent wars of Islam. These choices were to accept Islam, pay tribute, or fight. Damascus surrendered in September 635. The decisive battle was fought a year later in August 636 in Yarmuk, between Heraclius and Khalid. The Arab victory forced the Byzantine emperor to leave all of Syria and Palestine to the Muslims. Syria fell in 637 and Jerusalem in 638. Thus, in four short years, the Arabs had become masters of the best Byzantine provinces in the Fertile Crescent.

Amr ibn-al-As, who apparently was familiar with Egypt, led a detachment there with the reluctant permission of Umar. By 639 he reached the border and pushed on to Pleusium and Heliopolis. After receiving reinforcements he moved down the Nile to the famous city of Alexandria and received its surrender in September 642.

While these campaigns were going on in the west, Sa'd ibn-Waqqas, a third general of Islam, moved toward Iran with some 6,000 troops. In three major battles, the fate of the Sasanian Empire was sealed. The first took place on a hot, windy day in June 635 at Qadesiya, in which the Iranians, under the command of Rostam, were defeated. Two years later, with the aid of Arab tribes along the Euphrates, Sa'd laid seige to Ctesiphon, the capital of the Sasanids. The famed capital fell in 637. The wealth of the city must have been beyond the imagination of the Arab soldiers, and they looted Ctesiphon to their heart's content. The Sasanian king Yazdgerd III, with a remnant of his army, met the Arabs at Nahavand, near modern Hamadan, and was defeated in 641. The shah himself was murdered by a greedy miller somewhere in the region of Marv, thus bringing to an end the Sasanid rule which had started in A.D. 226.

Thus, in the course of some eight years, desert Arabs had overrun a territory extending from western Egypt to central Iran, and from the southern borders of Asia Minor to the Arabian Sea. Even though they had not conquered it entirely, the victory was nevertheless very impressive. What Iran and Byzantium could not do to each other, the Arabs did to both.

Problems of Expansion and Administration

The rapid expansion of the Islamic arms had brought on many problems of logistics, administration, and justice that the Koran had not foreseen. Abu Bakr's method of administration was similar to Muhammad's in its simplicity and personal application. With the acquisition of vast territories, the administrative problems connected with them could not be handled as before. New policies were needed, and Umar was equal to the occasion. The fact that he is regarded as the "second founder" of Islam is due as much to the success of his administrative policies as to his conquest of new territories for Islam.

It may be safely assumed that, given Umar's devotion to Muhammad, he would follow the latter's principles as closely as possible. Indeed, among the policies attributed to Umar can be distinguished those which mirror Muhammad. For the first time the new Islamic community encountered the problem of dealing with conquered non-Arab peoples and seeing some of these non-Arabs accept Islam. The problem of what to do with the non-Arab conquered peoples was not as difficult as the problem of how to deal with the non-Arabs who became Muslims.

To guide him, Umar had a number of principles and facts that had been taught by the Prophet. He knew that Muhammad was an Arab, sent by Allah with a message for the Arabs. He also knew that this message could not be withheld from the non-Arabs. He believed that the Islamic community, ummah, was a brotherhood of all Muslims, not of all mankind. Furthermore, with the vast territory under his control, Umar saw the necessity of establishing a solid base, preferably in Arabia, where nothing would prejudice the solidarity of this brotherhood. With the above principles in mind, Umar interpreted Islam to be a brotherhood of Arabs who had accepted the message of Muhammad. The non-Arab Muslims could join the Muslim ummah, but would not be part of its inner circle—an honor that would remain the prerogative of Arabs.

In the first place Umar drove all non-Muslims out of Arabia. To this day, non-Muslims are not considered permanent residents of the country. Second, he prohibited Arabs from owning land in the conquered territories. Without a land of their own, "home" would always be Arabia. Third, he frowned on intermarriage, even with converts, in order to keep the blood pure and the Arab military aristocracy intact. And fourth, to prevent the Arab warriors from fraternizing and mingling with the conquered peoples, he ordered the establishment of military cantonments. Among the Muslim encampments, some of which became cities later on, were Fustat in Egypt, Ramlah in Palestine, and Kufa and Basra in Iraq.

Consequently, the work of cultivation, trade, and the administration of districts was left in the hands of the inhabitants who, theoretically, were laboring for the "benefit of Muslims." In Christian territories local bishops were put in charge of affairs, while in Iran country squires took over the administrative responsibilities.

One of Umar's cardinal principles was that all immovable property and land in conquered territories belonged to the umma. The income of the state, in cash and in kind, came from different sources. One source was one-fifth of the booty, which had been instituted by Muhammad. Another was the *jizya,* head tax levied on non-Muslims. A third source was the land tax levied on all non-Arab cultivators. The total income was so large that the Arabs were exempt from paying Zakah. Since all proceeds belonged to the

ummah, whatever remained after defraying the expenses of war, administration, and public welfare was distributed among the Arabs. For this, Umar
ordered a census taken and established a bureau for the purpose of distribution. The above policy strengthened the Arabs, all of whom were members
of the inner circle of the Muslim ummah. All Arabs were elevated to the
rank of the privileged class, and—only because they were Arabs—they received an annual stipend in addition to exemption of payment of Zakah.

As a result of the census, all Arabs were classified according to rank
based on the length of their faith in Islam, service to the Prophet, and
position in the tribe. It started with the family of the Prophet, whose members received an annual stipend of 12,000 dirhams (about $3,000) and went
down to the lowest soldier, who could collect an annual stipend of 600
dirhams. Contrary to the claims of a number of modern historians, the
Arabs did indeed use Islam to bolster their position. Arabism was identified
with Islam, at least by Umar and his followers if not (and this is by no means
certain) by Muhammad himself. This policy of Arab superiority, however,
could not stand the test of time. Sooner or later the large number of non-
Arabs who, for whatever reason, had accepted Islam would insist on a
broader interpretation of the Koran as meaning Muslim brotherhood rather
than Arab-Muslim brotherhood.

UTHMAN

If the policies of Umar disintegrated sooner than expected, it was because
his successor was one of the worst administrators in the annals of Islam.
Uthman ibn-Affan was past seventy, and, like Ali, was a son-in-law of
Muhammad. He belonged to the aristocratic Umayyad clan of the Quraysh,
whose leader at the time of Muhammad, Abu Sufyan, was bitterly opposed
to the Prophet. After the capitulation of Mecca to the religious and political
demands of the Prophet, the Umayyads, thanks to Muhammad, had
emerged unscathed.

The Umayyads settled in Medina and exerted leadership over different
aspects of the Islamic state. Perhaps it was through their efforts that Uthman
was elected. As it turned out, it was the Umayyad family rather than Uthman that actually took over the reins of the state. The mild-mannered,
unenergetic old man preferred reading the Koran to public affairs and
trusted the administration of the state to the members of his family. Soon his
Umayyad relatives replaced old and tested warriors as governors of conquered provinces.

Not through the initiative of Uthman, but mostly because of the momentum of the Islamic movement, the military campaigns continued. The
Muslim armies advanced through the Berber territory in North Africa and
captured Tripoli and ancient Carthage. Uthman permitted the Berbers to
have the privileges of the "people of the Book." The campaign in Syria was
under the leadership of Mu'awiya, another member of the Umayyad family.
Muslims under his leadership won their first naval battle in the capture of
Cyprus and later pushed on to Rhodes. In the north, the Muslims took

Azarbaijan and parts of Armenia; and in the east, they advanced to the vicinity of Kabul, the capital of modern Afghanistan.

More and more, however, the attention of the leaders of Islam turned inward, especially to the mismanagement of Uthman. In addition to widespread nepotism, it was reported that Uthman had become so corrupt that he would sell governorships for cash or gifts of beautiful slave girls. Many of the Prophet's close companions were against him. It was an open secret that these feelings were encouraged by Ali and his supporters. Uthman, who lacked administrative ability, did not lack personal courage. When the most important members of his clan opposed Muhammad, he became a Muslim. He also showed courage in undertaking the canonization of the Koran, which instigated an uprising against him and which culminated in his death. The scholars in Kufa accused Uthman of tampering with the text of the Koran by suppressing verses that were against the Umayyads. The uprising, started in this tumultuous city, encouraged the friends of Ali in Egypt to rise in protest against Uthman. The Egyptians went a step further and sent a detachment of 500 soldiers to Medina in 656 and surrounded the caliph's house. Apparently Uthman was oblivious to these events. It is reported that he was reading the Koran when the soldiers broke in and killed him. According to Muslim historians, his assassin was Muhammad, the son of Uthman's friend Abu Bakr, the first caliph of Islam. Thus he was the second caliph to meet a violent death.

ALI

A week after the murder of Uthman, Ali assumed the office of caliph, to the satisfaction of all those who believed that he was the only rightful heir to the Prophet. The caliphate, which had been "wrested" from him three times, had at last, so it was claimed, been conferred upon the right person. But unfortunately for Ali and his followers, the position of caliph had, by this time, attracted many aspirants.

Twenty-four years after the death of Muhammad, a new generation had grown to manhood. This generation had experienced almost continuous victory, traveled far and wide, had tasted power, had partaken of new pleasures, and had inherited great wealth. The days of the simple life of the desert were gone and with them the awe and respect formerly held for those who had been close to the Prophet. Ali's caliphate was hardly begun before two of his closest associates, Talha and Zubayr, refused to acknowledge him.

In the course of three decades, interested Muslims had brooded over the problem of succession. Three opinions had emerged. One group believed that the successor of the Prophet must be from the Quraysh tribe. This was a development of the original argument between the Meccans and the Medinese immediately after the death of the Prophet. The first three caliphs had held this opinion. Abu Bakr had been chosen by an unpremeditated gathering of some of the leaders from rival parties. Umar had been appointed by his predecessor, and Uthman had been elected by a committee appointed by Umar. Apparently these methods were acceptable. Since all members of the Quraysh tribe were eligible for the caliphate, there was a good deal of rivalry among the different families.

The second group, commonly called the "legitimists," believed that the caliphate was a divine office and the appointee had to assume office by divine ordinance. Since no one questioned the fact that Muhammad was Prophet-King by divine ordinance, they argued that successorship would legitimately belong, by divine designation, to the family of the Prophet. According to this theory, Ali, as the son-in-law, cousin, and adopted son of Muhammad, was the legitimate successor and after him, leadership would go to his sons—i.e., Muhammad's grandsons—and so on down the line. The legitimists were known as *Shi'at Ali* ("partisans of Ali") and later on as simply *Shi'a*.

The third group, which comprised a minority of Muslims, believed that the caliphate did not belong to a particular family. They believed in the dictum of the Koran that greatness was based on piety and not on blood. They went so far as to say that even a slave could become a caliph. In their social ideals and personal life they were puritans and loved the simplicity of the prophetic message. At first they sided with Ali, very likely because of his piety, against his enemies. Later they left him and became known as *Kharijites* ("seceders"). They became the self-appointed warriors for the purity of Islam and were thorns in the flesh of all caliphs.

Very likely Ali's associates, Talha and Zubayr, rose against him because they were afraid that Ali would establish the caliphate in his household to the exclusion of the rest of the Quraysh. Ayisha, the young wife of Muhammad, had a personal hatred for Ali and joined the insurgents at Basra.

Thus the first civil war in Islam, which was by no means the last, was fought outside of Basra on December 9, 656, twenty-four years after the death of Muhammad. On one side was the son-in-law of the Prophet and on the other the Prophet's favorite wife. In the battle of the Camel, so called because Ayisha rode on a camel and aroused the warriors, Ali was the victor. He was quite magnanimous to Ayisha and sent her to Medina.

With this crisis out of the way, Ali began to rule, with Kufa as his capital. He dismissed most of Uthman's appointees and inaugurated reforms that favored the simpler patterns of the Prophet. He had not reckoned, however, with a more formidable foe. Mu'awiya, governor of Syria and a relative of Uthman, refused to acknowledge Ali. One Friday Mu'awiya exhibited the blood-stained shirt of the murdered caliph, Uthman, and accused Ali of being an accomplice in the murder. In this way the Umayyads challenged the succession of Ali.

The struggle, however, was over other issues as well. By the time of Ali's caliphate, the Muslims had created a large empire. The contact of the relatively uncultured, but zealous peninsula Arabs with the cultured and sophisticated peoples of Syria and Iraq had a tremendous effect on the Muslims. They were dazzled by so much wealth and by so much learning. Moreover, in a very practical way, they needed the help of the conquered peoples to administer the vast new empire. Thus the ostensibly inter-Arab war was, in a real sense, also a rivalry between the former dependencies of the Byzantines and the Sasanids. Should Syria, representing Greco-Roman culture, be supreme, or should Iraq, representing Iranian culture? (Medina, the center of the Muslim-Arab empire, had already lost its preeminence.)

The two armies, Ali with his Iraqis and Mu'awiya with his Syrians, met at Siffin on the Euphrates in July 657. The Syrians averted certain disaster by lifting copies of the Koran on their lances and asking for arbitration. Ali, whose valor and piety overshadowed his political acumen, accepted arbitration based on the Koran.

The arbiters took their time in arriving at a verdict. In the meantime, a large number of Ali's followers were disgusted with him for accepting arbitration. They seceded with the slogan, "There is no arbiter except God." Ali fought and defeated these Kharijites in 659 on the banks of Nahravan Canal.

It is difficult to ascertain what went on in the arbitration meetings. There are charges and countercharges. Whatever the facts, Ali, the acknowledged caliph, had wittingly or unwittingly questioned his own right to the caliphate by accepting arbitration. Mu'awiya, only a governor, had won by appearing to have a legitimate claim to the caliphate. It is said that the arbiters "deposed" both, which in reality meant that they deposed Ali, for Mu'awiya was not a caliph. They did not, however, propose means of electing a new one. In January 661, Ali was wounded by a Kharijite while on his way to the mosque and died two days later. In May 661 Mu'awiya had himself proclaimed caliph in Jerusalem.

The downhearted followers of Ali proclaimed his eldest son, Hasan, as caliph. Hasan, however, did not relish the inevitable struggle ahead. Mu'awiya prudently agreed to pay him a royal pension and protection if he would retire to his villa near Medina. This Hasan did and Mu'awiya became the undisputed ruler of Islam with Damascus as his capital.

Thus ended the period of the Orthodox Caliphs. This period has been idealized as the time of pure theocracy, when the law of Allah was the law of the land and the *sunna* ("way of the Prophet") was the path that everyone tried to follow. Most of the religiously oriented Muslims of the twentieth century always refer to this period as the best illustration of Islam at work and yearn to go back to it. Some European historians of Islam have called this period both "republican" and "democratic." Republican it may have been in that there was no attempt, except in the case of Ali, to establish a family dynasty. Democratic it certainly was not. At best it was an oligarchy. In theory, the caliphate was a prerogative of the Quraysh, but in practice it was decided by a very small and powerful group within the tribe.

Chapter Five
The Umayyad Dynasty and Its Development

THE SUFYAN BRANCH

Mu'awiya I (661–680)
Yazid I (680–683)
Mu'awiya II (683)

THE MARWAN BRANCH

Marwan I (683–685)
Abd al-Malik (685–705)
Walid I (705–715)
Sulayman (715–717)
Umar II (717–720)
Yazid II (720–724)
Hisham (724–743)
Walid II (743–744)
Yazid III (744)
Ibrahim (744)
Marwan II (744–750)

With the establishment of Mu'awiya in the caliphate, a new era came into being in the world of Islam. Mu'awiya organized the dynasty after the manner of the Byzantines and the Iranians, abandoning the "republicanism" of the Medinese period. For the sake of placating the traditionalists and preserving appearances, however, he took his son, Yazid, around to different tribes in Arabia and let them acknowledge him as his successor. But this practice was soon abandoned, and the succession went to the oldest son or to whoever was the strongest in the family. Even so, no caliph was undisputed and the Umayyad dynasty, as a whole, was not stable. As is apparent in the list of Umayyad caliphs, the average length of reign was only six years. Only four ruled for over ten years, while the rest ruled less than five. Among the latter there were three who did not last even a year.

Our information concerning the Umayyads comes almost entirely from Abbasid historians, who were prejudiced against that dynasty and depicted its rulers as nothing but pleasure-loving and hard-drinking usurpers of the caliphate. True as this description may be about a number of them, it is evident that not all of them were hard-drinking and pleasure-loving. Even some of those who were did much to strengthen the empire and advance its frontiers. The Umayyad caliphs were confronted with a vast empire with diverse religious and cultural elements and with manifold problems of administration. Given the circumstances, the Umayyads did not do badly.

It took Christianity and Buddhism each about 300 years of struggle and development before a Christian state became established under Constantine or a Buddhist state came into being under Ashoka. This was not so with militantly aggressive Islam. Even during the lifetime of Muhammad, people joined it for diverse and sometimes contradictory motives. There were, to be sure, those whose acceptance of Islam represented a total conversion of life and attitude. They formed the nucleus of the believers and their number grew with the passage of time. They were zealously on guard to protect the purity of the faith. The early Kharijites were among them and sided with Ali for the preservation of the faith proclaimed by Muhammad.

There were those who accepted the message of Islam for purely opportunistic reasons. The Meccans under the leadership of Sufyan, the scion of the Umayyads, certainly belonged to this group. When they found fighting against Muhammad futile, they joined him and remained in political and economic control of the new movement. They observed the laws of Islam and performed its rituals, but they were not converted men and would not think of sacrificing their personal gain for the sake of the faith.

There were still others who were brought into the realm of Islam by coercion. Most of these were the bedouin tribes of Arabia, who were subdued by Muhammad but who had had to be reconquered by Abu Bakr. They were interested in fighting and booty; and as long as they were kept busy fighting outsiders, they did not hamper the authorities in Medina. The Umayyads, like their predecessors, employed these tribesmen in wars of expansion and also used them against their rivals for the throne. The puritans of Islam hated the Umayyads and considered them a disgrace to the Islamic ummah. These zealots for the purity of Islam took advantage of every opportunity to destroy the power of the Umayyads. The Umayyads, on the other hand, had control of the government and were able to win successive struggles against other claimants to the caliphate.

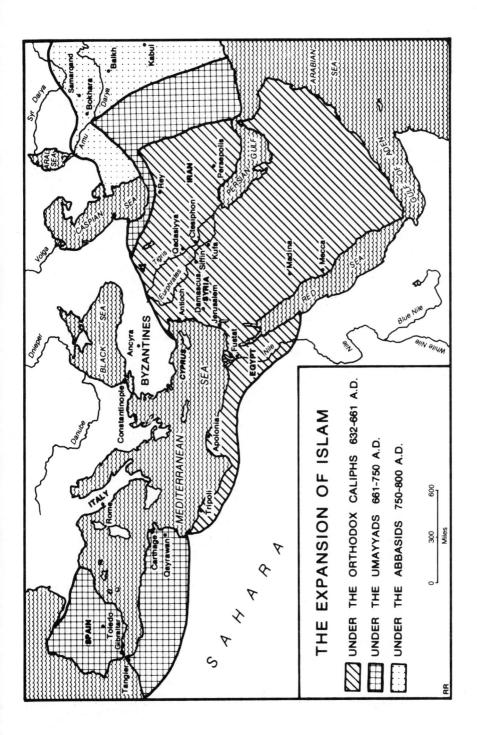

THE EXPANSION OF ISLAM

UNDER THE ORTHODOX CALIPHS 632-661 A.D.

UNDER THE UMAYYADS 661-750 A.D.

UNDER THE ABBASIDS 750-800 A.D.

RR

57

THE EXPANSION OF THE EMPIRE

The unfinished job of conquest, as far as the Arabs were concerned, was still the Byzantine Empire. Its riches beckoned the fighters of Islam, and the possibility of its conversion kindled the hopes of many Muslims.

Soon after he secured his position as caliph, Mu'awiya opened hostilities against the Byzantines and laid siege to Constantinople in the winter of 668. The fortifications, however, proved impregnable and the emperor, Constantine IV, too energetic for the Arabs to make any headway. The siege was discontinued but the expedition turned out to be of political value to the caliph. Yazid was recognized as the hero of the siege, which made it easier for Mu'awiya to proclaim him heir-apparent to the caliphate.

The Arabs attacked Byzantium twice after this, once in 717 and again in 782 during the Abbasid regime. Despite these attempts, the Arabs were never able to gain a foothold in Asia Minor. The Byzantine Empire lasted, in one way or another, until 1453, when it was destroyed by the Ottoman sultan Mehmed the Conqueror.

In 670 the Arabs had built the garrison city of Qayrawan in Tunisia as a base for the conquest of North Africa. In the ensuing thirty years, the Arabs tried to oust the Byzantines from the region and to subdue the rebellious Berber tribes. By the end of the seventh century, the Muslim capture of Carthage terminated the Byzantine rule.

The Berbers of North Africa are an Afro-Asian people. Those living in coastal cities had become Christians and had produced a number of early Christian scholars, one of the most famous being St. Augustine. For the majority of the Berber tribes living in the hinterland, Christianity did not seem to offer an attraction. Although the Berbers resisted the penetration of Muslim Arabs, in the end they became adherents of Islam and joined the Arab armies for further conquest.

In 711, Tariq, a Berber lieutenant, crossed into Spain at the head of an all-Berber raiding party. Tariq established his base near a rock that bears his name, Jabal al-Tariq ("Mount of Tariq"), now known as Gibraltar. His adventure reveals the confused state of affairs in that country. What started as a raiding party in the spring of 711 resulted in the conquest of half of Spain by the end of the summer.

Gradually, the Muslims finished the conquest of Spain, which they called Al-Andalus (perhaps "the land of Vandals"). By 718, they crossed the Pyrenees and raided the French countryside and churches. It was not until 732, the hundredth anniversary of the death of Muhammad, that the Muslim army under Abd al-Rahman was defeated in the celebrated battle of Tours by Charles Martel. Despite later Muslim raids and occupations of French cities such as Avignon and Lyons, the Muslims were not henceforth considered a permanent threat to the security of western Europe.

The Muslims stayed in Spain for nearly 800 years. In 756, the Umayyads, having been ousted from Damascus, established a rival caliphate in Spain with their capital in Cordoba. For centuries, Spain was the channel through which Islamic influence flowed to the West. Spain is the only country conquered by the Arabs the majority of whose inhabitants did not become Muslim. It is also the only country that was reconquered totally by the Christians and the only country in which no Muslim community has remained. The story of Islam in Spain is a fascinating one, but it is outside the scope of this volume.

The Umayyads, in addition to their struggle against the Byzantines and their conquest of North Africa and Spain, were able to pacify, at least for a time, the rebellious inhabitants of Iraq and Iran. They also penetrated into modern Afghanistan and later took Bokhara and Samarqand in the modern Soviet Republic of Uzbekistan. Another contingent marched toward India and, by 712, conquered the territory west of the Sind River.

With the downfall of the Umayyads, the almost continuous expansion that had been started by Abu Bakr came almost to an end. The result was an immense empire extending from the Amu Darya to the Sudan. Remarkable as this achievement was, the empire started to disintegrate almost as soon as it reached this immense size. By the time the Abbasids came to power, the vast empire had already been divided. It was fragmented still more in the course of centuries, leaving behind only a dream of a united Islamic empire.

LIFE AND LEISURE

Emerging from the harsh and barren life of the desert into the glitter and sophistication of Byzantine and Iranian urban centers; falling, as it were, into the lap of luxury from the tent of poverty; being the recipients of so much wealth; and becoming masters of so many slaves, male and female: all this could not but leave its imprint upon the manners and mores of the Arabs. The simple virtues preached by Islam as practiced by Muhammad and the Orthodox Caliphs were too confining to be practical for these affluent Arabs. Accordingly, they satisfied themselves by paying lip service to these virtues and, while observing the outward rituals of piety, immersed themselves in their newly found paradise of pleasure. Beginning with Uthman, who was not inattentive to the demands of the good life, and especially the Umayyad caliphs and their lieutenants, these conquerers of the vast domain could have paraphrased a statement attributed to Pope Leo X (1513–1521) to read, "Allah has given us the empire, let us enjoy it."

Abul Faraj al-Isfahani (897–967), who claimed lineal descent from Marwan II, the last Umayyad caliph, wrote a book called *Kitab al-Aghani* ("The Book of Songs"), which became a veritable best seller. People enjoyed reading the book as much as the author must have enjoyed writing it. Painstakingly, if not perhaps in a scholarly fashion, he went about collecting anecdotes, songs, stories, poems, games, pastimes, habits, jokes, and anything about the Arabs of the Umayyad and Abbasid periods that "entertained the hearers." He was a combination of anthropologist, literary and musical anthologist, and a keyhole observer. Ibn Khaldun, the great Muslim historian, regarded the book as the social register of the Arabs.

No one, caliph or commoner, escaped Isfahani's scrutiny. He relates how Mu'awiya entertained himself in the evenings by listening to stories and poems and drinking rose sherbet. Isfahani, as well as others, describes the wine drinking habits of the caliphs. It is said that Yazid drank every day; Walid I, every other day; Hisham, every Friday after prayers; Abd al-Malik, once a month; and the champion of them all, Walid II, used to swim in a pool of wine gulping at every stroke.

The wealthy Arabs loved to hunt and race horses, as both sports were native to Arabia. Yazid I had hunting dogs with gold anklets, and each dog had a special caretaker. The less wealthy used to enjoy cockfights and games of dice. Games of chess, originally from India, and backgammon were brought from Iran.

The most revealing information given by the author of *Kitab al-Aghani* is the transformation of the holy cities of Mecca and Medina into centers of leisure, pleasure, and vice. A large number of Arabs who received very lucrative pensions went "home" to the central cities of Arabia to enjoy themselves. There were clubs and cabarets, houses of ill-repute and elegant salons, belly dancers, serious musicians, and songsters, from all parts of the empire. Slave girls by the scores waited to entertain their masters, who reclined on cushions and drank wine from silver or golden goblets—all within a stone's throw of the Ka'ba and the tomb of the Prophet.

No less a personage than Sukayna, the daughter of Imam Husayn and the great-granddaughter of the Prophet, was the center of attraction in Medina. Her dazzling beauty attracted numerous husbands, all on her terms; her charms captivated many; and her wit and practical jokes were the talk of the town. She was the patroness of music (a profession denounced by the Prophet) and an arbiter of fashion. Her hairdo was imitated by the ladies of the realm.

Not to be outdone, the summer resort of Taif, near Mecca, had its own attraction in the person of Ayisha, whose father was a companion of the Prophet and whose mother was the daughter of Abu Bakr, the first caliph. She did not marry as often as Sukayna, but she did the unusual by refusing to veil herself on the grounds that people should see her beauty and praise the handiwork of Allah.

The thousands of pilgrims who poured into the two cities enjoyed these pleasant opportunities and contributed to the gaity. There were, no doubt, those who gaped in bewilderment at the shocking spectacles and shook their heads in disapproval.

ADMINISTRATION

Beneath the glittering surface of leisure and gaity there were many problems. Among these were governing the provinces, collecting taxes, regulating land tenure, maintaining public order, and preserving the loyalty of Arabs and non-Arabs to the central government in Damascus.

Since Arabs generally considered agriculture to be beneath their dignity and had little concern for the complexities of settled life, Mu'awiya and his successors had to recruit administrators from the ranks of the conquered peoples. The empire was divided into five provinces; each province was governed by a viceroy who was appointed by the caliph. The viceroy had complete control of the affairs of his province. He appointed agents and judges and was responsible for the administration of the province. Judges held court only for Muslims. Non-Muslims maintained separate courts according to their religious laws. Judges also administered the religious charitable foundation, *waqf*, which was financed by the faithful.

Muhammad, as we have seen, had established a system of taxation consisting of Zakah paid by the Muslims and the jizya (head-tax) paid by non-Muslims. During the years of expansion, however, and the acquisition of enormous booty, the Arab Muslims were exempt from paying taxes. Islam did not have a definite policy of land tenure. The status of cultivators, who during the Umayyad period were almost all non-Arabs, was not changed at all. Both Muslims and non-Muslims paid the same land tax that was prevalent under the Byzantines and Sasanids.

This system of land holding, however, did not remain as simple as the Arabs had hoped. In the first place the law prohibiting Arabs from holding land outside of Arabia was both impractical and unpopular. Uthman looked the other way when members of his own family began to acquire land. The practice continued to increase to the point that during the Umayyad period Arabs not only acquired land of their own but "leased" land under public domain from the government and sold it to others as private property. Being Arabs and Muslims, they did not pay taxes on private property.

In the second place, the early Arab leaders were caught between the demands of Islam for egalitarianism among all Muslims regardless of nationality, and their own nationalistic feelings. They could not decide whether all Muslims should be exempt from taxation or whether only Arab Muslims should be so privileged. The early Umayyads believed in Arab superiority and tried to secure special privileges for them. As long as the advancing Muslim armies continued to send booty back to the capital, it did not make much difference who paid taxes and who was exempt. The ruling class had enough wealth, with some to spare. But during the first quarter of the eighth century, when expansion slackened and economic conditions were stabilized, the government began to feel the pinch. Dissatisfaction was rampant in many parts of the empire, especially in Iran, and contributed in no small way to the downfall of the Umayyads.

Either the Umayyads could not or did not care to develop their political and social institutions in response to new circumstances. The use of military power had gained them an empire, and they continued to use it to solve their domestic problems. The more they used force, the more the opposition resorted to armed revolt and disturbed the peace.

CLAIMANTS FOR THE CALIPHATE

Two problems gnawed at the institution which the Arab conquest had created. One was the perennial question of succession, which was complicated by rival claimants to the high office. The death of Ali and the subsequent accession of Mu'awiya to the caliphate had settled the question in the minds of most Muslims that only a member of the Quraysh tribe could aspire to the high office. The fact that a majority upheld the Quraysh claim did not solve the problem, for there were rivals among the Quraysh, each of whom considered himself best suited for the position. It was generally agreed among the Quraysh tribesmen out of power that the Umayyads were the least deserving to occupy the caliphate.

Added to this animosity towards the Umayyads was the resurgence of native Arab tribalism. This had been temporarily eclipsed by loyalty to Islam, although it had been allowed to reassert itself by Uthman and had come into full bloom by the time of the Umayyads. In the new society, this tribal loyalty took the form of a bitter rivalry between north Arabs and south Arabs. The struggle between the two was long and bitter. The later Umayyad caliphs stood for one side or the other, depending upon which side their mothers belonged, and generally acted as heads of feuding families rather than as leaders of an empire.

The death of Ali did not end the claim of his partisans—namely, that the caliphate belonged to the descendants of the Prophet through his daughter, Fatima. Consequently, the two sons of Ali, Hasan and Husayn, became rallying points for the opponents of the Umayyads. Hasan, the older brother, was persuaded by Mu'awiya to retire for life to a villa outside Medina with an annual stipend of 5,000,000 dirhams. He was allegedly poisoned in 669. The Shi'is, however, believe that he was killed by Mu'awiya and consider Hasan to be an Imam (a successor of Muhammad) and a martyr.

The younger brother, Husayn, was of a different mettle. He was ambitious and gave vigorous leadership to the opposition, which had its center of strength around the town of Kufa at the head of the Persian Gulf. In 680, when Yazid became caliph, Husayn refused to acknowledge him and secretly left Medina to join his own followers in Kufa, who had already proclaimed him caliph. Unfortunately for Husayn, the plot was discovered and the small band, including women and children, was ambushed in Karbala, an oasis south of modern Baghdad. Most of the men were killed. Husayn, the grandson of the Prophet, was beheaded; and the women and children were taken captive.

This was the culmination of a series of unsuccessful political moves on the part of the partisans of Ali to secure the caliphate. Very likely in any other situation, the ambush at Karbala would have been recorded as another political failure. Indeed, at the time the incident did not create much excitement. In the subsequent history of Islam, however, the ambush at Karbala assumed important religious significance. Ali and Husayn became more formidable foes of the established caliphate through their deaths than through their lives. Husayn came to be considered the prince of martyrs, and the anniversary of his death on the tenth of Muharram (680) became a rallying occasion for opponents of the caliphate. Religious processions commemorating the event are similar to the processions and self-mortifications that were held in Mesopotamia for the death of the god Tammuz. With a cause and three martyrs, the followers of Ali separated themselves from the main body of Islam and formed a religio-political community with a theology and philosophy of its own.

The house of Ali was not the only claimant for the caliphate. One of the persons disputing the caliphate with Ali was Zubayr, who died in this attempt. His son, Abdullah (the nephew of Ayisha, the wife of Muhammad), at first sided with Husayn. After the latter's tragic death, he claimed the office for himself.

Yazid sent an expedition against Abdullah to Medina and Mecca in 683, two cities in which Abdullah had strong support. Mecca was besieged and bombarded, causing the Ka'ba to be burned to the ground and the Black Stone to be split into three pieces. In the meantime, Yazid died, and the expedition was inconclusive. Abdullah was acknowledged as caliph in Hijaz, Iraq, and Egypt. To the population, tired of the bloody feuds, Abdullah ibn-Zubayr was a happy compromise between the unpopular Umayyads and the extremist claims of the house of Ali. Furthermore, the death of Yazid had sparked rivalry within the Umayyad camp. Had Abdullah been willing to remove his capital from Medina to Damascus, he would have been acknowledged even in Syria. He belonged, however, to that group of Muslims who believed that Mecca and Medina should remain as the spiritual and political centers of Islam. He was not willing to move the center of power to Damascus, a non-Arab city.

In the meantime, Marwan, the founder of the Marwanid branch of the Umayyads, had come to power in Damascus with the help of the southern Arabs. Abdullah, however, continued as caliph in Hijaz until 692, when he was defeated in the second siege of Mecca. With the death of Abdullah, the influence of the old-school Muslims came to an end, and with it the supremacy of the Arabian peninsula, "the Cradle of Islam."

ARABS VERSUS OTHER MUSLIMS

At the bottom of Muslim society in the newly formed empire were slaves—white, black, and yellow—who were brought from territories extending from Turkistan to Central Africa and from Iran to Spain and France.

The next level above the slaves was occupied by the *dhimmi*, members of tolerated religions—Jews, Christians, and Sabians—as mentioned originally in the Koran. Later, when the Arab leaders realized that they could not possibly kill all those who were not considered "people of the Book" by the Koran, the privilege was extended to cover the Zoroastrians of Iran and Berbers of North Africa.

Next were the non-Arab Muslims, called "clients." It was their status vis-à-vis the Arab Muslims that became the bone of contention and the source of so much discontent and rebellion. These people, who had accepted Islam out of either conviction, force, or expediency, naturally placed the broadest interpretation on the egalitarian statements of the Koran. The Arabs, on the other hand, following the leadership of Umar I, were inclined to interpret the Koran from a more limited point of view. Umayyad society was based on the supremacy of the Arabs, and the new plutocrats hardly wanted to share their new privileges with converts. That the Arabs could not manage without the converts in anything except perhaps in military matters caused them to have a feeling of uncertainty. They tried to compensate for this uncertainty by asserting Arab national superiority and by forcing the notion on the conquered peoples. The non-Arabs were taxed heavily, forbidden marriage with Arabs, and humiliated in many ways. These humiliations, of course, were bitterly resented by all the clients, especially the Iranians. As a result, the Iranians espoused any cause, be it Shi'a or Kharijite or whatever, provided it was against the Umayyads.

Around 740 the Abbasids, descendants of Abbas, an uncle of the Prophet, claimed their right to the caliphate. In a short while, the Shi'is, the Iranians, and all others who, for one reason or another, were dissatisfied with the Umayyads, rallied to the Abbasids. In 747, the legendary young Iranian, Abu Muslim Khorasani, unfurled the black flag of the Abbasids. Two years later, Iraq was taken; and on Thursday, October 30, 749, Abul Abbas, the great-great-grandson of Abbas, was proclaimed caliph in Kufa. Marwan II, the last of the Umayyads, met the insurgents in January 750 and was decisively defeated. In April of that year, Damascus fell.

Members of the Umayyad Dynasty and their relatives and friends were hunted down and put to the sword. However, at least one prince, Abd al-Rahman, the grandson of Hisham, escaped and reached Spain after a series of harrowing experiences. Here he established the Umayyad caliphate of Spain with Cordoba as his capital.

The coming of the Abbasids ushered in a new era. The dream of Umar I to create a United Arab Empire had failed. The victory of the Abbasids resulted in the creation of two rival empires. Even the Muslim ummah had been broken by war and strife. The center of gravity moved from Syria to Iraq and Iran. Kufa, on the border of Iran, became the new capital. Non-Arabs felt a sense of liberation, and Iranians occupied the chief positions in the new government. The idea of Arab supremacy receded into the desert with the Arabs, not be heard of again until it was resurrected in a more inclusive form called "pan-Arabism" in the twentieth century. The Arabs went but Islam remained; and under the guise of Islam marched many ideas and systems, sometimes Iranian, sometimes Ottoman, and sometimes Indian.

Chapter Six
The Abbasid Empire: A New Era

The Early Abbasids and Their Relation to Muhammad and the Quraysh Tribe

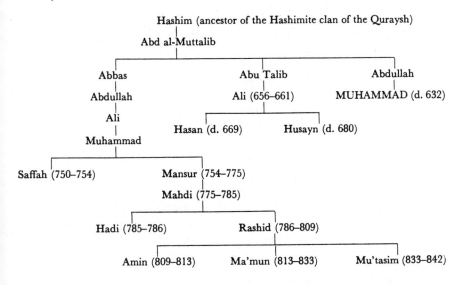

The Abbasids inherited most of the vast Umayyad Empire and all of its problems. In addition to the difficulties encountered by the Umayyads in the fields of taxation, land tenure, loyalty, and local peace, they also had to cope with a booming world trade and its tendency of making the rich richer and the poor poorer. "Military" towns such as Kufa, Fustat, and others were in the process of becoming urban centers and acquiring all the accompanying urban problems. The Abbasids had come to power with the help of diverse groups such as Shi'is, orthodox Sunnis, non-Arabs, and other dissidents by making the right promises to each group. Not only did they fail to fulfill the revolutionary ideals of these groups but they also failed to integrate the society either politically, economically, or even religiously into structures supported by appropriate institutions. Much like their descendents in the twentieth century who cannot cope with the sudden prosperity caused by the flow of petrodollars, the Abbasids failed to take advantage of the wealth that was pouring in from all parts of the world and allowed their empire to be fragmented partly because of that prosperity. Like their predecessors, they failed to support the concept of ummah by appropriate political and social institutions. Even though there was an Abbasid caliph in Baghdad until 1285, autonomous principalities began to appear simultaneously in all parts of the empire from 800 A.D. on.

No sooner was the new caliphate established than the Abbasids began to rid themselves of those who had been their allies against the Umayyads. In typical style, the Abbasids sided with one group to get rid of others. One of the last and most important of these allies was the legendary Abu Muslim Khorasani.

ABBASID RELIGIOUS POLICY

One of the most important issues that won the Abbasids the support of the orthodox segment of the population was the alleged lack of religious zeal on the part of the Umayyads. The Abbasids promised a more theocratic Muslim state as opposed to the worldliness of the Umayyads. This promise they proceeded to fulfill. To be sure, the Abbasids were not any less worldly than their Umayyad cousins, but they did keep the pretense of religiosity. They catered to the wishes of the religious leaders, imposed Islam upon the masses, became dogmatic, and were the first in Islam to organize an inquisition. As a token of their religiosity, the Abbasid caliphs used to wear the mantle of the Prophet on ceremonial occasions and for Friday prayers. The weaker the Abbasid caliphs became politically the more pretentious they became religiously. True to the practice of empty piety, the caliphs after Mu'tasim added the word *Allah* to their names, such as *al-Mu-tasim Bi-Allah* (pronounced "billah").

At the time of the shift in power to the Abbasids, a large segment of the population of the Iranian plateau and North Africa, especially in the rural areas, was still non-Muslim. With few exceptions, the Umayyads believed in Arab supremacy. The Abbasids, however, having put aside Arab supremacy, emphasized religion and began to impose it upon the masses of the population. These joined the various groups who had been thwarted in their aims, and they all turned against the established order. The strongest

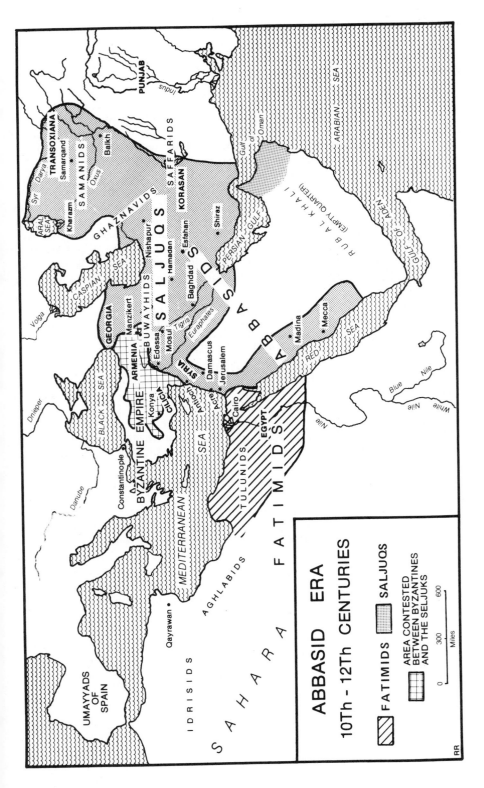

ABBASID ERA

10Th – 12Th CENTURIES

FATIMIDS   SALJUQS

AREA CONTESTED
BETWEEN BYZANTINES
AND THE SELJUKS

0   300   600

Miles

PUNJAB

TRANSOXIANA
Samarqand
SAMANIDS
Balkh
Kharazm
Oxus
SAFFARIDS
KORASAN
GHAZNAVIDS
Nishapur
SALJUQS
Esfahan
Shiraz
Hamadan
Baghdad
Tigris
Euphrates
BUWAYHIDS
Manzikert
GEORGIA
ARMENIA
Edessa
Mosul
SYRIA
Damascus
Jerusalem
Antioch
Acre
Cairo
EGYPT
TULUNIDS
FATIMIDS
ABBASIDS

ARAL SEA
Syr Darya
CASPIAN SEA
Volga

ARABIAN SEA
Gulf of Oman
RUB AL KHALI (EMPTY QUARTER)
GULF OF ADEN
PERSIAN GULF
Mecca
Madina
RED SEA

Nile
Blue Nile
White Nile

BLACK SEA
Dnieper
Danube
Constantinople
BYZANTINE EMPIRE
Konya
CILICIA
MEDITERRANEAN SEA

UMAYYADS OF SPAIN
Qayrawan
AGHLABIDS
IDRISIDS
SAHARA

RR

and the most numerous among these groups were the Iranians, who became one of the chief opponents of the Abbasids, as they had been of the Umayyads. Iranian opposition took three forms: religious, political, and literary; but the central aim remained unchanged—namely, freedom from Arab rule.

The first form of Iranian opposition was religious. Since the Abbasid religious policy uprooted the life and mores of the masses, the common people protested through the only means at their disposal. They engaged in a number of religious uprisings. The most famous of these uprisings was led by a man by the name of Muqanna, the "Veiled Prophet of Khorasan," who rebelled against the caliph in 776. His followers, who numbered in the thousands, wore white garments and were called "White Shirts." They robbed caravans, destroyed mosques, and killed those who gave the call to prayer and those who responded to the call. Muqanna claimed that Abu Muslim was god and had been reincarnated in himself, the Veiled Prophet. His rebellion was so destructive that the Caliph Mahdi had to send several expeditions against him. Most Muslim historians devote several pages to the Veiled Prophet.[1]

If the uprising of the Veiled Prophet was bizarre and confused, the rebellion of Babak Khorramdin was orderly and serious. Even though some sixty years had passed since the murder of Abu Muslim, Babak used this incident to arouse his own followers. Babak's religion was a mixture of Zoroastrianism and the economic ideas of Mazdakism. His followers were called "Red Shirts" because of their uniform. His movement was socio-economic, and for over twenty years he was a thorn in the flesh of the two caliphs, Ma'mun and Mu'tasim.

Babak had probably been a shepherd from Azerbaijan. The caliphs had sent many expeditions against him. It was not until 840 that Afshin, an Iranian general in the service of Mu'tasim, captured Babak and brought him to Samarra, the residence of the Abbasids. Babak was placed on an elephant and paraded in the city. The caliph ordered him decapitated.

Another form of non-Arab opposition to the Abbasid power was literary. It was called the *Shu'ubiyya* movement. It was started during the Umayyad dynasty by non-Arab Muslims to combat the claims of national superiority on the part of the Arabs. Most of the proponents of the movement were the non-Arab secretaries in government offices. They wrote both negatively against the Arabs and also positively extolling the achievements of their own nationality. For example, the Umayyad caliph Hisham (724–43) ordered Isma'il b. Yasar to be thrown into a tank of water because he had boasted his Iranian descent in verses like the following:

> Princes were my ancestors, noble satraps, of
>   high breeding, generous, hospitable,
> Comparable to Khosrow or Shapur, and to Hormozan
>   in renown and consideration;

[1] In St. Louis and Kansas City, Missouri, there is a fraternal organization called The Veiled Prophets of Khorasan. They believe that the Veiled Prophet was a mythical figure in the "never-never land of Khorasan." Perhaps this organization gets its name from Thomas Moore's story "Lalla Rookh," whose hero is the Veiled Prophet of Khorasan.

Lions of the war-hosts, when they rushed forth
  on the day of battle. . . .
Then, if thou askest, will thou learn that we are
  descended from a race which excels all others.[2]

Under the Abbasids, the Shu'ubiyya eventually became an Iranian literary movement whose purpose was, through original writing and especially the translation of Persian-language books, to revive the spirit of the Iranian culture and to reestablish the Iranian social structure and tradition. They were avant-garde literary critics who encouraged a spirit of skepticism in religion and morals and espoused heretical causes. There is no doubt that some of them were anti-Islamic in subtle ways. Two of their members, the literary genius ibn-Muqaffa and the blind poet, Bashshar ibn-Burd, were executed for heresy by the caliphs Mansur and Mahdi, respectively.

GOVERNMENT AND ADMINISTRATION

The administration of the Abbasids was a far cry from the simple practices of the early caliphs. The Abbasids had become imperial, with a complicated and costly bureaucracy commensurate with the pretentions of an empire. At the very beginning Saffah instituted the office of grand vazir. The grand vazir acted in all matters for the person of the caliph and had practically unlimited power. A dictum of the Abbasids said that he who obeys the vazir has obeyed the caliph and he who obeys the caliph has obeyed God.

The first grand vazir was Khalid ibn-Barmak, the head of a remarkable family that held the grand vazirate for over half a century. Khalid was an Iranian from Balkh whose father was a priest, or *barmak*, in a Buddhist monastery. Though Iranian and a Shi'i, Khalid, his son Yahya, and Yahya's sons Fadl and Ja'far were successive vazirs under the first five caliphs. The power of the Barmakids, and their generosity, wealth, and sumptuous living, are part of the stories of *The Thousand and One Nights*. They had charge of civil and military affairs and appointed and deposed governors and generals at will. Even candidates for the position of chamberlain to the caliph had to meet their approval. Allegedly, Harun al-Rashid could not withdraw money from the treasury without their approval. A caliph of Harun's temperament, however, could not share power with anyone. Harun, his sister Abbasa, and Ja'far, the son of Yahya, had grown up together and were boon companions. Nevertheless, the power of the Barmakids and their Shi'a faith, coupled with a probable scandal involving Abbasa and Ja'far, bought an end to their house. Ja'far was executed and Yahya and Fadl died in prison. However, this was not the end of the vazirate or of the Iranian influence.

Neither Saffah nor Mansur felt secure in Kufa. Saffah moved to nearby Hashimiya and Mansur decided to build a new capital on the site of a little village on the Tigris named Baghdad, meaning "God-given." This city, with its numerous parks, beautiful gardens, spacious palaces, thousands of

[2]Edward G. Browne, *A Literary History of Persia*, I: 266.

mosques, and public baths, became world famous as the center of power, learning, commerce, and leisure, as well as the scene of the stories of Scheherazade (Shahrzad) in *The Thousand and One Nights*. All roads led to Baghdad, and one could literally see people from all parts of the known world of the time in the streets of Baghdad. The city was rich and gaudy, and the caliphs and their vazirs spent money in unprecedented quantities. For example, Zubayda, the wife of Harun al-Rashid, would not serve food except on gold plates and would not wear shoes unless they were studded with precious stones. Once she spent three million dinars for a pilgrimage to Mecca. At the wedding of the heir-presumptive, Ma'mun, and his bride, Puran, a thousand matched pearls were showered upon the couple as they sat upon a bejewelled golden divan. Gifts of several slave girls at a time and thousands of gold pieces to poets, jesters, and other flatterers were quite common.

Abu Nuwas, the libertine poet and close friend of Harun, was telling the truth when he sang:

> Youth and I, we ran
> a headlong race of pleasure
> No recorded sin
> but soon I took its measure.

Very likely Harun was present when his comrade sang:

> Come, Sulaiman, sing to me
> And the wine, quick, bring to me!
> Lo, already dawn is here
> In golden mantle clear.
> Whilst the flask goes twinkling round,
> Pour me a cup that leaves me drowned
> With oblivion, how'er, so high
> Let the shrill muezzin cry!

Harun had also his critic in another poet, Abu al-Atahiya, who saw doom in all that glittered and warned the caliph:

> Live securely as you wish;
> the palace heights are safe enough.
> With pleasure flooding day and night,
> and the smooth proves sweeter than the rough.
> But when your breath begins to clog
> in sharp contractions of your lungs,
> Then know for certain, my dear Sire,
> Your life was vain as idle tongues.[3]

Foreign dignitaries seeking audience with the caliph were so dazzled by the wealth and beauty of the rooms that often they would mistake the office of

---

[3]The three poems are found in *An Anthology of Islamic Literature*, ed. by James Kritzeck, pp. 86–88.

the chamberlain as the audience hall. In such surroundings did the early Abbasids govern their far-flung empire.

The country was administered by a council presided over by the grand vazir. The members of the council were the heads of different administrative departments (sometimes called vazirs), the chief justice, and the commander of the army. One of the most important departments of the administration was the Department of Taxation. There were taxes on different types of land with loopholes for different categories of landowners. Other sources of revenue were the head tax from non-Muslims, tribute, and sometimes booty. The practice of extortion was quite common; indeed, there was a Bureau of Confiscations. Each official from the caliph on down would confiscate the property of a person below him who was guilty of some charge or who had fallen out of grace. Theoretically, the public treasury had two accounts, one for the caliph and one for the state, but in reality the caliph had control of both. In theory also, all taxes received from Muslims were to be spent for the benefit of Muslims such as the poor, orphans, strangers, and war. But in practice the main purpose of taxation was to enrich the treasury and strengthen the central government.

Two of the most important items of expenditure were the royal household and the royal bodyguard. The precarious position of the caliph is shown by the fact that in 867 the cost of the bodyguard was 200,000,000 dinars, or twice the annual land tax of the whole empire. The wealthy citizens were made to pay the difference. Other items of expenditure were the care of the holy cities, frontier posts, stipends for members of the Hashimite clan, and salaries for personnel.

Another important department was the postal service, an institution inherited from the Sasanids by Umayyads and enlarged by Yahya Barmaki to serve the public. Trunk roads connected important centers of the empire, caravanserais dotted the roads, and a postal timetable was kept in Baghdad for the whole realm. Interestingly enough, one of the functions of the post office was intelligence service. Then as now, the service used merchants, travelers, and vendors for espionage, internal and foreign. Perhaps the only difference was that the Abbasid chief of intelligence employed a large number of old women.

The Abbasids, like the Umayyads, were confronted with the ever-present problem of succession. The Umayyad practice of appointment by the caliph continued, but it did not help the Abbasids any more than it had the Umayyads. The most serious incident occurred after the death of Harun al-Rashid. He had designated both of his sons to succeed him in order of age, first Amin and then Ma'mun. The two brothers did not get along and civil war ensued. Amin was assassinated, and Ma'mun marched into Baghdad and assumed the caliphate.

COMMERCE, INDUSTRY, AND AGRICULTURE

The bedouin disdained agriculture but not business. The Prophet himself was a successful merchant, and Islam has always had a high regard for merchants. With ports like Baghdad, Basra, Siraf, Alexandria, and Cairo, there was brisk business activity within the empire as well as with the outside world. Chinese ships were not an uncommon sight at the wharves of Baghdad. Caravan routes connected the four corners of the empire, distributing products from one section to another. Processions of caravans carried goods such as rice, linen, silk, wine, brocades, pearls, glass, metal, fruit, perfume, marble, carpets, tables, cushions, frying pans, trays, bowls, drugs, and countless other commodities. Foreign trade with all parts of the world, with the exception of southern Europe, was brisk and profitable. Muslims established a colony of merchants in China from where they brought porcelain and silk. From India they imported spices and dyes. They traded in fur with Russia and in ivory with Africa. The discovery of Abbasid coins in Russia and Germany attests to the existence of an international trade.

Industry had to produce in order to keep pace with such a flourishing commerce. Pearls from Bahrain, steel swords from Yaman, wine from Shiraz, tiles from Kashan, and rugs from all parts of Iran were world famous. Paper making had been learned from the Chinese, and the Abbasids had several paper mills in operation in Iran, Iraq, and Egypt. The economy of the empire as a whole, however, was agrarian. The early Abbasids built dams, canals, and irrigation ditches in Iraq, Khorasan, and other parts of the realm. The whole region was more fertile then than it is now. It produced and distributed more wheat, rice, dates, cotton, fruits, nuts, oranges, melons, and vegetables. Also, one must not forget that one of the most lucrative institutions of the empire was slavery.

FOREIGN RELATIONS

By the time the Abbasids came to power, the vigor of the Arab conquest had spent itself and the Arab warriors had either gone back to the desert or had been assimilated. The Abbasids added very little to the territory they had inherited. Except for the bodyguard which remained in Baghdad, they did not even maintain a standing army. Consequently, most of their foreign relations depended upon the sending of emissaries and in the giving and receiving of gifts.

An exception to this general situation, however, was their relation with Byzantium. The riches of Constantinople were still inviting, and the conquest of Asia Minor had become a challenge. Emperor Constantine V (741–775), taking advantage of the civil war between the Abbasids and the Umayyads, had pushed back the Arab invaders all along the southern borders of Asia Minor. In 782, Mahdi sent an expedition under the command of his son, Harun, which advanced to the Bosporus. Queen Irene sued for and concluded peace with the payment of tribute. The Byzantine Empire was weak enough to excite the expansionist tendencies of the Arabs, both Umayyad and Abbasid, but strong enough to withstand their attacks. Consequently, the Arabs were happy to receive money and make peace, which in turn gave the Byzantines a breathing spell.

Later Emperor Nicephorus I (802–811) broke the treaty. Harun was so enraged at hearing the news that he wrote the famous letter quoted by practically every historian of Europe. "From Harun, the Commander of the Faithful, to Nicephorus, the dog of a Roman . . ." Harun sent an expedition that, true to form, exacted the tribute and returned. Arabs were not destined to master Asia Minor. Islam, however, conquered it by means of the Turks.

European writers have made much of the fact that Harun al-Rashid and Charlemagne were contemporaries and have recorded that Charlemagne's envoys brought gifts from "Aaron, the King of Persia." Muslim writers, however, are silent about such a relationship. It is quite plausible that the Abbasid caliph would want the friendship of Charlemagne against the Umayyad caliphate of Spain, and that Charlemagne could profit from the hostility between Baghdad and Constantinople. Nothing substantial, however, came of it except the exchange of gifts.

ABBASID SOCIETY

One of the most important transformations during the Abbasid period was the fact that Arab segregationist policies were discarded and society became international. Thanks to the vastness of the empire and the existence of good communications, and more especially, thanks to slavery and concubinage, Arabs, Iranians, Syrians, Egyptians, Berbers, Turks, and Indians comingled, at least in urban centers. Muslim writers like the author of *Aghani* describe mainly the life and leisure of the caliphs and upper classes. As for the common people, we know that they had ample opportunity to use the numerous public baths (as in modern times, even small towns and larger villages claimed such accommodations). Strangers were cared for in hostels; those who were poor could always sleep in the mosques. Women were segregated; their duty was in the home and in the rearing of children—except slave girls, who would amuse men with their songs and dances. Polygamy was permitted, to the extent of four legal wives. It being a slave society, we may assume that the men of the upper and middle classes availed themselves of the opportunity and had at least half a dozen slave concubines if not four wives. Tables and chairs were never used in the Middle East. The upper classes sat on raised divans covered with mattresses and cushions and the lower classes on mats. Food was served in large circular copper trays. Families that could not afford individual plates would sit around and eat from a common tray.

A large part of the population, especially in the rural areas and among the lower classes, had not become Muslims. During the early Abbasid period, the majority of non-Muslims were Zoroastrians; next in number were the Nestorian, Orthodox, and Coptic Christians. The number of Jews was quite small. The Abbasids were wont to keep a pretense of religiosity and, to please the Muslim theologians, persecuted non-Muslims. Caliphs such as Harun al-Rashid, Mutawakkil, and others were especially harsh. The dhimmi could not build places of worship, and all that were built after the Arab conquest were ordered demolished. They had to wear special attire, and some were even branded on their foreheads. Their homes could not be taller than those of Muslims, and their testimony against Muslims was not admitted in court.

Away from the capital, where everyone was at the mercy of the local governor, the dhimmi were required to pay the head tax in a prostrate position and, in lieu of a receipt, were given a seal, which they hung around their necks. Under such circumstances, conversions to Islam were numerous. Notwithstanding all this, there was tolerance in Islam. Many Christians and Jews held positions of honor as businessmen, court physicians, philosophers, and even vazirs. We do not, however, know of any Zoroastrians who were so honored or tolerated. It is safe to assume, therefore, that the brunt of persecution was borne by Zoroastrians and lower-class Christians and Jews. The Arab supremacy preached by the Umayyads caused resentment among the aristocrats and intelligentsia of Iran and Syria, while the religious zeal of the Abbasids persecuted the majority of the rural population. Perhaps it was their cry that the author of *Aghani* recorded:

> Oh, that the tyranny of the Umayyads would return
> Oh, that the justice of the Abbasids would go to hell.

FRAGMENTATION OF THE EMPIRE

The house of the Abbasids was built with propaganda and bricks of empty promises on a soil that was basically hostile to it. The different segments of society, some of which had based their hopes on the ascendency of the Abbasids, were now disgruntled. Their hopes had been changed into resentment.

The Arabs were dissatisfied because they had been cast aside; the Syrians because they had lost their power; the Shi'is because they had been deceived; the Iranians because they had been disinherited; and the non-Muslims because they had been humiliated. The Kharijites constantly opposed the official establishment. During nearly a century of "honeymoon" that the Abbasid caliphs enjoyed, they did not use their enormous wealth and power to keep the empire intact, let alone to weld a nation. To be sure, there were some exceptions—for example, during the twenty years of Mamun's reign; but on the whole the caliphs were interested in power and pleasure and maintained themselves with the aid of their executioners and their Turkish bodyguards.

The caliphs became more insecure with the passing of time. Their Khorasan bodyguards had been weakened or had left in disgust. The north and south Arabs, who had continued their feuding, were not inclined to save the caliphs from the obvious designs and machinations of the Iranians. To protect himself, Mu'tasim (833–842) brought in Turks to act as his bodyguard. The Turks were as brave and obedient as they were uncouth and unlettered. They could be used as a lever, so the caliph hoped, to let the Arabs and Iranians destroy each other. The fact that Mu'tasim's own mother was a Turkish slave may have contributed to the move.

In any event, the stalwart Turkish bodyguards that replaced the Khorasanis proved to be a kind of Frankenstein. In a few years their rowdyism and debauchery caused so much trouble in Baghdad that the caliph moved his capital to nearby Samarra and took them with him. The caliphs did not return to Baghdad until fifty years later. But whether the capital was in Samarra or in Baghdad the difficulty continued.

A few years after the Turks entered the service of the caliph, they began to take charge of state affairs. By 861 they felt strong enough to kill Mutawakkil and replace him with his son. From then until 941 the Turks made and unmade caliphs and became virtual rulers of whatever was left of the empire. Soon their leader became the grand vazir and was given the title of commander-in-chief. The hapless caliphs, however, were not allowed to languish in their insignificant status. Three of them were blinded and were seen begging in the streets of Baghdad. With such a situation in the capital it is not surprising that governors in practically all parts of the empire carved out principalities for themselves and became independent.

In addition to the weakness of the central government there were other causes of the Abbasid decline. A perennial one was the religious differences between the Shi'is and Sunnis. The Shi'is, who felt that they had been unjustly banned from leading the ummah of Islam, tried in every way possible to assume power. The important Shi'i principalities included the Idrisids of Morocco (788), the Aghlabids of Tunisia (800), the Fatimids of Egypt and Syria (900), and the Buyids of Iran (945). Of the above, the Fatimids were the most important. Fatimid leaders assumed the title of caliph and ruled until 1171, when they were defeated by Saladin, who became famous during the Crusades. They established the famous Azhar University in 972 in Cairo. (Azhar University was later taken over by the Sunnis; it remains in operation to this day and is perhaps the oldest university in the world.)

Religion alone was not the only reason for the establishment of these petty kingdoms. In North Africa there were at least three other factors that promoted their independence from Baghdad. One was gold. Between the ninth and twelfth centuries, the mercantile interests of Italian and other European city-states developed a gold-based currency, which in turn caused a boom in the gold trade. The North African principalities were soon challenging West African control of the Niger River gold trade. Muslim merchants and caravaneers vied with each other over the markets and towns of the western Sahara to meet the demands of the European city-states.

Second, the decline in southern European food production between the ninth and twelfth centuries created an interest among the North African principalities and merchants for staple crop production. Thus, large tracts of village land and cultivated coastal plains from Rabat to Tunis, which were rich in wheat, barley and tree crops, came under the control of the petty rulers. They, in turn, forced the Berber and Arab cultivators to turn over a large portion of their harvests to the merchants for export to southern Europe.

A third factor in the strengthening of the petty principalities was the efforts of merchants in establishing trading posts in West and Central Africa. They gathered information on land usage, crop production, road security, and labor resources, which were important to them. This knowledge was also utilized by the rulers, who formed diplomatic and commercial alliances with the Niger River towns and kingdoms. These became useful in the post-twelfth-century wars on the North African littoral. Thus, the emergence of these principalities was tied to the commercial and agricultural conditions of southern Europe on the one hand and the expansion of the West African kingdoms on the other.

The desire for national supremacy provided a strong motivation for self-rule, especially among the Iranians in the east. Here as in North Africa there were other factors that made self-rule possible. One was the standardization of commercial and agricultural exchange by the Abbasids and the security of overland routes from Central Asia and the Iranian plateau to the Fertile Crescent and the Mediterranean. The building of Baghdad as the Abbasid capital brought commerce and politics closer to the Iranian plateau, the Central Asian steppes, the Persian Gulf, and the Indian Ocean. The requirements of commerce, together with the intelligence needs of the government, produced a virtual explosion of information about the region. Merchants, sea captains, travelers, geographers, and historians in the ninth and tenth centuries provided detailed written accounts about the commercial and agricultural potential of the Iranian plateau and the market towns of Central Asia and the Persian Gulf.

The influx of goods and wealth not only heightened the prosperity and luxury of Baghdad, but bolstered the local nobility of the Iranian market towns of Shiraz, Esfahan, Kerman, Mashhad, and Tabriz. Shiraz and Kerman benefitted from the emergence of port towns on the Persian Gulf such as Siraf and Kish Island. Items such as spices, cotton cloth, perfume, precious stones, timber, gold, rice, and wines were usually exchanged in Siraf's markets or trans-shipped over land routes to Shiraz, Esfahan, and Baghdad. Such maritime and land trade did not escape the notice of the local nobility or the military strongmen of the Iranian plateau, who were trying to improve their own conditions at the expense of the Baghdad caliphs. Therefore, a number of petty principalities along the commercial routes began to emerge.

Foremost among the many principalities of the ninth and tenth centuries were the Samanids of Khorasan (874–999), established by a Balkhi landowner, and the Saffarids of Sistan (867–903), founded by a coppersmith who controlled the trade from the Persian Gulf to Esfahan and Hamadan in Iran and to Ghazneh and Herat in Afghanistan. In the tenth century other principalities arose along the northern Iranian trade routes, such as the Kharazmshahs of Gorgan (995–1015) and the Buyids of Mazandaran (936–1062)

The influx of Turks added to the number of petty principalities. The stream of Turks that started moving toward Baghdad in 830 grew in volume by the middle of the century, and some of them started kingdoms of their own. Among the Turkish principalities, two deserve special mention. One was the Ghaznavids (892–1186), whose greatest king, Mahmud, took the banner of Islam to northern India. The other group of Turks, known as the Saljuqs, was even more important. The Saljuqs arrived on the scene around the year 1000, and by 1055 their leader had been made commander-in-chief of the caliph in Baghdad. The Saljuqs eventually separated into three kingdoms. One kingdom was headed by the Saljuqs of Iran (1037–1194), who had their capital in Maragheh in northern Iran; another was headed by the Saljuqs of Syria (1094–1117), who had their capital in Aleppo in northern

Syria; and the third was headed by the Saljuqs of Asia Minor (1071–1299), with their capital in Konya in central Turkey. The Saljuqs of Iran, like the other Turkish principalities of Iran, became Persianized in time and used the Persian language in their courts. Similarly, the Saljuqs of Syria, together with other Turkish kingdoms, became Arabized and used the Arabic language. Only the Saljuqs of Asia Minor continued to speak Turkish, and they became the forerunners of the Ottoman Turks.

Looking back over the period of principalities, which lasted some 300 years, it may be noted that on the whole the petty kingdoms of the west were established for dynastic and religious reasons. In the east, however, religion did not play a great part. The motivation there, in addition to personal ambition, was primarily Persian patriotism. The Iranians were consciously anti-Arab and did much to revive Persian domination. They resisted the pressure of Arabization and refused to speak Arabic. Because of the prestige given to it by Islam and the attraction it had for the intelligentsia, Arabic continued to be the language of learning and commerce almost until the advent of the Mongol era. But Persian, which had always remained the spoken language, also became the language of administration, even of the Turkish principalities, from the time of the Saffarids in 867.

The question may be asked, "How was it, then, that the Abbasid caliphs lasted so long?" As a matter of fact, the caliphate, as an institution, was intentionally kept alive by a succession of strongmen, or "princes." The principal reason for this was the prestige of the office and its high position in the mind of the Muslim population. It was customary for these princes to receive an order of "investiture" from the caliph. This was probably to placate the populace and especially the religious leaders. Such letters of appointment were readily given by the caliphs, mostly out of fear and sometimes for a price.

Another reason that the caliphs were allowed to survive was the concern for legitimacy. The majority Sunni party believed that the caliph should be a member of the Quraysh tribe. The warring princes could not possibly make such a claim. Some of them did try, through marriage, to connect themselves with the house of Abbas. Even the Shi'is, who did not believe the Abbasids were legitimate caliphs, were afraid of popular sentiment.

Thus the members of the house of Abbas survived, even after the destruction of Baghdad, until 1517. At that time the Ottoman Sultan Selim I put an end to the pretense when he defeated the Mamluks.

Chapter Seven
Religion and Law under the Abbasids

Culturally speaking, the Arab conquest of the Fertile Crescent and Iran was a barbarian invasion of the advanced civilizations of the Byzantine and Sasanid empires. In the history surveyed thus far, four significant periods of this cultural movement may be distinguished. The first two have already been discussed in Chapters 4 and 5.

1. The period of the Orthodox Caliphs, when the chief activity was the consolidation of military conquest and the preaching of the simple faith brought from the desert.[1]

2. The period of the Umayyads, which was still very close to the primitive bedouin culture and was plagued by civil wars. It nevertheless brought the faith in contact with the Byzantine and Iranian cultures and raised many questions concerning faith and conduct in the community of Islam.

3. The early Abbasid period of borrowing in which the best available writings of the non-Islamic world were collected and systematically translated into Arabic.

4. The period of creativity during the decline of the Abbasids and the rise of principalities, when Muslim theologians, scientists, philosophers, and others produced original works built upon the knowledge that they had acquired.

A brief discussion of the period of translation, or borrowing, is necessary in this topical approach to Islamic culture, because without it, the cre-

[1]Muslim historians have always applied the adjective "Rashidin" to the first four caliphs.

ative contributions of scores of Muslim scholars would not have been possible. Furthermore, it serves to remind the student of the Middle East that this culture was an amalgamation of Egyptian, Greek, Iranian, Syrian, Indian, and Chinese sources and was a far cry from the original simple faith brought out of the Arabian peninsula. It will be seen, however, that this original simple faith was never discarded. All knowledge, contradictory as this may seem, was related to the central faith.

Most of the translations were done during the reign of the early Abbasids, especially Harun al-Rashid and Ma'mun. It was the latter who established the House of Wisdom, whose principal activities were the collection and translation of works from all parts of the world. It should be said, to the glory of the early Abbasids, that even though they squandered large sums of money on extravagant pleasures, they also supported intellectuals. Some of the caliphs did not hesitate to ask their enemies, the emperors of Byzantium, for books. As the records indicate, members of the Bureau of Translations were some of the highest paid intellectuals in the history of the world.

They translated all kinds of works, without bothering to be selective, from Greek, Pahlavi, Latin, Sanskrit, Chinese, Syriac, Nabataean, and other languages. Going over a list of scores of translations, it is possible to generalize that from Greek they translated works of philosophy, logic, medicine, and mathematics; from Persian, history, government, medicine, and literature; from Sanskrit, mathematics, medicine, and astronomy; and from Nabataean, agriculture and magic.

Almost none of the translators were Arab and some were not Muslims. Three of the most important translators, each from a different faith, who left an imprint on Islamic culture in different fields are, in chronological order: ibn-Muqaffa (d. 757), a Zoroastrian; Hunayn ibn-Ishaq (809–873), a Christian; and Thabit ibn-Qurrah (d. 901), a Sabian.

The sincerity of ibn-Muqaffa's conversion to Islam was doubtful. For a time he acted as secretary in the court of the last Umayyad caliph and then continued with the Abbasids, though not for long. One of his most important translations is the *Book of Lords*, which was rendered into Arabic as *Attributes of the Kings of Iran*. This became a model of historical writing for later Muslim historians. The most famous of his translations, however, is the ancient Sanskrit classic *Panchatantra,* which had been rendered into Pahlavi as the *Fables of Bidpay*. He translated it into Arabic as *Kalila wa Dimna*. This is a delightful animal story in which the animals take on the characteristics of humans and discuss all sorts of philosophical and moral ideas. Each idea is introduced by a parable involving even more animals. This has become a classic in the literatures of most of the nations of the world. Inasmuch as both the original Sanskrit and the Pahlavi versions are lost, the debt to this gifted translator is the greater. Ibn-Muqaffa was a Shu'ubiyya[2] leader and is reported to have claimed that his Arabic was much better than that of the Koran. He was suspected of being a Zoroastrian at heart, which he probably was, and was burned to death by the order of Mansur, the second Abbasid caliph.

[2]See p. 68.

The second eminent translator was Hunayn ibn-Ishaq. He was a Nestorian Christian who had training in medicine but became famous as a translator. As a Nestorian Christian, his mother tongue was Syriac and he did not know Arabic very well. But he must have improved tremendously, for Ma'mun used to pay him in gold the weight of the books he rendered into Arabic. Among his translations are Galen, Hippocrates, Plato's *Republic*, Aristotle's *Categories*, and others.

The third luminary in the field of translation was Thabit ibn-Qurrah, a Sabian (836–891).[3] He belonged to the star-worshipping Sabians and, together with his subordinates of the same faith, translated most of the then-known works in mathematics and astronomy from Greek. Among his translations are works by Archimedes, Apollonius of Perga, Euclid, and others. He established a school of translators, most of whom were, like that of Hunayn, members of his own family. In about the second generation, the family was converted to Islam, as seems to have been the case with the family of Hunayn.

THEOLOGY AND RELIGION

The simple creed of Islam, "There is no God but Allah and Muhammad is His Messenger," together with a few rituals and rules of conduct, seemed adequate for life in the desert. Catapulted into the mastery of an empire and drawn into close relation to and in competition with other religions, and involved in a variety of questions about life and eternity, the old faith seemed shamefully naked. Furthermore, the turbulent history of the period, with its bloodshed, civil wars, assassinations, disputes over succession, Umayyad worldliness, and a host of other problems, raised theological questions that rocked the new religious society of Islam.

One of the first groups to form definite opinions and separate themselves from the main body were the Kharijites.[4] These seceders were most liberal in their interpretation of the Koran and adamant in their belief that the office of the caliphate, the burning question of the time, was open to all Muslims no matter what their racial origin. "Even a slave can be a caliph," they insisted, provided he was righteous, honest, and went about doing good. They developed the doctrine of salvation through works and gradually came to the view that anyone could be saved through good works regardless of his faith. As has happened so many times in history, the Kharijites went about with drawn swords killing those who would not agree with their liberal ideas. By the tenth century, they had become virtual anarchists and got much of their support from Berbers and bedouins.

On the other side of the theological controversy were those who believed in salvation through confession. They believed in the suspension of human judgment concerning the acts of men and left it to God. Hence, they are known as Murji'ites. Their belief was an attempt to accommodate the

[3]See p. 10.
[4]See p. 53.

reality as well as the worldliness of the Umayyads to Islam. They said that once a man confessed his faith in Islam, as certainly the Umayyads did repeatedly, he was a true Muslim no matter what his actions. In between these two views came that of the Mu'tazilites, who formed a dominant school of religious thought for some time. They believed that when a major sin is committed by a Muslim he has separated himself from the community, ummah, but has not become an infidel. They also believed in free will, against those who followed the predestinarian pronouncements of the Koran.

The main interest of the Mu'tazilities, however, was in other questions that Greek rationalism had raised. One of these had to do with the names of Allah. Traditionally, there were some ninety-nine of them. To the Mu'tazilite rationalists, the anthropomorphic connotations of these names were disturbing. Furthermore, they believed that such names negated the unity of God emphasized in the Koran. Consequently, they separated the name of "Allah" from divine attributes, and, to preserve the unity of Allah, said that God and His attributes were not coexistent. The other question of great importance had to do with the Koran itself. The orthodox notion was that the Koran was the uncreated word of God and coexistent with Him. The rationalist Mu'tazilites could not accept this and announced that the Koran was created and, therefore, not eternal. Many of these rationalists were executed by the Umayyad Hisham (724–743) for teaching the creation of the Koran and for believing in free will.

During the reign of the Abbasids, however, the Mu'tazilites became strong and Ma'mun himself joined them. Under their influence he made a special proclamation of the dogma of the creation of the Koran. This caused a great deal of turmoil among the orthodox, but the Mu'tazilites had the upper hand. These former champions of freedom of thought induced Ma'mun and two of his successors to set up an inquisition to persecute anyone who would not subscribe to the new dogma.

It was not until the middle of the tenth century, however, that orthodoxy found its champion in the person of Abul Hassan Ali al-Ash'ari. He rejected free will and instead claimed that man was responsible for his actions only because God willed it. He declared the eternal nature of the Koran. As to God and His names, he said that every name attributed to God has a meaning that is different from the meaning of the same name when applied to man. Consequently, God is removed from the knowledge of man and the two have nothing in common.

Greek and other systems of thought continued in Islam, and the scholastic school that Ash'ari founded tried to reconcile Islam with these. This task was accomplished to the satisfaction of the orthodox by the prince of Muslim theologians, Abu Hamid al-Ghazali (1058–1111). He was born in Tus, Khorasan, and after a tumultuous life died in his birthplace. He studied every philosophy and religious thought and was converted to some of them in turn. His autobiography reads like the confessions of St. Augustine and, in much the same way as the Christian saint, Ghazali taught orthodox Islam at the Nizamiya college in Baghdad, and then quit to spend his days in contemplation. In his famous book, *The Revival of the Sciences of Religion*, he tried to combine Islam, rationalism, and mysticism into one harmonious unit. According to Ghazali, knowledge is of two categories: knowledge connected with theology and knowledge not connected with theology. Of the latter, he recommends medicine, mathematics, and crafts, and permits the study of poetry and history. His works were translated into Latin; and he is considered to be one of the important influences on Saint Thomas Aquinas, who also attempted to harmonize Christian revelation with Greek rationalism. Whereas medieval Thomism was challenged by the Protestant Reformation and subsequent philosophical systems, the medieval house in which Ghazali and others placed Muslim orthodoxy has remained intact. In this sense it is not correct to talk about the "end of Medieval Islam," for the so-called medieval scholasticism of Islam was not even challenged until the beginning of the twentieth century and remains unchanged.

SHI'ISM

These theological movements and many others did not cause permanent rifts in Islam. The movement, however, that eventually split Islam permanently into two camps was Shi'ism. It will be remembered that the partisans (Shi'a) of Ali banded together on the question of the caliphate. Failing to establish their claim by politics or by war, the Shi'is separated permanently from the majority and founded a religion of their own, complete with theology, philosophy, government, and ethics. Religiously, Shi'ism has supplied Islam with mysteries, saints, intercessors, belief in atonement, and a spirit of high cult—all of which are repugnant to the majority of Sunnis. The Sunnis and Shi'is both consider the Koran infallible, but the Shi'is place infallibility also in a man, the Imam, who is sinless and is considered to be man-God. The martyrdom of Husayn, the third Imam, at Karbala has afforded the Shi'is the opportunity to pour out their religious feelings in processions, all sorts of self-mortifications, and passion plays and poetry that depict his death as redeeming the sins of the world.

Ali, the first Imam and the "rightful heir" to the Prophet, claimed to have received the light of prophecy from Muhammad and to have passed it on to his descendant-successors. This enables the Shi'is to claim that Muhammad is truly the last Prophet, whose mission is perpetuated in his descendants through Ali. They believe in this so strongly that they are not satisfied with the witness of Islam, "I believe that there is no God but Allah, and Muhammad is the Messenger of Allah." To this they always add a third sentence, "I believe that Ali is the regent of Allah."

This doctine of the Imamate forms the heart of the political theory of the Shi'is, which is purely theocratic. No Muslim, Sunni, or Shi'a questions that Muhammad was the head of the state as agent of Allah. Since, according to the Shi'is, his powers both spiritual and temporal have passed on to Ali and successively to the other Imams, then it follows that the legitimate government belongs to the Imam. All other governments not under the Imam or his agents, including all Sunni caliphs, are usurpers. Consequently, the first three caliphs of Islam, Abu Bakr, Umar, and Uthman, are considered "usurpers" by the Shi'is.

The Shi'is believe in the doctrine of the Return. This belief has many things in common with the return of the deliverer in Zoroastrianism, the coming of the Messiah in Judaism, and "second coming" of Jesus in Christianity. The majority of Shi'is believe that there were twelve Imams and that the twelfth, the Mahdi ("messiah") has disappeared and shall reappear at the end of time, when he will bring justice to the whole world. The twelve Imams are shown below.

```
                        1. Ali (d. 661)
        ┌───────────────────────┴─────────────────┐
2. Hasan (d. 669)                        3. Husayn (d. 680)
                                         4. Ali Zayn al-Abidin (d. 712)
                          ┌──────────────────────┴───────────┐
                        Zayd                     5. Muhammad al-Baqir (d. 731)
                                                 6. Ja'far al-Sadiq (d. 765)
                    ┌───────┴──────────────────────────┐
              Ismail (d. 760)               7. Musa al-Kazim (d. 799)
                                            8. Ali al-Rida (d. 818)
                                            9. Muhammad al-Jawad (d. 835)
                                           10. Ali al-Hadi (d. 868)
                                           11. Hasan al-Askari (d. 874)
                                           12. Muhammad al-Muntazar
                                               (The Mahdi) (d. 878)
```

One Shi'ite sect is called Zaydi, for its members stop with Zayd, the grandson of Husayn, and regard him as their leader. They do not believe in the doctrine of the Return.

Another and more important sect among the Shi'is is the Ismaili, or the Seveners. The sixth Imam had two sons, Ismail and Musa. He first appointed Ismail; but because of Ismail's alleged drinking habits, he later transferred the succession to Musa. Ismail predeceased his father. Nevertheless, this sect considers Ismail to be the seventh Imam. They introduced esoteric mysteries around the number seven and had the best-organized missionary activity in all Islam. One of their leaders founded the Fatimid caliphate. It was one of the Fatimid caliphs, Hakim, who claimed deity and had a following called Druze, who may be found in Lebanon and Israel today. Another offshoot of the Ismaili was the Qarmatians. They were accused of practicing communism—even to the sharing of wives. This was a fraternal organization with secret mysteries. They caused havoc among the Muslims. In 930 they succeeded in removing the sacred Black Stone of the Ka'ba, which was not returned until twenty years later.

A better-known branch is called the Assassins. Their founder Hasan Sabbah (d. 1124) established his headquarters in the high and inaccessible redoubt, Alamut, in the Alborz Mountains northwest of Qazvin. Sabbah's activities were basically political and apparently anti-Sunni. Indeed, even collaborators of the Sunnis were opposed. Nizam al-Mulk was a strong Sunni, and he established several Nizamiya colleges especially to teach Ash'ari doctrine. Naturally, he was one of the targets of the Assassins. Successive expeditions against Alamut failed, and it was left for Hulagu, the Mongol conqueror of Baghdad, to destroy Alamut also.

SUFISM

Sufism—Islamic mysticism—is yet another development in the field of religion. Practically every religion has produced its particular form of mysticism. In Islam, Sufism was also a reaction to the Ash'ari theology of the separation of God and man. According to the Sufis, the world is a manifestation of God, and there is a true resemblance between the attributes of God and man. The Christian monastic orders and the mystical nature of the Gospels impressed the Sufis. Rumi says that "the monastery of Jesus is the place for the people of the heart." Orthodoxy, so the Sufis believed, had placed Islam in a shell. The Sufis broke the shell but thought it a necessary evil.

The Sufis, like the early Christians, called themselves "people of the way." The idea is built around the claim that the soul of man has been separated from its Maker and has a longing to return and be lost in Him. Attar in his exquisite allegory, "The Conversation of the Birds," tells the story of the birds (humanity), who went out to seek *simorgh* (God), who was their king and lived beyond the mountain, *qaf*. They had to pass seven valleys (conditions) of (1) search, (2) love, (3) understanding, (4) detachment, (5) communion, (6) wonder, (7) union and/or extinction. Of the thousands who flew to seek the king, only thirty birds—in Persian, *si* ("thirty") *morgh* ("bird")—arrived. The rest perished on the way and many even killed each other to save themselves. The bedraggled thirty birds who arrived were severely tested by the vazir of the king. Having passed the test, the portals opened and the veil was rent asunder. They entered and found peace. But when they looked at each other, they realized that they were the *simorgh* (God) and that *simorgh* was none other than they the *simorgh*, thirty birds. Detached from the outer world they saw themselves as they were in the beginning!

Jalal al-Din Rumi (1207–1273) of Khorasan, who lived and died in Konya, Asia Minor, is considered the prince of all the mystics. His book of poems, *Masnavi*, is full of anecdotes taken from everyday life to show the way to union with God. A pure and polished heart can reflect more clearly the beauty of God. He founded the order whose habit of dancing to music gained for them the name of "whirling dervishes."

Hafez of Shiraz, a more joyous and cheerful mystic than Rumi, used wine, roses, and love both as an allegory and as aids to spiritual life. To him life was supremely joyous and, like the wine that he enjoyed, also bitter. He could see the "light of God in the Magian house of worship," and the "countenance of [his] beloved in a cup of wine." Like all the Sufis, he believed in the supremacy of the heart over the mind. "The stage of love is much higher than that of the intellect. He can kiss the [former's] threshold who is ready to endanger his life."

It was Ghazali (1058–1111), however, who had tried Sufism and later became a theologian, who gave the mystics a place in the orthodox scheme so that they were tolerated. Consequently, the Sufis never separated from the Islamic community. They organized orders and had their own hierarchy of leaders but remained within Islam, both Sunni and Shi'a. One of these orders was *Bektashi*, to which all of the Ottoman sultans belonged. Another was a Shi'a fraternity, the *qizilbash,* "red heads," of which the Safavid shahs of Iran were leaders. Most of the Sufi orders, however, did not have anything to do with politics and war.

LAW

It is not difficult to say which is more important in Islam, faith or law. Muslims on the whole have spent more time and thought on the ramifications of law than on faith. Actually, law and faith are two sides of the same coin. Law is the will of God, and Islam is the terms of submission to it. It is the Muslim belief that Jews and Christians had corrupted and complicated the law of God and that Allah had sent Muhammad to clarify the confusion. In the medieval period, Judaism, Christianity, and Islam were closer together than at any other time in history. All three had the same conception of God as one Who was the ruler of the universe, Who demanded obedience, and Who had given mankind the law. In Judaism, He had given it to Moses and the priests; in Christianity to the Church of Christ; and in Islam, to Muhammad and the community (ummah) of believers.

The most important foundation of Islamic law is the Koran. But, the expanding community soon discovered that the Koran did not contain all the situations and questions that came up for decision and judgment. Furthermore, the political and religious controversies led Muslims to ask, "What would Muhammad have done?" or "What did the Prophet do?" In the early years there were many who had known the Prophet personally, and they narrated (*haddatha*) the practice (*sunna*) of the Prophet. Thus, *hadith,* or tradition, is the description of a saying or action of the Prophet or an action of his companions of which Muhammad approved, provided it is verified by a trustworthy chain of witnesses. It was used to make a difficult decision, to settle a religious or moral controversy, to solve a delicate legal problem, to advocate a new idea, and to do a thousand and one other things. The practices of the Prophet in all matters, from weighty and legal questions to the way he brushed his teeth or ate watermelon, became the norm. A typical hadith is the following taken from the collection by Bukhari:

> Abdullah ibn-al-Aswad told me; Al-Fadl ibn-al-Ata told us; Isma'il ibn-Umayya told us on the authority of Yahya ibn-Abdullah ibn-Sayfi that he heard Abu Ma'bad, the freedman of Ibn Abbas, say, "I heard Ibn Abbas say: 'when the Prophet, the blessings of Allah be upon him, and peace, said Mu'adh to the Yaman, he said to him . . .' "

There are six authoritative collections of hadith. These collections are second only to the Koran and their authority cannot be questioned. The Koran and the hadith formed the totality of the law of God, shari'a, which became the foundation of Islamic jurisprudence.

Islam, however, expanded very quickly and there were civil, criminal, fiscal, and other cases that varied in different countries and raised problems. To solve those problems two other principles were added. One is analogy, which is used when the principles established by the Koran or hadith are no longer applicable. The other is consensus of the community, which became an excellent expedient for introducing novel ideas and institutions. The jurists resorted also to private judgment, but it never received authoritative sanction. It must be pointed out that analogy and consensus were resorted to only when the Koran and hadith could not be of any assistance.

Schools of Law

Different interpretations of the Koran and the hadith, together with varying circumstances both in time and place, led to the formation of both Sunni and Shi'i schools of interpretation of law. There are four Sunni schools, each named after its founder:

The Hanafite School. It emphasizes analogy and the principle of equity, which is based on natural law. It is the most tolerant of the legal schools of Islam. It is said that the founder believed that the Koran should be translated into the vernacular and that prayers should be conducted in languages other than Arabic. The Hanafite system was used by the Ottoman Turks and is prevalent in India, Afghanistan, and Central Asia.

The Malikite School. It introduced the formula of consensus of the community for the first time. It is more conservative than the Hanafi school and is followed by the Muslims of North Africa, exclusive of Egypt.

The Shafi'i School. Between the conservatism of the Malikites and the liberalism of the Hanafites, came the Shafi'i school. As a mean between the two extremes it is believed to have influenced all schools. This school is followed in Indonesia, Egypt, East Africa, and Lebanon.

The Hanbali School. It is the champion of Islamic fundamentalism. It rejects consensus, analogy, private judgment, and in fact anything that is outside the letter of the Koran and the hadith. Too conservative to be popular, this rite has only about 3,000,000 followers. They are among the Wahhabis of Arabia.

There are three Shi'i schools of law interpretation:

The Ja'fari School. It is also known as the Imami school. It is the most important Shi'a system of jurisprudence. It rejects analogy, consensus, and private judgment. It believes that the hidden Imam is the true head of the state. In his absence he rules through his spokesmen who are called *mujtahids* and *ayatollahs*—that is, interpreters of the will of the Imam. There are usually several of these mujtahids at a time. They are not chosen but simply acknowledged by the consensus of the community to be learned, pious, and qualified to issue opinion, *fatwa,* which is as binding to the faithful as a papal bull is to Roman Catholics. All the Shi'i Twelvers follow this school.

The Ismaili School. This is named after Ismail, son of the sixth Imam. The difference between this school and the Ja'fari is that there is only one spokesman for the Imam, in whom there is an indwelling spirit of the Imam, and in whom is reflected the light of the Imam. Consequently, it is as liberal or conservative as the leader. The office is hereditary. The most famous leader is the recent one, the Agha Khan (1877–1957), who traced his lineage to Hasan Sabbah. He appointed his grandson, Karim Khan, as the new leader. The Ismailis are scattered in India, Iran, and East Africa.

The Zaydi School. This is named after Zayd, the son of the fourth Imam. They do not believe in a hidden Imam. They are dominant in Yaman.

ETHICS

Ethics is connected with law (Shari'a) and Shari'a regulates the life of the Muslim in all its aspects. Everything that is not governed by the Shari'a is left for man to decide for himself according to the mores of his society if he is a Sunni. The Shi'i, however, must emulate the ayatollah or mujtahid of his choice. For the Muslims all conduct falls in one of five categories:

1. Obligatory. The performance of these acts brings reward in heaven and neglect brings punishment.
2. Meritorious. Acts that are recommended. Commission is rewarded but omission is not punished.
3. Permissible. Acts that are legally neutral, being neither rewarded nor punished.
4. Reprehensible. Acts that are disapproved but not forbidden. Omission is meritorious but commission is not punished.
5. Forbidden. Acts for which the culprit is punished.

Some moralists in Islam believe that it is possible for the same act to go through the above categories. For example, lying and killing are forbidden within the Islamic community and yet become increasingly permissible until they are obligatory in war with the infidel.

Chapter Eight
The Sciences
and Humanities
under the Abbasids

To the early Muslim mind, philosophy was a "foreign science" and as such it presented a challenge to Islamic theology. The Muslims, however, were forced to take up this challenge because a large number of the neo-Muslims who were familiar with Greek philosophy began to think of Islam in philosophical terms. Some manifestations of this type of thinking among groups such as the Mu'tazilites have already been discussed. What interested the Muslims most was, of course, the Shari'a, which could not be enforced without a state, and the state could not be held together without a caliph. As has been noted, it was the caliphate that was the main problem of the new community; and this problem became more difficult as the caliphs became weaker and rival caliphs appeared. Consequently, Muslim philosophers have interested themselves in *political* philosophy. To be sure, they have dealt with other branches of philosophy, but their main concern was government. Plato's *Republic* and Aristotle's *Politics* have held more fascination for them than other works. Even Islamic theology is political in nature and expression.

In order to better understand the succeeding centuries of Middle Eastern history, including the contemporary period, it should be stated here that Muslim political and historical philosophy is derived from four streams. One is the Koran and the "political theology" incorporated in it. The second is the contributions of Muslim political philosophers. The third is what might be called "practical precepts" written for the guidance of princes, which might or might not include the two above. The last stream consists of Irano-Turkish theories, which are more or less secular in nature. All Muslim governments of the later periods reveal various combinations of two or three or all four of the above sources. The Koran and the theological-political problems related to it were discussed in Chapter 3. What follows is a brief discussion of Muslim political philosophy and a few words about the "practical precepts."

Ya'qub ibn-Ishaq al-Kindi, who lived during the last half of the ninth century, was the first philosopher the Arabs produced. As he was the only one throughout the medieval and early modern periods, he has certainly earned the title of Philosopher of the Arabs. Unfortunately, however, most of his works have been lost, and there is not much that can be said about him except that he combined the views of Plato and Aristotle.

One of the foremost political philosophers of Islam was Abu-Nasr al-Farabi (870–950), a Turk who gained the reputation of being the "second teacher," Aristotle being the first. He set out to try to resolve the dilemma created among the learned Muslim community by the challenge of the Greeks, who wanted a philosopher for a king, while Islam had already had a prophet as head of state. To the Greeks, law was the product of the human mind, while to the Muslims, law was the will of God. Who made the best ruler of a society—the prophet or the philosopher?

In his book, *Opinions of the Citizens of the Virtuous City,* Farabi resolves the dilemma between philosopher and prophet by combining the two. He considered prophecy to be a function of the imagination and philosophy a function of the intellect. Since both intellect and imagination were both natural phenomena, a man with intellect as well as imagination would be both a prophet and a philosopher. Only such a man could rule a state.

Farabi was followed by Abu Ali Husayn ibn-Sina (980–1037), an Iranian from Bokhara. Commonly known as Avicenna, he was undoubtedly one of the great geniuses of all time. He was familiar with Farabi's work and admits indebtedness to him. In his encyclopedic work, called *Shafa,* he modified Farabi's position. Rather than linking intellect with philosophy and imagination with prophecy, he stated that both philosophy and prophecy were the results of the highest human intellect. Consequently, he concluded that in the absence of a prophet, it was still possible to develop a good society.

Insofar as orthodox Islam was concerned, these ideas were considered heretical, and the two gentlemen were accused of heresy. There was no one, however, with enough power to suppress heresy. These individuals, their contemporaries, and those who followed them were influenced by the social and political movements of their time. It will be remembered that the most important political reality in this period was the decline of the caliphate and the rise of rival principalities, especially those of Shi'a persuasion. During a century of Umayyad and Abbasid power and affluence, there had grown up a string of large cities throughout the empire from Cairo to Transoxiana. The merchants, artisans, and entrepreneurs of these urban centers were affluent and cosmopolitan, and they were fascinated by new ideas. The masses, as usual, bore the brunt of the extravagances of the weak caliphs and were extremely dissatisfied.

The Shi'is in general, and especially the Ismailis, had a well-conducted missionary organization that fanned the grievances of the masses against the caliphs. Furthermore, in order to reach the intellectuals, they established schools in urban centers and encouraged the integration of Islam with Hellenic and Iranian cultures against the orthodox Sunnis. Farabi flourished under the Shi'a Hamdanids in Aleppo. Avicenna was perhaps a Shi'i and was brought up in an Ismaili home.

The secularization of Islam, which was started by Farabi and Avicenna on the philosophical level, was carried on by an already flourishing semisecret fraternity called the "Brethren of Sincerity." These philosophical "study clubs," mostly encouraged by the Ismailis, were established in urban centers and carried on semipolitical activities against the government.

Not fifty years after the death of Avicenna there appeared a number of books written to teach the princes the ways of government. These books are generally referred to as "Practical Precepts" or "Mirrors to Princes." Among these, the most important are *Qabusnameh*, written for the Ziyarid principality in about 1082, and *Siyasatnameh*, written for the Saljuqs in about 1092. In these books, the art of government is taught through anecdotes, maxims, and examples, all taken from Sasanian kings. These books are regarded as still another influence in the shaping of Muslim political philosophy, which is neither Greek nor Islamic. In *Qabusnameh*, for example, we read that it is the duty of the prince to improve cultivation because "good government is secured by an army; an army maintained with gold; gold is acquired through taxation of country squires; and country squires are sustained through justice and fairness to the peasantry."

Quite obviously, the conclusions of Farabi and Avicenna were not acceptable to the orthodox. To both, prophecy, rather than being a gift of God through revelation, was a natural phenomenon attained through imagination and/or the "active intellect." According to them, it was possible to establish the "virtuous city" without a prophet or, particularly, without Islamic revelation. Sustained through the power of the Saljuqs, the orthodox bestirred themselves against these heretical ideas; the Shafi'is started schools like those of the Ismailis. Nizam al-Mulk, the grand vazir of the Saljuqs and the most effective champion of orthodox theologians, placed orthodox civil administrators in all departments of the government. These orthodox bureaucrats were in an excellent position to apply the Muslim shari'a to every aspect of the machinery of government and society. It was for his activities in the cause of Sunni orthodoxy that Nizam al-Mulk was murdered by an agent of the Assassins, who belonged to the Ismaili sect.

The orthodox, however, could eradicate neither the influence of the philosophers nor the realities of the situation. Even Nizam al-Mulk incorporated non-Muslim Persian traditions and ethics in his book. Ghazali was teaching in the Nizamiya college in Baghdad at the time of the Saljuqs. In his attempt to keep the unity of the ummah intact, he stated that piety was the only qualification for the office of the caliphate. Consequently, power may legitimately be placed in the hands of the sultan, who rules for the caliph. The fact that the caliph's name is mentioned in Friday prayers and is engraved on coins, insures, according to Ghazali, the unity of the ummah.

Later on, Ibn-Taymiyya (1263–1328), who belonged to the fundamentalist Hanbali school but lived under the Mamluks when there was no caliph at all, offered an even more dangerous compromise. He said that anyone who had the power to coerce and seize the government was a legitimate ruler, provided he obeyed the Shari'a. To him, "religion without a sultan, army, and money is as futile as a sultan with army and money but without religion." From this it was but only a short step to the claim that a sultan (not a caliph) rules by the authority of Allah. The Ottomans took that step.

THE SCIENCES

True to the tradition of learning in the medieval period, the Muslim scholar had a wide variety of knowledge. It was quite common for a philosopher to be a famous physician, and at the same time be able to solve mathematical equations and write learned treatises on music and astronomy. Some philosophers, like Omar Khayyam, wrote poetry for relaxation. The Muslims considered science to be of two kinds: "religious" and "physical." The humanities included poetry and prose, the latter being mostly moral stories. In between these two categories were geography and history.

Medicine. The great Sasanid medical center and hospital in Gundi Shapur in Iran was in operation during the Arab occupation. The hospital that Harun built in Baghdad was modeled after this. Both physicians and pharmacists had to pass special examinations. There is evidence that physicians were bound by an oath. The head of the hospital in Gundi Shapur was Jibril ibn-Bakhtishu, a Christian. He and his family served as court physicians for the Abbasids. Among translators of Greek and Persian medical works into Arabic, as well as being distinguished physicians in their own right, were Hunayn ibn-Ishaq (809–73), Yuhanna ibn-Masawayh (777–857), an ophthalmologist, and Tabari, only to name a few.

The most original work in medicine, however, was done by two Iranians, Razi and Avicenna. Muhammad ibn-Zakariya al-Razi (865–985) was born, as his name shows, in Ray, near Tehran, the capital of modern Iran. Most of his life he lived under the patronage of the princes of the Samanid principality and, for a time, was the chief physician at Baghdad. He was a very prolific writer; and some of his works, including his major one, *Comprehensive Work in Medicine*, were translated into Latin and later into French, German, and English. He invented the seton in surgery and reported his clinical studies on kidney stones, smallpox, and measles. For his philosophical writing on the side of rationalism, he was maligned by the orthodox and had to defend his own philosophy and private conduct.

Avicenna, who has already been introduced as a great philosopher, was also a very distinguished physician. He also wrote on mathematics, art, and music. At sixteen years of age he was a full-fledged physician and was called upon to treat the Samanid prince. At eighteen he "had exhausted all these sciences," meaning philosophy, logic, mathematics, medicine, and the like. This man, who claimed that medicine "was not a difficult science," wrote a famous encyclopedia on medicine called the *Qanun*. This replaced all other works in medicine and was used as a text in the schools of Europe until well into the seventeenth century. He wrote about contagion and the spread of diseases by water and earth. He wrote a volume on *Materia Medica*, in which he classified and commented on hundreds of drugs. Avicenna died in Hamadan and was buried there in 1037.

Mathematics and astronomy.   In the field of mathematics and astronomy, the Muslims drew from Greek and Indian sources. The most important contribution of the Muslims to mathematics is the system of "Arabic numerals," which they learned from the Indians. One of the giants in the field of astronomy was Muhammad al-Kharazmi, the translation of whose work introduced the "Arabic" numerals, and algebra. "Algorism" is named after him. Another scholar in astronomy and mathematics was Abu Rayhan Biruni (973–1048). On the basis of the rotation of earth on its axis, he calculated the latitude and longitude of many cities in the Middle East. Omar Khayyam, of *Rubayiat* fame, was actually a brilliant mathematician-astronomer who revised the calendar that is in use in Iran today. Hulagu, the Mongol victor of Baghdad, built an observatory in Azarbaijan where Nasir al-Din Tusi of Khorasan, one of the last of the famous astronomers, invented intricate astronomical instruments such as the armillary sphere, mural quadrant, and solstitial armil. His astronomical tables were in standard use for many centuries. Many observatories were situated at different centers. Most of the astronomers assumed the earth was round and measured the size and circumference of the earth with astonishing accuracy.

Muslim scholars were also interested in chemistry, physics, biology, zoology, and botany. They maintained laboratories for experimentation. One of the important chemists was Jabir Ibn-Hayyan, who described calcination and reduction and knew of evaporation, sublimation, melting, and crystallization. The Arabic origin of such words as chemistry, alcohol, antimony, and others shows the degree of European indebtedness to medieval Muslim scientists.

Geography.   Muslim conquests and commerce brought an awareness of the world. The Abbasid period produced a number of globetrotters, merchants, and scientific geographers who wrote down their observations. Theoretically, they were under Ptolemy's influence, but in their travels they saw things differently and produced a mass of descriptive material about India, Ceylon, China, and Russia. Kharazmi drew a map of the world that was in use until the fourteenth century.

Ibn-Khordadbeh was postmaster of western Iran in about 848. His book *Roads and Countries,* described in detail the four main commercial routes of the period, among other things. One went from Spain, southern Europe, and Asia Minor to the Caspian. Another connected North Africa with India through Syria and Iran; the third went along the eastern Mediterranean to the Persian Gulf; the fourth was a sea route that went through the Red Sea and the Indian Ocean to Ceylon and China. Ya'qubi of Khorasan, who flourished in the ninth century, wrote *The Book of Countries,* which discusses topography and especially economic geography.

Two other geographers of the period were Estakhri of Persepolis (c. 950) and Muqaddasi of Jerusalem (c. 980). The former produced what is probably the first colored map of the world, and the latter wrote down original geographical observations from more than twenty years of travel in most of the Muslim world. A more famous geographer who lived in Sicily in the twelfeth century, was Idrisi (d. 1166). Idrisi summed up the contributions of Muslim geographers before him; he believed that the earth was a sphere, and his maps are remarkably accurate. To him the lands north of China and Russia were called Gog and Magog. His maps are the reverse of modern maps, in that north is at the bottom and south at the top of the page. This account of geography should not be concluded without mentioning the remarkable Greek slave, Yaqut ("ruby") (1179–1229), who, after being given his freedom, roamed wherever his fancy took him, supporting himself by copying and selling manuscripts. His copious notes resulted in his famous *Dictionary of Cities*, in which the names are arranged alphabetically.

THE HUMANITIES

History. Islam is a revealed religion and revelation involves time, place, person, and event—all of which form the stuff of history. In Islam, as in other revealed religions, history was a divine plan closely tied up with the ummah. Furthermore, Muhammad's claim that he was the last prophet in the Judeo-Christian tradition called for a knowledge of the lives of prophets in the Old and New Testaments.

Muslim historians, on the whole, were interested only in the accounts of the Bible and the religio-political events of Islam. They were not interested in the history of China, Rome, or any other nation not dealt with in Biblical history. Even in their "universal" histories, which normally began at the creation of the world and continued up to the author's time, they ignored non-Biblical and non-Islamic activities and did not deviate from the stereotypical pattern. Having been trained in the science of hadith, they wrote history chronologically, with direct quotations from the usual chain of authorities. Later, during the period of principalities, the writing of local history gained ascendency, a practice that was a welcome relief from the norm and that left posterity a wealth of local historical material. The stereotype, however, did not die. Even in the twentieth century, "history" books have been published that begin with the story of Adam.

Of the two historians of the Arab conquest, one is the Egyptian, ibn-Abd al-Hakam (d.870), who described the conquest of Egypt; and the second person is the Iranian, Ibn-Yahya al-Baladuri (d. 892), who wrote a comprehensive narrative of the Arab expansion. Of the two most important writers of "universal" history, one is Muhammad al-Tabari (838–923) from the province of Tabarestan on the south coast of the Caspian Sea. In addition to a standard commentary on the Koran, he wrote the *History of Apostles and Kings*, in which he has arranged his carefully collected material complete with chains of authorities, year by year from the creation of the world until A.D. 915. This work became the standard for later historians.

Another person equally famous as a historian and geographer was Abul-Hasan Ali al-Mas'udi (d. 956), the globetrotter from Baghdad. He is one of the few who deviated from the stereotype. His famous book, *The Golden Meadows and the Jewel Mines,* is a topical history of civilization. He deviated even farther from the norm by writing about Indians, Iranians, Romans, and other heathens. Furthermore, his book abounds in historical anecdotes, which he, no doubt, collected in his travels.

The greatest Muslim historian was Abd al-Rahman Ibn Khaldun of North Africa, who lived in the thirteenth century. His *Muqaddimah,* or *Introduction to History,* antedates the best of the social and political histories of the West by about 500 years. Ibn Khaldun discusses the importance of social and psychological factors in history, and his historical methodology in research and interpretation has won him a place among the major historians of the world. Arnold Toynbee, the twentieth-century English historian, considers Ibn Khaldun's prolegomenon to be "the greatest work of its kind that has ever yet been created by any mind in any time or place."

Ibn Khaldun's philosophy of history, was built around the concept of *asabiyya.* This concept has been translated by some as "nationalism," by others as "group solidarity," and by still others as "social solidarity." Civilizations rise and fall in direct proportion to the strength of this solidarity among the people who govern. Group solidarity is the most important factor in laying the foundation of a civilization. The same civilization, however, is an important cause of the weakening of this solidarity and, therefore, is a cause of the decline of that civilization.

Literature. In the field of literature, the Prophet Muhammad did not have a high regard for poets and poetry but had no objection to storytelling.[1] As it turned out, his followers throughout the centuries did not produce much fiction but may have written more poetry than the writers of any other culture in the world.

Aside from the *Book of Songs* (see Chapter 5), there was not much serious literary production in prose. The most famous on the lighter side, however, is *The Thousand and One Nights.* This was prepared by one Jahshiyar (d. 942) from the Persian original called "A Thousand Tales." The translator added a few stories of his own, using the original plot and the same heroes and heroines, including Shahrzad. Over the centuries, as individuals copied the book they added more stories from all parts of the world, but always keeping the same plot. It apparently took final form in the late Mamluk period in Egypt and is known in English as *The Arabian Nights.* It has been translated into most languages of the world.

The nature and content of pre-Islamic Arabic poetry was discussed in Chapter 1. The Umayyads perpetuated the pre-Islamic content of Arabic poetry. One of the most famous desert love stories sung by Arab and Iranian poets repeatedly is that of Layla and Majnun. The two loved each other, but the parents of Layla forced her to marry someone else. This drove Majnun to the desert, where he wandered for the rest of his life. Three other love

[1]Koran, Sura 26:224.

stories that were very popular concerned Joseph and Zolaykha (Potephar's wife), Vis and Rameen, and Shirin (a queen) and Farhad (a stonecutter). In the discussion of Sufism a number of Iranian poets such as Rumi, Attar, Hafez, and others were mentioned. The greatest epic poet of Iran was Abul Qasem Ferdowsi, who wrote the history of Iran in verse from mythological times up to the Arab conquest. *Shahnameh*, or *The Book of Kings*, is one of the most stirring poems in Persian literature. Even a brief discussion of Persian literature must include another luminary of Shiraz, the city of poets: Sa'di, whose collection of short anecdotes in prose and poetry, *The Rose Garden*, is a textbook in every Iranian school.

Poets were supported by the patronage of caliphs and princes, who were more interested in flattery than in science or literature. Consequently, the bulk of Persian and Arabic poetry contains a great deal of bombast and the clever use of words for flattery. The poets had to do this in order to make a living, and some of the better ones became very rich indeed. Every poet sought a patron and it became customary for each prince to have his own coterie of poets. Some of the princes in the period of principalities vied with each other in attracting certain able poets. Writing poetry became a means of livelihood; and evey occasion—be it birth, death, marriage, war, victory, the construction of a palace, or a successful hunt—became a suitable subject for poetry. It was customary for nobles to commission poets for suitable verses. Sometimes the poets sent the same poem to more than one patron and received a fee from each. If a proper fee or suitable gift was not forthcoming, the poet ridiculed the patron with satire and maligned him, always in exquisite poetic form. The power of the word in possession of poets was sometimes as potent as the power of the sword in the hands of princes. Nevertheless, some of these same poets who wrote so much sweet flattery and bitter satire also wrote—on their own time—some lasting poems that take the reader's soul to heights of artistic experience.

ARCHITECTURE AND THE ARTS

Some modern Middle East artists have stated that the term "Muslim art" is misleading, for Islam as a religion forbade sculpture and pictorial representation and frowned on others. While this is true, it is also a fact that the followers of Muhammad did not obey him in this any more than they did in the reciting of poetry, which the Prophet disliked, or the drinking of wine, which he had expressly forbidden. The Arabs did not bring much else into the arts besides a wealth of tribal melodies that were later incorporated by composers and singers in their works. But, coming as they did into the midst of the Christians of Byzantium and the Zoroastrians of Iran, two religious groups who used the arts as handmaidens, the Arabs could not long remain aloof. Consequently, the arts developed outside the inner religious circle of Islam and have never had its support.

Architecture is a possible exception to the above generalization, for Islam needed mosques and mosques had certain needs that were peculiar to Islam. Hence, the artistic talents of the new converts were directed toward the construction of mosques. The architectural needs of Islam were few and simple. A fountain or pool was constructed in the courtyard of the mosque for the purpose of ablutions. Consequently, the normal approach to a mosque from the street is not to the inside of the building but to a large courtyard with pools and fountains. Also, the Muslims needed a preferably high place from which the muezzin could give the call to prayer. For this they constructed tall circular or square columns, that were attached to the mosque. These were called *minarets*, from the Hebrew *minorah*.

Islam had two requirements for the inside of the mosque. One was the direction to Mecca, which is called *qibla*. The mosque had to be built so that the worshipper could face Mecca for prayer. As this had to be exact, it became customary to build a prayer niche. The other requirement was a pulpit, a staircase-like construction, often portable, from which the preacher spoke while sitting on the top step.

Most of the mosques and palaces built during the Umayyad and Abbasid periods have been destroyed. The best examples of Umayyad architecture that have survived are the Umayyad mosque at Damascus and the Dome of the Rock at Jerusalem. Of the Abbasid buildings, nothing is left except the ruins of the mosque in Samarra and the better-preserved Friday mosque at Esfahan, built around 760. Most authorities agree that, in general, Umayyad architecture shows Byzantine influence, while Abbasid architecture shows Iranian influence. The Sasanids had developed ovoid and elliptical domes, and arches and spiral towers, which the Muslims copied. City planners used domes and arches in building covered bazaars and open squares, usually in the proximity of mosques. Indeed, the art and architecture of the period reflect the close interrelationship between the commercial and religious realms of the empire.

Because of the interdictions against pictorial representation, mosques were decorated with colored tiles. The decoration on the tiles would sometimes consist of intricate geometric or floral designs of great beauty. Talented artists expressed themselves through calligraphy, a branch of the arts that had the support of religion, in copying the Koran or writing Koranic verses on tiles for the decoration of mosques. Even though Islam forbade the representation of animate objects, painting was patronized by the caliphs; and one of them, Mu'tasim, had the walls of his palace at Samarra decorated with nudes. During the period of principalities, artists illustrated books. Ferdowsi's *Book of Kings*, with its myths and stories, was a fertile ground for artistic expression. This was the beginning of miniature art for which the Iranians became famous.

The only branch of music that received approval from Islam was the chanting of the Koran. This, however, became stereotyped and it has not changed for centuries. Scholars, in imitation of the Greeks, wrote on the theory of music, but there was very little development of serious music. There were composers, singers, instrumentalists, and dancers; but, as has already been noted, they were used mostly for merrymaking.[2]

The paradox that the foregoing survey of culture reveals is that the

[2]See p. 57.

period of greatest creativity occurred during the period of principalities (c. 900–1200), when the caliphs were weak and princes driven by diverse motives were fighting each other. The reasons for the continuity of progress, despite war and strife, are not hard to find. In the first place, the Arab conquest acted as a catalyst to tired societies that had been in a rut for some time. Neither did the religion that the Arabs brought with them have a new elixir for the production of thought that the existing religions of the Middle East did not have, nor did Arabic as a language have a hidden capacity for the expression of culture that other languages did not possess. The fact remains, however, that Islam and the Arabic language became the instruments of the awakening and, in the process, were themselves renovated and enriched. The peoples of the Middle East, who were revitalized by the conquest, started again where they had left off and continued in spite of instability and war.

In the second place, the weakness of the central government in Baghdad was an indirect aid to the process of creativity. As we have seen, the Abbasids were committed to upholding religious dogma and did not shun persecution and inquisition to carry out their purpose. The weakness of the caliphs freed the philosophers and scientists in their investigations, without which they could not have been creative. The independent princes, who either did not understand the dogmas or did not care, vied with each other in patronizing the intellectuals, whom the religious divines in Baghdad continued to accuse of heresy. It is doubtful whether a strong caliphate would have allowed such creativity. This is borne out by the fact that after the Saljuqs restored the power of orthodoxy and Ghazali wrote his book, scholarship and creativity began to languish. The "Middle Ages" of the Middle East started with the restoration of the power of orthodox Islam. Its Renaissance started perhaps during the first decades of the twentieth century, and its Reformation has yet to occur.

Chapter Nine
Islamic Lands on the Defensive

One of the most striking differences between Islam and other religions such as Christianity or Buddhism is the fact that Islam, unlike the other two major religions, was founded upon conquest and for nearly a thousand years drew its lifeblood from war and expansion. To be sure, both Christianity and Buddhism became oppressive and perpetrated war; but the fact remains that both were minority communities for 300 years and both experienced persecutions that have left indelible marks upon each. Islam, on the contrary, did not know persecution and did not experience the feelings of a minority community, but rather experienced victory over other societies. These facts have influenced the attitude of Muslims.

The attempts of some historians—mostly Europeans or Europeanized Middle Easterners—to divide the Islamic movement into "religion," "empire," and "culture" as three distinct entities and then to imply that "Islam the religion" was not dependent upon imperial expansion is to distort the whole history of the period. To be sure, these historians' intentions are good. For centuries Islam and its Prophet were maligned by the West; the tendency of modern Western historians is to make amends and to right the wrong interpretations of the past. Since in their own minds the idea of a religion being propagated by wars of expansion is repugnant, they have tried to imply that the Islamic wars of conquest were not for the propagation of the Islamic religion but rather for the establishment of an Islamic empire.

Muslims, be they theologians or historians, do not share this view. To them empire, religion, and culture were one; the wars of expansion were ordered by Allah; and the soldiers were fighting for His cause. The early Muslim writers, as well as later historians, described in detail and with great pride the battles in which the Prophet himself had participated. The picture of Muhammad with sword in hand is not at all incongruous to a Muslim, whereas a painting of Christ or Buddha wielding a sword would shock a Christian or Buddhist soldier, even on his way to war.

From the battle of Badr (624), in which Muhammad participated, until the last years of the eleventh century, the armies of Islam did not suffer major defeats, and the advance of Islam was not effectively checked. The Saljuqs and the other Turkish tribes who gained supremacy over the Arabs came as devout Muslims and helped to strengthen orthodoxy and the unity of the ummah under the caliph of Allah. Every victory convinced the Muslims that Allah was with them and every conquest made them feel more invincible. Even though Asia Minor proved too high a wall to scale, they never gave up the attempt. When in 1071 the Saljuqs defeated the Byzantine army in the battle of Manzikert and established a kingdom in Asia Minor, hopes ran high. In the same way that Muhammad the last Prophet had proclaimed Islam the last religion, the Islamic Empire under the caliph would be the first to bring the whole world under the aegis of Allah and his Prophet.

THE CRUSADES

The first attack on this psychological and spiritual buildup came from Europe in the form of the Crusades. Europeans defeated the armies of Islam on their home ground and produced such a shock among the Muslims of the Fertile Crescent that the event still arouses strong emotions of resentment and disgust. As a matter of fact, the Crusades in themselves were only a passing phase in the history of Islam. They only momentarily halted the advance that was later begun again with the Ottomans. Nevertheless, in the minds of most Muslims, the Crusades are a blemish on the body politic of Islam.

The Crusades joined the history of Europe with that of the Middle East. Naturally, they affected these two regions differently. The Crusades were caused by many factors. In the first place, they may be considered as a reaction of the Christian West to the persistent aggression of Muslim Middle East. Second, the continuous strife between the Sunni Saljuqs of Syria and the Shi'a Fatimids of Egypt had made it very dangerous for Christian pilgrims to visit the holy places in Palestine. Third, the destruction of the Church of the Holy Sepulchre by the Fatimid caliph, Hakim, did arouse genuine religious concern in Europe. Fourth, the growing power of the Saljuqs in Asia Minor threatened the lucrative trade that cities like Genoa, Pisa, and Venice had been carrying on with the East. These trade centers helped the Crusaders in the expansion of their commerce. Fifth, Islam had already shown signs of weakening in Europe. In 1050, Castile and Aragon

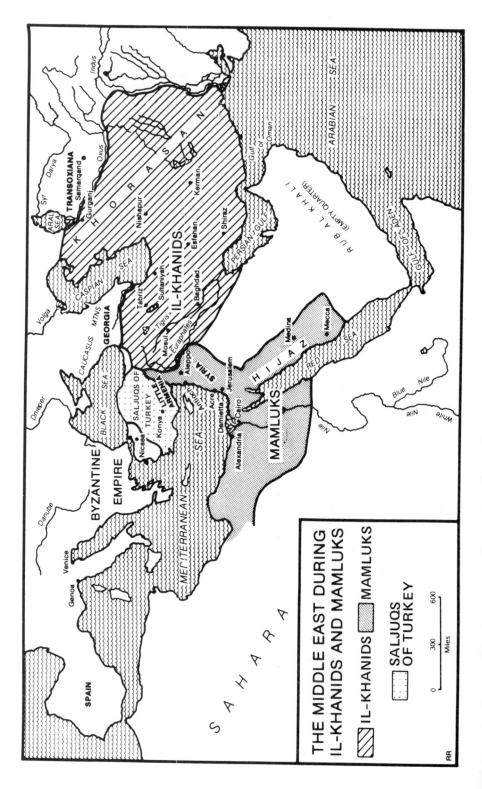

THE MIDDLE EAST DURING
IL-KHANIDS AND MAMLUKS

IL-KHANIDS ▨ MAMLUKS

SALJUQS
OF TURKEY

0   300   600
Miles

RR

had taken Andalusia from the Muslims of Spain. In 1060, the Normans had taken Sicily. By 1080, the Muslims had all but lost command of the Mediterranean. Furthermore, the reports of the pilgrims about weakness and dissension in the Muslim camp spread throughout Europe and did not fall on deaf ears. Sixth, there was a genuine religious motivation among the Crusaders. They wanted to free the birthplace of Christ and to convert the Muslims. That they were doing it with the sword bothered only a few people like St. Francis of Assisi. Seventh, there were many landless European knights, princes, and nobles who wanted domains of their own. Eighth, many Crusaders went for the adventure of seeing the world and perhaps gaining part of the fabled riches of the East. Ninth, there were masses of people in Europe who were oppressed and bored and wanted change. Finally, when Emperor Alexius Comnenus, who was beleaguered by the Saljuqs of Asia Minor, sent his appeal in 1094 to Rome for help, things began to happen: Pope Urban II made his famous call to arms in 1095 and most of Europe responded as though it was waiting for such a summons.

By July 15, 1099, the Crusaders had fought their way to Jerusalem, stormed it, and massacred Muslims, Jews, and even the Christians whom they had come to liberate. Godfrey, one of the leaders, became king of Jerusalem. The other territories that had been won were organized along European feudal lines into small kingdoms. In a region already torn by petty principalities, the creation of a few new ones did not change the general picture. In time the Christian kingdoms, following the example of their Muslim neighbors, started fighting among themselves. Sometimes Muslims and Christians went so far as to seek each other's aid against their own coreligionists.

In the meantime a new star had arisen among the Muslims, this time a Kurd, in the person of Salah al-Din ibn-Ayyub (Saladin), who captured Cairo and put an end to the Fatimid rule. Being a good Sunni, he stopped mentioning the Fatimid caliph's name in prayers and substituted the name of the Abbasid caliph, who probably did not know Saladin existed and cared even less. In 1175 he declared his independence in Egypt and formed the Ayyubid principality. He gained fame in defeating the Crusaders in the battle of Hittin on July 4, 1187, and soon after that retook Jerusalem, Antioch, Tripoli, and Tyre.

The fall of Jerusalem signaled the Third Crusade (1189–1192). The fact that three powerful monarchs of Europe, Frederick Barbarossa of Germany, Richard the Lion-hearted of England, and Philip Augustus of France, led this one, added more luster than achievement. They took Acre after a siege of two years and made peace in 1191. Soon after this, Saladin died; and his kingdom was divided among the members of his family, who fought against each other, a pattern that had become characteristic of all these dynasties. The Crusaders took advantage of the situation, and by 1229 they had recaptured Jerusalem, as well as the coastal cities.

The weakness of the Ayyubids set the stage for the rise of another principality. This was accomplished in Cairo by a slave, Aybak, who founded the Mamluk (slave) kingdom of Egypt in 1250. The fourth "slave-king," Baybars (1260–1277), started a series of campaigns, took several cities in

Palestine, and captured Antioch in the north. His successors continued the pressure, and by 1291 the last of the Crusaders had been driven out.

The Crusades, which spanned nearly 200 years, were only a phase in the history of the Middle East. They did not change the pattern of the era of the principalities. The periods of peace were more numerous than times of war, and in peace there was much social contact between Christians and Muslims. The Crusaders, who had come with a definite feeling of superiority over the Muslims, were forced to change their minds quickly. The Franks, as they were called by the Muslims, soon recognized the higher culture of the Muslims and emulated them in practically everything but religion.

As the Crusaders returned home with these newly acquired tastes, traders took advantage of the situation, and soon the marketplaces of Europe displayed such exotic merchandise as sugar, pepper, cloves, ginger, rugs, tapestries, muslin, velvet, satin, mirrors, rosaries, and perfumes of many kinds. In the art of war the Franks learned the use of carrier pigeons from the Muslim, and the latter learned the use of crossbows and the wearing of heavy mail from the Franks.

Two hundred years of intermittent warfare built a reservoir of ill will on both sides, and war propaganda was rampant. A good deal of misinformation about Islam in Europe dates from this period. And yet there were also people of good will—scholars who translated manuscripts, and Muslim physicians who cured the sick among the Franks and wondered at their superstitious medical beliefs. There were also people like St. Francis of Assisi and Raymond Lull, who believed in approaching Muslims in love instead of war. There were also intermarriages, as is evidenced by the large number of blue-eyed blonds in Lebanon, Syria, and Palestine.

THE MAMLUKS

This strange and unique oligarchy of slaves ruled Egypt from 1250 to 1517. The Mamluks who drove out the Crusaders were not a dynasty, for seldom did a son succeed his father. It was an oligarchy of slaves in which the average reign lasted not more than five years. At the death (often violent) of a strongman, the remaining slaves in the oligarchy fought each other for the top position. To remain in power, the slave sultan gave land and privileges to the amirs, who themselves were slaves and owned slaves of their own.

The Mamluk sultans are usually divided into two groups. One is called the Bahri ("sea"), who ruled from 1250 to 1390. They were mostly Turkish and Mongol slaves. The other is the Burji ("citadel"), whose rule from 1382 to 1517 slightly overlaps that of the Bahri. They were mostly Circassian slaves, with the exception of two who were Greek.

Two of the most famous Mamluk sultans were Baybars (1260–1277) and Qalawun (1279–1290). Baybars checked the advance of the Mongol Hulagu and dealt a crushing blow to the Crusaders. Qalawun controlled Syria and built one of the most advanced hospitals of the time in Cairo. It is a strange paradox that in the midst of so much bloodshed and turmoil, Egypt became an important center of learning in the world of Islam. Cairo was also a thriving commercial center for the East-West trade that brought goods by ship to the Red Sea and then by caravan to the Mediterranean. Some of these slave sultans who did not take the trouble to learn Arabic apparently encouraged the development of literature and art. Perhaps to perpetuate their own memory, they fell into the habit of constructing mausoleum-mosques and in this way contributed to the architectural development of the Islamic world. One of the most exquisite of these mausoleums is the one built by Kaitbay, who died in 1495.

In order to add prestige and an appearance of legitimacy to his rule, Baybars found a scion of the Abbasid family and installed him as Caliph al-Hakim. Hakim and his descendants became puppets of the Mamluks in Cairo. Their duties were to administer the religious endowments and to crown each succeeding Mamluk sultan.

THE MONGOLS

While the Muslims in the western Middle East were struggling against the Crusaders, the Muslims in the east were attacked by a new force that was more formidable. The Mongols, who roamed the uplands of Outer Mongolia around Lake Baikal and who had penetrated the Great Wall of China and overrun that civilization, had spread westward until they had come to the eastern-most boundaries of the Muslim principality of Kharazm.

Ti Mu Chin, who later assumed the title Chengiz Khan, was born between 1155 and 1162 to a minor clan leader among the Mongols who inhabited Outer Mongolia. By courage and cunning he rose to prominence, united the different tribes, and stormed the Great Wall that the civilized Chinese had built against these marauders from the north. Chengiz became the founder of an important dynasty in China and did not destroy the civilization that he conquered. As heir to the Chinese empire, his rule extended to Tibet and Sinkiang in the west.

It is not quite certain why he ordered the westward move so far from his base. It is likely that Chengiz, as the emperor of a settled and civilized China, had difficulty controlling his restless and warring Mongol tribesmen and had to keep them busy fighting, which was about the only occupation they relished.

In any event, the Mongol avalanche started in 1219 in Sinkiang. By the time its initial fury was over in about 1224, the Mongols had overrun the Iranian plateau and were approaching Kiev in the Ukraine. In its wake the chain of cities on the plateau such as Balkh, Bokhara, Samarqand, Marv, Harat, Nishapur, and Ray were looted and burned, and the majority of the inhabitants were slaughtered. One eyewitness, not finding words to describe the horror which he experienced, writes of the Mongol invasion: "They came, they looted, they killed, they burned, and they left." And yet with all their destructiveness, their actions were as nothing compared to the saturation bombings of World War II. Cruel as they were, the Mongol raids were almost humanitarian compared to the slaughter of Europeans, particularly of the Jews, under the Third Reich, or the liquidation of the Russian kulaks by the Soviets, not to mention the atom bombing of Hiroshima and Nagasaki or the atrocities committed by both sides during the Vietnam War.

Chengiz Khan died in 1227, having conquered and organized the largest empire the world had ever known, an empire that extended from the Vistula to the Pacific. Chengiz Khan was one of the greatest military geniuses of all time. His army was held together by strict discipline. As the whole army was entirely made up of cavalry, it was very mobile. Each soldier had one spare horse, and sometimes two. As a Mongol, he had perfected the art of surprise and of feigning retreat. Perhaps from the Chinese he had learned the use of explosives and had organized a demolition corps for the purpose of destroying fortifications. He usually asked cities to surrender before each attack. If a city surrendered without fighting, a tenth of all property was confiscated and a tenth of the population taken into slavery. The rest were put at the mercy of the Mongol governors. If a city resisted, then the looting and slaughter were more indiscriminate.

After his death, the empire of Chengiz Khan was divided into three parts. First was the mother region with its capital in Peking, whose ruler had the title of Khaqan with titular authority over the whole empire. The second part lay in what is now in Russia, with its capital at Kazan on the banks of the Volga. (In Russian history the Mongols are known as the "Golden Horde.") The third part was in Iran, with its capital in Maragheh in Azerbaijan. (In Persian history the Mongols are known as the "Ilkhan.")

The founder of the Ilkhan Dynasty was Hulagu, the grandson of Chengiz Khan. In 1252, Hulagu began to unite what Chengiz's Mongol generals had conquered and held after his death. The most tenacious resisters were the Assassins, whom the earlier Mongol avalanche had not consumed. In 1238 the Grand Master of the Assassins in Alamut had sent emissaries to the kings of England and France to ask for aid against the Mongols. From both he had received noncommittal responses. In 1256, however, Hulagu destroyed the strongholds of the Assassins and captured their famous redoubt, the fortress of Alamut. Two years later, Hulagu and the Mongols were at the gates of Baghdad. There was nothing that the weak and beleaguered caliph, Musta'sim, could do except to ask for mercy. His predecessors had saved themselves by bestowing honors on such strongmen; but Hulagu, being a pagan, was not moved by such considerations. Neither was he impressed by the warning that killing the caliph would "disturb the natural order of the universe." The caliph and his retinue were put to death and the city was given over to plunder. Compared to the destruction of the Iranian cities, Baghdad did not fare badly at all.

Thus ended the reign of the Abbasids. The Abbasid Dynasty had had thirty-seven caliphs, about eight of whom had ruled in reality and most of the rest had reigned as puppets for 508 years. Some Middle East historians have overrated the significance of the fall of Baghdad, as some European historians have done in the case of the fall of Constantinople some 200 years later. Each was anticlimax and did not greatly alter the existing situation.

Hulagu's garrison advanced into Syria but was checked by the Mamluks, a feat that saved Egypt from the ravages of the Mongols. The Ilkhanid territory extended from the Caucasus to the Indian Ocean and from the Euphrates to the Amu Darya. The immediate descendants of Chengiz Khan became patrons of civilization and learning. The Iranians, who influenced the Turkish principalities, began to educate the Mongols in the arts of government and culture. The Ilkhans relied on Iranians for every aspect of their administration. As part of a large empire, Iran was linked to China by well-traveled routes kept open and safe by a peace that was imposed by the Mongols. There were commercial and cultural exchanges between Iran and China. The famous Persian miniatures that were created in this period show definite Chinese influence. Marco Polo, a member of a Venetian merchant family, traveled through Iran to Peking around 1272, and spoke of the thriving industries of Tabriz, of the silk of Kashan, and the embroideries of Kerman.

The Mongols were pagans, and for a time the Ilkhans of Iran seesawed between Christianity and Islam. Indeed, as early as 1245 Pope Innocent IV sent two embassies, one of which under the Franciscan, Jean Plavo de Caprini, all the way to Karakorum in Mongolia for the purpose of opening religious missions in their domains. Actually, from the Ilkhanid period on, Iran began to attract embassies from European countries for political, religious, commercial, and cultural purposes continuously to the present time.

In the contest between Christianity and Islam for the allegiance of the Ilkhan kings, Islam was the victor. Ghazan Khan (1295–1304) became a devout Muslim and severed his relation with the Khaqan in China. He was one of the greatest of the Ilkhans and restored peace to war-torn Iran. Under him the abused and downtrodden peasantry began to prosper. Ghazan Khan instituted an equitable tax system, proclaimed rules of conduct for government officials, and strengthened internal communications. Ghazan was a Muslim with Shi'a leanings. He forced many of the Mongols to follow him and with the zeal of a convert destroyed not only "heathen" temples but also Christian and Jewish houses of worship. He did much to strengthen the Shi'a dervish orders which influenced the social and religious life of Iran and out of which arose the Safavid Dynasty.

After the utter destruction wrought by the Mongols, it is surprising that any kind of initiative was left in Iran. And yet, the Mongol invasion gave rise to one of the most culturally productive eras in Persian history. It is a tribute to the Iranians that they not only restored their own culture but also civilized the Mongols and, indeed, used their conquerors to improve their own lot. The struggle for survival on the part of the Iranians was purely individualistic and was carried out in three ways.

In the first place, as they had done in the case of the Arabs, the Iranians influenced the Mongols and assimilated them into Iranian culture. During the Umayyad and the Abbasid reigns the Iranians organized political revolts, fomented religious uprisings, joined forces with rival Arab factions, and used personal sacrifice in order to gain their ends. During the Mongol period, however, there were no signs of collective revolt, no uprisings, and no manifestations of personal bravery. Indeed, there was every sign of abject submission. Individual Iranians in all walks of life, by the use of their talents and cunning, worked their way into the confidence of the Mongols and led them toward the cultural rebirth of Iran rather than simple political domination by barbarians. It must be stated that the assimilation of the Mongols was made easier because of the vast distance which separated them from their native base in Mongolia. Lacking knowledge of a sedentary life, the Mongols had no one from whom to learn except the people they had conquered.

The second way the Iranians survived during the Mongol period was by means of artistic creativity. The first Arab invasions had suffocated the Iranians' artistic sensitivity. Islam destroyed the values which the Iranians cherished, and its strict iconoclasm forbade representational art and put artists under severe limitations. Artists were alienated from their surroundings, and were pushed into seclusion. Later they expressed themselves in abstract art by means of geometric designs and calligraphy. But they always created a border on their canvases or rugs and shut themselves up, as it were, in the central medallions. The Mongols also destroyed values but, not having any religious dogmas of their own, they did not impose any restrictions. Artists could indulge in representational or any other form of expression to their hearts' content. It was indeed the power of the once-barbaric Mongols that freed Iranian culture from the limiting influences of Islam and bought Iran into contact with the cultures of Asia and Europe. "Persian miniature" paintings are a mixture of Chinese and Iranian styles. Artists were free to illustrate any of the numerous episodes in the books that the copyists handed to them. It is interesting to note that Iranian artists painted borders around the miniatures, but sometimes the pictures inside extend beyond the borders at different points, reflecting the artists' freedom to move about.

The third way in which the Iranian spirit withstood the onslaught of the Mongol invasion was through Sufism, a form of mysticism by which many Iranians minimized the significance of the real world that had crumbled about them. Sufism enabled Iranians to avoid the rigors of Mongol domination, and also gave rise to some of the greatest Iranian creative talents. Sufism was a reaction to the Iranians' awareness of the transitory nature of life—an awareness that was heightened by Mongol destruction—so that the mystic experience (i.e., union of the self with God) became a means by which to free the soul. Some of the greatest Iranian poets and writers such as Rumi, Hafez, Sa'di, and others belong to this period. Christian mystics of the thirteenth and fourteenth centuries, having experienced the transitory nature of the world as a whole, decided that they could not enjoy any part of it and became ascetics. Iranians, on the other hand, disavowed the world as a whole but at the same time enjoyed the parts that were within their reach.

By the time the Crusaders were driven away and the Mongols had been absorbed, a pattern emerged in the Middle East that had been forming since the decline of the Abbasids at the beginning of the tenth century. The pattern was not new, but was quite traditional to the Middle East.

In the first place, Iran was separated from the Fertile Crescent by the Tigris River, the Shatt-al-Arab, and the Persian Gulf. Such had been the case during the Sasanid rule. Even though the people on both banks of the rivers had a common history and culture, neither side felt attached to the destiny of the other. This tendency had already started in the last decades of the ninth century and was subsequently strengthened. During the Crusades, the Saljuqs of Syria repeatedly asked the aid of their kinsmen the Saljuqs of Iran, but their pleas fell on deaf ears. Similarly, when both the Iranians and the Turks in the east were attacked by the Mongols, the powers in the Fertile Crescent did not come to their aid. The same division, which was the pattern in the pre-Islamic period, continued after the coming of the Mongols. Apparently, a common confession of faith makes no more difference in the Muslim world than it does elsewhere among different nations that have the same religion.

In the second place, during the Ilkhan period and afterward, the Persian language replaced Arabic in everything except the recitation of prayers and the reading of the Koran. It has been mentioned how the Saffarids and the Samanids started the revival of the Persian language. Throughout the period of principalities, Persian came to be used more and more, but still the learned wrote their serious works in Arabic. After the coming of the Mongols, however, Persian came into its own in every field. All writing—poetical, philosophical, or scientific—was done in the Persian language. The vast majority of the Iranians, however, continued to say their prayers and read the Koran in Arabic without understanding them. Consequently, the history of Iran from the Ilkhans to the present is an independent one. Including it with the rest of the Middle East is about as difficult as dealing with the history of England in a survey of European history.

It must be observed in this connection that the Mongol invasion proved to be a blessing for Iran in that it freed the Iranians spiritually and created a form of cultural unity. They were not bound by laws of religion nor inhibited by a sense of inferiority to the Arabs. Furthermore, the invasion freed the notables of the countryside from domination by the urban military and merchant elites. A new cultural nationalism replaced the old political struggle for supremacy. Once a cultural identity had been established, political unity followed a century and a half later in the founding of the Safavid dynasty.

In the third place, after the Crusades, the Fertile Crescent, Arabia, and Egypt also fell into the traditional patterns of the past. The Arabian Peninsula, which began to lose its importance with the advent of the Abbasids, had long been isolated. Its inhabitants retreated to their traditional desert life as readily as they had emerged from it. The relationship between the Fertile Crescent and Egypt also fell into a pattern that was familiar to students of the ancient Middle East. Egypt and the Fertile Crescent could not get along on equal terms then, and they are not able to do so now. Either one had to rule the other or both be ruled by a third power. At the end of the Crusades, it was Egypt under the Mamluks that ruled the Fertile Crescent except Iraq.

The history of the Middle East from the fall of Baghdad until the middle of the nineteenth century, however, is the story of neither the Arabic-speaking peoples nor of the Iranians. The main actors were actually the Turks. These were the Ottoman Turks, who replaced the Byzantine Empire, and the Persianized Turks in Iran, who established the Safavid Empire. Of the two, the Ottomans were by far the more influential and to them we shall now turn.

Chapter Ten
The Ottoman Empire

OTTOMAN SULTANS

Osman I (1299–1326)
Orhan (1326–1360)
Murad I (1360–1389)
Bayezid Yilderim (1389–1402)
Mehmed I (1412–1421)
Murad II (1421–1451)
Mehmed II (1451–1481)
Bayezid II (1481–1512)
Selim I (1512–1520)
Suleiman (1520–1566)
Selim II (1566–1574)
Murad III (1574–1595)
Ahmad I (1595–1603)

In the almost continuous struggle between the Muslim caliphate and the Byzantine Empire, Turkish soldiers proved to be an effective advance guard for Islam as we have seen. It was they who won the battle of Manzikert north of Lake Van in Armenia and took the Emperor Diogenes prisoner in 1071. This victory opened Asia Minor to Muslim settlement and enabled Turkish tribesmen to penetrate westward as far as Smyrna. The Saljuq Turks who had accomplished this feat were eventually separated from their kinsmen in Iran and organized the Saljuqs of Asia Minor. Through a series of wars the Saljuqs occupied most of Asia Minor and ruled in reality or in name until 1302. During most of this time, their capital was in Konya (Iconeum). During the last half of the thirteenth century and the first half of the fourteenth century, the Turks had a number of effective princes who attracted the Muslim intellectuals to their capital and were strong enough to provide safety for commerce. Perhaps the most important change wrought during the 300 years of Saljuq rule was the Turkification of a large segment of Asia Minor. Some of the nomadic Turks, influenced by the influx of the Turks of the western Caspian, had become settled farmers in the villages of Asia Minor.

With few exceptions, the Turkish tribes who came into contact with Islam accepted the Sunni faith and were fanatically loyal to its tenets and institutions. The nature of their attachment to Islam was more emotional than rational; it sprang more from a sense of loyalty than from understanding. Under these circumstances, it is not surprising to see the rapid growth of Sufi orders among them, because Sufism emphasized loyalty and extolled devotion. Sufism, which started as an attempt to attain union with God, took on a social aspect among the Turkish tribes. Mainly to practice their devotion, the adherents to Sufism banded into brotherhoods. These brotherhoods grew among both the Sunnis and the Shi'is. The loyalty of an individual to the person of a leader was more acceptable to Turks than loyalty to an abstract idea.

These groups, which later came to be known as "dervish" orders, gave a sense of solidarity and belonging to the Turks, who found themselves among strangers. Into these orders they brought the tradition of their tribes, such as strict discipline, loyalty to the leader, and patience in privations. There were numerous orders, and each one had a leader who had attained his position through spiritual insight, discipline, piety, and wisdom. Each order had a headquarters, and each headquarters had a leader, called an Elder. *Shaykh* (Arabic), *dada* (Turkish), or *peer* (Persian) all of which mean "elder." The novice shaved his head and followed a life of rigid self-discipline, study, prayer, and night vigil until he was pronounced "enlightened." At religious services they sat in a circle and repeated loudly a phrase of the Koran until overcome by emotion. In some orders there was music and the singing of Sufi poems until, in their state of ecstasy, the dervishes would dance and lose themselves in God. Upon enlightenment, some let their hair grow long and engaged in missionary activities.

Attached to these orders were lay brothers, who had an association called *akhi*, which resembled an economic guild. They accepted the leadership of the Elder and adhered to the virtues preached by the order, even though they were engaged in business. Another group of laymen attached to the order was a militant one, *ghazi*. Their purposes were war against non-Muslims and the capture of booty and slaves. In much the same way that the discipline of the contemplative order of Zen Buddhism encouraged the growth of the Samurai warrior in Japan, the rigid self-discipline of the Sufi orders produced the ghazi warrior who followed a set of rules and virtues as earnestly as he blindly obeyed the wishes of the leader. Members of orders were recognized by a special badge that they wore on their turbans or by a special article of clothing. In the absence of a strong central government, these orders offered political and economic security and religious satisfaction and motivation. In these orders religion, commerce, and war were joined together; and societies bound by a set of rules and obedience to a leader were established. The founders of both the Ottoman Dynasty of Turkey and the Safavid Dynasty of Iran belonged to Sufi orders, the former Sunni and the latter Shi'a.

The origin of the Ottomans is mixed with legend, and need not concern us here. All that is certain is that the founder was a ghazi leader by the name of Osman.

Osman began around 1300 and in twenty-six years he had carved out a little principality for himself in Asia Minor in the region of modern Bursa. Before he died, he had declared himself a prince, independent of the sultan of Konya. Similar small ghazi principalities had been established in like manner, only to lose strength after the first or second generation. The house of Osman, however, was destined to be an exception. Thirty-seven of his descendants were to rule one of the largest empires of the world for 622 years. His descendants never forgot him. They were proud to call themselves Osmanlis—hence "Ottomans"—and each one, upon ascending the throne, was girded with the sword of Osman as a symbol of power.

One is tempted to search for the causes of such a long existence, but here one is confronted with one of those intangible aspects of history where there are no satisfactory answers. Certainly one reason is the fact that the warrior ghazis had an economic base in the akhi; and they, together with the spiritual section of the order, were all one closely knit group who were loyal to each other and to the leader. Another reason frequently mentioned is the general disarray in the world of Islam and the crumbling domain of the Byzantines. Although this weakness contributed to the ascendency of the Ottomans, one must not conclude, however, that the Ottoman victories were easy. The city of Bursa was under siege for almost nine years. A unique aspect of the Osmanlis, however, and one that certainly contributed to their power, is the fact that for over eight generations spanning 200 years, one after the other of Osman's descendants were men of resolution, good administrators, and leaders in their own right. By the time the sultans began to show signs of weakness, the empire was so large that it took another 200 years for it to disintegrate. During these last years, the "sick man of Europe" was kept alive because it was in the interest of the rival powers of Europe to let him live.

The important city of Bursa was taken by Orhan while his father Osman was dying in 1326. Orhan made the city his capital and continued the expansion of the principality. The ghazi brotherhood was not based on ethnic grounds but on loyalty and action. Consquently, they accepted all comers provided they became Muslims and were loyal to the leader. With this spectacular success, other small ghazi bands joined Orhan and his power grew. Furthermore, Orhan quite wisely changed the prevalent ghazi tradition of destroying the enemy after he was defeated or forcing him to become a Muslim. He adopted the Muslim tradition of permitting Christians and Jews to live as "people of the Book" and pay the usual head tax. This policy brought stability rather than destruction, and urban centers as well as rural areas, which under the weak Byzantines or warring bands had had a precarious existence, found new security. Before his death in 1360, Orhan ruled a principality of considerable size. Orhan and his son Murad I, instituted the practice of taking boys from their Christian subjects and training them as soldiers in their new army, which became known as Janissaries.

Murad I succeeded his father in 1360. Two years later Edirne (Adrianople) fell into his hands, and it was to serve as the capital of the enlarged state for a century. Murad I was shrewd enough to ally himself with one Christian prince against others and in the end, finish them all. He conquered Bulgaria, Macedonia, and parts of Serbia. In Asia Minor he used diplomacy, aided by show of force, and captured Ankara. Perhaps his greatest battle was that of Kossovo (1389), which subdued Serbia and opened up southeastern Europe. Murad was killed in battle and it fell to his successor, Bayezid I, to finish the victory.

Bayezid (1389–1402) was the first Ottoman to put on the airs of a monarch. In addition, he was shrewd, cruel, vain, and ambitious. One of his first acts was to have his brother, Ya'qub, strangled in order to rid himself of a possible rival. He forced the religious leaders to justify the act through the Koran. This practice gradually became a regular procedure among the Ottomans for nearly three centuries. His ruthlessness and quick action caused his subordinates to call him *Yilderim* ("thunderbolt").

Under Bayezid Constantinople was completely blocked by land, but the Ottomans did not have enough sea power to close the city from the sea. Bayezid started a navy in 1390, with the help of seafaring ghazis who had joined him. By 1396 his navy was raiding the shores of the Adriatic and his army was advancing by land into Nicopolis, an area of what is now Bulgaria.

Bayezid, however, had his heart set on Asia Minor. He wanted to be the recognized ruler of a Muslim state. The subduing of Asia Minor, however, was against ghazi tradition. The ghazis were not willing to fight against fellow Muslims, especially against ghazis of brother orders. Murad had advanced to Ankara mostly through diplomacy, but Bayezid did not have such patience. He had to bring in Christian mercenaries in order to fight against Muslims, and this embittered the ghazi states of Asia Minor. To save themselves from Bayezid, some of them appealed to the Mamluks of Egypt and others sought the aid of a new conqueror Timur, who had appeared on the eastern horizon.

TIMUR (1336–1404)

Timur was born in Transoxiana in 1336. An arrow in one of his earlier battles wounded his leg and made him lame (*lang*), and so he was known as "Timur Lang," which in European annals became "Tamerlane." He was one of those adventurers who enjoyed cutting pretentious princes down to size.

He fought and destroyed and was seldom defeated. It is doubtful whether he had any plans for founding a dynasty, let alone a stable empire. He, like most of the post-Mongol sovereigns, did not have much regard for human life. Some were more sadistic than others. Timur liked to build pyramids of human heads, a practice that was imitated by a few who followed him. Nevertheless, he was a patron of art and literature and was magnanimous at times—even to his enemies. His one great love was the city of Samarqand. He wrought destruction practically everywhere else but built Samarqand and neighboring Bokhara. His tomb is still in Samarqand but not much else has survived.

Timur led campaigns in Russia and Iraq and wrested all of Syria from the Mamluks of Egypt. He was then in a position to aid the ghazis against Bayezid. Timur's last campaign was against Bayezid. It was perhaps his greatest campaign, for in all others from Central Asia and India to Iran and Syria, Timur had not encountered such a strong state as the Ottomans had established. The engagement took place on July 21, 1402, and Bayezid was defeated and taken captive. Timur overran all of Asia Minor, going as far west as Smyrna. Then he went to Samarqand, taking his famous captive with him. Bayezid died on the way and it is not known if his body ever arrived in Samarqand.

With the coming and going of so many petty kingdoms in the Middle East of this period, one might think that with the capture of Bayezid, another principality started by Osman had come to an end. But this was not the case. In spite of the slaughter and pillage wrought by Timur, the political situation in Asia Minor reverted to nearly what it was before the ill-fated campaign of Bayezid. The Ottoman army was still the strongest in the region, and the Ottomans had not lost their important political and economic ties with the akhi. Furthermore, their sources of revenue in Europe were still intact. All these factors made it possible for them to retain control. The sons of Bayezid, however, fought each other for the throne. In a fratricidal struggle that lasted a decade, Mehmed won and was proclaimed sultan in 1412.

With the aid of a strong fighting machine and efficient organization, Mehmed was able to subdue the independent leaders of Asia Minor and reunite the kingdom. His untimely death in 1421 was kept a secret until his successor Murad II had a chance to come to Edirne and assume control. Compared with his forebears and in contrast to his son, Murad II was a peaceful sultan. He devoted a good deal of time to the development of the Turkish language and to the education of his children.

Mehmed II ruled for thirty years and was engaged almost incessantly in war. He experienced one famous victory and two defeats. He is known, however, for his one great victory and has been given the title of "conqueror" for taking Constantinople. Almost as soon as he became sultan, he started preparing for the capture of the city. The siege began on April 6, 1453, and lasted for fifty-three days. On May 29, 1453, the Turkish columns entered the city through a breach in the wall. Emperor Paleologus, who had incurred the wrath of the citizens by agreeing to become Catholic if the pope would send him aid, was slain; and on the same afternoon Mehmed entered the city, went straight to Hagia Sophia, the great cathedral, and ordered it changed into a mosque.

Mehmed must have decided to make Constantinople (Stambul to its citizens), his capital, for he did not allow the customary pillage to last very long. Gradually the name was Turkified into Istanbul. Most of the churches were converted into mosques. He caused the city to be settled by Turks and Christians. Since the patriarch of the Orthodox Church had died, he ordered the election of a new patriarch and gave him a jeweled cross as the Byzantine emperors used to do. As has been pointed out, the fall of Constantinople, like the fall of Baghdad, was an anticlimax. The Turks felt that they had to take it, not because it blocked their commercial or military or political interests, but because it was the symbol of empire.

Mehmed developed the economy of the empire to pay for his military conquests. He encouraged cottagee industries and the production of cotton, silk, and wool. He also encouraged craftsmen's guilds. In addition, he devalued the coinage and created government monopolies of salt, soap, candles, and other articles, and gave them to the highest bidders. He died in 1481.

In the now-familiar struggle for power and the bloodbath that followed the death of the sultan, the Janissaries supported Bayezid II, and he became sultan. His rival and brother, Jem, sought the aid of Pope Innocent VIII and King Charles VII of France, but could not gain the throne and died in 1495. By Ottoman standards, Bayezid II was not a warlike individual, though in a great naval engagement at Navarino the Ottomans defeated the Venetians and put an end to the latter's hopes of supremacy in the Mediterranean. Bayezid II was troubled by border disputes with the Mamluks of Egypt and more importantly with the rising star of Esma'il, the founder of the Safavid dynasty of Iran. It was left to Bayezid's successor, however, to deal with both.

The sickly Bayezid II could not cope with his three sons, who started fighting him and each other while he was still alive. The Janissaries had become a real power behind the throne and sided with the most warlike of the sons, Selim, who became sultan in 1512. In his short reign of eight years he added more territory to the empire than had any other sultan.

The activities of Shah Esma'il in Iran, his use of the many Shi'is of Asia Minor against the Ottomans, and his alliance with the Mamluks forced Selim to act. He defeated Esma'il in August 1514 but the result was not conclusive. What was more significant, and what gained the Ottomans territory and prestige, was his victory over the Mamluks of Egypt two years later at Marj Dabiq.

Aside from the fact that Selim was bent on conquest in the east, he had a good excuse for war because the Mamluk sultan, Qansawh al-Ghuri, had allied himself with Shah Esma'il. Ghuri, therefore, had no choice but to fight Selim. A famous battle took place at Marj Dabiq, north of Aleppo, on August 24, 1516. The Mamluks were routed and all Syria fell to the Ottomans. The Turks entered such cities as Aleppo, Damascus, Beirut, and Jerusalem more as deliverers from the excesses of the Mamluks than as conquerors. Selim continued his victorious advance southward; in January 1517 he met the new Mamluk sultan, Tuman, and defeated him outside Cairo. All Egypt, as well as the holy cities of Arabia, now fell into his hands. The Ottomans became heirs of both the Byzantine emperors and the Abbasid caliphs, with a vast empire to match their new position. Their subordinates referred to the Ottoman sultans as "caliphs" and met with no objection. Gradually everyone took it for granted. So far as is known, the title was first mentioned officially in the Treaty of Kuchuk Kainarji between the Turks and the Russians in 1774.

Suleiman, the only surviving son of Selim, became sultan in 1520 and ruled for forty-six years. Under him the Ottoman Empire reached its pinnacle of power and glory, and he has been called "the Magnificent" by Europeans. In Ottoman history he is known as Qanuni ("lawgiver"). Suleiman decided to carry out the plans of his great-grandfather, Mehmed the Conqueror, and take Belgrade and Rhodes. Europe was then much stronger than at Mehmed's time, but Suleiman's contemporaries, Charles V, Francis I, and Henry VIII, were fighting each other and were too involved in the Reformation to have time to deal with Suleiman. Belgrade fell on August 8, 1521.

Four years later, Suleiman started out with 100,000 men toward Vienna. The Janissaries had been getting restless from inaction. On August 31, 1526, the sultan won a major battle at Mohacs, Hungary, which enabled him to capture Buda and Pest on both sides of the Danube. He did not have enough men, however, to take Vienna and had to return to Istanbul. Suleiman tried it again in 1529 but his march was impeded by rains and he did not reach Vienna until the end of September. On October 12, the Ottomans breached the wall of Vienna and launched a strong attack, but were beaten off. The Janissaries were not interested in continuing the war because of the approaching winter. A council was held in the field and the Ottomans retired on October 15. Suleiman let it be known that since the Holy Roman Emperor Ferdinand I was not in Vienna, the sultan had lost all interest in taking the city. This was the farthest advance of the Ottomans in Europe.

Suleiman's rule was the most glorious in Ottoman history, and its length gave it an aspect of permanence and luster. Nevertheless, Suleiman's reign marks the beginning of a long decline in imperial power and influence. Powerful as he was, Suleiman could not cope with the greed of his own retinue or the ambitions of his own officers. The Janissary corps had grown too large to be manageable and was taking an increasingly active part in the political affairs of the state. The old ghazi virtues became things of the past. Suleiman himself broke the time-honored tradition of promotion by merit and made his boon companion, Ibrahim, the grand vazir. Ibrahim happened to be an able administrator, but it soon became customary for sultans to appoint their own favorites without regard to ability. It was customary also that the sultan preside over the meetings of the Divan (Council). Suleiman delegated this important duty to his grand vazir.

The causes of the Ottoman decline were not all internal. This was the age of exploration in Europe and the development of maritime technology. With the improvement of shipping, merchants were traveling all over the world in search of markets and trade. The establishment of the British and Dutch East India companies encroached upon the commercial activities of the Ottomans. Their reliance on sea trade freed them from paying numerous "protection taxes" and enabled them to undersell the Ottomans, who relied on land routes. The Europeans were also beginning to modernize their weapons and improve their general fire power.

For one reason or another, Suleiman ordered the execution of two of his sons. The only one left to assume power was Selim II, who was debauched and a drunkard. Selim's short rule of eight years did not arrest the disintegration of the Empire. The Ottoman Empire was based on the principle of absolute monarchy. The glory of the empire was a reflection of the ability, courage, and wisdom of the supreme ruler. Such an empire could not last long with uninterested and weak monarchs.

Chapter Eleven
Society and Culture under the Ottomans

The Ottoman Empire was not a homogeneous society by any means. There were diverse nationalities, each with a different language, and there were Jews and Christians as well as Muslims. Most of the Christians, being of the Orthodox persuasion, were divided along national lines, such as Greek, Bulgarian, and Russian. The Ottoman rulers, as we shall see, applied the Islamic principle of allowing the "people of the Book" freedom of worship and developed the millet system. The concept of millet was applied to people of the same religion, except that the Ottomans subdivided the Christian millet into national linguistic groups, defined by geographical location. It was not a pluralistic society but a patchwork of different social and religious groups that enjoyed some measure of autonomy. All of them were held together by the might of the army and the person of the sultan.

THE ARMY

The Ottoman Empire was primarily an army encampment. Fighting was its most important business. At the heart of the army was the corps of Janissaries. This became the empire's most important fighting force and was dreaded by all its foes. It has already been noted that the ghazis took all comers who espoused their cause and accepted Islam. Gradually in battle they took slaves and forced them to become Muslims and soldiers. In fact the Abbasids and the Saljuqs recruited their armies in this way. The Ottomans, however, expanded and institutionalized the practice, with the sanction of religious leaders. Generally every five years the Christian population of the kingdom was made to contribute a certain percentage of its male population as tribute. Christian children in their teens or younger were completely severed from their Christian families and were brought up as Muslims. They were not allowed to marry, though later this rule was relaxed, and their loyalty was to the person of the sultan. Those more able were trained as pages for the court and educated to become administrators. The rest were given military training in the Janissary corps, which may have been the first well-trained standing army in Europe. These, being "slaves" of the sultan, were under his personal command, and he could deal with them as he pleased without reference to the religious leaders.

The Janissaries were closely connected with the Bektashi order of dervishes, as was the sultan himself. Their uniform was like that of the Bektashis. Their headgear was made of white felt, with a piece of white cloth hanging from the top of the hat to the shoulder. A spoon was embroidered on this cloth as a symbol of the fact that their livelihood came from the sultan. Every soldier prized his food kit and its loss to the enemy was considered a disgrace. Until Suleiman, sultans accompanied the army and took their pay as Janissaries, their names being first on the role. Later, when the weapons of war changed, the Janissaries were trained as riflemen and artillery men.

The provinces supplied the Ottomans with irregular infantry as well as the bulk of the cavalry. Inasmuch as ultimate title to all land belonged to the sultan, he could keep large parcels for himself or assign arable land to his officers as fiefs. These individuals would collect land revenues as salary, and their obligation was to provide the sultan with armed cavalry according to the size of their fiefs. In time the army needed cash to train men in the use of new firearms and could not depend upon fief holders to fulfill the need. Consequently fiefs were broken up into tax farms to provide cash for the government.

ADMINISTRATION

The old formula that was written in "Mirrors to Princes"[1] was repeated over and over again by Ottoman counselors: "No government without an army, no army without money, no money without subjects, no subjects without justice." In true Mongol fashion the absolute commander of this military encampment was the sultan. Unlike the Mongols, however, the Ottomans were Sunni Muslims, and as such their government was a theocracy. This meant that the power of the sultan was limited by the law of Allah. The Ottoman Empire was dedicated to the advancement of Islam. It was the land of Islam and soldiers fought for the cause of Islam. This naturally limited

[1]See p. 90.

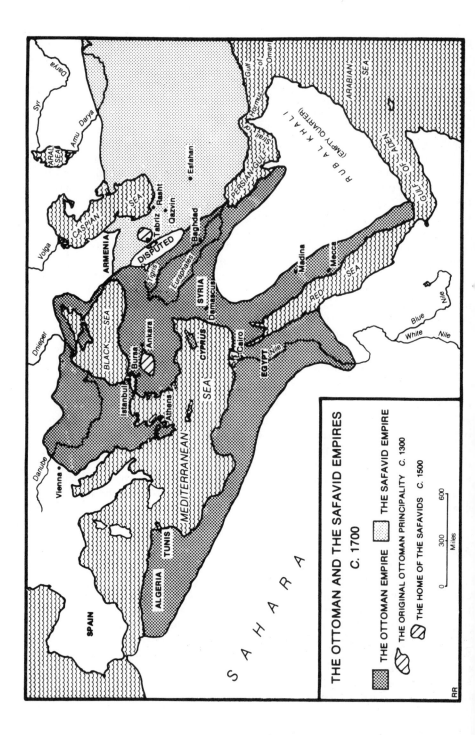

THE OTTOMAN AND THE SAFAVID EMPIRES
C. 1700

THE OTTOMAN EMPIRE

THE ORIGINAL OTTOMAN PRINCIPALITY C. 1300

THE SAFAVID EMPIRE

THE HOME OF THE SAFAVIDS C. 1500

0   300   600
Miles

the power of the sultan. The balance between an absolute monarch and an absolute God was very delicate. It always wavered. It is safe to say that all Ottoman institutions and laws were attempts to find a balance between the two.

Already a good deal of work had been done on determining this delicate balance during the time of the Abbasids and the period of principalities. By force of both circumstance and the writings of persons like Ghazali and ibn-Taymiyya, anyone with sufficient might could legitimately rule over the Muslims, provided he was with the Shari'a.[2] The natural step to believing in the divine right of kings was taken by Jalal al-Din Dawwani (1427–1501), who in his *Ethics of Jalali* wrote: "The sultan is a person distinguished by divine support . . . sovereignty itself is a gift of God and his [the sultan's] divine right will not be affected by his conduct." The Ottoman Sultans tried to use their prerogatives as much as they could without doing away with the Shari'a. They certainly used titles: "Vicar of God on Earth," "Successor of the Prophet," "Pontiff of the Muslims," "Refuge of the World," "Shadow of God," and, in unbecoming modesty, "Servant of the Two Sanctuaries" (i.e., Mecca and Medina).

In order to govern, the sultan leaned on a body of administrators that grew in number as the empire expanded. These administrators were acquired by the same method as the Janissaries. This was the practice of taking Christian boys as tribute, called *devshirmeh*. Most of the children were trained as Janissaries. The brighter ones were trained as pageboys at the court and received rigorous training in administration. At the age of twenty-five, they were sent away as minor officials in the provinces. Some rose to positions as prominent as the grand vazirate. All of the boys brought through the devshirmeh were given Muslim educations and converted to Islam. Even though they were slaves, they enjoyed special prerogatives. They could marry, acquire property, and have servants, among other individual rights. Nevertheless, they were slaves and as such they and everything they owned belonged to the sultan, who had complete power over them without interference from the religious leaders.

For purposes of administration the empire was divided into two regions. The region east of Istanbul went by the name of "Anatolia," and the region west of the capital was called "Rumeli." Each region had its own commander, judge, and treasurer. Each of these chief administrators had his own appointees at the provincial, county, and city levels. The decision-making body of the administration was the Council, presided over by the sultan. The usual members of the Council were the grand vazir, the two commanders of Rumeli and Anatolia, the two judges, the two treasurers, and the chancellor. Later the admiral of the navy and the commander of the Janissaries were added to the membership.

The collection of revenue was one of the most important activities of the administration. As we have seen, Islamic law had already provided for the collection of taxes. These were the head tax paid by non-Muslims, the Zakah paid by all Muslims, one-tenth of all agricultural products, municipal

[2]See p. 91.

taxes paid by craftsmen and merchants, and taxes on livestock and mines. In addition to the above, the Council had the prerogative of levying such extra canonical taxes as a household tax, a cultivation tax, custom duties, as well as fees of all sorts.

Parallel to the organization of the civil administration was the institution of religion. Its task, in addition to the performance of religious services, was the administration of justice, education, and religious endowments. The members were drawn from the Muslim population who were, of course, free. They had studied in special schools. The curricula of such schools included Islamic religion, Islamic education, and more importantly, Islamic law. Out of these schools came the future preachers, mosque scribes, muezzins, dervishes, teachers in both lower and higher schools, readers of the Koran, qadis, and muftis. Since Islam theoretically has neither a priesthood nor a hierarchy, the above offices would generally correspond, in Christian traditions, with ministers/priests, monks, schoolteachers, and lawyers. All scholars studied the Shari'a and, with the possible exception of some of the dervishes, were devoted to it and believed in the social and political institutions that were based upon it.

The Ottoman courts from the lowest to the highest were run by these people. As in their administrative organization, the Ottomans had two chief judges, one for Anatolia (Asia Minor), and one for Rumeli (Europe). True to the military nature of the Ottoman Empire, each of the chief judges was called Chaplain of the Army. At the pinnacle of this vast religious organization was the Shaykh ul-Islam, who was close to the sultan and was his chief advisor as to the intricacies of the Shari'a. In the history of the Ottoman Empire these men were sometimes very powerful individuals.

One of the responsibilities imposed by the institution was the administration of the *vaqf* (or *waqf*), the religious endowment. The *vaqf* had complete charge of the expenditure of funds and management of land and other properties that had been given by the pious for charitable and religious purposes. The chief duty of the judges, however, from the small-town mufti to the Shaykh ul-Islam, was to study each case, determine its relation to the Shari'a, and give an opinion, or *fetva*. The issuance of an opinion usually settled the case. The fetva of the Shaykh ul-Islam had, of course, national importance. At least eleven sultans were deposed by fetva. On all matters the Shaykh ul-Islam, representing the Shari'a, had veto power over the decisions of the sultan. In practice, the implementation of such an arrangement depended upon the power of the sultan and the courage of the Shaykh ul-Islam. In some cases the religious leaders showed courage and good judgment, as when the Shaykh ul-Islam vetoed Sultan Selim the Grim's decision to kill Christians who refused to learn Arabic. At other times these leaders went along with the wishes of the sultan, such as giving religious sanction to the practice of fratricide whenever a new sultan ascended the throne.

There were naturally clashes of interests between the sultan and Shaykh ul-Islam. Since the Shari'a had not foreseen all the problems of a large and complex empire, and could not be expanded, the sultan resorted to at least three other devices to meet new problems. These were *adet, urf,* and *qanun.* Adet was the custom of each community, which was different among the varied nationalities of the empire. Urf was the nonreligious law, which might have emanated from the will of the sultan and/or the judgment of the leaders of the community. Urf was usually introduced when Shari'a did not find a solution. Qanun was the official decree of the sultan, which superseded adet, urf, and other qanuns. The ulama were against all three because these did not emanate from the Shari'a. Furthermore, these devices gave more power to the sultans, who were tempted to contravene the Shari'a even more. During the period of reform in the nineteenth century, the ulama and the constitutionalists became allies (even though they were opposed in ideology) against the power of the sultan.

NON-MUSLIMS

As a Muslim state, the Ottomans early gave up the ghazi practice of forced conversion to Islam and instead adopted the toleration allowed to the "people of the Book" by Islam. The Turks referred to the non-Muslim religious communities as *millets,* and the whole practice became known as the *millet system.* Since the Christian subjects of the Ottomans were almost all members of the Orthodox Church and as such had national ecclesiastical organizations, the Ottomans treated each of them a separate millet. Each millet, whether Armenian, Syrian, Greek, Serbian Orthodox, or Jewish, was under the jurisdiction of its own religious organization and was subject to its laws. This arrangement had two effects. One was that the religious communities under this system were freer than those under most Christian rulers. As ecclesiastical bodies they became prosperous and powerful. Second, members of the top echelons of these millets, who had privileged positions, became as reactionary as the ulama, and they also were against change in the empire. It was only after the interference of European nations in the affairs of the Ottomans and their use of the Christian minority as a tool of their imperialism that the Ottomans became suspicious of these millets and ceased to be tolerant as they had previously been. The institution of the millet system should not, however, be taken to mean that non-Muslims were the equals of Muslims in the eyes of the law.

ARABIC-SPEAKING REGIONS

On the whole, the Turks were not colonizers, and certainly they did not try to colonize Syria and Egypt. The Arabic-speaking peoples were the largest single component of the empire. Either because the Arabs were their coreligionists or for other reasons, the Turks did not bring the Fertile Crescent and Egypt under the direct administration of Istanbul. Under Selim, who conquered the area, and subsequent sultans, local amirs continued to rule and pay tribute to the government. The Ottomans were content to send a *pasha,* or governor-general, just to keep an eye on the affairs. For nearly 400 years, Ottoman rule gave Syria a tranquility that it had not enjoyed since the Umayyad period.

The Arabic-speaking Muslims were never slaves; in fact, many reached high positions, especially in the religious administration. Indeed, the Ottomans treated the Arabs much better than they did the Anatolian Turks, who were called "*eshek Turk*" or "donkey of a Turk." The myth generally circulated by modern Arabs to the effect that 400 years of Ottoman rule suffocated Arab progress cannot be supported by the evidence. The Turks honored the religion of the Arabs, the language of the Arabs, and the laws that the Arabs had established. Certainly in these and other fields the Arabs were freer than some Turks, and the fact that Arabic-speaking peoples did not show greater progress should not be blamed wholly upon the Ottomans.

The situation in Egypt became intolerable not because the Ottomans wanted it that way but because their policy of leaving the local authorities in power had bad results. The Ottomans were interested only in tribute and in not much else. These local officials and their underlings confiscated property and looted the country as before. The Turkish pashas were helpless. Some of the pashas who could not overcome local amirs joined them in the plunder. In about 250 years of direct Ottoman rule, there were more than 100 pashas. Quite often an emissary of a local amir came riding on a donkey to the residence of a pasha at the citadel and cried out, "Descend, O Pasha," and this was usually enough for the pasha to pack his bags and go home to Istanbul.

The amirs became so strong that in 1769 Ali Bey proclaimed himself sultan. They were not eliminated until the coming of Napoleon and the rise of Muhammad Ali.

CULTURAL LIFE

First and foremost, the Turks were soldiers; more specifically, they were soldiers of Islam, whose aim was to propagate the faith and advance its power. In this role they felt their important tasks were to uphold the Shari'a as judges and to maintain law and order as administrators. The wealth of the Turk consisted of land, either as farmer or landlord, or the salary he received for his services. Christians and Jews were left with the more lucrative tasks of conducting the domestic and foreign commerce of the empire.

Islam owes a great deal to these soldiers, and it is difficult to imagine what would have happened to the faith had the Turks not appeared on the scene. The Saljuq Turks were the first to establish Islam in Asia Minor, and it was they who advanced the banner of Islam as far as the gates of Vienna.

Even though they very likely spoke Turkish in their homes, the Saljuqs of Iran and Syria adopted Persian and Arabic respectively and did not try to elevate Turkish as the official language of their respective kingdoms. The Saljuqs of Asia Minor, however, propagated the Turkish language as well as Islam in their kingdom. Perhaps the fact that the Mongol invasion isolated the Turks of Asia Minor had something to do with it. They had brought with them a Turkish grammar that a certain Muhammad Qashqai had prepared in 1074. The written Turkish language that developed contained many words borrowed from Arabic and Persian. The renowned Sufi poet, Jalal al-Din Rumi, who had made his home in Konya in the thirteenth century, wrote his famous book, *Masnavi,* exclusively in Persian. But his son, Sultan Veled, also a poet, wrote in both Turkish and Persian.

The Ottomans continued the use of Turkish. Murad I directed that the chronicles of his Ottoman ancestors be written in Turkish. He himself was a poet who wrote in both Turkish and Persian. For several centuries Arabic was the language of religion and Persian the language of poetry and decreasingly that of communication. Turkish, however, was the lingua franca and the language of military command.

The Turks excelled in many branches of learning. Mulla Khusrev was a distinguished jurist under Mehmed the Conqueror, and his works became standard. During the reign of Suleiman the Magnificent, ibn-Kemal was considered the greatest scholar in Islam. Perhaps because of the needs of war, the Turks produced a large number of eminent physicians. They were famous in Central Europe for their surgery and ophthalmology. While in medicine they used Turkish, in historiography the more popular language was Persian. Turkish historiography began with official chronicles and includes accounts of campaigns and conquests. Most of the historians, in imitation of their Abbasid predecessors, wrote comprehensive histories. A few, however, wrote monographs on biography, methods of administration, palace life, and even on causes of the decline of the empire.

In literature, the Turks followed the Persians in both style and language to such an extent that, as one writer has said, "Turkish literature has become a true depository of ideas from Islamized Iran." There were talented poets who wrote in Turkish like Fuzuli (d. 1556) and Ahmed Nadim (d. 1730). The masses who frequented coffee houses listened to professional and itinerant storytellers, who regaled their audiences with vernacular tales, interspersed with lines of poems. The influence of Europe in the nineteenth century and the need to have the participation of the masses, forced the writers to use simple Turkish rather than the Persianized Turkish that had been in vogue.

The Ottoman sultans maintained large harems made up of slaves, who were practically all Christians, and who were guarded by eunuchs headed by the chief of the women's bureau. Suleiman had some 300 women in his harem. According to custom, the girls lined up every day and the sultan, after reviewing them, gave his handkerchief to the one he desired. Girls who failed to attract the attention of the sovereign by the time they reached the age of twenty-five were usually married to the officials and soldiers.

According to written observations of European visitors, the trade routes were kept in good repair and there were caravanserais along the route. In large cities, there were public baths for men and women, and for a mere four aspers (about one cent) any Turk could spend an hour in the bath. Then, as now, the food of the common citizen consisted of black bread, rice, fruit, and sometimes mutton. There was not much wine drinking in the home out of deference to Islamic law, but there were taverns, which were managed most likely by non-Muslims. It is reported that card playing was unknown among the Ottomans, but this is very doubtful, for in Iran during the same period the practice was well known. Apparently, all European visitors were impressed with the policing of the cities, and some declared that Istanbul was safer than any other capital in Europe.

THE ECONOMY

The economy of the Ottoman Empire during the sixteenth and seventeenth centuries was basically agrarian, supported by craft industries and commercial trade in towns and urban areas. These varied greatly in different parts of the empire, necessitating considerable organization by local notables, merchants, artisans, and officials.

The agrarian sector was the most important source of revenue. Land belonged to the sultan, who leased it to the cultivators, through the notables or officials, to plant and harvest staple crops. The harvest was then divided among the sultan, the local notables and officials (who received it in lieu of a salary), and the farmer. On the whole, a small portion of the land was used for cash crops such as tobacco, coffee, silk, or cotton.

During the sixteenth century, there were three kinds of land-tenure systems. One was communal lands held by entire villages. The second was state lands leased to officials and notables in lieu of salary. The third was land held by the religious endowment office for charitable purposes. Toward the end of the seventeenth century, however, the local notables and commanders began to pay less and less of the revenues to the sultan, which enabled them to build up personal military forces and seize segments of state lands for their personal use. This made it difficult for the sultan to prevent the rise of rebellious and independent local centers of anti-imperial groups.

Dependent on a variety of resources, labor, and capital, the Ottoman craft industries flourished during the sixteenth century. They were organized into guilds for the purpose of regulating prices as well as setting up standards of quality. Sometimes different millets had their own guilds, and sometimes a single guild had members from different millets. Carpets, shawls, gold and silverware, and other metalwork were the most important products, while silk, wool, and cotton goods became increasingly important for the European markets toward the end of the seventeenth century. Ottoman crafts and goods were present in one form or another among the pastoral herders, village cultivators, and town artisans. From the sixteenth to the eighteenth centuries, an increasing number of merchants tried to bring all three under their control, avoiding local notables and government officials. In the Balkans and Egypt such incorporation proved very successful; the sultan's treasury was deprived of revenue, and an independent merchant class began to form.

Unlike the strictly regulated cultivators and crafts men, the merchants were relatively free. Itinerant merchants traveled within regions or within the empire and gradually grew in power and influence. By the seventeenth century they were dealing with the expanding world economy of Europe. Centers like Bursa, Istanbul, and Cairo became entrepôts for goods passing from Central Asia, India, and Arabia to Europe. Slaves, gold, and ivory were collected in Cairo and Alexandria for shipment to other parts of the empire. As principal traders of manufactured goods and foodstuffs, the merchants gained considerable wealth, but not much of this wealth got sent to the sultan's treasury.

The Ottoman sultans during this period had three main sources of revenue. One was taxes on rural and urban products. The second was tribute from industries, transit trade, and roads. The third was custom duties on imported and exported goods. For the collection of the above revenues, they had become dependent on the military, local notables, and merchants. This dependence, as we shall see, caused them a great deal of trouble during the eighteenth and nineteenth centuries.

SOCIETY

Ottoman society contained many different levels. On the first level was the court and all its intricate branches. In addition to the royal family, the court included imperial administrators and military units. Members of the court all spoke Ottoman Turkish, read Persian and Arabic literature, and were schooled in the disciplines of computation, philosophy, and composition.

Second, Ottoman society consisted of many local linguistic and religious communities. From the fifteenth to the eighteenth century, Arabic-, Armenian-, Assyrian-, Greek-, Hebrew-, Kurdish-, and Slavic-speaking peoples considered themselves to be members of the Ottoman system. Whether they functioned as merchants, artisans, traders, policemen, soldiers, or tax collectors, they defined themselves in political terms rather than in religious or linguistic terms. For their social and cultural identification they found solace in their millets and allowed themselves considerable latitude under the protective political "umbrella" of the Ottoman Empire.

Third, Ottoman Society consisted of vast numbers of people who rarely identified themselves as "Ottomans." Balkan villagers, like their Turkish, Kurdish, Armenian, and Arab counterparts in other sections of the empire, found their identity in their religion, language, customs, and occupations. Their difficulties as cultivators were with the local landlords and officials who sometimes belonged to their own millets. The Ottoman court and higher officials in Istanbul were remote and often inoffensive figureheads. In struggles between the court and local notables, the cultivators often would side with the court.

From the middle of the nineteenth century, however, the situation changed. As we shall see in Chapter 16 various reform movements caused the villagers to choose new alliances and identifications. No longer did Armenian, Turkish, and Kurdish villagers find a common cause; instead, each group rallied behind the banner of its own religious and linguistic identity and sometimes confronted each other. Christians and Jews sought out European support, while Muslim peoples drew greater distinctions between themselves. It was in reaction to the increased polarization of the Ottoman society and empire that the pan-Islamic, pan-Turkish, and pan-Arab political movements arose. The volatile eruptions at both the local and regional levels from the mid-nineteenth century to the end of the Ottoman Empire in 1923, stemmed primarily from the disintegration of the old Ottoman society under the pressures of new local, regional, and international interests and interventions.

Chapter Twelve
The Safavids and Their Imperial Institutions

SAFAVID SHAHS

Esma'il I (1500–1524)
Tahmasp I (1524–1576)
Esma'il II (1576–1578)
Khodabandeh (1578–1587)
Abbas I (1587–1629)
Safi (1629–1642)
Abbas II (1642–1667)
Soleimam (1667–1694)
Hosein (1694–1722)
Tahmasp II (1722–1731)
Abbas III (1731–1736)

The map of the Middle East at the beginning of the seventh century was (see page 118) not so very different from what it was a thousand years later. In the seventh century two powers dominated the area. The Byzantine Empire had control of Asia Minor, most of the Fertile Crescent, Egypt, and North Africa, and ruled from Constantinople. The Sasanids of Iran dominated the area from the Tigris to the Indus and from the Persian Gulf to the Caucasus and the Urals. These two empires fought each other to a standstill and weakened themselves so much that they fell easy prey to the Arabs of the desert. A thousand years later, we find the Middle East again dominated by two powers residing in the same areas as before: the Ottomans in Asia Minor and the Safavids in Iran. These two empires, like their predecessors, fought each other to a standstill. It is quite tempting to conclude, as some have done, that as the mutual weakening of the Byzantines and the Sasanids played into the hands of Arabs, the mutual weakening of the Ottomans and the Safavids played into the hands of Europeans. Whether such a conclusion is valid or not depends upon many imponderables that are beyond the scope of this survey. The question in itself, however, is very intriguing.

As a result of the Mongol invasion, the Iranians, on the whole, gave up political activities, immersed themselves in Sufism, and whiled their time away in all sorts of eclecticism. They kept their language and culture alive. Though they were not interested in political and dynastic activities, they influenced those who were. The Mongols and diverse Turkish tribes who formed principalities in Iran took on the culture of the Iranians and, with few exceptions, adopted the Persian language and institutions.

From the Mongol invasion until 1502, Iran did not enjoy a unified and stable government. The Ilkhans, after vacillating between Christianity and Islam, accepted the latter and, like the Turks of Anatolia, attached themselves to Sufi orders. Ghazan Khan settled the question of religion and became a Muslim. He came under the influence of a Sufi by the name of Shaykh Safi Gilani (d. 1334), who had organized an order in Rasht, a provincial capital near the Caspian Sea. By the fifteenth century, the Safi order of Sufis had joined the Shi'a sect and, like the Sunnis, had laymen who engaged in business activities and soldiers who were zealous to advance the cause of Shi'ism by the sword. The military followers of the Safavids wore red headgear and were called *qizilbash* ("red heads").

SHAH ESMA'IL

Members of the qizilbash were known for their absolute devotion to their leader. They were at constant war with Sunni ghazi states and later with the Ottomans ruling in Asia Minor. There were large numbers of Shi'a sympathizers in Asia Minor who were thorns in the flesh of the Ottoman body politic. Esma'il, the direct descendant of Safi, was a boy living in Iran where his father, Shaykh Haydar, was leader of the order. Haydar was killed in 1490. With a number of his father's followers, Esma'il went to Ardabil in 1500. He was then thirteen. In two years this remarkable boy conquered all of Shirvan, Armenia, and Azarbaijan, and declared himself shah.

The Safavids claimed that they were *sayyids* (descendants of the Prophet) on their father's side and descendants of the Sasanid princes on their mother's side. That they were either is unlikely. They were probably members of a Turkish or Kurdish tribe in Azarbaijan, and their early followers were Turkomans. Esma'il's mother tongue was Turkish and he also wrote poetry in that language. Indeed, when the Ottomans gloried in using Persian, Esma'il's court used the Turkish language. The Safavids, however, were Iranianized at a rapid pace. Like the heads of other principalities, they assumed the title and culture of the Iranians and were known to outsiders as Iranians.

Esma'il conquered all of Iran and forced the inhabitants to become Shi'i. He was a bitter enemy of all Sunnis and encouraged the Shi'is of Asia Minor to revolt against the Ottomans. Shi'ism became the state religion of Iran. This thwarted the ambition of the Ottomans, especially of Sultan Selim I, who wanted to be the supreme ruler of the Muslim world. Also, Shi'ism prevented Iran from being swallowed up by the Ottomans. Even though the Safavids were Turks, they identified themselves with Iranians, and the Safavid Dynasty certainly brought about a national independence.

In any case, Shah Esma'il at the age of twenty was master of most of Iran and stirred up a number of revolts against the Sunnis of Asia Minor. Bayezid II and Selim I were contemporaries of Shah Esma'il. Selim I, who was suspicious of Esma'il, decided to follow a conciliatory course. After all, the Ottoman sultan was not interested in taking Iran, and Bayezid would be satisfied if Esma'il were to direct his conquest eastward and let Asia Minor alone.

The growing power of Esma'il was a direct threat to Asia Minor, especially with the large number of Shi'i sympathizers who were living there. Furthermore, as defenders of Sunni orthodoxy, the Ottomans could not remain indifferent. When Selim II became sultan, Esma'il did not send him a congratulatory message but continued to devastate eastern Anatolia and undermine Ottoman authority in the region. Selim had no choice but to lead a campaign against Esma'il. Selim had a long way to go. By following a scorched earth policy, Esma'il tried to draw the Ottomans into the interior of Iran. The Ottoman soldiers were not happy in eastern campaigns. Perhaps the heat, the inhospitable terrain, and the fact that they had to fight Muslims had something to do with it. Even the Janissaries were unhappy. The sultan, however, persisted in his march and in killing Shi'is wherever he found them in his own domain. It is estimated that he destroyed some 40,000 Shi'i Sufis. The first engagement took place at Chaldiran, in the area of Lake Urmia on August 24, 1514. The victory of the Ottomans was definite though not conclusive. Selim occupied Tabriz for a time. Shah Esma'il, who was twenty-eight years old, became rather despondent at the defeat and took to wine. The battle of Chaldiran is important in the history of the Middle East because, first, it was the first of many engagements between the two protagonists—namely, the Ottomans and the Safavids—that would take place over the next 200 years. Second, it convinced the Safavids of the importance of modern weapons. The tendency of both Turkish and Iranian historians to exaggerate makes it difficult to ascertain the number of troops involved. What is certain, however, is that the Ottoman cavalry and infantry were equipped with muskets and the all-important artillery. The Safavid army was made up entirely of qizilbash cavalry armed with spears, bows, and swords. They were all religious devotees of Shah Esma'il and fought bravely with the encouragement of their women, who, apparently, accompanied them. But they found out that fanatical courage was no match against guns, and it was the Turkish artillery that won the day for the Ottomans at Chaldiran, as well as at Marj Dabiq two years later against the Mamluks. The Safavids purchased firearms and were able to avenge Chaldiran in later years.

Shah Esma'il died at the young age of thirty-seven. In spite of the Chaldiran defeat, however, he laid the foundation of an empire based on two principles: First, it was Shi'i, and second, it was Iranian. Shah Esma'il and his son, Shah Tahmasp, were more interested in the former, while Shah Abbas and the later Safavids emphasized the latter.

Having become masters of all of Iran, Shah Esma'il and his qizilbash devotees enforced conversion to Shi'ism at swordpoint and created a centralized state based on Shi'i doctrine. The Iranians, who had become tired of wars and bloodshed, accepted the suzerainty of the Safavids and the Shi'i sect without much resistance. Shi'ism separated the Shi'i Turks of Iran from the Turks of Asia Minor, who remained Sunnis; and the gap has not been breached to this day. Shi'ism also separated the Sunnis of the Ottoman Empire from the Sunnis of Central Asia and defeated the hope of the Ottoman sultans to rule as caliphs over a unified Islamic world.

YEARS OF UNCERTAINTY

From the death of Shah Esma'il in 1524 until the accession of Shah Abbas the Great in 1567, the Safavids under three shahs, Tahmasp I, Esma'il II, and Mohammad Khodabandeh, turned their eyes eastward and carved out an empire that stretched from the Persian Gulf to both sides of the Caspian Sea and from the Tigris to Transoxiana. They held their own against the Ottomans, reoccupied Tabriz, and fought back and forth against the Ottomans over Baghdad in the south and Armenia in the north. It was their aim to establish a Shi'i theocracy with the shah as the sole leader. The fighting order of the qizilbash was the backbone of the state. The country was divided into districts, and each district was under a leading qizilbash who ruled it as a fief. In return, he provided the shah with soldiers in time of war and with a portion of the revenue. Otherwise, he was free to do as he pleased. It was through these qizilbash feudal lords that the whole country was forced to become Shi'i. In towns and villages all across the land, people were asked to curse the first three caliphs—that is, Abu Bakr, Umar, and Uthman. Those who refused were summarily executed.

Because the Safavids controlled a large territory in the east and Tabriz, their capital, was too close to the Ottoman border to be safe, Shah Tahmasp moved the capital to the city of Qazvin, in north central Iran. The qizilbash leaders became so rich and powerful that they tried to interfere in the question of succession, which had generally become the most acute and perennial question in the whole Islamic world—whether Arab, Ottoman, or Iranian. The qizilbash fought each other over the succession and gradually revolted against the "most perfect leader" of the qizilbash order, the shah himself. Very much like the Boyars of Russia, the qizilbash lords preferred an oligarchy in which they wielded power collectively rather than a centralized government under an autocratic shah. They became especially trouble-some at the time of the mild-mannered ascetic shah, Mohammad Khodaban-deh, and tried to influence him to choose a weak successor. To insure the success of their scheme, they executed most of the Safavid princes, including the heir-apparent and his mother.

SHAH ABBAS

A younger brother of the crown prince, however, was rescued and taken secretly to Khorasan. Some years later, this young prince, with the help of the more loyal qizilbash, defeated the quarrelsome leaders and assumed the throne as Shah Abbas (1587). Under Shah Abbas, Iran reached its zenith of power politically, economically, and culturally. After the passage of a thou-sand years, a territory as extensive as during the time of the Sassanids was, once again, called Iran. It is no doubt for this reason that the Iranians remem-ber Shah Abbas with pride and affection and have given him the title of "the Great." Fortunately for Shah Abbas, he ruled during the time when the Otto-mans were at their weakest. He was a contemporary of no less than five sultans. Russia to the north was going through its "time of troubles" after the death of Ivan the Terrible. Shah Abbas was the contemporary of Ivan the Terrible, Boris Godunov, and Michael, the latter being the first in the line of the Romanovs. Consequently, Shah Abbas extended his territory at the ex-pense of both the Ottomans and the Muscovites and had little difficulty in penetrating into Transoxiana to the north and the Indus Valley in India.

One of the first things Shah Abbas did in asserting his power was to curb the power of the qizilbash feudal lords. His enmity toward them was both personal, in that they had killed his mother and brother, and political, in that they desired an oligarchy rather than a strong central government. He had them executed without mercy. He still maintained a qizilbash corps, but they were armed with the traditional antiquated weapons. To offset their prestige, he organized two armies: one made up mostly of Christian subjects from Georgia and Armenia, and the other composed of Iranians. He equipped them both with modern muskets and artillery.

The destruction of the qizilbash also weakened militant Sufism. Shah Abbas was not a fanatical Shi'i like his predecessors. While Shah Tahmasp would not allow Christians to come to his court because, as "infidels," they would defile it, Shah Abbas went out of his way to welcome foreigners and to be good to his Christian subjects. No doubt, as will be seen, he was politically motivated in his dealing with Christian nations; nevertheless, he could not have done all that he did without some liberal convictions.

To his new capital in Esfahan he brought a large number of Armenians from their home in Jolfa. Across the Zayandeh Rud (river) in Esfahan, he built the New Jolfa and settled the Armenians there. More Armenians mi-grated voluntarily to all parts of Iran. Perhaps Shah Abbas brought the Armenians with the idea of using them as hostages to keep the Armenians in Asia Minor under his control. Nevertheless, once there, the Armenians were given freedom and had a liberalizing effect on their Muslim neighbors. They could own their own houses, could ride on a horse, and could wear any kind of clothes they pleased, a privilege that non-Muslims did not have before or for long after Shah Abbas until modern times. Silk, which was one of the most important exports of Iran as a trade, became a monopoly of the shah, and Armenian merchants administered it for him. In being kind to the Christians and giving permission to Catholic missions to establish themselves in Iran, he hoped to ally himself with Europe against the Ottomans, to take advantage of the presence of so many European ships in the Persian Gulf, and to take trade away from the Ottomans. Indeed, by subtle remarks and hints, he had led some of the Christian monks from Rome to believe that he was just about ready to become a Christian. At one time, he even let it be known that any Muslim in his realm could become Christian if he so desired.

Shah Abbas, of course, was a Shi'i Muslim and continued the policy of strengthening that religion in Iran as a counteraction to the Sunnism of the Ottomans. In the course of years, the nationalism of the Iranians took on a religious flavor and Shi'ism and Iranian nationalism became one and the same.

Shah Abbas built a beautiful mausoleum over the tomb of the eighth Imam, Ali al-Rida, in Mashhad and made a vow to walk from Esfahan on a pilgrimage at the completion of the edifice. He fulfilled his vow, and pilgrimage to Mashhad became about as important as the pilgrimages to Mecca and to Karbala, the tomb of Husayn. The honorary title of "Mashhadi" was bestowed on anyone who had gone to Mashhad and became as important as *haji* for going to Mecca, and *karbalai* for going to Karbala. Safavid kings, to show their subservience to the first Imam, Ali, referred to themselves as the "dog of the threshold of Ali."

Shah Abbas did much to revive commerce and industry. He built numerous caravanserais and guest houses all along the trade routes. He was most harsh in his treatment of dishonest government officials in all parts of the country and, no doubt for this reason, was very popular among the common people. Like most sovereigns of his period, he was also a tyrant and had many executioners at his command. He had five sons. Of these, two died naturally and of the remaining three, one was executed and two blinded by his order, all on baseless charges. Like his contemporary Ivan the Terrible, when Shah Abbas died in 1629, there was no worthy successor left, for he had killed them all.

The Shi'i theocracy, like that of the *Sunni*, was championed by the Iranian ulama. Corresponding to the Shaykh ul-Islam of the Ottomans, the Safavids had the *Molla Bashi*, who was the chief of all the clergy. He, together with three or four others, was a mujtahid; that is, they had the right to give their opinions as representatives of the hidden Imam, who was the true head of the state. In this way the Shi'is, unlike the Sunnis, were not limited by the Shari'a, though this did not make them any less conservative. Shah Abbas was strong enough to limit the ulama to the field of law and preaching and did not let them interfere with his political and international affairs. When foreign ambassadors arrived, the ulama did not usually attend the reception given in the ambassadors' honor. Sometimes they did attend such meetings but usually left the banquet before wine was served or musicians had begun to entertain the guests. But the descendants of Shah Abbas gradually lost their power to the ulama. Shah Sultan Hosein was so superstitiously religious that he would not move without the advice of the ulama. This weak and indecisive Shah lost most of his empire to the Afghans. Tahmasp II was not much better, and were it not for the rise of Nader, the soldier of fortune, the whole empire would have disappeared. Even though Nader's accomplishments did not last very long, they came at an opportune time to give Iran a continued existence and bring it to the eighteenth century still with a strong government.

ADMINISTRATION

The Safavid religious, social, and administrative institutions are similar to those of the Ottomans insofar as they are Islamic and Turkish. They are different in that they are Shi'i and Iranian. Unlike the Ottomans, the Safavids did not organize an armed encampment (although they did, of course, maintain an army), and their institutions were not tied to the military. Inasmuch as a number of the institutions started by the Safavids in Iran lasted until World War I, it is important that these be explained. The Safavids, being Turks themselves, used the same names such as Shaykh ul-Islam, but not for the same positions. Perhaps for the purpose of belittling the Ottoman officers, the title of the highest personages in the Ottoman Empire were given to lower functionaries in the Safavid governmental organization. For example, among Iranians, sultan was the name given to the lowest provincial administrator and Shaykh ul-Islam was not anywhere near as important an office among the Safavids as it was among the Ottomans.

Concerning Islamic Shari'a, the Safavid shahs were free agents compared to the Ottoman sultans. With the Sunnis, the Shari'a was meticulously defined by the four orthodox schools. Deviation or innovation that went beyond the limits of the four schools was frowned upon. The Ottoman ulama gave their opinions based on the Hanafite school of religious law and the sultan was bound by those decision, which were published as fetva. Even though the Shi'is considered the Shari'a of great importance, the spokesmen of the hidden Imam, who was the true ruler of the empire, could interpret the law according to the needs of the time. There was the belief that these spokesmen, mujtahids, were inspired by the hidden Imam to make the interpretation. This procedure identified the opinion of the mujtahid with that of the Imam and made it binding.

Furthermore, among the shahs of Iran, only the early Safavids occupied a special position as "the most perfect leader" (that is, of the Sufi order). As the alleged descendants of the Prophet, and the actual leaders of the Sufi order, they exercised a certain religious power. The Safavid shahs, especially the early ones, combined in their persons not only kingship but also religious leadership. As such, they had religious as well as political power, and the more liberal among them followed an independent course. In a sense, all power belonged to the Imam, whose spokesmen were the mujtahids. In the early Safavid period, however, the shah, as "perfect leader," assumed religious power and acted as the spokesman for the Imam.

Later, when the power of the shah declined, the mujtahids assumed more and more power. Furthermore, in Iran the religious organization had complete charge, under the shah, over justice and religion; but, unlike the Ottomans, it did not have a voice in the administrative councils of government.

The shah, as the supreme leader, was the director of the administration. In order to stay in power, his task was to manipulate and keep in balance the two branches of government. One branch was the palace, or imperial household, called *dargah*; and the other was the chancery, or state administration, called *divan*. The first was run by the superintendent of crown properties and the second was directed by the grand vazir. Even though each had its own separate organization, the twenty-six officers in both branches were interdependent as well as rivals in receiving the favor of the shah. Each was jockeying for a position closer to the monarch, even though it sometimes meant walking over the fallen bodies of colleagues. Such actions sometimes resulted in promotion and sometimes in the loss of the individual's life, depending upon the mood and the plan of the shah.

The administrative affairs of the empire were under the general supervision of the grand vazir, who sat at the right hand of the shah, signed orders, and acted on behalf of the shah. He was not salaried. His income was from fiefs and gifts.

Under him the administration branched out into two sections. One had to do with the provinces. These were governed by a hierarchy of four officers. At the top was the provincial governor. Next to him was the district supervisor, who was aided by what might be called the county commissioner (khan), who in turn had under him local supervisors called sultans. All of these officers had fiefs commensurate with their rank. It was their job to collect taxes, pay the salary of soldiers in their locality, and send a specific amount of money each year to the shah. In addition to money, they also sent gifts to the shah. Each one of these officers had someone close to the shah who, in return for appropriate gifts, spoke well of him and caused him to be favored.

The second section of the administration oversaw the army, the court, and the finances of the empire. The main strength of the early Safavids came from the qizilbash tribes. These were represented in the government by two individuals. One was called the chief caliph, who headed the caliphs (spiritual leaders of the Sufi order) of the different tribes. In the eyes of the Sufis, the chief caliph was assistant to the perfect leader—i.e., the shah. The second representative of the qizilbash was the paymaster who was the lay leader of the tribes and who paid the warriors. Both of these men received salaries in addition to their fiefs.

THE ECONOMY

The major souces of wealth in Safavid Iran were land, trade, and taxes. From the time of Shah Abbas to the mid-eighteenth century, land tenure systems were generally of four kinds: (1) state lands, (2) crown lands, (3) religiously endowed lands, and (4) communal village lands.

State lands. The Safavids frequently granted state lands to high-ranking nobility or military officers in return for services. The state-owned mines, fisheries, and silkworm farms, and the collection of custom duties were given out to individuals for set periods of time to be returned to the state at its discretion or whim.

Crown lands. Crown lands, which had been seized by the Safavids in the initial conquest and domination of Iran, were the private domain of the royal family and court attendants. Shah Abbas expanded the family's private domains to undercut the growing power of the qizilbash and local nobility, either through outright confiscation or temporary seizure of the lands in return for compliance with Esfahan's wishes. By the end of the seventeenth century, it was difficult to distinguish between state and crown lands. Revenues from both tended to be confused as the Safavid court and high-ranking notables increasingly exacted more and more taxes from the local nobility, merchants, and pastoral lords. Sometimes the tax increases were passed onto the peasantry, artisans, and pastoral herders.

Religiously endowed lands. Religiously endowed lands were insignificant in the sixteenth century. With the emergence of a more politically active clergy, however, endowed lands grew in size. The local notables, merchants, and middle-level Safavid administrators passed on more and more of their own land to religious leaders for "pious purposes," sometimes retaining partial control of the gift for the benefit of a local mosque or religious school. With the increase in endowed lands came an increase in religious leaders' political leverage in local and imperial matters. Furthermore, such land holding gave religious leaders an enormous amount of autonomy in local affairs, thereby increasing their political involvement in the eighteenth-century economy and society.

Communal village lands. Communally held village lands and the rights to fertile range lands were as diverse as the country itself. The villagers of northern and northwestern Iran, because of favorable climatic conditions, were in a better economic situation than their counterparts in central and southern Iran. On the whole, however, the Safavid Empire fostered the rise of local aristocracies and strengthened older families. In economic terms, such assistance was frequently translated into private, inheritable property, which in turn, signalled the emergence of landlords. Lords of the Caucasus and Ottoman notables coveted and frequently fought over the northern and northwestern regions of Iran—as much for their fertile lands and usable products as for their commercial and military importance. The constantly expanding and changing trade routes between the Ottoman, Safavid, and Russian empires made the northern and northwestern Iranian lands and towns highly desirable and therefore frequent centers of conflict.

Trade, as has been mentioned, was another source of wealth during the Safavid period. The pre-Safavid trade routes, major market towns, and merchant-trader "associations" remained the basis of overland commerce under Safavid rule. Shah Abbas, more than any other Safavid ruler, placed special emphasis on the commercial sector of the empire's economy. Esfahan became a major trading center for Iran, as well as the principal administrative city of the empire. Following his conquest of the southern Caucasus at the beginning of the seventeenth century, Shah Abbas returned to Esfahan with Armenian merchants and traders from Jolfa; he then set them up in "New Jolfa," across the river from Esfahan, as merchants and craftsmen protected by royal patronage. The Armenian craftsmen greatly expanded the gold and silver craft industries, while the Armenian merchants were given the monopoly over the production and export of silk.

At the same time, Shah Abbas sought ways of expanding foreign and domestic trade. Following the reconquest of the port of Hormoz in 1622, Shah Abbas established a larger and more strategically located port on the Persian Gulf–Kerman trade routes. Naming the port Bandar Abbas, he concluded a series of unilateral grants to the English and Dutch East India companies to lease land and to trade in Bandar Abbas. Later the French joined the English and the Dutch in establishing trading houses in the ports of Bandar Abbas and Bushehr and in the hinterland trading centers of Shiraz, Kerman, Yazd, and Esfahan. As long as the grants to lease and trade were forthcoming, the European joint-stock companies maintained a steady flow of textiles, foodstuffs, and medical products into Safavid Iran in exchange for Iranian carpets, shawls, brocades, and processed and semiprocessed silk, cotton, and wool.

While catering to Dutch, English, and French interests in southern Iran and the Persian Gulf, the Safavid rulers initiated a variety of contacts with the English Levant and Muscovy companies to trade in northern and northwestern Iran. In time, the opening up of the Safavid economy to the European trading companies created greater problems than the rulers had anticipated. Already by the beginning of the eighteenth century, such trade had whetted the appetites of European political as well as commercial interests. In part, the Treaty of Turkmanchai, which initiated the nineteenth-century pattern of "enforced treaties" and the legalization of extraterritoriality to European merchants and individuals, was a continuation of the previous centuries' practices as Safavid control disintegrated and as European intervention escalated.

Finally the elaborate tax system established by the Safavids in addition to the existing systems became, during the seventeenth and eighteenth centuries, increasingly harsh and arbitrary. Local notables and pastoral lords in the northern and southern regions of Iran created their own tax systems in order to extract greater surpluses from the peasantry and artisans of the smaller towns and villages. It was not surprising, therefore, that frequent protests against local notables turned into widespread uprisings against the Safavid tax system by the mid-eighteenth century. Small traders and military officers joined pastoral lords and imperial notables in seizing lands, capturing major trading towns, and confiscating local tax revenues for themselves.

Rulers such as Karim Khan Zand stemmed the wars to a considerable extent and offset the fears of the Iranian and European merchants with renewed privileges and protective measures. Karim Khan Zand, in particular, sought various ways of enticing Iranian, Arab, and Indian merchants and artisans to return to post-Safavid Iran. Furthermore, he established Bushehr as a a major Iranian port by means of a bilaterial commercial agreement with the British East India Company in 1763. Such measures led him, in time, to renew the Safavid conquest of the major Persian Gulf port towns between 1765 and 1779. While successful in rejuvenating the Iranian economy and restoring the Safavid basis of wealth, Karim Khan's death in 1779 reactivated the old internal wars, which lasted until the establishment of the Tehran-centered empire of the Qajar princes at the turn of the nineteenth century.

Chapter Thirteen
Society and Culture under the Safavids

The conquest of Iran by the Safavids at the beginning of the sixteenth century proved to be a mixed blessing for the country. On the one hand, the Safavids unified Iran for the first time since the Arab conquest and expanded its boundaries to about what they were under the Sasanids. It is quite likely that the Safavids saved Iran from being incorporated into the Ottoman Empire. On the other hand, in that they made Shi'ism the state religion and imposed it on the population, they prevented the free exchange of ideas and stifled innovation in many fields of endeavor.

As we have seen, Iran's cultural golden age began in the ninth century, when the Abbasid caliphs did not have the power to impose orthodoxy, and the petty principalities lacked the power and, in some cases, the incentive to do so. Consequently, the resulting intellectual freedom advanced Iranian culture in all fields for some 800 years; this advance was unabated, save for about forty years following the Mongol invasion. Indeed, the Shi'is, being a minority group, were often at the forefront of this advance. As soon as Shi'i heterodoxy was made the state religion, however, it became more interested in advancing the new orthodoxy than in learning. Consequently, Iran experienced a barren period in many fields of knowledge and art. This decline actually started with the rise of the Safavids in 1500, but the momentum of the previous advance lasted long enough to give Shah Abbas, who had liberal tendencies, an opportunity to use it to good advantage. After him the decline became more precipitous under the weight of the Shi'i status quo orthodoxy.

SHI'I THEOLOGY

Shi'ism has influenced the life and culture of Iran to such an extent that Shi'i leaders were able to take over the entire government without the aid of a shah in 1979. It is essential, therefore, to take a closer look at some of its main doctrines. While we cannot discuss all the salient points of Shi'i theology, we shall mention three that have great political and social significance.

The Doctrine of the Imamate. The Doctrine of the Imamate is at the center of all Shi'i political theory. The reader will recall that Ali was the first Imam, and after him his direct male descendants for twelve generations. The twelfth Imam, by the name of Muhammad, who bore the title of *Mehdi* ("deliverer" or "messiah"), disappeared. He is in a state of occultation until his reappearance, when he will conquer the world and establish true Islamic rule. Even though the twelve Imams, with the exception of Ali, never presided over the affairs of state, nonetheless, they were the true rulers. It was quite natural, therefore, for them to consider all the caliphs of the Umayyad and Abbasid dynasties, and after them the Ottoman sultans and kings of the petty principalities that arose all over the Muslim world, as usurpers. Consequently, the twelfth Imam, even though absent, is the "Leader of the Age" and the only true ruler in the world. Hence there is a built-in distrust of government in Shi'i thought; *all* governments are illegitimate unless they rule according to the will and dictates of the Hidden Imam. But how is one to know the will of the Hidden Imam?

The Doctrine of Ijtihad. The answer to this question brings us to the second point in Shi'i theology—namely, the Doctrine of Ijtihad, or the right to interpret the Koran and the Tradition. The Twelvers, who follow the Hidden Imam, believe that they can know the will of the Imam through mujtahids, or those who have the right of interpretation. Even though a mujtahid is the spokesman of the Imam, he is not the Imam and therefore not infallible. No one appoints or elects a mujtahid. He is sometimes declared to be one by a recognized mujtahid, but more often he "evolves" and is accepted as one because of his maturity, intelligence, faith, justice, and experience. Sometimes, however, mujtahids do not agree with one another. A liberal mujtahid might give a different opinion on a given subject than a conservative one. These different and sometimes opposing interpretations, however, have not diminished the validity of Ijtihad in the minds of the Shi'is any more than the different and sometimes opposing interpretations of the Bible have diminished the validity of the guidance of the Holy Spirit among Protestant Christians.

The Doctrine of Taqlid.   There is a corollary doctrine that gives the Doctrine of Ijtihad practical importance, and that is the Doctrine of *Taqlid,* or imitation. According to Shi'i theology, all believers are divided into two groups: a small number whose job is to interpret and be "sources of imitation"—i.e., mujtahids; and a majority whose duty is to imitate. It must be emphasized, however, that the believer is not asked to accept the mujtahid's opinion in matters of faith without proof. In matters of practice and implementation of the faith, however, he must either be a mujtahid himself or imitate one. In the course of time this distinction has often been overlooked, and many mujtahids have demanded and received blind obedience from imitators.

It is incumbent upon each believer to choose for himself a "source of imitation." Some mujtahids lead hundreds, some thousands, and some millions. Since it is forbidden for anyone to follow a dead mujtahid, there is a continuous, living, and close relationship between the individual and his source of imitation. Because the mujtahid is a landmark or sign for the believer in matters of practice, he is also known as *ayatollah,* which means "sign of God." It is hard to exaggerate the power of ayatollahs for good or evil, for freedom or suppression, and for modernization or reaction.

Under these circumstances there has existed in the history of Iran from the advent of the Safavids until today, a constant tension and a struggle for power between the shah on the one hand and the mujtahids on the other. In this struggle the shah had the power of the sword and the mujtahids the devotion of the believers. Since mujtahids are not elected, some shahs built up the reputation of friendly clergymen by openly asking their opinion and thus "elevated" them to the position of mujtahid. Since there were always a few mujtahids around, some shahs were clever enough to set one against the other and get by with a great deal of innovation and deviation, both of which are anathema in Shi'i and Sunni Islam alike.

The history of Iran cannot be understood without an awareness of this tension. For nearly five centuries power has swung back and forth; sometimes more or less evenly, as during the early Safavids and late Qajars; sometimes on the side of the clergy as during the late Safavids and early Qajars; and sometimes on the side of the shah as during Nader Shah's reign and the Pahlavi period. During all this time the mujtahids were satisfied if they were the dominant power in the court of a subservient or even friendly shah. But, as we shall see, in 1979 the clergy, under the leadership of Ayatollah Khomayni, broke away from the "norm," ousted the shah, and grasped complete political power on behalf of the clergy.

SOCIETY

In many ways Iranian society under the Safavids contained the same differences and similarities found under the Ottomans. The great majority of people under the Safavids were either villagers or pastoralists, with a small portion living and working in the ports and hinterland towns of the Iranian plateau and mountains.

Pastoralists herded their sheep, goats, camels, and horses from one fertile rangeland to another, alternating their settlements of tents and herds according to the seasons. Tightly organized into clans, the pastoralists depended on their own resources for nearly all their goods and food, planting crops and harvesting tree and bush crops in their lowland settlements and highland encampments. Constantly hunting for better lands and deeper wells, pastoralists occasionally came into conflict with villagers, raiding their herds and robbing them of gold and salt. As long as the Safavid rulers maintained close ties with the pastoralists by employing them as irregular cavalry and armed militia, villagers and townspeople suffered only an occasional raid from the migrating herdsmen. As soon as the pastoralists severed their ties with the Safavids, however, both villagers and townspeople were at the mercy of the land- and water-hungry herders.

The majority of rural people were, however, villagers. Their major occupation was the cultivation of crops. In northern and northwestern Iran, the villages were densely settled and in close proximity to each other. In central, eastern, and southern Iran, the villages were sparsely settled and separated by great distances; they produced minimal harvests and maintained elaborate subterranean canal systems for irrigation.

Many peasants owned no land and worked for other peasants or for landlords in return for a share of the crop or settlement of debts. A smaller number of peasants held communal rights to the use of the land on the basis of their kinship ties with villages. A third group of peasants fulfilled other functions within the village, such as acting as representatives of landlords, or earning their living as craftsmen, traders, or herders.

In times of trouble, which were frequent, villagers of the coastal plains and in the mountains and plateau had several courses of action open to them. They either fled to the nearest mountain cave, impenetrable valley, or nearest island, or rose up in arms and defended themselves as best they could against intruders.

Some who lived in larger towns belonged to notable families who owned large tracts of land or held high political office. A greater number of families served the administrative and commercial interests of the empire or produced more menial goods and services. The Shi'i clergy were similarly divided into high-, middle-, and low-ranking families, reflecting the social structure of the Safavid towns.

LIFE IN THE CAPITAL AND LARGER TOWNS

The court of the shah had a bevy of officers, from chief of protocol, private secretary, physician, and astrologer, to gatekeeper, valet, stable chief, and a host of others too numerous to be named. The chief chamberlain was in charge of the shah's harem. The Safavid harems, like those of the Ottomans, were guarded by eunuchs, usually black. Iranian women seemed to have had more freedom than their sisters in the Ottoman Empire. The Safavids took their wives with them to wars; some of the women were good marksmen and actually participated in battle. In cases of defeat and general or hasty retreat, the eunuchs had orders to behead all the women. Sometimes there was "women's day" at the bazaars. No men except storekeepers would be allowed. On such days harem women mingled with town women. After Shah Abbas completed the boulevard in Esfahan, he inaugurated a women's evening. There the ladies promenaded up and down the tree-lined streets. The women were also given a special place from whence they could enjoy the frequent fireworks and lamp-lighing ceremonies, which were favorite pastimes of the shahs.

Most men spent their leisure hours in coffeehouses. Whereas the Ottoman sultan Murad IV, a contemporary of Shah Abbas, had ordered all coffeehouses closed, Shah Abbas encouraged them in Iran. He used to frequent them himself and on several occasions took foreign visitors to them. These coffeehouses were centers for the dissemination of news. To these also came travelers who recounted their experiences, and dervishes who for a price regaled their audiences with stories of the heroes of Iran from the *Shahnameh*. The Safavids encouraged the observation of many of the pre-Islamic Iranian festivities such as those held at the equinoxes and the solstices. The spring equinox, bringing the new year, was and still is the most important festival in Iran. There was also the rose festival, the water festival, and others that gave the common man an opportunity to escape from the drudgery of his routine life.

Other pastimes engaged in by the populace were cock, wolf, and bull fights; card games; acrobatics; tightrope walking; puppet shows; and, for the aristocracy only, polo. Formal physical exercise was a common practice in Iran before the Safavid period and has continued into modern times. A brotherhood was formed of those people who spent their leisure in physical exercise, and these brotherhoods have existed to the present. Their center was called "the house of strength," and they had a hierarchy with special codes of honor. They exercised to the beat of the drum. Usually the drummer was a man with a good voice who sang the story of the adventures of Iranian heroes from the *Shahnameh*.

Islam, especially Shi'i Islam, did not bring many festive days into the life of its adherents. With the exception of the anniversary of Mohammad's receiving the call and festival of sacrifice (enjoined by the Koran and celebrated throughout the Muslim world), the rest were occasions for mourning. There were mourning services for the death of Ali and Hasan, and the all-important tragic event in Karbala where Husayn lost his life. In their zeal for Shi'ism, the Safavids encouraged the observance of these events, and the common people crowded to the mosques to hear and weep at the recounting of the stories by the mollas and to participate in the numerous processions.

The event at Karbala on the tenth of Muharram (the first month in the Muslim lunar calendar) was the most important. Everywhere in the country there were processions. City districts vied with each other in the excellence of their processions. In these processions, they paraded corpses draped in blood-stained shrouds, and a headless body of Husayn. The Umayyad caliph, Yazid, whose troops ambushed and killed Husayn, was always impersonated in these parades; and this gave the onlookers opportunity to curse the Sunnis. Hundreds of individuals were involved in each procession. Some beat their breasts. Others beat their bare backs with a cluster of chains. On the tenth, when religious feelings had reached a climax, a new group joined the procession. These individuals wore white shrouds; and each held a short sword in his right hand, while with his left hand he held his companion's belt. They marched sideways inflicting wounds on their heads.

In the late Safavid period, "passion plays" came into vogue. Traveling troupes of actors with complete wardrobes and makeup performed in village and town squares, depicting different episodes, real and embellished, of the scene at Karbala.

Given the many differences between the pastoralists, villagers, and townspeople, it speaks well of both the Ottoman and Safavid empires that their administration and commerce functioned exceedingly well for over 200 years. But internal differences were rarely curbed, and by the end of the eighteenth century, conflicts were breaking out in towns and between pastoralists and villagers with increasing frequency. As with Ottoman society, so too with Safavid society, imperial disintegration accelerated by the beginning of the nineteenth century; the decline was due as much to the actions of independent-minded local nobility, merchants, and administrators as to intrusions by Europeans.

LITERATURE AND ART

From the literary and intellectual point of view, this was a relatively sterile period. Shi'ism was considered a heterodoxy during the Abbasid caliphate and as such, attracted all types of freethinkers. Unhindered intellectual inquiry was usually found among the Shi'is. During the Safavids, however, Shi'ism became the state religion and was transformed into a most rigid and fanatical orthodoxy. It is indicative of the sterility of the intellectual life that since 1500 Iran has produced only two philosophers of any note: Molla Sadra of Shiraz (d. 1641) and Haji Molla Hadi of Sabzavar.

Literature under the Safavids suffered unle it was religious. From 1519 to 1670 many important Iranian poets mig, .d to India because of the liberal patronage of the Moghul court, whose language was Persian. Iranian poets went to India because, to put it in their own words, "There exist not in Iran the means of acquiring perfection." Some experts have called this period the "Indian summer" of Persian poetry.

Many poets devoted themselves to religious poetry that described the virtues and suffering of the Imams. The Safavids encouraged it. As a result there is a wealth of collections with descriptive names such as "Garden of Martyrdom," "Deluge of Weeping," and "Mysteries of Martyrdom" from which professional reciters and writers of passion plays drew.

The Safavids endowed theological schools, and there are many religious treatises from this period. The most popular theologian was Molla Mohammad Baqer Majlesi (d. 1700), who made a huge compilation of Shi'i traditions on all sorts of subjects, including moral conduct, sexual behavior, and personal hygiene—all based on the counsels of the Imams. After decades of obscurity, Majlesi has come into his own in the present Islamic Republic of Iran.

Among the customs continued by the Safavids was that of bestowing titles such as the "pillar of the realm," "steward of the kingdom," and a host of others. Sometimes these titles were hereditary, and sometimes they were taken away from one individual and bestowed on another. Since most title holders were also important leaders of the state, the historian is always at a loss to distinguish father from son or grandson or from half a dozen others who have been given the same title.

The Safavids had their own historians. One of the most important sources for the reign of Shah Abbas is the *History of Abbas*. Such books, however, like their Ottoman counterparts, are daily chronicles of the activities of the shah and are always flattering to the shah and his policies. Fortunately, some of the many European visitors to Iran wrote about their experiences and have described the life of the people among whom they lived. It is through their reports that it is possible to penetrate the façade built by the official historians.

Shah Abbas had a great passion for building. He provided Esfahan with beautiful mosques, palaces, bridges, and parks. The majestic shrine of Imam Reza in Mashhad is the result of his endeavor. There is hardly a place in Iran where we cannot find a caravansarai, perhaps in ruins, built by Shah Abbas.

Chapter Fourteen
Two Centuries of Relations with Europe

The Mongol invasion and the subsequent fall of Baghdad brought Iran into contact with Europeans of all types: priests, merchants, diplomats, and adventurers. The Crusaders became conscious of the differences existing between Iran and the rest of the Muslims to the west, and they tried to cultivate the rulers of Iran against Syria. The Ilkhans and the Timurids were approached by the Europeans seeking an alliance against the Ottomans. The relations became mutually profitable and were intensified by Shah Abbas the Great.

This is not to say that there were no trade or diplomatic relations between the European countries and the Ottomans. Many countries of Europe had vied with each other to trade with the Ottomans. This attitude, however, changed when the Turks became more belligerent and threatened the independence of western European countries. In peacetime there were diplomatic relations and exchanges of embassies. Venice continued trade relations with the Ottomans the longest, in spite of frequent wars. These relations, however, either were broken by war or were always in danger of being broken. Usually the ambassadors from the countries against whom the sultan had commenced hostilities were thrown into prison. Furthermore, the Ottomans were always conscious that they were commissioned by Allah for the propagation and expansion of Islam. Consequently, whatever relations existed were precarious and were not on mutual terms.

In the case of Iran, however, the situation was quite different. The

Safavids, even in their most fanatical mood, never had the idea that they were commissioned by Allah to convert the infidels. On the contrary, if they felt commissioned at all, it was for the conversion or the destruction of Sunnis. It did not make any difference to them who destroyed the "heretical" Ottoman power, they or the "infidel" Christians. Since the aim of the Europeans was also the destruction of Ottoman power, the Iranians and the Europeans approached each other on a basis of equality. The Europeans needed Iran, or at least thought they did, to counteract the pressure of the Ottomans. The Iranians needed Europe to engage the Ottomans in war and, more important, to monopolize the commerce of the Middle East.

The spectacular victories of the pagan Mongols over Islam encouraged Europeans to seek a rapprochement with them both to counteract the aggressive nature of Islam and also to attempt to convert the Mongols to Christianity. As was mentioned in Chapter 9, Pope Innocent IV sent two embassies to the Mongols. Louis IX (1226–1270), king of France, was friendly to the Mongols and also sent them an embassy.

After the fall of the Abbasids, Europeans felt welcome in Iran and they came in great numbers for religious and commercial purposes. One of the most famous of these was Marco Polo (1254–1324), the record of whose adventures did much to encourage more Europeans to make the journey eastward. In the formative years of the Ottoman Empire, the Europeans were wary of this new antagonist and preferred to do business with Iran. During the reign of Ghazan Khan (1295–1304), Iran, rather than the blockaded Constantinople, was the center of commerical exchange between Asia and Europe, and Tabriz was an important center of business.

The Spanish rulers of Castile, sent an embassy to the court of Timur. It arrived when Timur was leading a campaign against Bayezid in Ankara. The Spanish embassy witnessed the battle and later went with the victorious Amir to Samarqand. The accounts of the experiences of this and other embassies are excellent sources for studying the life and culture of the Middle East of that period.

The Safavid policy toward the Ottomans was based on animosity. They separated Iran from the rest of the Muslim world and courted the friendship of Europe. Shah Abbas was especially helpful to the Christian Armenians whom he had brought to Esfahan. He built churches for them and gave them commercial privileges and religious freedom. They were exempt from paying import and export duties. Portuguese, Spanish, Dutch, English, Russian, French, and Indian merchants did business in Iran. Even the Ottoman merchants found it more profitable to carry on commercial activities in Iran during peace periods.

PORTUGAL AND SPAIN

Economically, it was an opportune time for the Iranians because trade routes were beginning to shift from the Mediterranean. Europeans were seeking other routes. Henry the Navigator of Portugal was using the Cape route to capture the trade of East Africa from the Mulsims and establish trade with India. It was not long before the Portuguese were bringing spices from India and had established themselves in the Persian Gulf.

In 1507, during the reign of Shah Esma'il, the Portuguese fleet under Admiral Albuquerque landed at Hormoz on the Persian Gulf. They set up trading posts in Hormoz, Bahrain, and Muscat. By the middle of the sixteenth century, Hormoz was one of the most famous marts of the world. Milton has recorded its glory in *Paradise Lost*. The Mamluks of Egypt and the merchants of Venice who had profited by the overland trade to the Mediterranean were indignant at being passed by and threatened to stop it.

Even though the threat bore no results, one must not conclude that the overland trade was inactive. Throughout most of the sixteenth century, Aleppo still remained an important business center as the main caravan depot for silk, spices, dyes, and drugs from the East. This, however, did not last. By the end of the sixteenth century and throughout the seventeenth century, the main trade route was by water, and the eastern Mediterranean experienced an economic decline.

Shah Esma'il also opposed the Portuguese capture of Hormoz but after a year of negotiation signed a treaty with Albuquerque in 1508. In return for Iran's recognition of the Portuguese establishment in the Persian Gulf, the Portuguese offered to help Iran in the occupation of Bahrain, and in subduing piracy on the shores of Baluchestan and Mokran. They also agreed to help each other against the Ottomans.

Even after Portugal was eclipsed by Spain, the trade installations and factories on the Persian Gulf continued. Philip II of Spain (reigned 1556–1598) sent an embassy to Iran with three requests: (1) that Iran give religious freedom to Catholics; (2) that Iran give special privileges to Spaniards; and (3) that Iran not make peace with the Ottomans. Apparently, all of these were in accord with Safavid policy. An Iranian ambassador was sent back to Spain; but, unfortunately, the ship, *Bon Voyage*, was lost on the way.

In 1598 two Portuguese monks arrived in Esfahan and were received by Shah Abbas. These monks were allotted land for building a church and parish house, and continued religious work for many years. Spain was especially anxious to incite Iran against the Ottomans, and Shah Abbas wanted Spain to harass the Ottomans from the sea. He also asked Philip to send a consul to mediate differences among the Christians. He also was willing to export all of Iran's silk by way of Hormoz under certain conditions.

THE SHERLEY BROTHERS

There came to Iran at the time of Shah Abbas two young Englishmen, Anthony Sherley and his eighteen-year-old brother, Robert. They were adventurers with military training and knowledge who were not connected with any business enterprise. Shah Abbas was attracted to them as persons and, no doubt, saw in them means of improving his army and getting closer to the Europeans. They were employed by the shah as military advisors, and both took part in battles against the Ottomans. Robert Sherley married an Iranian Christian woman and spent all his life in Iran.

In 1599, Shah Abbas sent a large embassy to Europe. The Iranian ambassador, Hosein Ali Bayat, accompanied by Anthony Sherley, had letters to the rulers of Russia, Poland, Germany, France, Spain, and England, and also to the pope. In the letters the shah introduced Anthony as a "dear brother" who had come to Iran voluntarily and with whom "we ate food from the same plate and drank wine from the same cup." The whole party included one *molla* (Shi'i clergyman), two or three Catholic monks, five interpreters, fourteen servants, four guards, and thirty-two camel loads of gifts.

It took them a month to travel the 500 miles to the Caspian Sea and another two months to cross the sea. In Russia they were guests of Boris Godunov and, after six months of unpleasant experiences, went to Europe via Archangle. In the fall of 1600 they reached Prague and were received by King Rudolph II. Venice did not receive them because they had made peace with the Ottomans and were entertaining a delegation from Istanbul. In Rome, Sherley and Bayat quarreled and were received by Pope Clement VIII separately.

Bayat and Sherley separated there. Sherley went to Spain and from there to England, and never returned to Iran. Bayat went to Spain and planned to return to Iran by ship. Prior to leaving Spain, however, a fanatical Christian stabbed the Muslim molla to death. Worse than this, in the minds of the Iranians, three members of the embassy became Christians. One was Ali Qoli, the nephew of the ambassador, who was baptized with King Philip as a godfather, and given the name of Don Philip. The second was the chief secretary of the embassy, Uruj Bey, who was baptized with the queen as his godmother, and became known as Don Juan of Persia. The third was Bonyad Bey, who was baptized as Don Diego. What happened to the ambassador and the rest of his party is not certain. Very likely, being sure that he would be put to death for such a miserable record, he prudently decided not to return to the shah. An Iranian historian, however, relates that in 1613 an Iranian envoy returned from Europe, together with a Spanish ambassador, and the envoy was summarily put to death. Later Shah Abbas explained his action to the Spaniards by saying that the Iranian ambassador had "behaved so ill towards the attendants who accompanied him, and vexed them so much, that several of them adopted the Christian faith and remained in Europe in order to escape from his [the executed ambassador's] tyranny. . . ."

Having had no results from the first embassy, Shah Abbas sent Anthony's brother, Robert Sherley, in 1608. The main objective was England. The British, who had formed the British East India Company in 1600, were set to expand their trade and responded favorably to Shah Abbas. In 1616 English ships arrived at the Persian Gulf, and the company established headquarters in Esfahan. By 1622, an Anglo-Iranian force expelled the Portuguese-Spanish traders from Hormoz and Bahrain and later from Muscat and Basra as well. The English also tried to enter the Levant trade but, rather than compete with the French who had the upper hand there, they established a branch in Baghdad. In Iran, Hormoz was replaced by Bandar Abbas, a new port built by Shah Abbas; the English did most of their business there and maintained branches in Esfahan, Shiraz, Kerman, Basra, and Baghdad.

THE DUTCH

In the meantime, the Dutch had appeared on the scene in 1581 and by 1602 had federated their various enterprises into one, the United East India Company. In 1623, the Dutch also opened a trading house in Bandar Abbas. Their arrangement with the shah was to barter Dutch merchandise for Iranian rugs, wool, silk, and brocade. This affected the English trade unfavorably, causing a great deal of rivalry between English and Dutch merchants. By the time of the death of Shah Abbas in 1629, there were a number of foreign stores in the bazaars of Esfahan and Shiraz. In the reign of Shah Safi (1629–1642), Dutch business was flourishing and the Dutch had practical control of the Iranian trade. By the time Shah Abbas II ascended the throne, the Dutch had a virtual monopoly of trade in Iran. They were exempt from paying import duties but instead had to buy 600 loads of silk annually. In addition to silk, they exported Persian rugs, fruit, and wine. The Iranian merchants, however, did not like to deal with the Dutch. The complaint was that the Dutch dickered and the Iranians, past masters of the art themselves, did not want to deal with wary and knowledgeable competitors!

THE END RESULTS

Most European countries had good reason to be on unfriendly terms with the Ottomans. But because of the long distance, the difficulties of communication, and the fact that some European countries wanted to maintain diplomatic and commercial ties with the Ottomans, the grandiose plan of Iranians and Europeans combining their forces against the Ottomans never materialized.

During the Safavid period, a large number of Europeans worked in Iran and received high wages. Shah Abbas, consistent with his policy of attracting Europeans, was lavish in his entertainment of foreign ambassadors. More often than not, he himself went out of the city to welcome them. The visitors were received by an honor guard with full dress uniforms and military bands. Slaves were also around with wine and ice water for the guests. To impress the Europeans with his tolerance of non-Muslims, Shah Abbas invited the leaders of the Christian, Jewish, and Zoroastrian communities to the receptions. Most unusual of all, twenty-five women were trained to entertain the foreign guests. These ladies, contrary to custom, were all unveiled. Shah Abbas went so much out of his way to be friendly to the monks that they thought he was ready to become a Christian, and the shah did nothing to discourage them. One year, when Christmas fell in the fasting month of Ramadan, the shah, as was his custom, went to the Armenian quarter of Esfahan for a reception. There he drank wine and then whispered in the ear of the Spanish ambassador, who is the narrator in this case: "When you see the pope in Rome, tell him how in the month of Ramadan in the presence of the qadi and the mufti and the heads of government I served wine. Tell him that even though I am not a Christian, I am worthy of praise."

In addition to social amenities, the Europeans enjoyed special trade privileges. All the provincial governors and administrators had strict orders to facilitate travel arrangements for European businessmen. Europeans were also given the courtesy of being subject to their own laws while in Iran. The Safavids were not alone in giving such extraterritorial privileges to Europeans. The Ottomans also extended them to the French. These privileges, given by Sultan Suleiman the Magnificent, recognized the jurisdiction of the French consul over all Frenchmen. It must be noted that such privileges were given as a courtesy and on the basis of equality. In their minds it was the extension of the millet sytem to the "people of the Book." Later it was used as a means of European imperialism over all the Middle East. This practice, later called "capitulations," continued until the second decade of the twentieth century.

Beginning with the last decade of the seventeenth century, trade in the Persian Gulf began to slacken. For one thing, European traders had found greener pastures and better profits farther east in Asia. Furthermore, the political situation in Iran was worsening and the weak Safavid shahs could not maintain peace and security. The Afghan invasion of Iran in 1722 curtailed the Dutch and English trade in that country. The war with England and France had also weakened the Dutch. Nader Shah was not pleased with the English because they had not helped him in his Ottoman campaign, while the Dutch had. After he became shah, however, he changed his attitude and renewed the past agreements with the British without signing new ones. Karim Khan Zand had difficulty with the English in 1769 over the control of ports and customs on imported goods. As a result, Bushehr on the Persian Gulf was closed and Basra became the port. By the middle of the eighteenth century, any semblance of equality between the Europeans on the one hand, and the Iranians or the Ottomans on the other, had come to an end. In 1780 the English helped Suleiman Pasha to secure his pashalik in Basra and in 1789 helped to determine the fate of Bushehr in the same way. The era of European imperialism had begun.

It is significant to note that two centuries of contact with Europe had not created much intellectual reaction either in Iran or in the Ottoman Empire. Both Turks and Iranians copied from the West the technique of making cannon and mortars, but that seems to be about all. As early as 1481, in the reign of Bayezid II, the Jewish refugees from Spain wanted to set up a printing press but were refused permission. The Shaykh ul-Islam ruled against it for fear that the Koran might be printed. Later, in 1493, however, the Jews were allowed to have one, provided they printed in Hebrew only. In the middle of the sixteenth century, the Armenians were permitted to have a printing press under the same conditions as the Jews, and in 1627 the same type of permission was granted the Greeks. It was not until 1721 that the sultan allowed anything to be printed in Turkish. All other things from Europe were forbidden, including clocks, as they were deemed to interfere with the work of the muezzin, the individual who called the faithful to prayers.

Even though the Iranians were more liberal in such matters than the Ottomans, there was not much to show for it. Shah Abbas imported a printing press, but there is no evidence that he used it at all. Shah Safi, in addition to having European gunmakers, had a watchmaker, a goldsmith, a diamond cutter, and a painter. Shah Abbas II brought two painters from Holland, and some portraits of the monarchs are still in existence.

Intellectually, both Turkey and Iran remained impervious to the West. Islam, as a religion of successive dispensations, believed itself to be the last and, therefore, the most complete. Consequently, the Muslims, be they Shi'i or Sunni did not think that they could learn anything from a religion such as Christianity, which was believed to be less complete than Islam. In the Ottoman Empire the Shaykh ul-Islam and most of the ulama never had any intellectual relationship with Europeans and did not allow any. In Iran the Shi'i religion had been mingled with Iranian patriotism and had formed such a fanatical and dogmatic shell that not much could penetrate it. Furthermore, the European intellectuals who had come to the Middle East were mostly monks. These individuals, on the whole, had a medieval mentality and were both unaffected by and opposed to the Reformation that was going on in Europe. They, like their Muslim colleagues, had closed minds and did not have much to offer to medieval Islam. Hence, neither side felt inclined to approach the other. The subsequent interaction between Middle East and Europe went over the heads of most of the leaders of Islam and did not begin to have an effect until the second half of the nineteenth century.

NADER SHAH AND KARIM KHAN ZAND

As was mentioned, the Afghan invasion was the straw that broke the back of a weakened Safavid dynasty. The country, however, was saved by the rise of Nader Shah (1736–1747). He was a Turk related to the Afshar tribe, which was one of the Turkish tribes loyal to the Safavids. He was born in 1688 and was an officer in the Safavid army. The weakness of the Safavids caused the Ottomans to encourage the Sunni Afghans to attack Iran. Their success whetted the appetites of both the Russians under Peter the Great and the Ottomans under Ahmed III. The Russians halted their plans because of the death of Peter in 1725, but the Ottomans continued the hostilities, and it was Sultan Mahmud I who defeated Shah Tahmasp II in 1731. In the peace treaty of 1732, Iran gave up five cities in the Caucasus.

Nader did not like what was going on, so he led a revolt against the shah and chose the latter's infant son, Abbas III, as shah with himself as regent. He then tore up the treaty and fought against the Ottomans. The infant shah died in 1736; and Nader, instead of assuming power himself, gathered together the leaders of the tribes and representatives of the population from all walks of life and caused them to request him to become shah. He was crowned on March 21, 1736.

Nader Shah was neither a Shi'i nor a Sunni, but a freethinker. His main purpose was to break the power of the Shi'i ulama and to protect himself, at least temporarily, from the Ottomans while he was busy in the east. In 1738, he led a campaign against the Moghul Empire of India. He took Ghazneh, Kabul, and Lahore. On March 20, 1739, he defeated Mohammad Shah of India and entered Delhi. In this campaign, in addition to gaining two fabulous thrones, one of them the famous peacock throne, he brought with him so many other riches that it was possible for him to exempt Iranians from paying taxes for three years. He led successful campaigns against the Russians and the Ottomans, but these did not last long, for his character had also changed and he became suspicious and ruthless. He blinded his own son. He was assassinated on June 20, 1747.

Ironically enough, the cause of his assassination was not his change of character but his religion. Nader Shah was a freethinker and wanted to unite all religions. He ordered that the Old and New Testaments be translated into Persian. He also had the Koran translated into Persian. He gathered the representatives of all religions in Iran and told them that if there was only one God, there should be only one religion. He was interested in uniting Islam. To achieve this goal he made a five-point proposition to the Ottoman sultan, Mahmud I:

1. That Shi'i doctrine be recognized officially as the fifth school of thought in Islam;[1]
2. That the Shi'is should have special accommodations in Mecca;
3. That every year there should be a special leader of pilgrimage, *Amir al-Haj*, from Iran;
4. That Ottomans and Iranians should exchange prisoners of war;
5. That Ottomans and Iranians should exchange ambassadors.

The Shi'i leaders in Najaf were greatly perturbed over this news. They opposed these measures and led a revolt against Nader Shah that culminated in his assassination. The failure of Nader Shah shows how deeply committed to Shi'ism the Iranians had become.

The death of Nader Shah was the signal for more confusion and warfare. For a brief period it seemed that an Iranian dynasty in Shiraz under Karim Khan Zand might save the situation, but his untimely death gave the opportunity to the Turkish Qajar tribe from the north to take control under Agha Mohammad in 1779. The history of Iran during the Qajar rule belongs to the period of European imperialism in the Middle East and will be treated later.

---

[1]See p. 86.

Chapter Fifteen
Imperialism
and the Ottomans

At the beginning of the eighteenth century the world of Islam lay sprawled from Central Europe and Morocco to Central Asia and the Bay of Bengal. Its destiny over 300 years had been in the hands of men of Turkish origin— namely, the Ottomans in the west, the Safavids in Iran, and the Moguls in India. The people of these three empires had more in common than Turkish lineage. They all were Muslims, recited the same Koran, prayed toward Mecca, and they honored the religious law of Islam, Shari'a. Furthermore, the literate among them loved Persian literature and corresponded mostly in that language; a "cultured" person was judged by his knowledge of the literature, history, art, and mores of the Iranians.

And yet these three empires never united or even cooperated in any project. Long distances and lack of communication were partially responsible. The main reason, however, was the fact that Safavid Iran was Shi'i in religion, and her geographical location separated the two Sunni empires of the Ottomans and the Moguls. On the other hand, religious differences aside, there was a good deal of cultural and commercial intercourse between Iran and India, and except for occasional raids from the tribes of Central Asia, their borders were quite peaceful.

The fanatical religious enmity between the Safavid and Ottoman empires was heightened by disputes over the control of the Shi'i holy places of Najaf and Karbala in southern Mesopotamia, and over the Shi'i settlements in eastern Asia Minor. Economically, the Ottoman Empire lay athwart the traditional trade routes connecting Iran with the Mediterranean and the Straits of Dardanelles and Bosporus. It was to break this barrier that the Safavid shahs tried to ally themselves with different potentates of Europe against the Ottomans. When that proved impossible, the trading parties bypassed the Ottoman barriers in the Mediterranean and the Levant, and opened up brisk commerce in the Persian Gulf. There is no doubt that the European nations benefited by this intense rivalry, for throughout the seventeenth and part of the eighteenth centuries, the Ottomans and the Iranians vied with each other in giving special economic and commercial privileges to the merchants and nationals of Europe.

Language differences were perhaps more important than economic rivalries in keeping the Ottomans and the Safavids at odds. The vast majority of the inhabitants of Azerbaijan and northwestern Iran were Turkish-speaking people. Intermittent wars and religious fanaticism, which made the wars personal, helped separate the two Turkish-speaking peoples and distinguished one as "Iranian" and the other as "Turk." If the Shi'is ever had as their goal the expansion of the frontiers of Islam against non-Muslims, the Safavids discouraged it. Instead, they tried to destroy the Sunnis, especially Ottoman Sunnis, wherever they found them, and required the Shi'is to curse the "usurpers" of the Imamate—namely, the first three caliphs of Islam.

The eighteenth century, which ushered in the cultural, political, and economic rejuvenation of most European countries, marked the beginning of stagnation in the world of Islam. The Mogul Empire was in an advanced state of decay and fell prey to merchant adventurers of the West. The Safavids were in decline; and the Ottomans, though still strong if only because of their size, were not far behind the Safavids.

Having flourished by military conquests, the Ottomans launched their last campaign against Vienna, which had escaped their grasp so often. It was carried out by Mehmed IV and Kara Mustafa, the grand vazir, in 1683. Kara Mustafa laid siege to Vienna in mid-July and for two months bombarded the city. The defenders of the city under the command of Count Starhemberg were greatly weakened, and Kara Mustafa expected the city to surrender. But King John Sobieski of Poland came to the rescue with 70,000 soldiers. The fateful encounter occurred on September 12, 1683. The Ottoman army was routed and the Austrians and Poles pursued their victory. The Ottomans deposed Mehmed in favor of his brother Suleiman II (1687–1691). In desperation, Suleiman called on Mustafa Köprülü to be the grand vazir. He was able to hold the line for a while, but the Ottoman Empire had lost its resilience and its ability to recoup. The crushing blow was dealt by Prince Eugene of Savoy in 1697 at the battle of Zenta. Two years later the Treaty of Karlowitz was signed.

Karlowitz marks the beginning of the end of the Ottoman Empire. It was the first of many dictated peace treaties that the Turks were to sign. European diplomats knew that henceforth the Turks would not threaten the integrity of Europe. The Ottomans, on the other hand, slowly realized that their domain was at the mercy of the countries of Europe. Furthermore, the

Ottomans were to realize that Europeans considered the rule of the sultan-caliph over an empire in which the Christian "minorities" outnumbered the Muslim "majority" an anomaly and were not willing to allow it to continue.

THE PERIOD OF DISINTEGRATION

It must be noted that Europe alone was not the cause of the downfall of the Ottoman Empire. The disintegration had already begun, and the empire would have fallen apart because of its own weakness. European countries happened to be there to pick up the pieces. Had it not been for the rivalry of European nations, the Ottoman Empire would not have lasted the next 200 years. Some of the learned men in the Ottoman Empire saw the handwriting on the wall and gave warning, but no one paid any attention to them.

One of these learned men, Koji Bey, wrote a report on the state of the empire in 1630, when Sultan Murat IV had reached the age of twenty-one. In unusually clear language Koji Bey described the degeneration of the empire and enumerated the causes in his report. Among other things, he mentioned that the sultan had made himself "invisible," preoccupied, as he was, with his harem. Because of the influence of the harem, "the sultan no longer governs himself and neither is the grand vazir allowed to do so; power is actually in the hands of negro eunuchs and purchased slave girls." He reported further on the economic decline of the empire and blamed it principally on heavy taxation and corruption in the administration. Another writer in the same century, the celebrated historian Haji Khalifa claimed that the state was sick and diagnosed the reasons for the illness as high taxation, oppression of the masses, and the sale of offices to the highest bidder.

It is futile to set an exact date for the onset of decay in an empire or to argue for a single cause. It seems to be a process for which philosophers of history have advanced many theories. Very likely if Ibn Khaldun had lived to analyze the Ottoman decay, he would have applied his own theory—namely, that the *asabiyyah,* the original material from which the early Ottomans had built their civilization, had lost its vigor.

We have mentioned that the decay of the empire began with Suleiman the Magnificent, when the empire's power was at its height. This was because Suleiman gradually refused to go to war with his troops, as his ancestors had done, and to preside personally at Council meetings. His successors, with few exceptions, gradually distanced themselves from the affairs of the state. Grand vazirs ruled in the name of the sultan; in time, they moved their residence to the palace and called it "the exalted portal" or simply "the Porte," as used by Europeans. For a system that was based on the army and loyalty to the person of the sultan, such practices were debilitating. The attitude of most of the sultans remained "business as usual" and the usual business of the sultan continued to be life in the harem and the sale of offices to pay for that type of living. The few sultans who did care found that the world had rapidly changed. Economic, social, political, military, and international problems were so new and overwhelming that the most intelligent of the sultans could not understand them, and not even the strongest could cope with them.

The Ottoman Empire remained a military encampment that was strengthened by well-organized levies of troops, supported economically by peasants, merchants, and craftsmen who depended on the army for the safety of the roads, and sustained by the ecclesiastical organization (ulama) that interpreted the Shari'a. The empire was administered by a burgeoning bureaucracy headed by the sultan himself. By the beginning of the nineteenth century, both the organization and methods of administration were hopelessly out of date. In Europe, growing liberalism, democratization, industrialization, and secularism had destroyed feudalism, decreased the power of the church, and nationalized the armies. Even though Ottoman religious, military, and feudal systems were not like those of Europe, nevertheless the Ottoman institutions could not cope with the problems of the century, such as the power of Western nations and their aggression, the nationalistic struggles of non-Turkish peoples, and the restless quest of the Turks themselves for progress and change.

In addition to being out of date, the Ottoman institutions had become corrupt. The provincial and local governorships, which in previous times were given in lieu of service, were now for sale to the highest bidder. As long as the governor, or pasha, sent the annual revenue agreed upon to Istanbul, the sultan did not care how the money was obtained. The *pashalik* ("governorship"), therefore, was the objective of ambitious men in the empire. The facts that it could only be obtained by cash and that cash was scarce limited the number of buyers. Those who could borrowed money from Greek, Armenian, or Jewish moneylenders and literally mortgaged their pashalik at high interest. In order to insure payment, often the moneylender appointed his agent as "secretary" of the pasha. The secretaries were more merciless than the pashas. They extorted enough from the helpless peasants and merchants to insure income for the sultan, the pasha, the moneylender, and themselves.

Even though pashas had the power of life and death over the inhabitants and maintained courts and harems in imitation of the sultan, they were not all-powerful. There were local strongmen who often refused to obey the pashas; and in the struggles between the two, the inhabitants suffered even more. In Anatolia there were hereditary warlords, probably descendants of ghazi leaders, who at the zenith of Ottoman power were obedient enough, but who now took advantage of the weakness of the central government and revived their old independence.

More notorious than the warlords were the Greek phanariotes. Under the millet system, the Greek Orthodox patriarchate in Istanbul was the head of all the Orthodox Christians in the empire. These men, all of whom were Greek, exploited the non-Greek Orthodox of the empire, such as Rumanians, Serbians, Bulgarians, and the rest. Later, when the rule requiring all officials of the empire be Muslims was slackened, these men became official interpreters in the increasing international involvement of the empire. In these positions they wielded great influence and amassed fortunes for themselves and for their Greek compatriots. All of this adversely affected the economy of the country. Caravan routes became unsafe, roads and bridges fell into disrepair, and local wars and brigandage paralyzed commerce.

The organization of the government, however, remained intact. The sultan, the vazirs, the bureaucrats, the ulama, and the moneylenders used their relatively short terms of office for amassing as much wealth as they could. In the nineteenth century, the Ottoman sultan could no longer depend on the Janissaries, who had grown in number and in arrogance. This once-effective force that had guarded the power of the sultans became a club in the reactionary hands of the ulama against any sultan who dared to change the status quo. During the nineteenth century, Egypt revolted, the Wahhabis of Arabia challenged the religious authority of the caliph, the Druzes and the Maronites of Lebanon set up autonomous governments, national groups in the Balkans agitated for independence, and the very pashas sent there to quell the rebellions rose against the central government.

Moreover, the economy of the empire declined. The financing of the wars resulted in general inflation. The villages were depopulated in favor of cities and towns, where there were not enough jobs for everyone. The guilds, which formed the backbone of the Ottoman craft industry, had become so entrenched and rigid that they could no longer compete in the international market.

More destructive to the economy of the empire than internal disorders were the events in Europe. Trade routes had shifted. With the discovery of new ocean routes and progress in shipbuilding, European trade, which had been most active in the Mediterranean, moved to the Persian Gulf for a few decades and from there to East Asia. With the increased number of manufacturing centers in Europe, the demand for the handmade products of the Ottomans slackened. Furthermore, the flow of silver and gold from the New World shifted the center of finance from the Mediterranean coastal cities to northern and central Europe. In all this the Ottoman trade suffered; and the merchants of the empire, even if they had been free from corruption, would not have been able to compete with the corporations and cartels that had been established in the West.

Notwithstanding all this, the Ottoman Empire lived on. To contemporary observers, it seemed that the empire could not last a day longer, but in the process of history it does not seem so amazing that the empire lasted so long. During the centuries, a system had been established that benefited the sultan as the commander-in-chief and those whom he wished to favor. As long as the sultan was strong and alert, he shifted his favors from one segment of society to the other and, in the long run, all were at peace, relatively secure, and satisfied.

But during the two centuries when the power of the sultanate was at a low ebb, the system did not disintegrate. Instead, it remained and benefited an oligarchy of which the sultan was often a member. The categories of beneficiaries became fixed. There were the sultans, who were influenced by the women of the harem, who in turn were under the strong and ambitious hands of eunuchs. There were the military commanders, the ulama, the pashas, the moneylenders, and the influential leaders of the various non-Muslim millets. These profited from the system by exploiting the masses under them, both Muslim and non-Muslim. The fact that they often vi-ciously fought against each other was part of the contest. But as soon as the system was threatened by external force or internal desire for reform, they united and supported each other to ward off the attack. No sooner would the "danger" pass than they would be at it again and also at each other.

EUROPEAN RIVALRY

The Ottoman system would, nevertheless, have fallen of its own weight and corruption had it not been for the fact that European nations—sometimes singly and often together—gave the tottering empire enough blood transfu-sions to keep it alive. The essence of what in European history is called the "Eastern Question," was the Western inability to divide the property once the sick man died. No single European power was strong enough to subdue the others and annex the empire. Meanwhile, each was fearful lest another power take the advantage. Ruthlessness, intrigue, secret agreements, duplic-ity, and war were all part of the diplomatic game. As soon as one country or any combination of countries got the upper hand, the rest came to aid the Ottomans until the "balance" was restored. When it became evident that the empire had to be kept alive in order to uphold the European balance, some of the European countries, such as Britain, France, and later Germany, joined the Ottoman oligarchy in the exploitation and perpetuated the sys-tem. Austria-Hungary was too unwieldy to be effective, and Russia had too much of a Messianic obsession to be practical. Indeed, even after World War I the European powers tried to keep the Ottomans alive; and they would have succeeded, had it not been for the Turks themselves, who practiced euthanasia and buried the corpse.

The major European countries involved in the affairs of the Ottoman Empere were six: Austria-Hungary, Russia, Britain, France, Germany, and Italy. Austria and Russia were primarily interested in the European holdings of the Ottomans. As such their interests often clashed. The Hapsburgs had borne the brunt of the Ottoman pressure since the fourteenth century and felt that they had the first option in the choice of territory. More especially, they wanted control of the Danube and the approaches to the Adriatic and Aegean seas. They, however, had difficulties which were not unlike those of the Ottomans. The Austrian and Hungarian ruling classes were made up of Germans and Magyars, while the population over whom they ruled was predominantly Slavic. The religion of the ruling classes was Roman Catholic, while that of most of the subjects was Orthodox. Like the Ottomans, the Austro-Hungarians were not able to weld the diverse groups of their empire into a nation. The growing spirit of nationalism in Europe in the nineteenth century encouraged movements for independence and adversely affected the Austro-Hungarian Empire.

The Russians, on the other hand, were more homogeneous. Their spirit of nationalism transcended their boundaries and reached the Slavs of the Balkans, who were under either the Ottomans or the Austrians. Further-more, as the only independent Orthodox country, the Russians had already claimed protection over the Orthodox subjects of the Porte, a fact that was not welcomed by the Hapsburgs, who also ruled over Orthodox people. Economically and politically the Russians felt hemmed in, as the Ottomans controlled the outlets to the great rivers of southern Russia. They continually justified their attempts to expand by ascribing their need for warm-water ports. In all these objectives they clashed with the Austrians. Neither of them alone was strong enough in the eighteenth century to put an end to the Ottomans, nor could they afford to unite in the effort. By the nineteenth century, when the Russians could deal with the Ottomans, the British and the French had become interested in the fate of the Turks and intervened on their behalf.

The main interests of Britain and France in southeastern Europe were economic and the upholding of the European balance of power. Any territorial ambitions that they might have had were not of highest priority. Their territorial interests were concentrated in the African and Asian dependencies of the Ottoman Empire. The imperial policy of Britain was built around the protection of India and the main routes leading to it. In the Middle East this meant the Persian Gulf and the Red Sea and the lands surrounding them.

France was interested mainly in North Africa and the Levant. Inasmuch as the boundaries of the Levant were always in doubt, she and Britain clashed. Otherwise the interests of France in the rest of the Ottoman Empire were economic and religious. She was one of the first to conclude a commercial treaty with the Ottomans, and this was renewed many times in the course of centuries. French businessmen, industrialists, and financiers had invested heavily in the Ottoman Empire. In religion, the French had the same interest and claim over the Roman Catholic subjects of the sultan as the Russians had over the Orthodox. Since both the Orthodox and the Roman Catholics wanted control of the Christian shrines in Palestine, Russia and France clashed.

Germany and Italy were latecomers to the scene. German interest were mainly economic and the gaining of influence at the Porte in order to thwart the plans of Russia and England. Italy's role was insignificant, but it managed to gain control of Libya while others were involved elsewhere.

The relationship of the European powers to each other and to the Ottoman Empire does not, however, follow a logical pattern. It was dictated by opportunism. France and England joined together against Russia and Austria as readily as France and Austria collaborated against Great Britain and Russia.

The first serious attempt of Russia to gain Ottoman territory was by Peter the Great in 1711, but he was not very successful. It was during the reign of Catherine the Great (1762–1798) that the Ottomans became involved in her plan for the partition of Poland. In 1768, Mustafa III (1757–1774) joined the "confederation" made up of Austria, France, and Sweden to safeguard the integrity of Poland against Russian aggression. Mustafa was persuaded to commit his unprepared army in a war against Russia. Catherine welcomed the opportunity, even though her armies were not prepared either. The Russian master plan included the sending of the Russian fleet around Europe to the Mediterranean and the contacting of Arab dissidents within the Ottoman Empire; the plan also counted upon the uprising of the Greek Orthodox and the Balkan Slavs against the Turks. In the early spring of 1770, a Russian squadron sailed through the Mediterranean and reached the shores of Turkey. The insurrection of the Christian population, however, did not materialize. It should be noted that under the Ottoman millet system the Christian population was relatively autonomous and it was not willing to give this up in exchange for Russian control. In the nineteenth century, when the peoples of the Balkans did rise against the Ottomans, it was not for the purpose of joining the Russians but for their own national independence.

The Russians won great victories and annihilated the bulk of the Ottoman fleet. But even though the fleet was reinforced, the Russians were not able to reach Istanbul. The war dragged on. The death of Sultan Mustafa in January 1774 weakened Turkish resistance. In the same year a peasant uprising against Catherine, led by Pugachev, assumed alarming dimensions. Both sides instituted direct negotiations and in July 1774 signed the Treaty of Kuchuk Kainarji.

Under the provisions of this famous treaty, Crimea became autonomous and Russia annexed Kerch and the territories between the Bug and the Dnieper rivers. Russia also received the privilege of free navigation on the Black Sea with the right of passage through the Straits. The Porte retained Moldavia, Wallachia, and the Greek Islands but had to pay an indemnity of 4,500,000 rubles.

This treaty is considered particularly significant because of articles VII and XIV. In the latter, Russia was given permission to build a public church in Istanbul which "shall always be under the protection of the ministers of that [Russian] Empire. . . ." In article VII, Russia received very vaguely defined rights. Later on the Russians used these articles to claim protectorship over the Christian subjects of the Porte. Other than these two articles there was not much new, however, in the treaty. The Ottoman Empire was in the habit of giving capitulatory privileges to foreign countries, as we have seen. These were mainly for trade privileges but religion was also nearly always mentioned. The last treaty of capitulation had been obtained by France in 1740, under which all Roman Catholics were put under French protection. Even though the agreement meant to imply the foreign Roman Catholics residing within the empire, the French acted as though they were also the protectors of the Roman Catholic subjects within the Ottoman Empire. The difference, however, between the former capitulations and the religious and economic capitulations in the Treaty of Kuchuk Kainarji was that the former capitulations were granted freely by the Porte either to bolster trade or to compete with similar privileges granted by the Safavids of Iran. The capitulations in the Treaty of Kuchuk Kainarji were forced upon the Porte as a penalty of defeat. Even though "the Sublime Porte promises to protect constantly the Christian religion and its churches. . . ," Russia as a victor could use the agreement as a convenient pretext to interfere in the domestic affairs of the Ottoman Empire.

After a series of characteristic maneuverings that combined pleasure, diplomacy, and intrigue, Catherine, in violation of the Treaty of Kuchuk

Kainarji, annexed the Crimea in 1784. Three years later she invited her friends, among them Emperor Joseph of Austria, to a spectacular party in the Crimea to celebrate the annexation. The military and naval maneuvers staged by Potemkin alarmed Sultan Abdul Hamid I (1773–1789), and war broke out in 1787 between the Ottomans and the Russian-Austrian alliance.

As usual, Russia was not prepared, but fortunately for her the Ottomans, also as usual, were even less prepared. This war also was a protracted one; and in the end international complications, such as the French Revolution and the death of Emperor Joseph II (1790) weakened the alliance. Pressure from England, Prussia, and Holland persuaded the new emperor of Austria, Leopold, to make peace with the Porte on August 4, 1791, without any gains. A few months later (January 1792) Catherine signed the Peace of Jassy and advanced her territory to the Dniester River, thus confirming the annexation of Crimea.

TRADITIONAL REFORMS

When Sultan Selim III succeeded to the throne in 1789, the Ottomans were at war with Russia and it became his task to sign the Treaty of Jassy. He was a well-educated young man who was convinced that without reforms the empire could not regain its lost initiative. Like many of his Turkish contemporaries, restoring the prestige of the empire meant the reorganization and revival of the armed forces. He therefore introduced and executed a series of reforms that were far reaching and considered radical. He separated the administrative and the military functions in the army, established new hierarchies, and subjected both officers and men to examinations in order to weed out the undesirable and the dishonest. He established military drills under foreign advisers and tried to reduce the number of Janissaries, whose ranks had been swollen by a large number of relatives and friends who drew pay from the government.

Finding the Janissaries too slow and reluctant to accept the reforms, Selim created a new corps, called the "New Order," gave them the latest weapons, and employed teachers for them from France and England. He separated the new corps from the rest of the army both in command and financing. Reforms along the same lines were instituted in the navy and artillery. He modernized the existing cannon foundries, but it was rather late in his reign (1795) that he established both land and naval and engineering schools where privileged young men were trained in both theoretical and practical aspects of warfare.

The reforms of Selim, even though radical for the army, did not encompass the social, economic, and governmental sectors of the empire. Neither he nor, apparently, his advisers saw the need of such a program and its relation to an efficient fighting force. Impressed by the Austrian and French reform movements initiated by their autocrats, he tried to make the old institutions work better and more honestly. He discouraged nepotism and established a hiring system based on ability.

Notwithstanding the limited scope of the reforms, Selim found himself surrounded by trouble. The Janissaries turned their soup kettle upside down, which was a sign of revolt, and the Shaykh ul-Islam issued a fetva deposing Selim in 1807 and elevating his submissive cousin Mustafa IV to the throne. Many, however, were not satisfied with this arrangement; and after a short period of confusion, Mustafa was deposed in favor of his younger brother Mahmud II (1807–1839), who was the only male heir left in the house of Osman. He was one of the more effective and forceful rulers in the Ottoman line and inaugurated reforms of far-reaching consequences in the empire.

Mahmud's more pressing task, however, was to deal with the Janissaries. By the beginning of the eighteenth century the Janissary corps had become a heavy burden on the Ottoman Empire. With the passage of time it had also become a stumbling block to progress and a threat to the sultanate. The Janissaries had become so powerful, corrupt, and indolent that they deposed and elevated sultans at will, beheaded grand vazirs, and opposed every attempt at reform. Sultan Selim had lost his life in a vain attempt to subdue them. Mahmud, however, prepared the ground before he took the vital step. He formed a new artillery group with modern weapons and brought thousands of these soldiers to Istanbul. Then he ordered the Janissaries to adopt the European form of military drill. The Janissaries, refusing to change their ways, rushed toward the palace, whereupon they were mowed down with grapeshot. They took refuge in their barracks and the artillery bombarded the barracks until almost all were destroyed. They were hunted in every city of the empire and were killed mercilessly. Then the sultan issued a decree abolishing the corps. The importance of this event in the history of the Ottoman Empire cannot be exaggerated, for it not only opened the way for military reorganization but for all other reforms. The reactionaries of the empire who had depended upon the Janissaries had been rendered impotent.

GREEK INDEPENDENCE

The exultation of Mahmud was dampened by the Greek uprising. Tsar Nicholas I (1825–1855) of Russia was anxious to turn the Greek revolt to Russian advantage. The British and French were forced to intervene by the great pressure of public opinion in favor of the Greeks expressed by Lord Byron in England and Chateaubriand in France. They were also afraid Russia might use this as a pretext to wreck the Ottoman Empire. So the three powers, Britain, France, and Russia, jointly asked the sultan to negotiate with the Greeks. This Mahmud refused, whereupon the combined fleet of the three European powers destroyed the Ottoman fleet at Navarino on October 20, 1827.

The sultan asked for indemnity and Russia retaliated unilaterally by declaring war in 1828. As usual the Russians were slow, but the Ottomans had not had time to organize a new army after the destruction of the Janissaries. After a year, the Russians had advanced perilously close to Istanbul by capturing Edirne (Adrianople). The European powers intervened and brought pressure upon Mahmud to sue for peace. By the Treaty of Adrianople (September 14, 1829), the Porte recognized the independence of Greece under the "Three Powers" guaranty, granted autonomy to Serbia, and ceded the mouth of the Danube to Russia.

For nearly a quarter of a century after the Treaty of Adrianople, the attention of the Porte was directed toward either internal struggle with Muhammad Ali of Egypt or attempts to reform, both of which will be discussed in subsequent chapters. The Porte was relatively at peace with its European neighbors. In the meantime, Europe went through the convulsion of a social and economic revolution in 1848 that had repercussions in the Middle East. In the same year, Marx and Engels published *The Communist Manifesto*. In the course of four years, France, through a series of revolutions, changed from a monarchy to the Second Republic and then to the Second Empire, with another Bonaparte, Louis Napoleon, as dictator.

THE CRIMEAN WAR

Louis Napoleon, who had helped the pope in his difficulties and in turn had been assisted by the Vatican in his coup to become emperor, was eager to prove himself a faithful son of the Church. He could do this by reasserting France's interest in the Roman Catholic subjects of the Porte and gain special privileges for the Vatican in the care and administration of the Christian holy places in Palestine. Furthermore, such a move would check the ambitions of Nicholas I, who had not accepted Napoleon III as a "brother" monarch, and would enhance the prestige of France.

There had always been friction between the Roman Catholics and the Orthodox over the right to control the holy places. Ever since the Ottomans came into possession of Palestine, the Porte had made decisions favoring sometimes one group and sometimes the other. To avoid bloodshed, sometimes Muslims were given custody of and the key to these places. There was friction again in 1850, and by 1852 Sultan Abdul Mejid (1839–1861) very reluctantly decided in favor of French control. Nicholas I, who considered this a great blow to Russian honor, sent Menshikov to persuade and cajole the sultan to change his decision. The sultan, with the open support of the French and the surreptitious encouragement of the British, gave a formal refusal to Russia in 1853.

It is very difficult to determine who started the Crimean War. Russia was committed to upholding her prestige, was "certain" of the neutrality of Britain, and was confident of her success. Nicholas I suggested that Russia and Britain cooperate in dividing the property of the "sick man" who was about to die. France was committed to holding her gains and apparently did not expect Britain to stay neutral. For the Ottomans, this seemed to be the opportunity they had been awaiting, because the sultan was confident that he would have the assistance of both Britain and France. In Britain the intense popular dislike for the autocracy of Nicholas I and the fear of the government for the safety of access to India combined to make British involvement in the war a certainty.

The main antagonists in the Crimean War were Russia against the Ottoman Empire, Britain, and France. Later, Austria and Prussia made a defensive alliance with each other and the former joined Britain and France in 1854. The Treaty of Paris ending the war was signed in March 1856. The Ottomans, who had become involved in the power politics of Europe, suffered as a result. They lost, even though they were part of the victorious alliance. In the treaty, the interested European powers virtually assumed responsibility for protecting the Ottoman Empire by declaring that anything which endangered the integrity of the empire would "be considered a question of European interest."

DISMEMBERMENT OF THE EMPIRE

For nearly 200 years the Ottoman Empire had been humiliated and defeated, had lost vast territories, but at least the Porte was economically free from foreign domination. The Ottoman sultans had many ways of meeting their deficits. They depreciated currency, they expropriated the wealth of their subjects, and they borrowed money from native moneylenders. They were not in the habit of borrowing money from foreign banks and governments. Insofar as can be ascertained, 1854 was the first time the Porte borrowed money from Britain and France to buy weapons and meet the needs of the Crimean War. Once the door had been opened, the sultans continued borrowing. Local bankers and European investors made such a good profit that they encouraged the practice. Loans with discount rates as high as 55 percent and interest rates of 12 percent were indeed profitable. By the time Abdul Hamid II became sultan (1877–1909), the country was virtually bankrupt. The Ottoman defeat in the war of 1877 against Russia imposed an indemnity of $100,000,000 on the Porte. By 1881, the whole empire went into receivership. The British, French, Dutch, German, Austrian, and Italian creditors set up the Council of Administration of the Ottoman Public Debt and took control of certain revenues to insure payment.

European investors found a gold mine in the vast and underdeveloped territory of the empire, both in raw material and in opportunities for development. The Ottomans needed roads, railroads, city lights, water, and public works of all types. The Europeans were ready to lend money and receive concessions. In 1870, Bismarck did not think that all the Balkans were worth the "bones of a single Pomeranian grenadier." Twenty years later the Germans, under Wilhelm II, were not only selling armaments to the Turks, but were also busy building railroads in Anatolia. In 1898, the Kaiser paid a second visit to Istanbul and this time went to Damascus and Jerusalem. The *Drang nach Osten* ("expansion to the east") was inaugurated; and the famous Berlin-to-Baghdad railway, financed by the Deutsches Bank, introduced German imperialism into the Middle East. This frightened the British, French, and Russians to such a degree that they forgot their differences and cooperated to block the German push eastward.

During the two decades following the Treaty of Paris, the Europeans were busy with their own struggles, wars of unification, and much else. This should have given the Ottomans some respite, but it was not so. The ideals of the French Revolution and the emergence of national states in western Europe had aroused similar feelings among the subject peoples of the Balkans. Serbs wanted independence, Greeks desired more territory, Bosnia and Herzegovina were seething with revolt, and there were uprisings in Rumania.

Educated liberals in western Europe were aghast at the speed and severity with which the Ottoman soldiers dealt with the revolters and were clamoring to have the Turks punished. The governments and industrialists of western Europe, on the other hand, had profitable investments to protect and did not care for such humane considerations. The Russians and Austrians saw in this a chance to settle accounts with the Turks. Representatives of European powers assembled in Istanbul to reach a solution. Abdul Hamid II, who had just been elevated to the throne by the reformists (August 31, 1876) agreed to constitutional reforms. This pleased the British but not the Russians, who were bent on war. France was still licking her wounds from defeat at the hands of the Germans; Bismarck was not interested in the Balkans; and in Britain public sentiment was too critical of the Turks to permit the leaders to go to war on the side of the Ottomans.

In the war of 1877–78, the Turks fought bravely but could not hold the Russians, who reached the village of San Stefano (Yeshilkoy), only ten miles from Istanbul. Abdul Hamid signed the Treaty of San Stefano (March 13, 1878), which dismembered whatever was left of the Ottoman Empire in Europe. It gave independence to Montenegro, Serbia, and Rumania, and gave autonomy to Bosnia and Herzegovina. The heart of the treaty, however, was the creation of a large Bulgaria, extending from the Black Sea to the Aegean Sea. Furthermore, in eastern Asia Minor the Porte had to cede considerable territory. In addition to all this, the demoralized sultan agreed to an indemnity of some 300,000,000 rubles.

There were immediate protests from the Greeks, who saw an end to their territorial ambitions; from the Serbs, who resented seeing so many Serbs become subjects of a large Bulgaria; from the Austrians, who felt that their advance to the east was blocked; and from the British, who, led by Prime Minister Disraeli, turned against Russia. All of these countries, together with Germany, brought pressure to bear upon Russia and convened the Congress of Berlin (June 13, 1878) to reconsider the Treaty of San Stefano.

The Treaty of Berlin replaced that of San Stefano and was full of double dealing that did not settle the Balkan problems. The nineteenth century came to an end with the Ottomans under the political and economic domination of European powers. Abdul Hamid II used all his cunning to wrest himself free, but the case was hopeless. By the time of World War I, the sultan had lost practically all his European holdings; and his control over the Fertile Crescent and North Africa was only nominal.

Chapter Sixteen
The Ottoman and Turkish Awakening

The history of the Middle East over the past 200 years, whether it be of Turkey, Iran, or the Arabic-speaking world, is largely the story of the reaction of the governments and peoples of the region to the challenges of Western civilization. These challenges have been political, social, religious, economic, literary, and artistic. The peoples have reacted to these in different ways, and it is quite likely that the reaction will not be resolved before the end of the twentieth century.

One thing is certain, however, and that is that the encounter of the peoples of the Middle East with Western civilization has created two types of revolutions. Actually these two revolutions are two aspects of the same phenomenon called nationalism. One is revolution for independence from a colonial power and the other is revolution for change. The revolution for independence is relatively short and always spectacular and cohesive. Since the blame for all the ills of society is almost always placed on the outsiders, all elements of society usually unite. The anti-imperialist who has the courage of his convictions and a certain amount of charisma is often a popular hero.

The revolution for change, on the other hand, is long, tedious, and divisive. Since the hero must, of necessity, be a reformer, he must criticize and sometimes destroy the established norm, whether it be political, social, economic, religious, literary, or artistic. Such an activity causes dissension and civil strife. The contending parties try to gain power by any means available and the struggle goes on for a very long time.

Since Turkey and Iran have never been ruled directly by a European power, they have not been involved in a revolution for independence from colonial rule. Instead, they have struggled for independence from imperialistic domination. In these two countries this struggle and the revolution for change have gone on hand in hand. The Arabic-speaking countries, however, spent many years in their struggle for independence and did not fully succeed until after World War II. This is not to say, however, that the Arabs took no steps toward modernization while under imperial rule, but that it could not have been a planned and direct attempt.

Inasmuch as "nationalism," "colonialism," and "imperialism" have been and are being used in reference to the Middle East, a working definition of these terms is in order. Professor Boyd Shafer, in his comprehensive book *Faces of Nationalism,*[1] does not attempt to define nationalism. He rather identifies ten statements that "taken together . . . describe its basic attributes, both real and mythical." These may be abridged as follows: a shared sense of belonging to a land, a shared culture, shared social or religious institutions, a shared political state, a shared history, a shared destiny with others of the same group, shared pride, shared hostility, shared devotion, and shared hope.

European domination of the world in recent centuries has taken three forms. One is "colonization," where Europeans have settled a land by pushing the natives aside, such as in the New World and in South Africa. The second is "colonialism," where a land has been occupied and governed directly by a handful of European military and civilian administrators for political and commercial advantages; examples include India, Egypt, and Malaya. A third is "imperialism," where a country has been left nominally independent but is indirectly dominated politically and economically; Iran and Thailand are two examples. In the case of the Ottomans, we must bear in mind that in the eighteenth and nineteenth centuries they were forced to relinquish what they had taken by force during the previous centuries.

TANZIMAT

On November 3, 1839, Sultan Abdul Mejid (1839–1861) gathered the notables of the empire and had his foreign minister read a statement that has come to be known as the "noble rescript." Seventeen years later, on February 18, 1856, the same sultan issued another statement that is known as the "imperial rescript." Both were issued under pressure and were made partly to appease European governments. Nevertheless, they did inaugurate and endorse an era of reform in the Ottoman Empire that is called *Tanzimat.* It must be noted, however, that Tanzimat was as much the result of upheavals in the eighteenth century as it was the cause of changes in the nineteenth and twentieth centuries.

[1](New York: Harcourt Brace Jovanovich, 1972), pp. 17ff.

Tanzimat was the culmination of a series of reforms along Western lines that started during the reign of Ahmed III (1703–1730). This was a period of comparative peace, known as the "Tulip Era," when the sultan and the elite of the empire became interested in imitating the superficialities of French life and amusements. In the midst of the frivolities, a few serious aspects of Western life were also adopted, among them the printing press. With the permission of the Shaykh ul-Islam, only books on military and scientific subjects were published. Ahmed III lost his throne partly because of his westernizing activities. This was followed by the New Order, which was inaugurated by Sultan Selim III, who also lost his throne. Mahmud II, who followed Selim and who destroyed the Janissaries, was no liberal. Like some of his contemporaries, he was an enlightened despot, but wanted to be obeyed. He forced the Shaykh ul-Islam to write a book on the necessity of complete obedience to the sultan. In his *Summary of Reasons for Obedience to the Sultan,* the religious dignitary produced no less than twenty-five hadiths to prove the point. Mahmud II seemed to have abandoned the idea that the Ottoman Empire existed for the propagation of Islam. He was probably secularized enough to believe that reform was possible in the context of power but not in the context of religion. He is supposed to have said, "From now on I want to know my subjects as 'Muslims' only in the mosque, as 'Christians' only in the church, and as 'Jews' only in the synagogue." All of this culminated in the proclamation of the Tanzimat.

To say that the two royal rescripts in the Tanzimat period were charters of individual liberty is to exaggerate, for both Mahmud (who prepared the way) and Abdul Mejid (who made the Tanzimat possible) were autocrats. On the other hand, to state that the rescripts were made solely for the purpose of complying with the demands of the European powers is to miss the point. Tanzimat contained the germs of individual liberty and constitutional government. It was used to mollify the liberal elements among European powers, but it also sprang from the intellectual and administrative ferment that had been going on within the Ottoman Empire for some time. Tanzimat was a "palace revolution" that strengthened the position of the bureaucrats who were in power. Almost all the changes in the machinery of the government were designed to give more power to the bureaucracy.

The old system of administration, which had been dying gradually, was discarded altogether. There was a council of ministers now headed by a prime minister, and the "new" military system was under the order of the council of ministers. These ministers were served by a bureaucracy that comprised the secular literate elite in the empire. Some of the members of the bureaucracy might have been anticlerical, but practically none were anti-Islamic. They ignored the ulama as often as they possibly could. They did not disband the religious schools but opened up secular schools beside them. The religious schools continued to train religious lawyers, but the secular schools trained civil servants, doctors, engineers, and army officers as well as lawyers. From 1840 to 1879 the judicial system of the empire was gradually modeled after that of France. By 1869, when the civil laws were codified, only personal status laws—i.e., marriage, divorce, inheritance, and personal property—were under the Shari'a.

In addition to the above, during the Tanzimat period the government encouraged the sending of students to western Europe, chiefly to France. The first high school for girls was opened in 1861. Two years later, the American Congregationalist missionary, Cyrus Hamlin, opened Robert College. At first, only Christian students of Bulgarian, Greek, and Armenian origin attended, but soon the Muslims patronized the college as well. This institution and the American College for girls have played important parts in the modernization of Turkey. In 1862, the Ottoman Scientific Society was formed, and many more similar organizations followed. In gatherings of this sort, young men who had returned from Europe discussed their observations, and poets and writers expressed their thoughts.

The Tanzimat period produced a new school of Turkish writers who transformed Turkish literature in both style and content. Among these writers was Ibrahim Shinasi, who spent five years in Paris. After a few years in the Turkish Ministry of Education, he worked on the staff of the *Terjumani Ahval*, the first nongovernment newspaper, which was founded in 1860. Later, in 1862, he edited his own paper, *Tasviri Efkar*, which was issued until 1925, when it was suppressed by Mustafa Kemal Atatürk. He was a forerunner in freeing the language from its pompous style and, through his translations, showed that it was possible to express foreign and sophisticated ideas in simple Turkish. He was followed by Ziya Pasha, who translated Rousseau and Molière, Ahmad Midhat, the short story writer, and Ahmed Jevdet, who started a movement to expunge Arabic and Persian words from the Turkish language.

In 1839, the noble rescript decreed by Sultan Abdul Mejid had recognized the sovereignty of law, the equality of all subjects, and the universal application of justice. In the enthusiasm of the period, Turks shaved their beards, wore European tunics and trousers, listened to Western music and exchanged the turban for the fez. In 1856, the imperial rescript decreed by the same sultan, which was mostly a product of foreign pressure, was more extensive. It eradicated, at least on paper, the differences that existed between Muslims and Christians, and extended to Christians all the rights and privileges that were enjoyed by Muslims. This meant equality in taxation, military service, and education. It also envisaged the founding of banks, and fiscal and agricultural reforms.

But these reforms and pronouncements were not without their opponents. The ulama did not sit idly by and in many instances were assisted by some of the members of the bureaucracy who had become established and did not want to change any further. The foreign powers, who espoused reforms to satisfy the liberal elements in their own countries, did not help the Turkish reformers. They were more interested in the political and economic exploitation of the weak empire than in strengthening it with modern institutions.

The members of the religious hierarchy appointed by the sultan under the millet system were not enthusiastic, for under the new equality they would lose power in their communities. The rank and file of the Christians had to serve in the army for the first time and pay the same tax as Muslims. A large number of them wanted both equal rights and also wanted to retain the privileges that they enjoyed under the millet system. As a Turkish writer puts it, when the Tanzimat people brought the ideas of democracy and nationalism from Europe, the Turks chose democracy while the Christians chose nationalism. The evidence for this is the series of independence movements by Greeks, Serbians, Rumanians, and others that characterized the political history of the empire during the last part of the ninteenth century.

THE YOUNG OTTOMANS

The most important opponents of Tanzimat were the young Turkish critics who accused the bureaucrats of being more interested in imitating the West than in creating a new Ottoman society. Most of these young men were part of the same bureaucracy, and some of them had worked in the translation bureau of the Porte. They were familiar with the West and were anxious to shape the destiny of the Ottoman Empire. A number of them formed a secret society in 1865 by the name of "Patriotic Alliance," along the lines of similar groups prevalent in Europe at that time. They were the forerunners of a new breed of young men who were not satisfied with modernizing the machinery of the state, but wanted to establish a constitutional monarchy and revitalize Islam. They may properly be called "Young Ottomans" to distinguish them from the Tanzimat that preceded them and the "Young Turks" who came after them.

The name is significant because these men, unlike the bureaucrats of Tanzimat, had accepted the principles of nationalism as well as of democracy. The only "nation" that they knew was the Ottoman Empire; and they set out to weld a nation, a task that had been neglected for five and a half centuries. The problems were insurmountable, especially since the non-Turks in the empire had already started their independent nationalistic programs. But the Young Ottomans were undaunted. It was quite natural that they should choose Islam as a spiritual-ideological base for their nationalism. By emphasizing Islam they probably knew that they could not attract the non-Muslim populations of the empire, but most of these peoples were in revolt anyway. On the other hand, they hoped to gain support among the non-Turkish Muslim subjects of the empire. They believed in a limited form of pan-Islamism that would be welded together by the power of the Ottoman Empire. Indeed, a considerable number of the literate elite among the Arabic-speaking subjects of the empire were attracted to them; and for a time "Ottomanism" was discussed and written about in Arabic literature. But, as we shall see, it did not last long, for the Arabs had also drunk of the cup of nationalism and were reluctant to throw in their lot with the Turks.

The Young Ottomans, like many similar intellectual groups of Europe, were vague about their methods. Some were in favor of terror, others supported infiltration into the government, still others voted for converting the sultan. Divergent as their ideas and their methods were, they managed to meet in secret societies and work together. The Young Ottomans used an Islamic vocabulary. Whereas the intellectuals of the medieval Ottoman Empire based their ideas on such diverse works as the Koran, Islamic political philosophers, the *Practical Counsels*, and the Turko-Iranian secular legislation,[2] the Young Ottomans based their ideas almost entirely on the Koran. Like many Muslim reformers who came before and after them, they wanted to go back to the time when Islam was "pure"—i.e., the time of the Medina Caliphate, which was idealized and used as an illustration time and time again.

Perhaps the most important intellectual, theoretician, and writer of the Young Ottomans was Namik Kemal (d. 1887). He was an effective critic of Tanzimat, which in his opinion had achieved a degree of modernization but had not freed the individual from internal tyranny, nor freed the nation from foreign domination. All his life he tried to blend Islam and the ideas of the Enlightenment. He wrote extensively in the newspaper *Hurriyet*, which was the organ of the Young Ottomans and which aproached problems from the Islamic point of view. Unlike the Young Turks who came after him, he was not interested in the Turks as Turks or in the pre-Islamic Turks of Central Asia. Unlike the Tanzimat bureaucrats who preceded him, he talked about the importance of the Shari'a and the observance of the basic principles of Islam. He was an Ottoman and is credited with having used the words "fatherland," and millet, "nation," in their modern sense. Soon the former was used throughout the Middle East and the latter mostly among the non-Arabic-speaking peoples.

The Islamic leanings of the Young Ottomans attracted some of the ulama to their groups, but their number was insignificant. On the whole, the Young Ottomans were suspect in the eyes of Sultan Abdul Hamid II. Their headquarters were raided by the police. Nevertheless Young Ottomans such as Namik Kemal, the liberal statesman Midhat, the journalist Zia, and others, were influential in bringing Abdul Hamid II to the throne in 1876. The wily sultan, in order to rid himself of the Conference of European Powers gathered in Istanbul to review the future of the Balkans, ratified the constitution that was drawn up by the Young Ottomans on December 3, 1876. He appointed Midhat Pasha as prime minister and promised to appoint Namik as his personal secretary. Almost as soon as the Conference of European Powers adjourned thinking that they had a liberal sultan in Abdul Hamid, the sultan shelved the constitution and exiled Midhat and Namik Kemal. Soon he suspended the assembly, and one by one the rest of the leaders were jailed or sent into exile. By 1878, the Young Ottoman movement had come to an end.

The Young Ottomans were perhaps the first ideologists of Islam in modern times who tried to take the "best" of the West and graft it onto Islam. They failed because their picture of the "purity" of the Medina caliphate was a figment of their imaginations. Furthermore, they distorted Islamic theories to make them fit the concept of democratic popular government. For example, the practices of allegiance and consultation were applied, respectively, to the modern concepts of "popular sovereignty" and "government by the people." In Islam the principle of paying allegiance to a newly elected caliph was a prerogative of only a few, and the idea of consul-

[2]See p. 90.

tation was to strengthen the government *for* the people and not *by* them. It goes without saying that in Islam, government is most certainly of God and not *of* the people. Hence the idea of a "government of the people, for the people, and by the people" does not fit Islamic teachings. The phrase must be changed to "the government of Allah, by His designated representatives, and for the people."

Even though the Young Ottomans failed to graft Western ideologies to the body politic of Islam, they were successful in introducing new values to the Turks. Time and time again, Ottoman writers, in imitation of the men before them, had counseled the sultans with advice that should be familiar to the reader by now. "No government without an army, no army without money, no money without subjects." Toward the last third of the nineteenth century, the Young Ottomans used the same format as above, but the content was different and replete with new values. They wrote, "No security without freedom, no endeavor without security, no prosperity without endeavor, no happiness without prosperity."

THE YOUNG TURKS

From 1878, when the sultan put aside the constitution, until 1908, when he was forced to reinstate it, Abdul Hamid II was the central figure on the Turkish scene. This man, who was destined to influence events in one of the most critical periods in Ottoman history, was full of contradictory characteristics. His character was shaped by his long reign, the radical changes that were occurring all around him, the pressure and intrigues of foreign governments, and his idiosyncracies. He started as a reformer who followed constitutional lines. When that failed he decided to carry out reforms by autocratic means. His opposition to Armenian nationalism and his espousal of pan-Islamism made him unpopular with European powers, who referred to him as "Abdul the Damned." To the Young Turks, who were the victims of his oppression, he was called "the hangman." He apparently did generate support among his Turkish and Arab subjects. It seems that he was consistent in two things. He was suspicious of everything and everyone. He had a whole army of spies scattered all over the empire, and others to watch the spies. He had agents in foreign capitals, not to gather diplomatic information, but to spy on his own subjects. His second consistent characteristic was in being autocratic. He was against all movements that in any way limited the power of the sultan. He had not learned from his father's reformist inclinations any more than his fellow monarch Alexander III of Russia had learned from his father.

The autocratic sultan with his network of spies was not able to prevent the new crop of Turkish patriots from meeting inside and outside of the country, or to stop the rising nationalistic aspirations of the non-Turkish elements within the empire. Among these, the Armenians and Kurds were more troublesome, mainly because they were located in eastern Asia Minor, in the heart of the empire. Of the two, the Armenians were more menacing because they were Christians and had friends among the

European powers. Indeed, there was an article about their protection in the Treaty of Berlin (1878). Like the other millets, the Armenians had their own social classifications. The more wealthy among them chose the patriarch of the Armenian church and had a vested interest in the preservation of the Ottoman system.

A number of the Armenians were influenced by nationalism and demanded an autonomous state of their own. From 1880 to 1890, they had their own secret nationalistic societies with different approaches to the common goal of independence. In 1890, some of the Armenian societies were federated into one nationalist movement known as Dashnaktzoutun. The Roman Catholic and American Protestant missionaries had gained converts among the Armenians, and they were probably the only millet in the Ottoman Empire who had advocates among the Greek Orthodox, Roman Catholic, and Protestant powers of the West. Abdul Hamid was afraid of them, and with good reason. He set the restless Kurds against the Armenians and their unchecked excesses resulted in the massacre of 1894. The Armenian leaders retaliated and seemed to needlessly expose their coreligionists in order to attract the attention of Europe. During three years, some 100,000 Armenians lost their lives and Europe did not intervene. On the contrary, in 1898 Kaiser Wilhelm paid his second visit to the Ottoman sultan. On his way to Palestine he laid a wreath at the tomb of Saladin and, in the garb of an Arab shaykh, promised to defend Islam. One can imagine that the picture was not so amusing to the kaiser's grandmother, Queen Victoria, who herself had over 100,000,000 Muslim subjects.

In the meantime, the ideological heirs of the Young Ottomans had banded together and were plotting the overthrow of the sultan. In 1889, a group of students in the medical college under the leadership of Ibrahim Edhem (Temo) formed a society that later became known as the Committee of Union and Progress, which was destined to grow and wield great influence. By 1892, the sultan's spies discovered the plot and the members fled into exile. One group went to Egypt, where one of their members, Murad Bey, published the newspaper called *Mizan*. Another group went to Paris, where one of them, Ahmad Reza, published another newspaper. Eventually these two papers represented two points of view. Murad Bey was closer to the ideas of the Young Ottomans. He was of pan-Islamist persuasion and felt that Islam was a liberal enough entity to unite all the Muslims under one roof. His solution was to remove the sultan, restore the constitution, make Islam the cornerstone of the empire, and bring the nationalities under the aegis of the Ottoman Empire. About this time, Abdul Hamid met the pan-Islamic agitator Afghani and became aware of the broader possibilities of pan-Islamism with himself as sultan-caliph. Whether Afghani, who was living in Istanbul at the time, was or was not responsible is uncertain, but Murad Bey and a number of his followers defected from the revolutionary ranks and made their peace with the sultan in 1897.

Ahmad Reza, however, had different ideas. Although he never rejected Islam, he was a disciple of Auguste Comte, and did not think in terms of pan-Islamism. The positivistic philosophy of Comte led him toward secularism and the espousal of Turkish rather than Ottoman nationalism. A number of his followers were freemasons and they established lodges in Turkey.[3]

The revolutionaries in Paris were aided by the escape of Damad Mahmud Pasha, the brother-in-law of the sultan, and his two sons Sabah al-Din and Lutfullah. The arrival of the royal fugitives in Paris in 1899 created quite a commotion in both Turkey and Europe. Damad Mahmud Pasha did not live to see the fruits of his labors, but his son Sabah al-Din, together with Ahmad Reza, called the first congress of Ottoman liberals in Paris in 1902. The forty-seven members present included Albanians, Arabs, Armenians, Circassians, Greeks, Jews, Kurds, and Turks. Sabah al-Din presided. The only point on which they all agreed was the deposing of the sultan. The national minorities wanted attachment to foreign powers, the non-Muslims did not care for the dynasty, and even the non-Turkish Muslims had become nationalistic. Sabah al-Din was for a federal union, while Ahmad Reza was for Turkish nationalism. It was the latter who won.

Perhaps because of Reza's influence, but independently of him, a group of graduates of the military school formed a society by the name of *vatan* in 1906. Among the members was a young officer named Mustafa Kemal who, after World War I, became Atatürk, the first president of modern Turkey. But at the time, leadership was in the hands of Talat Bey, Enver Bey, and Jemal Bey. They spread their revolutionary ideas through student groups, masonic lodges, and dervish orders. In 1907, the different societies that had been formed merged under the old name of Committee of Union and Progress. In 1908, they led a successful coup d'etat against the sultan. The people accepted the coup not only because of the misrule of Abdul Hamid, but also because they were afraid of what Russia and England might do. Their traditional enemy, Russia, had joined the Triple Entente in Europe and had divided Iran into spheres of influence with Great Britain in 1907. The Turks were afraid lest their turn come next.

The wily Abdul Hamid, however, was not ruffled by the coup. He welcomed it and reinstated the constitution of 1878. For a few weeks there was much rejoicing. Muslims, Christians, and Jews rejoiced together, Muslim ulama and Christian priests embraced, and Enver Bey proclaimed the equality of all. Perhaps the Young Turks would have been able to build a viable nation had they been given a chance, but they were not. In the same year, Austria-Hungary annexed Bosnia, and Ferdinand of Bulgaria proclaimed himself king. On April 13, 1909, the counterrevolution, which had been organized by Abdul Hamid, proclaimed the supremacy of the sultan and the Shari'a. The army, however, stood by the revolution and on April 27, Abdul Hamid was deposed in favor of his brother Mehmed V.

This was not all. Albania revolted in 1910, and Italy occupied Tripoli in 1911. Turkey fought against Italy and lost. In 1912, Bulgaria, Serbia, Montenegro, and Greece united against the Ottomans and started the First Balkan War. The defeat of the Ottomans in 1913 did not end the war, for the victors fought against each other. This involved the Ottomans once again in the Second Balkan War. Peace came late in 1913, and all that was left of the

---

[3]At about the same time, freemasonry was also introduced in Iran. See Chapter 21.

Ottoman Empire in Europe was a little under 11,000 square miles of territory. A year later World War I began, which involved the Ottomans once again and annihilated the empire.

And yet it is doubtful whether the Young Turks could have succeeded had they had peace. The parliament that convened after the abdication of Abdul Hamid was presided over by Ahmed Reza, who had been called from Paris to preside. The country was dominated by a triumvirate made up of Talat, Enver, and Jemal. Ottomanism of the older generation and federalism of Sabah al-Din had given way to the Turkish nationalism of Reza. The Young Turks wanted to unite the empire on the basis of the Turkish language and the ideal of pan-Turanianism, which connected the Turks with the Tatars of Central Asia and the great Chengiz Khan. They started the program of Turkification and established Turkish Ojak (hearth), where intellectuals and writers like Ziya Gökalp, Helide Edib, and others lectured on the history of Turan and the virtues of the Turks. This program, however, was oppressive to non-Turks and was doomed to failure. The non-Turkish elements, mainly Arabic-speaking, who as Muslims still had some sympathy with the empire, lost it altogether in the face of the pressure to give up their language in favor of Turkish. The great war of 1914–1918 ended the dream. Jemal Bey went to Afghanistan to become a military advisor, Talat Bey was assassinated by an Armenian in Germany, and Enver Pasha, a pan-Turanian to the end, was killed for the cause in Turkestan.

The development of the Turkish awakening, which had started in the Tanzimat, went through the successive steps of Ottomanism, pan-Islamism, and pan-Turanianism. It was left for Mustafa Kemal, the soldier-reformer, to reject them all and succeed with the simple Turkism of the Turks of Asia Minor.

Chapter Seventeen
Imperialism and the Arabic-Speaking Peoples

The expedition of Napoleon to Egypt in 1798 is usually regarded as an important landmark in the history of the European penetration into the Arabic-speaking world. It acted as a catalyst in arousing the interest of Europeans in the "hinterland" of the Ottoman Empire, and in opening the eyes of some Muslim leaders to the possibilities of Western civilization. Both France and Britain had some familiarity with the area. Ever since the time of the Crusades, France had been interested in the Levant, both for its flax and silk trade and also because of the Maronites, who were Roman Catholics and had French sympathies. In the intermittent struggles between the Maronite Christians and the Druzes, France always came to the aid of the Maronites. The British, who also had holdings in the Middle East and were rivals of France, took the side of the Druzes. In the seventeenth century, the British East India Company had penetrated the Persian Gulf and had established trade centers in Basra, Baghdad, Damascus, and Aleppo. In 1770, Warren Hastings, the governor of the British company in Bengal, sent an expedition to Suez. The purpose was to use it as a base for the shipment of goods overland to the Mediterranean. In 1778, the British were able to conclude a treaty with the Mamluk ruler of Egypt to secure the Red Sea shipping.

The rivalry between France and Britain in the Middle East, as well as in India, was heightened by the French Revolution and the rise of Napoleon. While the main scene of the struggle between France and England was in

Europe, it was part of Napoleon's grand scheme to harass Britain from all directions. Certainly the trade route to India was one of the most vulnerable. His expedition was based on fairly accurate knowledge of the social and political situation in Egypt, and he took with him scholars and scientists to learn more. In Egypt, Napoleon posed as the liberator of the masses from the tyranny of the Mamluks. He proclaimed himself a friend of Islam and of the Ottoman sultan. But Egypt belonged to the Ottomans, and the Porte did not like Napoleon's intrusion. The British were not slow to point this out, and the sultan sent an expedition which, with the help of the British, forced the French army to surrender in 1801.

THE RISE OF MUHAMMAD ALI

Napoleon failed in his attempt to harass the British or even to increase his own fame. He had returned to France long before his army surrendered. Everything probably would have gone back to normal had it not been for a by-product for which Napoleon was not responsible. It happened that in the expeditionary force sent by the sultan to Egypt was a young man, Muhammad Ali, who changed the history of Egypt. Napoleon's expedition revealed the might of Europe, but Muhammad Ali was one of the few who understood the source of that might and attempted to bring Egypt into the modern world by borrowing from the West.

Muhammad Ali was born in Albania in 1769 and was an important officer in 1799 when he went with the Albanian contingent to Egypt. After the defeat of the French army in 1801, it was Muhammad Ali who filled the vacuum. By 1805, he was appointed pasha of Egypt. From then on Muhammad Ali's star shone brighter with the passing of the years. Before long the British suspected that they had saved Egypt from France only to put it into the hands of Muhammad Ali. The French, on the other hand, felt that perhaps Muhammad Ali could accomplish what they had failed to do and gave him every assistance.

Muhammad Ali, however, did not become a puppet of the French. He was shrewd enough to see the supremacy of European arms, technical knowledge, and education. He asked the French to teach his followers. Bringing French naval and military experts to Egypt, he created a new army and navy with the latest weapons. Opening schools on the French model, he also had French books translated into Arabic. He brought in agricultural experts and by 1815 had monopolized trade in cotton, hemp, indigo, and sesame. And he built ships and harbors. By the time of his death in 1849, Muhammad Ali had overhauled the administration and revitalized the economy of Egypt. He created a hierarchy of officials who oversaw the collection of taxes, controlled irrigation, and maintained public order.

Muhammad Ali controlled all the land that had been confiscated from the Mamluks. Parts of this he gave to his family and friends. The rest was state property, which was leased to tenants. By 1858 these lands were registered in the name of the "owners" and came under the Islamic law of inheritance. This meant that the land remained in the hands of families, thus creating a class of landlords. He organized state monopolies for the export of cotton, tobacco, and other products. The government bought all products at low prices and sold them at great profit. In nearly forty years of his rule the cultivated area of Egypt rose from 3,200,000 acres to 4,150,000; revenue rose from £1,203,500 to £4,200,000; and exports from £200,000 to £2,000,000.

Muhammad Ali also built factories, but these generally failed because of a lack of trained technicians, fuel, and spare parts. The financial loss was staggering, but the iron determination of Muhammad Ali kept these factories going despite the loss. What spelled the doom of Muhammad Ali's industrial empire was the Anglo-Ottoman Commercial Treaty of 1838, which outlawed monopolies and trade controls and gave the British the right to buy directly from the people. This treaty was enforced in Egypt and thwarted Ali's plans to industrialize the country. It is doubtful whether the reforms of Muhammad Ali raised the standard of living or improved the health of the masses, but they were a remarkable beginning.

He obeyed the summons of the sultan to send an expedition to Arabia and quell the religio-political rebellion of the Wahhabis in 1818 (see Chapter 20). A few years later, in 1824, after the Greeks revolted for independence, the sultan again asked Muhammad Ali for help. Ibrahim, the son of Muhammad Ali, went with 10,000 troops and would have been successful had not European powers intervened and destroyed the Egyptian fleet at Navarino in 1827.

In 1831, Muhammad Ali decided that the time was ripe to execute his plan of grasping ultimate power by invading Syria. He claimed that the sultan had promised him the pashalik of Syria as a reward for going to the aid of the Porte in the Greek rebellion. Again he sent well-equipped troops under the command of his son, Ibrahim. The Egyptian troops overran Syria without much difficulty and by 1833 were in Asia Minor, where they defeated the Ottoman army at Konya. The Ottoman sultan, Mahmud II, was so alarmed that he asked the aid of Russia. The tsar, hoping for an opportunity to expand Russian influence, gladly accepted the invitation and sent troops to Istanbul. The French, who had been encouraging Muhammad Ali all along, became apprehensive and asked their protégé to make peace with the beleaguered sultan. Muhammad Ali decided to comply and in return was given the pashalik of Egypt, Syria, and Crete on an annual basis, in return for an annual tribute of £150,000. The Russians, however, before evacuating Istanbul, signed the Treaty of Hunkyar Iskelesi, which gave them the right to sent troops to Turkey whenever internal conditions warranted.

Thus Egypt and all the Fertile Crescent were drawn into the maze of European power politics. The British were unhappy when the Egyptians in Syria threatened their access to India. The French, who had aided Muhammad Ali, were alarmed at the turn of events and, like the British, feared the consequences of the Hunkyar Iskelesi treaty. The sultan could not bear defeat at the hands of his vassal and prepared for war. Muhammad Ali was thus thwarted in his attempt to destroy Mahmud II, whom he held in contempt. But for eight years Ibrahim ruled Syria with ability and enlightenment and broke down the economic isolation of the region. His enlightenment, however, was more self centered than people oriented. His heavy-handed policies and his imposition of a much-hated conscription upon the people united Muslims, Christians, Druzes, and Jews in rebellion against him.

With such universal dissatisfaction, conflict could not be prevented. The sultan's army, which had been trained by the Prussian colonel, Von Moltke, crossed over into Syria in 1839 and was soundly beaten by Ibrahim at Nazib. A few days after that battle, the sultan died, and his death was followed by the surrender of the Ottoman navy to Egypt in Alexandria. The new sultan was willing to accede to Muhammad Ali's demands, and once again the European powers were vigorously active. In the end Britain was able to persuade Russia, Prussia, and Austria to agree to a treaty in 1840, according to which Muhammad Ali would be given the hereditary pashalik of Egypt and lifetime control of south Syria. Muhammad Ali refused and British troops landed in Syria. With the aid of their friends, the Druzes, the British took Beirut and defeated Ibrahim. France suffered a diplomatic defeat. Muhammad Ali was defeated in his purpose and was content to accept the hereditary pashalik of Egypt. The Hunkyar Iskelesi treaty was replaced by the "Straits Convention" in 1841, which closed the Straits to the warships of all nations. Thus ended the first major attempt in the long history of the Ottoman Empire to unseat the house of Osman. The attempt failed, but it had far-reaching repercussions. It brought Egypt out of its miserable stupor; it opened Egypt and the Fertile Crescent to direct European imperialism; and, perhaps most important of all, it gave the Arabic-speaking world a taste of what European technology could do.

Muhammad Ali died in 1849. Like many other reformers who came after him in the Middle East, he had two major weaknesses. One was that he had to do everything himself because he did not think that others were capable. The second resulted from the first. Since he had to do everything himself, he was in a hurry lest death overtake him. Both resulted in wastage and the use of force.

Unfortunately for Egypt, the successors of Muhammad Ali were mostly incompetent and extravagant. His immediate successor, Abbas, was a religious fanatic who refused to receive the French advisers whom Muhammad Ali had brought. His short misrule of six years was of little consequence, and his murder in 1854 brought the glutton Sa'id to power.

SYRIA-LEBANON

Religious rivalries and wars have been part of the history of Syria-Lebanon for a long time. There were not only Muslims, Christians, and Druzes fighting against each other, but there was strife among the different sects within Islam and Christianity. When Ibrahim and his Egyptian troops entered the region, Lebanon was part of the pashalik of Syria, ruled by Bashir II (1788–1840). He was a scion of the house of Shihab, which had been in power since 1697. In the struggle among the three religions, the dynasty managed to belong to all three. They changed their religion whenever the situation demanded. Bashir II was baptized a Christian, but his mother was a Muslim. At the time of the Egyptian occupation, he happened to be a Druze. He cooperated with Ibrahim, even though a number of lesser shaykhs of different religious persuasions remained loyal to the sultan. With the encouragement of Ibrahim, Bashir opened Lebanon to the West. In addition to French businessmen and British ships, French and American missionaries came into the region.

With the defeat of Ibrahim, the rule of Bashir ended and he was exiled to Malta. European rivalry became dominant in the area. On the whole, the Maronite Christians sided with the French, the Orthodox with the Russians, the Druzes with the British, and the Muslims with the Ottoman sultan. Since neither the sultan nor the Russians had much power in the Fertile Crescent, the main protagonists were the French and the British acting through their protégés, the Maronites and the Druzes, respectively.

For a time the Porte sent governors to rule the area under the aegis of five European powers. When this scheme failed, the powers developed a dual control, the Maronites in the north and the Druzes in the south. Skirmishes between the two groups led to open warfare in 1860, when the Druzes massacred some 14,000 Maronites. The French sent an expedition to help the Maronites, but by the time the troops arrived the Ottomans had managed to pacify the area. The French, with the support of Russia, wanted to declare a protectorate over Lebanon. The British, with the support of the Porte, opposed the move. By June 1861, the European powers and the Porte were able to sign the "reglement organique" in Istanbul. According to this, Lebanon was declared autonomous under a Christian governor designated by the Porte. This arrangement lasted until World War I.

THE PERSIAN GULF

We have already seen that under the Safavids the Spaniards came to the Persian Gulf for trade. They were followed by the Portuguese, the Dutch, and finally the British. The rivalry between the British and the Dutch lasted until the middle of the eighteenth century, when the British were able to oust the Dutch from Hormoz with the help of the Persians and from Muscat with the help of the Arabs. The main interest of the British in the Persian Gulf was not only trade with Iran, but the defense of India and the opening of communications and a trade route via the Persian Gulf and the Red Sea.

The British East India Company established a residency in Bushehr, Iran, in 1763. By the beginning of the nineteenth century, almost all of their rivals had faded away. In 1827 they surveyed the possibilities of a Persian Gulf-Baghdad-Aleppo route but later abandoned it in favor of a Red Sea-Suez route. Goods would be brought from London by water to Alexandria and then by railroad to Cairo. This railroad, which was the first in the Middle East, was built during the rule of Abbas I, the successor of Muhammad Ali. The remaining eighty miles of desert from Cairo to Suez was traversed by caravan, which necessitated the building and provisioning of stations along the route.

The basic problems of the British in the Persian Gulf were piracy and the intermittent fighting among the Arab shaykhs along the southern shores of the Gulf. They solved the first by bringing in a naval patrol. To deal with the second, the British signed treaties with the different shaykhs all along the gulf. One of the articles in these treaties required that each shaykh be "frozen" in his locality. This minimized warfare and raiding. In another article the shaykhs promised not to allow representatives of any country to settle in their territories without permission of the British political resident. A third article dealt with the prevention of piracy. The British also tried to abolish slavery; but they were not very successful, as slavery was practiced in certain parts of the Arabian Peninsula until after World War II. In all cases the British "sealed" the agreements by providing the shaykhs with regular cash subsidies.

The British were always wary of the power of Muhammad Ali in Syria. So, in order to protect their interests, they established a residency in Baghdad. To protect the Red Sea route, they established protectorates in Bab al-Mandab and Aden in South Arabia. The Wahhabis, whom Ibrahim, the son of Muhammad Ali, had defeated, were not altogether vanquished. Their banner was taken up by a certain Muhammad ibn-Sa'ud, whose son, before becoming master of all Arabia, received a regular subsidy from the British. That account will be dealt with in a later chapter.

THE SUEZ CANAL

Sa'id, the successor of Abbas, had many European friends, among them the talented Ferdinand de Lesseps, son of the French political agent in Egypt. Almost immediately after the accession of Sa'id, de Lesseps came to Cairo and received a concession to dig the canal. While much of the world paid scant attention to the news, a small minority in France became very enthusiastic, while Britain was incensed and did everything in its power to stop it. The concession needed the approval of the Porte, who could ill afford to antagonize an ally such as Britain in the Crimean War, which was going on at the time. It was not that England did not appreciate the commercial possibilities of Egypt. Indeed, Egypt traded more with Britain than with any other country. In 1869, British trade accounted for 41 percent of Egypt's imports and 49 percent of Egypt's exports. England, however, was obsessed with the idea of protecting India. The canal, it was true, would shorten considerably the distance between London and Bombay; but by the same token it would also make it easier for other powers to threaten the British hold on India, and for rivals to compete with its trade in Egypt and in the Persian Gulf.

But de Lesseps was able to raise the necessary capital in France, the Netherlands, Spain, and Italy. By 1856 he formed the Compagnie Universelle du Canal Maritime de Suez. For giving the concession to the company for ninety-nine years from the date of completion, Sa'id received preferred shares that gave him 15 percent of the net profit. For the building of the canal he promised to provide four-fifths of the labor. Founders of the company and influential individuals who could be of assistance to the company received shares that returned 10 percent of the profit. There were also 400,000 shares of common stock at 500 francs per share. The digging started in 1859 without the sultan's permission, though by 1863, the year of Sa'id's death, not much had been accomplished.

Sa'id's travels, public works, and high living had incurred a debt of some £3,000,000. This did not bother Sa'id's spendthrift successor, Isma'il, for these were prosperous times for Egypt. Because of the Civil War in the United States, Egyptian cotton was in great demand, and Isma'il's revenue from cotton rose to five times above normal. While the digging of the canal was going on, Isma'il gave vent to his craze for building. He erected public buildings, installed gas and water mains, extended railroads, and built expensive factories that could not be used. He almost doubled the annual tribute to the Porte and in return received the title of khedive, with the law of succession established in his line.

When the Suez Canal was finished in 1869, Isma'il spent upwards of £1,000,000 for entertainment. The canal was 93.5 miles long, from 96 to 110 yards wide, and 35 feet deep. It began at Port Sa'id on the Mediterranean and continued to Suez on the Red Sea. Among the thousands of guests were Princess Eugénie of France, Emperor Joseph of Austria, and the crown prince of Prussia. In the opera house that Sa'id had built, Verdi's *Aïda,* based on ancient Egyptian history, was performed for the first time in 1871.

The cost of the canal to Egypt was 11,500,000 francs, not counting the tremendous cost in forced labor and human life. The company did not begin to show a profit until 1875. In 1873 an international conference set a schedule of tariffs for the passage of ships through the canal, and agreed that the canal would be open to ships of all countries. In 1888, the Constantinople Convention was drawn up and signed by Austria, France, Germany, Britain, Italy, Holland, Russia, Spain, and Turkey. It stated that the canal should "always be free and open in time of war as in time of peace, to every vessel of commerce or of war, without distinction of flag." Britain was to violate the above agreement during World War I by refusing free access to its enemies. The commercial operation of the company, however, remained intact and worked smoothly until the nationalization of the Suez Canal in 1956. It was the strategic position of the canal and the rivalry for its control and protection that was an important factor in placing Egypt under the influence of European powers.

EUROPEAN INTERVENTION AND BRITISH OCCUPATION

Isma'il had fallen into the habit of indiscriminate spending; so when the end of the Civil War in the United States brought cotton prices down, he borrowed large sums of money from unscrupulous bankers of Europe at onerous terms that included high discounts, generous commissions, and exorbitant interest rates. By 1875 the combined foreign and domestic debt reached nearly £100,000,000. The interest charges alone amounted to the burdensome total of £51,000,000 per year. The per capita public debt was £14, with an annual service charge of £1/15s/10d, which was perhaps the highest in the world. Undaunted, Isma'il raised the taxes of the fellahin to pay for his new schemes. When this source was exhausted, he sold all of his ordinary shares of canal stock to Britain for £4,000,000, thereby providing the formerly antagonistic England with an economic as well as a political interest in the canal.

This money was a paltry sum compared to the indebtedness of the khedive. His creditors were alarmed and pressed their demands. At the instigation of Bismarck, joined by England and France, the Porte was persuaded to dismiss Isma'il in favor of his mild-mannered son, Tawfiq. Isma'il's departure from Alexandria in his yacht foreshadowed the way his grandson, Faruq, was exiled from the same port in 1952. The European bankers followed the change of khedives by foreclosing the mortgage on Egypt and taking control. They acted through two controllers—hence Dual Control : a Frenchman, who was in charge of Egypt's expenditures; and an Englishman, who was to supervise the collection of taxes.

The Dual Controllers, who had become the actual rulers of Egypt, passed the Law of Liquidation in 1880. This law fixed the debt of the country at £98,377,000 and 4 percent interest. Out of the annual income of the government a certain sum was set aside for the needs of the budget; all the rest was designated for the liquidation of debt. There was nothing left for development. No matter how hard the people worked, their income, beyond subsistence or less, went to pay the debt.

THE FIRST EGYPTIAN REVOLT

The reduction of expenditures meant that a large number of employees, including army officers, were dismissed or retired. But at the same time the foreigners were drawing handsome salaries, and the financial retrenchment did not involve the high army and administrative officers, who were either Turks or Circassians. Heavy taxes, the incompetence of government officials, the presence of foreigners who seemed to be allied with Turks—all aroused animosity among the Egyptians. For the first time in centuries, the junior officers of the army, who were all Egyptians, arose in protest. Their leader, Colonel 'Urabi, a former student of Azhar University and a son of a fellah, headed the resistance movement. The resistance was neither well organized nor well thought out beyond vague ideas concerning a constitution. In its ranks were only some educated Egyptians, theologians, civil servants, and junior army officers. Tawfiq accepted the demands of the officers against the advice of the Dual Control. Due to the deep anger of the people, demonstrations broke out in Alexandria and some Europeans and Egyptians were killed.

The powers used this as a pretext to intervene. The Porte remained neutral. This was the opportunity Britain had been waiting for. Its great rival, France, due to a change of government and also out of fear of German designs in North Africa, withdrew as a neutral, hoping perhaps that Britain would do the same, and that they would try to come to terms with 'Urabi.

This left Britain in the role of sole deliverer of Europeans of all nationalities in Egypt who felt themselves in danger. It also made Britain the undisputed ruler of Egypt.

In any case, on July 11, 1882, the British bombarded Alexandria. In September of the same year, in the battle of Tel al-Kabir, north of Cairo, the British contingent defeated 'Urabi's forces and became masters of Egypt. 'Urabi was banished to Ceylon. The revolt failed but, nevertheless, a genuine, even though disorganized, movement had been started—a movement that gained momentum until 1952, when another group of junior army officers under another colonel, Gamal Abd al-Nasser, forced out the last of the non-Egyptian rulers and took full control.

In sending troops to Egypt the British had promised to withdraw "as soon as the state of the country and the organization of proper means for the maintenance of khedival authority will permit it." The fact that the British troops stayed on Egyptian soil until 1956 may be defended on, perhaps, admissible grounds. In the mind of the Egyptians, however, as well as most of the Asians, it was another neat trick in the imperialist trade.

EGYPT UNDER THE BRITISH

The direct and indirect British rule, which lasted until 1936 (according to some Egyptian historians, until 1952), was a mixed blessing. The Egyptians were under both the Ottomans and the British, but the Ottomans themselves were under the British. In this double-decker imperialism, the British were certainly more efficient than the Ottomans. They were anxious to create a viable Egypt for the safety of the route to India, for purposes of trade and, incidentally, for good public relations as well.

The pretense of the Dual Control was abandoned. As the sole power responsible for Egypt, the British sent the very able and astute Lord Cromer, the former Major Evelyn Baring, as proconsul. Nominally the Ottoman sultan was the ruler and his representative was the khedive, but the actual power was in the hands of Lord Cromer. He ruled through a "legislative" assembly of thirty members—sixteen elected and fourteen appointed—which was, in reality, consultative. For each Egyptian minister there was a British adviser and for each governor a British inspector.

Cromer abolished forced labor, revised taxation in favor of the fellahin, cut down the national debt, and improved irrigation, sanitation, and other services. These reforms were capable of being carried out by administrative action, and Cromer made them in an orderly and efficient manner. He did not concern himself, however, with reforms that would have to be carried out through social revolution, such as land tenure, waqf, education, and the like. Under Cromer, Egypt became economically solvent and maintained a balanced budget. Per capita income rose and with it the standard of living. Furthermore, peace and order advanced Egyptian agriculture and foreign trade. At the turn of the century, cotton prices rose and the terms of trade were in Egypt's favor. On the other hand, the British relied on a one-crop agricultural policy and ignored the problem of population growth.

While they encouraged mining, they were consciously against industrialization. By 1916, the total number of industrial laborers in Egypt did not exceed 35,000.

The positive and negative aspects of the proximity of Egypt with Europe could not help but create collaborationists as well as antagonists, evolutionists in social change, as well as revolutionists. It may be safely stated that any manifestation of the spirit of nationalism was frowned upon by the increasingly imperious Lord Cromer. His successors, Sir Eldon Gorst in 1907 and Lord Kitchener in 1911, were more or less of the same opinion, but these men were less efficient. Lord Cromer kept the number of British officials to a minimum, but under Gorst and Kitchener they increased in number and decreased in quality. Great Britain could not afford to relax control. Not only the safety of India was at stake, but also the Suez Canal and heavy economic investments. So the history of Egypt during the first half of the twentieth century is the story of the growing desire of the Egyptians for change versus the reluctance of the British to offer the opportunity.

Chapter Eighteen
Religious and Political Movements in Islam

The history of the Middle East in the nineteenth and twentieth centuries is the story of the reaction of the people in the area to the political, economic, social, and cultural pressures of the West. This reaction, both hostile and friendly, has manifested itself mostly in Islamic terms. Like any other religion, Islam has many faces and many spokesmen. Each believes itself to be the "true Islam." In the name of Islam, Western civilization has been rejected by some and accepted by others. Between the two extremes have been those who have advocated a restatement of Islamic principles in the light of modern conditions, and those who have accepted Western values and have tried to integrate them with Islamic beliefs. The tidal waves generated by the onslaught of Western civilization have not settled as yet, and it is difficult to determine what the final result will be.

Interestingly enough the first reaction occurred in India in the seventeenth century. Here the Muslims, a minority among the majority Hindus, had been challenged by Portuguese religious and commercial interests. A new order of Sufis by the name of Naqshbandi started a religious revival that brought new life to Indian Muslims. The disciples and missionaries of this order carried the message to the Middle East and established centers in Palestine, Damascus, and Baghdad.

Purely religious revivals, however, especially when they are tinged with a Sufi emphasis on the inner life, are generally not given a cordial reception by orthodox Islam. The Koran stresses religious observance and performance of social duties rather than the quality of the inner life. Instead of individual devotion, Islam relies more on political organization and law to uphold the faith. Consequently, the reaction of Islam to the West has been, in the main, both political and militant.

WAHHABISM

An indigenous movement that arose from the soil of the Arabian Peninsula was started by Muhammad ibn-Abd al-Wahhab (d. 1792). This movement in both its purpose and method was so similar to the movement started by Muhammad in the seventh century that some have called it "the second coming of Islam." It is difficult to understand Islam's reaction to the West without considering the Wahhabi movement.

Muhammad ibn-Abd al-Wahhab traveled in different parts of the Ottoman Empire and observed a tottering and sick society. Some years later, an Ottoman intellectual named Zia Pasha also traveled in Europe and the Ottoman Empire. He wrote, "I roamed in the lands of the infidels and have beheld their cities and mansions. I also traveled in the realm of Islam and all I saw was ruins." While later Muslims were to compare the world of Islam with Europe and find the former wanting, ibn-Abd al-Wahhab, on the other hand, compared the world of Islam with what it should have been according to the Koran and found it wanting. He did not go to Europe because he was sure the infidels had nothing to teach Islam. Instead, he went back to the Koran and the time of the Prophet and denounced every influence, religious, social, and intellectual, that did not have its justification in the Koran. These influences, according to ibn-Abd al-Wahhab, included the Sufi belief in the immanence of God, the rationalism of the intellectuals, and the practices of the common people in visiting the tombs of saints and asking the intercession of the Prophet and the Imams. He was a strict Muslim in that he thought that innovations such as belief in the power of saints, shrines, tombs, rosaries, trees, and jinns were against Islam. He was an Arab in that he preached that Islam had been polluted by non-Arabs, especially Persians and Turks. He was also the first to challenge the legitimacy of the sultan-caliph.

His followers called themselves *Muwahhidin* ("unitarians") in contrast to the rest of the Muslims, whom they called "polytheists." They idealized the times of the Prophet and his early companions and advocated the strict observance of the laws of the Koran and the Sunna of the Prophet according to the Hanbali School of Law. Quite in keeping with the tradition of early Islam, they took to the sword and went about converting the polytheists. In 1765, a tribal chieftain by the name of Muhammad ibn-Sa'ud accepted this message and dedicated his sword to the new cause. By 1773, the city of Riyad was captured; and by the beginning of the nineteenth century, the Wahhabis, as others called them, took Mecca and Medina in the west and were threatening Karbala and Najaf in the north. To them the Arabs had fallen into a second period of ignorance (*jahiliyya*), and they were set to revive Islam in its purity and save the Arabs.

The sultan-caliph could not let the challenge go unnoticed, but at the same time did not have the power to quell such a rebellion in a remote corner of the empire. Consequently he appealed to Muhammad Ali of Egypt, who responded to the call in 1811. In a series of campaigns that lasted several years, Ibrahim, the son of Muhmmad Ali, had subdued the Wahhabis by 1818 and recaptured Mecca and Medina. The Wahhabis fought against the representatives of the sultan throughout the nineteenth century until 1891, when Muhammad ibn-Rashid took Riyad and drove ibn-Sa'ud's family into exile in Kuwait. It was from here on January 16, 1902, that twenty-year-old Abd al-Aziz ibn-Sa'ud, the shaykh of the Wahhabis, stole into the Rashidi palace in Riyad, killed the governor, and from there went on to eventually become master of all Arabia.

Even though Wahhabism did not take hold outside the Arabian Peninsula, its religious revivalism influenced other regions and its basically Arab nature contributed to the pan-Arabism of the middle twentieth century. By the end of the eighteenth century, we witness similar movements in Yaman and North Africa that disputed the use of analogy in the interpretation of the Koran and held the Koran and the Sunna to be the only source of doctrine and law.

PAN-ISLAMISM

We have already mentioned that some of the Young Ottomans, such as Namik Kemal and others, thought in terms of a limited form of pan-Islamism within the Ottoman Empire. Abdul Hamid II encouraged the idea partly to gain the loyalty of the non-Turkish elements of his own realm and partly to neutralize the pressure from European powers, some of whom had large Muslim populations of their own. Since the Arabic-speaking peoples were the largest Muslim group in the Ottoman Empire and, because of their language, were best suited for the propagation of pan-Islamism, the sultan gathered a number of these around him.

One of the most important of the pan-Islamists invited by Abdul Hamid was Shaykh Abul-Huda of Aleppo, who gained a great deal of influence in the Ottoman court. He was against Wahhabism and believed that the institution of the caliphate was essential to Islam and the person of the caliph was the executor of God's decrees. The faithful should be "thankful if he [the caliph] does right, patient if he does wrong." Abul-Huda's pan-Islamism was limited to the Muslims of the empire, and his main purpose was to strengthen the claims of Abdul Hamid.

JAMAL AL-DIN AL-AFGHANI

Without doubt the most famous pan-Islamist of the nineteenth century, one whose horizons were not limited by the confines of the Ottoman Empire but included the whole ummah of Islam, was Jamal al-Din al-Afghani (1839–1897). His life was so tumultuous, his writings so flamboyant and incendiary, and his projects for the revival of the glory of Islam so varied and sometimes contradictory that it is difficult to appraise his character. He claimed to be from Afghanistan, though he was actually an Iranian. He paraded as a Sunni though he was a Shi'i. There are those who believe that he was the forerunner of the Iranian Constitutional Revolution, but it is evident that he was not a constitutionalist. All his life he looked for a strong Muslim ruler as whose prime minister he could revive and unify Islam. He wrote vituperatively against the British Empire and considered it to be the main enemy of Islam. Nevertheless, there are those who believe that he was a British agent.

Be this as it may, Afghani (or Asadabadi, as he is known in Iran) was an able, effective, and restless agitator. He was much more interested in philosophy than in theology and more interested in politics than in philosophy. In politics, he was an activist rather than a theoretician. Like most activists, he had a tendency to oversimplify his concepts and set right against wrong. Like the Wahhabis, he idealized the period of the first four caliphs and believed in transcendentalism. Unlike the Wahhabis, Afghani believed in the importance of reason in Islam. According to him the Koran contained hidden references to modern scientific discoveries such as the steam engine and electricity as well as to modern political and social institutions.[1] All man had to do was to apply his reason to truly understand the word of God. But more important, to Afghani Islam was power and only incidentally a faith.

A favorite phrase of his was "Islam needs a Martin Luther" and perhaps he believed that in himself Islam had found one. But the sword of the crusader was more to his liking than the pen of the reformer. To bring about the union of Islam, he wanted the shah of Iran to recognize the Ottoman sultan as caliph. In turn, the sultan should recognize the "independence" of Iran and cede the Shi'i holy cities of Karbala and Najaf to that country. Having done this, he wanted all Muslim countries to send their "political" leaders for a conference in Istanbul for the purpose of declaring jihad against the European powers.

Afghani in Iran

Pan-Islamism, with all its religious and political connotations, was unpopular in a Shi'i country like Iran and was unacceptable to the Iranian ulama, who wanted to keep their own brand of Islam isolated from the contaminating influences of the Sunnis. The pan-Islamist Afghani, however, being a forceful and charismatic person, had a small number of followers in the lay circle close to the shah of Iran. During his active adult life, Afghani went to Iran only two times. Both times he was the guest of an important merchant in Tehran, and most of his visitors were laymen and not the clergy. Both times he had an audience with Naser al-Din Shah.

Afghani's first visit to Iran occurred in 1886. His vituperous utterances so infuriated the shah and his courtiers that his host, Haji Amin al-Zarb, was asked to take him out of the country. The latter took Afghani with him to Russia. In 1889, during his third trip to Europe, the shah saw Afghani in

---

[1] In the middle of the twentieth century, the spiritual heirs of Afghani claimed that the Koran contained references to the radio, television, atomic energy, and space rockets.

Munich. Afghani claims that he was sent on a special mission to Russia and the shah asked him to return to Iran after that. According to Afghani's own account, he went to Petersburg in behalf of the notorious Amin al-Sultan, the prime minister, to assure the Russians that the recent concession for the Karun River navigation and bank given to Britain would be matched by corresponding concessions to Russia. The fact that Afghani would consent to go on such a mission, which was detrimental to Iran, perhaps reveals his opportunism as a political agitator. The fact that the shah, who had known Afghani, would invite him once again to visit Iran, perhaps reveals the confusion in the mind of the monarch.

The second visit was not much different from the first. Perhaps Afghani once again insisted on his plan for the union of Islam, with autonomy for Iran under the Ottoman caliph. This time the shah was so infuriated that Afghani, to save himself from expulsion, took sanctuary in the nearby shrine of Shah Abdul Azim. Shortly afterward he was forcibly expelled from Iran.

The year 1890, in which Afghani was expelled, was also the year in which the notorious tobacco concession was granted to a British company. Perhaps because most Iranians smoked, this concession aroused the hostility of the whole country without Afghani having to do anything. To the ulama, this concession was another breach in their isolationist wall. They had led sporadic riots against the concession, unassisted by Afghani. Only after Afghani was rebuffed by the shah did his hatred for the monarch become so complete that he made common cause with the ulama whom he had attacked until then. He wrote letters against the shah and the concession to the mujtahids in Samarra and Shiraz. Since one of the letters was addressed to Haji Mirza Mohammad Hasan-e Shirazi, who had issued the famous fatva against smoking, Afghani has been credited with having played an important role in the tobacco strike and in the awakening of the Persians that subsequently resulted in the revolution of 1906. The defeat of the concession showed that the Iranians could, with concerted action, control the activities of the king. As such it was an important step toward the establishment of a constitutional monarchy.

Afghani, however, went to Istanbul and continued his anti-shah activities. The pan-Islamic group in Iran was very small and was led by Shaykh Ahmad Ruhi, a poet from Kerman. His poetry denouncing Naser al-Din Shah and praising Abdul Hamid as the "Sultan of Islam," leaves no doubt about the plan of Afghani for the union of Islam and the position of Iran in such a union. Eventually one of Afghani's pan-Islamic disciples, Mirza Reza of Kerman, assassinated Naser al-Din Shah in 1896.

It was evident that Afghani, as an activist agitator, was willing to use any and all means to attain his purpose. He preached the unity of Islam, he argued for its supremacy over all other religions, and he endorsed the death of those who he thought stood in the way. For a time he actually tried to gain the cooperation of the British and later he sought the assistance of the Russians. Since his Shi'ism was a hindrance, he claimed to be from Afghanistan so that everyone would take it for granted that he was a Sunni (most Afghanis are of that persuasion). He went to Paris, London, and Petersburg in the hope of enlisting aid in the rejuvenation of Islam. In the Islamic world he searched for a strong political ruler, anyone strong enough to unite Islam. He went to the khedive of Egypt, the shah of Iran, and the sultan of Turkey. Each one used him for a while and then let him go. He was more attracted to Abdul Hamid than to anyone else. He went to Istanbul again; but since Afghani's ultimate loyalty was to Islam and not to the Osmanli Dynasty, the wily sultan kept him under honored house arrest, where he died of cancer in 1897.

"The ambiguities of his words thus left a peculiar legacy, in which Jamal ad-Din is claimed as a precursor by the widest variety of persons—all the way from leftists who cite with favor his anti-imperialism and his reported vague words advocating Muslim socialism, to groups like the Muslim Brethren who want primarily to preserve Muslim traditions from Western encroachments."[2]

MUHAMMAD ABDUH

Another pan-Islamist of great influence was Muhammad Abduh (1849–1905). He was a disciple of Afghani but more of a thinker, and he had greater influence. Unlike his itinerant teacher, Abduh was rooted in the life and culture of Egypt. Although he was drawn for a time into Afghani's political activities, his heart was not in them and he spent his fruitful years in education and reform. He agreed with his teacher that there was aggression against Islam but disagreed with him that the aggressive force was the Christian religion. He believed Islam was misunderstood mostly because of the conduct of the Muslims themselves. Abduh believed that Islam should respond to the challenge of the West not so much through a return to political power, but through reform within Islam. Consequently, Abduh founded the first benevolent social service society in the modern Muslim world and spent his energies in educational reform in Cairo at Azhar University, and in social and religious reforms in Islam. He rejected the purely political intrigues that Afghani was promoting in the capitals of the Muslim world and instead angered his former teacher by suggesting that he should persuade the rulers to inaugurate educational reforms.

He also followed the Wahhabis in idealizing the "purity" of Islam in the first century, but unlike them accepted modern science, new methods of education, and even modern patterns of philosophy in expounding Islam. He was opposed to *taqlid*, imitation of past writers, and believed that the door of *ijtihad*, interpretation of the Koran, was not closed. This last was a heretical belief in Sunni Islam. But neither was he for imitations of European educational aims. He felt that Muslims must borrow European methods and go through the same sacrifices as the Europeans had in the evaluation of their aims. He held Islam to be a universal religion; and his important commentary on the Koran is tolerant, moral, and pragmatic. It is inclined toward both a voluntarist and an activist ethic.

[2]Nikki R. Keddie, *Sayyid Jamal ad-Din "al-Afghani"* (Berkeley, CA: University of California Press, 1972), p. 422.

Most of his life he had to defend himself against attacks from orthodox Muslims who were devoted to the tradition passed down to them. "What sort of a shaykh is this," they complained, "who speaks French, travels about in Europe, translates Western books, quotes from Western philosophers, holds discussions with their scholars, issues fatwas on things that not one of the ancients would have known about, takes part in benevolent organizations and collects money for the poor and the unfortunate? If he is a doctor of religion, let him spend his life between his home and the mosque. If he belongs to the secular world, we are of the opinion that he is more active in that sphere than all the rest of the Muslims."

Abduh was an Egyptian and took part in the nationalist 'Urabi rebellion against the khedive and the foreign powers. He was proud of the glories of ancient Egypt and as such his ideas may be a slight modification of the supranationalism of the Muslim ummah. He considered the unity of Muslims in one country as a strong link in the chain of the unity of all Muslims. This was orthodox pan-Islamism, but the modification introduced by Abduh was that when both Muslims and non-Muslims belonged to the same nation there should be unity between them regardless of differences in religion. On the other hand, he was critical of doctrinaire nationalistic thinking.

For Abduh, as for countless Muslim thinkers after him, there was always a tension between the demands of Islam that men should live according to the dictates of God, and the irresistible demands of modern civilization, which forced them to live in a different way. He maintained that the two were not incompatible. Whenever they did differ, he believed that the moral and doctrinal imperatives of Islam could not be compromised. Nevertheless, the tension was ever-present; and in time he was rejected both by the orthodox because he had gone too far, and by the modernists because he had not gone far enough.

SALAFIYYAH

One of Abduh's followers who exerted a great influence in all parts of the Muslim world was Rashid Rida of Syria (1865–1935). This restless soul joined the Sufi order of Mowlawis in search of the inner light. After his disappointment with that, he joined Afghani and Abduh. He founded the periodical *Al-Minar,* which enjoyed a wide circulation until his death in 1935. Like his mentors he believed that a properly understood and obeyed Islam leads to progress and prosperity. Inasmuch as the Koran had created a great civilization in the past, it could do so again, provided there was adequate leadership.

Gradually he separated himself from Abduh and joined the Hanbali school and sided with the Wahhabis, but he did not go all the way with them either. Somewhere along the line he founded a new religious and political party called Salafiyyah, which indicated a return to the ancestral forms of Islam. The Salafiyyahs were modernists in that they rejected the authority of the medieval schools and fundamentalists in that they rejected Western liberalism.

Rashid Rida believed that the ulama should prepare a new set of laws, based on the Koran, that would fit the new conditions. He introduced the doctrine that "necessity" makes certain practices valid even though they do not conform strictly with the Koran. For example, a caliph of Islam should not only be a member of the Quaraysh tribe but should know Arabic. The Ottoman sultans did not fulfill either requirement, but he recognized them as caliphs because prevailing conditions made it necessary. It was the same in the case of usury. Islam forbids the charging of interest; but being under the pressure of Western capitalism, it became necessary for Muslims to build their economic life on the same basis as the West. He had similar ideas regarding the law of apostasy, jihad, women, and other matters.

THE MAHDIYYAH MOVEMENT

Three other religious movements, one in the Sudan, one in India, and a third in Iran had opposing ideologies, and each had its influence on the Muslims of the Middle East.

The Mahdiyyah movement in the Sudan was a fundamentalist Islamic revival that had a threefold purpose: (1) to drive out the foreign rulers (Turkish, Egyptian, and British); (2) to restore the Islamic form of government as practiced by the Prophet; and (3) to export the revolution with the purpose of purifying the whole Islamic world. The idea of a *Mahdi,* or deliverer (Messiah), has its roots in the tradition of Islam as well as other monotheistic religions. The idea is more prevalent among the Shi'is, but the Sunnis also have a somewhat similar tradition. According to Ibn Khaldun, the eminent Muslim historian, the Mahdi will appear at the end of the age. He will be of the lineage of the Prophet, will establish justice, and will restore the unity of Islam. The appearance of the Mahdi is connected with eschatological events in which Jesus will come, kill the antichrist, and participate in public prayer in which the Mahdi is the Imam.

The person who claimed to be the Mahdi was born in 1844 and was given the name Muhammad Ahmad. He was a descendant of the Prophet. He joined a Sufi order and gained a reputation as an ascetic. He became one of the leaders of the order, but he left it because he thought the order's tolerance of music and dancing to be against the laws of the Prophet. In his travels he saw the misery of the people, the oppression of the Turks, the misrule of the Egyptians, and the acquiescence of the ulama with these conditions. There were also merchants who had lost business because of the ban on the slave trade, and cattle nomads who did not want to pay taxes to colonial authorities. In 1844 he proclaimed that he was the Mahdi who had been commanded by the Prophet to rid the Sudan of infidels and establish true Islam. He invited the people to revolt, and Sudanese from all walks of life joined him. After a series of victories over the Egyptians and the British, Muslim delegations from Arabia, India, Tunis, and Morocco came to visit him. Following his victory over the British general Charles Gordon, the Mahdi entered Khartoum. He was considered to be the apostle of the Prophet who had commanded a jihad, and his followers considered themselves to be soldiers of God.

Although he died five months after the capture of Khartoum, he had succeeded in bringing most of the Sudan under his sway. His successors, however, were not able to establish an Islamic state, nor were they able to export the revolution to Egypt let alone other parts of the Islamic world. The main reason for this was that they were not united. The cultivators and merchants who were settled along the Nile could not get along with the nomadic warriors of the desert. Even though one of the nomads, Abd Al-lahi, was chosen to succeed the Mahdi, the two factions never ceased to undermine each other's efforts. Furthermore, they were ignorant of the conditions of the outside world and too rigid in their ideology to be able to compromise. Also in the nineteenth century, it was impossible for them to maintain their independence in the face of rival European powers that were active in the area.

Their expedition to Egypt, where they expected the public to rise up in support of their cause, failed in 1889. The last engagement between the Mahdiyyah and the British took place in 1899, when the successor of the Mahdi was killed and the movement came to an end.

The Aligarh Movement

At practically the opposite end of the Islamic world and with an opposite point of view from the Mahdiyyah movement, was the Aligarh movement in India. It was started by Sir Sayyid Ahmad Khan (1817–1898), who agreed with Abduh that Islam and science were not incompatible and stated further that any idea that was in conflict with the laws of nature and science could not be regarded as authentic Islam. He founded Aligarh University in 1875 to promulgate his ideas. The ulama were naturally against him and so was Afghani, who attacked his ideas as pure materialism.

One of his followers who gained a great deal of popularity was Sayyid Amir Ali, a Shi'i intellectual. In 1891, he published his book, *The Spirit of Islam,* in which he presented Muslim doctrine in terms of Western thought. A large number of intellectuals were attracted to him. He presented Islam as a progressive force, in contrast to the backwardness of medieval Europe, and emphasized the debt that the West owed Islam. He commends some of the social teachings of Islam such as prayer and almsgiving and admits the weaknesses of others such as slavery, polygamy, and divorce for which he blames the ulama for their wrong interpretation. He even went so far as to say that the Koran was written by Muhammad, an idea that was rejected by the majority of modernists who considered the Koran to be the literal word of God.

Babi-Bahaism

Even a very brief survey of the Islamic religious movements of the eighteenth and nineteenth centuries is not complete without a description of the Babi-Bahai movement that occurred within Shi'ism. It was not a reform movement but a bringer of a new revelation.

Babi-Bahaism was an offshoot of the Shaykhi sect within the twelve Imamate Shi'a. According to this school, the twelfth Imam, who is hidden and shall someday appear, keeps in touch with believers through one person, who is called the *Bab*, or "gate." In 1844, the leader of the Shaykhi group, Mirza Ali Mohammad (1821–1850) of Shiraz in south Iran, claimed to be the Bab. Later he said that he was the "Point of Revelation" and the Hidden Imam himself. It is not certain that he really did claim to be the Hidden Imam, because in his book *Bayan*, the Bab uses mystic terms, calling himself a mirror, and speaks of "Him whom God shall manifest." It seems certain that he thought he was inaugurating a new age and a new kingdom with a new calendar, in which the numbers 9 and 19 had mystical qualities.

The fact that these claims gained a ready following in all parts of the country is perhaps indicative of the opposition of the people toward the power of the ulama and toward conditions in general. Typical of most Islamic movements, the Babis, as they were called, took up arms and set out to establish the new kingdom. Soon Kerman and Yazd in south Iran became Babi centers. The shah forbade it, and the ulama preached against it, but the movement grew. Fighting broke out in many parts of the country and the Babis of Zanjan resisted a siege for a year.

The Bab himself was arrested and eventually executed in Tabriz by a government firing squad. Soon after, two of his followers made an attempt on the life of the Iranian monarch, Naser al-Din Shah. In retaliation, there were mass arrests and severe persecutions. The courage, fortitude, and selflessness that the Babis exhibited as they went to their deaths reciting poetry was by far more effective in spreading the faith than the teachings of its leaders.

Among the leaders of the Babis after the Bab's execution were two half-brothers from Mazandaran in north Iran. One of them, Yahya, was designated by the Bab as the leader of the group and was given the title *Sobh-e Azal*, the "Morning of Eternity." The other, Hoseyn Ali, was given the title *Bahaullah*, the "Splendor of God." Both brothers and a number of Babis were exiled to the Ottoman Empire. In 1866, Bahaullah claimed that he was "Him whom God shall manifest," as foretold by the Bab. Yahya did not submit to his authority, and the ensuing conflict between the two groups caused the Ottoman government to separate the two brothers. Sobh-e Azal was sent to Cyprus and Bahaullah to Acre in Palestine.

Bahaullah, however, won the struggle and Babism was replaced by Bahaism. The further dissension among the Bahais after the death of Bahaullah in 1892 and the eventual growth of the "Bahai World Faith," with centers in many parts of the world, is not part of this story.[3] Whether Babism could have become a national religio-political movement in Iran is not certain. Bahaism, however, under Bahaullah and especially his son Abdul Baha, became too devoted to internationalism to be in sympathy with the constitutional movement in Iran or to be attractive to the Iranian nationalistic revolutionaries. The Shi'i religious leaders who were opposed to Bahaism and westernization identified the two with each other. They denounced Bahaism because it was preaching new doctrine, and they rejected every-

---

[3] The center of the faith in the United States is in Wilmette, Illinois, where their nine-sided temple is a well-known landmark.

thing new from attire to ideas by charging that they were "Bahai." Even though the Bahais were not particularly interested in westernization, they were accused of it, and all modern concepts were attributed to them. There is no doubt that the Iranian Bahais were more receptive to new ideas, even though they were not the originators of them. By the end of World War I, however, Bahaism lost its "new look" and ceased to be a modernizing influence. It is difficult to estimate the number of Bahais in Iran, as they were being persecuted as late as 1954 and even more so in the Islamic Republic of Iran.

Chapter Nineteen
The Arab Awakening

In the discussion of the various Islamic movements in the previous chapter, two trends become apparent. One is the difficulty of discussing a purely religious movement in Islam without getting involved in politics. Of course, every religious movement has social and political implications, but in Islam there is always a tendency of political involvement. This is to be expected because Islam does not separate religion from government. Almost all Muslim religious reformers have encouraged their followers to return to the Islam of the days of the first four caliphs. In this call, they mean not only a return to theological and moral purity, but perhaps even more, a reestablishment of the political dominance of early Islam.

The second trend is the presence of Arabism in Islam, which modern Arab nationalists call *urubah*. Islam was born in Arabia, the Prophet was an Arab, and the Koran was revealed in Arabic. Consequently, despite the genuine universality of Islam, there is an abiding link between it and Arabism. Certainly Umar, the second caliph, considered the Arabs to be above all other Muslims, who were considered to be only "clients." The Umayyads intensified this sense of Arab superiority and imposed the Arabic language on all who became Muslims. As the political power of the Arabs waned, Arabism as a political phenomenon disappeared; but Arabism, insofar as it was connected with the language, remained. Strict Muslims have generally believed in the proposition that "whoever loves the Prophet loves the Arabs, and whoever loves the Arabs loves the Arabic language in which the best of the books was revealed." It is a common saying among the Muslims everywhere that "Arabic is the language of the angels."

This is not only the sentiment of Arabs but also of non-Arab Muslims. When Pakistan was carved out of British India because of the Islamic majority of its population, a number of the ulama in that country suggested that Arabic become the official language of the realm. In the Islamic Republic of Iran, one of the first moves was to make the study of Arabic compulsory from first grade through college.

THE BEGINNINGS OF ARAB NATIONALISM

The original concept of Arabism developed, in the twentieth century, into the idea that anyone who spoke Arabic was an Arab and a member of the "Arab Nation," which had a right to be united and independent. After the downfall of the Abbasid caliphate, Muslim jurists questioned the legitimacy of Muslim rulers who did not belong to the tribe of the Prophet. Some sort of explanation was necessary, and one of the last theories was offered by ibn-Taymiyya who stated that anyone who could command sufficient power to rule was legitimate, provided he followed the Shari'a. The Ottoman sultans gradually assumed the title of "caliph" on the ground that they were upholding the holy law.

In the eighteenth century when the Turks had drunk of the cup of nationalism and democracy, Young Ottomans like Namik Kemal based their ideas almost entirely on the Koran and the creation of an Ottoman nation. While this movement did not attract the non-Muslims of the empire, it was not unattractive to non-Turkish Muslims. Arabs, who formed the bulk of the non-Turkish Muslims of the empire, found themselves between a rock and a hard place. On the one hand, they had to admit that the Ottoman sultans had protected Islam and had expanded its territory. On the other hand, they failed to see how a Turk could be the successor to the Prophet, who was a Quraysh Arab. Consequently, their espousal of pan-Islamism with Sultan Abdul Hamid as caliph was at best equivocal or, according to Rashid Rida, an acceptance rooted in "necessity."

The advent of the Young Turks and their acceptance of all Ottoman subjects without regard to religion did not attract the Arabs either, because the Young Turks advocated a strong Turkish nationalism. By that time the Arabs, as well as the Armenians, Greeks, and others, had become nationalistic themselves and did not want to join Turkish nationalists. The first Arabic-speaking peoples who espoused Arab nationalism and revived the Arabic language as a tool of modern political thought were Christians of the Fertile Crescent. In this they were encouraged by the American Protestant missionaries.

Most of the Christians of Syria-Lebanon, unlike their Muslim neighbors, felt no loyalty toward the Ottoman Empire. To gain Muslim support for his program of pan-Islamism, Abdul Hamid completed the building of the Hijaz railroad to make pilgrimage easier, repaired the buildings of the holy cities, appointed Arabs to high office, and chose Arab soldiers for his bodyguards. The Christians, however, were left out of such generous considerations. Precisely because of their lack of loyalty, the Christians were more receptive to Western ideas and institutions. There were generally two groups of Christians: one that depended upon Europe for its welfare; and another that was nationalistic and wanted to be free of Europe and Istanbul. The religious interest of the French Catholics in the Maronites of Lebanon and the missionary zeal of American Protestants brought the benefits of Western civilization. In religious matters, neither mission proved very successful, but their cultural, social, and indirect political influence was of utmost importance.

There was an unspoken rivalry between the Catholic and the Protestant missions. Both opened schools and hospitals, both established printing presses, and both founded universities with faculties in medicine, engineering, and other branches of knowledge. The French influence was more limited in that the Roman Catholics were most interested in educating and strengthening the Maronite Christians. Furthermore, being interested in the propagation of French culture, they stressed French language and literature. The American Protestants, on the other hand, used the vernacular to preach the Christian Gospel to Arabic-speaking peoples. In 1834, they established the first Arabic press in Beirut and set about, as all pioneering Protestant missionaries have done, translating the Bible into Arabic. Cornelius Van Dyke, who became a great Arabic scholar, was in charge of the project and was assisted by two Lebanese, Butrus al-Bustani (1819–1883) and Nasif al-Yaziji (1800–1871). Yaziji wrote on Arab history and literature and exalted classical Arabic in his poetry. It was he who, in 1868, perhaps for the first time, announced that they should work for freedom from the Ottoman yoke. Butrus became a school teacher and a very productive writer. In 1870, he founded the first Arabic periodical, *Al-Jinan*, which for sixteen years presented modern themes to the Arabic-speaking world.

The students and alumni of the Syrian Protestant College, later called the American University of Beirut, founded in 1866, spearheaded a renaissance that not only rediscovered the versatility of the Arabic language but also introduced Western religious, social, scientific, and political thought. These pioneers started literary and scientific societies, and it was in these societies that the Arab national movement was launched.

Of the two most influential Arabic-language periodicals published in the last half of the nineteenth century, one was *Al-Muqtataf*, founded in 1876 by two graduates of the Syrian Protestant College, Ya'qub Saruf and Faris Nimri; the other was *Al-Hilal*, founded by Jurji Zaydan in 1892. The editors of both of these, as well as of other publications, later fled the heavy hands of Adbul Hamid's agents and went to the freer atmosphere of Cairo. These men and a host of others, among them Shibli Shumayyil (1850–1917) and Farah Antun (1874–1922), were in general agreement on certain points.

First and foremost was Western science. This was believed to have a universal value all its own and to hold the key to the secrets of the universe. It was the basis for the unity of all being. To express this unity they used *tawhid*, the same awesome word that in Islam denotes the oneness of God. Most of them were impressed by social Darwinism, and the idea of progress was as much a reality to them as it was to the writers of Europe whose works were being translated into Arabic.

Second, they believed in the unity of the nation and the equality of all its citizens, regardless of religious differences. For "nation" they sometimes used *watan* ("fatherland"), sometimes *qawm* ("people"), or sometimes *ummah*, the word used by pan-Islamists to denote the whole Muslim community. Those words were to be specifically defined in the twentieth century. But what mattered then was that Muslims, Christians, Jews, and Druzes were members of the same ummah, qawm, or watan.

Third, they believed that the new science embodied in itself new laws and new relationships. Complete subjugation to the laws of the past, be they the Shari'a of Islam or the canon law of Christianity, was regressive. Furthermore, it would divide the people and create inequality and strife.

Fourth, they believed in the separation of religious institutions, Muslim or Christian, from the temporal. Any mixture of the two would corrupt both, and putting religion at the basis of nationality would curb the freedom of thought and the liberty of the individual. Most of them, not all, were religious people and some of them, even though they were Christians, went so far as to say that Islam, as an historical expression of the Arabs, should be given an honored place.

By demanding the creation of a secular state, the Christians were asking not only for equal rights with the Muslims but also for an equal and active share in the social and political responsibilities of society. For the Muslims, on the other hand, acceptance of the same principle meant giving up the preferred position that they had enjoyed all along. For the pan-Islamist, even for a person as tolerant and moderate as Abduh, it was the denial of the supremacy of Islam over all religions.

But as more Muslims came into contact with the ideas and institutions of the West, and as they became disenchanted with the policies of the Ottoman sultan, they became more receptive to such ideas. The Young Turk revolution of 1908 and its Turkification program forced the Arabic-speaking Muslim youth to make common cause with the Christians. Some joined existing Christian organizations; others founded Muslim groups such as the al-Fatat, which demanded complete independence. Still others, who could not go quite that far, championed a dual monarchy, Arab and Turk, like that of Austria-Hungary. These societies grew in number and had their meetings in secret or in Cairo or in Europe. During World War I the British took advantage of this desire for independence for their own ends.

EGYPTIAN NATIONALISM

The Ottomans governed most of the Fertile Crescent as a unit, with the exception of Lebanon and parts of the Arabian Peninsula under separate governments. Egypt, as we have seen, was distinct both geographically and politically. The advent of Muhammad Ali and the subsequent history of Egypt widened the gap between the Egyptians and the peoples of the Fertile Crescent. Thus it was easier for the intellectual elite and the political activists of Egypt to think of themselves as a separate nation. The European contacts that the reforms of Muhammad Ali provided made it easier for them to adopt European nationalism. The cry "Egypt for the Egyptians" was raised in the Egypt of 1882, though there was no corresponding cry, "Syria for the Syrians" or "Iraq for the Iraqis."

On the other hand, Al-Azhar University in Cairo, as the largest center of Islamic studies, was very influential; and its teachers, like Afghani and Abduh, were proclaiming the demands of Islam. Furthermore, because of the fact that there was more freedom in Egypt than in the other parts of the Ottoman Empire, many writers from Syria and Lebanon moved to Cairo and published their papers and books there. Hence, Egypt became the center of all sorts of movements that were active in the Ottoman Empire. Pan-Islamists were there as well as pan-Arabs. There were the Muslim traditionalists as well as secularists. There were also Egyptians who thought of themselves as a "nation" and had nothing to do with the others, though they spoke Arabic or were Muslims or both. To make the picture even more confusing was the fact that in each of the three groups (i.e., pan-Islamists, pan-Arabs, and Egyptian nationalists), there were different degrees of relationships and loyalty to the Ottoman sultan.

One of the first individuals to apply the liberal thinking of the Young Ottomans to Egyptian nationalism was Rafi al-Tahtawi (1801–1873). He was an Azhar University graduate and was appointed imam (chaplain) of the Egyptian students whom Muhammad Ali had sent to France. He spent five years in that country, learned French, and read books on history, philosophy, and other subjects. He was attracted to eighteenth-century French writers such as Voltaire, Rousseau, and Montesquieu.

He returned to Egypt in 1831 and wrote on the ideas of the French Enlightenment. He believed that people should be educated to participate in government. The simple idea that laws which may have been useful at one time may not be useful at other times, was quite revolutionary when applied to the laws of the Koran. He taught that the causes of rise and fall of a state can be found in the spirit of the nation and that therefore love of country should be the basis of national life. He published his observations of life in France and translated many French books.

He still held his Islamic views, however, but believed that the ulama should interpret the Koran in the light of modern needs. To be able to do this, the ulama needed to understand Egyptian society and its needs. He believed that the education should teach love of country, the duties of citizenship, submission to law, and the knowledge of individual rights. To Tahtawi "love of country" was love of Egypt, and Egypt was the continuation of the civilization of the pharaohs.

The economic collapse of Egypt and subsequent supremacy of foreign creditors brought different elements together in the national party, *hizb al-wataniyya*, which resulted in the 'Urabi revolt. Even though Abduh was not happy with the principles underlying the revolt, he nevertheless joined it. They were banded together not as Ottomans or as Arabs or even as Muslims, but as Egyptians. A Muslim (Abdullah Nadim), a Christian (Adib Ishaq), and a Jew (Ya'qub Sanu) emphasized "national"—i.e. Egyptian—unity.

Later on, when the British won and established order, many joined the new civil service, while others, like Abduh, devoted their time to the development of education and other reforms. A new generation came into being that had not known the condition of Egypt before the arrival of the British. To them Britain was not the savior of Egypt from bankruptcy, but a foreign country imposing its rule. It is quite likely that the British attitude goaded these young men into action. The British, through Lord Cromer and others, stated that Egypt was not a nation and consequently the idea of a patriot, whether a Muslim or not, was not capable of realization. On the other hand it was possible, said Cromer, for the diverse elements in Egypt to be fused together into "one self-governing body." But such an ideal would take "years—possibly generations—to achieve...." It was, of course, implied that the British would remain for years—possibly generations—until it was achieved.

To the challenge that Egypt was not a nation, Mustafa Kamil (1874–1908) answered that it was. He was a controversial figure—to some a hero and to others an impostor. His premature death at the age of thirty-four has made him a hero in the eyes of his countrymen. He believed that Egypt was a nation, but part of a larger whole that was at once Ottoman, Muslim, and Eastern. For the time being, however, the last three had to wait until Egyptians had asserted their national identity. For a time he sought the aid of the French to oust the British and did not oppose the annexation of Algeria by the French. He and many other Egyptians denounced Arabism and especially disliked the Syrians. He believed that the basis for nationality was neither language nor religion nor tribal descent but land. Egypt would be a nation when the Egyptians could say "Egypt my country."

At the beginning of the twentieth century, there were three parties in Egypt. First was the People's (ummah) Party to which belonged Abduh and his friends, who, as pan-Islamists, were Muslims first, Egyptians second, and perhaps Ottomans or Arabs third. The second was the Constitutional Reform Party, founded by the friends of the khedive with the blessings of the British, for the safeguarding of the status quo. The third was the National Party, which was led by Kamil, for whom Egypt came first and Islam and Ottomanism took less significant positions. It was the spirit of the National Party that prevailed. Egyptianism was the driving force of Egyptian nationalism until the second half of the twentieth century.

Chapter Twenty
Imperialism and the Iranians

The Anglo-French struggle for supremacy in the Arabic-speaking world was repeated in Iran, but it was not anywhere as vigorous as the Anglo-Russian rivalry in that country. Because of its perennial excuse of needing warm-water ports, Russia was interested in the Caspian Sea and the Persian Gulf region. It is not definitely known whether Russia was seriously considering the annexation of India. If it had such a plan, it could have been accomplished either by way of the Persian Gulf or through Afghanistan. Consequently, the cornerstone of British imperial policy was to prevent Russia from taking Iran, which, in the early years of the nineteenth century, included Afghanistan. After the defeat of Napoleon, the political interest of France in Iran practically disappeared and the history of Western imperialism in Iran became the story of Anglo-Russian rivalry in that country.

Although the assassination of Nader Shah in 1747 ended the glory of the Safavid Empire, Iran was still a power to be reckoned with in western Asia during the short-lived Zand Dynasty (1753–1794), and was important enough to be wooed by European rivals. During the whole of the nineteenth century, when Europe was in the throes of industrial revolution, imperial expansion, ideological change, and intellectual advancement, Iran, like her neighbor the Ottoman Empire, was ruled by monarchs who were almost entirely oblivious of these developments. Practically every king in the Qajar Dynasty, which lasted from 1794 to 1925, was inept, unimaginative, superstitious, and selfish. Not only were they ignorant of the impact of developments in Europe, but they also neither acted nor lived according to the traditions of their own country. The result was that they were caught between the power of Russia in the north and the pressure of Britain in the south.

Agha Mohammad, a scion of the Turkish Qajar tribe from Mazandaran in northern Iran, was a cruel, shrewd, shrivelled-up young man. He was a hostage in the court of Karim Khan Zand in Shiraz and was treated with kindness by that ruler. Upon the death of Karim Khan, Agha Mohammad fled to Mazandaran; after years of warfare, in a struggle for power, he gained the throne of Iran in 1794 with Tehran as his capital. No sooner had he succeeded in controlling the country when the Russian army by order of Catherine the Great invaded the Caucasus in 1796. When the empress died that same year, the new tsar, Paul, who was opposed to his mother's policies, stopped the campaign. A year later, Agha Mohammad was assassinated by his own servants.

His nephew and successor, Fath-Ali Shah (1797–1834), known for his unusually long beard and a progeny of numerous princes and princesses, had most of his uncle's bad traits. Almost from the beginning he was called upon to make decisions on international problems for which he was not prepared. He was wooed by Britain, France, and Russia. Napoleon persuaded him to sign a treaty of alliance with France against Russia in 1807; in return Napoleon sent a large military mission for the purpose of training the Iranian army and setting up foundries for making cannon and other weapons. All this came to naught, however, because of the treaty of friendship between Napoleon and Tsar Alexander I at Tilsit in 1807.

Taking advantage of this opportunity, the British sent a mission under Sir Harford Jones in 1808 and signed a treaty of alliance with Iran against France and Russia. The treaty had provisions to train the Iranian army plus a "subsidy" of £120,000 for the shah. This was followed by a large mission under a representative of the East India Company in 1810. It must be noted that there was a long-standing rivalry between the British government and the East India Company. Each sent its own mission and the two sometimes worked at cross-purposes. Neither the shah nor any of his advisers took advantage of this or of the other rivalries and wars among the Europeans.

Ever since 1804 the Russians had carried on a campaign of expansion at the expense of Iran in the Caucasus. The campaign slackened whenever Russia became involved with the struggle against the Ottomans or with any of the European countries. The Iranian army was under the command of Abbas Mirza, the crown prince, who was considered the most able man among the Qajar princes. This army was trained along European lines, sometimes by the French and at other times by the British. From all accounts, it seems that the command was not uniform and the soldiers were confused. In any case, the major battle of this prolonged and slow war was fought in 1812 at Aslanduz. Since Britain, in its struggle against Napoleon, had once again come to an understanding with Russia, most of the British officers commanding in the Iranian army were withdrawn. How much confusion this caused in the Iranian ranks is not known, but the Russians gained a great victory. The British used their good offices, and the Iranians signed the peace treaty of Golestan on October 12, 1813. According to this treaty, Iran lost five cities in the Caucasus and gave up its claims to Georgia and Daghestan. For its part, Russia promised to support the claim of Abbas Mirza to the throne.

The crown prince, in accepting the support of Russia, was all but inviting the latter to interfere in the internal affairs of Iran. Britain, not to be outdone, joined Russia in this support. After this, every Qajar crown prince, except the last, was accompanied to the capital by the Russian and British ministers when he ascended the throne. The involvement of Russia in the Napoleonic wars prevented her from becoming firmly established in the new territory in the Caucasus. It was quite apparent that the Iranians did not consider their defeat conclusive and had every intention of regaining their lost territory.

While Russia in 1812 was fighting for her life against Napoleon, Britain tried to strengthen its position in Iran. The British representative, Sir Gore Ousley, concluded the Definitive Treaty with Iran in 1814. According to this agreement, Iran promised to break her alliance with any European power at war with Britain; to prevent any army hostile to Britain from entering Iran; and to induce the khans of Kharazm, Tataristan, Bokhara, and Samarqand (who paid tribute to the shah) to deny access to an invading army destined for India. On the other hand, Britain promised to help Iran settle her boundaries with Russia; to come to Iran's aid in case of war with a European country; not to interfere in any struggle between Iran and Afghanistan; and to pay Iran an annual subsidy of £150,000.

During the decade between 1815 and 1825, Fath-Ali Shah was involved in securing his throne against internal enemies, forcing Afghanistan to pay tribute, and warring against the Ottomans from 1821 to 1823. This latter was the last campaign in the long and fruitless strife between the two empires that had started with the battle of Chaldiran in 1514. Since the Ottomans had their hands full with the Greek rebellion, the Russians encouraged Abbas Mirza to attack the Turks and regain his prestige, which had suffered at the hands of the Russians. The Turko-Iranian War, like so many before it, was inconclusive and ended in 1823 with the Treaty of Erzerum, which involved no territorial changes.

Soon after, Russia renewed its offensive against Iran in 1825, when it occupied Gokcha in the region of Erivan. At first the Iranian forces were very successful and regained many of the lost cities in the Caucasus. Fath-Ali Shah, however, whose avarice was as notorious as his long beard, hoarded gold rather than spending it for defense. The arsenal was empty and a good deal of the army disbanded because of lack of pay. The British, who were supposed to come to the aid of Iran according to the treaty of 1814, refused to so do on the claim that Iran was the aggressor. The fact of the matter was that Britain had just signed a treaty of friendship with Russia. Consequently, the Iranians, who nevertheless were waging some successful campaigns, could not sustain a long war and had to retreat. By 1827 even the major city of Tabriz was occupied. The Iranians sued for peace and had to sign the Treaty of Turkmanchai in 1828.

The defeat of Iran was complete. It lost all its territory west of the Caspian Sea. The boundary followed the Aras River to the forty-eighth parallel, south to include Lankaran, and east to Astara on the Caspian Sea. Furthermore, duty on Russian imported goods was limited to 5 percent, and Iran accepted the principle of extraterritoriality and the payment of an indemnity amounting to £3,000,000. The Treaty of Turkmanchai ushered in a new era, because from that date on Iran was not altogether independent. This fact was not lost on the British, who had failed to aid Iran. With the payment of £150,000 to the penniless crown prince, the British were able to cancel that portion of the Definitive Treaty of 1814 in which Great Britain had promised to aid Iran if the latter were attacked by a European nation.

Abbas Mirza, the crown prince, died in 1833; and his father, Fath-Ali Shah, died a year later at the age of sixty-eight. The new heir was Mohammad, the son of Abbas Mirza, but there were many other claimants. The young Mohammad Shah marched to Tehran with an army commanded by the British general, Sir Henry Lindsay Bethune, and was accompanied by both Russian and British ministers. This was enough to dishearten most of the rivals, even though some were foolish enough to persist for a time.

The Iranians, who claimed suzerainty over Afghanistan and the territory east of the Caspian Sea, wanted to strengthen their positions there in order to offset their losses to the west of the Caspian Sea. The British, however, were against this because they did not think that the Iranians were strong enough to stop the Russian advance. Furthermore, the British rightly believed that the Qajar kings had Russian sympathies and might enter into an agreement with them for a campaign against India. Consequently, the main trend in the military and political history of Iran from 1828, the date of the Treaty of Turkmanchai, until about 1900, is the story of the slow but sure advance of Russia from the northeast and Britain from the southeast. That most of Iran was spared outright annexation was due less to the strength of Iran and more to the unwillingness of Russia and Britain to allow the other complete control of the country.

Mohammad Shah spent most of his thirteen years as king trying to strengthen his position in Afghanistan. The Qajar kings, who were not endowed with much ability themselves, could not even endure able grand vazirs for long. Mohammad Shah ordered the death of the very able Abol Qasem Qa'em Maqam, and gave the office to his tutor, Haji Mirza Aghasi, whose superstitions, ignorance, fanaticism, and avarice accelerated the ruin of the country even more. One of the important events in the reign of Mohammad Shah was the advent of the Bab, the founder of the Babi religion, which has been discussed.

Mohammad Shah died in 1848; his son, Naser al-Din, was escorted from Tabriz to Tehran by both the British and Russian ministers to become shah. Naser al-Din was one of the better Qajar kings, but during the fifty years of his reign did not leave much of a constructive legacy. The story might have been different had he not, like his father, ordered the death of his grand vazir, Mirza Taqi Khan Amir Kabir, who was, without doubt, the most able individual in Iran to reach that high office in the entire nineteenth century.

Naser al-Din was sixteen years old when he ascended the throne in 1848. After a series of political maneuvers by both Iran and Britain in Afghanistan, Iran occupied the city of Herat. This action was considered serious enough by Britain to declare war on Iran the same year. A British army marched on Herat while other British forces, after occupying Bushehr on the Persian Gulf, took the city of Mohamareh (later called Khorram Shahr), at the confluence of the Karun and Shatt al-Arab rivers. Later a British flotilla went up the Karun and occupied Ahvaz. Most of this was done without much resistance on the part of the Iranians, and the little resistance they did offer was disorganized.

A treaty of peace was concluded in Paris in 1857. According to this treaty, Iran agreed to evacuate Afghanistan and recognize its independence. Iran also agreed to use the "good offices" of Britain in any future disputes with Afghanistan. A few weeks after the conclusion of this treaty, the famous "Indian Mutiny" broke out, and the British used their troops in quelling that uprising. Following the "mutiny," the British government took over the formal control of India, and the securing of its western and northwestern approaches became all the more important. The defense of India was made easy by Britain's dominance in Afghanistan, which also included the Hindu Kush mountains. It was not necessary for the British to leave the safety of the mountains and go farther north. This left Central Asia and the land east of the Caspian Sea open for the Russians to do as they pleased.

But after its defeat in the Crimean War (1853–1856) and the death of Nicholas I, Russia was in no position to carry on campaigns of expansion. Furthermore, Alexander II was busy freeing the serfs and trying other internal reforms. But the wars of Italian and German unification in Europe, added to a relative stability at home, allowed Alexander to try his hand again in Turkey and, more especially, in the area east of the Caspian. A full account of the campaigns would be too tedious to repeat here. Suffice it to say that the Russian troops occupied Bokhara in 1868, Khiva in 1873, and Khokand in 1876. With the capture of Marv in 1884, Russia became master of the territories east of the Caspian and all of Central Asia. Iran was forced to accept the Atrak River as the new boundary, thus ceding to Russia the most fertile land north of the river.

The envelopment of Iran by Russia and Britain was now complete. Just as Britain did not find it necessary to interfere with the Russian advance to the Atrak River and the northern borders of Afghanistan, the Russians did not mind the British annexation of Iranian territories south of Afghanistan to the Persian Gulf. The British used means other than military campaigns to gain their ends. From 1870 to 1903 there were minor revolts in Baluchestan and boundary disputes with Afghanistan. In all these, Britain was there to offer its "good offices." For example, there were the Mokran Boundary Commission of 1871, the Sistan Arbitration Commission of 1872, and the Irano-Baluchestan Boundary Commission of 1892. By the time of the Second Sistan Commission of 1903, the western boundaries of British India had expanded considerably at the expense of Iran. Just as in the northwest of Iran, Azerbaijan had been cut into two parts—Russian and Iranian—so in the southeast, Baluchestan was cut into two parts—British and Iranian.

The Anglo-Russian rivalry in Iran that had started with the defeat of Napoleon in 1812 ended its annexation phase with the beginning of the twentieth century. Neither country allowed the other to annex any more territory. Long before the end of the nineteenth century, however, the rivalry had entered its second phase, namely economic, which lasted from about 1870 to 1921. During this long period, Iran was avowedly a buffer state in which Russia and Britain wielded political and economic power without having to assume any responsibility for the welfare of the inhabitants.

An immediate cause of what might be called economic imperialism in Iran was the "Indian Mutiny." Both in the course of the struggle in India and afterwards when the British government assumed full responsibility for India, speedy communication became of utmost importance. To connect London and Delhi by telegraph, it was necessary to pass through Iran. Signed in Istanbul in 1863, the Overland Telegraph Convention connected the capital of the Ottomans to Baghdad. In 1864, the British made arrangements with the shah to extend the line to Kermanshah, Hamadan, Tehran, and Bushehr. The Indo-European Telegraph Company was formed in 1870 to extend telegraph services and connected Tehran with Tabriz and Odessa. No doubt the establishment of these lines was a great boon to Iran. It not only made effective control of the provinces possible by the central government, but also ended the isolation of Iran and helped to bring her closer to the ideas and institutions of Europe. At the same time this first concession opened the way for other concessions, not only to the British but also to the Russians, who demanded equal treatment. The telegraph concession in 1870 was the first of many concessions given to both Britain and Russia for a period of forty years. These concessions and loans gradually put the resources of the country under foreign control and culminated in the most far-reaching concessions of all—those concerning oil—which were given to the British in 1901 and to the Russians in 1911.

In 1872, Baron Julius de Reuter, a naturalized British subject, received a seventy-year concession from Naser al-Din Shah for a gigantic monopoly for the building of railroads, the exploitation of mines, the establishment of a bank, the building of water works, the regulation of rivers, and so on, in exchange for the customs receipts and most of the other resources of the country. The next year, when the shah made his first trip to Europe, largely on the funds advanced by de Reuter, he found out that the Russians were against the concession and, on his return, was forced to cancel it. The shah was soon to learn the bitter lessons of the "debt clause" in subsequent concessions.

In 1888 the British received a concession to develop the lower Karun River for navigation. In the following year, the shah, in partial compensation for the cancellation of the previous concession, gave Baron de Reuter a new one for the establishment of a bank, to be known as the Imperial Bank of Persia, with the right to issue bank notes. This was matched in 1890 by the founding of the Banque d'Escompte de Perse by Russia. The Imperial Bank printed paper money that was negotiable only in cities designated on the bill. Travelers going from city to city had to pay a commission to exchange their money for the money accepted in that city, as though they were in a different country.

The most notorious of all concessions was the Tobacco Concession of 1890, which gave the British a monopoly on the production, sale, and export of all tobacco in Iran. In return, the shah was to receive an annual payment of £15,000 plus one-fourth of the profits. The concessionaires, according to their advertisement for the sale of shares, expected a profit of £500,000 per annum. It is of interest to note that in 1884 the Ottoman Empire had given a somewhat similar, but more limited, tobacco concession to the French for a flat payment of £630,000 per annum. While the Iranian concession was all-inclusive and was to be effective for fifty years, the Turkish concession was for internal consumption and of thirty years' duration. Whereas the French monopoly went almost unnoticed by the populace, the one in Iran aroused vehement antagonism among the people. In a country where a large majority of men and women smoked, such an antagonism could not be ignored. The people could not understand why they had to buy from the British the tobacco that they themselves had grown. The ulama, who were against Western and non-Muslim encroachments in Iran, took the side of the people and asked the government to cancel the concession. The shah responded by imprisoning the opponents of the concession. The controversy dragged on until early December 1891, when the respected Shi'i mujtahid, Haji Mirza Hasan Shirazi, issued a fatva from his residence in Samarra, Iraq, making it unlawful for Iranian Muslims to smoke until the concession was withdrawn. The obedience to this religious rule was so total that the shah was forced to cancel the agreement.

The cancellation, however, cost Iran £500,000 in damages, which was borrowed from the newly established British-controlled Imperial Bank at 6 percent interest and paid to the company. The customs of the Persian Gulf were pledged for the payment of the interest, and the capital was to be paid at the end of forty years. This was the first foreign loan contracted by Iran. There were many others to follow, and eventually most of the resources of the country were pledged to British and Russian creditors.

In 1896, Naser al-Din Shah was celebrating his jubilee, according to the lunar Muslim calendar, as the "King of Kings." On Friday, May 1, 1896, just a few days before the celebrations were to begin, the shah went to the shrine of Shah Abdul Azim, some ten miles south of Tehran. There he was shot to death by a certain Mirza Reza of Kerman. The assassin was a disciple of Sayyed Jamal al-Din al-Afghani, the pan-Islamist agitator, who had been ousted from Iran by the late shah in 1891. Afghani was residing under the protection of Sultan Abdul Hamid II, whose hope of becoming the caliph of a unified Islamic world was no secret. Pan-Islamism was not a popular movement in Iran, and the murder does not seem to have been the result of the unrest caused by the tobacco fiasco. The hope that the shah would be killed was expressed by Afghani more than once; and a devoted disciple, who also had his own personal grudges, carried out the wish.

Thus came to an end the life of the last autocratic king of Iran. In a dynasty of inferior kings he was perhaps the most able. He made three trips to Europe, in 1873, 1878, and 1889. The country did not gain anything by these visits. If he did apprehend the serious movements going on in Europe, he did not think them to be useful for Iran, because he discouraged, with growing harshness, every attempt at westernization.

The heir-apparent, Mozaffar al-Din, who lived in Tabriz, came to Tehran accompanied by the British and Russian ministers, and was crowned king. He was forty-three years old and rather sickly. He had been advised to go to Europe for cure, and now as shah he was impatient to make the trip. But there was no money in the treasury and the Belgian customs advisers, headed by M. Naus, who had been employed by the late shah, could not produce the funds soon enough. The Russian bank, however, lent the shah £2,400,000 at 5 percent interest against the customs receipts of the whole country except the Persian Gulf. To make Russia the sole creditor, the loan was made on condition that the £500,000 debt to the Imperial (British) Bank, incurred because of the tobacco fiasco, be paid. After the payment of this debt, discounts, and commission, enough was left for the shah to depart for Europe in the summer of 1900.

Two years later, the shah arranged for another loan of a little over a million pounds from Russia at 4 percent. Attached to his loan was the concession to construct a road from Julfa on the Russo-Iranian border to Tabriz, Qazvin, and Tehran.

The heavy burden of these unproductive loans, the quarrel between the corrupt Russophile Iranian officials with the equally corrupt Anglophile officials, the harsh treatment of the people by the grand vazir, and the general awakening culminated in the Constitutional Revolution of 1906.

IRANIAN OIL: THE FIRST PHASE

The discovery of oil was to become a tool of imperialism and the battle cry of Iranian nationalism. It was of great importance in the social, economic, and political upheavals that rocked Iran in the twentieth century and will be discussed in four phases in later chapters.

The presence of oil in the Middle East was known to the people in ancient times. Noah's Ark was made seaworthy by the use of pitch, which is an oil product; and the Zoroastrians of Iran built some of their religious fire temples around ignited natural gas. In certain parts of southwestern Iran, the seepage of oil to the surface had formed small pools, and the distribution of this crude oil had become a small industry in the nineteenth century. In 1872, when Baron de Reuter was granted the comprehensive concession by the shah of Iran, oil was one of the many items mentioned. In 1892, Professor Jacques de Morgan, head of the French archaeological expedition on the site of ancient Susa in western Iran, wrote an article claiming the existence of oil in that part of the country. Later, Ketabchi Khan, an Iranian customs official, was impressed by this article and tried to interest French capitalists in the exploitation of oil. Failing in this, he approached Sir Henry Drummond Wolff, the former British minister in Iran, with his plan. The latter placed Ketabchi in touch with his friend William Knox D'Arcy, who was a British gold prospector in Australia.

D'Arcy, whose name has been immortalized in connection with oil, never went to Iran. He sent geologists there and, after receiving favorable reports, sent his representative Alfred Marriot to negotiate a concession. In 1901, a concession was signed by Mozaffar al-Din Shah for Iran and by Mr. Marriot for D'Arcy. The extent of the concession included all of Iran except the five provinces of the north. The term of concession was for sixty years, after which time all the machinery, buildings, and installations would revert to Iran without compensation. The concessionaire agreed to pay the Iranian government £20,000 in cash and £20,000 in paid-up shares, plus an annual royalty of 16 percent of the net profits.

After seven years of hard work and heavy expenditures, when D'Arcy and his associates were about to abandon the whole project, oil in commercial quantities was discovered in the region of Masjed-e Solaiman, northeast of Ahvaz. The memorable date was May 26, 1908. A year later the Anglo-Persian Oil Company (APOC) was formed, with a capital of £2,000,000. By this time the Iranian Constitutional Revolution was two years old. The proceedings of the first session of the Iranian parliament reveal that the deputies discussed the oil concession but were not aware of its tremendous importance in the economic and political life of the country. By 1914, the APOC had drilled some thirty wells, and had built a pipeline to the nearby refinery that had been constructed on the island of Abadan in the Persian Gulf. After 1908, the company had the assistance of the British government in coming to terms with the Bakhtyari tribesmen who owned land in the oil fields, and with the warlord, Shaykh Khaz'al, who claimed jurisdiction in the area of Abadan.

By the beginning of World War I, the British Admiralty had converted the British Navy from coal to oil. Both for the purpose of obtaining oil at a low price and for preventing other countries from having a share in the rich deposits of Iran, the British Admiralty arranged to purchase enough shares in APOC to become its major and controlling partner in May 1914. A month later, the House of Commons approved the agreement. With the investment of £2,200,000, the British government gained control of APOC and, through two representatives on the APOC board, had veto power over the policies of the company and all its subsidiaries. From this date until the nationalization of the Iranian oil industry in 1951, the British Navy bought oil from the APOC at a "special" price. The company never revealed what this price was nor whether the British Navy paid anything at all for the oil.

The rivalry between Britain and Russia in Iran was the main reason for exempting the five northern provinces from the D'Arcy concession. Apparently the Russian government, probably because of the Baku oil fields, did not demand a similar concession in northern Iran. In 1916, however, a Russian entrepreneur, A. M. Khoshtaria, with the help of the Russian government, received a concession from the prime minister of Iran. The concession was for the exploitation of oil in three of the northern provinces—Gilan, Mazandaran, and Astrabad—for a term of seventy years. The rest of the provisions of the concession were similar to those given to D'Arcy. According to Iranian law, all concessions had to be ratified by the Iranian parliament, a condition that did not apply in 1901 when D'Arcy obtained his concession. The Khoshtaria concession was never ratified and so was considered null and void. Later the Russian Revolution and the Bolsheviks' renunciation of all concessions obviated the whole issue. The Iranians thought the matter was closed, but they were mistaken.

Chapter Twenty-One
The Iranian Awakening

In the history of the Middle East, the Iranians were the only major group conquered by the Arabs who consistently kept their identity as a people. As we have seen, the Iranians almost always kept themselves apart. They thought of themselves as different from the rest of the Muslims and thereby consistently aroused the hostility of others. This sense of identity was sometimes expressed religiously, as in the revolts of the Black Shirts, White Shirts, and Red Shirts during the early Abbasid period. Sometimes it was expressed through literature, as in the Shu'ubiyya movement and in the poetry of Ferdowsi. It was also at times expressed politically, in, for example, the partially successful revolts of the Saffarids, Samanids, and others, who established autonomous principalities. Sometimes it was expressed culturally, as during the Mongol period, when the Iranians developed a culture of their own that was distinct from the Arabic-speaking Muslims.

Even though the Iranians thought of themselves as special or unique, they were at least in and part of the Muslim world. They participated in the various activities of the community (ummah) of Islam. They compiled the first complete grammar of the Arabic language, even though they refused to speak it. They had a large share in writing a systematic theology of Islam, even though eventually they refused to follow it. They participated in the history of Islam and wrote about it for posterity—but somehow did not feel part of it. Much of what is commonly known as "Islamic," or erroneously as "Arab," culture in the fields of art, literature, philosophy, medicine, mathematics, astronomy, physics, chemistry, history, geography, and theology, was contributed by Iranians. Their poets and architects were invited to India and their art adorned the mosques and buildings of the Ottomans. From the thirteenth century to the end of the sixteenth century, from Istanbul to Delhi, most art was Iranian and the sign of culture was the ability to speak Persian.

Not only were the Iranians very different in actuality from the Arabs and the Turks, but they were very conscious of these differences and made themselves obnoxious and were shunned by others for boasting about themselves. During the Safavid period, the establishment of Shi'ism as the official religion isolated the Iranians even more. Notwithstanding the extensive commercial and political relationships between Iran and various European countries during the Safavid period, there was no known intellectual interaction. Culturally Iran was also isolated from many world communities, and by espousing Shi'ism it set itself apart from the rest of the Muslim world. Iran was in the world of Islam but certainly not one with it. As the power of the Safavid and other kings decreased and the influence of the Shi'i ulama increased, Iran's isolation became more complete. Various movements in the nineteenth and twentieth centuries in Iran can best be understood in the light of this isolation. These movements attempted to destroy the cultural and political wall surrounding the Iranians. The purpose of the very insignificant pan-Islamist group in Iran, encouraged by Afghani, was to destroy the inner wall that separated the Iranian Shi'is from the rest of the Muslims. The Babi-Bahai movement shook the foundation of Shi'i Islam and, in its Bahai form, "leapt the outer wall," as it were, to the outside world. The aim of the "constitutionalists" was to raze the wall that isolated Iran from the rest of the world. In all cases the vast majority of the Shi'i ulama and their followers tried to prevent both of these walls from crumbling.

The strong sense of identity that the Iranians had developed became very useful in the process of nation-building in the 1900s. As early as the tenth century Ferdowsi expressed the sentiment, "If there is no Iran, then let me not be." While most students of nationalism in the Middle East credit the Turkish writer of the nineteenth century, Namik Kemal, with the use of *vatan* ("fatherland") in the modern sense, we find the Iranian poet Sa'di (d. 1291) using the phrase "love of fatherland" to criticize a sentiment that is quite modern. He says "O Sa'di, love of *vatan* is a noble sentiment. But one just can't die miserably [for it] because one is born there."

It is considered erroneous to identify these sentiments as "nationalism," although one is at a loss to know what to call them. But the fact of the matter is that the Iranians built their modern nationalism, which they borrowed from Europe, on the consciousness of their own political and cultural identity. The Turks and the Arabic-speaking peoples had difficulty in adapting the European concept of nationalism to such identities as Islam, Ottomanism, Arabism, and Turanianism. The Iranians did not have such difficulties. It is important to note that while the Turks and Arabs were—and in a sense the Arabs still are—in search of a cohesive identity, the Iranians had a fairly developed one.

INFLUENCES FROM THE WEST

The relative isolation of Iran was broken directly by encounters with the West and indirectly through Ottoman Turkey and Moghul India. As in the case of the Ottoman Empire, the first borrowing was of military equipment and training. During the reign of Fath-Ali Shah (1797–1834) and during the Russo-Iranian wars (1796–1828), foreign officers commanded Iranian troops; but it was Mirza Taqi Khan, the astute grand vazir under Naser al-Din Shah, who put modernization on a sound basis.

This remarkable man, who is commonly known by the title "Amir Kabir," was the son of a cook and a protégé of Qa'em Maqam, the able vazir under Mohammad Shah (1834–1848). When Naser al-Din was crown prince and governor of Azerbaijan, Amir Kabir was his chief officer and close enough to him to marry his sister. When Naser al-Din was crowned in 1848, Mirza Taqi Khan was made the grand vazir. During his three short years in office he did more than any other individual to direct Iran toward modernization. He was familiar with the Tanzimat of the Ottoman Empire and had observed much on his visit to Petersburg. He was convinced that the salvation of Iran was to reform along Western lines.

He reorganized the government, facilitated commerce with Europe, built bazaars and warehouses, and reorganized the army. Perhaps his greatest accomplishment was the establishment in 1851 of the *Dar al-Fonun,* ("Institute of Arts and Sciences"), which became an important center of learning for the sons of the aristocracy. To this center were brought teachers from Europe who taught Western science, history, and technology. But Amir Kabir was not allowed to continue in office. His most powerful enemies were the ulama, who had found an effective ally in the person of the queen mother. She had great influence over her son and was a mortal enemy of her son-in-law. By the end of 1851, Mirza Taqi Khan was dismissed from office and a year later was executed in Kashan. About the only person who stood by him until the end was his devoted wife, the shah's only sister.

Western influence came to Iran also through students who as early as 1815 had been travelling to Europe. They returned to become teachers, newspaper publishers, translators, and authors. The first newspaper in Iran was published by Amir Kabir as a weekly government gazette. Because of censorship, newspapers were published abroad and smuggled into Iran. Of the two most important newspapers, one was *Akhtar,* published in Istanbul from 1875. For a while it advocated pan-Islamism under the influence of Ruhi, but later became a proponent of westernization and was very popular in Iran. The other paper was *Qanun,* published in London in 1890. Its editor, Malkom Khan, was very close to Naser al-Din Shah and acted as his envoy to England. But Malkom's progressive ideas could not be tolerated by the shah, who saw westernization as a danger to his position and wanted to keep his people so ignorant of Europe that they would not know whether, to quote the king himself, "Brussels was the name of a city or a kind of cabbage." Malkom Khan wrote on social and political subjects in simple Persian, always emphasizing the necessity of the rule of law. He also tried to revise the alphabet and introduced freemasonry.

The publication of books played an important role in introducing Western ideas. The Institute of Arts and Sciences became the center for translation and the publication of books on scientific, technical, literary, historical, and social subjects. Two authors who had a more direct influence on the revolution are Abdul Rahman Talebof and Zeynul Abedin Maragheyi, both merchants from Azerbaijan. Talebof, who had spent long sojourns in the Caucasus, was interested in chemistry and physics and wrote extensively on these as well as social and political subjects. A book of his that became very popular was *The Book of Ahmad*. It is a dialogue between a father and his little boy, Ahmad. In a child's simple language the father discusses the progress of Europe and the backwardness of Iran.

An even more popular book than *Ahmad* was the *Travels of Ebrahim Bey* by Maragheyi. Ebrahim was the son of an Iranian merchant residing in Cairo who went to see what Iran was like. His varied experiences and involvements reveal the misery of the people, the deceitfulness of the clergy, and the cruelty of the officials. This book caught the imagination of the people, was read by those who could, and was read aloud to the illiterate, as was the custom, in tea houses.

Schools also played an important role in the awakening of Iran. The Dar al-Fonun was about the only important school opened by the government in the nineteenth century, but liberal merchants in Azerbaijan, Gilan, and other provinces opened schools along Western lines. The models for these were the schools that had been established by American, British, and French missionaries. The French Lazarite mission established a school in Tabriz in 1839 and later opened schools in other parts of the country. The Americans began their work in Urumiyeh (later Rezaiyeh), Azerbaijan, in 1839 and the British in Esfahan in 1870. Both established hospitals as well as schools. One of these schools, Alborz College in Tehran, became an especially important educational institution in the country. Its long-time and beloved president, Dr. S. M. Jordan, is the only American, perhaps the only foreigner, in all the Middle East to have a commemorative statue erected by an appreciative people. The Americans were the first to establish schools for women. They were also the first to publish a magazine for women. *The World of Women*, edited by Mrs. Arthur Boyce with the assistance of the graduates of the American girls' school in Tehran, continued publication for twelve years and was the forerunner of many similar modern magazines for women. From 1860 onward, Iranian merchants, especially from Azerbaijan and Gilan, traveled north to Russia. The annual fair at Nizhni Novgorod attracted many Iranian visitors. Furthermore, the shortest route to Europe lay through Russia. Toward the end of the nineteenth century, thousands of Iranians worked in the oil fields of Baku and in other industries in Russia. All of them came back impressed not only with the progress of Russia compared to that of Iran, but also with the ideas that led to the revolutions of 1905 and 1917 in Russia.

THE IRANIAN CONSTITUTIONAL REVOLUTION

The Iranian constitutional revolution is perhaps unique among the revolutions of the twentieth-century Middle East, in that the military did not have much to do with it. No strongman, military or civilian, had complete or even partial charge of it. The revolution was directed, somewhat haphazardly, by the merchants, the educated elite, the moderate-to-liberal ulama, the tribesmen, and the ethnic groups. The merchants in the bazaars of different cities had been organized into guilds from Safavid times and wielded great influence. They have been an effective force in every movement in the twentieth century and are still a power to be reckoned with. Iranians who had been to Europe or who had come under the influence of Western education formed the educated elite, who wanted to have a constitutional monarchy patterned after those of European countries. There was a constant struggle for power between the shah and the Shi'i ulama throughout the late Safavid and Qajar periods. Theologically, government was claimed to be the sole prerogative of the Hidden Imam, and any person who assumed power was considered a usurper. Since the aim of the revolution was to limit the power of the shah, the moderate clergy considered it a step in the right direction and helped to bring it about. The tribes and the ethnic groups in Iran, who wanted some measure of autonomy, saw in the constitutional movement a way of achieving their goal. The Bakhtyaris among the tribes and the Azarbaijanis among the ethnic groups were of tremendous help to the revolution. Insofar as the religious minorities are concerned, only the Armenian Christians contributed fighting men and leadership to the revolution. The Zoroastrians contributed leadership after the parliament had been formed. The Jews and the Assyrian Christians assumed a neutral role throughout the revolutionary period.

The accession of Mozaffar al-Din Shah in 1896 did not change the situation in Iran. The opportunist grand vazir, Amin al-Sultan, was in charge and sided with the British or the Russians as the situation demanded. The sickly and weak-willed shah was obsessed with the desire to go to Europe, both to be cured (he was suffering from a kidney ailment) and to be wined and dined by the crown heads of Europe. The heavy expenses of the two trips that the shah took increased the indebtedness of Iran to both Russia and Britain, as we have seen. The new pro-Russian tariff agreements arranged by the Belgian director of customs had raised the price of sugar. Furthermore, there was a shortage of silver coins in the country, as speculators had bought up large quantities and sold them to India to be recoined as rupees. Consequently the mint in Tehran was closed for lack of silver, and merchants refused to honor the flood of paper money printed by the British-owned Imperial Bank of Persia. On December 11, 1905, a group of merchants called a strike in protest and closed the bazaars. The government retaliated by flogging the merchants. On December 13, some 2,000 clergymen and merchants headed by two moderate mujtahids, Sayyed Mohammad Tabataba'i and Sayyed Abdullah Behbahani, took sanctuary at the nearby shrine of Shah Abdul Azim. There they demanded a "house of justice."

In July 1906, a large number of the ulama and their followers took sanctuary in the important shrine of Qom some sixty miles south of Tehran. At the same time, 13,000 westernizers, merchants, tradesmen, and others took sanctuary in the grounds of the British legation in Tehran. The taking of sanctuary was an honored institution in Iran, but the usual places of sanctuary were shrines, mosques, the palaces or stables of the shah, and, of late, the provincial telegraph office, which presumably had a line connecting it to the shah's palace. Taking sanctuary in a foreign legation was an innovation, but it was done with the consent of the British. In the rivalry between Russia and Britain the revolutionaries sided with Britain because of its liberal and democratic institutions. Britain, for its part, joined the revolutionaries because such a policy would hurt Russia. On the other hand, Russia was against the constitutional movement because the tsar himself was in the midst of a struggle against constitutionalists in his own country and did not want the idea to spread. On August 5, 1906, Mozaffar al-Din Shah finally granted a constitution and a parliament, the *Majles*. Election to the first Majles was based on membership in different sections of society, such as princes, ulama, nobles, landlords, merchants, and guilds. The first Majles contained representatives from all segments of society except the peasants. Almost its first act was to reject a joint Anglo-Russian loan of £400,000, and this action was followed by compelling the shah to dismiss the Belgian customs officials.

The death of the shah on January 8, 1907, placed the young revolutionary movement in grave jeopardy. The new shah, Mohammad Ali, was known to be a puppet of Russia and against the revolution. Even though at his coronation he swore to uphold the constitution, practically everything he did worked against it. One of his first acts was to recall the reactionary Amin al-Sultan and name him prime minister.

The granting of the constitution had brought with it freedom of the press. The number of newspapers increased by the month, and by 1911 their number had reached over 400. As the new shah increased his anti-Majles activities, the newspapers lampooned him and the reactionaries in poetry, prose, satire, humor, and cartoon. Songs were written on the love of country, freedom, equality, justice, and democracy. Everywhere in the country troubadors who played at weddings sang these songs, which spread the message and encouraged the people to oppose the reactionaries.

Perhaps the best evidence that the constitutional movement was not the monopoly of a "very small European-educated elite" is the appearance of the *Anjomans* ("councils"). All over the country there arose literally hundreds of Anjomans to carry out some aspect of the revolution. These Anjomans each had from half a dozen to 100 members. Some were religious groups, others supported education and conducted literacy classes, still others became pamphleteers, and a few were terroristic, assassinating a number of antirevolutionary leaders. There was no central committee of the revolution to direct the activities of the Anjomans. Each had its own rules. The terroristic Anjomans, which were similar to the contemporary nihilist and social revolutionary groups in Russia, chose their own victims. One of the first was Amin al-Sultan, the pro-Russian prime minister, who was assassinated on August 31, 1907.

On the same day as the assassination, an Anglo-Russian convention was signed that had a far-reaching influence on the fate of the Iranian Revolution. The convention was a result of the inability of the Western powers to get along among themselves. With the advent of a unified Germany on the European scene and with the avowed interest of Kaiser Wilhelm in the problems of the Middle East, Russia and Britain wanted to show a "united front" against the newcomer. They came to an agreement concerning Iran, Afghanistan, and Tibet. In the case of Iran, in which both Britain and Russia were interested, they designated "spheres of influence" (see map). Such an uneven division shows that Britain was still obsessed with the defense of India and that the oil in southwest Iran had not yet been discovered. The Iranians quite correctly viewed the agreement as a violation of the independence of their country. The Iranian revolutionaries, who had hoped for so much from "democratic" Britain, believed they had been betrayed. This belief was also true, as they were to learn more fully in 1911.

In the summer of 1907, however, the revolutionaries did not have much time to brood over the betrayal, for the reactionary shah was closing in on them. After a series of moves and countermoves, a Cossack regiment, under the command of Colonel Liakhanov, bombarded the Majles by order of the shah. A large number of revolutionaries were arrested, their leaders were executed, and the rest fled the country. It seemed that the constitutional movement was over, but the movement had supporters among the people. Three centers rallied in defense of the constitution: Tabriz, Esfahan, and Rasht.

The Tabrizis, under the leadership of Sattar Khan and Baqer Khan,[1] refused to allow the government forces to enter the city and were besieged by the shah's and Russian troops for over nine months. Mr. Howard Baskerville, a young American teacher at the mission school in Tabriz, resigned his post and joined the revolutionaries. He trained some of his own students and led a sortie to bring food to the starving population. He was killed on April 21, 1909, and his grave became a shrine of the revolution.

The gallant resistance of Tabriz gave time and encouragement to the nationalists in other centers. The Bakhtyari tribe under their chief, Sardar-e As'ad, declared for the constitution and moved toward Tehran. In Rasht in the north, an army of volunteers, including a large number of Armenian nationalists, also moved toward Tehran. The Rasht contingent was under the nominal command of Sepahdar and the actual command of Sardar Mohi and the Armenian military officer, Yefrem Khan. The two armies from the north and south converged on Tehran and took the capital on July 13, 1909. The shah was deposed and his young son Ahmad was declared king on the next day.

The siege of Tabriz was lifted and constitutionalists were in power

---

[1]"Khan" is not a surname but an honorific title assumed by practically all Iranians. Its use was forbidden in 1934, when all titles were abolished.

again, but they were faced with many problems. With the intervention of the Russians and the British, the ex-shah was reluctantly pensioned and gladly sent to Europe. Furthermore, neither Sardar As'ad, the Bakhtyari chieftain, nor Sepahdar of Rasht was a serious constitutionalist. In addition to this, the differences between the ulama and the European-trained nationalists came to the surface. When the second Majles opened on November 15, 1909, there were two distinct groups, one revolutionary and the other "evolutionary." The former were known as Social Democrats; they believed in the separation of temporal and religious powers, land reform, compulsory conscription, universal education, and division of land. The other group, called Social Moderates, included the ulama and most of the nobility and landlords, who opposed only the excesses of Mohammad Ali Shah.

This division was seen at the outset in the Supplement to the Constitution, which was passed October 7, 1907. While the nationalists wanted a constitutional government based on laws passed by the elected representatives of the people, the ulama wanted the rule of the Muslim Shari'a. The two were poles apart but the compromise they reached is apparent in the Supplement to the Constitution. Article II of this document requires that five representatives of the ulama be present in the Majles with veto power over any legislation that they consider to be against the tenets of Islam. The fact, however, that Article II was never implemented shows that the secular nationalists were not without influence.

During the second Majles, the rift between the two groups became open and fierce. The ulama from Najaf excommunicated the Social Democrats while, on the other hand, a number of moderates were assassinated by secret Anjomans. Most of 1910 was spent by the Majles in looking for money to run the country. Since they were against borrowing from Russia and Britain and were unable to borrow from Germany, the Majles authorized an internal loan. This was received with enthusiasm by the population and many women sold their jewels to provide the money.

In the meantime, the Majles realized that it needed expert financial advice from abroad. To ask for such aid from Russia and Britain was unthinkable. Its experience with other European nationalities had not been satisfactory. But the influence of the American missionaries, the martyrdom of Baskerville, and the general policy of the United States made it natural for the Iranians to seek such aid from the United States. Morgan Shuster, together with a number of assistants, arrived in Iran as treasurer-general and was invested with very extensive powers.

Shuster was very popular among the Iranians and in sympathy with the aims of the Social Democrats in the Majles. This probably disappointed the Bakhtyaris and the moderates, who wanted to use him for their own purposes. Shuster realized that the country would have sufficient revenue if taxes were paid regularly. One method employed by some landlords to avoid paying taxes was to declare themselves "under the protection" of Russia or Britain. The treasury forces, however, confiscated the properties while the owners were taking refuge in the foreign legations. The Russians protested, and it was evident that the British sympathized with them.

A series of incidents resulted in the Russian government sending its first ultimatum on November 29, 1911, asking the Iranian government to dismiss Shuster. A second ultimatum followed, requiring Iran not to employ foreign advisers without the sanction of Russian and British governments. A third came soon afterward, demanding indemnity for the troops that Russia had dispatched to Iran. The British, to whom the Iranians had appealed, not only advised compliance with the Russian ultimatum but strengthened Indian troops who were already occupying south Iran. Many people responded by boycotting Russian and British goods, closing the bazaars, and demanding resistance. The finest hour of the revolution came when the members of the Majles, in a roll-call vote, unanimously rejected the ultimatum.

The cabinet, however, under the leadership of Samsam al-Saltaneh Bakhtyari, closed the Majles and dismissed Shuster on December 24, 1911. Aref Qazvini, the popular songwriter of the revolution, composed a song that continued to be sung long after Shuster's departure.

> Shame on the host whose guest unfed doth from the table rise
> Rather than this should happen, make thy life his sacrifice
> Should Shuster fare from Iran forth, Iran lost in sooth
> O let not Iran thus be lost, if ye be men in truth.[2]

Thus came to an end this phase of the Iranian Constitutional revolution. It failed because of the rift between the ulama and the nationalists, lack of unity among the nationalists, and lack of experience in government and administration. It also failed because of the interference of Russia and Britain. During World War I, the Iranians were afraid that in case of an Entente victory, Iran would certainly be divided between Russia and Britain. So they sided with the Central Powers. The Entente won, but Iran was not divided, mainly because Russia was temporarily taken out of the rivalry by the Revolution of 1917.

---

[2] Translation by the late E. G. Browne.

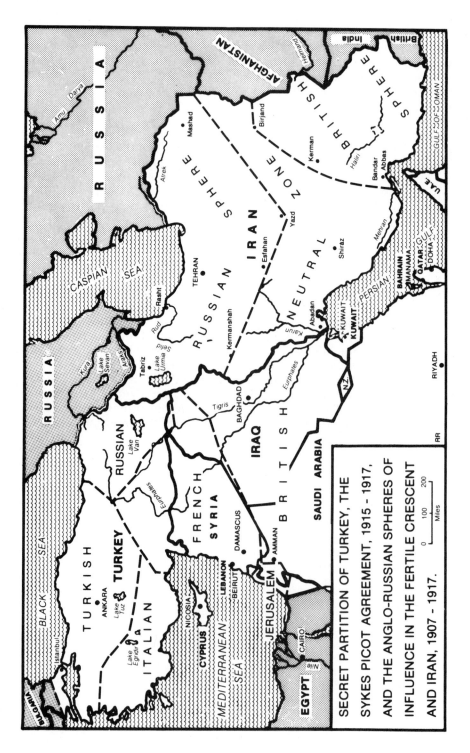

SECRET PARTITION OF TURKEY, THE
SYKES PICOT AGREEMENT, 1915 - 1917,
AND THE ANGLO-RUSSIAN SPHERES OF
INFLUENCE IN THE FERTILE CRESCENT
AND IRAN, 1907 - 1917.

Chapter Twenty-Two
The Middle East in World War I

When World War I broke out in 1914, all of Egypt, the Fertile Crescent, and portions of the eastern and western Arabian Peninsula were officially, if not actually, part of the Ottoman Empire and therefore involved in the war. Iran, even though nominally independent, had become the scene of intense rivalry between the Russian and British empires.

EGYPT AND LORD CROMER

Britain had ruled Egypt ever since 1882 but tried to maintain the fiction that the occupation was temporary, since Egypt was legally an Ottoman province. On December 18, 1914, a few months after the beginning of World War I, Britain abandoned the pretense and declared a protectorate over Egypt. Fortunately for Britain, Khedive Abbas Hilmi, who was anti-British, was in Istanbul at the time. He was deposed in absentia and his uncle Husayn Kamal was chosen in his place. The new ruler was not called khedive but was promoted to "sultan."

The British took great pride in their record in Egypt. They had brought peace to a country ridden with strife and prosperity to a bankrupt people. They had also given the Egyptians an efficient administration. But there were also failures, and the younger generation of Egyptians saw only these. Social change was too slow to be effective. Turko-Egyptians still constituted the ruling class. It was they and their relatives who owned most of the land. The *fellahin,* or peasants, still lived in squalor, paid the taxes, and supplied forced labor. The ulama administered the sacred law, which seemed to have less and less to say about either the struggle of the poor or the idleness of the rich. Banking, business, shipping, and finance were in the hands of foreigners—British, French, Italians, Greeks, Armenians, and others—who, because of their foreign passports, enjoyed capitulatory (extraterritorial) rights and had all the advantages but ran practically none of the risks. Indeed, the British government was there to safeguard their interests.

Egypt was relatively prosperous and orderly; and the more it became so, the more reluctant the British became to relinquish their hold. The famed British commissioner, Lord Cromer, and his successors had a condescending attitude toward the Egyptians, believing that they had a "tendency to shirk their responsibility" and could not be trusted with the administration of Egypt. Under Cromer the administration was efficient and paternalistic. His successors, however, Gorst and Kitchener, did not impress the Egyptians with their efficiency. Positions that were filled by Egyptians under Cromer were given to Englishmen, and with bigger salaries. Foreign concession seekers, profiteers, and usurers flooded the country and took advantage of capitulation privileges. The pan-Islamists and the ulama in general bemoaned the British "Christian rule." Educated civil servants, professors, lawyers, and newspapermen took pages out of the books of European liberal writers and politicians and used them against the British. For the Egyptian nationalists, it was an exhilarating experience to quote British authors against British imperialism.

Almost all Egyptians who were politically aware joined the anti-British movement. They were not united in purpose except to oust the British. They were journalists, small landlords, older bureaucrats who hated to work under young Englishmen, pan-Islamists, frustrated politicians, and nationalists who hoped for an independent Egypt. Khedive Abbas Hilmi was demanding independence and, for a time, worked hand-in-hand with some nationalists against the British. A younger generation had appeared that had not experienced the condition of Egypt before the British occupation in 1882 and did not appreciate what the British had accomplished. Furthermore, they did not have the patience of the older generation and were more aggressive in their attitudes.

The war years, however, were relatively peaceful. There were thousands of British, Australian, New Zealand, and Indian troops in Egypt. Martial law was proclaimed and the army was supreme. Throughout the war Rushdi Pasha was prime minister. If the Egyptians were on the side of the Central Powers, they did not show it. But though the presence of so many foreign soldiers must have wounded the pride of the nationalists, they did not try to sabotage the British war machine. With so much military spending there were severe shortages and rocketing inflation, but no riots. The British commandeered forced labor for their Palestine expedition. What bothered the peasants was the use of flogging to requisition their grain and animals. Sultan Husayn Kamil died in 1917 and his brother Fuad succeeded him.

THE HUSAYN-McMAHON CORRESPONDENCE

The entry of the Ottoman Empire into World War I on the side of the Central Powers threatened the British imperial line of communication to India. Consequently, from their bases in Egypt and the Persian Gulf, the British tried to secure that lifeline. The Germans, on the other hand, who were the main advisers of the Ottoman armies both in the field and on the general staff, wanted to harass the British in their bases all the way to India. They advised the Turks to curtail shipping through the Suez Canal and proclaim a jihad against the Entente. The main purpose of the jihad was to insure the allegiance of the Arabic-speaking Muslims of the Ottoman Empire and to arouse feelings of animosity against the British among the Muslims of India. Jihad was proclaimed in all its solemnity by the sultan-caliph on November 23, 1914, without effect. With the exception of Yaman, a few tribal shaykhs in south Arabia, and several Indian pan-Islamists, most of the inhabitants of the Fertile Crescent reacted to the jihad by doing nothing. Some actually took up arms against the caliph.

In a previous chapter we discussed the evolution of nationalism among the Arabic-speaking peoples of the Fertile Crescent. The Young Turk revolution of 1908 had reasserted the supremacy of Turks over non-Turks. Arabic-speaking peoples were not adequately represented in the Ottoman parliament. Furthermore, they were not willing to give up Arabic in favor of Turkish. Consequently, a number of Muslims began to be attracted to the pan-Arabist ideas of their Christian friends. At first they formed purely Muslim societies; later they established mixed groups in which Muslims, Christians, and Druzes joined in advocating the formation of a secular state with freedom of religion. There were more than a dozen of these societies from Baghdad to Beirut, and some of them were formed by Arab officers in the Ottoman army. In 1913, twenty-four representatives of secret nationalist societies held a congress in Paris, in the wake of the Balkan wars, and called for independence from Ottoman rule. During the early years of the war Jemal Pasha, a member of the Turkish triumvirate, was commander of the Turkish forces in Syria. His ruthlessness against the Arabs increased the popularity of the secret societies.

The British knew about these movements and naturally took advantage of their anti-Turkish feeling. Furthermore, the British campaign under General Allenby in the Sinai was not going well in 1915, and a British army of 13,000 men under General Townsend surrendered in Mesopotamia on April 25, 1916. The Ottomans did not expect an Arab revolt, but the British desired to foment one. The secret societies in different cities of the Fertile Crescent were not strong enough to offer armed resistance to the Turks who controlled the cities. There were, however, two Arab leaders who at the time had enough influence and freedom to lead a revolt against the Turks. One of these was ibn-Sa'ud, the leader of the Wahhabis, who had regained his patrimony and was ruling Najd, the eastern section of the Arabian peninsula. The other was Husayn, appointed sharif of Mecca by the sultan in 1908. He was the scion of the clan of Hashim, the same to which the Prophet Muhammad belonged, and was virtual ruler of Hijaz, the western part of the Arabian peninsula.

In our discussion of imperialism in Iran, we have mentioned the rivalry that existed between the British East India Company, which was the virtual ruler of India, and the British government in London. After the Indian Mutiny of 1857, the British government abolished the company and itself assumed control. Because of India's importance, it was governed through a separate department and was not part of the colonial office. There was a secretary for India in the British cabinet, and in the course of years those Englishmen who administered India developed a special point of view that examined every policy in the light of the defense of India. As was mentioned, a main interest of Britain in the Middle East was to safeguard the route to India. Because the British government personnel in India were on the spot and claimed special knowledge of Indian problems, they believed that they knew much better than the "London government" how to deal with the "natives." London, however, was reluctant to relinquish policy matters to New Delhi. There was rivalry between the London government and the "India government" until the disbanding of the latter in 1947, when India became independent. Sometimes this rivalry extended to British policy in Iran and the Fertile Crescent.

At the beginning of World War I, there was a difference of opinion between London and New Delhi over the policy to be pursued in the Fertile Crescent. Indian Muslims had great respect for the caliph of Islam, who happened to be the Ottoman sultan and at war with Britain. The "India government" expected Muslims of the Fertile Crescent to have the same respect for the person of the caliph as the Indian Muslims had. So it was against instigating a revolt among the Arabs. It concluded treaties of friendship with the shaykhs of the Persian Gulf and recognized ibn-Sa'ud as king of Najd. It paid subsidies to all of them and kept them friendly throughout the war.

The London government, however, knew about the nationalistic sentiments of the Arabs against the Turks and pursued the policy of fomenting open revolt. The British were aware of Husayn's anti-Ottoman feeling and also of his personal ambitions. His second son, Abdullah, had visited Lord Kitchener, the British pro-consul in Egypt, before the war to sound out the British position. In 1915 Lord Kitchener, as secretary of war, advised Sir Henry McMahon, the high commissioner in Egypt, to approach Sharif Husayn of Mecca. In the meantime, Sharif Husayn sent his pro-Ottoman third son, Faysal, to Damascus to assure the Turks of his loyalty and also obtain the opinion of the Syrian leaders. It was on this trip that Faysal was converted to the cause of Arab nationalism without distinction of religion. He became a member of the Fatat secret society and discussed with its leaders the feasibility of revolt against the Turks and the possibility of British assistance. These leaders gave Faysal a document, known as the "Damascus Protocol," which contained the conditions under which such a revolt should be launched. The subsequent negotiation between Sharif Husayn and Britain was based on the contents of this protocol.

From July 14, 1915, to March 10, 1916, Sharif Husayn, who claimed to represent the Arabs of the Crescent, and Sir Henry McMahon, representing Britain, exchanged ten letters which are known as the "Husayn-McMahon

Correspondence." This correspondence, in general terms and language, dealt with two principle points. In one, Husayn promised to recruit soldiers and fight against the Ottomans; and Britain promised, in case of victory, to "support the independence of the Arabs." In his correspondence, Husayn reveals the secular influence of the Syrian nationalists when he insists that "there is no difference between a Moslem and a Christian Arab, they are both descendents of one forefather." Furthermore, the term "Arab" or "Arab nation" in the view of Husayn or the Syrian nationalists did not include the populations of Egypt, North Africa, or possibly south Arabia and Najd.

The second point of the correspondence dealt with the boundaries of the "independent Arab Nation." On this point the correspondence, especially on the side of McMahon, is very ambiguous. Britain limited the boundary of the Arab nation by saying that "portions of Syria lying to the west of the district of Damascus, Homs, Hama, Aleppo cannot be said to be purely Arab, and should be excluded from the limits demanded." Sharif Husayn understood this to mean the area of modern Lebanon and the coastal region to the north of it, especially in the light of the fact that McMahon had mentioned the interest of France in that region. In his reply, Husayn stated that his acceptance of the above limitations was only temporary and expressed the hope that after the war Britain would help him in his negotiations with France.

After the war, the Husayn-McMahon Correspondence and especially the geographic meaning of the above limitation became a subject of bitter controversy. The main issue was whether the description "west of the district of Damascus . . ." included Palestine or not. The Arabs have forcefully maintained that Palestine was to be part of the Arab nation, and successive British governments since 1922 have repeatedly affirmed that the above sentence meant the whole Mediterranean coast from Sinai to Turkey, which includes Palestine.

Six months after the close of the Husayn-McMahon correspondence, the British government discarded its entire pledge to the Arabs by signing the Sykes-Picot Agreement. But this was part of the Triple Entente secret agreements, and the Arabs did not know about it. Partly on the strength of McMahon's pledge, the Arabs declared war on the Ottomans on June 5, 1916. In November 1916, Sharif Husayn made good his intentions by declaring himself king of the Arabs. Arab troops under the command of Prince Faysal with the advice of the famous Colonel T. E. Lawrence fought against the Turkish garrisons and conducted guerrilla activities all along the Turkish lines of communication. Most of the Arab officers were members of the Fatat secret society of Syria, and the Ahd society of Iraq. They took the port of Aqaba in July 1917, which made it easier for General Allenby to capture Jerusalem in December 1917. Faysal and his troops made a triumphant entry into Damascus on October 1, 1918. Remembering the Sykes-Picot Agreement, the British government ordered General Allenby to go to Damascus and counteract the activities of Faysal and Lawrence. Faysal, however, proclaimed the formation of an "Arab Constitutional Government, fully and absolutely independent." He then went in pursuit of the Turks and captured Homs and Hama in the north. On October 29, 1918, the Turks surrendered on the plain of Marj Dabiq, the same place where Sultan Selim I had conquered Syria in 1516.

THE SYKES-PICOT AGREEMENT

During World War I, there were three secret agreements among the members of the Triple (Britain, France, and Russia) Entente that dealt with the Ottoman Empire. One was the Constantinople Agreement of March 18, 1915, which divided northern Syria, Asia Minor, and Iran among the member countries. The second was the London Agreement of April 26, 1915, which was arranged when Italy joined the war and demanded its share of the spoils. In these two agreements, the Fertile Crescent was left to Britain and France.

On October 21, 1915, the British informed the French about the Husayn-McMahon Correspondence and suggested that they get together and discuss their interests in the Fertile Crescent. Accordingly, Sir Mark Sykes of Britain and Charles Georges-Picot of France reached an agreement by February 1916. Later this agreement was ratified by Russia and Italy. Without regard to the pledge to the Arabs, the Fertile Crescent was divided into three parts. At the insistence of Russia, Palestine, because of its holy places, was made international. The rest was divided by a line extending from the Mediterranean coast north of Haifa in a northeasterly direction to the Iranian border south of Mosul. The region north of this line was to go to France and south of the line to Britain. Furthermore, the northern region was divided into two parts, one under direct French control and the other under its "influence." Similarly the southern region was divided into two parts, one under the direct British control and the other under its "influence."

The Sykes-Picot Agreement was secret, but the Bolsheviks made it public property in November 1917. Jemal Pasha of Turkey sent the agreement to King Husayn and proposed a separate Turko-Arab peace. Husayn asked the British for an explanation and they, on three occasions, assured him that they would help in the establishment of an Arab state. The Arabs believed these assurances, perhaps because they wanted to believe them. With the Ottomans losing on practically all fronts, a Turko-Arab treaty did not have any meaning. The Arabs could not do much else but to hope for the best.

ZIONISM AND THE BALFOUR DECLARATION

The fledgling Arab nationalism of the Fertile Crescent faced many problems from the beginning. In addition to the formidable imperialist power of Britain and France, Faysal and his Arab nationalist advisors had internal adversaries. The Christians of Syria-Lebanon, especially the Maronites, wanted separation from the Muslims and the protection of a foreign power. There were pan-Islamists encouraged by the local ulama who were against the "Arabism" of the liberals and wanted an Islamic state. There were the bedouins in both Hijaz and the Fertile Crescent who were basically nomadic and did not particularly care for any kind of state. No doubt Arab nationalism, given peace and time, could have solved some of these problems were it not for the fact that it had to deal with a new and strong rival—Jewish nationalism—which appeared on the scene toward the end of 1917.

Jewish nationalism, or Zionism, had some of its roots in Hebrew religious history. Of the three religions—Judaism, Christianity, and Islam—that have theological and historical ties with each other, Judaism alone was exclusive. It believed its people to be different from all other peoples by birth, by heritage, and by virtue of a special covenant that God had made with them through Abraham and Moses. Furthermore, God had designated a particular territory, known in ancient times as Canaan and in modern times as Palestine, to be the special land where this people could live and practice their religion without danger of intermarriage with others. Notwithstanding the promise of God, the Jews were never the exclusive settlers of Canaan. The original inhabitants, who were defeated by the army of Joshua, were not wiped out but remained a minority in the land.

In the course of centuries, two trends developed in Judaism. One was the priestly trend, which was ritualistic and usually segregationalist and literal in its interpretation of the law of Moses. The other was the prophetic trend, which was against ritualism and usually integrationalist and spiritual in its interpretation of the law. Beginning with the Babylonian captivity in 586 B.C., and especially in the later Roman period, the Jews were gradually scattered to all parts of the world. Wherever they went, they carried these two schools of thought. The prophetic school of thought followed the admonitions of Jeremiah, Isaiah, Micah, and other prophets, who had advised the dispersed Jews to "build houses . . . plant gardens . . . take wives and beget sons and daughters" in the lands they had settled "for in the peace thereof shall you have peace." But the priestly school followed the admonitions of people like the author of Psalm 137, who had said, "If I forget you, O Jerusalem, let my right hand wither, let my tongue cleave to the roof of my mouth, if I do not remember you, if I do not set Jerusalem above my highest joy." The prophetic school considered the Temple as a "house of prayer for all people," while to the priestly party it was exclusively for the Jews. According to one group, the Messiah would establish the Kingdom of God, while according to the other group he would establish the Kingdom of David.

What is relevant to this discussion is the fact that the followers of the priestly school were in the majority. Generations of Jews were taught to consider themselves "strangers" in the land where they were living. All of the Jewish festivals, with the exception of *Yom Kippur*, or the Day of Atonement, are quasi-national festivals. Jewish families at the end of Friday evening prayers drank a toast, "Next year in Jerusalem," and every Jew turned toward Jerusalem when he prayed. But the festivals, the toast, and the direction of prayer did not mean that the majority of Jews wanted to go to Canaan or Palestine to live, any more than a Muslim praying toward Mecca desired to live there. Some went to Jerusalem for pilgrimage and came back, but the city and the land were not forgotten. Whenever there were persecutions, and there were many, the desire for the "Return" and the "Kingdom of David" would come to the surface.

Political Zionism

Rapid changes in Europe, such as the political and social revolutions of the sixteenth to eighteenth centuries, profoundly affected the position of Jews. Ghettos disappeared and religious Jews, who had come under the influence of scientific thought and method, revived the prophetic school of interpretation and introduced Reformed Judaism. The Reformed Jews of the nineteenth century in Europe and the United States spoke of the "Kingdom of Truth" and considered themselves "no longer a nation, but a religious community, and therefore expected neither a return to Palestine, nor the restoration of a sacrificial worship under the Sons of Aaron, or of any of the laws concerning the Jewish State." In the nineteenth century, however, the majority of the Jews lived in the ghettos of Eastern Europe and Russia where the ideas of Enlightenment had not penetrated. They were victims of Christian fanaticism and periodic pogroms. Even though a number of them had been deeply influenced by Marxism, the bulk of them were strictly orthodox Jews who expected that someday the Messiah would lead them to Palestine, the Promised Land, and would once again establish the Jewish state.

In 1894, Theodor Herzl, a Jewish intellectual and journalist, was covering the famous Dreyfus trial for his Vienna newspaper. A crime committed by a member of the French aristocracy was blamed on Captain Alfred Dreyfus of the French army chiefly because he was a Jew. The conviction of Dreyfus and his imprisonment in a penal colony created a wave of anti-Semitism throughout France. Even though some of the liberals exposed the fraud and fully cleared Dreyfus of any guilt, the lesson was not lost on Theodor Herzl. If in France, the center of Enlightenment, in spite of all its stress on liberty and religious freedom, there was such an undercurrent of anti-Semitism, then the only hope for the Jews was to leave Europe and organize a state of their own. In 1895, he embodied this idea in his book, *Der Judenstaat* (*The Jews' State*) and launched the modern Zionist movement.

Zionism, from the beginning, merged two trends in nineteenth-century Jewish thought. One was the religious longing for the "return to the Promised Land," intensified because of the anti-Jewish pogroms and the urgency of escape from persecution. The other was the nineteenth-century liberal and romantic nationalism that exalted "statehood" and saw in it a panacea for the ills of humanity. The secular Jews, following the current thinking of the late nineteenth century, concluded that only by the creation of a Jewish state could anti-Semitism be destroyed. This also appealed to some non-Jewish liberals of the day who were as ashamed of anti-Semitism as the Jews were afraid of it.

There were bitter conflicts between orthodox and liberal Jews in the early days of Zionist organization. To the orthodox Jews, the return to Palestine was all-important, while to the secularists, statehood was essential and not the locality. Theodor Herzl, who belonged to the secularists, and some of his associates suggested Argentina, Australia, Africa, or anywhere else that was available. In the first World Zionist Congress held in Switzerland in 1897, the delegates reached the conclusion that Palestine had an emotional appeal to the devoutly religious Jew and Christian alike, which another locality would not have. Once Palestine was decided upon, religious and agnostic Jews worked together for the realization of the common goal.

Jewish Colonization

Palestine was part of the Ottoman Empire; and its conversion into a Jewish state did, of necessity, require the colonization of the land by mass transplantation of Jews from Europe. Colonialism and imperialism were accepted institutions in late-nineteenth-century Europe. It is not surprising, therefore, to find the Zionists having the same general attitudes and using the same methods as the rest of their fellow Europeans. For example, for the purpose of financing and supervising the colonization of Palestine, the Zionists formed commercial and political organizations such as the Jewish Colonial Trust, the Colonization Commission, the Jewish National Fund, the Palestine Office, and the Palestine Land Development Company. Having heard of the bankruptcy of the Ottoman Empire, Herzl arranged an interview with Sultan Abdul Hamid II and proposed that a Jewish financial syndicate would assume all the foreign debts of the empire if the sultan would grant a charter for the Jewish colonization of Palestine. Abdul Hamid refused the offer, although he said he would allow a limited number of Jews to settle in Palestine, provided they became Ottoman citizens. Herzl and his friends appealed to practically every government in Europe and offered Jewish loyalty in return for the Zionist colonization of Palestine.

Toward the end of the nineteenth century, it became evident to the Zionists that Britain was the power to deal with. Herzl tried to persuade Cecil Rhodes in 1899 and Joseph Chamberlain in 1902, without result. Herzl died in 1904; a few years later the mantle of Zionist leadership fell on the able shoulders of Dr. Chaim Weizmann, a chemist and a naturalized British citizen. While Herzl and his associates had failed to entice a number of British governments to accede to their requests, developments during World War I set the stage for an alliance between the Zionists and Britain. The first announcement of this alliance was in the form of a letter by the foreign secretary, Arthur Balfour, to Lord Rothschild, a Jewish financier, on November 2, 1917. This letter is known as the "Balfour Declaration."

In the course of two short years, from November 1915 to November 1917, Britain had solemnly made agreements with three different parties that were contradictory to each other. It is probably incorrect to assume that Britain did this out of either stupidity or willful malice. Neither is it possible to dismiss the whole matter as an "unfortunate mistake" in the confusion of war. Each step was calculated to strengthen the British Empire. But when unforeseen complications arose, changes were made that best served the empire and without regard to the anguish it might cause others. This was a rule of the game of imperialism.

In 1915, it was the British policy to supplant the Ottoman Empire by an independent Arab state in the Fertile Crescent in which Britain had special privileges. If the situation had not changed, it is quite likely that Britain would have honored its promise. But there were pressures from other European powers, especially France, who insisted in sharing the control of the post-Ottoman Fertile Crescent. The only way that Britain could control the southern part of the area was to give the northern section to France. This was the essence of the Sykes-Picot Agreement in 1916. Russia complicated the matter by insisting on the internationalization of Palestine because of the Russian Orthodox Church's interest in the area. Internationalization involved the French, who also had an interest in the holy places. This alarmed the British policy makers, especially the "India government," which did not want the French so close to the Suez Canal. The Zionists had been arguing all along that a Jewish national home in Palestine required the presence of Britain in the area, and a grateful Zionist government in Palestine would always remain an ally of the British Empire.

The strongest opposition to this convenient alliance with the British government came from the anti-Zionist Jews of Britain, France, and the United States. This became clear in the text of the Balfour Declaration. "His Majesty's government view with favor the establishment in Palestine of a national home for the Jewish people, and will use their best endeavors to facilitate the achievement of this objective, it being clearly understood that nothing shall be done which may prejudice the civil and religious rights of existing non-Jewish communities in Palestine, or the rights and political status enjoyed by Jews in any other country."

The last phrase was inserted to allay the fears of anti-Zionist Jews, who saw the solution to the Jewish problem as integration rather than self-imposed segregation and did not want the creation of a Jewish state to prejudice their nationality status in the countries of their birth. "National home" in the first sentence was understood by the Zionists, and perhaps by Balfour, to be the same as "national state." The first World Zionist Congress in 1897 had decided to use "home" instead of state, "in the interest of opportunism," to quote Dr. Max Nordau, one of the famous leaders of Zionism. Perhaps the Zionists believed that they could settle in Palestine without prejudice to the civil and religious rights of the Palestinians. The later Faysal-Weizmann agreement confirmed their belief.

King Husayn was perplexed when he learned about the Balfour Declaration. Britain sent Commander Hogarth of the Arab Bureau to Cairo on January 4, 1918, to assure him that a Jewish settlement in Palestine would be allowed only if it were "compatible with the freedom of the existing population, both economic and political." The British also advised King Husayn to accept the Zionists because "the friendship of world Jewry to the Arab cause is equivalent to support in all states where Jews have a political influence." A few days later, a joint Anglo-French proclamation promised the Arabs a government "freely chosen by the population." Both King Husayn and Faysal were encouraged by these assurances and accepted them as they had done in the case of the Sykes-Picot Agreement.

IRAN AND THE BRITISH-RUSSIAN RIVALRY

During World War I, Iran was the scene of numerous battles between the Entente and the Central Powers, even though it had declared its neutrality. Russians and Turks fought in Azerbaijan; the British formed an Iranian militia in the south known as the South Persia Rifles; and the Germans tried to arouse the tribes against the Entente through adventurous agents such as Niedermayer and Wassmuss. In the meantime, the young monarch, Ahmad Shah, having come of age, was crowned in July 1914; and Iran began to have some semblance of parliamentary life. The government was in the hands of a coalition of political moderates, tribal leaders, and landed aristocracy, a large number of whom had been against constitutional government a few years before. Ever since the closing of the Majles in 1911 when Shuster was dismissed, the liberal Democrats had been scattered. Since the liberals believed that in case of an Entente victory, Iran would surely be divided between Russia and Britain, their sympathies lay with Germany and Turkey. Most of those who had fled to Europe gathered in Berlin, from where Hasan Taqizadeh, one of the foremost liberal constitutionalists, edited a paper called *Kaveh*[1] until 1921. Other constitutionalists who had remained in Iran made the long trek to Istanbul to make common cause with the Ottomans.

The Soviet Republic of Gilan.   Neither in Berlin nor in Istanbul did the Iranian liberals affect the course of events in Iran. There were, however, a few liberals who took matters into their own hands, gathered a small number of armed men, and set up revolutionary governments in Azerbaijan, Gilan, and Khorasan, the northern provinces of Iran. The most important of these was the one led by Mirza Kuchek Khan in the province of Gilan, south of the Caspian Sea. He and his followers had vowed not to shave or cut their hair until foreign troops had withdrawn from Iran. Living as they did in the forests of Gilan, they came to be known as *Jangali* ("jungle men") and supported themselves in Robin Hood fashion. For a time, German, Austrian, and Turkish officers trained the Jangali volunteers to harass the British and Russian lines of communication in the midst of World War I. After the Russian Revolution, the Bolsheviks, moreover, got in touch with the Jangalis through Ehsanullah Khan, a Communist and a friend of Kuchek Khan.

The relationship between the Jangalis and the Communist Central Committee in Moscow was never stabilized. On the one hand, the Bolsheviks were not sure whether Iran was ideologically "ready" for revolution. On the other hand, only Ehsanullah was a radical Communist among the Jangalis, and the leader, Kuchek Khan, could not bring himself to cooperate wholeheartedly with the Bolsheviks. Nevertheless, in the spring of 1920 he did accept the aid of the Bolsheviks in forcing the British soldiers, who had occupied northern Iran after the Russian Revolution, to evacuate Gilan. The Soviet Republic of Gilan was established in Rasht, the provincial capital, but

---

[1]Kaveh was the name of the legendary Iranian blacksmith who, by raising his leather apron, led a revolt against the tyranny of the non-Iranian Zahhak.

soon there was a rift among the Jangalis. Kuchek Khan, as an Iranian nationalist, would not allow Gilan to become part of Russia, and as a moderate socialist, would not agree to the complete dispossession of Iranian landlords and merchants.

It has been mentioned that Moscow was not certain as to what policy to follow. At the same time that a Soviet republic was being formed in Gilan, Moscow was negotiating a treaty of friendship with the Iranian government in Tehran. Eventually Lenin decided to let the situation in Iran develop until it was ready for a Marxist revolution. He withdrew his support from the Jangalis and recalled the Soviet troops. Mirza Kuchek Khan, thus left alone, could not cope with the Iranian government forces. His troops were defeated and disbanded and he died of exposure as a fugitive in the mountains of Gilan.

THE PARIS PEACE CONFERENCE

At the end of World War I, interested parties in the Fertile Crescent, Egypt, and Iran sent delegations to be admitted to the conference in order to plead their separate causes. They regarded President Woodrow Wilson of the United States as their champion on his Fourteen Points, especially the article on self-determination, as their main goal.

The Fertile Crescent

Three groups were contending for supremacy in all or part of the Fertile Crescent. The first and the most powerful was the Anglo-French group. But Britain and France were not in agreement. Since France had not done any of the fighting in the east, British troops occupied all of the Fertile Crescent and they were reluctant to leave. On the other hand, France insisted on carrying out the Sykes-Picot Agreement. They landed some 20,000 troops in Lebanon and demanded British evacuation. The British, on their part, wanted modifications in the the agreement concerning the oil-rich province of Mosul and the internationalization of Palestine. While speeches to determine the peace of the world were going on, the intense in-fighting between the two imperialistic rivals led to accusations and recriminations.

The second group that was contending for a part of the Fertile Crescent was political Zionism. The Zionists were more powerful than the Arabs because they had men of influence in the powerful countries to advance their cause. They did not want the Balfour Declaration to remain a private agreement between themselves and Britain. They wanted to incorporate it in all policies pertaining to the Middle East. There were Jews, however, who strongly opposed the Zionist plan because they believed that Zionism was endangering their status and causing more anti-Semitism.

The third and weakest contenders for the Fertile Crescent were the inhabitants of the area represented by Faysal and the Hashimites of the peninsula. The Arabs wanted the independence promised to them by Britain. They also pinned their hopes on Woodrow Wilson and his principle of self-determination. The Arabs were further weakened by disagreements among themselves. The Christians in general and Maronites in particular were afraid to be a minority in a predominantly Muslim state. France, as an old-time protector of the Maronites, organized a group called the "Syrian Commission," which went to Paris and opposed Faysal and the union with the Muslim Arabs. Furthermore, there was rivalry between the Arab leaders of Baghdad and Damascus. Some wanted a united kingdom and others preferred a federation of two states.

Faysal went to London and for the first time became fully acquainted with the Sykes-Picot Agreement. The British told him to accept the French, and the Zionist leaders gave a banquet in his honor. Faysal continued to talk about self-determination, freedom, and justice, but he had become aware that the realities of politics did not pay attention to such ideals. Perhaps it was this realization that induced him to sign an agreement, in January 1919, with Weizmann, the head of the World Zionist Organization. In this document Faysal accepted "the immigration of Jews into Palestine on a large scale," provided "the Arab peasant and tenant farmers shall be protected in their rights." For their part, the Zionists agreed "to send to Palestine a commission of experts to make a survey of the economic possibilities" of Palestine as well as "the Arab state." Faysal's signature was conditional upon the creation of the "Arab state," which was not created. A complete implementation of this agreement might have averted a great deal of subsequent bloodshed, had it not been for the Sykes-Picot Agreement, which was against the creation of an Arab state.

In the meantime, President Wilson took the view that the great powers, in accepting his Fourteen Points, had automatically nullified their secret agreements. To minimize tension, a compromise was reached with the introduction of the mandate system of the League of Nations. This was based upon the idea that the Arabs were not ready for self-government and would be tutored in the art by a mandatory power. President Wilson accepted this principle because it was not a rejection of the principle of self-determination, but only a postponement of it. But difficulties arose on the question of which powers should have mandatory rights over what specific areas. Wilson proposed to send a joint commission to the Fertile Crescent to ascertain the wishes of the people. France refused to join, Britain abstained, and the Zionists opposed the proposal. But President Wilson sent the King-Crane Commission to the area in August 1919. By the time the commission was ready with its report, Wilson was a defeated and sick man. Every one of his Fourteen Points, save one, had been modified or rejected or its enactment postponed. The one remaining point, the League of Nations, became a reality but was rejected by his own country. The report of the commission was not published until three years after. It reported that a great majority of the Palestinians wanted to remain part of Syria and that they would accept a temporary mandate if it were under the United States or Britain. Although the report considered some of the aspirations of the Zionists to be praiseworthy, it warned against the "extreme Zionist programme for Palestine of unlimited immigration of Jews looking finally to make Palestine a Jewish state."

By the end of the Paris Peace Conference, Britain and France had come to an understanding on the Sykes-Picot Agreement, Palestine, and the mandates. The Zionists had succeeded in turning the Balfour Declaration from a private correspondence into an international proclamation. The Arabs, however, found themselves serving two European Christian masters in place of the one Turkish Muslim master against whom they had rebelled.

Egypt and Britain

The foundations of Egyptian nationalism and the independence movement, which were laid in prewar years, were sparked anew by Woodrow Wilson's Fourteen Points. The latent influence of the United States on the minds of leading nationalists of the Middle East, through the liberal views of President Wilson, cannot be exaggerated. All of them wanted to send delegations to the Paris Peace Conference in the hope that Wilson's presence and influence would gain them a hearing and recognition.

The Egyptians also wanted to go, and the person who assumed leadership was Sa'd Zaghlul Pasha (1857–1927). He was a friend of Abduh and one-time student of Afghani. As a judge he was active in reforming the laws of Egypt according to modern needs. In 1906 Zaghlul was made minister of education under Cromer, with whom he was on good terms. Perhaps because of his dislike for Gorst and Kitchener, Zaghlul resigned in 1912 as minister of justice and was elected a deputy to the Egyptian Assembly. In November 1918 he sought permission of the British authorities to lead a delegation (*wafd*) to the Paris Peace Conference. He was not permitted to do so. Then he asked to go to London and put Egypt's case before the British authorities, but this was also denied. The British argued that Zaghlul had not been "elected" by the Egyptians to represent them, which was true, but they failed to recognize that he was voicing what was in the minds of most of the nationalists. Zaghlul persuaded the prime minister, Rushdi Pasha, to ask to go to Paris. Rushdi was also refused permission and he resigned the premiership. In the meantime, during the first months of 1919, Zaghlul had formed the Wafd Party and, with this backing, he tried to prevent the sultan from appointing a new prime minister. The British responded by arresting Zaghlul and a few of his associates. Zaghlul was exiled to Malta. By this time, the idea of sending a delegation had become a *cause célèbre*, and thousands rushed to join the Wafd Party. Zaghlul's exile ignited a conflagration. Riots, general strikes, the burning of foreigners' houses, and the killing of British soldiers became the order of the day. This was the first of the many uprisings that united Muslims and Christians and involved even women and the peasantry. Such revolts continued to shake Egypt until well after World War II.

The British, who were preoccupied with the defense of the empire, reacted by tightening their grip even more closely. But the leaders of the general strike insisted on the "Delegation." Lord Allenby, the conqueror of Jerusalem, was sent to Cairo to maintain order. In the end there was no other way out but to free Zaghlul and let him lead his delegation to Paris. He did not accomplish much in Paris or later in London. But he had become very popular at home and returned in triumph.

Iran and Britain

The Bolshevik Revolution in Russia affected Iran in diverse ways. One of them was that it, at least temporarily, ended the Anglo-Russian rivalry over the country. The revolution had rendered obsolete the Anglo-Russian Convention of 1907 by which the two countries had divided Iran into spheres of influence. With the absence of Russia it was only natural for Britain to fill the vacuum and bring all of Iran under its influence, thereby controlling the land and sea approaches to India as well as the newly discovered oil wells. It was the dream of Foreign Secretary Lord Curzon to create a "chain of vassal states stretching from the Mediterranean to the Pamirs" in which Iran was the "most vital link." In 1919, the veteran British diplomat, Sir Percy Cox, was minister in Tehran and he was given the task of implementing the above policy.

The year 1919 also was the year of the Paris Peace Conference to which Woodrow Wilson's doctrine of self-determination had attracted so many small nations. Iran had also sent a delegation with a set of demands. The British were against admitting Iran to the conference. Wilson was for admitting all delegations. In the case of Iran, France and Italy were favorable, but Britain would not consent. By August 1919 it was announced that Britain and Iran had signed an agreement, negotiations for which had been going on secretly for some time. Representing Iran in this ill-famed agreement were Prime Minister Hasan Vosuq al-Dowleh and Prince Firuz, who had been appointed foreign minister by his cousin the shah.

The agreement was so obviously on the side of Britain that it aroused the wrath not only of Iranian liberals but also of countries like the United States and France. After the usual promise to respect absolutely the independence and integrity of Iran, the agreement went on to stipulate the following:

1. Britain would provide advisors for as many Iranian departments as considered necessary. Iran would agree to pay the cost and to endow the advisors with "adequate powers."
2. Britain would organize and train an Iranian army at the expense of the Iranian government.
3. A loan of £2,000,000 at 7 percent was arranged to pay for the above, and collateral was to be "all the revenues and customs receipts" of Iran.
4. Britain would improve communication in Iran by "means of railway construction and other forms of transport."

The agreement was designed to bring Iran under the tutelage of Britain; in many ways it was similar to the unilateral agreement imposed upon Egypt in 1922.

The reaction to the agreement was immediate and negative. Not so much by the opposition of the Iranians, as by that of the United States, the agreement was abandoned. It must be stated that combined with the idealism of Woodrow Wilson was the desire of American oil companies to gain concessions in Iran. The companies did not like the monopoly that such an agreement gave to the fledgling Anglo-Persian Oil Company while consolidating future British claims to oil in the region. The British, on the other hand, were so sure of themselves that even before the agreement was ratified by the Majles (it never was), they dispatched three chief advisors to Iran. The scuttling of the agreement was a blow to British prestige, but soon they found another scheme to regain their influence in Iran. In view of the impossibility of direct control, a strong anti-Russian government in Iran that was friendly to Britain would serve the purposes of the empire. They proceeded to bring about such a change.

Chapter Twenty-Three
The Making
of Modern Turkey

It was perhaps inevitable that the Ottoman Empire should enter World War I on the side of the Central Powers. Russia was an old enemy; and experience had shown the Turks that they could not always depend on the British and the French, especially when they were allies of Russia. On the other hand, Germany was a new power with whom they had not had adverse experiences. The Germans had extensive commercial enterprises in the empire, and the kaiser's trips (in 1889 and 1898) had made favorable impressions. Furthermore, the triumvirate, Jemal, Enver, and Talat, who were running the empire, were pro-German; and many a Turk believed that the coming of Germany would neutralize the power of Russia and Britain.

The war, however, brought the Ottoman Empire to the verge of destruction. The bravery of the Turkish troops in numerous battles and their victory at Gallipoli were not enough to overcome the inner weaknesses of the empire. Long before Germany was brought to its knees, the defeat of the Ottomans was a certainty. The term "verge of destruction" is used advisedly, because after the Armistice of Mudros, on October 30, 1918, the Allied powers, especially Britain, did not want to utterly destroy the Ottoman Empire. A weakened and subservient Ottoman state would serve the same purpose and would be just as effective a buffer against the new designs of a Russian state with communist ideology. The "sick man of Europe" was still useful and was to be kept alive in a nursing home administered by the

Western powers. It was during the struggle for independence between 1919 and 1923 that the Turks decided to destroy the sick man altogether and start anew. Consequently, the four years after World War I are more significant to modern Turks than the four years of the war itself.

For the defeated Ottomans, there was only President Woodrow Wilson's word that "The Turkish portions of the present Ottoman Empire should be assured a secure sovereignty." In secret agreements during the war (1915–1917) the Allies, without the knowledge of the United States, had divided Asia Minor among themselves. Subsequently the Treaty of Sèvres on August 10, 1920, made new arrangements for the territories given to Russia in the secret agreements. In the west, the Straits were internationalized under the League of Nations, but Istanbul remained under Turkish sovereignty. In the east, almost exactly the same territory that had been given to Russia was declared the independent state of Armenia. Furthermore, local autonomy was granted to the Kurds with a provision of a plebiscite and possible independence within a year. The Kurds did not get their autonomy nor was there a plebiscite. The Armenians, however, established a republic in 1918, but they were abandoned by the British. Later Kemalist Turkey and the USSR aborted the scheme altogether.

In addition to the territorial dismemberment, the Turkish army was limited to 50,000 and subject to the advice of the Allied or neutral states. A financial commission representing Britain, France, and Italy was given control of all financial affairs of the state. Extraterritoriality was continued and the Turks had to give assurance as to the rights and privileges of the minorities within their boundaries. Humiliating as this treaty was, some historians believe that the Turks might have accepted it had not the Greeks been given a share of the spoils. Greece had been under Ottoman rule for nearly three centuries. To see them brought back as masters was too bitter a pill for the Turks to swallow. Not only did the prospective gains of the Greeks arouse the Turks, but also the creation of Armenia, Kurdish autonomy, capitulations, and financial control, all of which were included in the Treaty of Sèvres. All of this, however, might have been forced upon them had it not been for one person. He was Mustafa Kemal Pasha, later known as Atatürk, who united the Turks and led them to victory.

Mention has already been made of Mustafa Kemal, who as a young officer had joined the Committee of Union and Progress. He did not take an active part in the coup d'etat of 1908, and at no time was he identified with the policies or practices of the Young Turks who had control of the government. He had his disagreements with the triumvirate but he was too good an officer to be pushed aside. His defense of Gallipoli won him national acclaim. Toward the end of the war, however, he was a disillusioned officer on the Syrian front. Whether it was by accident or by design will probably never be known, but in May of 1919 he was appointed inspector of the Third Army in Anatolia. On May 19, 1919, he landed at the Black Sea port of Samsun in northern Anatolia. This date became a national holiday in all Turkey.

Almost immediately after landing, he began to arouse the nation against the severe limitations which, thanks to the Bolshevik disclosure, everyone knew would be imposed on Turkey. In two conferences, one in Erzerum in July 1919, and the other one in Sivas in September of the same year, he organized the Committee for the Defense of Eastern Asia Minor. He sent a telegram to the sultan asking him to dismiss the prime minister and to call for a new election to the Ottoman parliament. This the sultan proceeded to do. It must be remembered that Mustafa Kemal was a well-known hero. More important than this, the Third Army of Anatolia was intact and the Ninth Army under General Bekir, which had been carrying on successful campaigns in the Caucasus, had joined the nationalist cause. Mustafa Kemal was strong and the sultan was cognizant of this.

The result of the elections was a clear victory for the supporters of Kemal, and deputies from different parts of the country converged upon Istanbul. The British realized that it would be hard to cope with the decisions of such a parliament and so they arrested the deputies and sent some of them to Malta. The sultan was forced to denounce the nationalists. The Shaykh ul-Islam, in what was to be the last fetva of any Shaykh ul-Islam, declared that the whole nationalist movement was against Islam. Not to be outdone, Mustafa Kemal gathered the clergy of Anatolia, and they issued a counter-fetva denouncing the Shaykh ul-Islam. In place of the disbanded Ottoman parliament, the nationalists established the Grand National Assembly in Ankara, April 23, 1920.

With the creation of the Grand National Assembly, there were virtually two governments in Turkey, but the more powerful and popular one was the nationalist government in Ankara. Mustafa Kemal made excellent use of the opportunities which presented themselves. One of these was a quarrel among the Allies. After the war, the British and the French had serious misunderstandings in the Fertile Crescent, which led to recrimination and hostility. Furthermore, the French had much larger economic investments in Turkey than the British. French bondholders were afraid that the Turkish nationalists might cancel all debts the way the Bolsheviks had done. The Italians were not satisfied with the coming of the Greeks. Furthermore, Count Sforza, the Italian commissioner in Istanbul, predicted a nationalist victory. Both France and Italy wanted to gain as much as they could without going to war, and they did not mind wounding Britain in the process. Thus Italy and France made agreements with Mustafa Kemal, ceding their territories in return for economic concessions.

Perhaps the most important ally of Mustafa Kemal was the Soviet Union. Even though the doctrinaire Marxists among the Bolsheviks looked to Europe for the predicted proletarian revolution, there were enough "Asia firsters" among them to pay some attention to Iran and Turkey. As early as November 8, 1917, the Bolsheviks annulled all of the annexations of tsarist Russia. In 1919, the Bolsheviks were very friendly to Mustafa Kemal and his revolution. Some of them went so far as to write that there was not much difference between the red flag of Turkey and the red flag of Russia. Mustafa Kemal was never a communist, but he played along with them. In 1919, the Turkish communist, Shefi Degmer, founded the Socialist Workers and Peasants Party, which in 1922 became the Communist Party. In the World Communist Congress of 1922 there was one Turk in the executive committee. But when Mustafa Kemal became master of the situation in Turkey, he outlawed the Communist Party and arrested many, including Degmer.

The Bolsheviks were involved in a civil war of their own and were not in a position to give military assistance to Mustafa Kemal. But friendship with Lenin's government was good for Turkish morale and secured them from attack from the east. When the nationalist army under General Kiazim Bekir captured Kars from the Armenians, the Bolsheviks welcomed it. On December 3, 1920, they officially ceded Kars, Ardahan, and a large portion of eastern Asia Minor to the Turks. On March 16, 1921, Mustafa Kemal signed a treaty of friendship and collaboration with Russia against the Western powers.

THE GRECO-TURKISH WAR

The Greeks were the protégés of the British and were used by them as agents to defeat the plans of the nationalists. The Greeks, furthermore, were overjoyed by the fact that their ancient enemy, the Turks, had been subdued and humiliated. In this they saw a great opportunity to establish their power in Asia Minor and perhaps even take control of Istanbul as the rightful heirs of the Byzantines. The Greeks landed in Smyrna on the western shore of Asia Minor on May 15, 1919.

British plans for the control of the Ottoman state were blocked by the resistance of Mustafa Kemal. Many of the British people, who had just finished a long and bloody war, were in no mood to fight against the nationalists in Turkey. Besides, informed and liberal public opinion in England did not support fighting against a people who were demanding self-determination. Under the circumstances, the best that Prime Minister Lloyd George could do was to help the Greeks to destroy Mustafa Kemal. The Greeks were only too eager to take advantage of this opportunity.

In June 1920, the Greek army moved eastward from Smyrna and won several victories; it advanced slowly until it reached the vicinity of Ankara by the summer of 1922. In August 1922, the Turks were able to launch an offensive that swept everything before them; within two weeks the Greeks were thrown back to the sea. Atrocities were committed by both sides—by the Greeks as they were retreating and by the Turks when they took Smyrna. The Greek dream was shattered and Mustafa Kemal moved toward Istanbul.

THE TREATY OF LAUSANNE

Lloyd George sent a plea to his former allies to help defend the Straits against the nationalists. But France and Italy responded by withdrawing their forces from the Straits. Britain was not in a position to fight and Mustafa Kemal did not want to provoke the Western powers. Consequently, the convention of Mudania was signed, according to which eastern Thrace and Adrianople were ceded to Turkey, and Mustafa Kemal accepted international control of the Straits.

Turkey was the only defeated power to force the Allies to scrap their dictated Treaty of Sèvres. Another conference met in Lausanne in 1922 to write a second treaty of peace. The chief antagonists were Lord Curzon for the British, and General Ismet Pasha, later known as Inönü, for Turkey. The imperious Curzon was reluctant to accede to the wishes of Turkish nationalists. Ismet Pasha, on the other hand, felt that time was on his side and was persistently patient. The main issues were the oil-rich province of Mosul, which the Turks demanded, and the principle of extraterritoriality, which Lord Curzon did not want to relinquish. The conference was at last suspended, resuming again in July 1923. This time Lord Curzon was not present, and the Treaty of Lausanne was signed. Turkey was recognized as master of all of Asia Minor, the Straits, and eastern Thrace. Extraterritoriality was abolished. The Straits were internationalized under the League but the chairman of the commission was to be a Turk. The Straits were also demilitarized, but Turkey was allowed to keep a garrison of 12,000 in Istanbul. The Turks and the Greeks agreed to an exchange of population, with the exception of the Greeks of Istanbul and the Turks of western Thrace. The question of Mosul was left to arbitration by the League of Nations. Mustafa Kemal and his associates had achieved their goal after four years of perseverance, sacrifice, diplomacy, and war. Kemalist Turkey was much smaller than the Ottoman Empire; it was, however, more homogeneous and manageable and a strong viable state.

THE TURKISH REFORMS

For Mustafa Kemal, independence from foreign interference was not an end but only a means to give the Turks the opportunity to build a new Turkey. This could be done by far-reaching reforms in practically every aspect of life. Most of the reform programs launched by the nationalists under Mustafa Kemal had been proposed and discussed by scores of Turkish intellectuals and reformers from Tanzimat on. The most important contribution of Mustafa Kemal was not so much originality of ideas but the ability to choose a set of interrelated, consistent, and relevant ideas and build them into a practical program. He was more a child of the Young Turks than of the Young Ottomans and more a Turkist than a pan-Turkist. His idea of Turkification was not the imposition of Turkish language and culture on non-Turks, but getting rid of non-Turkish elements, including territories with non-Turkish populations.

Some of these ideas had been systematized by the famous sociologist Ziya Gökalp (1876–1924), whose writings influenced many a Turkish nationalist, including Mustafa Kemal. Gökalp separated culture and civilization and proposed to "graft Western civilization in its entirety" to the Turkish national culture. The mistake of all past reformers, according to him, was their attempt to reconcile Western civilization with that of the East. Civilizations, according to Gökalp, are incompatible with each other and do not mix. The thing for the Turk to do was to divest himself of Eastern civilization, revive his Turkish culture, and then graft Western civilization onto it. To

Gökalp, "Turkish culture" was a combination of somewhat idealized folk mores, Islam, and some modern concepts, provided they were all expressed in Turkish. Turkism in religious matters meant reading the Koran and giving the call to prayer and praying in Turkish. In law it meant establishing "modern law," and in morality it meant going back to the early "democracy" of the Turks. Turkism was defined as a "scientific, philosophical, and literary movement," but not as a political movement. Turkism, however, supported the "Peoples' Party . . . of our great Mustafa Kemal . . ." because he "delivered the country from invasion and, at the same time, called our state, nation, and language by their real name, . . ." that is, Turkish. Gökalp may be called the philosopher of a latter-day Turkish nationalism of which Kemal Atatürk was the executor and inspirer.

The Committee for the Defense of Eastern Asia Minor, which had called the conferences at Erzerum and Sivas in 1919, gradually developed into the Republican Party in September 1923. This party had a six-point program that came to be known as the "Six Principles of Kemalism." It was not until 1937 that these were incorporated into the Turkish constitution. All reforms, however, before the proclamation of the six principles and after, were based on them. These principles were:

1. Republicanism, which asserted the idea that sovereignty was vested in the people.
2. Nationalism, which claimed Turkey for the Turks and rejected jurisdiction over territories with non-Turkish population.
3. Populism, which did away with the millet system and proclaimed the equality of all classes of people before the law.
4. Statism, which accepted the necessity of the constructive intervention of the state in the national economy.
5. Secularism, which established the principle of the separation of religion and state.
6. Reformism, which emphasized the determination to change and bypass tradition and precedent if they do not serve national purpose.

It is important to note that notwithstanding violent vicissitudes, the death of Atatürk in 1938, and World War II, the above principles have remained without much modification. Furthermore, these and all the reforms carried out under them have been directed toward one major objective—namely, the replacement of an Eastern civilization with that of a Western one. While the other countries of the Middle East have tried to reconcile the two civilizations, the Turks have attempted to turn their backs on the East and think of themselves as members of the European community.

Since Islam rejected the principle of separation of the spiritual and the temporal, it penetrated all aspects of life and controlled all things by laws. Not only prayer and pilgrimage, but government and commerce, peace and war, sex, marriage and divorce, and even food and attire were regulated either by the Koran and the hadith or by mores and customs that had become almost as binding. Consequently, all of the reforms which are discussed have some relationship to Islam. From 1922 to the death of Atatürk in 1938, the major activities of the government and people of Turkey consisted of abolishing institutions or laws or ways of life and substituting others in their place.

The abolition of the sultanate.   Soon after the military victory against the Greeks and the political victory against the British, the Grand National Assembly, on November 1, 1922, deposed Sultan Mehmed V. Perhaps in the mind of Atatürk the sultanate was doomed from the beginning, but he did not reveal this. The fact of the matter was that many of the nationalists in Ankara did not want the dissolution of the Ottoman Dynasty, but only a different sultan subject to a constitution. Even as the sultan and his family were boarding a British ship into exile, his cousin, Abdul Mejid, was designated caliph. Almost a year later, on October 29, 1923, the Grand National Assembly declared Turkey a republic and chose Mustafa Kemal as its first president.

The abolition of the caliphate.   If the abolition of the sultanate offended many a Turk, the abolition of the caliphate offended all Sunni Muslims everywhere. This decision also was reached cautiously. Atatürk studied Islam and used to impress the Ankara clerics with his knowledge of it. He even tolerated the calling of a pan-Islamic conference at Sivas in February 1921. One-fifth of the members of the Grand National Assembly were clerics. Many of Atatürk's associates wanted a liberal but Islamic state. Perhaps Atatürk, who had a reputation of being an agnostic, believed that if the state was Islamic it could not be liberal. In the public mind, however, Abdul Mejid the caliph could not be distinguished from Abdul Mejid the sultan. It had always been that way. To those who had some knowledge of Islam, the office of the caliph without the power of the sultan was an anomaly. The question was debated in the assembly and, on March 3, 1924, the office of caliph was abolished. Abdul Mejid and the other members of the family of Osman, the founder of the Ottoman Empire, were banished from Turkey. The Ottomans had ruled 625 years. The institution of the caliphate was not replaced by anything.

The abolition of Islamic law.   The abolition of the sultanate and the caliphate did not affect the daily life of the average Turk. The end of the caliphate, however, marked the beginning of far-reaching reforms that affected every individual and rocked the country. One of the most important of these was the abolition of Islamic law, Shari'a. The judicial reforms of 1926 swept aside the religious courts and replaced them with Swiss civil and Italian penal codes. This act disqualified the ulama, who had had virtual monopoly of the legal profession. Only those who had studied Western law could pass the bar examination. Practically all of the schools for the teaching of Islamic law were closed. The department of Islamic theology at the University of Istanbul was so small that it was combined with the department of literature. The office of Shaykh ul-Islam was abolished; in its place all religious matters were administered by two bureaus attached to the office of the prime minister. One of them was the Bureau of Religious Affairs, which licensed preachers, censored sermons, and gave occasional advice on the intricacies of the Shari'a. The second was the Bureau of Religious Foundation, which administered all religious endowments.

The abolition of the Islamic calendar. In the same year (1926) that Shari'a was put aside, the Muslim calendar was replaced by the Christian calendar. For many years Turkish business firms were in the habit of using both Muslim lunar dates and the Western solar dates. All Muslim festivals and religious observations took place according to the Muslim calendar. The state, however, adopted the Western calendar and ordered citizens to use it exclusively; this constituted another step away from the East and toward the West. With the change of calendar came also the change of capital. Istanbul was too Ottoman and "foreign" to suit the new mentality. Ankara was located in Anatolia, where the "real" Turks lived. Istanbul had numerous mosques, but in the new city built next to the old town of Ankara, no mosques were erected. Furthermore, since Ankara's location was in the center of a farming district, the officials of the government could not, like the old Ottomans, avoid the Turkish peasants who lived all around them.

The abolition of the Arabic alphabet. Even though all Muslims had not adopted the Arabic language, as had been hoped by the early conquerors, all Muslims, no matter what their language, had adopted the Arabic alphabet. The main purpose of education was to be able to read the Koran even if the words could not be understood. In 1928 the Turkish Assembly replaced the Arabic alphabet with Latin symbols adapted to suit the needs of Turkish language. Atatürk ordered the Koran to be translated into Turkish and published it in the new alphabet. He also ordered the call to prayer to be given in Turkish and tried to persuade the people to pray in Turkish. Not all Muslims were persuaded to pray in Turkish, but with the change of alphabet a new generation of Turks did not read the Koran in Arabic. Only the very devout took the trouble to teach their children the rudiments of the Arabic alphabet.

Atatürk's purpose in changing the alphabet was not to prevent Turks from reading the Koran. He wanted to reduce illiteracy and develop a uniform and logical Turkish language. He rightly concluded that it was easier for a Turk to learn to read and write using the Latin alphabet. He and the members of the assembly each took a blackboard to the villages and towns and proved that the Latin alphabet was an easier medium. The introduction of a new alphabet was a staggering undertaking in the printing of books for the growing schools of the country, but it was done. Turks everywhere knew for the first time how a word was to be pronounced from the way it was written.

The abolition of titles. The continuation of titles, such as bey, pasha, and others, was against the principle of populism, which asserted the equality of all classes of people before the law. In later Ottoman times, titles had been sold to the highest bidder and had created a false class stratification. In 1934 all titles were abolished and Turks were ordered to choose family names.

Many were encouraged to choose purely Turkish names. It was in conformity with this law that Mustafa Kemal was given the name Atatürk, "Father of the Turks," by the assembly.

The abolition of Turkish attire for men. Like Peter the Great of Russia, Atatürk, in his program of westernization, forced the Turks to wear European clothes. No doubt both men thought that a change in attire might change the people's outlook. If a person wore a European hat, he might be persuaded to think like a European. The Turks might not have minded the change to European coats and trousers if they had been allowed to wear the fez, but Atatürk insisted on the wearing of European hats. The Turks had forgotten that the fez itself was introduced in the nineteenth century as a sign of modernization. The fez, however, was compatible with Muslim practice in a way that the hat was not. In prayer the Muslims used to cover their heads. Since one of the postures of prayer is prostration and touching the forehead to the ground, European hats presented a problem. But the Turks changed, and the faithful learned to pray with bare heads or with a cap turned backwards.

The abolition of the veil. If a Muslim woman wanted to follow the general directions of the Koran, she dressed somewhat like a Roman Catholic nun. The origin of the veil is obscure. But, un-Koranic as it is, the custom has been identified with Islam and followed it wherever it went. As the first step toward the emancipation of women, the veil was abolished; and Turkish women began to take part in all aspects of national life. In 1934 they were given the right to vote. Polygamy was abolished; and soon women were seen as teachers, lawyers, doctors, office workers, and even members of the Grand National Assembly.

The abolition of mosque schools. In the Ottoman Empire, all education had been under the control of the ulama. Beside each mosque there was usually a school. In small towns, the mosque was used as a school the main purposes of which were teaching children to read the Koran, to pray, and to perform the basic rituals of Islam. Those who wanted to go further attended special schools that trained the ulama. From Tanzimat days in the middle of the nineteenth century, European-type schools began to appear, though their number was not large. Under the republic, education was taken away from the ulama. The government built Western-type schools, and education was proclaimed to be universal and free. It was easy to make education free, but to make it universal would take decades to accomplish.

The abolition of Friday as a day of rest. This was accomplished in 1935. The rationale for it was theological, cultural, and economic. It was argued that the main purpose of the three main religions of the Middle East— Judaism, Christianity, and Islam—was the same—namely, that there should be one day of rest during the week. The fact that Jews had Saturday, Christians Sunday, and Muslims Friday was just an accident and irrelevant to the main issue. Furthermore, since all Western nations observed Sunday and the

Turks wanted to be like the Europeans, they might as well adopt Sunday. Keeping Friday as a holiday, it was pointed out, had dire economic consequences. Most of the business of Turkey was with Europe, which was closed on Sunday. If Turkey insisted on closing on Friday, she would then lose three days in the week, since the Saturday in between would also be sacrificed. Turkey could not afford so much leisure. Turkey has remained the only Muslim country in which Friday is not a national holiday.

The abolition of non-Turkish words.   The Turkish language had borrowed heavily from Arabic and Persian. Turkish writers and intelligentsia had written and spoken for each other. The bulk of the population, who did not know Arabic or Persian, could not understand them. In a genuine desire to reach the masses and in a surge of understandable nationalism, the nationalists discarded as many Arabic and Persian words as they could and replaced them with "Turkish" words. Almost every week newspapers published a list of these words. Where they could not find a Turkish word, they preferred a European word to an Arabic or Persian one. In the same spirit, they also changed many place names, such as Izmir for Smyrna and Edirne for Adrianople.

One of the most important programs, and one that caused the Turkish republic more trouble in later years, was in the field of economics. Many of the above reforms were not popular among the Turks, but the principle of government interference in economic matters was even less popular. In the Ottoman days, most of the commerce was in the hands of Greeks and Armenians. With the exchange of population with Greece, and the general flight of Armenians during World War I, the republic was faced with a great shortage of trained businessmen. It was deemed all the more necessary for the government to intervene.

In the 1930s, French experts advised the government in all aspects of economic life. New banks were established to help in agriculture, industry, mining, commerce, and finance. The government took control of all planning; and state monopolies were established in tobacco, salt, liquor, matches, playing cards, and munitions, among other things. Roads were built, factories were established, and foreign investment and trade were encouraged. The gradual nationalization of the railroads was accomplished. The purpose was to make Turkey economically independent, and to do this the Turks were required to work and to sacrifice.

None of these reforms, religious, social, or economic, was easily accomplished. If it had not been for the power and popularity of Atatürk, not much would have been achieved. In the constitution adopted in 1924, democracy was proclaimed and it was declared that sovereignty was vested in the nation. In practice, however, Atatürk was a dictator whose word was law. Some of his associates criticized him on his dictatorship. Others objected to some of the reforms. In the purge of 1926, some lost their lives and others, like General Kiazim Bekir, the hero of the war against the Greeks, and Halide Edib, the novelist and perhaps the first Turkish woman to serve as a soldier in the front lines, were banished. In the general election of 1927, when Atatürk's Republican Party had won, partly for encouragement and partly in self-justification, Atatürk gave a speech that lasted six days. He began with, "On May 19, 1919, I landed at Samsun," and ended with, "Our nation cannot die; if that ever happens, the world cannot support the bier." Atatürk was a benevolent dictator, one who was not aloof. His dictatorship was similar to that of a coach training athletes. In 1930, he asked one of his friends to organize an opposition party, but the venture failed. The Republican Party remained the only party; but in 1935, sixteen independent deputies were elected. Without the use of power, the reforms would have failed. Perhaps the effectiveness of Atatürk's dictatorship can be shown by the fact that in 1926, had there been a free choice, most of the reforms would have been rejected. In 1947, however, when there was a free election, most of the reforms were endorsed.

In foreign policy, Turkey followed a cautious and peaceful attitude. Its relationship with Russia remained correct, but the issue of communism drew them apart. Atatürk was closer to the countries of Western Europe and the United States. He had to compromise on the Mosul question. Turkey was given 10 percent of the oil royalties for giving up its claim on that territory. He was successful in his negotiation with the French on the port of Alexandrata (Iskandrun) on the Mediterranean; the French ceded it to Turkey over the opposition of the Syrians. The question of the Straits eventually was settled to the satisfaction of Turkey. On July 20, 1936, the Montreux Convention was called, in which the Soviet Union was also a participant. The specter of Hitler and the growing friendship between him and Mussolini persuaded Britain and France to accommodate Turkey. In peacetime and in a war in which Turkey was neutral there would be freedom of passage for all. If Turkey was belligerent, only vessels of countries not at war with Turkey enjoyed freedom. More important than these and other provisions were the abolition of the International Straits Commission, which restored the jurisdiction to the Turks, and the permission for the Turks to militarize the Straits.

On November 10, 1938, Atatürk died of cirrhosis. His death was premature and was aggravated most likely by overwork, overdrinking, and overindulgence. He had created a strong and viable state out of the ruins of the Ottoman Empire. A grateful people mourned him sadly.

TURKEY AND WORLD WAR II

Turkey declared its neutrality in World War II and was able to maintain it almost until the end. Turkish attitudes toward the major countries of Europe can be explained under three headings. Historically the Turks were conditioned not to trust Russia, economically they favored Germany and valued its trade, and culturally they were attracted by the institutions and mores of Britain and France.

When the Russo-German nonaggression treaty was signed in 1939, the Soviets wanted Turkey to close the Straits and promise not to participate in a war against Germany. Turkey could not accept this and instead signed a treaty of mutual assistance with Britain and France, under which Turkey was under no obligation to open hostilities against the Soviet Union. Even though Turkey was under obligation to assist Britain and France in case war spread to the Mediterranean, it saw fit to ignore its treaty obligations and remain neutral when Mussolini entered the conflict.

When Germany attacked Russia in 1941, Hitler's armies took control of the Balkans, and Turkey was hard-pressed by Germany to cancel its treaty with Britain and France and close the Straits to the USSR. Rather than risk the displeasure of the apparent victor in World War II, Turkey signed a pact with Germany in June 1941 and closed the Straits to the USSR, in contravention of the 1936 Montreux Convention.

During most of the war, Turkey was the center of spying and intrigue, as citizens of all the belligerent nations were free to come and go. Economically the war was a strain. All the products of Turkey, such as chrome, oil, mohair, and tobacco, had ready customers among the antagonists. There was a large supply of foreign exchange in the country, which could not be used for imports. This caused inflation and budgetary deficits. Furthermore, Turkey had to maintain a large army and in order to raise money levied a special tax based on the income of individuals. Special committees in each province were given power to determine the amount.

Turkish leaders had shown good sense, patience, and perseverance in keeping Turkey out of the war. By 1944 it was evident which side was going to win, and the Turks could afford to relax. In February 1945, they declared war on Germany, Italy, and Japan in order to become charter members of the United Nations.

Chapter Twenty-Four
Modern Turkey: The
Ordeal of a Democracy

The rich and varied legacy that Kemal Atatürk left to his people may be divided in two parts. One has to do with the way Turks looked upon themselves in relation to the other nations of the world. The second pertains to the way the Turks looked upon themselves as a nation independent of other nations. President Atatürk left his deep impress upon the Turks in both of these questions. To perpetuate his ideas and policies, he organized the Republican Peoples' Party in 1923. The party was both the symbol of "Kemalism" and the instrument to implement his principles.

THE TRUMAN DOCTRINE

During World War II, Turkey, due to geographical and political circumstances, was able to maintain its neutrality until nearly the end of the war. Immediately after the war, however, Turkey found itself practically cut off from Europe. All of the Balkans, except Greece, came under the direct or indirect rule of Moscow. The success of the separatist movement in Iranian Azarbaijan, with possible autonomy for the Kurds, would have resulted in Turkey's being almost completely surrounded by the USSR. The Turks had no reason to believe that the policies of the Soviet Union towards modern Turkey would be much different from those of tsarist Russia toward the Ottoman Empire.

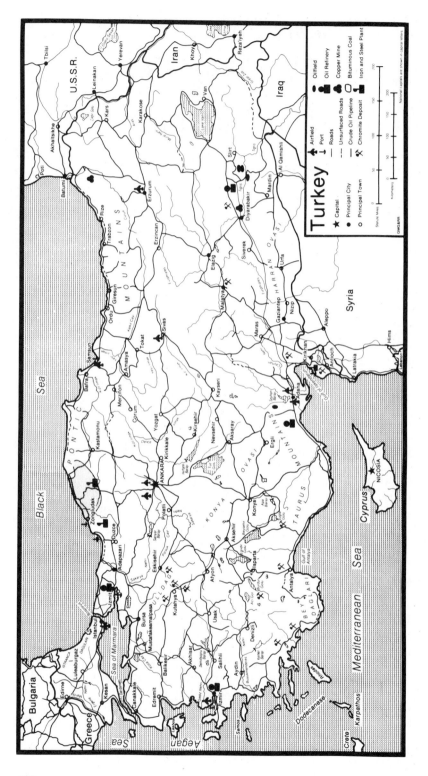

Turkey

Key

- ★ Capital
- ● Principal City
- ○ Principal Town

- ⚓ Airfield
- ⚓ Port
- — Roads
- -- Unsurfaced Roads
- Crude Oil Pipeline
- ✗ Chromite Deposit

- ● Oilfield
- ▮ Oil Refinery
- ✦ Copper Mine
- ▮ Bituminous Coal
- ▯ Iron and Steel Plant

252

Indeed, the Turks did not have to wait too long to find this out. In 1945, before the war was actually over, the Soviet Union demanded Kars and Ardahan, mountainous regions in eastern Turkey. They coupled this with demands for bases on the Straits. The Turkish ambassador in Moscow refused both demands outright and then reported to his government.

But the Russians tried to reach the same perennial goal in another way. Article 29 of the 1936 Montreux Convention on the governing of the Straits provided that each signatory was entitled to initiate a revision of the agreement at the end of five-year intervals. Inasmuch as 1946 marked the end of the second five-year interval from the signing of the treaty, the three powers (the Soviet Union, the United States, and Britain) agreed to revise it. Consequently, the United States, in agreeing to participate in the revision of the Montreux Convention, proposed four points for consideration. These were that merchant ships of all nations be permitted passage through the Straits; that warships of Black Sea nations be permitted passage at all times; that except with the consent of Black Sea nations, the warships of other countries not be allowed passage; and that necessary revisions be made to update the treaty.

All of the countries concerned accepted these changes. The Soviet Union, however, in a note of August 1946, accepted the American proposal but added two points of its own for consideration. These points were that the regime of the Straits be controlled by a committee made up of Black Sea powers; and that the defense of the Straits be a responsibility of the Black Sea powers—that is, Turkey, Bulgaria, Rumania, Ukraine SSR, and the USSR. This would mean four votes against one and, if accepted, Russia would control the Straits. As usual, Turkey was apprehensive, and Britain did not have the strength or the means to aid Turkey in refusing Russian demands. To withstand Soviet pressure Turkey was obliged to keep almost a million men under arms. The Soviet Union, in its plan to encircle Turkey, also exerted pressure on Greece. On March 12, 1947, the American Congress proposed an historic resolution that came to be known as the Truman Doctrine. It appropriated $400,000,000 to strengthen Turkey and Greece to resist Russian pressure. For the majority of American congressmen the main purpose was to "contain communism," but in the context of Middle East history, the United States had replaced a weakened Britain and France and was ready to prevent Russia from controlling Istanbul and the Straits.

TURKEY AND THE WEST

The Truman Doctrine provided the financial and military security that Turkey needed and, at the same time, opened the way for it to join the European block as a "European" nation. In 1950, when the United Nations formed an international army to defend the Republic of South Korea against the communists from the north, Turkey was one of the first to dispatch 5,000 soldiers to fight under the command of General MacArthur. The gallantry of Turkish soldiers in battle gained them worldwide acclaim and took them a step farther into the European camp. Indeed, the Turkish desire for identity with Europe was so strong that the government declined an invitation by Prime Minister Nehru of India to send delegates to an "Asian Conference." When the Western European countries and the United States formed the North Atlantic Treaty Organization (NATO), Turkey applied for membership. Izmir became the eastern headquarters for NATO, and important naval and air bases were built in Turkey along the perimeter of the Soviet Union.

Only after Turkey had joined United States-Western European alliances such as NATO and the Council of Europe did it enter into agreements with the countries of the East. Perhaps it was doing so as a European power that had common regional and defense problems with its neighbors to the east. In April 1954, Turkey entered into a mutual cooperation agreement with Pakistan, and on February 24, 1955, filled the defense gap by joining Iran in the Baghdad Pact. This pact was one of a series of mutual defense agreements encouraged by the United States. The members were Iran, Iraq, Turkey, Pakistan, and the United Kingdom. After Iraq's withdrawal from the pact the name of the agreement was changed to Central Treaty Organization (CENTO); there was now a line of defense on the "northern tier" of the Middle East from Turkey to Pakistan.

THE MULTIPARTY EXPERIENCE

A second aspect of Atatürk's legacy to his people had to do with the internal development of the nation. This legacy was expressed in the Six Principles of Kemalism, which became the main guide of the Republican People's Party that ruled Turkey. These principles were: republicanism, nationalism, populism, statism, secularism, and reformism.[1] They formed the understructure of Turkish government and society. At different times one or another of the principles was emphasized but none was repudiated.

During Atatürk's lifetime the principle of "populism," which included the concept of democracy, was reiterated but not practiced. Reforms were considered essential; but given the level of education in Turkey, no reform could have been enacted had the people been consulted in a democratic way. President Atatürk experimented by allowing the formation of another party to act as "loyal opposition" to the government and debate issues with the Republican People's Party, but this did not work. The concept of loyal opposition was new and debate soon degenerated into diatribe. Atatürk had to abandon the idea and ruled through the one party. Soon after his death in 1938, Turkey had to face the dangers of war and experience the economic difficulties of a war-torn world.

The cost of Turkish neutrality during World War II was high. Citizens were subjected to food shortages, inflation, and badly administered taxation. They blamed the party in power, even though it was Atatürk's party. The mantle of leadership had fallen on Ismet İnönü, and he was not as strong as Atatürk had been in checking corruption. When the war was over, President

[1]See p. 244.

Inönü was liberal enough to allow the formation of political parties to contest in the election of 1946. Four of the leaders of Atatürk's Republican People's Party—namely, Celal Bayar, Adnan Menderes, Fuat Köprülü, and Refik Koraltan—left the party to form the new Democrat Party. There was not enough time for much discussion of issues in the election of 1946. The Democrats won only 60 seats out of the 487. During the next four years there was freedom for opposition parties to organize. Some of the dissidents from the Democrat Party formed a political party of their own called the Nation Party. There was healthy political activity in the country. To the surprise of many observers of the Turkish scene, and in one of the rare occurrences in history, a one-party dictatorship was allowing open criticism of its policies and taking the chance of being defeated at the polls.

The Republican Party had been in power for such a long time that it attracted a great deal of criticism. In addition to reports of real and imaginary corruption in the government, the businessmen of Turkey were dissatisfied because of wartime controls; the urban people were unhappy because of high prices; the non-Muslims felt the injustice of the confiscatory taxes of 1942; and the peasants felt neglected because the country was being industrialized at their expense. The major issues, however, which divided the nation concerned two of Atatürk's principles. These two were statism, which dealt with economic policies, and secularism, which had to do with religion.

The opposition parties, whose leadership had aided Atatürk in the revolution, were not against these principles but claimed that the Republican Party had misinterpreted them. The Republican Party was criticized for having made statism and secularism ends rather than means toward prosperity and progress. Businessmen in urban centers wanted more private enterprise than they enjoyed and less restrictive laws imposed by the bureaucrats in Ankara. The Democrat Party accused the government of misinterpreting the principle of secularism and of espousing a program of "enmity toward religion." In 1947, there were doubts within the Republican Party whether they had not gone too far in implementing secularism and alienated the peasants, who were concerned with the question. Consequently, the government permitted religious education in schools upon written request of the parents. It further allowed a limited number to make the pilgrimage to Mecca, organized special courses for the training of imams, established a theological faculty at the University of Ankara, and opened the mausoleums of Ottoman sultans and other religious and political leaders of the Ottoman era. These measures, however, did not save the Republican Party. In the election of 1950 the Democrats won by a landslide—416 out of 487 seats—and the government changed hands in an orderly manner.

TURKEY UNDER THE DEMOCRATS

The new National Assembly elected Celal Bayar, the head of the Democrat Party, as president, and Adnan Menderes as prime minister. The new government had the cooperation and good will of the Western European democracies and was held up as a model to emerging nations. Here was proof that a nation could be educated in the ways of democracy and become mature enough to change governments without coups and bloodshed. There are those who believe that such confidence and enthusiasm were premature because of the subsequent military coup d'etat of 1960. But in the context of Turkish history it may be equally premature to announce the failure of democracy in Turkey.

The Democrat Party was able to poll decreasing but nevertheless impressive majorities in the elections of 1954 and 1957. During the decade of its rule, between 1950 and 1960, its main preoccupation was the reinterpretation of secularism and statism and the implementation of the new interpretation. Of the other four principles, republicanism and nationalism were so entrenched that no one, except perhaps a small number on the fringes of Turkish society, challenged them. The principle of populism, which was to advance representative democracy and which was neglected during the Republican People's Party regime, had come into its own by the will of the same party. It must be remembered, however, that part of the mounting opposition to the Democrat Party, which had come to power on the principle of populism, was its repeated attempt to destroy it. In the light of the multiparty system developed after the election of 1946, the principle of reformism—i.e., the right of government to inaugurate reforms by force—was both unnecessary and impractical. Henceforth, it was probably impossible, except in emergency cases, to force change in Turkey the way it had been done in the days of Atatürk. The two questions that have generated national debate and are likely to do so for some time to come are the questions of religion and economics.

TURKISH SECULARISM

Secularism was one of the most important principles of Atatürk's revolution. To Atatürk, the term meant the virtual exclusion of religious influence from public life. Even though a number of Atatürk's associates were against the interference of religion in public questions, they did not approve of Atatürk's measures that made it difficult for individuals to practice their religion. In 1924, Atatürk followed the formation of the Progressive Republican Party as a "loyal opposition." But he disbanded it mainly because this party criticized the government for going "too far" in limiting individual religious freedom. Perhaps the most contentious debate in Turkey for a long time to come will be where to draw the line. If complete religious freedom is granted, then there is fear of the resurgence of the ulama, Islamic law, and a general return of all the institutions and practices that the Turkish reform movement had abolished. To Atatürk the solution was simple: prevent the corporate and private practice of religion in public. Even Atatürk could not forbid people to pray in mosques nor prevent them from giving the call to prayer. But he virtually forbade the call by ordering that it be given in the Turkish language, penalizing those who used Arabic, as Islamic usage prescribes.

After the advent of the multiparty system in the election of 1946, the Republican People's Party, which had held fast to Atatürk's interpretation of secularism, felt the pressure of dissent, especially in rural areas, so it relaxed the laws and allowed religious education in schools, pilgrimage to Mecca, and other practices, to go on unmolested. The Democrat Party, however, in the election of 1950 had as one of its main planks the recognition of "religious freedom . . . as a sacred human right." During the election the Democrats had discovered that the issue of religion was one of the grievances of the rural population against the government.

Almost the first act of the new government under the Democrat Party was to abolish the penalty for using Arabic in the call to prayer. This was followed by allowing the celebration of fasting in the month of Ramazan, publication of religious books, the liberalization of laws concerning religious orders, increasing the number of schools for the training of imams, and the building of mosques. It is estimated that during the decade of its rule the Democrat government built 5,000 mosques and about the same number of public schools.

Nevertheless, it was not the intention of Democrat Party leaders to abandon the principle of secularism or to bring back the situation that existed before the formation of the Turkish Republic. When groups and individuals voiced such ideas, the government tried to suppress them. The criticism of the secularists was precisely that relaxation of laws restricting religion would encourage return to the old ways. Indeed the Nation Party, which was organized in 1948, went further than the Democrat Party in this matter. It advocated respect for the religious tradition of the nation and demanded freedom for everyone to worship in any language. It also asked that the religious endowments be turned over to the ulama. Religious orders that had gone underground came out in public; and some wrote and spoke against westernization and nationalism. Some even advocated that Turkey should fight on the side of the Arabs in Palestine. Most of these people and groups were suppressed, but the debate continued. No one was sure what this "resurgence" of religion signified: the utilitarian use of religion by political parties, or the restoration of the old system, or the expression of religious freedom, or the betrayal of the tenets of secularism, or the renaissance of a new and reformed Islam.

THE NEW STATISM

More immediate and more complex than the issue of secularism was the new government's economic policy. The shortage of consumer goods, inflation, and lack of economic expansion in the decade before 1950 brought about conditions that made people desire change. Furthermore, during a quarter century of stable government there had emerged in Turkey a new class of businessmen, entrepreneurs, capitalists, industrialists, and managers who welcomed the economic changes promised by the Democrat Party. The postwar situation of Turkey, the Truman Doctrine, and the promise and expectation of massive capital investment made the leaders of Turkey use this unprecedented opportunity to develop the country by rapid industrialization.

The nature of American investment in the Middle East, especially in

Turkey and Iran, was economic and military and for the purposes of the Cold War. Moreover, most American organizations administering capital investment in both countries were controlled and advised by American military personnel. The Congress of the United States appropriated funds annually, and it was known that failure to spend appropriated funds one year would result in smaller appropriations the next. The temptation, therefore, was to spend the money building factories and expanding industries. For the American agencies such expansion insured renewed appropriations from Congress, whose sole purpose was to "stop communism in the Middle East"; for the Turkish public the factories signified "development"; and for the party in power it meant more votes.

Development, however, is a long-term process. Under favorable economic circumstances it takes at least five years to realize the capital invested in the building of a factory. In many cases the Turkish government did not have enough capital to start production after construction was finished. So, in the expectation of foreign aid, the Menderes government embarked on a program of deficit spending. By 1960 it had incurred a debt of $1,354,604,636.

This is not to say, however, that little was done. Roads were built, agricultural methods were advanced, and many infrastructural projects were carried out. But on the whole, rapid industrialization and the excessive construction program overtaxed the economy. Prime Minister Menderes did not like planning, ignored economic realities, invested in nonproductive projects, carried on construction for political gains, and guided the country to the brink of economic disaster. Some of the guilt, however, should be borne by those who continued to provide Turkey with the necessary funds. The U.S. financial and military programs fueled excessive waste, overspending, and uneven growth.

THE COUP D'ETAT OF 1960

Some Turks were alarmed at the resurgence of religious power. Businessmen were frustrated at the disparity between external and internal prices, which made it unprofitable for them to export and expensive for them to import. The Turkish public was angered at the shortage of consumer goods, which caused inflation. These problems were enough to defeat any government, but what caused the coup d'etat was the suppression of the principle of populism, through which the Democrat Party had come to power. No sooner had that party come to power than it started, by a gradual process, to make itself the only party in the country. In 1953, the government retired all judges who had served twenty-five years or more, providing opportunity for political appointments. It also banned political activity on the part of university professors and confiscated the assets of the Republican People's Party. In the election year of 1954, the government banned "political propaganda," established censorship, and suspended opposition newspapers for "damaging public confidence" in the government. In the election year of 1957, the government passed a law forbidding the coalition of parties and gave any party winning the majority vote in a given province all the deputies allotted to that province. Even with such tactics they did not win more than 47.7 percent of the votes, while the Republican Party polled 40.9 percent.

The disintegration of the economic situation in Turkey encouraged the Menderes government to stay in power through repression. In 1959, the first violence took place when former president Ismet Inönü, the leader of the Republican People's Party, suffered physical harm. This and similar incidents caused the government to bring in an army detachment to prevent an uprising. In February 1960, the opposition party questioned the government on a number of irregularities. On April 2, police tried to stop Inönü from entering the city of Keyseri. He tore up the order and remained on the train. When people heard about this, they came and kissed his hands. At another occasion soldiers stopped his car at a bridge. Inönü got out of the car and walked toward the soldiers, who remained standing at attention and let him pass.

The first student demonstrations took place at the University of Istanbul on April 28–29 and soon spread to Ankara. Students built barricades, hurled stones, and shouted "freedom, freedom, Menderes resign." NATO was meeting in Istanbul in May, and students increased the tempo of demonstration to embarrass the government. On May 20, Prime Minister Nehru of India had come on a state visit and the crowd in Ankara jeered Menderes.

Frightened by student and worker militancy and cognizant of the general unrest, the military took matters into its own hands. The actual coup d'etat, sometimes called a revolution, took place on May 27, 1960, and lasted for only four hours. Strategic buildings in the capital were occupied and President Celal Bayar and Prime Minister Menderes were arrested. The coup was led by the army under the command of General Cemal Gürsel, former commander of land forces. He was the head of a junta known as the National Unity Committee. One of their first acts was to commission a number of political science and law professors from the universities of Istanbul and Ankara to write a new constitution. The junta appointed a seventeen-man cabinet, fifteen of whom were civilians, and announced a fifteen-point program that dealt with all kinds of subjects, including economic matters, religion, freedom of the press, the importation of coffee, ease of foreign travel, property transfer, and financial transactions.

During the seventeen months of its rule, the National Unity Committee retired 5,000 officers and 147 university professors, and brought to trial some 600 members of the Democrat Party. The trial lasted eleven months. The Court passed death sentences on fifteen, gave life imprisonment to thirty-one, acquitted 138, and gave jail sentences of different lengths to the rest. The death sentences of all except Prime Minister Menderes, Foreign Minister Zörlü, and Finance Minister Polatkan were commuted to life. The purpose of the trials was to impress upon Turks that the crimes of any regime would not go unpunished. Observers believe that the trials had both positive and negative results, but they did not diminish the popularity of Menderes and the Democratic Party, especially among the peasants. Some of the new political parties did not hide their adherence to the principles of the defunct Democrat Party in order to capture the votes of its followers.

The constitution was ready, and in January 1961 the Constituent Assembly met to approve it. On July 9, 1961, the new constitution was put to a general referendum, and over 60 percent of the people approved it. The 1924 constitution was for a republic in which power was invested in the National Assembly. It did not have enough checks and balances. Under the new constitution, the Turks tried to close the loopholes that permitted individuals to become strong. It provided for a multiparty system and more checks and balances. Of the six principles of Atatürk, the new constitution mentioned only four. Reformism and statism were not mentioned. The constitution declared that "The Turkish Republic is a nationalist, democratic, secular, and social state." Among the fundamental rights, the controversial religious education in schools was "subject to the individual's own will and volition." The constitution provided for the right of the state to plan and the right of individual ownership. Workers were allowed to organize, and intellectual associations and other societies were allowed to function.

THE SECOND TURKISH REPUBLIC

As a result of the newly found freedom and the euphoria it caused, some eleven parties registered and carried on a lively campaign. In the election on October 15, 1961, only four parties were able to win seats in the Assembly. The Republican People's Party won 173 seats, the Justice Party 158 seats, the New Turkey Party 65 seats, and the Republican Peasants' National Party 54 seats. Inasmuch as the Republican People's Party did not have a majority, it arranged a coalition with the Justice Party. The Assembly elected General Gürsel as president and Ismet İnönü as prime minister. A year later internal disagreement in the coalition caused the People's Party to arrange a coalition with the other two parties and leave the Justice Party out of the government.

No one was surprised that the Republican People's Party got more votes than any other. Aside from being Atatürk's party, it spearheaded the opposition to the excesses of the Democrat Party. What surprised observers, however, was the strength shown by the Justice Party. Generally it was composed of conservatives who believed in lower taxes and the transfer of state monopolies to private industry; the party was for the abolition of governmental control, all state planning, and land reform programs. Comprised of merchants, industrialists, and big landlords, it is not surprising that, on the whole, the Justice Party captured the votes of followers of the Democrat Party.

The New Turkey Party was made up of economic, liberal, and political progressives who someday might be the chief opponents of the Republican People's Party. They were strong secularists and advocated the right of labor to strike. The Republican Peasants' National Party advocated social conservatism and had antisecularist tendencies. It and the Justice Party generally appealed to the rural areas, while the Republican and the New Turkey parties had their followers among the urban dwellers.

The indecisive results of the 1961 election led to the formation of coalition governments. Since the members of the coalitions did not trust each other, different alignments were made and unmade during the decade of the 1960s. The army was also divided between the high command and the junior officers. The contradictions within these groups eventually led to the "coup by memorandum" of March 12, 1971.

The Republican People's Party, which had headed the coalition governments since 1961, was defeated in the election of 1965 by the conservative Justice Party under the leadership of Suleyman Demirel. He had the confidence of the army and business interests but was hampered in his actions by the conflict of personalities and dissension within the party. He did away with the requirement that government officials declare their wealth and thus opened the way for tax evasion. Capitalists were allowed to form monopolies, thereby placing small businessmen at a disadvantage. Inflation was becoming a major problem. In the election of 1968, the Justice Party won by a smaller majority. By 1969, however, even the big industrialists were angry and dissidents became strong enough to defeat Demirel's budget in 1970. These dissidents were provincial notables and landowners who opposed Demirel's agrarian policies.

ECONOMIC ACTIVITIES

Following the coup of 1960, the military created OYAK (Armed Forces Mutual Fund) in 1961. All regular officers within the military were required to invest 10 percent of their salaries in the fund, with the promise of future reimbursement. The fund, in the meantime, became the largest industrial and commercial conglomerate in Turkey; it maintained controlling interests in an insurance company, food and cement factories, the International Harvester's Turkish automotive industry, and shares in Renault, Goodyear, and Petkim, a petrochemical corporation. By 1972, OYAK's assets had grown to $300 million.

The net result of the 1960 coup was essentially to redirect the attention of the bourgeoisie toward industrial capitalist development and away from the agricultural planning so dominant in the Democrat Party period of the 1950s. The landlords and import-export merchants lost in the coup of 1960, while the industrialists and financiers won. The military began to assume a more active and dynamic role in the new industrialization of present-day Turkey through OYAK; arms sales to Turkey also increased during the 1960s and 1970s. The State Planning Board (SPB) confirmed its commitment to the redirection of Turkey's capitalist development. The plan was to focus principally on industrial, financial, and military expansion through massive loans ($6 billion) from the United States, other NATO nations, and the International Monetary Fund. Between 1968 and 1970, however, the economic malaise of the late 1950s returned to plague Turkey once more with greater consequences and more serious confrontations than ever before.

The State Planning Board inaugurated the first five-year plan in 1962. The principal of planning, both economic and social, was incorporated in the constitution. The purpose was not only economic recovery but also equitable distribution. The plan, however, met with obstacles. Although everyone seemed to approve of the goals, they disagreed on the way to achieve them. The result was that the SPB did not become a means of development but rather a tool in the hands of the vested interests.

Land reform did not fare much better. In 1960 some 80 percent of Turks worked on the land, but produced only 40 percent of the GNP. On the whole, sharecropping and absentee landlordism remained operative. In 1960 12.72 percent of the people owned 46.31 percent of the land, while 87.28 percent of the people owned 53.69 percent of the land. A mild attempt at land reform was opposed by landlords.

In the same year as the reconsolidation of the Turkish state and the establishment of the military fund (OYAK), a movement emerged from the dust of the 1950s that represented the first political efforts of Turkey's workers. This movement consolidated their own radicalization and their opposition to the bourgeois leadership and the direction of Turkey's economy and society. The first Turkish workers' political organization, Turk-Iş, came into being in 1953, organized by the Democrat Party. By 1961, however, with the removal of the DP from Turkish politics (later to reemerge as the Justice Party under Suleyman Demirel) and the intensification of the industrialization of Turkey under the new industrialist-financier-military Second Republic, the grass-roots workers' movement established the Workers' Party of Turkey (WPT). By 1965, the WPT had become a left-dominated workers' movement. It was a rival of the Turk-Iş organization, which was more moderate and sought to influence the state bureaucracy in the interests of its members. In 1967, the Marxist-oriented Confederation of Progressive Workers' Union, or DISK, was established to more clearly oppose both the state-operated union of Turk-Iş on the one hand and the proliferation of right-wing political parties and state politics on the other.

Between 1968 and 1970, the evidence of growing economic malaise was enormous. High unemployment in the industrial, agricultural, and service sectors plagued the Second Republic. Increasing numbers of industrial workers demanded strikes for better pay and safer jobs. The peasantry streamed into squatter settlements ringing the major towns and cities of Turkey. A large number of Turks prolonged their stays in Europe as "guest workers" of Germany, France, Italy, and Belgium. Turkish universities and high schools rapidly became combat zones between organizations of the left and the right. Rising food prices and housing costs only exacerbated the worsening economic and social conditions under the five-year plan. Between 1968 and 1969, most universities were formally closed by the state in order to stem the rising tide of political warfare. On June 15 and 16, 1970, a general strike took place in Istanbul and Kocaeli that halted all production in those two industrial regions. The strike was called by DISK to challenge the state's amendments of the Union Law, which in essence forced workers to join the state-operated Turk-Iş through a complicated system of requirements.

Even though DISK did not get more than 4.7 percent of the votes, its influence was greater than the size of its membership. Under the leadership of Bülent Ecevit as general secretary, the Republican People's Party veered to the left in order to pre-empt the Marxist elements. Soon the RPP gave up the attempt and the struggle was polarized between the Marxists on the one hand and the right-wing National Action group on the other.

The Demirel government could not cope with the situation. Demirel had fragmented the right and could not get along with the working class. He also failed the nationalists, who opposed the presence of the United States fleet. He blamed the constitution for the malaise. In 1970, the dissidents, which were made up of landowners and industrialists, formed a party of their own; and Demirel lost his majority in the Turkish Assembly. On March 21, 1971, he was forced out.

COUP BY MEMORANDUM

The military intervention of March 1971 did not come as a surprise. To understand the disintegration of the Turkish economy and society and the cyclical dominance of the military, we must consider four major factors in modern Turkish socioeconomic history. (1) Since the emergence of the Young Turks in 1908, the dominant classes (landlords, factory owners, import-export merchants, and bankers) have tried to create a stable capitalist economy by alternating industrial capitalist development with agricultural capitalist development (or Atatürk's statism). (2) Broad-based support within Turkey for such development plans had been established through the elimination of minority issues, class wars, and political dissent and the creation of a Turkish ideology acceptable to the upper and middle classes (Atatürk's populism and nationalism). (3) By means of capitalist development and a "unified" state, the Turkish bourgeoisie hoped not only to preserve Turkey's image as a European state but to serve as an intermediary between European and United States industries and agricultural production on the one hand and the Middle East on the other. Such an intermediary role was not only to be commercial, financial, industrial, and agricultural but military and strategic as well. (4) Since the emergence of Mustafa Kemal Atatürk, the military has played a major role in creating a capitalist economy and in imposing a dominant and unifying ideology; it had played a regional role as intermediary between advanced capitalist and Middle Eastern states.

By the 1960s, however, capitalist development in Turkish industry, trade, and agriculture had produced not only a bourgeoisie but also created a prosperous middle class, or petty bourgeoisie, of small factory owners, import agents, and middle-scale farmers. These developments in the 1960s were accompanied by a radicalized working class in the industrial sector, a militant professional class in the service sector, and a politicized retail class in the commercial sector. The events in the decades immediately following World War II had accelerated social and political change and had culminated in the first military coup of 1960. This coup did not signal the dominance of the military in the state politics of Turkey as much as the expansion of the military within the economic and political realms of modern Turkey.

The generals did not stop expanding their influence. The coup of 1971 was a further development of the military role within the Turkish economy and society; the economy and society deteriorated toward a state of perpetual crisis. The coup's proclaimed purpose was to save the country from anarchy and to reinstate Kemalist reforms. In an atmosphere of economic collapse and class war, the generals imposed martial law on eleven provinces, arrested members of the People's Liberation Army, banned the Workers' Party of Turkey, and imposed severe penalties for bank robberies, bomb or arms possession, and street demonstrations. DISK was severely weakened, with many of its leaders in prison or driven underground. By August 1971, a new alignment of the industrialist-financier-military bloc had emerged. On August 2, a notice appeared announcing the establishment of the Association of Turkish Industrialists and Businessmen, or TUSIAD. Its purpose was to organize the 114 leading industrialists, newspaper owners, and business-men into an effective lobby for industrialization; important regional groups were established throughout Turkey. The majority of TUSIAD supported the Justice Party while others were active in the RPP. In either case, TUSIAD represented a major effort on the part of the ruling coalition to prevent a repetition of 1968–1970 and to accelerate the expansion of the capitalist industrial sector within Turkish economy.

Nihat Erim was chosen by the conservatives to form a government. He tried to form a national government with the proclaimed purpose of carry-ing out reforms. Partly because of the opposition of the conservatives to reform and partly because of continued uprisings, the reform movement was overshadowed by a desire for law and order. Nihat Erim, however, did not last long and one coalition government followed another. In the elec-tions of 1973, the RPP won a plurality; and its leader, Bülent Ecevit, formed a coalition government with the small National Salvation Party. This was in effect a marriage of the secularist party of Atatürk with an avowedly Islamic party. Article 19 of the constitution was against the exploitation of religion and forbade "basing the fundamental social, economic, political, and legal order of the state on religious dogma." There was a great deal of misgiving on this account. What saved Ecevit's government, however, was the invasion of Cyprus.

CYPRUS

Perhaps the most potentially volatile aspect of Turkish foreign policy was the question of Cyprus, where a large number of Turks resided. Atatürk had not paid much attention to the Turks living in Cyprus or in any of the adjoining countries around Turkey. In 1950, however, Menderes thought that Cyprus was different. Since, from the Turkish point of view, there was danger of the annexation of the island by Greece, the Turks were in favor of partition. From 1956 to 1960 the case had been settled in London by provid-ing for joint rule. The president would be Greek and the vice-president Turkish. Education, welfare, and religious matters were administered sepa-rately. Both Turkey and Greece were allowed to maintain token forces on the island.

In 1963 President Archbishop Makarios, encouraged by the nationalist Greek Cypriots, tried to change the constitution in such a manner as to take away the veto power of the vice-president over all legislation. There was fear of war and the threat of both Greece and Turkey invading the island. The

United Nations sent a peace-keeping force to Cyprus and kept the adversaries apart for a while.

In 1967, however, fighting erupted again and both Greece and Turkey ordered a mobilization. With the intervention of the United Nations and the United States, the two sides were prevailed upon to avoid war. In 1968, Archbishop Makarios and Dr. Kucuk were re-elected president and vice-president respectively, and there was relative peace and economic prosperity.

In 1974 trouble flared up when the military junta in Athens overthrew Makarios. Fearing that this move would lead to the union of Cyprus with Greece, Turkey landed 40,000 soldiers on the island in July. A month later they had occupied 40 percent of the island. Ecevit became popular in Turkey because of his bold move in Cyprus. In full expectation of winning a large majority in the Turkish assembly, he called new elections in 1975. He failed to win, however, and the new prime minister, Demirel, called for a federated government for Cyprus. In 1976 Rauf Denktas was elected president of the Turkish Federated State of Cyprus. The new president declared that his purpose was not to create two sovereign states. After the death of Makarios in 1977, the Greeks chose Spyros Kaprianou as president. Neither party would unite nor would they declare independence. The United Nations's peace-keeping mission remained on the island to prevent hostilities from breaking out. Successive Turkish governments have been willing to relinquish some territory but have refused to give up the bizonal federation.

ETHNIC MINORITIES

According to the 1965 census, Turkey contained about 365,000 Arabic-speaking Muslims, 200,000 Christians, 125,000 Circassians, and 40,000 Jews. The largest minority, however, consists of about 2,370,000 Kurds, whom the Turks prefer to call "Mountain Turks." Their relationship with Turkey, like their relationship with neighboring Iran and Iraq, has not been always friendly. The history of modern Turkey is dotted with Kurdish uprisings. During the 1960s when Marxist activity increased in Turkey, a number of Kurds joined the Marxist parties. In 1977 the Kurdish areas were placed under martial law. In later years the Kurds split into Marxist and nationalist groups and have continued to be a problem in Turkey.

Even though the Armenians of eastern Turkey were replaced by the Kurds, the Turkish government has been harassed by Armenian nationalist-terrorist groups. Between 1980 and 1984 they bombed Turkish buildings or killed Turkish officials in the United States, Canada, France, Bulgaria, Britain, Iran, and Turkey itself. The major motive is revenge for the massacre of Armenians by the Ottoman Empire during World War I.

RELIGION AND GOVERNMENT

Since Islam and government have been intertwined from the beginning, the separation of religion from government has not been an easy task for Turkey, the first Islamic country to try it. The Kemalist reformers were confronted at every step of the way by Islamic restrictions on their reforms. Consequently the new government carried out its reforms by dictatorial means. In their zeal, the Kemalist reformers not only separated religion from government but interfered with the religious worship and practices of individual Muslims. In doing so, they alienated 98 percent of the population. Things went on without much difficulty until after World War II, when the one-party dictatorship was relaxed. The introduction of multi-party democracy, therefore, brought religion to the forefront.

By 1950 Islamic groups had gained enough strength to vandalize statues of Atatürk and to demand the return of the Arabic alphabet, the fez, and the veil. The Democrat Party, which had granted religious freedom, was still loyal to the Kemalist principle of the separation of religion and state and opposed the use of religion as an instrument of politics.

By the mid-1960s political parties vied with each other in their zeal for Islam. The logo of the Justice Party was an open book of law with an *A* and a *P* on either side, standing for *Adalat* ("justice") *Partisi*. In 1967 the Koran had replaced the book of law, and the *A* and *P* were said to stand for Allah and the Prophet. The attempt of fundamentalist Islamic groups to take over the government still continues. As late as March 1983, thirty-three Turkish Khomayni supporters were arrested by the government. Nevertheless the different governments that have come to power have not allowed Turkey to become an Islamic state in the true meaning of the term.

THE THIRD TURKISH REPUBLIC

Between 1974 and 1979, Turkey again underwent a severe economic recession and near bankruptcy of the state. This was accompanied by strikes and right-wing terrorism similar to that of the 1968–1970 period; and the collapse of the civilian leadership's programs to recreate the liberal and democratic experiences of the 1960s. Turkey had a poor balance of payments and unemployment was on the rise. The statism created by the early reformers had not encouraged creativity and resulted in a closed economy and monopoly. By 1975 Turkey had a most unequal distribution of wealth, inflation, increased debt, and high oil prices. All of this had exacerbated political infighting and instability.

Despite the efforts between 1975 and 1978 of the Nationalist Front governments to restore working relationships between opposing political blocs and to resist the growing economic malaise, Turkey was near bankruptcy in 1977. The austerity programs introduced in that year by Bülent Ecevit failed to satisfy the International Monetary Fund's requirements for credits to be extended to Turkey. Ecevit faced further problems in 1977 with the May Day massacre in Taksim (Istanbul's Trafalgar Square). Organized by DISK, the mammoth gathering of workers in Taksim on May 1 disintegrated amidst the riot police sirens, gunfire, and death. More fearsome and ominous, however, was the December 1978 attack by a right-wing youth organization, the UGD, on the funeral of two leftist teachers in the southeastern province of Kahramanmaras that resulted in the killing of the civilian population of the Alevi Kurdish district. The UGD continued its murder, looting, and plundering for two days before army and security forces restored order. Thirteen provinces were placed under martial law by Ecevit. This increased not only the dissatisfaction of the general public with the RPP and Ecevit, but also the displeasure of the generals.

On September 12, 1980, the third military coup in three decades was carried out swiftly under General Kenan Evren, chief of the general staff. In Military Communiqué No. 1, he announced that the military intervention was necessitated by the failure of state institutions, constitutional structures, and political parties to deal with the country's problems. Noting that Turkey had experienced martial law on the average of one year out of two over the last twenty years, Evren hinted that more severe measures would be taken in order to break Turkey's recurrent pattern of crises.

Between 1980 and 1981 some 45,000 people were arrested. Even though the victims included members from both the right and left, far more of the latter were detained. DISK, the leftist confederation of trade unions, was hit hard, while the larger confederation, the more moderate Turk-İş was encouraged. Strikes were forbidden and ceilings were placed on wages.

With minor adjustments, the military regime continued the same foreign policy. It was favorable to the United States military presence, and in March 1980 signed a new agreement for United States bases. U.S. military aid to Turkey increased at the expense of economic aid. In 1980 economic aid was $198 million and military aid $208 million. Four years after the military takeover in 1984, economic aid had dropped to $138 million, while military aid had soared to $716 million.

Turkey's relationship with the European Economic Community has been complex. The Turks wanted full membership, but France and Germany were reluctant to go along. Another point of friction was the visa requirements for Turkish workers in Europe, where they were not welcomed any longer. Saudi Arabia lent $250 million to Turkey, and at the last report some 84,000 Turks were employed in the Middle East.

Even though the military junta had stayed in power longer than previous juntas, it organized a constitutional assembly to write and ratify a new constitution. On August 17, 1982, the National Assembly approved a draft of a new constitution; and on November 7, 1982, a general referendum approved it. The new document safeguarded human rights, equality before the law, free elections, separation of powers, a free press, and the multiparty system of government. The new constitution also supported a strong presidency. The 1924 constitution had given excessive power to the majority party. To remedy this, the 1960 constitution went to the other extreme. The third constitution presumably contained a better balance.

General Kenan Evren was elected president of the republic on November 9, 1982. On November 13, 1983, a general election was held under the third constitution and the Third Republic. Only three parties were allowed to compete. They were:

1. The Nationalist Democracy Party, a right-of-center, law-and-order party led by a former general, Turgut Sunalp.

2. The Motherland Party, a free market economy party led by the technocrat economist Turgut Ozal.

3. The Populist Party, a left-of-center, social justice party led by Necdet Calp.

The Motherland Party won the election and Turgut Ozal became prime minister. During the four years of junta rule, the economic growth rate had risen 4 percent; inflation was down to 25 percent; and exports had increased to $5.7 billion (from $1.8 billion in 1978). The deficit had decreased from $3.3 billion in 1977 to $1.1 billion in 1982. The economy was deemed sound enough that Turkey was approved for a Euro-loan of $200 million.

Whether the new government can stem Turkey's growing long-term economic and political problems, and whether it can bridge the chasm between landlords, industrialists, import-export merchants, and the military on the one hand and the peasantry, workers, small shopkeepers, and professionals on the other, is difficult to determine.

Chapter Twenty-Five
The Fertile Crescent under Mandate

According to Woodrow Wilson and millions of other people in the world, World War I had been fought "to make the world safe for democracy"; the European victors, however, had other notions. At the Paris Peace Conference and later in the League of Nations, the contest was between the principle of self-determination for the peoples of the Middle East against the plan of Britain and France to dominate the area. In order to placate the liberals, the concept of *mandate* was introduced. It was proposed that since the "natives" of the Fertile Crescent were not yet prepared to govern themselves, Britain and France would be given mandatory powers over the region in order to prepare it for self-government. This facade enabled the two powers to continue their previous imperialistic activities, but now with the blessing of the League of Nations.

The mandate system did not change the nature of the Sykes-Picot Agreement. Britain and France had two difficulties with it: one concerned Palestine and the other concerned the oil-rich Mosul. Both of these problems were solved outside the Paris Peace Conference and were eventually settled at San Remo on April 24, 1920. Britain was recognized as the mandatory power over Palestine. Thanks to Zionist efforts, the League instructed Britain to implement the Balfour Declaration. Because of the presence of oil in the Mosul region, Britain tried to persuade a reluctant France to revise the Sykes-Picot Agreement on this point. The fact that Turkey claimed the territory further complicated the problem.

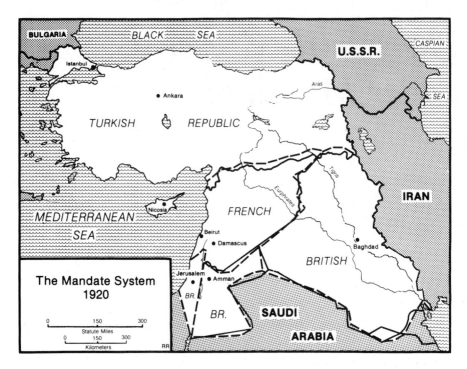

The Mandate System
1920

THE IRAQ PETROLEUM COMPANY

In ancient times oil was known to exist in northern Iraq, as it was in south-western Iran. In the late nineteenth century the Ottoman Empire was informed of the presence of oil in commercial quantities. A succession of foreign prospectors, from 1904 to 1912, showed interest in acquiring concessions. The Germans were involved through the Deutsche Bank; the British had an interest through D'Arcy's Anglo-Persian Oil Company; the Royal Dutch Shell Company was interested through its subsidiary, the Anglo-Saxon Oil Company; finally, the Americans had begun negotiating through the so-called Chester Group. While the approach of World War I prevented the different countries from receiving firm concessions, after the war, each company claimed that it had one.

Apparently neither Sykes nor Picot was aware of these negotiations in 1914, so that their division of spoils did not take oil into consideration. British officials, however, who knew about oil took it for granted that the concession to the Turkish Petroleum Company that had been given to the Germans by the Ottomans in 1912 was valid. But it was awkward to hold a concession for oil in a territory that was assigned to France. The British foreign secretary, Sir Edward Grey, introduced the difficulty to the French ambassador in a secret letter dated May 15, 1916. In December 1918, when the French premier, Clemenceau, visited London, the subject was brought up again. It was tentatively agreed that in return for a share in the Mosul oil and British support for French demands in the Ruhr, France might be willing to accommodate Britain. This became the basis of later negotiations between the two countries. According to the new agreement, France relinquished the province of Mosul to Britain in return for 25 percent of the shares in Turkish Petroleum that originally were to go to Germany. A new map was prepared to show the change, and the whole plan was incorporated as part of the San Remo Agreement of April 24, 1920.

The San Remo Agreement, however, did not altogether solve the oil problem. The interest of American oil companies in the oil of the Middle East and the claim of the Turkish nationalists over Mosul complicated the issue. An American observer at San Remo reported on the oil concession, and the United States government demanded a share in the enterprise for the American oil companies. The American argument was based on the fact that the United States had paid for the war against Turkey, even though it had not officially declared war. Furthermore, the monopoly of an oil concession by Britain and France was against the American Open Door Policy. Later, the United States introduced the Chester concession and argued that it was as valid as the one given to the Turkish Petroleum Company.

The argument dragged on until 1923 and was an issue at the Lausanne Conference. At this conference, Atatürk demanded the province of Mosul. For a time, the Turks and the Americans discussed an arrangment through which the Turks would give the Mosul oil to the Americans if they in turn would help the Turks to acquire Mosul. In the meantime the British became convinced that they could not keep the Americans out of the oil enterprise in Iraq as they had done in Iran. Because the Council of the League had resolved the Mosul question in favor of Britain, the Turks decided to come to terms with the British. So, with minor border adjustments and a 10 percent share in the royalty payments from the Mosul oil, the Turks withdrew their claim to Mosul. Under a new formula, the Iraq government gave a concession to the Turkish Petroleum Company, subsequently renamed Iraq Petroleum. The British, French, Dutch, and American groups each received 23.75 percent; the remaining 5 percent went to Sarkis Gulbenkian, the broker for the original 1914 concession, who somehow had had a hand in all subsequent negotiations.

FAYSAL AND THE FRENCH

As we have seen, the Paris Peace Conference adjourned without reaching firm agreements about the Fertile Crescent. Faysal and a small number of Arab leaders pinned their hopes on President Wilson's King-Crane Commission. But, as we have seen, no one paid any attention to the report.

The hopes of the Arabs, however, were shattered by the Anglo-French Agreement of September 1919, which showed that the Sykes-Picot Agreement still was official policy. French troops replaced the British and the protests of Faysal resulted in nothing. To counteract the Anglo-French policy, the Syrian Congress, led by the Fatat society, met in Damascus on March

20, 1920, and announced the independence of Syria (which included Lebanon and Palestine). They offered the crown to Faysal, and he accepted it. The British and French governments repudiated the action of the congress and continued their preparation for the San Remo Conference, which decided the fate of the Fertile Crescent.

The French and the Syrians prepared for war. General Gouraud, the French high commissioner for Syria, sent an ultimatum to Faysal demanding the immediate acceptance of the French mandate, French paper currency, French occupation of Aleppo, reduction of the Syrian army, abolition of conscription, and punishment of those responsible for anti-French demonstrations. The Syrians wanted to resist, but their army had ammunition for only a few hours. Faysal accepted the ultimatum, which must have surprised the French general, for he presented eight more stringent demands. It was evident that the French wanted to occupy all of Syria. War could not be averted. The battle of Maysalun on July 24, 1920, lasted half a day; and the French army of Africans, Algerians, Moroccans, and Senegalese advanced toward Damascus. They entered the city on July 25, and Faysal left Damascus twenty-two months after his triumphal entry, on October 1, 1918. The British had ties with the French and they did not want to break them for the sake of the Arabs. But they did receive Faysal in their territory with full honors.

The French mandate over Syria-Lebanon, and the British mandate over Palestine and Iraq were approved by the Council of the League of Nations in July 1922. The United States recognized the mandates in 1924.

SYRIA-LEBANON UNDER MANDATE

It is naïve to think that the French would go to so much trouble to gain the mandate solely in order to help educate the Syrians and Lebanese for self-rule. In Syria and Lebanon, French economic and social interest was of long standing. Over the years they had invested heavily in different economic enterprises. They had also persuaded a large number of Lebanese Christians to join the Roman Catholic Church as Uniate Catholics. This group became known as Maronite Christians and has played a very important role in the history of Lebanon.

It was the French prime minister Clemenceau who assured President Wilson that if France did not stay in Syria it would be a "national humiliation, as the desertion of a soldier from the battlefield." It is significant to note that General de Gaulle, exhibiting the same spirit, had to be driven out of Syria-Lebanon in 1946.

With such a national as well as imperial purpose, France was against Arab nationalism and in favor of strengthing the groups that might support France. These were to be found among minorities such as the Christians, Alawis, Kurds, and Armenians. Adopting the time-tested policy of divide and rule, General Gouraud, the French high commissioner, divided the little territory into five parts. These were: (1) Greater Lebanon, which included the Lebanon and Anti-Lebanon mountains and the sea coast from north of

Tripoli to Palestine; (2) Latakia, the Alawi seacoast territory north of Tripoli; (3) Aleppo; (4) Damascus; and (5) Jabal Druze, or the mountainous territory to the south of Damascus. This division proved impractical from the beginning. Different French high commissioners suggested federations of one sort or another, but in the end two separate administrations evolved: one for Greater Lebanon and the other for a combination of the remaining four sections, which was called Syria. Of these two, Lebanon was easier for France to administer, chiefly because of the Maronites who had always favored the French.

The history of Syria from the ousting of Faysal in 1920 until independence in 1946 is a story of riots, uprisings, and war. For this there were two main reasons. One was the fact that in comparison with any other part of the Arabic-speaking world, Arab nationalism was and remained strongest in Syria. It was in Syria-Lebanon that Arabism had its start and it was the Syrian Fatat society that proposed the idea of a united Arab kingdom as early as the Husayn-McMahon Correspondence. Under the Ottoman administration, the term "Syria" included Lebanon and Palestine. The Syrians were never willing or able to adjust themselves to the separation. Furthermore, the Syrians feel a special responsibility for Arab unity because of the fact that Damascus was the capital of the first and only united Arab empire, that of the Umayyads.

A second reason for Syrian resentment was the repressive administration by the French. On the whole, the French were proud, narrow-minded, inept, condescendingly paternalistic, and harsh. The division of the people according to religion was basic policy; but the military high commissioners, who probably did not share the traditional anti-clericalism of the French, went out of their way to aid the propagation of Roman Catholicism and favor the Catholic Christians over the rest.

The imperialism of France, on the one hand, and the desire of the Syrians for independence, on the other, led to the revolt of 1925. The immediate cause of it was the tactlessness of Captain Carbillet in introducing changes not sanctioned by the Druze chief, Sultan al-Atrash, and the harsh handling of the whole matter by General Sarrail, the high commissioner who invited the Druze leaders to a banquet and then arrested them. Atrash, who had not attended the banquet, attacked a French garrison in the Druze area. This was the signal for uprisings in Damascus, Homs, Hama, and other places. There was collusion between the Druze leader and the nationalists in these cities. General Sarrail was replaced by General Gamelin, who moved with armor and planes against Damascus in October 1925. He took the city but the insurrection dragged on, with great loss of life, until 1928. A lull came when France sent a civilian high commissioner who started negotiations. Syrian nationalist parties formed the Nationalist Block and demanded autonomy and unity of all the separate administrative areas except Lebanon. The years from 1928 to 1936 were interspersed with strikes and uprisings, while the nationalists and the French wrangled over the contents of a constitution, form of government, and degree of independence.

The same considerations that induced Britain to come to terms with the Egyptians—namely, the rise of Hitler and the campaign of Mussolini in

Ethiopia—forced the French to accommodate the Syrians. A treaty was signed between the two countries on September 9, 1936, with provisions similar to the Anglo-Egyptian treaty of the same year. The nationalists won the elections and chose Hashim al-Atassi as president and Jamil Mardam as prime minister. Apparently France was not serious, for it resumed its mandatory regime in Syria as though no agreement had been reached. The French parliament never ratified the treaty. Negotiations were started in 1936 between Turkey and France over the fate of the port of Alexandretta. Relations between Syria and France worsened when these negotiations culminated in the seizure of the port by Turkey. The Syrians were greatly annoyed over the loss of the port and the entire region of the Hatay; their president resigned in protest.

The situation in Lebanon, because of the presence of the French army headquarters and because of the French proclivities for the Maronites, was not as volatile as in Syria. There were nationalists in Lebanon—Christians, Muslims, and Druzes—who were members of the Syrian National Party and wanted union and independence. On the whole, however, the initiative for nationalist agitation was in Syria. As a result of the war of 1925 in Syria, the Lebanese gained some measure of independence. They established a republic and chose Charles Dabbas as president, but the French emphasized the fact that Lebanon was independent but not sovereign. It was not long before the French took away the "independence" and revoked the constitution. In 1936, a treaty similar to the Franco-Syrian one was arranged with Lebanon. But the French did not deal any better with the Lebanese than they had with the Syrians. They simply were not able to let their mandates go free and let the "civilizing mission" of France take its own course.

The approach of World War II ended the short-lived semi-independence of both Syria and Lebanon. After the fall of France in 1940, the puppet Vichy government that the Germans had created in France claimed suzerainty over the French colonial empire. Before the Vichy government sent General Dentz to Syria-Lebanon as high commissioner in November 1940, a number of French officers and soldiers had escaped to Palestine to join the Free French forces. With the arrival of General Dentz, Syria-Lebanon became an open field for Axis espionage against the British.

Syrians and Lebanese considered the fall of France as an opportunity to press for their immediate independence. The collapse of the French franc, and the economic hardship that resulted, gave the Syrians and the Lebanese occasion to carry on strikes, organize political demonstrations, and demand independence. The measures that General Dentz took to satisfy the nationalists were not effective.

British experience with the revolt in Iraq made them realize all the more the potential dangers of German concentration in Syria and Lebanon. Consequently, in June 1941, British and Free French forces, under General Wilson and General Catroux respectively, entered Lebanon and Syria. General Dentz offered a stiff resistance but could not prevent the Allies from entering Beirut and Damascus. In July, the Vichy French forces surrendered; those who wished were allowed to leave for France, and those who so desired were allowed to stay.

General Catroux, as representative of General de Gaulle, head of Free France, appointed new governors for Lebanon and Syria. This did not satisfy the nationalists, who clamored for national independence. In the meantime, the British, who had to supply the economic needs of Syria-Lebanon through their Middle East Supply Center in Cairo, revised the currency and brought the two regions under the sterling block. It was an open secret that the British were encouraging the nationalists in their demand for independence. In May 1943, the Syrians conducted an election and chose nationalist leader Shukri al-Quwatly as president of the new republic. The Lebanese followed the same procedure in August and chose their nationalist leader Bishara al-Khuri as president.

The Free French under General de Gaulle proved no different from other Frenchmen who had had jurisdiction over the territories. They were reluctant to relinquish power. This led to strikes and uprisings. The French arrested the president of Lebanon, and the Lebanese countered by repealing all French rights in the country. Britain and the United States supported the Lebanese and the Syrians. The United States and the Soviet Union recognized the two republics; they, in turn, by declaring war against the Axis in 1945, became charter members of the United Nations. Nevertheless, General de Gaulle insisted upon "French prerogatives"; the French army did not fully evacuate Syria until April 1946 and remained in Lebanon until December of the same year.

IRAQ UNDER MANDATE

The British mandate over Iraq was peaceful compared to the French mandate over Syria. This was owing partly to the British experience in the area. From the second half of the nineteenth century, the Persian Gulf region had become a preserve of Britain; and British agents had political and economic influence in lower Mesopotamia. Furthermore, a number of British officers had fought side-by-side with Arab officers in the Hijaz army in the war against the Ottomans, an experience that most French officers did not have. The Iraqi political parties were not dominated by extremists as were the parties of Syria. For the Syrians the motto was "all or nothing," a policy that the Arabs used time and time again in dealing with the question of Zionism. For the Iraqis the motto was "take and ask for more." This is not to say, however, that Iraq did not have its share of extremists and coups d'etat.

The British had difficulties in the beginning mainly because the affairs of Iraq were under the control of the government of India. As early as 1918 the "Anglo-Indians" were so sure that they were going to have control of Iraq that they moved in with their families and took over the administration as though they were going to stay forever. The British high commissioner, Sir Arnold Wilson, conducted a "plebiscite" which showed that the Iraqis preferred Britain.

Of course the Iraqis actually did not prefer the British, as the rebellion of July 1920 proved. The announcement of the San Remo Agreement of April 1920, coupled with the attitude of the Anglo-Indians, caused the outbreak of July 1920. It is significant that at this time Egyptian nationalists were challenging the authority of the British, Kemalists were resisting the "peace" imposed by the Entente, and the Syrians were fighting against the French. After landing some 65,000 troops, spending about $1,000,000, and suffering casualties on both sides, the British government in London took control. Sir Percy Cox, a man known and respected in the area, was made high commissioner. He announced the British intention of establishing a national Iraqi government.

The Cairo Conference in 1920, under the chairmanship of the then colonial secretary Winston Churchill, had a delicate problem in its hands. In the implementation of the Sykes-Picot Agreement, the general consensus was that Faysal would become king of Syria and his older brother Abdullah king of Iraq. Indeed, the Syrian National Congress, in choosing Faysal as king of Syria, had designated Abdullah as king of Iraq. Britain was not opposed to this. The French government, however, complicated the situation by expelling Faysal, which meant that the British had two "kings" on their hands. Of the two brothers, Faysal was the more popular, so Great Britain decided that he should be king of Iraq. Sir Percy Cox saw to it that there was an invitation from the leaders of Iraq to Faysal to become their king. He was enthroned on August 23, 1921. As for Abdullah, he was given the amirate of "Transjordan," a region conveniently created by the British on the east bank of the Jordan River, extending southward to the Gulf of Aqaba.

The idealistic nationalism of Faysal received several severe jolts during the three years after his decision to fight against the Ottomans in 1918. He tried to steer a course between the extreme nationalism of the Syrians and complete subservience to the British. Britain, having freed its Middle East policy from the influence of the India government, also became less rigid. Between 1922 and 1930 several treaties were negotiated and discarded. There was a tug of war in which the Iraqi nationalists demanded more than the British imperialists were willing to give. As an Arab, Faysal was not totally trusted by Britain and as a protégé of the British, he was not beyond suspicion by the nationalists. But he did keep a balance between the two sides until 1930, when a treaty was signed giving Iraq its independence. The treaty was a prototype for the Anglo-Egyptian treaty six years later and a model for the French as well. Britain was allowed to maintain a naval base in Basra on the Persian Gulf, and a base at the Habbaniya airfield near Baghdad. In time of war Iraq agreed to put its resources at the disposal of the British. Iraq was declared independent, and the last semblance of the mandate came to an end. By 1932, both Great Britain and Iraq ratified the treaty, and Iraq became the first Arab state to be admitted to the League of Nations.

Iraqi nationalists were not satisfied with the treaty of 1930. In their eyes, Iraq was not fully independent as long as it had ties with Britain. They also wanted to make common cause with the nationalists of Syria. On the other hand, the discovery of oil in Iraq and the conclusion of oil concessions made Iraq affluent. The concession was granted for seventy-five years, and Iraq received a royalty of four gold shillings per metric ton of crude oil.

There were those among the Iraqis who were reluctant to share this wealth with other Arabs. Furthermore, the Iraqi currency was secure because it was a member of the "sterling block"; it was a far cry from the fluctuating Syrian currency, which was tied to the French franc.

The ruling body in Iraq was divided into political factions, each built around influential individuals whose fortunes rose and fell with the number of votes they could muster in parliament. On the whole, they were divided into two groups: one in favor of alliance with Britain and the other against it. Among the former were the National Party, the Progressive Party, and the old Ahd Party of the premandate days, dominated by the personality of General Nuri al-Sa'id. Individuals who opposed Britain had formed the National Brotherhood Party, which was dominated by Yasin al-Hashimi and Rashid al-Gailani.

Lack of homogeneity among the people of Iraq made the solution of political and social problems more difficult. This was true of many countries in the Middle East and colonial powers were not responsible for it. The vast majority of the 5,000,000 inhabitants of Iraq were Muslims, but they belonged to three hostile camps: Shi'a and Sunni Arabs and Sunni Kurds. The Sunni minority, which ruled the Shi'i majority, were never sure of the latter's loyalty because of their Iranian proclivities. The Shi'is and the Sunnis spoke Arabic; but the Kurds, who were Sunni in religion, spoke Kurdish. Furthermore, they were part of the seminomadic Kurds who lived in Iran and Turkey and who aspired to national autonomy. Perhaps the most tragic group in Iraq were some 90,000 Assyrian Christians who spoke Syriac. They lived in the mountains of eastern Asia Minor. The British held before them, as they had done with the Armenians, the hope of national autonomy and had encouraged them to rise against the Turks. After the withdrawal of the Russian troops because of the Bolshevik Revolution, the Assyrians were pushed south to Mesopotamia. In the struggle of 1920, the British enlisted Assyrian soldiers to fight against the Iraqis, causing enmity between the groups. In the subsequent peace negotiations the Turks did not permit the Assyrians to return to their homes, which meant that the bulk of them were stranded in Iraq. In addition to these, there were 100,000 Jews who had settled in Mesopotamia from before the Christian era, a smaller number of Armenians, and sundry groups known as Sabeans and Yazidis.

After Iraq declared its independence in 1932, Faysal wanted to transform the various ethnic and religious groups into a nation. He wanted to strengthen the armed forces of the country, bring a rapprochement between the Sunnis and the Shi'is, open schools, encourage industries, solve the land problems, and reform the administrative system. For this purpose he tried to bring about a coalition government. He asked Nuri al-Sa'id to resign the premiership and eventually offered it to Rashid al-Gailani of the National Brotherhood Party. This party dominated the parliament from 1932 to 1936. Perhaps Faysal would have succeeded had he lived, but he died in 1933. His twenty-one-year-old son, Ghazi, was proclaimed king, but had neither the experience nor the prestige to check the antiminority actions of the National Brotherhood under Rashid al-Gailani and Yasin al-Hashimi.

In 1936, two widely divergent groups joined together and overthrew the government by a coup d'etat, the first of several in the history of Iraq subsequent to Faysal's death. One of these groups was the People's Party, made up of young intellectuals who professed a kind of socialist democracy. The other group was made up of army officers who advocated nationalism while preferring their own brand of political hegemony. The two groups got together through Hikmat Sulayman of the People's Party and General Bakr Sidqi of the army, and overthrew the government in October 1936. The inexperienced young intellectuals were no match for the army, and the latter took control under General Sidqi. Then the army leaders turned against each other, which led to the assassination of General Sidqi in 1937 and another coup d'etat. After a year, a third coup brought back once again General Nuri al-Sa'id. Such jockeying for power was only one of Iraq's problems; there were others. One was a new controversy with Britain over oil-rich Kuwait. Britain held a protectorate over the area, while Iraq claimed ownership. The fate of the Palestinians in the struggle with the Zionists was another problem that involved the Iraqis. There were also problems of reform and the question of Iraqi nationalism versus the larger Arab nationalism.

In the midst of this, young King Ghazi was killed in an automobile accident on April 4, 1939. Since he was popular and on the reformist nationalist side on all questions, it was difficult for many to believe that his death was only an accident. His four-year-old son, Faysal II, was proclaimed king with Abdul Ilah, his maternal uncle, as regent.

In 1939, the prime minister of Iraq was Nuri al-Sa'id, who had come to power as a result of the last in a series of five coups d'etat. He was inclined to cooperate with the British and had received £7,000,000 from Britain and the Iraq Petroleum Company in loans and advance royalty payments. Nevertheless he merely broke diplomatic relations with Germany and did not declare war. Anti-British feelings in Iraq and the possibility of German victory were too strong to permit even the Iraqi "pro-British" government to go very far in committing themselves.

Local politics in 1940 forced Nuri al-Sa'id to resign the premiership in favor of the nationalist Rashid al-Gailani. Iraq had become involved in the struggle in Palestine, partly because a "sister Arab state" was being "invaded" by an alien people, and partly because of the "Greater Syria Movement," which envisaged the unity of the Fertile Crescent under the Hashimites, to which the royal family of Iraq belonged. It will be recalled that Britain had invited Iraq to participate in the 1939 conference to find a solution to the Palestine problem. Furthermore, Haj Amin al-Husayni, the mufti of Jerusalem and leader of the anti-British Arab Higher Committee, who had fled to Lebanon, was given asylum in Baghdad. With Syria and Palestine under foreign control, Iraq had become the center of pan-Arabism. Haj Amin received a generous subsidy from the Iraqi government and began his activities for the independence of Palestine.

The nationalist prime minister, Rashid al-Gailani, quite naïvely tried to entice the British into discarding the Balfour Declaration and declaring the independence of an Arab Palestine. In return, Iraq would formally join the Allies and declare war against the Axis. The refusal of Britain to comply with such a request stengthened Gailani and his fellow nationalists in their hope that cooperation with the Axis might help them achieve their goal. Haj Amin was already in touch with the Germans. Gailani joined hands with him and established contact with Von Papen, the German ambassador in Ankara. The British could not tolerate such activities and asked the regent, Abdul Ilah, to dismiss Gailani. The premier refused to resign and there was confusion in the Iraqi parliament. Political pressure, however, forced Gailani out of office in favor of General Taha al-Hashimi. On April 4, 1941, Gailani executed a coup d'etat with the help of four army colonels. Regent Abdul Ilah and a number of moderate leaders, including Nuri al-Sa'id, escaped, taking the infant king with them.

Even though the Germans had a hand in the coup, they were too busy in Greece to be able to take advantage of it. The British landed troops in Basra, while the Iraqis surrounded the Habbaniya airfield. The Germans were able to land fifty planes in Iraq via Syria, which was under the pro-Axis French Vichy government, but it was too late. The Arab Legion from Transjordan came to rescue the British. The Thirty-Day War ended in disaster for Rashid al-Gailani, the mufti, Haj Amin of Jerusalem, and a number of their supporters. They fled to Iran and from there they found their way through Turkey to Germany. During the rest of the war, they—especially the mufti—worked for the Axis. After the war, Gailani escaped in disguise on board a French ship to Beirut and from there across the desert to Riyad, capital of Saudi Arabia, where King ibn-Sa'ud gave him asylum. The mufti was put under house arrest in Paris after the war. In May 1946, he also escaped in disguise on board an American military craft to Cairo, where he was given asylum by King Faruq.

For the remainder of the war, Nuri al-Sa'id was prime minister. By declaring war against the Axis, Iraq was the first Middle Eastern country to become a member of the United Nations. Iraq played a part in the transportation of war supplies to the Soviet Union. Like other countries in the Middle East, Iraq was rich in foreign exchange; but a scarcity of consumer goods caused inflation.

TRANSJORDAN UNDER MANDATE

The territory of Transjordan, over which Abdullah was asked to be the amir, was, for the most part, a desert that was inhabited by some 200,000 people, most of whom were bedouins. To make it palatable for Abdullah to rule over an empty land, the British arranged for a monthly stipend of £5,000. From 1921 until after World War II, Britain's influence in the area went unchallenged. From the confines of this preserve, the British could observe and hope to control the restlessness of Iraq, the struggle for power in Palestine, and the passage through the Persian Gulf. Through a subsidy of £100,000 per year, which by 1940 had grown to £200,000, the British organized an army that became the best trained and equipped in the Fertile Crescent. The Arab Legion, as the army was called, was commanded by Captain F. G. Peake until 1939 and from then on by the legendary Glubb Pasha (Sir John Glubb). The army was made up of volunteers from all parts of the Fertile Crescent, but was dominated by young men from bedouin tribes.

The nature of government in Transjordan was simple. The powers of legislation and administration were vested in the amir, who, in turn, had an executive council to assist him. Membership in the legislative council was based on proportional representation among the bedouins and other groups. The British residents stationed in Amman (Philadelphia of Roman times) supervised the administration and controlled the budget, army, and foreign affairs. After the death of King Faysal of Iraq, Abdullah became head of the Hashimite family that ruled Iraq and Transjordan. Abdullah tried to identify his ambitions for the family of Hashim with the desire for unity on the part of the Arabs of the Crescent and supported a program called the "Greater Syria Movement." The idea was a revival of the contents of the Husayn-McMahon Correspondence, which envisaged a united Fertile Crescent under the rule of the Hashimites. Against the plan were Saudi Arabia and Egypt, as well as the Christians of Lebanon, aided by some political parties in Syria and Iraq.

THE LEAGUE OF ARAB STATES

It will be recalled that Britain's traditional policy of maintaining the independence of the Ottoman Empire had a triple purpose. One was to use it as a buffer state against the southward expansion of Russia, a second was to use it for safeguarding the route to India, and a third was to maintain the balance of power in Europe. By the middle of the twentieth century, the protection of the vast oil reserves of the Middle East perhaps outweighed all these considerations. During World War I, Britain decided to continue its previous policy by replacing the defunct Ottoman Empire by a united or federated Arab state in the Fertile Crescent. The agreement embodied in the Husayn-McMahon Correspondence was a direct result of such a policy. The Sykes-Picot Agreement and the Balfour Declaration, however, prevented the implementation of this policy. Instead of a united or federated Arab state in the Fertile Crescent, five different states came into being, excluding Saudi Arabia and the Persian Gulf shaykhdoms.

During World War II, because of the defeat of France, British troops controlled all of the Fertile Crescent as they had done in 1917. The British still needed a buffer to stop the expansionist plans of the Soviet Union, and they still needed friendly people along the route to India. It was not surprising, therefore, to see Britain revive the old policy.

As early as 1939, the British government called a conference on Palestine and for the first time involved representatives of Arab states. On May 29, 1941, Anthony Eden, the British foreign secretary, announced the need for Arab unity and spoke of their desire for "a greater degree of unity than they now enjoy." In the same speech he also promised that "His Majesty's government for their part will give their full support to any scheme that commands general approval." The idea of pan-Arabism was in the ascendency among the Arabic-speaking peoples of the Fertile Crescent, so that

Eden's remarks fell on receptive ears. In direct response to this invitation, Nuri al-Sa'id of Iraq in 1942 proposed a union of Iraq, Palestine, Transjordan, Syria, and possibly Lebanon, with the possibility of others joining later on. This sounded very much like the Greater Syria Movement under the Hashimite family and was not acceptable. Nahhas Pasha of Egypt, who had not previously shown enthusiasm for pan-Arabism, invited one Arab government after another to "consultations on Arab unity." In consultations that lasted more than a year, Syria and Iraq favored a federative scheme; Transjordan championed union with Palestine, Syria, and possibly Lebanon within a greater Arab Union; and Egypt, Lebanon, Saudi Arabia, and Yaman favored a confederation of states.

How much the Biltmore Program[1] spurred the Arabs toward union or encouraged the British to bring it about cannot be determined, but it probably did have some effect. On October 7, 1944, the eight states mentioned above signed the Protocol of Alexandria in which they agreed to form an Arab League. The final pact of the League of the Arab States was signed in Cairo on March 22, 1945. It favored a confederative scheme and was inspired mostly by the Covenant of the League of Nations. Each state was sovereign and the decisions of the League were not binding. One of three annexes to the agreement dealt with Palestine. It considered Palestine "legally" an independent Arab state that could not as yet exercise its rights, and gave the League the right to choose a representative for Palestine until the time that it could do so. By the end of the war, Arab nationalism had, for the first time, a legally though loosely constituted body to represent it against the Zionist nationalism in Palestine.

[1]See p. 358.

Chapter Twenty-Six
Modern Syria and Lebanon

Out of the colonial period, there emerged political coalitions and parties whose leadership reflected the social and economic interests of the Fertile Crescent. The Ba'th parties of Syria and Iraq, the nationalist and socialist parties of Lebanon, Syria, Iraq, and Jordan, and the communist parties, particularly of Iraq, all had their roots in the colonial period (1922–1945). They were dominated by professionals such as teachers, journalists, lawyers, and doctors. The nationalist parties represented primarily either landed or industrial bourgeoisie, while the socialist and communist parties represented primarily the peasants and workers. All of these were usually based in the urban regions of the Fertile Crescent.

The French mandatory authorities in Lebanon and Syria succeeded in creating a number of institutions beneficial to French banking and industrial interests, such as the Banque de Syrie et du Liban. Similarly, the British rule in Iraq and Jordan prolonged British interests, particularly in the oil industry through the establishment of the Iraq Petroleum Company. In terms of internal politics and economics, the French and British colonial authorities managed to prevent the establishment of self-government based on any national consensus. Instead, the French and British colonial rule from 1922 to 1945 drove deeper divisions into an already fragile and splintered region. The Maronite-Druze split was fueled by French policies that favored the Maronites. The Kurdish-Arab hostilities in Iraq were exacerbated by British policies that extended promises to the Kurds while favoring the old Arab families of Baghdad in the governing of the state. The economics and politics of Syria, Lebanon, Iraq, and Jordan underwent significant changes—changes that are still evident in the Fertile Crescent today. Three principal factors plagued the states of the Fertile Crescent in the 1950s: (1) The colonial legacy of industrial capitalist development was dependent, to a considerable degree, upon the capital, technology, and advice of the former colonial powers. This prevented the nationalist aspirations for economic and political independence from being fulfilled. (2) Social divisions and the survival of the old landed families in regional politics remained an obstacle to social mobility and political realignment. (3) On the whole, each region continued to experience widely diverse political developments without the communality so essential to the pan-Arab aspirations of so many people in the Fertile Crescent.

THE MAKING OF MODERN SYRIA

Syria is one of the best examples of the Arabs' desire for unity and their difficulties in achieving it. Syria can rightly claim to be the home of modern Arab nationalism. The division of Ottoman Syria into four independent countries—Syria, Lebanon, Jordan, and Israel—with one of them an alien implant, has never been accepted by ardent Syrian nationalists. Nevertheless, Syrians have not been able to speak with one voice, for they are divided by religious, ethnic, and sectional differences. Syria's 85 percent Muslim population is divided into Sunnis, Shi'is, Alawis, Druzes, Isma'ilis, and Yazidis. The smaller Christian population is divided into a dozen denominations. About 10 percent of the population is non-Arabic-speaking, including Kurds, Turkomans, and Circassians. Another 10 percent are roaming bedouins, who cause more devisiveness than their number would indicate. Political and economic interests are usually centered in each of the four major cities: Damascus, Homs, Hama, and Aleppo.

During a given week, a Syrian as a Sunni could be against the rest of the Muslims; as a Muslim, against the non-Muslims; as a pan-Arab secularist, against the religious communalists; as a Damascene against all other sections of Syria; and as a Syrian against other Arab countries. If some Syrians somehow transcend all these barriers, their intense individualism still hinders their cooperation. Syria is the Arab world in microcosm; anyone who can rule Syria can unite the Arabs.

During twenty-five years since independence in 1946, Syria has had nearly a dozen coups d'etat and about as many constitutions. Each government undid whatever the previous government had done or wanted to do. From 1949 to 1950, perhaps as a reaction to the defeat in the Palestine War, three military coups d'etat rapidly followed one another. The last one, by Colonel Adib Shishakli, endured long enough to permit a constitution to be written and a foundation laid for a welfare state with far-reaching social and economic legislation. As a result of opposition from the landlords and conservatives, Shishakli staged a second coup in 1952, dissolving parliament and outlawing political parties, trade unions, and student organizations. He wrote a new constitution, organized his own Arab Liberation Party and got himself elected president and prime minister for a five-year term. In February 1954, however, Shishakli was ousted by a coalition of all dissident groups.

In the relatively free elections that took place after the coup of 1954, the Ba'th (Resurrection) Party gained fifteen seats. This was not very much in a 142-member parliament; but in the light of the role the party played in Syria, it was significant. The Ba'th Party was created in 1953 from a fusion of two parties that had been pan-Arab and socialist in their orientation. It advocated nationalization of industry, redistribution of land, and extensive social reforms. The party was led by Michel Aflaq, a Christian, and Salah al-Bitar, a Muslim. As true secular pan-Arabs, they believed in "one Arab nation with an eternal mission." Between 1954 and 1958, Ba'thists became influential and organized branches in Lebanon, Jordan, and Iraq. The main rival of the Ba'th in Syria, in organization, ideology, and influence, was the Communist Party.

The United Arab Republic

In 1956, the Syrian conservative and moderate politicians had come under the influence of Nasser[1] and hoped that he might save them from leftist domination. There was a split within the leftist camp; the communists favored collaboration with the Soviet Union and the Ba'thists were for independent action. The communists gained increasing influence in the army and brought General Afif Bizri, chief of staff of the Syrian army, to a pro-Soviet position. The more powerful the communists became, the more the Bat'thists thought of union with Egypt, which would save Syria from communism and would be a step toward the ultimate union of all Arabs.

In the beginning, Ba'thists considered Nasser as a military dictator and looked down upon the Revolutionary Command Council of Egypt as a group without ideology. But after the nationalization of the Suez Company and the Sinai war, Nasser had emerged with new ideas. The slogan of the R.C.C.—"Discipline, Unity, Work"—was changed to "Democracy, Socialism, and Cooperative Society." Nassar "Egyptianized" all foreign industry and property and at the same time nationalized many Egyptian-owned private industries. This endeared him to Ba'th's socialist eyes. They thought they would add an ideological dimension to Nasser's pragmatism and use his popularity and power for the union and socialization of all the Arab world.

In January 1958, the Ba'thists, who were afraid of a communist coup, went to Cairo and asked for union. The United Arab Republic was established after remarkably short negotiations. Having been disappointed with the confederation of the League of Arab States, the two countries set up a model at the opposite extreme: a totally centralized union. The union was hailed as the first step toward the unity of all Arabs. Nasser as the first president of the U.A.R. became the idol of all Arabs. Not to be outdone, the

[1]See p. 397.

Hashimite kings of Jordan and Iraq announced a federal union, but it did not impress even the citizens of those countries. The U.A.R. became the hope of Arabs for the future. But this hope was short-lived.

The Demise of the U.A.R.

Some groups in Syria, such as the moderates, conservatives, military, and small businessmen, gradually realized that Syria was becoming a province of Egypt rather than an equal partner in a union. Businessmen and shopkeepers suffered under economic restrictions that were based on Egyptian needs. The army was disgruntled because it had come under the control of the U.A.R. vice-president Hakim Amer, who acted as Nasser's proconsul in Syria. The Ba'thists, as the enthusiastic proponents of union, had suffered the most. They had accepted the disbanding of all political parties, including their own, confident that they would be given a free hand in building the new National Union Party of the U.A.R. But Nasser refused to give them that opportunity. Indeed, in the first election in 1959, the Ba'thists were pushed out of the government altogether. Perhaps the severest blow came when Nasser began to collaborate with such former enemies as Jordan and Saudi Arabia, against which both Nasser and Ba'thists had uttered so many vindictive statements.

For whatever reasons, Nasser did not take into account the existing agricultural, economic, and social differences between Syria and Egypt and forced upon Syria his "Arab socialism," which was devised for Egyptian needs. For their part, the Ba'thist ideologists of Syria did not take into account the pragmatism of Nasser, who introduced and discarded ideological principles as he went along.

The Syrians had had enough. On September 28, 1961, Syrian officers staged a coup and ordered Vice-President Amer and other Egyptian officials to leave. Nasser did not try to quell the rebellion and accepted the separation of Syria and Egypt. The leaders of the coup called an election; almost all the old parties won seats (though the Ba'thists won only eighteen), and undid most of what the U.A.R. had accomplished. Syria had not changed much in its desire for Arab unity. It signed a National Unity Charter, in which it advocated the creation of a "voluntary" Arab union. Neither had it changed much internally, for there was another coup in March 1962 that tried to reinstate some of the reforms of the U.A.R.

The Rise of Hafiz al-Asad

Following its break with Egypt, Syria experienced many coups and countercoups for the control of the important state institutions. In each of these coups the Ba'th Party went through a reorganization of its leadership; in March 1963, it took control of the government in yet another coup. Since the Ba'thists of Iraq had executed a coup a month before, there was talk of union between Syria, Iraq, and Egypt. It did not, however, get beyond the talking stage.

There was disagreement, however, between the Ba'thists and Nasser's followers in Syria, and also between the moderate and radical elements of the Ba'th Party. In January 1966, the radical faction, with the aid of the army, wrested control from the moderates and formed a new government. In the new Revolutionary Council, the chief executive and leader of the party, General Jadid; the minister of defense, Hafiz al-Asad; and the deputy prime minister, Dr. Makhus, were all Alawis.

The Alawis were members of a minority Shi'i group. One of the few avenues for advancement open to them was the army, and they took advantage of the education and promotion it offered and gradually gained control of it. They were also involved in the periodic reorganization of the Ba'th Party. Although Syria had lost the Golan Heights and the city of Quneitra in the Six-Day War against Israel in 1967, the defeat had strengthened Alawi military control and accelerated the centralization of the state.

By 1970, Hafiz al-Asad, the forty-year-old son of a peasant near Latakia, was in full control of the government as prime minister and presided over a council that included all parties. In 1973 a new consitution was ratified which stated that Syria was to be democratic and socialist, and laws were to be based on the Muslim Shari'a. Ba'th was designated as the leading political organization. Personal and religious freedom were guaranteed and the president was to have a seven-year term. In the general elections that followed, Ba'th received 70 percent of the votes and Asad was elected president. With Asad in power, Syria seemed to have ended the series of coups and countercoups that had plagued its political life for more then three decades.

The stability of government was shaken, but not destroyed, by the October War between Egypt and Israel in 1973, in which Syria took part. The early successes of the Syrian army were reversed when the Israelis counterattacked and came to within forty kilometers of Damascus. A ceasefire was declared on October 23. The "shuttle diplomacy" of the American secretary of state, Henry Kissinger, failed to bring peace. A United Nations peacekeeping force was stationed in Quneitra, and Syria was given aid to repair the destruction wrought by the war. President Nixon went to Damascus in 1974, and diplomatic relations between the United States and Syria were resumed after seven years. American and European companies were invited to explore for oil. Trade with the United States increased, even though Syria refused to enter peace negotiations with Israel. The Soviet Union replaced the weapons Syria lost in the October War and continued to give economic aid, even though Syria had outlawed the Communist Party.

Inter-Arab Relations

Perhaps the stability of the government would have contributed to economic prosperity had it not been for the presence of Israel in the Golan Heights, a sense of duty on the part of the Syrians to help the Palestinians to regain their lost land, and the jockeying for position in the inter-Arab rivalry. In September 1970, King Husayn of Jordan evicted Yasser Arafat and the Palestine Liberation Organization forces from Amman; a number of them went to Syria and joined the Sa'iqah branch of the PLO, which was being controlled more and more by Syria. The bulk of the PLO went to

Lebanon. Asad was instrumental in persuading the Arab nations gathered in Rabat in 1974 to recognize the PLO as the sole legitimate representative of the Palestinians.

The presence of the PLO exacerbated the already shaky situation in Lebanon and resulted in war among the different factions. To end the strife, Egypt, Kuwait, Lebanon, Saudi Arabia, and Syria gathered in Riyad in 1976 and authorized a peacekeeping force of 30,000, almost all from Syria, to prevent bloodshed until a conference of Arab states could propose a more lasting remedy. Even though these troops were to be under the command of President Sarkis of Lebanon, everyone knew that President Asad was in actual command.

The famous journey of President Sadat of Egypt to Jerusalem in November 1977 and the eventual Camp David Accords shattered the fragile unity of the Arabs, in which Syria was greatly involved. When the Soviet Union invaded Afghanistan in December 1979, Syria went against most of the Islamic world and supported the invasion. Furthermore, Asad who, as an Alawi, is part of the Shi'i group, not only approved of the revolution in Iran, but also sided with Iran over the Iraqi invasion of September 1980, alienating the Arabs of the Fertile Crescent and the Persian Gulf.

Economic and Internal Unrest

Following its separation from Egypt in 1961, and not because of it, Syria continued its nationalization policy, which had started with the Central Bank in 1956, by taking over its largest industries in 1965. This was followed by the establishment of a state monopoly of foreign trade in 1969. In the process, much of the Syrian economy came under state control, commerce and construction being the fastest-growing sectors. Finance, commerce, transportation, education, and health expanded from 62 percent of the GNP in 1950 to almost 72 percent in 1970. The fourth five-year plan (1976–1980) failed to meet its announced targets. Industrial growth rose only 2 percent, compared to the projected target of 15.4 percent. New projects, such as Deir ez-Zor pulp and paper mills and the Homs ammonia plant, and others, had to be closed because of lack of trained personnel. Inflation fluctuated between 15 and 20 percent.

On the positive side, the construction of a major dam on the Euphrates was started in 1973. It was expected to irrigate some 1.5 million acres of land. Because of the discovery of oil, the General Petroleum Organization was formed, and a 644-kilometer pipeline was built. In 1971, Syria produced 100,000 barrels of oil. The plan was for Syrian crude to replace Iraqi oil at Homs. On the whole, however, the reduction of aid that Syria was receiving from some of the Arab states, the drain of supporting troops in Lebanon, and the complete loss of Iraqi oil aggravated the already slow economic recovery.

By 1982, Syria's political isolation and economic malaise gave rise to internal dissent. Syrians objected to the Alawis' (who comprised 12 percent of the population) having all the power in the country. There were strikes by shopkeepers in Aleppo and Hama. A few Alawis were assassinated, and there was an attempt on the life of Asad himself. Inasmuch as the members of the Muslim Brotherhood were involved, its members were hunted down and brutally liquidated in the two cities.

No doubt the defeat of the United States' policy in Lebanon, the emergence of Syria as the most important power among the Arabs of the Fertile Crescent and the Persian Gulf in 1984, and the courting of Asad by some of the Arab states, made him popular in his own country and he was able to weather the storm of discontent. A fifth five-year plan was announced in 1981 that emphasized agriculture, improving the balance of payments, and increasing exports, the GNP, and employment. Whether it will be successful or not depends upon many imponderables, both internal and external. United States aid was completely ended because of Syria's disapproval of the 1979 Camp David Accords and its approval of the 1979 Soviet invasion of Afghanistan. Syria, however, has continued to receive aid from other countries, especially West Germany and the Soviet Union; in addition, aid from other Arab states has been resumed. In one of its first sessions, the second Islamic parliament of Iran approved the provision of oil to Syria free of charge. All these developments may mean a new day for Syria.

THE MAKING OF MODERN LEBANON

Bound by common economic, social, and political ties and developments, Lebanon and Syria have remained remarkably similar in the decades following their independence. Both developed capitalist economies and experienced a series of uprisings of various religious and linguistic minorities within their borders. Both were drawn more deeply into the continued Israeli occupation of Palestinian lands and its seizure of "border" lands in southern Lebanon and the Golan Heights. On the other hand, no two states in the Middle East after World War II were as diverse as Lebanon and Syria. Indeed, the experience of Lebanon was unlike that of any other state in the region. Lebanon never became a nation in the usual sense of the term, and neither did its inhabitants think of themselves as Lebanese. The people of Lebanon have been more loyal to their clans and religious communities than to the state. Consequently, Lebanon never formed a centralized state economy, nor did the military ever take over from the civilian government in running the affairs of state.

Lebanon and Arab Union

The almost even division in the population of Lebanon between Christians and Muslims gave it a peculiar position in the Arab world. The Maronites were usually pro-European, while the Muslims favored closer ties with the Arab countries. The Orthodox and other Christians tipped the scales in favor of Arabism. Nevertheless, the Christian minority was apprehensive about its life in a unified Arab Muslim country. When Lebanon became independent, first in 1943 and finally in 1946, President Bishara al-Khuri proposed the National Pact in order to ease the tension between Muslims and Christians. All government positions, from clerk to director general, were distributed among the various religious communities on a fixed ratio based on the census of 1932. The number of seats in the Chamber of Deputies, even though fluctuating, was always a multiple of eleven—a ratio of six Christians to five Muslims.

In the course of years, this unwritten National Pact began to wear thin. Muslims complained of second-class citizenship and demanded a new census that, they were sure, would show a Muslim majority in Lebanon. By 1956, when Nasser had become an Arab hero, the Muslims of Lebanon identified themselves with him, while the Maronites became more pro-European. President Chamoun of Lebanon was accused by Muslims and by some Christians of discrimination against non-Maronites. At the time of Nasser's visit to Damascus, as the first president of the U.A.R., hundreds of thousands of Lebanese went there to welcome him, and the desire to have Lebanon join the union was very strong. This, added to the general dissatisfaction concerning the Chamoun government and the rumors that Chamoun wanted to amend the constitution in order to serve another term, caused the Muslims to riot.

There were violent clashes between the government and the opposition. The Lebanese government charged that the rebels had received military supplies from Syria and took the matter to the Arab League. As the League did not take any action, Lebanon took the matter to the United Nations Security Council. The Security Council's team of observers, however, did not find anything to substantiate the charge. By midsummer of 1958, there was a virtual civil war in Lebanon, but it was not between Christians and Muslims. In this case, the Maronite patriarch opposed Chamoun's policies, believing that they might endanger the position of all Christians in the Arab world.

On July 14, 1958, a military coup d'etat in Iraq destroyed the Hashimite rule in that country. As it was reputed to be a pro-Nasser revolt, Chamoun became alarmed lest Lebanon be next and appealed to the United States to invoke the Eisenhower Doctrine. This controversial doctrine, passed by the United States Congress in 1957, was formulated to help Middle Eastern countries defend themselves against outside aggression. President Eisenhower complied with the request, and American Marines landed in Lebanon. It was not the last time that U.S. Marines would be sent to Lebanon to prop up a shaky Maronite-dominated government.

Settlement in Lebanon

The year of 1958 was a crucial year for Arab unity. In that year, the pan-Arabists experienced the joy of achievement in the creation of the U.A.R., and also the dismay of failure in the breaking up of that union. One of the first states to resume normalcy was Lebanon. The American troops did not engage in any fighting, but their presence quieted the opponents in the civil war. On July 31, 1958, the parliament elected the popular general, Fuad Shehab, to succeed Chamoun. The new president chose Rashid Karami, the Muslim leader of the opposition in the civil war, as prime minister.

A new "salvation cabinet," made up of an equal number of Christians and Muslems, carried on the work of rebuilding and pacification.

Events had probably convinced the majority of Lebanese that it was better for their country to resume its role of "neutrality" in the inter-Arab Cold War. The Arabs of the Middle East needed a "neutral Switzerland"; and Lebanon was qualified, both by the beauty of its landscape and by the aptitude of its people, to be such a place. The Lebanese seemed to be better off as the financial managers of the Arab world than as participants in inter-Arab rivalries. Almost all Arab countries had accounts in the numerous banks of Lebanon, and the banks in turn financed many industrial developments in those countries. Lebanon enjoyed many advantages. It was accessible by sea and air to trade centers in Europe, and it had practically no commercial or monetary encumbrances often found in other Middle Eastern countries. Consequently, almost all foreign enterprises that had invested in the Middle East, save Israel, had their offices in Lebanon; Chase Manhattan, Bankers Trust, and Citibank of New York are a few examples from the United States alone.

The rival politicians of the Arab countries needed a neutral Lebanon. As long as the coups and countercoups continued, as they seemed to, in Syria, Iraq, Yaman, and even in Saudi Arabia, the defeated needed safety and the rivals needed a neutral ground to iron out their differences. The oil-rich shaykhs of the Persian Gulf and Saudi Arabia found Lebanon as beautiful and more convenient than Switzerland. They built their palaces in the cool mountains of Lebanon and enjoyed the virtues and vices of Europe without the handicap of needing an interpreter. Beirut enjoyed over a dozen daily newspapers, almost all of them subsidized by one Arab country or another. All one had to do was to read the editorials in order to know the current policy of any Arab country.

The Nature of Lebanese Society

Lebanon is a fragmented dissonant society that has no national identity, a society formed by the circumstances of history. It is like a kaleidoscope, every time it is shaken, the colored pieces fall haphazardly to form a new design without evident reason. Even though the fragments that make up the society go by religious labels such as Christian, Muslim, or Druze (or their subdivisions such as Maronite and Orthodox, Sunni and Shi'i), the causes of the disagreements and war are not based on religion. Indeed, religious leaders have played a secondary role in the Lebanese struggle. The ordinary Lebanese, who is loyal to his religion, is quite likely not interested in the fighting. Those who order the fighting use religious symbolism, both Christian and Muslim, to further their own political and economic interests.

The Shi'is.   Shi'is form the largest community in the Lebanese kaleidoscope; at the same time, they are the most economically and politically disadvantaged. Musa al-Sadr, a charismatic Shi'i leader, founded the Movement of the Disinherited in 1974. A year later he organized AMAL, which is the Arabic acronym for "Battalion of the Lebanese Resistance." This was to be the military arm of the Movement of the Disinherited. These two organizations, especially AMAL, gained strength when Musa al-Sadr went to Libya in August 1978 and simply disappeared. This event galvanized the Shi'is. Furthermore, the Islamic Revolution in Iran of 1977–1979 provided inspiration for the Shi'is of Lebanon and, for some, an example to emulate. After the disappearance of Sadr, AMAL leadership changed hands; by 1980 a lawyer, Nabih Birri, was in charge. He emphasized the military and political functions of AMAL rather than the religious. A small group called "Islamic AMAL" influenced by the Iranian Revolution, was the only militant rival among the Shi'is.

In addition to AMAL, there were local notables and feudal families who wielded a great deal of influence and who were interested in improving the lot of the Shi'is without losing their own traditional prominence in the community.

In the 1983 reconciliation meeting in Geneva, Nabih Birri demanded a greater share of civil service jobs for the Shi'is. He also emphasized that Lebanon was his national home; for the Islamic AMAL, on the other hand, the Shi'i Islamic ummah supersedes nationality, a view that the Iranian volunteers in Lebanon had been preaching.

The Maronites. The 800,000 Maronites form the second largest group in Lebanon. By common consent, they provide the presidents of the republic; not by common consent, they control the army as well as many of the country's commercial and financial enterprises. They hold on to their power tenaciously and fear exploitation by the larger non-Christian groups that do not feel the same loyalty to Lebanese independence. The Maronites are also divided into rival clans that sometimes unite but often are antagonistic to each other. Some are willing to invest in a new, united Lebanon with political reforms. There are also hard-liners who command militias and have given up hope of a reintegrated Lebanon. They favor the cantonization of Lebanon without having considered the practicality of such a move in a small country.

Among the important Maronite leaders, there is Pierre Jumayyil, whose son Amin was elected president in September 1982 and commands a strong militia. Another leader is Sulayman Frangieh. He has close ties with Syria and is opposed to the Phalangist Party of Jumayyil. In the Geneva reconciliation meeting of 1983, however, he is reputed to have made peace with Amin Jumayyil. A third leader, Raymond Edde, has refused to form a militia of his own. A fourth leader is Camille Chamoun, who commands a militia of his own and who encouraged the coming of United States Marines in 1958. All of these leaders have been presidents of Lebanon; and all, except one, have had their own communal militia as well as being commander of the Lebanese army. They have opposed any reform before the withdrawal of non-Lebanese forces. It is interesting to note that in the reconciliation meeting in Geneva, all of them were present and they were the only representatives from all of the Christian groups.

The Sunnis. The 600,000 Sunnis form the third largest group in Lebanon. They are the most prosperous and the least militant of the Muslim groups. Traditionally they have provided Lebanon with its prime ministers.

They reside mostly in Beirut, Tripoli, and Sidon. Among the prime minis-
ters from Beirut have been men such as Saib Salaam, Tagi-al-Din al-Sulh,
Rashid al-Sulh, and Shafiq al-Wazzan. The leader of the Tripoli Sunnis,
Rashid Karami, has been prime minister several times.

Made up largely of landowners and bourgeoisie, the Sunni community
inhibits radical political demands. Economically and politically they have
more in common with their prosperous Christian compatriots than with
their Shi'i co-religionists. They also are divided into different clans. There is
a religious Sunni organization under the leadership of the mufti of Lebanon. True to Sunni tradition, the religious leaders do not involve themselves
in politics but are not without influence. The Sunni and some Shi'i representatives gathered at a conference on September 21, 1983. They called for the
withdrawal of all non-Lebanese troops, the disbandment of all militias and
armed organizations, and "equal opportunity for all Lebanese without discrimination." They declared Lebanon to be "a democratic, parliamentary
republic . . . committed to the free enterprise system."

The Greek Orthodox. The Greek Orthodox community of about 250,000
has its patriarchate in Damascus. Its members are more liberal than the
Maronites and have not participated in any of the civil wars in Lebanon.
Many have come under the influence of the Maronite factions. Others have
joined marginal political parties such as the Syrian Social Nationalist Party
and the Lebanese Community Party, both of which are headed by Greek
Orthodox Christians. It has been customary for a member of this community to be assigned the ministry of foreign affairs. The most famous member
is Charles Malik, who was ambassador to the United States and the United
Nations, president of the United Nations, and foreign minister of Lebanon.

Other Christian groups. The 150,000 Greek Catholics comprise another
Christian group. They are concentrated in Zahle in the Beqaa Valley. They
are not very militaristic except in the south, where the former major, Sa'd
Haddad, started the "Free Lebanon" movement in alliance with Israel.

The Armenians, who were transplanted from Turkey, number about
150,000. Unlike other migrant groups, they are naturalized Lebanese and
almost totally assimilated. While supporting the Phalangist Party in parliamentary elections, they have refused to take sides in the civil war. The
Armenian Church has been very active in helping its people socially and has
had a moderating influence on the Lebanese political scene.

Protestant Christians form the smallest group, numbering about 20,000.
They are nonpolitical and, on the whole, better educated. Like the Orthodox,
they are diversified in their outlook. In recent years some fundamentalists
from outside have entered Lebanese Protestant society and have established
"missions" in the south. Their literature promotes the idea that the establishment of the state of Israel is the fulfillment of Biblical prophecy.

The Druzes. During the early phase of Ottoman rule in the sixteenth
and seventeenth centuries, the Druzes, whose religion is an offshoot of Shi'i
Islam that has been influenced by other religious doctrines, were the rulers

of Mount Lebanon. By the eighteenth century, the Maronites had replaced them there, and the two groups have been antagonistic to each other ever since. The Druzes, like the Maronites, are parochial, ethnocentric mountain people. They number about 200,000, and their religious sanctuary is in the Hasbaya area. Of the two important Druze clans, the Arslans have favored the established government and have supported the ruling presidents of Lebanon. The other clan, the Jumblatts, have been more critical of the establishment. Their leader, until his assassination in March 1977, was Kamal Jumblatt. An erudite, cosmopolitan figure, he founded the Lebanese National Movement, which had a program for democratic reform. His son and successor, Walid Jumblatt, carried out a successful military offensive against the Maronites in the Shuf area in 1983. He is close to Syria, and it seems that the old animosity between the Druze and the Maronites has been revived. Being a small community, and having co-religionists in both Syria and Israel, the Druzes have had to be pragmatic and to adapt to new situations. They talk a great deal about socialism and progress, but they are not free from ethnocentric clan considerations.

The Palestinians. After the war between the Arab states and Israel in 1948, Palestinian refugees were scattered in different parts of the Fertile Crescent. The 100,000 Palestinian refugees living in fifteen camps in Lebanon caused considerable economic problems for the country. Because of the fact that Lebanon enjoyed a free society, the PLO leaders were able to take control of the camps and use them as bases for their raids against Israel. Also because of the fact that Lebanon was weak militarily, it became a general pattern that no matter from which Arab state Israel was raided, the retaliation would be, more often than not, against Lebanon. The Lebanese were divided on this point. Generally the Maronites wanted the government to subdue the PLO, and the Muslims wanted the government to strengthen the army and stop Israel.

The whole problem became more complicated in 1970 by the events of Black September, when King Husayn evicted the PLO military contingent from Jordan. As a result, the Palestinian resistance movement moved to Lebanon. When the PLO armed units joined with the refugees, Lebanon began to face a new minority of increasingly radical proportions in the 1970s. The arrival of the expelled PLO militiary forces exacerbated an already delicate political and economic situation. By 1973, a Maronite milita led by the Jumayyil family unsuccessfully attempted to provoke the Palestinian armed forces into combat. The provocation came in the form of unanticipated attacks on segments of the Palestinian community within the Beirut area.

Two events of 1974 further aggravated the right-wing Phalangist militia. The first was the October 1974 Rabat Conference decision concerning the legitimacy of the PLO as representing the Palestinian people's aspirations. The second was the November 1974 United Nations appearance of Yasser Arafat and the conferring of observer status on the PLO representatives at the UN. In April 1975, the Jumayyil Phalangist militia ambushed a school-bus loaded with Palestinian youth, thus beginning the Lebanese civil war.

Civil War

It must be noted that, unlike Syria whose dominant political leadership represented a force within the country's politics, Lebanon had no such dominant leadership. Rather, in 1969, the Druze leader, Kamal Jumblatt organized twelve various "radical" groups into a coalition called the Lebanese National Movement. By 1973, the LNM—which included the Organization for Communist Action, Jumblatt's own Progressive Socialist Party, the Independent Nasserite Movement, the Lebanese Community Party, and the Syrian Social Nationalist Party—had aligned itself with the PLO in challenging the old Lebanese landed, banking, and industrial families for control of the Lebanese state. Such an alliance between the LNM and the PLO clearly challenged the National Charter of the Lebanese government, which had continued to be dominated by the Maronite Chamoun, Edde, and Jumayyil families. By April 1975, the alliance of the LNM and the PLO was influencing village and industrial labor forces, such as union and strike organizations and village collectives, in very profound ways. To this may be added the increasing hostility of the Lebanese commercial sector to the continued dominance of the banking and industrial families, whose privileged position was supported by a large amount of foreign capital and many multinational corporate interests, particularly those of the United States. The Lebanese coalition of peasants, workers, shopkeepers, and professionals had become increasingly hostile toward the Maronite-dominated status quo. It had also become increasingly effective in mobilizing public support for both radical solutions and for the PLO and the Palestinian refugee camp communities ringing Lebanon's major towns, in particular Beirut.

Initially begun as an attack by Jumayyil Phalangists on a Palestinian schoolbus, the shooting incident of April 1975 quickly exploded into raging warfare between rival towns and militia groups. The angered PLO and LNM armed forces attacked the Phalangist districts of Beirut and surrounding towns, and the Phalangists attacked the Palestinian refugee camps. An unending number of cease-fire agreements were made, only to be broken as soon as the rival groups could organize themselves. The civil war was soon followed by the Syrian occupation of the Beqaa Valley at the behest of the League of Arab States, meeting in Riyad.

Described variously as an "invasion" and as "a peacekeeping expedition," the Syrian army clearly entered the Lebanese class and sectarian war in order to protect itself from a dangerously devisive conflict for its own political conditions. By initially supporting the government against the PLO and LNM, Syria was bitterly attacked for its pro-Phalangist politics. The position of Syria changed, however, to keep pace with the altered positions of the embattled parties. By 1982, Syria no longer supported the Phalangist militias, encircled as they were in 1977 by the PLO and LNM, but rather switched support to the PLO when the latter was being encircled within Beirut by Israeli forces.

The Israeli Invasion.   In the same year that Syrian troops entered Lebanon, Major Sa'd Haddad of the Lebanese army deserted with a contingent of Christian militia and took control of south Lebanon. In addition to arming and equipping this group, Israel also provided war materiel to the Maronite militia in the north under the leadership of Bashir Jumayyil. In 1978, about a year after Menachem Begin assumed power as prime minister, the Israeli army began its incursion into southern Lebanon. As a result of this, the United Nations sent a peacekeeping force to south Lebanon, which, with Haddad's forces, formed a buffer between the PLO and Israel. Both because of the criticism Syria was receiving for its pro-Phalangist policy and because of the Israeli march into Lebanon, Syria changed sides and began to help the PLO and other anti-Phalangist groups. By April 1981, a fierce clash between the Syrian troops and the Phalangists had erupted in Zahle; and Israel had assumed a more aggressive role on the side of the Phalangists.

With the appointment of Ariel Sharon as defense minister in 1981, Israeli policy became more bellicose. It was Sharon's plan to uproot the PLO and its armed forces and to help elect Bashir Jumayyil as president of Lebanon, who in turn would be persuaded to sign a separate peace agreement with Israel. The fifth war since the establishment of Israel was initiated by the Israeli invasion of Lebanon on June 6, 1982. The Lebanese civil war had become a regional war. Moreover, with the coming of United States, French, British, and Italian peacekeeping troops in 1983 and with Soviet troops nearby, the Lebanese civil war had become internationalized. In the end these interventions proved more fatal than peaceful.

The reaction of the world and, more especially, that of the citizens of Israel to the invasion and to Israel's use of cluster bombs and the destruction they wrought both in life and property, was very negative. The saturation bombing of Beirut in August 1982, followed by the Sabra and Shatila massacres in November, profoundly shocked the Israeli public. For the first time there were antiwar demonstrations in Israel; some Israeli field officers resigned their commissions. As for the Lebanese, some feared the dismemberment of their country; others welcomed the invasion because, in their view, Israel was the lesser of two evils—the other one being the PLO. For still others, however, the invasion represented the beginning of another conflagration in which Israel would be bogged down in the quagmire of Lebanon.

This last view was not too far wrong. Israel succeeded in uprooting the PLO military organization in Lebanon, but not entirely. Thousands of PLO soldiers, including Arafat, evacuated Lebanon. Shortly afterward, however, Arafat returned to lead the remnant of his forces in northern Lebanon against the Sa'iqah Palestinians under Syrian influence, and a number of his own followers who had joined the opposition. After the days of fighting in the outskirts of Tripoli, Arafat was forced to leave Lebanon again, but he has remained the acknowledged leader of the PLO. Insofar as Israel was concerned, enough Palestinian soldiers remained behind to harass the occupying Israeli army.

Israel was successful in influencing the election of the pro-Israel Maronite Phalangist leader, Bashir Jumayyil, to the presidency of Lebanon on August 23, 1982. Bashir, however, was assassinated on September 14 and was replaced by his more moderate brother, Amin Jumayyil, on September 21. With the United States as arbiter, Israel was able to sign a separate peace agreement with President Jumayyil on May 17, 1983. While it was true that

Jumayyil was the president of Lebanon, it was also true that he was the leader of the Phalangist militia that was fighting the other factions in Lebanon. The agreement was "ratified" by the Lebanese cabinet, but there were so many abstentions that it was made meaningless.

The United States, more than the European nations with troops in Lebanon, had maneuvered itself on the side of the Phalangists against other Lebanese factions and Syria. United States battleships bombarded anti-Jumayyil forces in Lebanon, causing more destruction and loss of life. The United States embassy in Beirut was bombed on April 18, 1983, killing 46 and wounding about 100. On October 23, 1983, a truck loaded with explosives demolished the United States Marine headquarters building, killing 241 Marines and wounding many others. On the same day another truck exploded in the French camp, killing 40 soldiers. Both trucks had been driven by volunteers who had sacrificed themselves for the cause. These volunteers were alleged to be members of the Islamic AMAL. By the spring of 1984, President Reagan was forced to withdraw the Marines from Lebanon. The British, Italians, and French did the same. These actions weakened the Jumayyil government, and he was forced to abandon the agreement with Israel.

Ariel Sharon himself was forced to resign because of the unfortunate massacre by the Phalangists of over 800 Palestinian women and children in the two refugee camps of Sabra and Shatila while the Israeli army occupied the area. On the whole, Israel did not gain much from the invasion. The Israeli army continued to occupy southern Lebanon; by mid-1984 several Israeli soldiers had become victims of intermittent attacks. Whether or not southern Lebanon becomes another West Bank remains to be seen.

The Fate of Lebanon

Lebanon's social and economic conditions had deteriorated to such a degree that its banking and industrial interests—so vital to European and United States corporations—could no longer maintain their increasingly vulnerable minority position. With the departure of the United States and European forces, Syria became the only arbiter in the latest Lebanese civil war, as well as the primary country confronting Israel on behalf of the Palestinians and the Arabs in general. As champions of modern Arab nationalism, Syria has not abandoned the concept of the "inseparability" of Lebanon and Syria. Furthermore, Syria sees its security linked with that of Lebanon. In the Syrian view, the Lebanese-Israeli agreement of May 1983 made Lebanon a puppet of Israel and could not be tolerated. Syria has said that it will leave Lebanon only after Israel withdraws. Syria insists that Israel invaded Lebanon, while its own presence in Lebanon had the approval of the Arab states, including Lebanon, and also that of the United States. Consequently, a simultaneous withdrawal of both forces would make Syria seem to be an aggressor like Israel.

As arbiter of the Lebanese civil war, Syria brought the leaders of the warring factions together in two "reconciliation" meetings in Switzerland. By mid-1984, a cabinet made up of those same leaders had been formed. While intermittent shooting continued, the cabinet sought solution to the problems of Lebanon. Some wanted cantonization; some desired a modification of the 1943 pact; and still others favored the elimination of sectarian politics and the secularization of Lebanese society.

Lebanon has not been able to defend its territorial integrity since 1970. By mid-1984, Israeli, Syrian, and Palestinian soldiers still occupied Lebanon. Even though in the reconciliation talks in Switzerland it was agreed that Lebanon was "Arab in its identity," it remains to be seen whether this concept will stand the test of time. As long as foreign forces occupy Lebanon, and as long as the Arab-Israeli problem, to which Lebanon is linked, remains unsolved, the factional leaders of Lebanon will be attracted to one side or the other, and Lebanon will remain a kaleidoscopic society.

Chapter Twenty-Seven
Modern Iraq and Jordan

During World War I, Sharif Husayn of Mecca and his sons took up the cause of Arab nationalism and negotiated with the British. Their aim was to create an Arab state encompassing all of the Fertile Crescent and the Arabian peninsula, with themselves as rulers and with jurisdiction over the holy cities of Mecca and Medina. The Balfour Declaration and the Sykes-Picot Agreement, together with the rising power of Abdul Aziz ibn-Sa'ud, whittled down both the territory and the ambitions of the Hashimite clan to what is known today as Iraq and Jordan. According to the Sykes-Picot Agreement, the whole area, including Palestine, was to be in the British sphere. Insofar as the British had the two sons of Sharif Husayn in their zone, they conveniently carved out a territory on the east bank of the Jordan River and called it Transjordan. They appointed the oldest son, Abdullah, amir of Transjordan (later to become "king" and the "Hashimite Kingdom of Jordan," respectively), and the more active son, Faysal I, king of Iraq.

These states had two things in common: One was the fact that they were under the British mandate and were subject to all the pressures and privileges relevant to such a relationship. The second was the close family ties that united them against rivals and movements which tried to dethrone them. By the end of World War II, the British had relinquished the region; and by 1958, the Hashimite Dynasty had been overthrown in Iraq, leaving the Jordan branch of the family to continue what was left of the original hope.

298

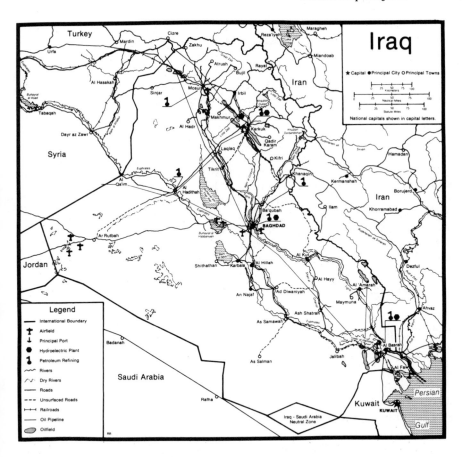

THE MAKING OF MODERN IRAQ

In the years after World War II, the government of Iraq was in the hands of an oligarchy of landlords, tribal shaykhs, military officers, and elder politicians presided over by the young king Faysal II. Even with the lush flow of oil royalties, the dismal poverty of the people was appalling. In 1951, thanks to Iran's nationalization of its oil industry, the Iraq Petroleum Company arranged a 50-50 sharing of profits with the Iraqi government. But not much of this sum trickled down to the masses. A Development Board was supposed to use the oil income for public projects, but most of these projects profited the landlords.

Egyptian land reforms created unrest among Iraqi peasants, and the 1956 Egyptian war made Nasser a hero in the eyes of the Iraqis. Insofar as coups were concerned the Iraqis were no match for the Syrians, but they were a close second. From 1934 to 1958 the Iraqis had eight coups with varying degrees of violence. The 1958 coup d'etat was a collaboration of several nationalist and leftist groups, with the army under the leadership of General Abd al-Karim Qasim. It differed from the Egyptian revolution in that it was not all military and was also much more violent. In July 1958, the protestors went into the streets of Baghdad, killing and looting. The leaders of the revolution did away with King Faysal, Crown Prince Abdul Ilah, and Prime Minister Nuri al-Sai'd. Ba'thists, communists, and members of a couple of other parties formed the civilian component of the revolution.

After overthrowing the Hashimite kingdom, the new Iraqi government under General Qasim seceded from the federation with Jordan, broke all ties with the Baghdad Pact, and recognized both the Soviet Union and the People's Republic of China. Nasser sent his congratulations and the Syrian Ba'thists urged their fellow party members in Iraq to join the U.A.R. This was the closest the Arabs had—and have—ever been to union. The union of Syria and Egypt was a reality, a seemingly pro-Nasser group had come to power in Iraq, a pan-Arab uprising had occurred in Lebanon, and even Yaman had tied itself by special arrangment to the U.A.R.

Qasim and Nasser

Qasim of Iraq did not prove to be the pan-Arab revolutionary that people thought he was. Neither was he the reactionary that he was accused of being by Nasser. He had come to power at the head of a coalition of communists and pan-Arab Ba'thists. He was, however, an Iraqi nationalist who, along with the non-pan-Arab elements of Iraq, did not want to share sovereignty and wealth with Nasser. He had used the Ba'thists and communists to come to power and then had used the communists to get rid of the Ba'thists. One of the leading pan-Arab nationalists, Colonel Abd al-Salam Arif, had been in Damascus two days after the 1958 revolution with Nasser, receiving the cheers of the population; three months later he was in a Baghdad jail under sentence of death.

For nearly three years the communists were free in Iraq. They were well organized and had numerous front groups. They established a field "people's court," in which they tried members of the former government. In these trials, sarcastic remarks were made against President Nasser of the U.A.R. In 1959, a U.A.R.-supported uprising against Qasim in Mosul was brutally suppressed. A few months later, an unsuccessful attempt on Qasim's life was attributed to Nasserites. The animosity between the two became stronger by the day. At the time when the pan-Arab nationalists were on the verge of attaining their goal of union, the ascetic-looking and ascetic-living General Qasim, helped by the communists, raised the cry, "Iraq for the Iraqis."

Nasser could not allow Qasim to continue imprisoning Iraqi Nasserites without challenging him. And he could not very well challenge him without the aid of Jordan and Saudi Arabia. In the summer of 1959, Nasser restored diplomatic relations with Jordan and received King Saud of Arabia as an honored guest in Cairo. Furthermore, it looked as though the Soviet Union was aiding Qasim against Nasser, and this drove the latter into closer ties with the United States.

A climax came in June 1961, when the British protectorate over Kuwait, established in 1899, was lifted and the oil-rich territory was declared independent. Qasim used the occasion to declare that Kuwait belonged to Iraq and prepared to annex it. The ruling shaykh of Kuwait immediately invoked the treaty agreement with Britain and arranged for British troops to defend his country against Iraq. Ideologically, the U.A.R. should have welcomed the annexation of a reactionary shaykhdom by a radical Arab, but Qasim was a sworn enemy of Nasser and could not be allowed to do this. Consequently, the Arabs witnessed the unusual spectacle of Nasser cooperating with the British to save Kuwait from the hands of Qasim. By mid-September, the British troops had left; and it was a combination of troops from Egypt, Jordan, and Saudi Arabia that stood guard over Kuwait against another Arab country.

In the meantime Qasim was trying to implement his brand of socialism in Iraq. In 1959, he inaugurated a four-year plan consisting of land reform, industrialization, housing, and transportation. By 1961, some 60 percent of the land had been redistributed.

Whatever enthusiasm existed in the immediate aftermath of the 1958 Iraqi Revolution soon began to dissipate. Qasim not only had opened up the political prisons but also had invited exiled Iraqis, including the Kurdish leader, Mulla Mustafa Barzani, to return to Iraq. By 1961, however, Barzani and his Pesh Merga had begun to fight once more for autonomy in northern Iraq for the Kurdish people. His demand for national cultural rights was agreeable to Qasim and the republican government. But the Kurds wanted more. Barzani demanded a federated Iraq in which an Iraqi Kurdestan would have complete autonomy. He also wanted a large share of the revenues of the northern Iraqi oil fields. These demands, however, were not acceptable. So the Kurds resumed their opposition in 1961, and a year later it had grown into a full-scale revolt.

The Kurdish uprising, the aborted Kuwait takeover, and the purging of the Communist Party from the offices of the republic had greatly weakened Qasim. He was open to a wide range of criticism from both the socialist and the nationalist camps. The military, which was the only force capable of challenging Qasim, had been politicized by the Communist Party. Under the circumstances, the Ba'th Party was the principal force for change. Consequently, the Iraqi branch of the Ba'th Party staged a coup against Qasim on February 8, 1963. The leader of the coup, Abd al-Salam Arif, whose death sentence had been reprieved by Qasim, ordered the death of Qasim and his leftist supporters. Nasser sent his congratulations to Arif. Michel Aflaq, the Syrian theoretician of the Ba'th Party, held long meetings with his Iraqi colleagues. On March 8, 1963, Syria had another coup that brought to power a number of military leaders, who, although not Ba'thist, were sympathetic to its ideas. Once again the three countries, Iraq, Syria, and Egypt, held meetings for union and every meeting ended in recriminations. In spite of all this, the Egyptian, Iraqi, and Syrian leaders still spoke of union and approved a flag design with three stars on it.

Conflict within Ba'th

It is generally accepted that the Ba'th Party was founded in 1940 by two Syrians, Michel Aflaq and Salah al-Din al-Bitar. It had a threefold aim: nationalism, unity, and socialism. By "nationalism," it meant the idea that all who speak Arabic are one nation. By "unity," it meant that all the Arab states should have one centralized government or form a federal union. By "socialism," it meant the achievement of social, economic, and political justice for all Arabs, irrespective of religious affiliation. Although all Arabic-speaking students of such subjects agree on these three goals, the existential realities under which most Arabs live contain contradictions that turn Arabs against each other. Local nationalisms work against the interests of a larger Arab nationalism. The integrity of each Arab state and the personal pride and ambition of its leaders prevent the union of the Arab states. Finally, what a Saudi Arab considers to be social justice may not be acceptable to an Egyptian Arab or to the Arabs of half a dozen other states. We have already seen the results of these contradictions in the futile attempts to form the United Arab Republic and the federal union of Iraq and Jordan, and we see it again in the Ba'th movements of Syria and Iraq.

Between 1963 and 1983 the Ba'th Party of Iraq managed to purge itself twice (1968 and 1979); in the process, it became the bitter enemy of the Ba'th Party of Syria. When the Iraqi Ba'th, under Abd al-Salim Arif, ousted Qasim in 1963, the National Council of Revolutionary Command was formed, with Arif as president and General Ahmad Hasan al-Bakr as prime minister. They began to arrest communists and Nasserites. Even though Barzani had supported the coup, the Ba'thist dealing with the Kurds was a continuation of Qasim's policies. The Soviet Union criticized Iraq for its treatment of the communists and the Kurds, and Nasser denounced the Iraqi leaders as traitors to Arab unity. (This in spite of the fact that one of the goals of Ba'th was Arab unity!) Under these circumstances, Arif evicted all non-Iraqi Ba'thists from positions of influence and took control himself by forming the Iraqi Arab Socialist Union.

Arif was killed in a helicopter crash on April 13, 1966; his brother, General Abd al-Rahman Arif, took his place. Most of the two years of his rule was taken up by the Kurdish question. As usual, he resorted to military means first and launched an offensive against Barzani. After he was badly defeated, he changed his tactics and announced his willingness to negotiate. He received a Kurdish delegation and announced amnesty for the rebels. He recognized Kurdish autonomy and promised the Kurds proportional representation in the cabinet, army, and other branches of the government. But a number of nationalist Iraqi officers, together with the disgruntled Ba'thists, carried out a coup in July 1968 and chose General al-Bakr as president and head of the Revolutionary Command Council. The new regime found itself between the right-wing anti-Ba'thists on the one hand, and the left-wing Ba'thists, supported by Syria, on the other. Nevertheless, the government was able to nationalize Iraq's major industries, negotiate an arms deal with France, and sign a Soviet-Iraqi friendship agreement in 1972.

The Rise of Saddam Husayn

In the midst of the Ba'thist restructuring of the republic's economy and politics, Saddam Husayn emerged as a leading figure in both the Ba'th Party and the Iraqi army. Saddam Husayn first came to public attention in the July 1968 coup and party purge, figuring prominently as vice-chairman of al-Bakr's Revolutionary Command Council. He was also secretary-general of the Ba'th Party and vice-president of Iraq.

Even though al-Bakr was president, it was becoming more and more evident that it was Saddam Husayn who was making all the decisions. Following the second major party purge of 1979, Husayn emerged as the single most important person within the country. He nonetheless carried on the previous policies of state control of every major industrial and financial enterprise. Meanwhile, he allowed the growth of private commercial and construction enterprises by following policies similar to those of the Syrian Ba'thist Party.

Saddam's rise to power coincided with the OPEC oil price rise. The Soviet Union lent Iraq $70 million to develop the Rumayla oil field in the north. The French received a concession to build a pipeline to the Persian Gulf terminal at Fao in 1970; and, a year later, Czechoslovakia was given the concession to build a refinery in Basra. The government nationalized the Iraq Petroleum Company in 1972. Soon after that, oil prices skyrocketed and Iraq's income rose with them. In 1971 Iraq's income from oil had been about $914 million; by 1976 it had jumped to $9.25 billion. A pipeline from northern Iraq through Turkey to Iskenderun was completed in 1977. As a result Iraq enjoyed oil outlets to the Persian Gulf and to the Mediterranean through Lebanon, Syria, and Turkey.

Iraq, as well as its neighbor Iran and many other developing countries, considered industrialization to be a panacea for almost all ills. Consequently, they paid little attention to the problems of agriculture, which was the principal occupation of the majority of their citizens. With the help of the World Bank and the Soviet Union, Iraq started building a twenty-five-mile canal connecting the Tigris and Euphrates rivers. Because the completion of the great dam on the Euphrates by the Syrians had reduced the northern water supply for Iraqi farmers, the government stepped up the completion of its own dam on the Euphrates, which it had begun in 1966. Other than these steps, however, and the fact that agriculture was always mentioned in five-year plans, not much was done, and many Iraqi farmers were forced to go to the cities in search of work.

The Kurdish Problem

It will be recalled that the government of Arif was overthrown because it had accepted the demands of Barzani for Kurdish self-determination. The new government of al-Bakr and Saddam Husayn continued the struggle against the Kurds. When another massive campaign against the Kurds in 1969 was not successful, the government accepted Barzani's terms. These were: the creation of an autonomous Kurdestan with its own language, that would be federated to Iraq; and proportional representation in all departments of the government. Serious fighting, however, resumed within a few months when Barzani accused the government of breaking the agreement. For their part, the Kurds were not totally united either. There were Kurds who were sympathetic with the Ba'th Party's first program. They joined the Kurdish Democratic Party, which was under communist leadership and fought against the nationalist Barzani. On the other hand, Barzani was being aided by Iran, which supplied arms and asylum when needed. It has been reported, furthermore, that both the American CIA and Israel helped Barzani through Iran by providing funds and Russian-made equipment that had been captured by Israel.

The inconclusive struggle continued until 1975, when the heads of OPEC nations were meeting at Algiers. There, Saddam Husayn, as vice-president of Iraq, signed an agreement with the shah of Iran settling their differences. One of the items of this agreement was a promise on the part of the shah that the government of Iran would not aid the Iraqi Kurds. Thus, the shah deserted the Kurds, alienating even further the Iranian Kurds in the bargain. This was not the first time the Kurds had been kicked around like a football. In the late 1920s when Reza Shah of Iran was having difficulties with the Kurds of Iran, the then Iraqi government supplied the Iranian Kurds with arms and asylum. Iraq deserted the Kurds, however, as soon as its dispute with Iran was settled. In the 1970s, it was Iran's turn to do the same. By the mid-1980s, however, Saddam Husayn had turned the tables and was helping the Iranian Kurds, who were fighting against the Islamic Republic of Khomayni.

Saddam Husayn took advantage of his newly found respite and tried to resettle a large number of Kurdish peasants away from their northern ancestral homelands to the marshlands of the south. The Kurds, however, did not sit idly by but increased the fury of their resistance until 1977, when Husayn rescinded the order.

Iraq and Iran

Iran has had more disputes with Iraq than with any other Arabic-speaking state. Partly this is because Iraq had been part of the Ottoman Empire which had had centuries of rivalry and war with Iran. The Ottomans and the Iranians had had boundary, trade route, and minority disputes that have come down to modern times. The problem of political boundaries has been exacerbated by the rural people, especially the Kurds, whose ancestral homelands had been divided by these powers against their consent. Their rural economies do not recognize boundaries and such modern contraptions as passports and customs duties.

Furthermore, for the Shi'i Iranians, the most sacred Shi'i shrine—the tomb of the third Imam, Husayn—and the most prestigious Shi'i school of theology and jurisprudence are both located in Iraq, in Karbala and Najaf, respectively. During the past centuries, every shah of Iran has either visited the shrine or showered it with gold and silver, or both. Because of the shrine, many Iranians go there on pilgrimage every year, and some of the old and the sick stay in the hope of dying there and being buried in the holy ground. Moreover, there is another fact that is not mentioned much but is nonetheless true: most Iraqi citizens are Shi'is but they are ruled by a Sunni minority. Inasmuch as Iran is the only Shi'i power in the Islamic world, the Shi'is of Iraq have sometimes shown pro-Iranian proclivities. To the above list we must add the fact that modern nationalism has revived old Arab-Iranian rivalries and desires to be the region's leading power.

Most of the above problems were supposedly solved in the agreement of 1937, which paved the way for the Tehran-organized Sa'dabad Treaty of Friendship in the same year, and which was followed by the Baghdad Pact of 1954. The problems, however, kept reappearing from time to time. One of them was the Kurdish problem, which has been discussed. The other was the Shatt al-Arab (Arvand-Rud to the Iranians) river dispute. The Shatt al-Arab is formed by the confluence of the Tigris and Euphrates in southern Iraq and flows for its last hundred miles south to the Persian Gulf. At the confluence of Karun River from Iran, the Shatt forms the boundary between the two countries. Iraq claimed the whole body of the river, while Iran felt that the boundary should follow the line of the *thalweg* (course of the main channel).

In the 1937 compromise, Iraq accepted the principle of the *thalweg* at certain places and Iran accepted the Iraqi claim at other places. The fees would be received by Iraq and would be spent for maintenance, dredging, and improvement of the river channel. The case lay dormant until the 1960s, when increased oil traffic in the Gulf and the activities of the Iranian navy reopened the whole question. Iran accused Iraq of breaking the agreement and sent its navy to control its side of the river all the way. Iran also aided the Iraqi Kurds to press its point. The problem was "solved" a second time by the Algiers Agreement, and in turn the shah abandoned the Kurdish leader, Mustafa Barzani. There was peace again between the two countries—for a little while.

The Iraq-Iran War

Unfortunately the peace did not last very long. Between 1977 and 1979, Iran was rocked by a great popular upheaval that forced the shah out of the country and established the Revolutionary Council headed by Ayatollah Ruhollah Khomayni. The reign of terror that followed the Islamic Revolution and the summary trials and executions of hundreds of political and military leaders had weakened Iran enough to tempt Saddam Husayn to try to take back what he had lost and some more. He felt that the easy victory that would certainly be his would serve several purposes: (1) It would give him the right to play the pan-Arab, Nasserite role of protector of the Arabic-speaking people in the oil-rich southeastern Iranian province of Khuzestan. (2) It would stop Khomayni's continued broadcasts into Iraq inciting the Shi'i population against the Ba'thist rule. (3) With Iran on its knees, Iraq would be the most powerful state in the Persian Gulf. (4) Iraq would occupy a place of leadership in the Arab world, especially now that Egypt had been banned from membership in the Arab League because of President Sadat's 1977 trip to Jerusalem and Syria was involved in the quagmire of Lebanon.

On September 20, 1980, Iraqi military forces crossed the Iranian border at three different points. Husayn proudly called it the "second Qadesiya," hoping to revive the memory of the first Qadesiya in 635 A.D., when the Arabs under Caliph Umar defeated the Iranians. By January 1981, Iraqi forces had advanced from ten to a hundred miles inside Iran. They captured Khorram Shahr and many towns and villages in Khuzestan. They shelled Ahvaz and many other towns but were not able to take the oil city of Abadan.

The Iraqi advance was, on the whole, slower than expected. By early 1982, the Iranians were able to launch a counterattack that proved to be the beginning of the end of Iraqi advance. Except for a small pocket, they retook all their territory and by April 1984 were inside Iraq and had captured the oil island of Majnun near Basra. The losses in life and property to both sides were enormous and economically disastrous especially to Iraq. Iraq was not able to export much oil to earn the necessary foreign exchange to buy war materiel. The Persian Gulf was closed to Iraqi shipping. Since Syria had declared itself on the side of Iran, it closed all the pipelines in its territory. The only outlet left to Iraq lay through Turkey to the port of Iskenderun. Having spent practically all its foreign exchange reserves for war, Iraq borrowed heavily from Saudi Arabia and other Arab states. Egypt sent military advisers; and Jordan, in addition to sending a contingent of soldiers, opened the port of Aqaba to Iraq. Before the war, Iraq was a boom country and foreign companies vied with each other for contracts. In mid-1984, however, Iraq was in grave financial trouble and in danger of defaulting on its bills.

Saddam Husayn was greatly humiliated when on June 7, 1981, Israel blew up the Tammuz-1 nuclear reactor. He lost prestige when the Conference of Nonaligned Nations that was to be held in Baghdad in 1982 was moved to India. Ironically, Iraq's defeat has strengthened Saddam Husayn and the Ba'th Party; Iraqi soldiers fought bravely to defend their land from Iranian attacks, as did the Iranians when the Iraqis were advancing in Iran.

The attempts of the United Nations and the Islamic nations to stop the war have been fruitless. Iran's conditions for peace are the complete evacuation of Iran by Iraqi forces, the payment of reparations, and the resignation of Saddam Husayn. Indeed, Iran has, with the help of some Iraqi prisoners of war and dissidents, formed the "Supreme Council of the Islamic Revolution of Iraq" and fully expects to form an Islamic republic in Iraq. The Arab countries, who are wary of Saddam Husayn's pretensions, might be willing to help Iraq pay reparations; but they are afraid that removing Saddam as a precondition for peace will give Khomayni too much power and prestige.

The Western nations, on the other hand, have not shown too much enthusiasm for ending the war. The Soviet Union, with 2,200 advisers in Iraq, has helped both countries; for the most part, however, it has adopted a "neutral" pose, while encouraging its Eastern European satellites to help Iraq. The French lent Iraq five Super-Etendard jets with Exocet missiles, while England increased its trade with Iran. The United States, which has had no ties with Iraq since 1972, gave $460 million for grain purchases in December 1982. On the other hand, it has not minded Israel's selling spare parts for American planes and equipment to Iran. In July 1984, the war had spread to the oil shipping lanes of the Persian Gulf. Inasmuch as there was an oil glut in the world market, the bombing of oil tankers only raised insurance premiums.

It has been a costly war for both sides but there are few signs of ending it. Four years of combat have resulted in over 500,000 military and civilian casualties, some 3 million displaced person, a financial debt on both sides of over $50 billion, and the enormous destruction of cities, towns, and industrial installations in both countries that will take decades to rebuild. In July 1984, Iraq was asking for peace while sinking oil tankers loaded with Iranian oil, and Iran was preparing 500,000 soldiers for a new offensive against Basra.

THE MAKING OF MODERN JORDAN

The establishment of Jordan in 1923 under King Abdullah was the beginning of another British-assisted state founded on monarchy, landed-family interests, and well-drilled military units. British-sponsored states in the years following World War I were typically centered around either a dominant family or a monarchy; furthemore, Britain trained the military units of Egypt, Saudi Arabia, Oman, Iraq, the Persian Gulf states, and Jordan. Jordan differed from the rest, however, in that it continued the British pattern well after World War II. British officers continued to direct Jordanian military and paramilitary units. Jordan also differed from other British client states in that its present monarch, King Husayn, was able to survive both Israeli and PLO military clashes with his own forces. King Husayn and the Royal Hashimite Kingdom of Jordan have proven to possess an uncanny amount of survivability. There are, of course, several explanations for Hashimite longevity in Middle Eastern politics.

Of all the princely states under British tutelage, none received such close attention as Jordan. The establishment of the Jordanian border patrol, which in time led to the creation of the Royal Jordanian Guard and the Arab Legion under Glubb Pasha, was a commitment that Britain made only to Jordan and not to any other client state in the years after World War I. Given Jordan's geographic position on the east bank of the Jordan River and within the Middle East, Britain's concerns were not entirely altruistic. The oil pipelines from Kirkuk and the later Trans-Arabian Pipe Line (TAP) from Saudi Arabia rendered Jordan strategic for oil exports. In addition, Jordan was geographically well placed for Britain's defense of the Suez Canal and Red Sea zone. It complemented the Palestinian mandate. Finally, the heavily subsidized Hashimite monarchy was of both practical and romantic interest to the British foreign office. The desert kingdom was still a British client.

The Expansion of Jordan

After the war of 1948 between the newly founded state of Israel and its Arab neighbors and the ensuing truce, the United Nations forgot that Palestine was originally to be partitioned between the Israelis and the Palestinians.

It also ignored the fact that in the original partition plan, Jerusalem was designated as an international city. Consequently, since the Israelis were allowed to hold the extra land that they had conquered, the United Nations looked the other way when King Abdullah of Jordan annexed half of Jerusalem and all of the Palestinian highlands (the West Bank) that had not been taken by Israel. This not only added the fertile land on the West Bank of the Jordan River to the Hashimite Kingdom, but increased the population of Jordan by one million. It also brought Jordan into close proximity with Israel over the haphazardly drawn border in the countryside and the streets and alleys of Jerusalem.

Two-thirds of the population of Jordan were Palestinians who were better educated and more politically aware than the bedouins who inhabited the East Bank of the Jordan River. These Palestinians, who were most bitter over the creation of Israel and frustrated by defeat, came to consider King Abdullah of Jordan as the main cause of their plight. They accused him of undermining the cooperative effort of the Arabs in the war against Israel in 1948. In July 1951, one of their members assassinated King Abdullah as he was attending the Mosque of Aqsa in Jerusalem.

Abdullah's son Talal succeeded him but had to abdicate, because of illness, in 1953 in favor of his eighteen-year-old son, Husayn. Resolute and courageous as Husayn proved to be, he had a difficult time balancing the Palestinian and bedouin elements in the country. The rise of Nasser was a beacon of hope for the Palestinians, who saw in him a sure way of defeating Israel and reoccupying their lost lands. Husayn was in a difficult position. He could not join the U.A.R. or make peace with Israel without losing his throne. If he were attacked by the U.A.R., then Israel might occupy the West Bank of the Jordan River as a "preventive" measure.

The fact that Husayn received military and economic aid from the United States did not make him popular with the Palestinian nationalists, but helped him stay in power. After the Iraqi revolution of 1958, Husayn was in real danger; he appealed to Britain, and some 2,000 British troops were brought in to protect Jordan against its Arab neighbors.

The heads of Arab states who met in Cairo in 1964 made a decision that proved crucial to the future of Jordan. It approved the creation of a Palestinian political entity that came to be known as the Palestinian Liberation Organization (PLO). It was made up of several groups such as Fatah under Yasser Arafat, who later assumed the leadership of the PLO; the Popular Front for the Liberation of Palestine (PFLP); and the Democratic Popular Front for the Liberation of Palestine (DPFLP). The PLO also received funds to create the Palestinian Liberation Army (PLA). Inasmuch as the majority of Palestinians were living within the political boundaries of Jordan, most of the recruitment and training of the PLA took place in Jordan. Indeed, there were two armies in the country, one under the command of King Husayn, and the other under the leadership of Arafat. Added to this potentially explosive situation was the fact that Jordan became a staging area for frequent attacks on Israeli-occupied lands, which resulted in more destructive Israeli retaliations.

The Aftermath of the Six-Day War of 1967

The Six-Day War of 1967, also called the June War, delivered a devastating blow to Jordan. Egypt and Syria lost the Sinai and the Golan Heights respectively. In addition to losing the populous and fertile West Bank, Jordan also lost control of the city of Jerusalem. This meant the loss of the potash industry of Jericho; the commercial, industrial, and financial revenues of Nablus; the enormous tourism revenues of Jerusalem and Bethlehem; and the agricultural products of the highlands and the Jordan Valley. Furthermore, there was the reversal of the Palestinian influx of postsecondary students since the 1950s. In the latter case, before 1967 Palestinian students had accounted for as much as 70 percent of Jordan's trained personnel and professional workforce; they also comprised a large majority in its colleges and universities. Following 1967, the Palestinians of the West Bank began to expand their own secondary schools and two-year colleges into universities, such as Birzeit University (1972), Najah National University (1977), and Bethlehem University (1973). In the case of markets, products, and manpower, Jordan lost all such resources with the Israeli occupation of the Palestinian highlands. On the other hand, the Israelis inherited a larger Palestinian population than they had done in the aftermath of the 1948 war, thus increasing their military and political problems.

There were two additional burdens that Jordan had to bear because of the war. One was the care of some 200,000 refugees from the West Bank, of which Israel allowed only 15,000 to return. In the second place, inasmuch as Israel allowed the Palestinians to continue as administrators and teachers under Israeli military authority, Jordan continued to pay their salaries, which was a drain on Jordan's treasury.

The Palestinian population under Israeli control created new problems for Jordan. The approximately 1.5 million villagers, refugees in camps, and townspeople of the West Bank and Gaza Strip resisted Israeli rule in different ways—from a three-month teachers' strike in the Ramallah/al-Bireh district to open confrontations with the Israeli authorities and army. All of these had repercussions among the Palestinians of Jordan. From 1968 on, a good deal of King Husayn's time was spent in arranging grants, loans, and military procurements from any source available.

Black September

The emergence of the PLO as the representative of Palestinians within Israeli-occupied territories became a dynamic reality to the Palestinians everywhere. This was illustrated by the battle of Karameh in March 1968. When the Israelis launched an air and ground attack on the village of Karameh located on the East Bank of the Jordan River, the village was successfully defended by the PLA. The United Nations censored Israel for the attack, which had become a *cause célèbre* among the Palestinians. This was regarded both a psychological and a military victory for the PLA. The PLO's prestige among Palestinians and within the Arab world skyrocketed. A series of airplane heists, political murders—including the killing of Israeli athletes at the 1976 Munich Olympics—confirmed the Palestinian leaders' deeply held belief that only a disaster or an armed confrontation would rivet European and American attention on the plight of the Palestinians. However, in spite of all the attention the Palestinians received for their violent deeds, the United States and the Western European countries did not change their policies nor draw any closer to the Palestinian point of view. Indeed, neither did the remonstrances of King Husayn constrain the PLO from carrying on raids, nor did the censors of the United Nations stop Israel from destructive retaliations. Then came "Black September" in 1970.

King Husayn became increasingly nervous with the ascendency of the PLO and their militant confrontations. Finally in September 1970 he intervened to end the Palestinians' free-wheeling control of Amman and the PLO's dominance in Jordan. With superior armed forces and the close assistance of Britain and the United States and the silence of Syria and Egypt, King Husayn crushed the PLO leadership in Amman. Hundreds of Palestinians were killed in the process, and thousands retreated to Lebanon and Syria. The battle of Amman and King Husayn's determination to win back his leadership of the kingdom closed the door to any further PLO-Jordanian cooperation. A new attempt was made in 1983, following the Beirut and Tripoli evacuations, when Yasser Arafat began to consider a possible federation of a Palestinian-Jordanian state.

The October (Yom Kippur) War of 1973

Having rid himself of the dominance of the PLO, King Husayn felt free to try a peace plan of his own. His twelve-point peace plan with Israel envisaged the creation of a "Federated Arab Kingdom" with two autonomous sections. The West Bank would have Jerusalem as its capital and the East Bank would have Amman. Both Israel and the Arab states rejected the plan, and, for a time, Jordan was isolated.

Perhaps it was his sense of frustration, or his remorse over having participated in the 1967 war that persuaded King Husayn not to join Egypt and Syria in the October, or Yom Kippur, War of 1973. According to Ezer Weizman, an Israeli minister of defense, Jordan made a mistake in entering the 1967 war and staying out of the 1973 war! Be that as it may, the passive reactions of King Husayn to the October War on the one hand and the active role of Jordanian troops and officers in the Dhofar province of Oman on the other, left him open to criticism. His enemies felt that leaving Egypt and Syria to themselves to battle the Israeli forces, called into question Jordan's commitment to the "anti-Zionist and anti-imperialist" aims of the Arab states. Furthermore, they argued that King Husayn's active participation in crushing the Dhofari uprising against Sultan Qabus of Oman indicated that Jordan was indeed fit and ready to fight against Marxist-Leninist uprisings but not against Israeli occupations.

The fears of Jordan concerning its relations with the PLO over the period from 1968 to 1974 were only heightened with the Rabat Conference of October 1974 and the appearance of Yasser Arafat before the United Nations General Assembly in November 1974. The Rabat Conference of

Arab leaders confirmed clearly the title of "sole and legitimate" representative of the Palestinian peoples upon the PLO and not upon King Husayn. The rebuff from fellow Arab states over the Palestinian question was reconfirmed by the warm reception that Yasser Arafat received after his address to the UN General Assembly and the subsequent observer status granted to the PLO. Thus the Rabat Conference decision on the status of the PLO received nearly universal acceptance. It would be with a note of irony that King Husayn would receive Yasser Arafat in Amman ten years later to discuss the possibilities of a federated Palestinian-Jordanian joint rule over the West Bank and Jordan. In the meantime, King Husayn publicly accepted the status of the PLO. He also fell into line with other Arab states in condemning both Anwar Sadat's 1977 visit to Jerusalem and the 1979 Camp David Accords.

In spite of the setbacks that King Husayn experienced in the decade ending in 1974, he began to rule over a fairly stable country during the following decade. He dissolved the Jordanian parliament in 1974 and ruled personally, aided by an advisory council, until 1984, when elections were held for a new parliament. He is presently commander of a very loyal army and has been able to equip it with grants and purchases from the United States, European countries, and the Soviet Union. He claims legitimacy both as a descendent of the Prophet and as one whose family led the Arab Revolt of 1916 against the Turks with the goal of forming an Arab entity. He is hard working and his dictatorship has not been unduly harsh.

The Jordanian Economy

Although Jordan has no oil fields, it has benefitted from Arab oil wealth. For one thing, Jordan has received generous aid from Saudi Arabia, Kuwait, and other Persian Gulf states. These states realize that Jordan is the only monarchy left in the Fertile Crescent with policies ranging from moderate to conservative. They can depend upon Jordan more than they can upon Syria or Iraq. The 1978 Arab summit meeting in Baghdad recognized Jordan as holding the frontline of defense against Israel, and therefore as being worthy of aid. They decided to give Jordan $1.25 billion in annual aid. Notwithstanding the fact that Libya and Algeria did not continue paying their shares, the aid received has been a tremendous boost to Jordan's economy.

Jordan has used the aid wisely in two five-year plans. The first plan (1975–1981) was used to build an industrial base and to improve the infrastructure and telecommunications. Under the second plan (1981–1985), investment has been evenly divided between public and private sectors. Emphasis has been on industry and mining, but there have been difficulties. Jordan's largest single source of natural wealth is phosphate, which is found in 60 percent of the country. In 1974 the price of phosphate had jumped from fifteen to sixty dollars a ton, but by 1984 it had gone down and the trend was continuing. Jordan has revived the production of potash, after losing a good deal of its capacity to Israel in 1967. Israel, however, is planning to build a canal connecting the Mediterranean with the Dead Sea. If such a plan is carried out, it will raise the level of the Dead Sea and will be certain to cause difficulties for Jordan.

In an arid country like Jordan, water is always crucial. One source is the East Ghor Canal. There have also been plans to go ahead with the Magarin Dam on the Yarmuk River; both Syria and Israel, however, have serious reservations about the project, and it may not be implemented. The latest project is pumping water from the Euphrates.

Since the civil war in Lebanon, many foreign companies have moved their offices to Amman. The presence of these companies has brought in much-needed foreign exchange. Another source of income has been tourism. Even though most of the tourist trade was captured by Israel in 1967, it still accounts for 15 percent of Jordan's income. The building of Aqaba as a winter resort and ancient sites such as Petra bring in about $1 billion a year. The Iraq-Iran War has proved to be an economic bonanza for Jordan. When requested, only Jordan immediately sent several divisions of volunteers and arms supplies to assist Iraq in its war against Iran. Since 1982, Egypt has supplied some officers; and the Pakistanis and Sudanis have sent limited numbers of troops and pilots. Nonetheless, Jordan remains the most committed to the support of its Arab neighbor. Perhaps the Hashimite connection, despite the bloody 1958 revolution, remains strong between Iraq and Jordan. With Iraq's Persian Gulf ports virtually closed, the Jordanian port of Aqaba has become Iraq's only source of supply.

This brief account of Jordan's economy would not be complete without mentioning Jordan's education "industry," which prepares skilled workers for "export." In 1984 some 310,000 Jordanian skilled workers and professionals were employed in the Persian Gulf states and were sending home $1.3 billion every year. Of the population of Jordan 60 percent are twenty-four years of age or younger and 37 percent of them are in school. There are some 120,000 unskilled laborers in Jordan from other Arab states, mainly Egypt. The balance of trade in the export of highly paid skilled workers and the import of poorly paid unskilled laborers is in Jordan's favor.

The Fate of Jordan

No matter how favorble its economic situation or how high its standards of living, the fact remains that Jordan is basically a dependent state. For example, because of the glut of oil in the world market, the original $1.25 billion annual aid approved by the Arab states in 1978 decreased to $850 million in 1983. As a dependent individual, King Husayn is virtually trapped and cannot act as freely as he would want.

Jordan's economic dependence on the Persian Gulf states may have to come to an end at any moment. It is dependent militarily on the United States for its supply of arms; however, U.S. arms have not been forthcoming. Fifty-six U.S. senators have signed a resolution prohibiting arms sales to Jordan because it is considered a potential enemy of Israel. King Husayn makes periodic trips to Moscow, but he is reluctant to become dependent on the Soviet Union. Politically, Jordan is caught between Israel and Syria; the former is supplied by the United States and the latter by the Soviet Union. The PLO and the unsolved Palestinian problem remain a potential danger.

The Reagan Initiative of 1982, which envisaged the formation of a West Bank-Jordanian entity based on United Nations Resolution 242 of 1967, encouraged the moderate Arab states and enticed Yasser Arafat to go to Amman and consult with King Husayn. Since the Reagan plan ignored Syria altogether, the Palestinians under the influence of Syria rejected it and Arafat backed out. Israel, which had rejected the plan out of hand, ignored the whole affair.

In the Iraq-Iran War, Jordan has been in the forefront of Arab assistance to Iraq. As an ally of Iran, Syria may become a potential enemy of Jordan. On the other hand, Jordan is not sure of Israel's intentions. According to Jordanian estimates, between 1980 and 1982 there were 300 land and 250 air violations of Jordan's sovereignty by Israel.[1] Furthermore, King Husayn is alarmed at the recent Israeli slogan "Jordan Is Palestine." If the idea takes root and wins the acceptance of the United States and, especially, of desperate Palestinians, then it may sound the death knell for the Hashimite family.

Notwithstanding all this, King Husayn has played the center stage successfully for decades. No Arab leader, so far, has proven to be as resilient as King Husayn to the fallout of the Palestinian and Israeli problems on the one hand, and as stable in the face of continuous Fertile Crescent turmoil on the other. Whatever the direction of Jordan's future, it is clear that the Palestinians and Israelis will have a considerable influence on the course of that desert kingdom.

[1]*Christian Science Monitor* (May 25, 1983), p. 1.

Chapter Twenty-Eight
The Arabian Peninsula and the Persian Gulf Shaykhdoms

The Arabian Peninsula and the Persian Gulf region underwent massive economic and political changes following World War I. In part, the changes resembled those of the Fertile Crescent economies and societies, such as the continued colonial presence of the British in South Yaman, Oman, the Trucial Coast (later known as the United Arab Emirates, or U.A.E.), Bahrayn Islands, Qatar, and Kuwait. The homeland of the Hashimites, Hijaz, and the central Saudi region of Najd were also under British protection, more semi-colonial than colonial, similar to Egypt. As in the Fertile Crescent, so too in the Arabian Peninsula and the Persian Gulf, the modern period inaugurated the establishment of national military, paramilitary, and police forces, a national bureaucracy, and European- and American-supported industrialization. But there were also many differences between the Fertile Crescent's twentieth-century history and that of the peninsula and the Persian Gulf.

Representing the largest landmass in the Middle East, the economy and society of the Arabian Peninsula and the Persian Gulf were primarily dominated by the rural peoples such as pastoral nomads, seminomadic herders, coastal and highland agriculturalists or peasants, and urban merchants and shopkeepers. The population along the coastline consisted of Arabic-speaking fishing, pearling, and shipping communities. They also managed the ports and nearby date plantations. The oasis economics of the peninsula and the gulf, indeed, bore a closer resemblance to those of North Africa and the

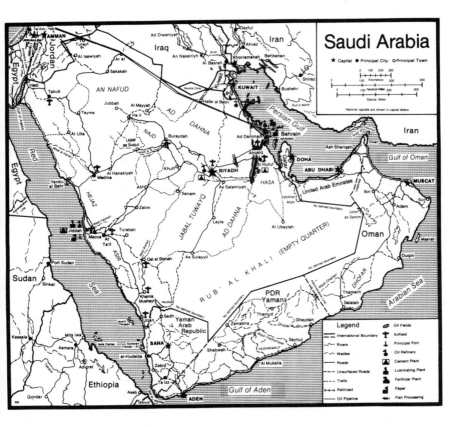

Sahara than to those of the Fertile Crescent. Known to many today for their oil industry, wealthy shaykhs, and desert areas, the peninsula and the gulf are equally remarkable for their enormous foreign labor force consisting of Koreans, Pakistanis, Indians, Filipinos, Baluchis, Iranians, and Palestinians. Both peninsula and gulf are also known for their strident worker movements, rural and urban poor, "instant" cities, the Trans-Arabian Pipeline (TAP), skyscrapers, and spectacular mountain ranges in Asir, Yaman, and Oman.

The peninsula and the gulf are equally important for their past and present rural and urban uprisings, coups, and revolutions; for their large U.S. military missions and trade commissions; and for their burgeoning educational systems. Finally, many today are familiar with the peninsula's holy places such as Mecca and Medina; some may be aware of the region's system of free schooling and health facilities. Few seem to know, however, that the illiteracy rate ranges between 60 and 80 percent and remains a major problem; that the peninsula's ethnic-religious, and linguistic minorities do not enjoy the benefits of the Saudi welfare state; that state censorship and Islamic fundamentalist laws abound; and that the mercenary military system of the peninsula and gulf continues to drain resources away from nascent social programs and the addressing of political inequalities.

The combination of transnational corporations (TNC), shaykhs, and oil continues to shape the direction and nature of the peninsula and gulf economies and societies. The present dominance of U.S. corporations, military and civilian advisors, and military forces such as the U.S. Rapid Deployment Force (RDF), are features of the colonial legacy left by Britain following World War II. It is no coincidence that the expenditure on arms is proportionate to the levels of oil production, insuring not only access to the region's oil-rich reserves by the advanced industrial states, but also the longevity of the fragile Saudi and Persian Gulf states as industrialization grows apace.

THE MAKING OF MODERN SAUDI ARABIA

In the confusion of World War I, claims and counterclaims in the Paris Peace Conference, and the revolts connected with the mandate regimes, perhaps the reader has forgotten about King Husayn, who had started the whole chain of events. Actually everyone else seemed to have forgotten and abandoned the venerable sharif of Mecca. He who had proclaimed himself "king of the Arab countries" in 1916 and had provoked the enmity of other hopeful claimants to such a title was reduced to being a king without a country. He kept up the pretense for some time without doing anything to secure his position. Events and developments passed him by while he insisted on being king. He did not clarify his relation with the British under the changed circumstances, and paid no attention to international meetings such as Versailles, San Remo, Lausanne, and the League of Nations. He had already aroused the hostility of Muslim groups in India by drawing his sword against the caliph of Islam. His anger, pride, and frustration led him, on March 7, 1924, to assume the title of "caliph of all Islam."

This announcement gave his rival, King ibn-Sa'ud of Najd, the pretext he had been waiting for. On August 24, 1924, ibn-Sa'ud led his Wahhabi fighters against Husayn, who was friendless and had no funds to raise an army. Husayn's sons, Faysal and Abdullah, probably were not in a position to help him, and he had served his usefulness to the British. The Wahhabis swept everything before them; and by January 1926, ibn-Sa'ud was master of the holy cities and of the major portion of the peninsula. Husayn fled to Cyprus, where he was received with great honor by the British and was invested in the Order of St. Michael.

It can probably be stated that ever since the rise of the Prophet Muhammad no such powerful and astute leader as Abd al-Aziz ibn-Sa'ud had arisen in the Arabian Peninsula. But the supremacy of the Wahhabis over the holy cities of Mecca and Medina created a very serious problem in the world of Islam. The Wahhabis were puritan fanatics and were opposed to the liberal practices of the rest of the Muslims, whom they called "polytheists." But revenue from the pilgrimages was the highest income of the Arabian government and ibn-Sa'ud did not propose to sacrifice this income. So on June 7, 1926, he called an Islamic conference in Mecca. His purpose was to allay the fears of the Muslims and to provide an opportunity for his Wahhabi ulama to meet others. The Muslim delegations were captivated by the personality and wisdom of the tall monarch. Pilgrimages, which had been sporadic during the war, resumed on a regular basis.

Next, ibn-Sa'ud clarified his relationship with Britain, which directly and indirectly controlled the territorities along the southern coast and parts of the eastern coast of Arabia in addition to Palestine, Transjordan, and Iraq to the north. A basic difficulty concerned Transjordan, partly because it was an expedient creation of the British to find a place for Abdullah, and partly because ibn-Sa'ud had a feud of long standing with the Hashimite family to which Abdullah and Faysal belonged. These and other questions were resolved by two treaties: One was the agreement of Hadda (November 2, 1925), which settled the border with Transjordan. The other was the treaty of Jiddah, (May 20, 1927), in which Britain recognized the independence of Saudi Arabia, and ibn-Sa'ud acknowledged the special interest of Britain in the Persian Gulf shaykhdoms. In reality, Saudi Arabia became the first relatively independent Arab state, as there were no special clauses for political privileges or any military bases. British trade had always been paramount on both the Red Sea and the Persian Gulf and continued to be for some time to come.

The main task for ibn-Sa'ud, like that of the Prophet Muhammad, was to break up the tribes and settle the rivalries and wars among them. He organized the Wahhabis in small *Ikhwan* ("brotherhoods") and settled them on oases across the land. He provided each settlement with agriculture, mosques, and schools. These settlements were very much like the military towns of the second caliph Umar. They were socioeconomic as well as military units, and all were loyal to the king. It took him years of fighting, firm administration, and justice to accomplish his task.

In the midst of the Saudi-Hashimite struggle over the leadershp in the peninsula, Major Frank Holmes, a New Zealand entrepreneur, began a series of geological explorations in eastern Arabia for oil. Between 1923 and 1925 Holmes failed to find oil in commercially exportable quantities to his satisfaction and that of King Abd al-Aziz. By 1932, the declining state revenues and the need for ready cash, as well as the news of an oil discovery in Bahrayn, prompted the king to renew his interest in oil. In May 1933, Standard Oil of California (Socal), still exuberant from its 1932 Bahrayn oil find, readily agreed to explore for oil within King ibn-Sa'ud's new realm. The Socal concession covered a sixty-year period, costing the oil company 35,000 gold sovereigns plus £5,000 per year until oil was discovered and a £100,000 loan against any future royalties from the exports of the newly found oil. Due, in great part, to its own lack of marketing facilities and the need to invest capital in its new venture, Socal gave half of its interest in the concession to Texaco. In 1936, Caltex (California-Texaco Oil Company) was formed. The venture paid off with the discovery of oil in 1938 at Well No. 7 in Dhahran. By 1941, on the eve of the U.S. entry into World War II, American oil companies held concessions for 42 percent of all the known oil reserves in the Middle East. Oil and shaykhs were to become integral parts of U.S. foreign policy, and Saudi Arabia was clearly becoming the lynchpin in the U.S. alliance system in the Middle East. At the same time, oil was to shape the politics and the economy of Saudi Arabia and the peninsula in ways not yet clearly understood. The establishment of the kingdom in 1932 and the discovery of oil at Dhahran in 1938 were the beginnings of modern Saudi Arabia.

From Desert Kingdom to Modern State

In the midst of World War II, Saudi Arabia's economy and politics underwent several important changes. Traditionally a rural society dependent on herding and agriculture, Saudi Arabia began to use its new-found industrial energy source of oil as a leverage to shift its labor force, capital, and economic planning towards commerce, finance, and industry. Lacking funds to continue supporting the personal luxury of the Saudi family and to reorient the economy towards greater imports, exports, construction, banking, and industrialization, ibn-Sa'ud asked for changes in the 1933 oil agreement. Caltex was faced with new demands for its oil in the midst of a world war but was not prepared to export and market Saudi oil in order to meet ibn-Sa'ud's $6 million demand.

By 1943, however, a United States treasury committee was established to assist in the distribution of lend-lease funds following President Roosevelt's determination that Saudi Arabia was "vital to the defense" of the United States. In the following year, the United States decided to establish a military base at Dhahran to protect its "vital" interests, and Caltex renamed itself the Arab-American Oil Company, or Aramco.

Following World War II, King ibn-Sa'ud pressed for greater royalties and more capital from the oil concession while Aramco opened discussions with two more U.S. oil companies for incorporation into the oil "jackpot." By 1948, Mobil and Exxon formally entered into Aramco following three years of discussions. Thirty percent of the royalties were to go on to Socal, 30 percent to Texaco, 30 percent to Exxon, and 10 percent to Mobil. In addition, Gulf Oil held a 50 percent interest in the new Kuwaiti oil concession, while Socal continued to operate the Bahrayn oil field. By 1950, under demands for increased shares in the Aramco revenues, Saudi Arabia demanded 50-50 sharing, in contrast to the previous 16-84 sharing system. In the midst of the heated controversy in Iran between AIOC and Dr. Mosaddeq, Aramco finally agreed to the 50-50 sharing system (see Chapter 34). With the cooperation of the U.S. Treasury, it was arranged that these royalties would be called "income taxes" (the Saudi government did not levy an income tax), thereby saving Aramco from paying any taxes to the U.S. government. The result of the 50-50 sharing agreement with Aramco was windfall profits for the oil company at the expense of the American people, whose government handed over $50 million annually in lost taxes while Saudi Arabia's annual revenues from oil exports jumped from $39.2 million in 1949 to 111.7 million in 1950. Such high-level bargaining within Aramco and between Aramco and Saudi Arabia allowed the kingdom to begin acting like a state. Capital was now available for infrastructure projects, industrialization, and construction work.

King Abd al-Aziz ibn-Sa'ud died in 1953. His heir, King Saud (reigned 1953–1964) was faced with a number of formidable problems. To begin with, the kingdom was finally economically solvent but had no structure for managing the new revenues. Ibn-Sa'ud had assembled no council of ministers, made no provisions for schools or universities, and taken little interest in training a skilled labor force. Ibn-Sa'ud's venture into foreign affairs had begun with formulating a policy toward the Persian Gulf and the other peninsula states. His first venture outside the peninsula had been made at the request of the British over the 1936 Palestinian uprising and national strike. In addition, little had been done to develop a national armed force.

Between 1953 and 1973 King Saud and his successor, King Faysal (reigned 1964–1975), altered the Saudi kingdom in several profound ways, beginning with a reorganization of the government, the establishment of the Central Planning Organization, and the creation of the National Guard and air and land forces. To begin with, the number of government officials in 1953 included 2,300 persons. By 1964, the number had increased to 100,000, due primarily to the tripling of oil revenues following the Aramco-Saudi profit-sharing agreement. The number of government officials had reached 250,000 in 1974. The few ministries established under King ibn-Sa'ud in the World War II period had expanded and in 1964 became consolidated in the Council of Ministers. In addition, Abdullah Tariki, the energetic director of petroleum affairs, had been instrumental in the creation of the Ministry of Petroleum and Mineral Resources. Due to his efforts, the Arab Oil Congress, begun in 1959, was soon transformed into the Organization of Petroleum Exporting Countries (OPEC). The latter organization was largely created by both Tariki and Perez Alfonso, his Venezuelan counterpart.

Known as a reformer, the strongly nationalistic Tariki had exemplified the new postwar government official. Trained as an oil technician at the University of Texas, Tariki had headed the Saudi oil affairs office before 1954, when he became minister of petroleum and mineral resources under King Saud. It was he who constantly argued for a Saudi-trained professional cadre in government affairs to educate the emerging postwar middle and working classes about the realities of the petroleum industry. Shortly after the establishment of OPEC, Tariki began to run into problems with the oil technocrats and the new directions of OPEC. Both ran counter to his own nationalistic (that is, pro-Saudi) Arabian positions. By 1962, Tariki had been replaced by the more management-oriented and less nationalistic Shaykh Zaki al-Yamani.

The example of Abdullah Tariki was not an isolated one. Prince Talal, a member of the Saudi family, also disagreed with the new directions of the post-ibn-Sa'ud state. He too rose to a high political position in the years following the death of ibn-Sa'ud and the succession of King Saud. Like Tariki, he was appointed to the Ministry of Finance and National Economy, while Tariki assumed the position of minister of petroleum and mineral resources. Prince Talal, as a member of the royal family, was privy to the difficulties the family was having with King Saud. In addition to being a notorious spendthrift, Saud had renewed U.S. base agreements, such as the one at Dhahran, supported the Eisenhower Doctrine, and concluded the informal Alliance of Kings (Saud of Arabia, Husayn of Jordan, Faysal II of Iraq) in 1957. A year later in 1958, the spectre of the U.A.R. and a revolutionary Iraq under Qasem loomed large on the Arabian horizon. In the midst of the February and July events in the Fertile Crescent, the royal family, already worried by possible economic destabilization, replaced Saud with Crown Prince Faysal in all legislative and executive affairs. Faysal's appointment, though seen as temporary, provided an opportunity for reformers such as Abdullah Tariki and Prince Talal to move more vigorously towards independent economic and political policies.

By 1960, Prince Talal and a small number of royal family supporters demanded further reforms in the structure of the modern kingdom. They recommended the establishment of a legislative body and certain constitutional reforms. Prince Talal's purpose was to give the kingdom broader controls over the near-absolute powers of the king. He wanted to involve the increased numbers of government officials and newly educated Saudis in the processes of government. Upon Crown Prince Faysal's failure to grant legislative and constitutional reforms, Talal continued to call for renewed reforms. Prince Talal was removed from the Council of Ministers in 1961. A year later he relinquished his royal title and went into exile to Cairo with three of his brothers. There they renounced their Saudi citizenship, formed the Arab National Liberation Front (ANLF) and became involved in anti-Saudi activities. Due in great part to the enormous power of Aramco, which feared that the Saudis might follow Dr. Mosaddeq of Iran and nationalize Arabian oil, and partly due to the lack of any alternative political organization within Saudi Arabia, Prince Talal and Abdullah Tariki failed in their efforts to push the Saud-Faysal coalition toward nationalist programs and reforms.

Crown Prince Faysal, as deputy prime minister and head of the Council of Ministers, appointed Shaykh al-Yamani as minister of petroleum and national resources. Following the revolution and civil war between the North and South Yaman in September 1962 Faysal moved to replace Saud's sons with his own sons in key positions of the armed forces and the defense and interior ministries. By 1964, the ambiguity of King Saud as titular head of the kingdom was resolved in favor of Faysal, as the royal family moved more clearly to preserve its absolutist control over all key government positions. By the end of 1964, King Faysal assumed full sovereign powers and consolidated the family's control as primary heads of the Saudi kingdom. At the same time the royal family accepted the prodigal Prince Talal, who returned and was content to work within the goverment. Shaykh al-Yamani did not seek the nationalization of Saudi oil production but instead "participation" and close cooperation with Aramco. In doing so, al-Yamani hoped to avoid the example of Iraq in its 1961 nationalization of the Iraq Petroleum Company and at the same time to moderate the OPEC hardliners on price increases on oil exports.

The Saudis and the Ruling Families

The period from 1953 to 1975 under Kings Saud and Faysal saw several important changes in the Saudi kingdom. The dominant ruling classes within Saudi Arabia—in addition to the Saudi royal family—were of three types.

1. The rural families of past renown and landholding powers such as the Jiluwi family of Hasa; the Thunayyi clan, which had married into ibn-Sa'ud's family; and the Sudeiri clan, which dominated the Ministries of Defense and Aviation.
2. The Hijazi merchant families, whose dominant position, particularly in the important trade and construction industries of Jiddah, had been established in the 1930s. These included the Ali Rizas of Jiddah and the four Sudayan brothers in Riyadh and Jiddah.
3. The Najdi religious families, particularly the al-Shaykh family, of the house of Muhammad ibn-Wahhab, and holders of key judicial and educational offices in Saudi Arabia.

Kings Saud and Faysal both utilized their control of the Saudi oil fortunes and their intimate contact with foreign corporations, particularly those of the United States, to fend off internal opposition and potential rivalries within the ruling classes mentioned above. The Sudeiri clan maintained near-dominance over the Ministry of Defense and Aviation. On the other hand, the Saudi family, through Prince Abdullah, maintained complete control of the rival military corps, the National Guard, which had been created from the crack British-trained White Army. In 1965, the armed forces comprised 35,000 army and 3,500 air force personnel, while the National Guard was 10,000 strong with jurisdiction over internal security through cooperation with the police and paramilitary units in the provinces. The Saudi family's marriage alliances with some of these clans enabled the sons of ibn-Sa'ud to share the power of the security forces as well as to control the major clans and their possible ambitions to rule the Saudi state.

The big merchant families of the Hijaz, particularly of the Ali Rizas of Jiddah, had already been prominent in Saudi economic affairs. Two brothers from the Ali Riza family had founded an import-export company as early as 1862; the company imported rugs, pearls, spices and other trade items from Iran, India, and Ethiopia by land and sea to the domestic Saudi market. They also had interests in steamship companies that transported pilgrims to Mecca and Medina. By the eve of World War II, they had exclusive dealerships for Ford, Westinghouse, ITT, and Omega and Tissot watches. From 1960 to 1980, members of the same family had partnerships or shares in a variety of companies, such as large public works, heavy equipment imports, real estate, services, modern transportation and petroleum exploration. The four Sudayan brothers used their inside information while working for the government to acquire knowledge of Saudi development plans, capitalizing on valuable land sales, construction contracts, and imports of necessary products such as prefabricated cement, aluminium, and elevators.

The Saudi family nurtured the friendship of these merchant families through liberal import-export licensing procedures, tax incentives, high-cost development projects, communication systems, and sophisticated arms purchases. From 1953 to 1975 the Saudi state gradually expanded its planning institutions. It began by forming the Saudi Arabian Monetary Agency (SAMA) and the Ministry of Economy and Finance. By 1965, the Central Planning Organization was launched, which, with the aid of technicians from the U.S., evolved into a planning team to work with U.S.-trained Saudis. The combination of favorable commercial and financial investments to foreign transnational corporations through joint-venture projects kept the big Hijazi merchants both prosperous and cooperative.

The third segment of the Saudi ruling class is composed of religious families, such as the al-Shaykh. They were dominant in the educational and judicial fields during the ibn-Sa'ud period. The al-Shaykh family was partially baffled by the numerous projects for reforms in education and the legal system. King Saud University in Riyadh was opened in 1957, while former palaces in Jiddah, Medina, and Riyadh were converted into schools. Private and public schools for girls and boys became a common feature of the 1960s and 1970s. In order to quell any misgivings of the religious establishment, the Saudi state opened the Islamic Shari'a College in Medina. The introduction of television had to be countered by more stringent Islamic measures against alcohol, Western music, and unveiled women. Rather than remove members of leading religious families from high offices in the legal and educational systems, the Saudi state mollified major dissidents by creating alternative ministries and by asserting Saudi leadership in Islamic observance. The Israeli annexation of old Jerusalem following the Six-Day War of 1967 prompted King Faysal to interject Saudi Arabia into a more active role in the Islamic world. Faysal organized the first Islamic Conference in Rabat in 1969. This was a summit meeting of all Muslim peoples to consider, among other matters, the burning of the al-Aqsa Mosque in old Jerusalem. The second summit was held in Jiddah in 1970, where an Islamic secretariat was created to promote cultural, economic, and political cooperation among its members and to regain control over old Jerusalem. By 1970, King Faysal had taken control of the courts, educational system, and the Ministry of Pilgrimage and Religious Endowments from the al-Shaykh family and given it to the Hijazi merchant families.

The Saudi concern for its Islamic role in contemporary Middle Eastern and peninsular affairs was clearly demonstrated in 1979. As the custodian of the holy cities of Mecca and Medina, Saudi Arabia is committed to protecting the many thousands of Muslim pilgrims who attend the ceremonies each year. A considerable part of Saudi political legitimacy rests on its ability to insure safe passage and the security of all Muslims seeking the spiritual and material benefits of the Hajj. On November 20, 1979, the first day of Islam's fifteenth century, 50,000 pilgrims in the Great Mosque of Mecca were preparing to begin their morning prayers. Suddenly Juhayman ibn-Sayf al-Otayba, a former member of the Saudi National Guard, and Muhammad ibn-Abdullah al-Qurayshi, a theological student at the Islamic University in Mecca, emerged to proclaim the latter as the Mahdi and the need to cleanse a corrupt Arabia. Thunderstruck, the pilgrims remained within the mosque while the ailing King Khalid (reigned 1975–1982) ordered his brothers, the ministers of defense and interior, to take charge of the military operation against the alleged Mahdi and the invaders. Fighting continued from November 20 to December 3, between the besieged rebels and the Saudi troops assisted by French and American antiterrorist squads. More than 100 were killed on both sides, many more were wounded, and 170 of the original 500 to 600 well-armed and well-trained rebels were taken prisoner.

The Great Mosque takeover spurred the replacement of the air and land force commanders, the governor of Mecca (a brother of King Khalid), and changes within the Saudi armed forces. Sixty-three of the insurgents were publicly executed on January 6, 1980, leaving a number of questions unresolved for the Saudi ruling families. Rapid industrialization, militarization, and burgeoning oil revenues had in great part solved many of Saudi Arabia's social, economic, and political problems. On the other hand, such profound changes had weakened the ruling family and the state through the growing influence of the bourgeoisie, technocrats, and foreign advisors. The masses of displaced bedouins, small peasants, and the increasingly disadvantaged low-level Saudi managers and professionals made the ulama and the fundamentalists the most natural leaders of the opposition. Indeed, beginning in 1953, and over the course of the next thirty years, various opposition groups had emerged, groups opposed to the rule of the Saudi family and to the widespread corruption and mismanagement accompanying the Saudi elite's open-door policy toward TNCs, arms dealers, foreign advisors, and Aramco.

The Saudi Opposition

Even under the leadership of King ibn-Sa'ud, the Saudi family faced opposition first to the creation of the kingdom and then to establishing the modern state. Initially, the opposition was rural-based, comprised primarily of pastoral clans of the Najd, the Hijaz, and the province of Asir. Following the Aramco-Saudi profit-sharing program in the oil industry, the Saudi family faced the first major opposition from oilfield workers. The shift from rural to urban skilled and semiskilled wage labor was a harbinger of newer and more complicated forms of opposition to the Saudi ruling families. The response of the Saudi families, in turn, was also more up to date and sophisticated.

The first Aramco oilfield strike of 1953 lasted for three weeks and involved 13,000 of the 15,000 workers. Their demands were primarily related to wages, living and working conditions, and the right to unionize. Other strikes followed in which workers reiterated previous demands for higher wages in the face of tripled oil revenues and doubled food prices. In addition, the oilfield workers demanded an end to the special privileges given to Aramco's American staff. Aramco remained a primary target of the increased labor militancy.

The major difficulties that the modern Saudi state was facing and that accounted for some of the grievances of oilfield laborers were:

1. The oil revenue boom for Aramco and the state without any major changes in the workers' wages or benefits.
2. The top-heavy, American-dominated oil industry.
3. Mismanagement of the oil revenues, corruption, wastage, and the excessive luxury purchases of the royal family such as the building of a $60 million palace.
4. The Iranian oil nationalization and the Egyptian revolution under Nasser, followed by the Suez Canal nationalization.

Saudi workers were aspiring to a better life and blaming their social and economic ills on the ruling families and the U.S. corporate presences in Saudi Arabia.

The Saudi response to the strikes was swift and brutal. Arrests and detentions followed each major confrontation between oil workers and the Saudi state. In addition, a royal decree of June 11, 1956 imposed a minimum one-year prison sentence on all those striking or inciting strikes. Other royal decrees followed forbidding adherence to any ideology other than Islam, or the formation of political parties. The government controlled the radio and television media while forbidding movies. It created the Ministry of Information to monitor the press, restricted the right to publish newspapers or periodicals, controlled editorial policies through forced resignations, and closed down offensive publications. Such measures rarely prevented the emergence of an opposition; rather they usually changed the direction and nature of the opposition. By 1966, the Saudi state was facing even greater internal problems.

In 1966, Arabian Peninsula People's Union (APPU) began to carry out a series of sabotage actions. APPU believed in the unity of the peninsula, including the Persian Gulf. At the same time, the union argued that it was part of the "unity of the Arab homeland." Again, Saudi internal security forces held fast. In June 1969, opposition was uncovered in the air force as well as within Petromin, the state-owned agency for the industrial development of petroleum and minerals. The opposition of 200 air force officers and the air force academy director in Dhahran signalled a new and greater danger to the Saudi ruling families.

The Saudi Communist Party was formed after the Aramco strike of 1953. It was active as part of the National Reform Front, which was comprised of civil servants, workers, and professionals. By 1963, it had joined the Arab National Liberation Front that was associated with Prince Talal and his brothers. The ANLF demanded a transformation of the country into a constitutional state, leaving the choice of a monarchy or a republic to a public referendum. Due in part to the coalition nature of the ANLF and in part to the lack of a broad base of support within Saudi society, the ANLF remained ineffective. Consequently, the Communist Party of Saudi Arabia (CPSA) was established in 1975 as an independent underground movement. It adopted a pro-Soviet position, believed in a "patriotic, democratic, and republican regime" that guaranteed civil liberties, parliamentary procedures, and freedom for political parties and unions; in addition, it advocated citizen equality, diplomatic relations with the USSR, and industrialization. By 1984, the CPSA, in spite of its efforts, had little mass support.

In addition to the APPU, the ANLF, and CPSA, there were a number of smaller groups associated in one way or another with the Ba'th Party of the Fertile Crescent, and the Arab Nationalist Movement, or the Nasserites, of Egypt. There were also other groups with varied ideologies. Due to their narrow ideological focus, their close association with non-Saudi political parties, and the strength of the Saudi family's association with the business community, the TNCs, and the American military, the opposition remained fragmented and without widespread support within Saudi Arabia. Nonetheless, the Saudi state, frightened by the activities of a number of these groups, carried out political arrests and internal administrative purges.

The Iranian Revolution of February 1979, the seizure of the Great Mosque in November of the same year, and the confrontation between 2,000 Saudi troops and the population of the Eastern Province in December, revived the Saudi family's fears of internal revolt. The demands of the al-Otayba rebels at the Great Mosque did not concern Islamic religious observances. Instead, they wanted:

1. The trial and expulsion of imperialistic agents particularly those of the United States.
2. Rejection of the domination of thought in favor of the right of self-expression.
3. An end to corruption and bribery and the wasting of the nation's wealth.
4. The trial and dismissal of "hypocrites" who speak in the name of Islam.

In stating their demands, the al-Otayba group of 500 to 600 well-armed and well-trained rebels asked in essence for a reconstitution of the Saudi state and an end of loyalty to the Saudi family.

Today, the Saudi royal family and the modern Saudi state remain as fragile and as vulnerable as they were in 1953. The increased purchases of small arms and crowd-control weaponry, and the growing number of "civil defense" advisors and police and paramilitary units suggest that the Saudi state is escalating its preparedness for future Great Mosque takeovers. However, the North Yamani revolution of 1962, the South Yamani National Liberation Front guerrilla movement in 1963, and the establishment of the Dhofari Popular Front for the Liberation of Oman guerrilla organization in 1965 in Oman—all contributed to a new set of jitters for King Faysal and his successors. Each event in the Yamans and in Oman had to be dealt with in time.

THE MAKING OF MODERN NORTH AND SOUTH YAMAN

Following World War I, North and South Yaman resembled each other more than ever before. Socially and economically, both were comprised of coastal agriculturalists, sea port merchants, shopkeepers, religious scholars, and hinterland pastoralists and cultivators. The majority of the people, who were bound to each other by kinship ties and local interests, were either peasants or pastoralists. The position of the Yamani ports made them strategic to the international trade on the Red Sea and Indian Ocean and to the overland trade of the peninsula; the merchant families of Hodeida and Mocha in North Yaman and Aden in South Yaman had a distinct advantage, therefore, in coastal politics. On the other hand, the Yamani mountain ranges skirting the coastal plains were the special reserve of the pastoral shaykhs and local sultans, many of whom exercised considerable control over the coastal communities lying outside the large and small towns dotting the fertile plains. The service-based commercial economies of the coastal and hinterland towns of the Yamans contrasted sharply with the agricultural and pastoral subsistence economies of the rural regions. This "divided economy" and the two dominant social groups of urban merchants and rural shaykhs determined, more often than not, the politics and dominant ideologies of the two Yamans.

In the midst of the rival factions of big merchants and semiautonomous pastoral shaykhs, there had emerged a third force—that is, the major religious families of Sayyids, whose support both the merchant and pastoral families sought. In North Yaman, the hereditary theocracy of the Zaydi-Shi'i Imam, located in the city of San'a, was the primary political, legal, and spiritual system of the hinterland clans and pastoralists. In South Yaman, the political epicenter was fragmented between twelve sultanates, eight shaykhdoms, two emirates, and one large confederation of pastoralists in the lowlands and mountain ranges. Interestingly enough, the more centralized North Yaman was deeply involved in a crippling civil war by 1962; while the more fragmented South Yaman emerged under the unified command of the National Liberation Front (NLF) by 1967. Both regions, however, were plagued throughout the period after World War I with internal rivalries and coups, stagnant economies, widely diverse social groups, high rates of illiteracy, low life expectancy, and a high susceptibility to outside intervention. Following World War II, the TNCS, oil workers' militancy, and trade union movements changed all that.

North Yaman before the 1962 Revolution

Following World War I, the 74,000 square miles of North Yaman gradually passed under the absolutist rule of Imam Yahya ibn-Muhammad Hamid al-Din (1904–1948) and the Hamid al-Din family. High in the North Yaman highlands were the Bakil and Hashid confederations of pastoral nomads specializing in herding, clan warfare, and steadfast loyalty to the Imam. Both the highland towns of San'a and Ta'iz were within the Imam's political realm. In contrast, Tihama peoples of the lowlands or coastal plains were predominantly cultivators or urban merchants in the major towns of Hodeida and Mocha. Until his death in 1922, Muhammad al-Idrisi of Asir Province maintained political control over the Tihama lowlands and Asir as well as control over Hodeida. By 1925, however, Imam Yahya was successful in defeating Ali al-Idrisi, son of Muhammad, for control of the port of Hodeida. The Tihama lowlands remained semiautonomous for another decade.

From the cessation of Ottoman rule over the Tihama lowlands and the Red Sea provinces of Hijaz and Asir, until 1948, Imam Yahya expanded his mountain realm into the lowlands at an unrelenting pace. He ended an intermittent war with ibn-Sa'ud over Asir and Hodeida in the Treaty of Taif. Asir went to ibn-Sa'ud and Hodeida passed once more under the control of the Hamid al-Din family. In that same year, Imam Yahya concluded a treaty with the British in the crown colony of Aden. The 1934 Treaty of San'a redrew the former Turkish-British border between North and South Yaman. As a result of the two agreements, the Hamid al-Din family became supreme in North Yaman, with Imam Yahya in San'a and his sons governors of the major cities.

The rule of the Hamid al-Din family was not without opposition. One group by the name of Society of Struggle started in 1934; it was against the Imam's monopoly of North Yaman's coastal commerce and hinterland subsistence farming. Another one, the Free Yamini Movement, arose during World War II. The two dominant aspirations of most North and South Yamanis were clearly being consolidated. The first was the unification of the two Yamans into one national state and the second was the end of British Colonial rule in the region. Two events in 1948 demonstrated that changes were in the making.

First in January 1948, the Society of Struggle and the Free Yamani Movement joined to form the National Holy Charter. In doing so, groups of reform-minded merchants, princely families, and migrant workers acknowledged the need to unite the Yamans in collective action against the Imam's absolutism and the vested interests of the old social groups of merchants and shaykhs. Second, in the following month, a coup took place in San'a against the Imam and the heir-apparent, Prince Ahmad. The leader of the coup was Abdullah al-Wazir, a member of a rival family. The Imam was assassinated and Prince Ahmad fled northward. Within months he returned, with the backing of ibn-Sa'ud, and beheaded scores of the rebels. This coup was followed by another in 1955 to remove the vestiges of Imam Yahya's rule; it was led by Prince Abdullah, a member of the Imam's family, and it also failed.

Prince Ahmad (1948–1962), obviously shaken by a coup led by a member of his own family, moved in two directions that departed from his father's policies. In the first place, he approved a number of lucrative trade agreements, such as the thirty-year concession to the American-Yaman Development Corporation to explore and export Yaman's mineral resources on a 50-50 profit-sharing basis. In the second place, he sought to establish a wide range of regional alliances.

This was not the first time that the United States had figured prominently in Yamani commercial agreements. Charles S. Crane, one of the authors of the King-Crane Commission on Palestine, visited North Yaman in the 1930s to advise Imam Yahya on the possibilities of development. Karl S. Twitchell, an American mining engineer, visited North Yaman on his way to Saudi Arabia in 1930. After the Saudi oil concession to Socal, Twitchell returned to North Yaman to assist in the building of bridges connecting San'a with its ports on the coast. Furthermore, in 1946, Colonel William Eddy negotiated the U.S.-Yaman Treaty of Friendship and Commerce. In the following year, North Yaman was admitted to the United Nations.

The activities of Prince Ahmad went beyond improving U.S.-Yamani relations. He sent a delegation to the 1955 Bandung Conference of non-aligned nations. A year later he signed the five-year Jiddah Military Pact with Nasser of Egypt and King Saud of Arabia. This treaty opposed the British protectorate in Aden and the Baghdad Pact in the Fertile Crescent, and called for regional cooperation among all Arab states. Trade missions were received from China, the Soviet Union, and East Germany, while a treaty of friendship was signed with Czechoslovakia. At the peak of North Yaman's new regional orientation in 1958, Crown Prince Muhammad al-Badr was sent to Cairo to sign a pact with Nasser creating the United Arab

States—that is, a federation of Yaman and the newly created United Arab Republic.

While Imam Ahmad was seeking medical aid in Italy in 1959, the crown prince, supported by remnants of reform-minded merchants, seized the capital, abrogated the imam's absolute authority, and instituted an advisory legislature. Imam Ahmad rushed home, arrested al-Badr, and, with the assistance of loyal shaykhs and highland clans, restored his rule. North Yaman's Imamate survived the third attack on its absolutism.

With the death of Imam Ahmad in 1962, a combination of events inside and outside of North Yaman finally succeeded in doing what previous challengers could not. Muhammad al-Badr succeeded his father as the new Imam with Colonel Abdullah al-Sallal, army chief of staff at his side. A week after the succession, on September 26, 1962, Sallal, with the assistance of a Revolutionary Command Council of seven others, bombarded the Imam's palace, announced the death of al-Badr, and declared the establishment of the Republic of Yaman. A broad-based coalition of princes, merchants, and professional leaders had toppled an absolutist regime. The event not only altered the history of North and South Yaman, but also sent a shock wave throughout the peninsula. The Revolution of 1962 was indeed a watershed event in the history of the region.

South Yaman before the 1962 Revolution

South Yaman, following World War I, remained as politically fragmented and economically stagnant as North Yaman. The sole port of Aden, occupied in 1839 by the British, had become an important British coaling station, communication center, and major trading entrepôt. Established as a crown colony by the British, Aden was not only a major economic center for British trade and shipping, but also a major political center for the expansion of British interests throughout the southern coastal plains of south Arabia. By the end of World War I, the twelve sultanates, eight shaykhdoms, two emirates, and one confederation of pastoralists that comprised South Yaman, had been divided into the protectorates of Eastern Aden and Western Aden, with Aden as the major port of trade and crown colony.

British colonial rule exacerbated the already existing "divided economy" of South Yaman. This was an economy of commercial services in the coastal towns of Aden and Mukalla, and of subsistence agriculture and herding in the lowlands, mountain ranges, and desert plateau. Following World War I, the British rulers in Aden invested its meager colonial revenues into the development of the port of Aden and the expansion of several key roadways connecting the port of Aden and the coastal hinterland towns with the fertile cash-crop regions in the mountains. In 1934, the British crown colony ended an interminable war over boundaries with North Yaman through the Treaty of San'a. A decade later, the port of Aden, so essential to the British war efforts, became the third-ranking port in the British Empire after London and Liverpool, as the Suez Canal and the Indian Ocean ports became more important to troop movements between Europe and Asia. The big merchants of Aden and the smaller towns did a thriving wartime business in British manufactured goods and food-stuffs as imports rose dramatically in Britain's wartime economy. On the other hand, small shopkeepers, low-level colonial administrators, a growing number of impoverished cultivators and herders, and South Yamani migrant laborers did not do so well.

By the end of World War II, South Yamani communities were to be found in places far away from their homeland. The crown colony in Aden funnelled South Yamani laborers into British factories, and these laborers established communities in many industrial cities of England. South Yamani workers had been recruited into Britain's shipping industry as stokers or donkeymen. Furthermore, Yamani workers had migrated to the United States to work in Detroit's automobile industry or in California's fertile valleys. Finally, South Yamani skilled and semiskilled migrant laborers moved northward into North Yaman to work in Imam Ahmad's nascent industrialization program of road construction, port expansion, and mining industries.

Due to the Iranian nationalization of oil and the resulting crisis for British revenues and crude oil processing, Britain searched its flagging empire for yet another appropriate location for the former AIOC operations. Aden, so central to British imperial interests in the Middle East and so well fitted as an export center for refined crude, was soon selected for the task of refining Britain's Asian oil. There, the newly named British Petroleum Company built a $150 million refinery in 1954. As in Saudi Arabia, the creation of the BP refinery in the Aden crown colony necessitated the recruitment of skilled labor and managers, in addition to the necessary capital. Not long afterwards, a series of labor disputes between Indian and Adeni workers and the British managers and executives signalled a new level of political consciousness and activism among the industrial labor forces. The establishment of the Aden Trade Union movement (ATUC) by the mid-1950s, the success of Nasser's nationalization of the Suez Canal in 1956, and the overseas organizing efforts of the Arab National Movement (ANM)—all contributed to new political movements within the crown colony of Aden and the coastal hinterland communities of South Yaman.

To accommodate the rapid politicization of the peninsula and its southern regions, London moved to reorganize the protectorates of Western and Eastern Aden into the Federation of South Arabia, complete with a new capital, al-Ittihad, near Aden.

By 1962, the swift movement of events in North Yaman, combined with the growing activism of South Yamani groups such as the ATUC and ANM brought an end to the British protectorate system and colonial rule. British efforts to rescue its colony and its refinery continued until 1967. So damaging were the activities of the National Liberation Front in South Yaman that the British withdrew its troops in November 1967, several months earlier than planned.

The Revolution of 1962 in North Yaman had finally achieved one of the major goals of the Yamani national aspirations—namely, the removal of the institution of the Imam. The resulting civil war of 1962 to 1969 drove thousands of South Yamani workers and activists out of North Yaman and back to Aden to participate in the National Liberation Front's armed uprising against the crown colony. In this regard, the Revolution of 1962 opened the way to the fulfillment of the second aspiration of the Yamani peoples; the end of British colonial rule in South Yaman and intervention in the region.

North Yaman's Civil War (1962–1969)

Contrary to rumors, Imam al-Badr was not dead. About ten days after the takeover by al-Sallal and the military junta, the Imam held a news conference in the northern Yamani highlands to announce his determination to fight the junta. With the aid of Prince al-Hasan, the royalist forces of the Imam, composed of highland pastoralists, began the long eight-year civil war. Assisted by Saudi Arabia, the royalists concentrated on the northern and eastern provinces for much of the eight-year period, while the armies of al-Sallal and his republican backers held firm in the lowlands and portions of the central and southern provinces.

From the beginning, the junta sought and obtained a five-year military agreement with Nasser. Before the civil war was over, Egypt had committed 30,000 men, at a cost of $300,000 to $500,000 per day. Before the start of the conflict, the Soviet Union, the United Arab Republic, and the United States had all recognized the Yaman Arab Republic (Y.A.R.), and soon afterwards it was admitted into the United Nations.

The increased Saudi assistance made it possible for the royalists to continue the war. Furthermore, the rugged terrain of the Yamani highlands made it difficult for the better-trained and equipped Egyptian troops, who were unused to mountain warfare, to maneuver, and therefore they were usually confined to the coastal plains. A United Nations Observation Mission was sent in 1963, at the insistence of the United States to forestall any radicalization of the republican movement, while following the policy of the Kennedy administration of establishing some working arrangement with radical regimes. Because of Egypt's defeat in the 1967 war against Israel, Nasser was prepared to end Egypt's support of the republican cause. At the Khartoum Conference in August of that year, Nasser agreed to withdraw his troops from Yaman. By December of the same year the last Egyptian soldiers had departed for Cairo.

A combination of events gradually reduced the intensity of the war. The Nasser agreement at Khartoum in August was followed by a bloodless coup in San'a in November. While al-Sallal was in Moscow seeking support for the revolution following Nasser's decision to withdraw his troops, a group of military officers swiftly replaced al-Sallal with Abd al-Rahman al-Iryani; and a government of civilians assumed control of the Y.A.R., only to be replaced a few weeks later by Major-General Hasan al-Amri and former al-Sallal officers. In addition, King Faysal began to speak of moderation, following the new role that the Saudi government had assumed in Khartoum. More importantly, Prince al-Hasan and the ailing al-Badr agreed to return to San'a to begin negotiations without prior conditions. When Saudi Arabia finally halted the flow of money and arms, al-Badr and his family gave up and left North Yaman. The establishment of the new Yaman Arab Republic was officially proclaimed in March 17, 1969, with al-Iryani as president and General al-Amri as prime minister. Ironically, South Yaman had already achieved independence by that date, although the process of independence had taken other directions.

South Yaman's Liberation Struggle

The Free Yamani Movement and the Adeni trade unions, together with various nationalist and socialist movements within South Yaman, joined forces to form the National Liberation Front (NLF) in 1963. Due to the influence of the North Yamanis and Nasser, another group was soon formed called the National Front for the Liberation of Occupied South Yaman (FLOSY). Between 1963 and 1967, South Yaman became a battleground not only between the South Yamani guerrillas and the British crown colony but also between South Yamani groups who were jockeying for position in anticipation of the eventual departure of the British. The most intense in-fighting centered on the differences between the NLF and the FLOSY organizations. This gave the British a brief period of respite while the two organizations fought over their differences.

The NLF focused its attention on British imperialism and the old social elites, primarily the big merchants in the service sector and the feudal and semifeudal rural lords in the agricultural sector. Thus, the NLF concentrated on recruiting its supporters and basing its struggle on the working class in Aden and on the rural poor in the countryside. The NLF was predominantly concerned with South Yaman as the area of liberation. Even though it benefited from the republican forces in North Yaman in terms of border sanctuaries and arms, it showed little interest in a joint Yamani struggle.

The NLF was predominantly a coalition of radical nationalists and Marxists; its leadership was in the hands of Qahtan al-Sha'bi and the radical nationalists. Marxism and Leninism were much discussed in the NLF Party Congresses; and in June 1969, there emerged a dominant Marxist-Leninist rather than radical nationalist leadership.

On the other hand, FLOSY focused its attention on a national coalition of all of South Yaman's classes, including the commercial bourgeoisie and the rural pastoral lords. It concentrated, more often than not, on the urban and rural elite and was supported strongly by Nasser, al-Sallal, and the North Yamani republican leaders. FLOSY's strategy was not only to eliminate the British colonial presence but also to unite with North Yaman under the leadership of the reform-minded nationalist elites, such as the merchants and shaykhs in the republican movement of North Yaman. Nasser and al-Sallal carefully cultivated close ties with FLOSY, preferring it over the NLF and offering special services to FLOSY in the midst of the more intense fighting around Aden and the immediate hinterland of the Western Aden protectorate.

While the initial date of independence had been set by Britain for 1968, the events in South and North Yaman precipitated a rapid British withdrawal and the emergence of a liberated—rather than an independent—South Yaman. The heating up of the guerrilla fighting in and around Aden, culminating in the battle of the Crater in the summer of 1967, coincided with the defeat of Egypt, Jordan, and Syria in the Six-Day War. The NLF military and political forces assumed complete control over much of the region of South Yaman, eliminated FLOSY from the scene, and emerged as the only opposition to the British. Furthermore, following Nasser's August agreement in ·Khartoum and the relegation of FLOSY's fragmented movement to the border fighting between North and South Yaman, the NLF appeared invincible. Britain advanced its planned departure to November 2, 1967, when the last of the British left the former crown colony, thus ending 128 years of colonial rule. Qahtan al-Sha'bi, the leader of the NLF, became president, prime minister, and commander in chief of the armed forces; and the new People's Republic of South Yaman was formally established.

North and South Yaman in the 1970s and 1980s

By 1969, both North and South Yaman had established control over their own internal political and military affairs. Economically, the Yaman Arab Republic in the north and the People's Republic of South Yaman faced similar problems. The closing of the Suez Canal hurt both of their port economies. With the decline in shipping revenues came a decline in imports and, for South Yaman, a decline in oil exports. The merchants, shopkeepers, and skilled laborers of both republics suffered from the decline in trade. Furthermore, the service sectors such as transportation, communication, and commerce faced continued setbacks as each republic reorganized its administration and renewed trade agreements with Europe, the United States, the Soviet Union, and China. Crop failures and recurrent drought plagued agricultural production, while it remained too early to measure the results of the much-discussed land reforms.

Three factors emerged, however, as most important for both republics as they braced themselves to face the 1970s: (1) internal disagreements on the nature and directions of their own governments; (2) disagreements between both republics as to the character of the much-desired union of North and South Yaman; and (3) outside intervention in their internal reorganizations, principally from Saudi Arabia. The increasingly violent and expanding Dhofari revolution in neighboring Oman created new problems for South Yaman. South Yaman, having come to the assistance of the Dhofari guerrillas from 1965 onwards in their attempt to "liberate" the southwestern province of Oman, thereby draining South Yaman of resources and people in that protracted war.

South Yaman. After achieving its independence in 1967, South Yaman joined the Arab League and the United Nations. Later, it joined the World Bank and the International Monetary Fund. Britain, the United States, and the Soviet Union recognized the People's Republic. Al-Sha'bi began a number of talks with the North Yamani republicans, while opening new talks with Moscow over arms and aid. In June 1969, however, al-Sha'bi was summarily removed from office and later executed by a five-man council headed by Salim Rubay Ali and Muhammad Ali Haytham. Partly due to the differences between the radical nationalist and socialist leadership within the NLF and partly due to a number of his decisions regarding personnel and development priorities, al-Sha'bi did not represent the needs of the rural poor in political affairs; more drastic measures were deemed necessary to solve basic economic problems. Salim Rubay Ali, therefore, inaugurated a period of more radical approaches to South Yaman's economic and social conditions, beginning with a new constitution in 1970, the establishment of the People's Supreme Assembly, greater stress on land reform, and closer ties with the Sino-Soviet bloc. The state was officially renamed the People's Democratic Republic of Yaman (P.D.R.Y.).

From 1969 to 1978, Salim Rubay Ali and Prime Minister Ali Nasser Muhammad Hasani remained the principal leaders of the republic. After overcoming internal differences within the state, South Yaman took a more forceful step toward mending its relations with other Arab states. Such moves were usually accompanied by much-needed funds to offset the precarious balance of trade and to overcome the problems left by the colonial economy. Relations with North Yaman and Saudi Arabia worsened until the two Yamans were at a virtual state of war. On the other hand, Oman escalated its counteroffensives against the P.D.R.Y.-supported Dhofari guerrillas, straining even further the poor relations between Oman and South Yaman. Closer ties with China, moreover, signalled a shift in the party's leadership under Salim towards a pro-Mao position in state planning and rural populism. It also made available arms for the Dhofari guerrillas and for the continued war against undesirable exiles and the FLOSY mercenaries on P.D.R.Y.'s northern borders.

Some of South Yaman's difficulties came to an end when peace negotiations were entered into by North Yaman to stop the border incidents. The reopening of the Suez Canal in 1975 and the normalization of relations with Saudi Arabia led to a $100 million grant and improvements in both port and petrochemical industry facilities. The P.D.R.Y. and Saudi Arabia exchanged ambassadors, and British Petroleum transferred the title of the refinery to the state.

With the end of the Dhofari guerrilla operations in Oman, the P.D.R.Y. was prepared to address its own internal difficulties once more. On June 26, 1978, Salim Rubay Ali and his followers challenged the rest of the NLF leadership in the streets of Aden. By the end of the day, Salim surrendered, was tried by a special tribunal that evening, and shot. The P.D.R.Y.'s Central Committee issued an explanation for the crisis and the death of the former president and announced that General Abdul Fatah Isma'il and Ali Nasser Muhammad would be the country's new leaders. The two problems of populism and too close ties with North Yaman were cited as reasons for the crisis.

The events demonstrated, however, that the P.D.R.Y. was going through another realignment of forces within the NLF leadership as the new government moved firmly towards a pro-Soviet instead of a pro-Chinese policy. At the same time, the administrative cadre within P.D.R.Y. was reorganized in order to raise productivity and efficiency. Whether the new P.D.R.Y. is any more successful than the 1969–1978 P.D.R.Y. remains to be seen.

North Yaman.   North Yaman, under al-Iryani as president and General al-Amri as prime minister, set out in March 1969 to rebuild a faltering economy, to mend a displaced and divided people, and to create a new republic without the worries of a civil war. Relations with Saudi Arabia were renewed in 1970, and a new constitution was accepted by the National Assembly in 1971. Al-Iryani was recognized as president and Muhsin al-Ayni, dismissed the year before, returned as prime minister. To rectify its grave economic problems, the Y.A.R. proceeded to create an "open door" policy and allowed some royalists to reclaim their lost lands. The port facilities of Hodeida and Mocha remained stagnant as long as the Suez Canal remained inoperative; but new relations with countries such as Saudi Arabia made available large sums of money to import foods, consumer goods, and equipment in order to overcome the immediate problems of the 1970 drought and widespread famine. The Central Planning Organization was established with the assistance of the World Bank and the Kuwait Fund. A three-year plan was begun in 1973 to develop the country's infrastructure. The government started a five-year plan in 1976, with the assistance of the United States Aid for International Development (AID) Britain's Overseas Development Ministry, the Kuwait Fund, and the Abu Dhabi Fund. The program encompassed building new port and road facilities and creating new irrigation systems and communication systems.

These small advances in the social and economic realms were not matched in the political realm. In June 1974, the military junta staged a bloodless coup, suspended the constitution, dissolved the National Assembly, and removed the state officials. A seven-man council led by Colonel Ibrahim al-Hamdi assumed control of the Y.A.R. The coup marked the beginning of stronger ties with Saudi Arabia and the United States, as evidenced by the structure of the 1976–1981 five-year plan. Under Prime Minister Muhsin al-Ayni, the new tilt toward Saudi Arabia produced the necessary funds to revive the economy. The annual remittances of $160 million from Yamani workers in Saudi Arabia created a new sense of stability.

The new relations with Saudi Arabia and the United States, however, were not viewed as a panacea. Some viewed the Saudi-U.S. connection as building a new dependency for the Y.A.R., while creating further obstacles for unification with the P.D.R.Y. Colonel al-Hamdi was assassinated in October 1977 by unknown assailants. Colonel Ahmad al-Ghashmi assumed command and continued al-Hamdi's policies until he too was assassinated in June 1978. The assassination triggered the downfall of Salim Rubay Ali, president of the P.D.R.Y., two days later. The new Y.A.R. president, Colonel Ali Abdullah Salih, has shown no intention of altering the economic and political policies of his predecessors. Nor does it seem probable that improved economic conditions, better social relations, a representative government, or renewed efforts for unification will occur in the near future.

Each Yaman, because of the type of ideology it espouses, is caught in a difficult position. Nationalist North Yaman is caught between Marxist-Leninist South Yaman and monarchical Saudi Arabia. On the other hand, Marxist-Leninist South Yaman is caught between nationalist North Yaman and monarchical Oman. The presence of the superpowers in the area complicates matters. Both United States and the Soviet Union are watching developments along the Horn of Africa, the Strait of Bab al-Mandab and the Strait of Hormoz. The United States is increasing its military aid to all members of the Gulf Cooperation Council, plus Egypt, Kenya, Somalia, Sudan, and North Yaman. The Soviet Union is forging stronger military ties with Afghanistan, Ethiopia, and South Yaman. North Yaman has tried to appease the Soviet Union by buying arms and relying on Soviet technicians. Similarly, South Yaman has tried to appease the Council of the Gulf by promising that South Yaman will not become another Afghanistan. Neither can make good its intentions because of internal disagreements. The future of the two Yamans and their desired union depend upon both of them agreeing on one ideology, which is a remote prospect at present.

THE MAKING OF MODERN OMAN

Oman (formerly Oman and Muscat), like the Yamans, is a country of sea ports and fertile coastal plains whose inhabitants have long been at war with its mountain pastoralists and peasants. Similar to North Yaman, Oman's Jabal al-Akhdar region, which extends from the northernmost point of Ras Musandum in the Strait of Hormoz to the southern Indian Ocean Cape of Ras al-Hadd, was the center of a Shi'i Imamate. The southern Omani plains extending from Ras al-Hadd to the border of South Yaman are dotted with small fishing villages, scattered cultivated oases, and port towns, the most important being Salalah in the southwestern province of Dhofar. Oman's merchant and maritime communities in the towns and its pastoral and peasant communities in the countryside had, since World War I, been under the near-absolute domination of the Bu Sa'idi sultanate. The mountain peoples, primarily pastoralists, with scattered village and small town populations, were, on the other hand, loyal to the Imam. The British intervened in 1920, and the Treaty of Sib ended several decades of sporadic warfare between the sultanate and the Imamate. This treaty gave the sultan full control over the coastal region in exchange for full autonomy of the Imamate on conditions of nonintervention in the sultan's affairs. This de facto partition of Oman continued until the 1950s.

Two events after World War II altered Omani history. One was the British oil exploration in the Buraimi oasis and Jabal al-Akhdar. The other was twenty years of spontaneous and then organized guerrilla warfare against the rule of Sultan Sa'id ibn-Taymur (reigned 1932–1970). The Buraimi crisis began in 1963 and centered on Omani and Saudi claims and counterclaims for the village and its oil. The area had been part of the undemarcated border between the Trucial Coast states and Oman. Its importance until 1953 lay more in its strategic position in the political contests of the region. Following an Aramco report of possible oil reserves, Oman, backed by the British, claimed the oasis in 1955. Saudi Arabia, aided by the United States, contested the claim vigorously. The political and legal conflict over the claims to the Buraimi oasis continued until 1974, when a decision to divide the region between Abu Dhabi and Oman was reached. More explosive, however, was the conflict between Sultan Sa'id ibn-Taymur and Imam Ghalib ibn-Ali in the Jabal al-Akhdar.

The penetration of British oil interests into the Omani interior, aroused the newly appointed Imam Ghalib ibn-Ali to challenge the Treaty of Sib and take up arms against the sultan. In the fall of 1955, troops headed by British officers occupied the town of Nizwa, the political and spiritual capital of the Imamate. The Imam began to organize the mountain pastoralists, including Dhofari leaders, into a coordinated and well-armed movement against the sultan, demanding the complete withdrawal of all British and Omani troops from the interior. In this the Imam was aided by Saudi Arabia, the Arab League and, in time, the Soviet Union. On the other hand, the British had organized the sultan's armed forces, made up of Baluchi and Omani troops headed by British officers. The struggle lasted until 1959, when, with the help of the Royal Air Force and Britain's special counterinsurgency troops, the uprising was suppressed. Saudi Arabia was supportive of the Imam at first, but the events in North Yaman and the emergence of the NLF in South Yaman caused it to hesitate. When Faysal replaced his brother Saud as king, he became a full supporter of Sultan Sa'id.

The Saudis had guessed correctly in viewing the Yamani revolutions of 1962 as a watershed in the relations with Oman. By June 1965, a guerrilla war had begun in Dhofar Province to remove both the sultan and the British from Oman. The Dhofaris had organized themselves into the Dhofar Liberation Front (DLF) and were aided by the Yamani NLF, as well as the defeated troops of the Imam. The emergence of the Dhofari rebellion signalled a far more difficult time for the Omani sultanate than the previous decades of insurgency in the Jabal al-Akhdar.

The Dhofari Liberation Movement

Initially, the Dhofaris were on the defensive. In June 1965, however, the DLF began their armed struggle by ambushing a government patrol in the mountains of central Dhofar. Better organized but more poorly armed than the Imam's army, the DLF carried out a series of attacks against the sultan's armed forces, culminating in an attempted assassination of Sa'id himself. The plot nearly succeeded when a group of DLF supporters within the sultan's army opened fire on the sultan during a troop inspection in Dhofar. At their second congress in 1968, the DLF inaugurated a more radicalized program of scientific socialism and a comprehensive strategy for the liberation of Oman and the Persian Gulf. Changing their name to reflect their new direcion, the DLF became known as the Popular Front for the Liberation of the Occupied Arab Gulf (PFLOAG). The PFLOAG mounted an intense military and political campaign in Dhofar from 1968 to 1970. They drove the British and the sultan's forces from most regions of the province. By August 1970, the sultan's provincial capital in Salalah was little more than a coastal enclave. During the same period, the PFLOAG mounted a rural educational program in health and literacy, published a number of ideological texts, sought the support of other liberation movements in the Middle

East, and focused on the unequal position of women within Dhofari village and herding communities.

Sultan Sa'id ibn-Taymur was overthrown in July 1970, and a more representative government was set up under Sa'id's British-educated son, Sultan Qabus. The political changes within the Bu Sa'id family were matched by plans to revive the faltering oil revenues of the Petroleum Development Company. This company was jointly owned by Shell Petroleum Ltd. and the Gulbenkian interests until 1967, when the latter sold most of their shares to the Compagnie Française des Petroles.

Sultan Qabus and the New Oman

Sultan Qabus and his advisors set out to accomplish three tasks: The first was to contain and then eliminate the Dhofari liberation movement with the increased assistance of Iran and Jordan. The second was to remove Sultan Sa'id's tyrannical imprint by opening the government to both Omani and Dhofari technocrats and professionals through a series of reforms. The third was to improve the Omani economy by establishing the Supreme Planning Council and a five-year plan focusing on harbors, roads, education, and the development of Oman's oil and mineral resources. The sultan offered a sweeping amnesty program to all repentent Dhofaris. At the same time, he launched operations to isolate the armed struggle from South Yaman. The PFLOAG counterattacked; but Sultan Qabus was able, with the assistance of 2,000 to 3,000 Iranian troops, to begin a massive and crippling campaign from 1973 onwards. In the end the Dhofaris, who had trimmed their aim and their name to PFLO, retreated into South Yaman. The fighting ceased in 1975.

The sultan began a series of internal reforms regarding land, government ministries, and education. He acquired 60 percent of the Petroleum Development Company in 1974, thereby raising the revenues so necessary for his political and economic reforms. In that same year, Canadian Prospecting Ltd. uncovered large deposits of high-grade copper and other valuable minerals in northern Oman. Also in the same year, Qabus granted permission to the United States to use Masirah Island as a temporary base.

While Britain remained Oman's major arms supplier, the United States' position clearly improved. Oman agreed to allow the U.S. military to use its "facilities" in return for more than $100 million in military aid. The presence of the U.S. Rapid Deployment Force off the coast of Oman increased the importance of Oman to American military forces. Convinced that the Dhofari uprising was over, Qabus set out in 1976 to devote more than half of the budget to development. He launched the second five-year plan in 1980, with a $21 million budget. Because of the discovery of major oil reserves in Dhofar and in northern Oman, the country now receives more than 90 percent of its revenues from oil production.

In February 1981, Oman, along with five other Persian Gulf states (Saudi Arabia, Kuwait, Bahrayn, Qatar, and the United Arab Emirates) formed the Gulf Cooperation Council (GCC). By May of that same year, a secretary-general was appointed, and headquarters were set up in Riyadh.

The inclusion of Oman, which was not a member of OPEC, in the development of the Gulf Cooperation Council was significant for Sultan Qabus and the Omani kingdom. In one sense, Oman's inclusion was the result of the social and political reforms Sultan Qabus had begun a decade earlier. The reforms went a long way in breaking Oman's regional isolation that had been so carefully preserved by his father, and to rehabilitate the sultanate in the eyes of other peninsular and Persian Gulf states.

GCC membership brought Oman closer to Saudi Arabia, which was in the midst of its worries over the Yaman Socialist Party and the policies of the P.D.R.Y. vis-á-vis the PFLO guerrilla movement and the Soviet Union. In another sense, GCC membership meant that Oman was now forced to take a more serious interest in the security of the Persian Gulf, as well as affairs in the Indian Ocean such as the U.S. base at Diego Garcia. Oman's ties with the Persian Gulf states on the one hand and with the United States on the other have become the major preoccupations of its foreign policy. If both Yamans are admitted into the GCC, that regional organization will certainly play a critical role in resolving some of Oman's present difficulties with the P.D.R.Y.

THE PERSIAN GULF SHAYKHDOMS

The cluster of small fishing villages and sea ports along the southern rim of the Persian Gulf seemed insignificant to the politics and economics of the Middle East after World War I. Known as the shaykhdoms of Kuwait, Bahrayn, Qatar, and the Trucial Coast,[1] the villages and ports of the region were dramatically transformed by the discovery of oil, urban militant movements, arms sales, and transnational corporations (TNCs). Nearly every feature of the pre-oil Persian Gulf shaykhdoms was reshaped and structured in ways similar to the making of modern Saudi Arabia and Oman.

The Trucial Coast shaykhdoms were a series of fishing, pearling, and trading communities centered around a port town and governed by the nearly absolute authority of a dominant family. Bound by kinship ties to the shaykh or head of the ruling family, the agricultural and pastoral communities traded goods, paid tribute, and fought in the family's wars. Qatar and Bahrayn both had a long history of fishing, pearling, date cultivation, and maritime commerce. Bahrayn in particular was the center of frequent conflicts in the eighteenth and nineteenth centuries. Due to its strategic position midway along the southern rim of shaykhdoms, Bahrayn was both a commercial and shipping entrepôt. In addition, Bahrayn was strategically located on the Persian Gulf sea lanes, possessed fertile pearl beds, and was the center of large date plantations. A cluster of small islands, Bahrayn, ruled by the al-Khalifah family, was the first of the Persian Gulf shaykhdoms to export oil in 1934 in commercial quantities. It was also the first shaykhdom to establish an oil refinery.

Kuwait, the wealthiest of the post-World War II shaykhdoms, was ruled by the al-Sabah family, which was related to the al-Khalifah family of

[1]Known also as the Trucial States and Trucial Oman and later to be called the United Arab Emirates (U.A.E.).

Bahrayn. Like the other shaykhdoms, Kuwait also operated under a British exclusive treaty whereby Britain extended military protection in exchange for exclusive rights to commercial, political, and land interests—exclusive, that is, of other European countries. Located at the northernmost reach of the gulf, Kuwait's advantageous geographical position near the Shatt al-Arab benefitted both its merchant and maritime communities as long as Persian Gulf trade prospered. The discovery of oil in 1938 transformed Kuwait's collection of tiny fishing and trading villages and desert communities into a prosperous welfare state. Oil, however, is not the only feature of the Persian Gulf shaykhdoms.

The Persian Gulf shaykhdoms share many characteristics with their gulf neighbor Saudi Arabia. Like Saudi Arabia, the shaykhdoms depend on oil exports for more than 90 percent of their annual income. Not all the states, however, produce oil. Fujayrah and Umm al-Qaywayn, for example, do not; while Ras al-Khaymah has discovered oil but does not produce enough for export. Again, similar to Saudi Arabia, the gulf shaykhdoms were associated in one way or another with the former British Empire. All were agricultural and pastoral societies whose populations were mostly rural, with a small percentage engaged in the commercial and maritime activities of the seaports. All were relatively small in population and geographical area. Thus, except for their size and vast oil reserves, the shaykhdoms were in many way mirror images of Saudi Arabia.

The Persian Gulf shaykhdoms also share many of Saudi Arabia's domestic and foreign problems. Like Saudi Arabia, the ruling princely families of the Persian Gulf remain hesitant to relinquish their control over their economies and politics. Such reluctance runs counter to the aspirations and, in time, the demands of the burgeoning working classes and a growing intelligentsia. Like Saudi Arabia, the shaykhdoms have experienced several decades of strikes, coups, and popular demonstrations. The policies of the shaykhs and the oil-rich families have led, in turn, to increased arms purchases, large police and paramilitary programs, and elaborate security systems. The shaykhdoms also devote much of their oil revenues to large industrial projects, hotels, shipyards, petrochemical plants, and processing industries. The opposition frequently claims that little has been allocated to health, education, and housing and that much of the revenues are wasted on unnecessary project duplications, widespread corruption, and cost overruns. Finally, unlike Saudi Arabia, the Persian Gulf shaykhdoms continue to seek British, Japanese, and Western European assistance in running their petrochemical and light industries, while they have inclined more in the last several decades toward the United States in military and political matters.

The establishment of the Gulf Cooperation Council (GCC) in 1981 and the creation of joint-venture projects, such as the 1982 Gulf Aluminum Rolling Mill Company, have brought Kuwait, Bahrayn, Qatar, the United Arab Emirates, and Saudi Arabia closer together. In light of the continual war between Iran and Iraq as well as the presence of the superpowers in the gulf and Indian Ocean, such cooperative efforts bode well for the future of the shaykhdoms and Persian Gulf security. The overall effect of these efforts has been to reduce factionalism among the Gulf states. At the same time that strong kinship bonds have been weakened, some ruling families have pressed for greater integration of the emerging industrial working class and the intelligentsia into the modern state system. The former Trucial Coast shaykhdoms are a good example of the new trends.

The United Arab Emirates

At the end of World War I, the seven Trucial Coast shaykhdoms (Abu Dhabi, Dubay, Sharjah, Ajman, Umm al-Qaywayn, Ras al-Khaymah and Fujayrah) had no boundaries, capitals, modern industries, bureaucracies, or national military forces. Each engaged in pearling, fishing, plantation, agriculture, grain-crop farming, and maritime trade. The size of their shipping fleets corresponded to the wealth and interests of the ruling families. Sharjah was the location of the British political resident; it boasted a small military force and an airstrip. Abu Dhabi was the largest of the shaykhdoms in land size and Dubay was the largest seaport. Ras al-Khaymah maintained, along with Dubay, the best port facilities. Ajman, Umm al-Qaywayn, and Fujayrah were the smallest in size and had the smallest seaports. All of the Trucial Coast shaykhdoms had pledged by treaty arrangements with Britain to maintain peaceful relations with each other and to give Britain exclusive rights over their foreign affairs, lands, and administrations. Due to the two treaties of 1820 and 1853, the seven shaykhdoms were referred to collectively as the Trucial Coast—that is, under truce with Britain.

The first oil discoveries. All seven states were primarily exporters of foodstuffs, pearls, and items for the peninsular transit trade. The peninsular transit trade linked the shaykhdoms to the southern Iranian coast, to each other, and to the Indian Ocean. Thus, many merchants, brokers, and moneychangers in the shaykhdoms were Iranian, Pakistani, or Indian. The British Oil Company, which had prevented U.S. companies from prospecting in the region, began to search for oil in the 1950s, after it lost control of Iran's oil fields. Exploration was started in Abu Dhabi by the Petroleum Development (Oman) Company (PDO), and the Murban fields were opened in 1960. With this discovery, British Petroleum, a key member in the PDO, arranged to begin offshore explorations. With the support of the Compagnie Française des Petroles, British Petroleum organized Abu Dhabi Marine Areas Ltd., keeping two-thirds of the shares for itself and giving one-third to the French company. Oil was soon discovered off Das Island near Umm Shaif. Dubay and Sharjah followed suit in 1967 and 1970, respectively, with oil finds in their territories.

As the Trucial Coast's first oil producer, Abu Dhabi faced the same problems in spending its oil revenues as had Saudi Arabia. Shaykh Shakhbut (reigned 1928–1966) spent much of the new wealth on his family, air-conditioned hotels, improved port facilities, and desalinization plants. Concerned about the reckless expenditure of oil revenues and Shakhbut's unwillingness to cooperate with Britain, Shaykh Zayd (1966–   ), his brother, replaced him. The coup could not have come at a better time for the interests of both the ruling family and Britain. Britain, in particular, was deeply embroiled in

Oman's hinterland uprisings and was on the verge of being forced out of South Yaman. Critical adjustments were needed to insure Britain's long-range interests in the Persian Gulf.

Almost immediately Shaykh Zayd, with the assistance of a British consortium, set out to reorganize Abu Dhabi's vast cash surpluses. In 1967, the Abu Dhabi Investment Authority was created. Plans were made to build a major gas production and oil refinery complex at Ruwais, improve the port facilities, and construct storage tanks and fertilizer plants. With the discovery of oil that same year in neighboring Dubay, the question of a confederation of the Trucial Coast states was inevitable, especially considering the inadequacies of the council of shaykhs and the development council. (These councils had been established in 1952 and 1965 respectively.)

The establishment of the U.A.E.   Britain's announcement in January 1968 to withdraw from the Persian Gulf by 1971 came as a surprise to most observers and gulf shaykhdoms. A month later, on February 18, 1968, Shaykh Zayd of Abu Dhabi and Shaykh Rashid of Dubay announced their intention to create a union following the expiration of the British protectorate treaties. The next three years found Bahrayn, Qatar, and Kuwait enmeshed in a series of heated discussions over the form and content of the proposed union. As the 1971 deadline for the termination of British rule approached, Iran renewed its past interests in controlling Bahrayn; while Kuwait, Qatar, and Bahrayn were reluctant to join Abu Dhabi and Dubay.

On November 2, 1971, Britain formally withdrew its protectorate rule. Iran, having withdrawn its claim to Bahrayn, invaded the Tunb Islands and the island of Abu Musa. The former had been under the jurisdiction of Ras al-Khaymah and the latter under Sharjah's control. A month later, six of the seven Trucial States—Abu Dhabi, Dubay, Sharjah, Ajman, Umm al-Qaywayn, and Fujayrah—announced the formation of the United Arab Emirates (U.A.E.). Ras al-Khaymah, which was reluctant at first, finally joined in February 1972, completing the political transformation of the Trucial States into the United Arab Emirates.

Within a week of the establishment of the U.A.E., the emirates were admitted into the Arab League and the United Nations. Shortly afterwards, the Provisional Constitution was approved, creating three different governing units within the emirates: the Supreme Council of seven emirs (shaykhs of the ruling families), the Council of Ministers, or cabinet, presided over by the prime minister, and the forty-member National Assembly. Each emirate largely controlled its own taxation and mineral rights; each had its own flag and police and military forces; and each oversaw its own internal affairs. Shaykh Zayd of Abu Dhabi became president and Shaykh Rashid of Dubay vice-president. Each was to hold office for five years. The Council of Ministers functioned as a cabinet of advisors, with key positions going either to Abu Dhabi's al-Nuhayyan family or to Dubay's al-Maktum family. The National Assembly was to be filled with appointed members only, and they were to have limited legislative powers. A number of issues arose soon afterwards, however, indicating the fragility of the union and the numerous problems the U.A.E. had to face in the 1970s and 1980s.

Political issues.   Representation in national politics became one of the major issues. After eight years of rule, the authority of the Supreme Council was challenged in April 1979. Discontent among the emerging technocrats and intelligentsia was coupled with the growing militancy of the oilfield workers. In addition to greater participation in the political system, the protesters also wanted stricter immigration laws, a shift away from large-scale development projects, and greater distribution of national resources. In April, a special joint session of the National Assembly and Council of Ministers presented a list of reforms to the Supreme Council amid street demonstrations. Upon the refusal of the council to address the grievances, the cabinet and assembly refused to meet any longer. The main issue was the continued debate over greater or lesser unification, as represented by Shaykh Zayd's centrist position and Shaykh Rashid's separatist position. Under pressure to compromise, Shaykh Zayd recognized Shaykh Rashid as vice-president and prime minister. In addition, greater efforts were made by both rulers to share the U.A.E.'s economic and political power, particularly with Shaykh Saqr of Ras al-Khaymah and a number of the leading merchant families of Dubay and Ras al-Khaymah. As of 1985, however, no further discussion has taken place over the reformers' demands, indicating that further confrontation between the technocrats, intelligentsia, and industrial workers may occur in the future.

Defense, finance, and foreign policy.   As for defense, finance, and foreign policy issues, the U.A.E.'s shaykhs differed little. Change was needed, however. So, in 1973, the Union Defense Force was established along American lines, with the possibility of U.S. military sales and training programs in the future. On the other hand, the U.A.E.'s population of 1,000,000, 70 percent of whom were foreign laborers, appeared to be benefitting from the oil exports; per capita income was estimated to be $13,000. By 1981, this had risen to $24,999. Such figures, however, masked many inequalities in the U.A.E.; shantytowns existed in most of the seaports and transnational migrants gained little from the benefits lavished on their U.A.E. counterparts.

Furthermore, much of the income from oil exports went to large-scale projects, such as international hotels, airports, and shipyards. The resulting duplication among the emirates of such large-scale projects increased the wastage so often criticized by the National Assembly and other gulf shaykhdoms. Following a slump in the economy between 1977 and 1979, the U.A.E.'s oil receipts reached nearly $19 billion in 1980. Taking into account expatriate remittances and overseas market speculation, the federation's overall cash surplus after other commitments, including foreign aid, came to $4.5 billion for that same year. With expected surpluses running at the same rate over the 1980–1985 period, the U.A.E. hoped to complete the Ruwais oil refinery complex, an iron and steel complex, and the exploration of the Upper Zakum offshore oilfield. By 1980, Dubay had completed its major deep water port complex at Jabal Ali, becoming the first free trade zone in the region. Finally, by December 1980, the U.A.E. created a central bank capitalized at $81.4 million with authority over domestic monetary affairs and tighter credit.

Finally, in foreign affairs, the U.A.E. joined the Gulf Cooperation Council and enjoyed a major role in the OPEC, OAPEC, and United Nations deliberations. While maintaining an aloof position toward the Iran-Iraq War, the U.A.E. sought ways to resolve that regional conflict and donated large sums (estimated to be $1.1 billion) to aid Third World countries. Increasingly concerned over the course of the Iranian Revolution, the U.A.E. considered itself to be neutral as regards fundamentalist Islamic politics, Saudi-Iranian conflicts, and the U.S.'s Rapid Deployment Force activities in the Indian Ocean. While relying more and more upon U.S. protection against apparent Soviet and regional opposition forces, the U.A.E. continues to prevent a "shahlike" relationship from developing. However successful the U.A.E. has been so far in keeping its distance and its political and economic stability, the later 1980s will surely prove to be a difficult period for the federation.

Qatar

Qatar was ruled by the al-Thani family at the end of World War I. Located midway along the Arabian Peninsula's Persian Gulf coast, Qatar was no more than a series of fishing and pearling villages with a port at Doha, which remains the principal city and capital to this day. Qatar's society and economy began to change dramatically with the discovery of oil in 1950. The next three decades witnessed an eightfold increase in its population (estimated to be 250,000 by 1981), a per capita income of $29,000, and a series of labor strikes and demonstrations. Like the U.A.E., Qatar's oil revenues accounted for more than 90 percent of its Gross National Product. Most of its food is still imported; and its major trading partners are Britain, Japan, Western Europe, and the United States. Like Bahrayn, Qatar remained outside the United Arab Emirates' federation. While Qatar shares most of the U.A.E.'s characteristics, its geographical position and historical ties with Bahrayn, Saudi Arabia, and Kuwait have set it apart from the U.A.E.

The Qatar Petroleum Company, a subsidiary of the Iraq Petroleum Company, began to prospect for oil in 1949. A year later, oil was discovered and exports commenced. Due primarily to the oilfields and petroleum exports (estimated to be nearly $6 billion in 1981), Qatar's labor force became a key political factor in the 1960s and 1970s. At the time of the oil discovery, Qatar's population numbered about 30,000, 20,000 of whom were related to, or in the service of, the al-Thani ruling family. With British assistance, the uprising was quickly suppressed but not without leaving a number of unanswered issues in its wake. The proportion of Qataris to foreign laborers had decreased even further in 1976, with 8,000 Qataris to 40,000 foreign workers and service employees. The large number of immigrant laborers, mostly from Iran and Pakistan, created special security problems for the Qatari rulers.

In February 1972, Shaykh Khalifa, who was deputy ruler and prime minister, deposed his cousin, Shaykh Ahmad, and assumed the throne. Khalifa has vacillated between more stringent immigration, property, and citizenship regulations on the one hand, and liberalization on the other. Anticipating the coming of independence, Qatar had announced, by 1970, a Basic Law that included a bill of rights. Qatar's Basic Law has not gone as far as the U.A.E.'s constitution in restructuring political power within the shaykhdom.

From the beginning of Shaykh Kalifa's reign to the present, much of the oil revenues have gone into petroleum and gas-related industries, infrastructure projects, buildings, social services, and light industry. By 1977, Qatar had assumed complete control over its oil production and marketing; it set up the Qatar General Petroleum Corporation to regulate and control the oil industry. A number of joint ventures with foreign firms expanded the port at Doha and the industrial and port facilities of Umm Said. Furthermore, Qatar bought into the Gulf Aluminum Rolling Mill Company in 1982 as a 10 percent shareholder. Qatar is also active in the Gulf Cooperation Council, the Arab League, OAPEC, OPEC, and the United Nations. In expanding its regional ties beyond its close relationship with Saudi Arabia and Kuwait, Qatar shared many of the economic and political problems of another shaykhdom of the Persian Gulf—Bahrayn.

Bahrayn

Under the control of the al-Khalifa family since the late eighteenth century, the Bahrayn Islands enjoyed a special role in the Persian Gulf. It was not only the home of the British political resident for Persian Gulf and Omani affairs but also the principal commercial center for the land and sea trade between the Najd (Saudi Arabia), the Persian Gulf, and the Indian Ocean. Under the usual British protectorate treaties (in 1820, 1861, 1892, and 1951), Bahrayn became increasingly important to the British after World War I. The principal reasons were: first, the U.S. oil companies' "invasion" of the Persian Gulf and peninsular regions following World War I; and second, the turbulent mandate periods in neighboring Palestine and Iraq that had made Bahrayn Britain's major military port for the region. During the Safavid period Iran had periodic control of the islands. Ever since 1820, Iran has contested the British control over the islands until 1974 when the Shah consented to a plebiscite and the Bahraynis chose independence.

The appointment of Sir Charles Belgrave (1925–1955) as advisor to Shaykh Hamad and the al-Khalifa family was the first of several significant events in recent Bahrayni history. In 1930, Socal and Texaco became the first U.S. companies to enter the Persian Gulf oil business. In that year, the two companies formed the Bahrayn Petroleum Company (Bapco) under Canadian licensing and began to explore for oil. By 1932, oil was found and two years later, exports commenced.

The discovery of oil in Bahrayn paved the way for Socal and Texaco to pursue an oil concession in Saudi Arabia, which in turn led to the discovery of the peninsula's largest oil reserves. Furthermore, the discovery of oil led to the building of an oil refinery in Bahrayn. Operated and owned by Bapco, the refinery processed not only Bahrayn's crude oil but also Saudi Arabia's. As a subsidiary of Caltex, Bapco's oilfield operations and refinery were the U.S. counterpart to the British-owned and -operated Iranian oilfields and refinery.

Like Qatar, Bahrayn's population increased rapidly primarily because of its petrochemical industries, the establishment of the Aluminum-Bahrayn smelter (Alba) in 1968, and the opening of the OAPEC-owned Arab Ship-building and Repair Yard in 1977. By 1975, Bahrayn's population had risen to 230,000, of whom 82 percent were Bahraynis and 18 percent foreign laborers. The total labor force numbered about 60,000, with 40 percent comprising the foreign labor sector. These figures conceal the high percent-age of Bahraynis of Iranian ancestry, the large number of Shi'i peoples, and the diverse number of skilled, semiskilled, and unskilled workers. The workers had immigrated to Bahrayn from India, Pakistan, Iranian Baluchi-stan, Palestine, Egypt, and Syria. The figures do, however, reveal the poten-tial problems Bahrayn has faced since the beginning of its oil production. Unlike Qatar and the U.A.E., Bahrayn has been shaken by repeated strikes and widespread unrest from World War II to the present. The volatile eruptions have been due in part to the large Shi'i segment within the Sunni shaykhdom and in part to the large concentration of workers in urban areas, which makes for better coordination among protestors.

Following a 1938 labor strike, protests began to occur under Shaykh Salman (reigned 1942–1961). Early demands for restrictions on foreign workers, the dismissal of the British political resident, and the right to unionize were not granted. By 1952, Bapco agreed to a 50-50 profit-sharing arrangement with the al-Khalifa family, thus forestalling labor militancy. As in Saudi Arabia, Bapco also hoped to increase participation in order to avoid nationalization.

Between 1953 and 1954, the protests began as religious conflicts be-tween the ruling Bahrayni Sunni community and the Shi'i merchant and industrial working classes. A general strike demanding sweeping political reforms prompted the establishment of a ten-man advisory council. In No-vember 1956, however, widespread rioting erupted over Britain's participa-tion in the invasion of Egypt following Nasser's nationalization of the Suez Canal. Demands were once more made for the right to unionize and for the creation of a popularly elected assembly. So severe were the riots that British forces were called in, and an emergency declared. By 1961, the al-Khalifah family moved to replace Shaykh Salman with Shaykh Isa (1961–) in an attempt to prevent further disruptions. Such political tinkering, however, did not work.

Because of Bahrayni worker antipathy to the unskilled and semiskilled foreign laborers, and because of Bapco layoffs, serious labor demonstrations occurred between 1965 and 1973. The high water mark of the protests, according to some, occurred in March 1965, when secondary-school students and teachers joined the general strike and street demonstrations. Influenced by the Arab National Movement, Ba'th, and the Nasserites, the labor demon-strations were assisted by a secret trade union, the Bahrayn National Libera-tion Front, and the beginnings of the Dhofari uprising. Again, British assis-tance was needed to quell the demonstrators; but no serious efforts were made to meet demands for unionization, stricter immigration laws, an end to the British presence, and an elected assembly.

The British decision in 1968 to withdraw its protectorate agreements with the al-Khalifahs and the declaration of independence on August 15, 1971, eased the situation to some degree. A constituent assembly of forty-four members was called by Shaykh Isa, and elections were held in December 1972. Nearly 89 percent of the eligible voters turned out, surprising both the ruling family and the opposition. The election, however, of a number of prominent opposition leaders disquieted the merchants and the ruling family, particularly when such leaders represented the Arab National Movement, Ba'th, and liberation movements. Disagreements over the May 1973 constitution set off another round of demonstrations by the workers, the intelligentsia, and the technocrats. The government moved to increase the membership of the councils and to end the 1971 U.S. naval base agreement. By 1974, Shaykh Isa rewrote the naval base agreement with a 600 percent increase in rent, gained 100 percent control over the Bapco oilfields and refinery, and announced the opening of a newly elected National Assembly of thirty seats.

Between 1974 and 1984, strikes continued to occur and Bahrayn's industry continued to grow. Protests in April 1980 over the death of a leading Shi'i leader in Iraq were followed by other protests in support of Ayatollah Khomayni in December of that year. An unsuccessful attempt on the life of Shaykh Isa in 1981 convinced the al-Khalifa family and the leading merchants that previous reforms and elections had gone too far. They decided that security against internal opposition forces and against Iran's Islamic fundamentalism had to be tightened.

In the meantime, Bahrayn's building programs and industrial development grew at a fast pace. In 1976, the Bahrayn National Oil Company assumed complete ownership of Bapco's operations, with the latter continuing as manager. In the following year, the OAPEC-owned Arab Shipbuilding and Repair Yard was completed in order to accommodate the largest crude tankers in the Persian Gulf. In 1982, the Gulf Petrochemical Industries Company and the Gulf Aluminum Rolling Mill Company began production. These bold new joint ventures between the Persian Gulf shaykhdoms and Saudi Arabia had their origins in sessions of the Gulf Cooperation Council. In addition, the location of these joint-venture programs in strategically situated Bahrayn reflected the deep concern of the ruling families over wastage and widespread duplication of large-scale projects. Finally, while Bahrayn has emerged as the center of Persian Gulf labor militancy as well as the centerpiece of gulf industrial cooperation, Kuwait is clearly the center for Persian Gulf finance capital.

Kuwait

Like Bahrayn, Kuwait came under the control of the al-Sabah family in the late eighteenth century. Related to the al-Khalifahs of Bahrayn, Kuwait's ruling family held land, controlled the port and land trade, and collected duties and tribute. In 1899, Britain signed a protectorate treaty with the al-Sabah family to curb German interests in the Persian Gulf through the proposed Berlin-Baghdad railroad project. With the rise of Shaykh Ahmad (reigned 1921–1950) as head of the al-Sabah family, Kuwait entered an era of modernization and fast change.

What with being a British political and military protectorate and the discovery of oil in 1938, Kuwait's recent history seemed to resemble that of other shaykhdoms in every way. Compared to other Persian Gulf shaykhdoms, however, there were several important differences in the making of modern Kuwait. Its vastly richer oil reserves allowed Kuwait to create a highly sophisticated banking system, particularly the Kuwait Fund for Arab Economic Development. Its overwhelming number of foreign workers did not, like others, prevent Kuwait from establishing a national assembly, writing fair labor laws, setting up an educational system, providing health facilities, and creating a liberal atmosphere for the press. Its relations with Saudi Arabia, unlike the U.A.E.'s, were close and, by the 1960s, included the Yaman Arab Republic. Its ties with the USSR, including commercial and military activities, set Kuwait apart from the other Persian Gulf states, (Kuwait saw no threat of Soviet military action or occupation.)

Kuwait's mercurial rise in the financial world began in 1934 with an oil concession to the Kuwait Oil Company (KOC), a consortium of British Petroleum and the Gulf Oil Company. Due to its independent position, Kuwait was the major focus of British Petroleum's oil search outside Iraq and Iran. The discovery of oil in 1938 in the Burghan oil fields more than compensated for BP's losses in Bahrayn and Saudi Arabia. Interestingly enough, BP and Gulf delayed oil production until *after* World War II, increasing exports in response to the Iranian nationalization of BP's Abadan oilfields. In addition, having learned a hard lesson from Iran, KOC agreed to a 50-50 profit-sharing plan. Between 1953 and 1966, Kuwait was the single largest producer of oil in the Middle East.

Having established its citizenship requirements in 1960, Kuwait declared its independence from Britain on June 19, 1961. One week later, Iraq invaded Kuwait, claiming that the Ottoman-British borders were invalid. The crisis passed but not without the arrival of 7,000 British troops to bolster the fledgling state and to protect the KOC oil operations. By 1971, Kuwait had invested more than $1 billion in the Arab world; it had given Egypt $100 million for reconstruction, and the PLO $14 million.

Following its independence, Shaykh Abdullah (reigned 1950–1965) agreed to a national assembly. The National Assembly met for the first time in 1963 and continued to meet until its suspension in 1976. It was restored in early 1981. Unlike the other shaykhdoms, Kuwait authorized the formation of labor unions for government workers, as well for those in the petroleum and financial sectors. The move complemented the establishment of the National Assembly. On the one hand, the al-Sabah family's liberal reforms opened the political doors to Kuwait's fast-growing numbers of intellectuals, technocrats, and industrial workers; on the other hand, through its regulatory powers the government maintained a tight control over emerging militancy within its borders. It was estimated, for example, that by 1965 foreign workers comprised 78 percent of the unskilled labor force and 100 percent of the skilled. By 1975, the proportion of foreign employees in Kuwait's private sector had grown to 97.4 percent, with Kuwaiti citizens earning as much as 25 to 30 percent more than foreign workers. Furthermore, by 1975, Kuwait's immigrants comprised over 50 percent of a total population of about 900,000, and as much as 70 percent of its economically active segment. Finally, to accommodate the increasingly literate portions of its growing population (about 71 percent by 1983), the al-Sabah family opened Kuwait University. Except for Al-Ain University in the U.A.E., Kuwait University remains the major institution of higher education in the Persian Gulf shaykhdoms. Furthermore, by 1982, 17,000 students were attending Kuwait University in all disciplines; and another 3,000 students were studying in the U.S., USSR, France, and Britain. In spite of its far-reaching reforms, Kuwait faced rising urban militancy in the 1960s and 1970s.

Martial law was declared for eight months in 1967. The threat of industrial strikes and urban demonstrations was temporarily removed. These drastic measures revealed the sensitivity of Kuwait to several factors. Foreign workers continued to flow into Kuwait, particularly Palestinian skilled and semiskilled laborers in the aftermath of the Israeli occupation of the West Bank. By 1975, Palestinians made up about 30 percent of the total population of Kuwait, thus making Kuwait more vulnerable than other gulf states to the vicissitudes of the Palestinian Question. Furthermore, the wide range of government-sponsored social welfare programs did not reduce the monopoly control over the revenues by the few privileged families. By 1971, nearly 90 percent of all Kuwaiti investments abroad were controlled by only eighteen families. When earnings on overseas government and private investments exceeded Kuwait's 1982 projected oil revenues, the social and political imbalance within Kuwait became clear. In response to the growing power of the privileged few, the National Assembly voted for nationalization rather than the continued participation of the koc. Shaykh Jabir (reigned 1971–) suspended the assembly.

With the British withdrawal from the Persian Gulf in 1971, Kuwait began to use its revenues for U.S. arms, internal security forces, and increased trade with the USSR and the Eastern European bloc. By 1983, Kuwait had purchased $2.4 billion of U.S. military equipment and sophisticated weapons, while continuing to rely on Britain as its main supplier. Some arms were also purchased from the USSR, while U.S. advisors and British, Pakistani, Jordanian, and Egyptian personnel supplied technical expertise on arms and security matters. While the 1964 commercial and technical agreement with the USSR opened the way for expanded political ties with Kuwait, the United States remains Kuwait's second largest supplier (after Japan). Kuwait, in turn, ranks fifth in the Middle East for U.S. goods and services. In 1981, Kuwait established the government-owned Kuwait Petroleum Corporation absorbing the previously owned koc, the Kuwait National Petroleum Company, the Petrochemical Industries Company, and the Kuwait Oil Tankers Company.

Kuwait, like the other Persian Gulf shaykhdoms, was surprised by the September 1980 Iraqi invasion of Iran's oilfields and Khuzestan Province. Initially supporting a quick cease-fire, Kuwait began to pump long-term loans into Iraq in order to forestall a possible Iranian victory. The latter became a possibility after the 1982–1983 Iranian counteroffensives. While several Persian Gulf shaykhdoms are clearly apprehensive over the emergence of Islamic Shi'i fundamentalism and Ayatollah Khomayni's bellicose announcements, Kuwait fears the economic implications of the "gulf war" between Iran and Iraq. Whether Iraq or Iran is the winner of that massively destructive war, Kuwait (and the other gulf states) will face a large oil-producing country's drive to rebuild its crumbling infrastructures, and be forced to reduce its own production of oil. In either case, Kuwait and the nine other shaykhdoms entered the 1980s with a number of uncertainties. Overall, however, the last four decades have meant long-term transformations barely foreseeable in the 1920s.

Chapter Twenty-Nine
The Struggle for Palestine

The Balfour Declaration and its eventual ratification by the League of Nations and other international bodies dealing with the Middle East initiated a bitter and prolonged contest between the Palestinians and the Zionists. Both claimed the same territory: The Palestinian Arabs claimed it belonged to them and their forefathers; the Zionists, on the other hand, claimed that it had been promised them by their God, Yahweh, and that they needed it to escape racist violence in Europe. The history of the six and half decades after the Balfour Declaration has been full of stories of courage, cowardice, compassion, tyranny, fear, prejudice, achievement, frustration, terrorism, war, political bickering, propaganda, and bitter controversy. Most points of difference in the struggle have not been settled; in spite of hundreds of volumes written on the subject, all the sources are not available to historians. It is difficult to give a full and impartial account. All that a contemporary historian can do is to sketch the main trends; but even then he or she will be criticized by one side or the other or, often, by both.

To understand this prolonged struggle, one has to understand—or at least take into account—the depth of the feelings of the protagonists. For the Zionists, it was a "Return" full of mystical significance. For the Palestinians, it was simply another invasion. For the Zionists, it was the end of homeless wandering. For the Palestinians, it was the beginning of homelessness.

One has to understand also the context in which this struggle has been and is being waged. This context is a world in which nations do not recognize the rule of law in international relations. Human beings over the course of millenia have come to acknowledge the usefulness of law, even though it limits their desires, and, with minor exceptions, abide by it. Individual nations, on the other hand, are laws unto themselves and have made such a fetish of national sovereignty that they do not recognize any law above their own. In such a situation, nations have resorted to the use of power, have made and broken alliances to gain more power, and still believe it is necessary to negotiate with each other "through strength."

Both Arabs and Zionists have resorted to the use of power to reach their ends. The Zionists have been able to muster the religious, moral, political, and economic power of the West and combine it with their own ability, as Westerners, to make use of modern weapons of war. The Arabs, on the other hand, have not been close to the centers of power and have not been able to obtain and have not been familiar with modern weapons of warfare. It has been easy for the Zionists, most of whom did not live in Palestine, to accept at different stages of the struggle whatever anyone has been willing to concede to them. The Palestinians, however, who resided on the land, have not been willing to compromise. They had as their motto "All or Nothing," while the Zionists followed the motto of "Take and Ask for More."

The Palestinians have relied on their family relations or on other Arab states, and placed the blame for many of their problems on Europe and the United States. The Zionists, on the other hand, have considered anyone who did not agree with them or criticized them to be anti-semitic. After some seventy years of struggle, neither side is ready to compromise, and each believes in the absolute rightness of its own claims. The end of this struggle is not in sight.

PALESTINE UNDER MANDATE

On April 25, 1920, the San Remo Conference gave the mandate over Palestine to Britain; two years later, the Council of the League of Nations confirmed it. Not only was the Balfour Declaration included in the text of the mandate, but also a number of points that the Zionist delegation had presented to the Paris Peace Conference. It recognized the Jewish Agency, which was to work with the administration in all "matters as may effect the establishment of the Jewish national home." It also recognized the Zionist organization "as such agency." Furthermore, the administration of Palestine was instructed to facilitate Jewish immigration and encourage Jews to settle on the land, "including state lands and waste lands not required for public purpose." The Jewish Agency was like a government within the administration of the mandate with wide responsibilities and powers. It is important to note that no such provision was made for the Palestinian Arabs. Indeed, the mandate articles do not refer to Arabs, except a few times indirectly, as the "non-Jewish" or "other sections of the population."

Soon after the San Remo Conference, Britain appointed Sir Herbert

Samuel as high commissioner. Perhaps because he was a Jew, Sir Herbert leaned over backwards to be fair and just to the Arab population. It is part of the irony of history that it was Sir Herbert who appointed Haj Amin al-Husayni as mufti of Jerusalem. The latter claimed descent from the Prophet, was educated in Azhar, and fought on the Turkish side during the war. As mufti, he was in charge of the religious endowments, which amounted to about $300,000 a year. He became the head of Supreme Council and later headed the intensely anti-British, anti-Zionist Palestine Higher Committee. The British put a price on his head during World War II when he broadcast anti-Ally and anti-Zionist speeches from Berlin.

The first anti-Zionist uprising broke out in Jerusalem in 1921. A local commission under the chairmanship of Sir Thomas Haycraft, chief justice of Palestine, reported that the Arabs had instigated the riots because of their fear of Zionist programs. Winston Churchill, however, as head of the colonial office, issued a lengthy statement that was designed to please both sides. He emphasized that it was not the aim of Britain "that Palestine should become as Jewish as England is English." He also stated that "the Jewish People will be in Palestine as of right and not on sufferance." During the thirty years of its mandate, Britain tried to carry out the two diametrically contradictory purposes of the Balfour Declaration—namely, to help establish a national home for the Jews and to safeguard the civil and religious rights of the Palestinians. Since they could not do both at the same time, they first did one and then the other, depending upon the situation. Zionists, however, insisted that Britain did not have dual obligations "of equal weight." They claimed that the safeguarding of the rights of the non-Jewish people was a "secondary and subordinate clause" and should not have been given the same importance as the main purpose of the document, the establishment of a national home.

After the riots of 1921 there followed some eight years of apparent calm. The mandate government allowed the formation of the Palestine Arab Executive Committee, which acted as an unofficial spokesman for the Arabs. This committee did not have the official sanction or the powers of the Jewish Agency, which was active in bringing up Jewish settlers and acquiring land. The Jewish Agency also introduced new industries into Palestine, and by 1939 some 90 percent of all industries in Palestine were owned by Jews. But industrialization did not cause as much friction as did immigration and the acquiring of land.

The Palestinian Arabs were apprehensive lest excessive and rapid immigration of Jews cause the Arabs to become a minority in their own country. This, of course, was precisely what the Zionists planned to do. In 1922, the year in which the first census was taken, the estimated population of Palestine was about 744,000, of which 83,000 were Jews. Between 1922 and 1930 the Arab population increased by 23 percent, while the Jewish population increased by almost 100 percent. The contrast in the rate of increase from 1931 to 1940 is even more striking. The Arab population grew about 30 percent while the Jewish population more than tripled. In 1920 the Jews formed about 9 percent of the population of Palestine, but in 1940 the ratio had increased to about 30 percent.

Insofar as immigration to Palestine is concerned, it is well to take note of the following points. First, the rate of Jewish immigration from the date of the mandate to 1932 was not large. Second, the bulk of Jews migrating were from Poland and Russia. Third, the majority of these migrants, in spite of inducements offered by the Zionists, did not want to go to Palestine but to the United States and other Western countries. Fourth, it was usually only when there were persecutions and other discriminations that the Jews thought of going to Palestine. For example, in 1925, the restrictive immigration laws of the United States reduced Jewish immigration to that country from 50,000 in 1924 to only 10,000 in 1925, which explains the sharp rise of immigration to Palestine in that year. Finally, one may surmise that were it not for Hitler's rise to power and his wanton and systematic annihilation of the Jews of Europe, Palestine might have remained a peaceful national home for the Jews rather than a turbulent national state.

On the Palestinian side, one can safely say that the increase in the Arab population of Palestine was due not just to an increased birth rate, but also to the possibility that Zionist enterprise had attracted many Arabs of the surrounding regions to migrate to Palestine.

Zionist labor practices. The large and rapid population increase in Palestine naturally caused economic crises and widespread unemployment among both Jews and Palestinians. The Zionists, however, had funds from outside and well-organized groups in Palestine to take care of their members. The most important economic and social organization created by the Zionists was the Jewish Federation of Labor, *Histadrut,* a trade union that not only controlled rural and industrial cooperatives for production and marketing, hospitals, schools, banks, insurance, but was also a paramilitary force. In some cases the Palestinians were not allowed to set up similar organizations and they experienced economic dislocation. The activities of Histadrut on behalf of labor did not help Palestinian laborers, except those who worked on the railroads and in the ports. These were not enough to offset the fact that in Zionist-owned industries, which were about 90 percent of the total, Palestinian laborers were not welcomed.

Zionist land policy. Immigration did not arouse the indignation of the rural Arabs as much as the land policy of the Jewish Agency. The question of land transfers became a thorny issue between the two groups. The Zionists had rightly concluded that they could not build a viable Jewish state without Jewish rural and agricultural settlements. Inasmuch as the mandate government did not put the state lands at their disposal, the Zionists bought land from the Palestinian owners at high prices. In an arid land like Palestine farmers were, of necessity, huddled together in villages where there was a spring. Often the land surrounding a village belonged to an absentee landlord who lived in Jerusalem, Beirut, or Damascus. Even though the landlord held title to the grazing land and water, these were used by all the village. The village was a social as well as an agricultural unit. The Palestinian landlord who sold the land made a good profit, but it was the Palestinian farmer who bore the brunt of this transaction.

It was the Zionist plan to purchase farmlands and encourage Jewish immigrants to settle on the land and become farmers. Thus, the purchase of land by Zionists meant that Palestinian farmers had to be evicted. Land bought by the Jewish National Fund, a subsidiary of the Jewish Agency, was declared to be "national land" and not transferable to non-Jews. Furthermore, the Jewish cooperatives, or whoever else received the land for cultivation, were not allowed to use Palestinian labor. The dislocated Palestinian farmer who went to the cities to find work faced difficulties partly because the Zionist industries were reluctant to employ him and those that did paid him lower wages. It must be mentioned, however, that most Palestinian workers were unskilled and had a hard time adjusting to modern industrial methods. Those Palestinian farmers who stayed on the land soon witnessed the rise of modern settlements next to their villages, against which they could not or were not allowed to compete. The people in these new settlements not only spoke a different language and followed a different religion, but used different methods of agriculture and held different social values. It is not surprising that the Palestinians could be readily aroused to try to expel the invaders.

One of the ironies of the Jewish settlement of Palestine was the fact that funds were contributed largely by the Jewish capitalists of Western Europe or the United States, who were firm believers in free enterprise, while the recipients of these funds were socialist or Marxist idealists of Poland and Russia, who had definite tendencies toward collectivism. Chief among these collective settlements were the *kibbutz* and the *moshav*. The kibbutz combined collective farming and collective living, with a common mess hall and common nursery. All profits went to the group, and individuals received weekly spending money from the treasury. The moshav, on the other hand, was a regular cooperative where each family had its own apartment and retained a good deal of freedom socially as well as economically.

In spite of all the encouragement given by Zionist organizations to return to the land, by 1943 only about 13.2 percent of the Jews were engaged in agriculture. Their efforts were more marked in the field of industry. By 1944, the Jews owned over 2,000 industries employing some 45,000 workers. Chief among these were the Palestine Electric Corporation, for harnessing the Jordan and Yarmuk rivers, and the Palestine Potash Company on the Dead Sea.

Zionist social organizations.   The Zionists established a complete Hebrew school system comprising elementary and secondary schools, trade, art, and music schools as well as a technical college and the Hebrew University. One of the most impressive achievements of the Zionists in Palestine was the revival of Old Testament Hebrew and the use of it in a modern industrial and technical society.

The Jews in Palestine had their own communal organizations composed of elected assemblies and enjoyed a certain degree of self-government. There were numerous political parties represented among the Jewish settlers of Palestine, ranging from communistic to capitalistic and from religious to secular. There were parties within parties. For example, the religious socialists and the secular socialists formed two separate parties although they agreed on economic issues.

Of even greater significance was the division of Jews in their ideas concerning the future of Palestine. Zionists were in favor of establishing a Jewish state in cooperation with the mandate administration. In their planning the Zionists ignored the Palestinians. Theodor Herzl, the founder of modern Zionism, in his book *The Jews' State,* does not mention the Palestinians at all. In an official report to the Anglo-American Commission of 1946, the Jewish Agency stated that the rights of the non-Jewish population of Palestine would be safeguarded "so far as might be compatible with" the establishment of a Jewish national home. David Ben-Gurion, the first prime minister of Israel, in his book *Rebirth and Destiny of Israel,* stated that "The State of Israel is a part of the Middle East only in geography. . . ." The enduring motto of the Zionists was Israel Zangwil's phrase, "a land without people for a people without land."

A group of Zionists who went by the name of Revisionists were opposed to the policy of moderation pursued by the main body of Zionists. They opposed the British mandate and wanted to create a Jewish state over the whole area originally demanded by the Zionists at the Paris Peace Conference in 1919. The map that they submitted at that time included most of Transjordan and a major part of Syria and Lebanon. Still another group among the Zionists organized the Union Party. Its purpose was union with the Palestinians. The proponents of this program were Judah Magnes, president of the Hebrew University, Martin Buber, the philosopher, and other intellectuals who favored the formation of a binational state in Palestine.

The Jewish Agency, which had organized vast agricultural, cultural, economic, political, and social enterprises, also commanded its own armed forces. In the late nineteenth century, small Jewish settlements in Palestine as well as Arab villages did not enjoy the best of security. Each Jewish settlement maintained its own guardsmen. In 1907, these guardsmen formed an organization that continued into the mandate period as an elite guard. In World War I, Jewish veterans in the British army who returned to Palestine formed a defense corps called *Haganah* to protect Jewish settlements during the numerous disorders. They trained clandestinely and kept arms illegally. They were financed by the Histadrut and the Jewish Agency. By 1936 the Haganah had tacit British recognition, and some of its members were accepted in the police force. Another paramilitary organization was the *Irgun,* the fighting force of the Revisionist Party, which fought the British and the Palestinians alike. Even more nationalistic than the Irgun was the *Stern Group,* "Fighters for the Freedom of Israel." Like Irgun they engaged largely in terroristic activities. The Jewish Agency criticized both the Irgun and the Stern and disavowed any relationship with them until the war with the Arab states in 1948, when all fighting forces came under one command.

Palestinian Organizations. Compared with the efficient Zionist organizations, the organized activities of the Palestinian community were insignificant. There were practically no comparable Palestinian groups in any field. There was the Supreme Muslim Council, which had charge of the Muslim religious courts and the religious endowments, but it was not concerned with political or social questions. The political activities of the Arabs were channelled through the union of several parties called the Arab Higher Committee, but they were sporadic and ineffective. Both the Muslim Council and the Higher Committee were headed by the mufti, Haj Amin al-Husayni, who was extremely anti-British and anti-Zionist. The Palestinians did not receive any aid from outside and could not boast of any thing comparable to what the Zionists had accomplished. Nevertheless, they opened a few schools of their own.

Palestinian Opposition Movements (1929–1940)

The first major Palestinian action against the Jews, starting in August of 1929 in Jerusalem, Hebron, and other centers, resulted in casualties on both sides. Sir Walter Shaw headed a commission of inquiry and his report, one of the first among many similar reports in the coming years, appeared in March 1930. It condemned the Palestinians but explained that their anger was caused by their frustration and suggested that the government should "issue a clear statement of policy on such matters as immigration, land purchase, and land transfer in order to alleviate the fears of the Arabs." The Zionists attacked the implications of the Shaw Report, whereupon Britain sent another mission under Sir John Hope Simpson to study the land problem. This report, which was the basis of the Passfield White Paper issued by the British government, upheld the legality of land purchase by the Zionists, but criticized the provisions that forbade non-Jewish labor on the purchased land and also banned its resale to non-Jews. On other points, the Passfield White Paper rejected both extremist Zionist and Palestinian views and asked all to cooperate.

The White Paper caused such resentment among the Zionists that Chaim Weizmann resigned as president of the Zionist Organization and the Jewish Agency. The protests from Zionists in Europe and the United States were so strong that Prime Minister Ramsey MacDonald of Britain wrote a letter to Weizmann to allay his fears on immigration and land purchases. Then it was the Palestinians' turn to protest against the prime minister's "black letter," and attack the Balfour Declaration once again.

From 1933 to 1936 there were numerous Palestinian uprisings, most of them directed against the British mandate. Trapped by its own contradictory promises, Britain could do nothing better than to send another fact-finding commission under Lord Peel in the autumn of 1936. The Peel Commission came to the conclusion that Britain could not "both concede the Arab claim to self-government and secure the establishment of the Jewish National Home." It recommended, therefore, that the country be partitioned into Jewish and Palestinian states with Jerusalem and Bethlehem under the direct administration of the mandate.

The reaction to this first proposal of partition was mixed, both among the Zionists and the Palestinians. There were a number of Zionists, among them Weizmann, who favored it because it recognized the Zionist desire for independent statehood. The Twentieth Zionist Congress in 1937, however, rejected the plan as infringing upon the guarantees made in the Balfour Declaration, but left the door open for further study. Among the Arab leaders, only Abdullah, the amir of Transjordan, counseled acceptance. The Arab High Committee was against it; and a Pan-Arab Congress held in September of 1937 in Syria rejected the plan outright and demanded the withdrawal of the Balfour Declaration.

Soon after the Syrian conference, rebellion broke out again and continued sporadically until the beginning of World War II. The British ordered the arrest of the Mufti of Jerusalem and other members of the Arab Higher Committee, but they fled to Lebanon, from where they directed the rebellion. In 1938, Britain, now seemingly acting by force of habit, sent the Woodhead Commission to report on the partition plan, but its report was rejected by the government. The Zionists, on the other hand, were under great pressure because of the rise of Hitler and the rising demand on the part of German Jews to immigrate to Palestine. There was virtual civil war in Palestine. The Haganah finally received permission from the mandate government to bear arms, and the underground, Irgun, became active once more in terrorism.

World War II

War clouds were once again gathering on the European horizon, and Britain had to think of the German threat. It did not want the Arabs to side with the Germans. The Egyptians and the Arabs of the Fertile Crescent were outwardly friendly but unhappy over Palestine, and there was no guarantee what effect concentrated German propaganda might have. Taking the possibility of a second world war into consideration, Britain issued a white paper on May 17, 1939. There was a definite reversal of policy in favor of the Arabs. It proposed the creation of an independent binational state of Palestine in ten years. It provided for about 75,000 immigrants to enter Palestine in the course of five years, after which further immigration would be conditional on Arab consent. Land sales were allowed in some parts, restricted in others, and forbidden in most of Palestine. Both sides rejected the proposal, though the Zionists were more vehement than the Arabs. There were Zionist demonstrations all over Palestine; and Ben-Gurion, chairman of the Jewish Agency executive, promised Zionist resistance to British policy.

Strange as it may seem, World War II calmed many strained nerves in the Middle East. For the Zionists the choice was clear. In a war between Britain and Hitler's Germany there was no question which side the Zionists would support. In the words of Ben-Gurion, "We shall fight the White Paper as if there is no war; and we shall fight the war as if there is no White Paper." The Zionists wanted the opportunity to organize a totally Jewish unit, but the British organized a Palestine Pioneer Corps and opened it to both Arab and Jewish volunteers. By 1944, however, the British relented and allowed the formation of a Jewish brigade with its own insignia and flag. The Palestinians, not having the same incentive to fight against Germany as the Zionists, were reluctant. Not more than 9,000 volunteered.

The Biltmore Program.

Perhaps the most important single event affecting Palestine occurred in the United States. The occasion was an extraordinary Zionist conference in 1942 at the Hotel Biltmore in New York City. In this conference the Zionist program was reformulated to meet the changing situation and has since been called "the Biltmore Program." The conference urged the fulfillment of the "original purpose" of the Balfour Declaration, which was interpreted to be the creation of an independent Jewish state. It rejected the 1939 White Paper, supported the creation of a Jewish army under its own flag, favored the unlimited immigration of Jews to Palestine, and urged that the Jewish Agency be given power and facilities to develop the state lands in Palestine for the use of Jewish refugees.

Most of the Biltmore Program was not new although some of the points, especially those on statehood, had not been previously emphasized so clearly. What was new and significant, however, was a change in the attitude of Zionism from dependence upon Britain to dependence upon the United States. Nearly thirty years of vacillating and uneasy British-Zionist cooperation was coming to an end. The entry of the United States into the war and its tremendous economic and military power were realities that the Zionists could not ignore. In the 1920s and 1930s the British Empire had served the Zionists' purposes. In the next decade the situation demanded that they look to the United States for support. As a result of this change of attitude at the Biltmore Conference, Zionist activity increased in the United States. Jewish and non-Jewish organizations in that country urged the implementation of the Biltmore Program, resolutions to this effect were introduced in both houses of Congress, and a pro-Zionist plank was part of the platform of both major parties for the election of national, state, and even local offices.

The reasons for such pro-Zionist sentiment in the United States were many. Fundamentalist Christians considered the return of the Jews to Palestine to be a fulfillment of Old Testament prophecy; liberals, both religious and secular, were rightly ashamed of the way Western civilization had dealt with the Jews and were eager to make amends. Unlike the British, the Americans at that time did not have Arab sensitivities to consider. On the whole, the Americans were ignorant of the situation in Palestine and did not know that Jewish immigration was hurting Palestinians. Finally, it must be pointed out that the Zionist lobby made it nearly impossible for members of Congress and other elected officials to take an anti-Zionist stance if they wanted to get elected.

There were dissenting voices against the Biltmore Program among the Jews. In Palestine, the opposition was voiced by members of the Union Party, mostly intellectuals led by Judas Magnus, president of the Hebrew University in Jerusalem, the philosopher Martin Buber, and others who opposed the idea of a pure Jewish state. Instead, they were for reconciliation with the Palestinians and supported the creation of a binational state. In the United States the Biltmore Program was opposed by the American Council for Judaism, whose members, all of the Jewish faith, believed that Judaism was not a nationality for political ends but a faith for spiritual rejuvenation. Among the non-Jews, the Arabs of Palestine, Christians and Muslims alike, were against the Biltmore Program. They, however, did not have a spokesman, especially since their leader, the mufti, had become a Nazi. Amir Abdullah of Transjordan appealed to President Roosevelt in 1944. A year later, after the meeting with King ibn-Sa'ud of Arabia, President Roosevelt wrote the Arabian monarch essentially what he had written Amir Abdullah, that the United States would make no decisions that would be hostile to the Arabs.

No discussion of wartime Palestine should fail to mention the plight of the Jews in Europe. The diabolical and systematic policy of the Nazis to exterminate European Jews stirred both Jews and non-Jews in many parts of the world. While it is true that the free countries of the West did not automatically open their doors to receive these victims, it is also true that Zionists used the plight of the refugees to advance their aim for statehood. Underground groups, some Jewish and some non-Jewish, smuggled Jewish refugees out of Europe and into Palestine. The British, who could have modified their stand, found themselves in the unenviable position of having to resort to violence in order to prevent Jewish immigration. Thousands of these refugees were arrested by the British and placed in camps in Cyprus, which must have reminded the victims of the Nazi concentration camps.

THE UNITED STATES AND PALESTINE

The defeat of Germany in 1945, coupled with the victory of the British Labor Party at the polls, gave new hope to the Zionists. Members of the Labor Party were generally pro-Zionist and had attacked the conservative government for issuing the White Paper of 1939, which had limited Jewish immigration in Palestine. The Zionists, however, were disappointed. As a member of the opposition party, the socialist Ernest Bevin had defended the rights of the Zionists, but as the new foreign secretary of the British government had to weigh his pro-Zionism with other problems. With the pressure that the Soviet Union was exerting on Turkey and Greece, the separatist movement in Iranian Azerbaijan, the Kurdish autonomy bid, and the independence movement in India, Britain could ill afford anti-British uprisings among the Arabs. Consequently, Beven continued the policies of his predecessors.

In August 1945, President Truman asked Prime Minister Clement Attlee for the immediate admission of 100,000 Jewish refugees into Palestine. Attlee countered by inviting American participation in the solution of the Palestine problem. The United States accepted and an Anglo-American Commission was dispatched to London, Germany, Austria, and Palestine to study the matter. In the meantime, the plight of Jewish refugees in Central Europe and West Germany was getting worse.

If the attitude of the British Labor government disappointed the Zionist leaders, it angered the Jewish Irgun and Stern terrorist groups in Palestine. The terrorists were able to receive money from the United States to buy weapons and coordinate their activities with the semiofficial Zionist force,

Haganah, while the Zionist political leaders publically denounced their terrorism. In any case, terroristic activity by these underground Jewish groups had started against the British as early as 1944. They bombed British police stations and killed civil and military officials. In November 1944, a member of the Stern group assassinated the British resident minister for the Middle East, Lord Moyne, in Cairo.

THE ANGLO-AMERICAN COMMISSION

The Anglo-American Commission carried on its investigation in an atmosphere of hostility and general insecurity. By the fall of 1945, even the Haganah-trained commandos (Palmach) were involved in anti-British activities. In October, they attacked a camp and freed over 200 immigrants who had been illegally smuggled in against the provisions of the 1939 White Paper. Later that month, they sank three British ships. During the rest of 1945, the Irgun and Stern underground groups tore up railroads, blew up oil refineries, raided arms depots, robbed banks, destroyed bridges, and ambushed British soldiers. The British retaliated but were not able to do much, mainly because the Jewish population helped the underground groups. The most infamous Irgun feat was the bombing of British military headquarters in the King David Hotel in Jerusalem, killing over ninety people.

The Anglo-American Commission presented its report on April 30, 1946. Its conclusions were not drastically different from the reports of previous commissions. It recommended that Palestine be neither a totally Jewish nor a Palestinian state, warned against partition, and favored a binational, bilingual state, safeguarding the rights of Palestinians and Jews alike. It did not find the situation ripe for independence and recommended that "Palestine be continued as at present under mandate pending the execution of a trusteeship agreement under the United Nations." In order to alleviate the suffering of the Jewish refugees in Europe, the commission recommended the admission of 100,000 Jews. On the evening of the day that the report was published, President Truman, singling out the one recommendation that interested him the most, asked that 100,000 Jews be admitted immediately. Prime Minister Attlee refused the request, stating that the report "must be considered as a whole in all its implications."

The British were caught in a dilemma. Perhaps the only friend they had among the Arab leaders was Abdullah of Transjordan, whom they had elevated to the position of king of the "Hashimite Kingdom of Jordan" on January 17, 1946, when they had terminated the British mandate. The Irgun and Stern groups were in open warfare against the British in Palestine. Furthermore, at the world Zionist Congress that met in Basle in December 1946, the pro-British Chaim Weizmann almost lost the presidency of the congress. The American Zionists, headed by Rabbi Hillel Silver, denounced British rule in Palestine as "illegal" and called Weizmann a "gradualist," an "appeaser," and even a "demagogue." Weizmann was elected president by a slim majority, but the American Zionists captured the leadership and cooperated with the more radical members of the Jewish Agency, led by Ben-Gurion.

THE UNITED NATIONS COMMISSION

In such an atmosphere of distrust, recrimination, sabatoge, and murder, it had become clear that the British were not able to solve the problem, if indeed anyone could. The hypocrisy and the inconsistencies of the promises of the First World War had eventually caught up with the British policy makers. On February 18, 1947, Foreign Secretary Bevin announced the decision of the British government to submit the Palestine problem to the United Nations. The General Assembly appointed a commission to study the situation and report in September. The United Nations Special Committee on Palestine (UNSCOP) was composed of representatives of eleven states: Austria, Canada, Czechoslovakia, Guatemala, India, Iran, the Netherlands, Peru, Sweden, Uruguay, and Yugoslavia. When the committee was in Palestine, the Irgun staged a daring attack on the prison at Acre and freed many Jewish prisoners. Perhaps also for the benefit of UNSCOP, the Zionists timed

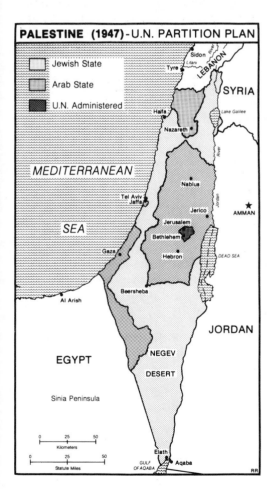

PALESTINE (1947)-U.N. PARTITION PLAN

Jewish State

Arab State

U.N. Administered

the arrival of the S.S. *Exodus* with about 4,500 Jewish refugees on board. It was seized by the British and sent back to France from where it had sailed.

UNSCOP was not able to present a unanimous report. Three countries, India, Iran, and Yugoslavia, presented a minority report, recommending a federated Palestine. The rest proposed partition of Palestine into Arab and Jewish states. The Zionists favored partition, while the Arabs rejected both plans. Consequently, the political committee of the United Nations considered the partition plan. It divided Palestine into six parts: three for the Arabs and three for the Jews. Even though the division was made according to the concentration of each group in a given area, there were 10,000 Jews in the Arab state and nearly 500,000 Arabs (48 percent) in the Jewish state. Fifty-six percent of the area of Palestine was given to the Jews, who constituted about 30 percent of the whole population, and 43 percent was given to the Arabs. The remaining 1 percent, the area of Jerusalem and Bethlehem, was to be under international control.

The naïveté of the proponents of partition was further shown by attaching the condition of a ten-year economic union to the plan. In this economic union, the Jewish state was obligated to assist the Arab state. But in the heat of the debate that followed, the economic union, which was a major justification for partition, was forgotten. At the United Nations, it was by no means certain that the partition plan would receive the two-thirds majority necessary for any recommendation of the General Assembly. Some countries were against the plan, especially the Philippines, whose representative, General Carlos Romulo, spoke eloquently against it. The final vote was scheduled for November 26, 1947, but there were delays partly because November 27 was Thanksgiving Day in the United States. During the delay great pressure was brought to bear, reportedly by American officials, on the countries who had planned to cast negative votes. One by one the reluctant countries were brought into line, and even the Philippines delegation received instructions to change its vote. The fact that three of the five permanent members of the Security Council were in favor of the plan helped the Zionist cause. The other two, Britain and China, abstained.

When the General Assembly convened on November 29, it was evident that the partition plan would pass. It was then that the Arab delegation proposed consideration of the minority report which they had rejected earlier. This sort of conduct became a regular habit of the Arabs in the years to come. They would vehemently oppose a resolution or an arrangement and then support it after all hope for its approval had disappeared. The partition plan was accepted by a vote of 33 to 13, with 10 abstentions. Britain announced that it would terminate the mandate on May 15, 1948, and would evacuate Palestine before August 1.

Chapter Thirty
The Establishment
of the Jewish State of Israel

The twentieth century has witnessed many catastrophic as well as constructive events, of which the unleashing of nuclear power and the conquest of space are but two examples. In either case, the establishment of the Jewish state of Israel is certainly one of the most unusual events of this century. Unfortunately, the establishment was preceded, accompanied, and followed by much bloodshed, destruction, dislocation, misrepresentation, and terrorism, not to mention five wars. Many years will undoubtedly lapse before anyone will be able to say for certain that the result was worth all the destruction.

WAR IN PALESTINE

Almost immediately after the United Nations vote, the sporadic violence escalated to a daily war between Palestinians and Zionists. The British troops did not intervene. They were interested mainly in their own orderly withdrawal and in the progressive abandonment of strongholds. The Palestinians were armed by neighboring Arab states and the Zionists by the United States and Czechoslovakia. Furthermore, Haganah, Irgun, and Stern groups continued raiding British depots for more arms. It is estimated that the Palestinians had about 5,000 men with little experience, under the distant direction of the ex-mufti of Jerusalem, who was in exile in Cairo. The Zionists, on the other hand, were better armed and better trained. A large number of their officers and men were veterans of World War II.

There were acts of violence on both sides. In January 1948, the Irgun blew up the Arab-owned Semiramis Hotel in Jerusalem; the Palestinians retaliated by blowing up the Jewish-owned *Jerusalem Post* building. In February, a bomb exploded in the crowded marketplace of Ramleh. Two days later, the Palestinians countered with an explosion in the crowded center of Tel Aviv. The most shocking incident was the massacre at the Palestinian village of Deir Yassin. It was occupied by the Irgun-Stern gangs, and they killed 254 Palestinian men, women, and children. A few days later, the Palestinians retaliated by ambushing a Zionist convoy bound for the Hadassah Hospital in Jerusalem and killed nearly 80 doctors, nurses, and students. There was panic among the noncombatants, both Palestinian and Zionist, but Zionists were not allowed to leave their homes without the express permission of the Haganah, while Palestinians did not have such protection. By the time of the termination of the mandate on May 15, there were already about 150,000 Palestinian refugees who had fled the battles and the bloodshed.

In the midst of all this bloodshed, two incongruous events were taking place thousands of miles apart. In the halls of the United Nations in New York, the United States underwent an apparent change of mind. It proposed that in view of the difficulties in implementing the partition plan, the United Nations should take over the trusteeship of Palestine. A special session of the General Assembly sat between April 16 and May 15 to consider this proposal amid the harsh criticism of the Zionists and their supporters. While the UN delegates were discussing the fate of the partition plan, Ben-Gurion and the members of the National Council of the Jewish State in Palestine gathered in Tel Aviv on May 14, 1948, and proclaimed the establishment of the state of Israel. In a matter of minutes, both the United States and the Soviet Union recognized the new state, while U.S. representatives were still debating trusteeship in the United Nations. Dr. Chaim Weizmann was chosen as the first president of the new republic and David Ben-Gurion as its first prime minister.

THE ARAB-ISRAELI WAR OF 1948–1949

On the morning of May 15, six Arab states (Egypt, Iraq, Jordan, Lebanon, Saudi Arabia, and Syria) attacked Israel. When one considers that a nation with a population of 650,000 defeated the combined Arab states with a population of 40,000,000, the result seems nothing short of a miracle. But when actual fighting forces are taken into consideration, a different picture emerges. The combined fighting forces of the six Arab states did not exceed 70,000. Of these only about 10,000 had adequate training. Facing the Arab armies were 60,000 fighting men of the Haganah. In this army there were 300 British-trained officers, some 20,000 veterans of World War II, and 3,000 specially trained commandos (Palmach). One should not in any way minimize the courage and tenacity of the Israelis, who had high morale and were fighting for their very existence. The Arabs, on the other hand, had neither the singleness of purpose nor a unified command. Most of their soldiers did not know what they were fighting for, and their leaders were not without their national and personal vested interests.

Both armies were unevenly equipped at the start, but the Israelis were supplied with necessary arms by Zionists in America and Europe, and with airplanes piloted by volunteers from England, the United States, and South Africa. The war lasted from May 15, 1948, until February 24, 1949. During these nine months there were two cease-fires. By the terms of each truce, the contending armies were to hold their positions and were not supposed to be reinforced with additional men or arms. Both sides ignored the second part of the agreement. The Arabs, however, were not able to circumvent the arms embargo on the whole area. But the Israelis were able to purchase great quantities of first-class armaments from Czechoslovakia. Flying fortresses from the United States and Beau-fighters from Britain were smuggled into Israel.

Count Folke Bernadotte of Sweden was sent by the United Nations as a truce mediator. He made proposals of his own for an armistice based on an economic union of both Palestine and Jordan and autonomy for a Jewish state. Both the Palestinians and the Israelis rejected the plan, and Count Bernadotte was assassinated by the Stern gang on September 17, 1948.

By October 31, the Israeli armies with air superiority had pushed the Egyptians out of the Negev and the "Arab Liberation Force" out of northern Galilee. In the meantime, the United Nations debated the Palestine question. Ralph Bunche of the United Nations Secretariat was chosen as acting mediator. At his headquarters on Rhodes he gathered Arab and Israeli representatives in separate rooms (the Arabs refused to sit with the Israelis in the same room) and went back and forth between the rooms until he obtained the first armistice between Israel and Egypt on February 24, 1949. Others followed: with Lebanon on March 23, with Jordan on April 3, and with Syria on July 20. A truce was achieved and Ralph Bunche received a well-deserved Nobel Peace Prize for his efforts, though there was no peace.

Boundaries.   Three important problems were left unresolved. The first was the question of boundaries. In all the armistice agreements, the final position of the opposing troops was used to designate "temporary" boundaries that would presumably be changed at the time of "ultimate settlement." The original partition plan of the United Nations was forgotten by everyone except the Palestinians. Israeli annexed 20 percent more Palestinian territory than it had been given in the partition plan. Jordan annexed the West Bank of the Jordan River, including Old Jerusalem, which its armies occupied at the time of armistice. Egypt assumed the governance of the Gaza Strip.

Jerusalem.   The second unsettled problem was the question of Jerusalem, Old and New. The city, together with nearby Bethlehem, was envisaged by the United Nations to be under international control. The war changed the status of the city from an international one to a divided one with barbed wires.

The Jordanians had control of Old Jerusalem and Bethlehem, where most of the shrines holy to Christianity, Islam, and Judaism are located. The Israelis occupied the greater part of New Jerusalem. Although the United Nations had not abandoned the idea of an international Jerusalem, it allowed the demarcation formula that had been followed in armistice agreements to apply to Jerusalem also. Consequently, the area occupied by Israel and Jordan became separate territories and Jerusalem remained a divided city.

The internationalization of Jerusalem remained on the agenda of the United Nations; every year during the first twenty years of Israel's existence, the delegates passed resolutions concerning the status of Jerusalem, but neither Israel nor Jordan paid any attention to them. As early as 1949, Israel proclaimed Jerusalem as its capital and moved the *Knesset* (parliament) and many of its ministries there. Diplomats assigned to Israel, however, did not recognize this fact and kept their embassies at Tel Aviv. Furthermore, Israel ignored the fact that Jerusalem was supposed to be demilitarized and held annual commemorative military parades in the city. After the Six-Day War of June 1967, and Israel's occupation of Old Jerusalem, the question of internationalization became a dead issue.

Palestinian Arab Refugees.   The third and the most vexing problem following the cease-fire agreements between Israel and the Arab states was the fate of the Palestinian refugees. By the end of the fighting early in 1949, there were approximately 750,000 Palestinian refugees scattered in Egypt (Gaza Strip), Jordan, Lebanon, and Syria. There have been conflicting reasons advanced as to why there were so many refugees. The Israelis and their supporters usually claim that the Palestinians were encouraged, via radio, by the Arab states to leave their homes, join the invading armies, and defeat Israel. Arab writers claim that the Israeli soldiers "drove" Palestinian men, women, and children out at bayonet point in order to make room for the Jewish refugees who were coming into the country. It seems that the bulk of the Palestinians, like so many people in countless wars, were in fear for their lives and sought refuge from the war, hoping to return when the shooting was over. At the end of the war, however, the Israeli forces did not allow them to return. Their homes were occupied by tens of thousands of Zionists who poured in from Europe, and their farms and orchards were appropriated by the conquerors.

Practically every year the United Nations reiterated the principle of the right of Palestinian refugees to return to their homes; but Israel, which considered the Palestinian refugees as potential fifth columnists, did not allow them to return. Nor did Israel offer to compensate them for the expropriation of their lands and properties unless the Arab states were willing to sign a comprehensive peace treaty. Most of the refugees lived in camps and were supported by the United Nations Relief and Work Agency (UNRWA), Friends Service Committee, World Church Service, and other charitable organizations. Egypt confined most of the refugees to the Gaza Strip and discouraged them from swelling their already overpopulated country. In Syria-Lebanon, the refugees were technically aliens, but the educated among them managed to get jobs and gain citizenship. A number of educated refugees went to Kuwait and Saudi Arabia as teachers and workers. Only in Jordan, which had occupied what was left of Palestine, were the refugees given full citizenship. Nevertheless, those who were in camps carried on an aimless existence and in the course of years became a sad part of the general mosaic of the Fertile Crescent.

ISRAEL: A ZIONIST STATE

Israel is perhaps unique among the states of the world in that it was established intentionally as a refuge. In a sense, the United States, Canada, Australia, South Africa, and some other countries that have been built up by immigration could be considered as places of refuge. But what makes Israel unique is that it is a place of refuge for a particular group, the Jews, and for no one else. Because Zionism had labored for a Jewish home and then a Jewish state, it was inevitable that Israel should prepare for the "ingathering" of all the Jews of the world. The state of Israel never denied admission to non-Jews, but its "Jewishness" was so emphasized that non-Jews felt them-

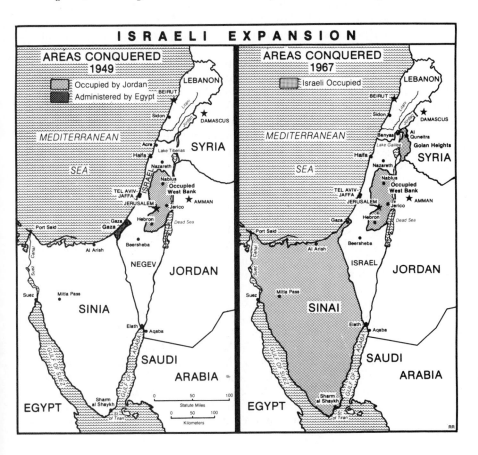

selves to be out of place. Not only did the Zionists invite the Jews, but they also helped transport them, house them in the new state, and find them jobs. Any Jew from any part of the world could—and still can—go to Israel and, in as long as it takes to fill out the proper papers, gain citizenship. Non-Jews could not do this.

Consequently, one of the burning questions in Israel was—and remains: "Who is a Jew?" The Israelis are more or less agreed that, at least legally, belief, faith, or ideology have nothing to do with being a Jew. There are in Israel devout believers in God and in the Torah, and also agnostics and atheists, but all are Jews. The most important (perhaps the only) criterion for being considered a Jew is birth. The courts of Israel have decided that a person whose mother was of "Jewish blood" can be considered a Jew. This emphasis on "Jewishness" is consistent with the claim and program of Zionism, but appears anachronistic when applied to a modern state. Regardless of belief, immigrants to Israel who cannot prove their Jewish descent are not considered Jews and therefore are not participants in the privileges and perquisites of the laws of the "ingathering." Such a state is likely to appear to its critics racist, exclusive, and self-centered.

The classic Zionist ideology was expressed by Prime Minister Ben-Gurion to the twenty-fifth Zionist Congress in December 1960. While the Jew in the diaspora is "subordinate to a non-Jewish authority in all his material and political life," only in Israel, "—the soil we walk upon, the trees whose fruit we eat . . . the schools where our children are educated . . . the landscape we see and the vegetation that surrounds us—all of it is Jewish." With such an all-pervasive Jewishness of the state, it is doubtful whether non-Jews can ever feel at home. There seems to be an attitude of "anti-Gentilism" in Israel which, ironically, is similar to anti-Semitism in other countries. It must be stated, however, that this is true of all countries that are based on a particular religion or "race." It is certainly true, in different degrees, that in some Islamic countries non-Muslims are made to feel like outsiders.

The Israeli Government

This is not to say that there is no democracy or freedom for the Jewish citizens of Israel. The government of Israel is based on democratic principles. The early Jewish immigrants brought with them the diverse political ideologies of Eastern Europe and have combined these with British parliamentary procedures. In the first election of 1949, 21 political parties competed for the 120 seats of the Knesset. People vote for a party and not for an individual. Parties send representatives to the Knesset in proportion to the number of votes they receive. Of the 21 parties in 1949, only 9 had enough votes (5 percent) to occupy at least one seat in the Knesset.

Over the course of years both the names and character of Israel's political parties have changed. For most of this period, however, the center stage has been held by the Israeli Labor Party or Mapai, which controlled the government from the creation of the state in 1948 until 1977, and is still a power to be reckoned with. Some of its leaders—men like Ben-Gurion—

were members of the Jewish Agency during the mandate. Perhaps its domination of the great labor and industrial organization, Histadrut, explains its power among the electorate.

There have been—and are—political parties both to the left and right of Labor that emphasize Zionism, socialism, and capitalism to various degrees. The parties to the left have generally been doctrinaire Marxists and make Zionism subservient to socialism. They advocated a binational (Arab-Jewish) state and were opposed to the Biltmore Program. For a long time they were the only parties that allowed Palestinians to be members. These parties of the left have generally been social capitalists whose interests have centered on a public-sector economy, collectivism, and neutrality.

The parties to the right of Labor have generally been dominated by conservative fundamentalist Zionists who have advocated a capitalistic private-sector economy. During the early years, the strongest party in this group was called the General Zionist Party. Later it was dominated by its right-wing offshoot, the Herut Party. These parties have been extremely chauvinistic and have advocated Israeli territorial expansionism. In the process, these parties have argued for the complete annexation of the West Bank and the Gaza Strip, as well as pre-emptive wars against the Arab states. In 1977, a new coalition of right-wing parties called Likud, under the leadership of Menachem Begin, a former leader of the terrorist Irgun, won control of the government.

Important among other parties are the religious groups. They believe that Zionism is rooted in the Jewish religion and therefore the Jewish religion should not be separated from Jewish nationalism. They are strong advocates of religious education and practices. Because no party in Israel has ever gained a majority in the Knesset, it has been necessary to form coalition governments. Perhaps because the religious parties do not challenge the economic principles of the other parties, they have usually been part of every coalition government in Israel. To obtain the cooperation of the religious parties, the Mapai has acceded to their demands for religious education, the observance of dietary and Sabbath laws, the control of marriage and divorce, and a ban on pig raising, among other things.

Social Integration

Because of the nature of the state of Israel and the circumstances under which it was established, it is beset by special social, economic, and political problems. The population of Israel in 1948 was about 650,000. Within the first eighteen months of its existence, the population was swelled by over 300,000 immigrants. As almost all the immigrants were refugees without financial resources, the problems of providing housing, jobs, and general social integration were staggering. After 1950, when immigration of American and European Jews (Ashkenazim) slackened, special efforts were made to bring in Oriental Jews (Sephardim) from the Arabic-speaking countries, Iran, Turkey, India, and elsewhere. Operation Magic Carpet brought in 45,000 Yamani Jews, and Operation Ali Baba transported 114,000 Jews from Iraq. By 1962, Oriental Jews comprised 55 percent of the population of Israel.

These immigrants brought with them different cultures, languages, prejudices, and religious beliefs; they also differed widely in physical appearance. They had to learn Hebrew and live and work together as one nation. In their native countries, they were known as Jews, but in Israel they were Germans, Poles, Rumanians, Iraqis, Yamanis, Egyptians, or Americans. The Germans disliked the Poles, and the Europeans looked down on the Orientals. For the purpose of integration the Israeli government established mixed cooperatives, but these were given up because social differences led to quarrels and violence.

On the whole, the Oriental Jews, because they are late-comers, less educated, less wealthy, less skilled, and simply "Oriental," suffer the most discriminations. Almost all the better-paying jobs are held by Europeans. The European Jews are conscious of the fact that they were the ones who established the state through years of work and sacrifice. They believe, therefore, that the Oriental Jews should go through some of the same experiences and should not expect to be treated equally. This may be logical to the European Jews, but to the struggling Orientals it is a bitter pill to swallow. Consequently, a number of Jews from non-Arab and non-European countries have left Israel.

The Israeli army, to which both men and women are conscripted, is the best amalgamator. Also, war with the Arab states tends to bring the different elements in Israel together. Nevertheless, social integration, especially in a limited geographical space, is a long and hard process.

The Israeli Economy

Between 1951 and 1952, the Israeli leadership attempted to gain access to long-range sources of capital. In 1951, a $500 million bond issue drive for capital development of all sectors of the Israeli economy was launched in the United States with disappointing results. In 1952, however, West Germany agreed to pay Israel $822 million in goods over the next fourteen years as a form of war reparations. Despite its political defeat over the Sinai invasion in 1956 and the nationalization of the Suez Canal, Israel maintained a steady growth in its economy, particularly in the agricultural and commercial sectors. On the other hand, in the thirty-five years of its existence, Israel's imports have usually been two and one half times its exports. Israel has depended almost entirely upon outside loans and gifts. Because of such loans and grants, Israel's present foreign debt is the largest in the world; at the same time, however, they help to forestall formal bankruptcy.

To offset such tremendous economic difficulties, the Israelis have taken bold steps. They have diverted water from the Sea of Galilee and carried it in 108-inch pipes to the Negev. They have built some 9,000 industries employing about 100,000 persons. They have developed the port of Eilat on the Gulf of Aqaba for tourism and trade with Asia and have built an oil pipeline from there to Haifi on the Mediterranean. They export citrus fruits, tomatoes, olives, and cucumbers to markets in Europe. They have developed tourism; and with the occupation of the West Bank in 1967, they have practically monopolized the tourist trade to the Holy Land. They have many projects for the future. Nevertheless, the Israelis will have a precarious economic existence as long as they occupy and exclusively exploit Palestinian lands; they can expect to have continuous internal conflicts with the 1.5 million Palestinians and unending wars with the Arab states.

Matters both economic and political worsened for Israel from 1961 to 1965. The average yearly unfavorable balance of trade was $371 million, going to well over $600 million by 1966. Israeli reports for the 1961–1965 period concluded:

1. that the Israeli economy continued to stress agricultural, commercial, and financial development over industrial development;
2. that the kibbutz movement, which counted for less than 4 percent of the total labor force, contributed little to the Gross Domestic Product and, on the whole, was inefficient and in decline;
3. that most Israelis aspired only to luxurious living;
4. that industrial wages were high for Israeli labor;
5. and that the Israeli standard of living was out of line with the country's actual production and resources.

By 1965, moreover, German war reparations had come to an end, charitable gifts from world Jewry had declined, and fewer Jews had been immigrating than ever before. In addition, the completion of the deep-water port of Ashdod in 1965 (it was begun in 1960 in order to provide another Mediterranean outlet in addition to Haifa) only exacerbated Israel's growing economic crisis due to high-interest loans and construction overruns. The opening of Ashdod did give Israel greater access to the world commercial markets (both capital and commodity goods) without, however, any major investment in production.

Israel negotiated $40 million in new loans to meet its economic problems, while the Knesset budget in 1966 was set at $1.1 billion. By 1977, the budget had reached $15 billion. Most of the capital was to come from U.S. government grants and loans. Funds from the United Jewish Appeal and other private sources of income were not included in the 1966 budget.

THE SIX-DAY WAR AND ITS AFTERMATH

The year 1967 began ominously. After a series of raids and retaliations, which are described elsewhere,[1] on June 5, Israel launched its blitzkrieg against Egypt, Syria, and Jordan; by June 10, it had completed its pre-emptive strikes. As a result, Israel more than doubled its territory; inflicted devastating blows on the collective military might of Egypt, Syria, and Jordan (including the two-hour strafing of the U.S.S. *Liberty*, an American intelligence-gathering ship, resulting in the deaths of forty-five American seamen); and gathered more than 1.5 million Palestinians into its fold.

[1]See p. 286 for the war's effect on Syria, p. 309 for Jordan, and p. 405 for Egypt.

The Six-Day War created as many problems as it solved. Israeli needs for military purchases and production were enormously expanded. Since arms manufacturing is generally thought to be nonproductive and costly and to have little impact on the general economic well-being of a nation, the war added to Israeli's economic burden. In addition there was the burden of 1.5 million Palestinians on the West Bank and the Gaza Strip. The majority of them were rural cultivators who lived in unimproved housing and relied on labor-intensive agricultural techniques. Jordan had done little between 1949 and 1967 to improve the lives of most Palestinians, whether urban or rural. Israeli rule would do no better and, in the areas of finance, education, and health services, much worse.

West Bank Settlements

While plagued with enormous political and economic problems resulting from the seizure of the West Bank and Gaza and the military supervision of 1.5 million people, Israel found that the occupation brought mixed results for its settlers and its construction industries. Drawing on the enormous pool of cheap labor made available for settlements and "security" purposes, the Israelis were to discover that the rising number of Palestinian day laborers bussed into Israeli construction sites and the creation of over 100 settlements between 1967 and 1983 brought mixed economic and political blessings. The Palestinians would not leave the West Bank or Gaza as Israeli policymakers had hoped. With the Israeli budget burdened with arms purchases and production on the one hand and the construction of settlements on the other, there was not much left over for social services to Israeli citizens within the pre-1967 borders.

From 1967 to the election of Menachem Begin as prime minister in 1977, 90 settlements were planned for the West Bank at a cost of approximately $350 million. With the election of Begin and the ascendency of the Likud coalition in government, the 32 existing settlements containing 3,200 Israelis were augmented by an additional 69 settlements with 17,000 settlers. Furthermore, Begin announced a plan to expand the settlements by another 4, and an expected Israeli settler population of 100,000 by 1984. Furthermore, by 1977, the Israeli-occupied portion of the West Bank amounted to more than 160,000 hectares (ca. 330,000 acres), or one-third of the total area of the West Bank. By 1984, with the announcement of a further 16 planned settlements, the overall Israeli ownership of West Bank lands exceeded one-half the total area of the West Bank.

Palestinian Inequalities

The number of Palestinian laborers working in Israel had increased from 12,000 in 1968 to 78,000 in 1974. The latter figure accounted for 49.8 percent of the total Palestinian labor force on the West Bank and Gaza. By 1972, certain labor practices regarding the Palestinians had become the norm. Palestinians working for Israeli contractors or factory owners received higher wages than those working on the West Bank or Gaza. Palestinian laborers, however, were not eligible to receive the same insurance benefits that were given to Israeli citizens, nor could they receive benefits, such as workers' compensation or retirement funds, although deduction for both were made from their wages. On the other hand, Palestinians did qualify for some health benefits. On the whole, Israeli wage laborers received 50 percent more on the average than did Palestinian laborers. Finally, between 1967 and 1983, the Palestinian unemployment rate fluctuated between 20 and 30 percent per year, while the Israeli unemployment rate ranged between 5 and 8 percent.

Such inequalities in employment were paralleled by others in the industrial, financial, commercial, and agricultural sectors. While differences occurred during the seventeen years of Israeli occupation, the West Bank and Gaza areas received no less than 90 percent of their total imports from Israel while Israel received 2 percent of its total imports from the West Bank and Gaza. When Jordanian rule on the West Bank collapsed in 1967 so did the Jordanian banking, health, and educational systems. The health and education systems were revived by the Israelis after some delays, while the banking system remained defunct except for the sole official presence of Bank Leumi throughout the West Bank. The Israeli bank was rarely used by Palestinians, who preferred to bank in Amman or to exchange currency on a day-to-day basis with West Bank and Gaza Palestinian moneychangers.

No sooner was the 1967 cease-fire negotiated by the United Nations than Israel annexed Old Jerusalem, and bulldozed a number of Palestinian homes in order to enlarge the area around the Wailing Wall to accommodate crowds of Jewish pilgrims. Abba Eban, the Israeli ambassador to the United Nations, declared that the future of Jerusalem was not negotiable.

The United Nations and Resolution 242

From June to the end of November, proposals and counterproposals were put forward in the United Nations in an attempt to bring about peace. In general, the United States took the side of Israel, while the Soviet Union, which had broken diplomatic relations with Israel, sided with the Arabs. In the end, on November 22, 1967, the United Nations was able to approve Resolution 242 with a unanimous vote. This resolution, even though not complied with, has become the major point of reference in all subsequent negotiations and pronouncements.

Resolution 242, after "emphasizing the inadmissability of the acquisition of territory by war," affirms in part:

1. "withdrawal of Israeli armed forces from territories of recent conflict"—i.e., the West Bank, the Gaza Strip, and Sinai;
2. "freedom of navigation through international waterways in the area"—i.e., the Suez Canal and the Straits of Tiran;
3. "achieving a just settlement of the refugee problem";
4. "guaranteeing the territorial integrity and political independence of every state in the area"—i.e., the recognition of Israel by the Arab states.

Although all the belligerent parties approved Resolution 242, peace remained as elusive as ever. Egypt did not open the Suez Canal to Israeli shipping as long as Israel occupied Palestine and other Arab lands. Israel established settlements on the West Bank and built a strong line of defense along the Suez Canal, known as the Bar Lev Line. From 1967 to 1973 there was sporadic fighting in the Sinai and the Golan Heights, as well as raids by the PLO.

Prime Minister Levi Eshkol, who had that office since 1963, died in 1969. He was a veteran politician who had a hand in the founding of Israel and was a key figure in the Six Day War. Golda Meir succeeded him on March 17. In the election of October 1969, the Labor Party won but, in order to form a majority, had to align itself with the National Religious Party and the right-wing Gahal Party. The coalition of Labor and other parties was weakening because of the tremendous problems Israel was facing after the 1967 war. Golda Meir formed what amounted to a coalition cabinet in which the opposition leader, Menachem Begin was a minister without portfolio.

THE OCTOBER (Yom Kippur) WAR OF 1973

Yom Kippur, a high holy day in Judaism, occurred on October 6, 1973. On that day Egypt and Syria launched an attack that took the Israelis by complete surprise. The Egyptian forces crossed the Suez Canal and broke the Bar Lev Line and the Syrians took the Golan Heights. Inasmuch as the Soviet Union and the United States were airlifting tanks, airplanes, and materiel to their respective clients, there was fear that the campaign would escalate into a full-fledged war between the two superpowers. The arrival of the United Nations Emergency Force between the Egyptian and the Israeli armies eased tensions. According to the disengagement agreement of January 1974, Israeli forces withdrew from the Suez, giving up the strategic passes of Mitla and Gidi. They also returned the Abu Rudeis oil field to Egypt, while the latter agreed to allow nonmilitary cargo to pass through the Canal. The UNEF was stationed between the two armies, while 200 American civilian technicians operated an early warning electronic system. In the north, the Israelis relinquished all the new territory they had gained plus the town of Quneitra, which had been seized in 1967.

Although the Israeli counterattack had been successful and some of its forces had crossed the Suez Canal and was advancing toward Cairo, while another contingent came to within thirty-five kilometers of Damascus, the war proved to be as much of a psychological defeat for Israel as it had become a psychological victory for Egypt and Syria. The loss of 2,400 soldiers, plus airplanes, tanks, and other equipment amounting to an estimated $7 billion, was staggering for Israel. Prime Minister Golda Meir resigned under pressure and Yitzhak Rabin, a former chief of staff and ambassador to the United States, took charge of the government.

ENTER MENACHEM BEGIN

The disengagement after the October War did not change the Israeli-Palestinian relations. The PLO, which had been driven to Lebanon, was launching commando raids in northern Israel; and the Gush Emunim, a fundamentalist Zionist group, was building more and more settlements in the West Bank. Israel was isolated. Many of Israel's African supporters broke off diplomatic relations; UNESCO censored Israel for changing the physical appearance of Jerusalem; and, most damaging of all, was the 1975 resolution of the United Nations declaring Zionism to be a form of racism. On the whole, the Israelis were discouraged and, for the first time, more people were leaving Israel than coming in.

There were charges of corruption and scandal within the government. In the elections of May 17, 1977, Rabin himself became involved in a scandal and was forced to resign the leadership of the party. Shimon Perez was chosen to succeed him. As a result the Labor Party was defeated for the first time since the birth of the state; and Menachem Begin, the leader of the Likud coalition, became prime minister. As a religious conservative, Begin always referred to the West Bank as "Judea and Samaria," recalling the Biblical names for the region, and encouraged the settlement of the West Bank by ardent Zionists. As a fiscal conservative, he abandoned the socialism of the Labor Party in favor of a conservative economic system that ended subsidies and raised taxes. To ease the pain of skyrocketing inflation, he broadened indexation and encouraged spending.

Mr. Begin went to the United States in July 1977 and in his meeting with President Carter accepted Resolution 242. On his return to Israel, however, he approved three new settlements in the West Bank; President Carter called the settlements "illegal." Begin declared that Israel would never negotiate with the PLO and would not allow the establishment of a Palestinian state on the West Bank. At the same time, the United States and the Soviet Union were planning to cosponsor a meeting in Geneva to consider the Palestinian question.

THE CAMP DAVID ACCORDS

President Anwar Sadat of Egypt announced his intention of visiting Israel in 1977. Begin and his government, initially caught off-guard by the announcement, warmly received Sadat in Jerusalem. The Egyptian leader spoke in the Knesset of the necessity of cooperating peacefully, and emphasized the need of the Palestinians for self-determination and their right to an independent state. The Israeli public received Sadat with mixed emotions. Some were enthusiastic and hoped for a major breakthrough in the twenty-nine years of war between Israel and the Arab states, while others remained skeptical about the possible benefits they would receive from the Egyptian leader's gesture. Between November 1977 and the March 1979 Camp David Accords, Israeli public opinion ran hot and cold on the Sadat initiative. The liberal segment of the Israeli public was enthusiastic and the conservative

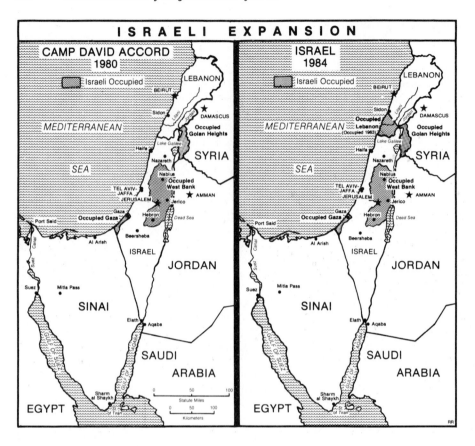

segment skeptical. The nationalist Zionists opposed the loss of the Sinai, especially its oilfields and its strategic position between the Suez Canal and the Gulf of Aqaba. On September 8, 1978, Israel experienced its largest public demonstration when 100,000 Israelis marched in Jerusalem in support of the Camp David Accords and the Begin-Sadat talks. Furthermore, 30,000 Peace Now supporters demonstrated in Tel Aviv against Begin's West Bank settlement plans.

Volumes have been written on the Camp David Accords, praising them for their accomplishments and condemning them for their failures. When President Carter invited Anwar Sadat and Menahem Begin to Camp David, he was determined to persuade these leaders to arrive at a peaceful solution. Both leaders, however, came to the conference with different purposes. Sadat wanted self-determination for the Palestinians of the West Bank and Gaza and the evacuation of Sinai by Israel. Begin wanted a separate peace with Egypt but no concessions on the Palestinian problem. President Carter hoped for peace between Egypt and Israel and the replacement of the Israeli military government on the West Bank and Gaza by Palestinians "with self-government [and] with full authority."

Inasmuch as the final outcome of the conference was a separate peace between Egypt and Israel, one must conclude that President Carter and President Sadat got half of what they wanted and that Prime Minister Begin got all of what he had planned for. The section of the Accords that deals with the Palestinians is called "Framework for Peace in the Middle East." It speaks about autonomy but leaves the definition of the term to be negotiated among Egypt, Israel, and Jordan. It provides for Palestinian participation only indirectly through Egypt or Jordan, subject to Israel's veto. It speaks about free elections by the "inhabitants" of the West Bank, without specifying whether the new Israeli settlers are to be included among the inhabitants. The elections, moreover, are to be held under Israeli military authority with no outside supervision. The status of Jerusalem is not to be within the jurisdiction of the projected "self-governing" authority. On the all-important issue of new settlements, a freeze was agreed upon. Soon after the conference, there was some disagreement as to whether the freeze applied only to the three-month period during which Israel and Egypt were to conclude a separate peace, or to the time it took Egypt, Israel, and Jordan to agree on a form for the self-governing authority. For the implementation of the above points there was to be a five-year transitional period.

Under these circumstances, it was not surprising that on the West Bank and in Gaza, the Camp David Accords were received with stony silence. Palestinians joined others in the Arab World in condemning the talks and attacking Sadat for his separate peace with the Zionist state. By July 1980, West Bank inhabitants learned of Military Order 854, which intended to put Israel in control over the eleven Palestinian institutions of higher education on both the West Bank and Gaza. The order would extend the controls Israel presently exercised over the primary, preparatory, and secondary government schools on the West Bank and Gaza. Opposition in the universities, colleges, and institutions immediately resulted in the closure of the universities and colleges for a number of months, lengthy prison detentions and house arrests of students and faculty, and the expulsion of approximately forty university faculty members and administrators. By 1984, the opposition to 854 was still as vehement and volatile as it had been in 1980.

As for the settlements, both Begin and his successor Shamir encouraged the building of apartment complexes and provided generous subsidies so that Israelis could buy them at low cost. By mid-1984, 40 percent of the land had been taken over by Israel for military purposes and civilian settlements. Many observers believe that the trend is not reversible and that the provisions of the Camp David Accords, let alone Resolution 242, have become irrelevant.

THE INVASION OF LEBANON

The brief Israeli intrusion into southern Lebanon had brought the United Nations peacekeeping mission and had resulted in a closer alliance between Israel and the Maronite Phalangists against the PLO and Syria. As the civil war in Lebanon increasingly became a regional war, few Israelis were surprised by the early morning announcements of June 5, 1982, of a full-scale, 50,000-man blitzkrieg of South Lebanon under the code name, Peace for Galilee. The consequences of the invasion, however, were not anticipated either by the Israeli planners of the invasion or the general Israeli public. The original announcement referred to a twenty-five-mile advance to make Galilee safe from PLO bombardment, but the Israelis were surprised to see their armies moving towards Beirut on the one hand and towards the Beqaa Valley on the other. Between June and August 1982, the Israeli Defense Force (IDF) shelled towns and refugee camps, and rounded up thousands of Palestinians and Lebanese into makeshift detention centers. It blew up countless homes of suspected PLO collaborators. Besieging Beirut, Sharon, the Israeli defense minister, announced his intention of crushing the PLO and proceeded to order round-the-clock saturation bombing of Beirut through August and September. Public outrage in the Arab world spread to Europe and the United States, and the attention of the United Nations was snapped once more toward Lebanon. Soon the Israeli public began to sense the destructive results of their government's actions. What was initially to be a limited invasion of South Lebanon was clearly becoming an occupation of Lebanon and the systematic destruction of the densely populated city of Beirut. In November 1982, amidst the regional and international debates over the appropriateness of the IDF's activities came the news of the massacres of Palestinians in the refugee camps of Sabra and Shitila. Prompted by the shock of the massacres, and the growing feeling that the IDF might be out of control, 200,000 Israelis demonstrated against both the invasion and Ariel Sharon in the largest antigovernment demonstration in Israel's history.

Throughout 1983 and early 1984, the repercussions of the Lebanese adventure continued to unfold. In the spring of 1983, a specially designated commission of respected Israelis investigated the charges of the IDF's alleged involvement in the refugee camp massacres. Its only finding was that Sharon had been clearly involved, and the Begin government accepted the commission's recommendation for his resignation. In August, Menachem Begin himself resigned as prime minister, as a result of personal hardships and continued criticism within Israel of the invasion of Lebanon. The political crises affecting the Begin government and Sharon also had an impact on the IDF as it continued its costly occupation of South Lebanon. The IDF withdrew its forces south of the Awali River, following the commission's findings on Sharon and the IDF leadership.

ISRAEL AND THE ARAB STATES

The social and economic problems of Israel are closely tied to its relations with the Arab states. The problems of passage through the Suez, or use of the Gulf of Aqaba, or the status of the Palestinians are symptoms of the basic issue, which is the establishment of Israel against the will of the inhabitants. Perhaps if the Arabs could view Israel as a "tiny nation," friendly and without design on its neighbors, a reconciliation could be worked out. But Israel's relationship with world Jewry and the expressed hope of Zionists to bring all Jews to Israel, transforms the state into a colossus in the eyes of the Arabs. To the Arabs, World Zionism is more dangerous than communism. So they fight it, they boycott it, and they are afraid of it. When, as a result of five wars in thirty-six years, Israel is master of all Palestine, south Lebanon, and a strategic district of Syria, it is understandable why the Arabs cannot regard it as a "tiny" nation. On the other hand, the fact that Israel is surrounded by Arab states on three sides produces a precarious political existence that contributes to an already quasi-chaotic economic life.

Israel, with its techniques of modern civilization, could be a great blessing to the neighboring Middle East countries as its technical aid missions have been to many emerging African states. Perhaps two conditions will have to be met before such a hope can be entertained. One is a modification in Zionist ideology that will transform Israel from an exclusively Jewish state into a pluralistic secular state where "race" or religion are not considered criteria for citizenship. The second is the abandonment of the attitude of superiority which Israel, as a European transplant, has shown toward the "Oriental" Arabs.

THE FUTURE OF ISRAEL

In the elections of July 23, 1984, the main contenders were the Likud Party, under the leadership of Prime Minister Yitzhak Shamir, and the Labor Party, headed by Shimon Perez; neither party won enough seats to form a government. Labor won forty-four seats and Likud forty-one, and the remaining thirty-five seats were won by thirteen small parties. Among these splinter parties were two new ones that were allowed to participate only at the intervention of Israeli Supreme Court. One seat was won by the Kach Party, whose leader, Rabbi Meir Kahane, an American citizen, believes that no Palestinian should be allowed to live in any part of Eretz (land) Israel. Two seats were won by the Progressive List for Peace (PLP) Party, led by Muhammad Miari, which is not Zionist and believes in self-determination for Palestinians and the Israeli evacuation of the West Bank and Gaza. If either of the two leading parties is able to coopt enough votes among the splinter parties to form a government, or if the two parties are able to form a national unity government, the result will be indecisive. It means that Israel's overwhelming problems will continue to cause unrest at home and in neighboring countries.

The occupation of Lebanon. Israel seems to be bogged down in Lebanon. The cost of the Lebanese occupation, both in money and lives, has been staggering. Israel failed to make a separate peace with Lebanon, and it failed to force Syria out of Lebanon; and although it knocked the PLO down, it was not able to knock it out. Inside Israel, public outcries against the Lebanon war began to be supplemented by refusals by IDF personnel to go to Lebanon. Concerts were held to raise money for the families of IDF soldiers serving in Israeli prisons for their refusal to serve in Lebonan.

Economic troubles.   Israel has been in serious economic difficulty for a long time. Its foreign exchange reserve is zero and its inflation rate had risen to 400 percent by mid-1984. The only protection Israelis have is an elaborate system of indexation that adjusts personal wages and pensions. Israel had a trade deficit of $51 billion in 1983. It has the largest per capita debt ($5,150), of any nation in the world. Its chief creditor is the United States, which continues to lend and give grants every year. Since 1948, the United States has given over $28 billion to Israel, over half in grants. The Israeli banking system nearly collapsed in November 1983, when the country's four major banking institutions closed for four days before reopening amid public alarm. Many Israelis are fearful of losing their economic independence.

The West Bank settlements.   On the question of the West Bank settlements, Israeli sentiment is almost evenly divided. Some 43 percent of the people are willing to concede some territory in return for a peaceful arrangement with Jordan. On the other hand, 41 percent are opposed to giving up any territory. The attitude of the Zionist settlers has been expressed thus: "Those who call themselves Palestinian Arabs should be grateful that we permit them to live in our homeland. . . ."[2] In March 1984, Prime Minister Yitzhak Shamir announced the establishment of sixteen more settlements. The 1.5 million Palestinians of the West Bank and Gaza do not enjoy full citizenship rights and feel no loyalty to the state. There are constant uprisings on the one hand, and brutal police reprisals and imprisonments on the other. This is an agonizing dilemma for Israel. If all the Palestinians were to be fully integrated into Israeli society and given equal rights, then in a very short time Israel would cease to be a Jewish state and would lose its Zionist underpinnings upon which it was established. If, on the other hand, the right of self-determination is not granted the Palestinians, Israel will increasingly become a police state in order to maintain control and, in the process, lose its soul.

Israel has changed greatly since 1948. Its agrarian economy has become industrialized; its military buildup has made it the fourth largest military force in the world; its pioneer vision has lost much of its luster; and its people have suffered a great deal; but in 1984, it seemed no closer to its stated aspiration for peace than it had been in 1948.

[2]*Time* (July 9, 1984), p. 34.

Chapter Thirty-One
Egypt: The Struggle for Independence

The spirit of nationalism and the desire for independence among the Egyptians increased in intensity even though their delegation (Wafd) to the Paris Peace Conference (1919–1920) did not accomplish much. The fire, once started, would not die down. For their part, the British were in a quandary. They did not want to relinquish their hold on Egypt, but they realized that the war had changed things to the point that they could not settle the problems of Egypt in London as peacefully as they were used to doing.

The British concluded that some sort of a compromise was necessary. In December 1919, they did what was to become a habit of theirs in periods of unrest between the two great wars—they sent a commission under Lord Milner to study and report. The Wafdists, on the other hand, set an example that was followed by most Arab leaders in Palestine until World War II— they boycotted the commission.

PARTIAL INDEPENDENCE

As a result of the Milner Commission's report, the British, on February 28, 1922, unilaterally terminated the protectorate and declared Egypt's independence. Fuad assumed the title of king. Thus Egypt became the first Arabic-speaking state to achieve at least partial independence. Not much actually changed under the new arrangement. The four points "absolutely reserved to the discretion of His Britannic Majesty's Government" were: (1) the security of imperial communication in Egypt, (2) the defense of Egypt, (3) the protection of foreign interests and minorities, and (4) control over the Sudan.

In 1923, King Fuad accepted a constitution that provided for a bicameral legislature, which granted great power to the king. He could dissolve the parliament, appoint and dismiss ministers, or rule by decree if he wished. He had veto power, which could be overruled only by a two-thirds majority. He was commander in chief of the armed forces and could appoint two-fifths of the members of the senate. At the same time the constitution was proclaimed there was also an announcement of general elections. Under the general amnesty proclamation, Sa'd Zaghlul returned to Egypt and in the election of January 1924, the Wafd Party won a landslide—199 seats against 27. Zaghlul was made prime minister and immediately pressed for the revision of the unilateral declaration of independence. He called for the complete sovereignty of Egypt and the Sudan. .

The Wafd Party dominated the political scene in Egypt until 1952. It had a wide base of support and was very popular. The Wafd not only negotiated but also led in strikes, riots, and even terrorist activities. During most of the time before 1952, it dominated the parliament. The premiership, the appointment to which was a prerogative of the king, usually went to an anti-Wafdist. Consequently, the cabinet and the parliament were at loggerheads and the winner of this conflict was usually the king or the British or both. There were other political parties in Egypt. One was the Liberal Constitutional Party, founded in 1922. It usually represented the aristocracy and landlords. Another was the Union Party, founded in 1925. It represented the interests of the palace. A third was the Peoples' Party, founded in 1930. This was formed on its founder's personality and did not have much of a following. In 1932, the Wafd Party split and the insurgents formed the Sa'dist Party. All of these parties were more moderate than the Wafd and were more willing to collaborate with the British or the king or both.

Nationalists in general neglected Egypt's economic and social conditions because they spent all their energies in trying to oust the British. Indeed, they tended to blame everything on the British and to believe that if the British left Egypt through one door, progress and prosperity would enter through another. Britain, on the other hand, was still interested in controlling the route to India, and in safeguarding foreign economic interests in Egypt. Aside from the needs of the empire, the British did not assume much responsibility except in maintaining law and order. Heavy taxes were imposed on the masses and small landowners. Since Egyptian long-staple cotton was the best in the world, more and more land went into cotton plantations to supply the needs of Britain's textile industry. In twenty years, from 1917 to 1937, the population of Egypt rose by a staggering 25 percent; the amount of land under cultivation, however, remained constant, and consequently the standard of living declined.

The riots of previous years were repeated in 1924, and on November 19 of the same year Sir Lee Stack, the British commander-in-chief of the Egyptian army and governor-general of the Sudan, was assassinated. The

British met this incident with strong reprisals and demanded punishment of the culprits, an apology, and an indemnity of $1,500,000. Furthermore, they forbade political demonstrations and ordered the withdrawal of Egyptian troops from the Sudan. They also demanded that British advisors be retained in the finance, justice, and interior departments. Perhaps most stringent of all was the threat to extend the area of cultivation in the Sudan's Gezira region. Such an act would channel Nile water for irrigation and decrease the flow into Egypt. Without the Nile there would be no Egypt. Since the flow of the Nile can be controlled from the Sudan, Egypt has always had a great interest in the government of the Sudan.

THE ANGLO-EGYPTIAN SUDAN

During 1881, Muhammad Ahmad had claimed to be the Mahdi (messiah) sent to deliver the Muslims. This started the famous Mahdi movement, which embroiled the Sudan for a number of years. Because of the 'Urabi revolt, the situation in Egypt was too chaotic for anyone (British or Egyptian) to contain the Mahdi. Meanwhile, his power grew and the Anglo-Egyptian garrison in Khartoum was in danger. In 1884, Lord Cromer sent General Gordon to evacuate Khartoum, but the latter delayed the operation and was cut down by the Mahdi's forces. For over a decade, the Mahdi had control of all the Sudan.[1] In 1896, Lord Kitchener took Dongola, the headquarters of the Mahdi, and two years later routed him in the battle of Omdurman. This led to an agreement between Britain and Egypt that is commonly called the Condominium. According to this document, which was signed on January 19, 1899, the Sudan was to be ruled by a governor-general chosen by the British but appointed by the khedive. Laws of the Sudan were to be made by the governor-general and the laws of Egypt were not valid in the territory. While Egyptian goods were free from import duties, no power was allowed to establish a consulate in the Sudan without the permission of the British government. Slavery was abolished and the Brussels Act of 1890 governed the import, sale, and the manufacture of munitions and liquors. Henceforth, the region was called Anglo-Egyptian Sudan, but as might be expected the voice of Egypt was even weaker in the Sudan than it was in Egypt.

Since the Condominium had already recognized the legitimacy of Egyptian interests in the Sudan, Zaghlul considered the British demand of 1924 that Egypt withdraw its troops from the Sudan outrageous. Many leading Egyptians looked upon the further threat of diverting the Nile's waters for the irrigation of the Gezira as an act tantamount to a declaration of war. In rejecting the ultimatum, Zaghlul resigned and Ziwar Pasha became prime minister. He then accepted the ultimatum. The British, however, implemented all the points of the ultimatum except that concerning the irrigation of the Gezira. As a result of the riots of 1924, the British got a stronger hold on Egyptian affairs, and Egypt lost all influence in the affairs of the Sudan.

[1]See p. 193.

EGYPTIAN INDEPENDENCE

Sa'd Zaghlul died in 1927, and leadership of the Wafd Party went to Nahhas Pasha. The change of leadership, however, did not make negotiations between the British and the Wafd any smoother. Basic problems remained. The British wanted a bilateral agreement that continued British dominance, and the Wafd wanted evacuation of British troops from Egypt and control of the Sudan. Negotiations ended in 1930 and were not resumed for five years. The position of the Wafd was weakened by the death of Zaghlul, the existence of other parties, and the open hostility of the king. Despite this weakened position, the Wafd won the elections again in 1929. King Fuad, rather than appoint a Wafdist prime minister, dissolved the parliament, appointed Sidqi Pasha, the leader of the Peoples' Party, as premier, and revoked the constitution of 1923. In the new constitution that Fuad promulgated in 1930, he gave himself more power and introduced a two-grade indirect voting system. As a result of these measures, he and Sidqi Pasha ruled without effective opposition until 1934.

The Italian invasion of Ethiopia in 1935 changed the complexion of Anglo-Egyptian relationships. The British were all the more intent on the defense of the Suez, because they were afraid of Italian propaganda in Egypt against the British. On the whole, the British were anxious to reach some sort of a bilateral agreement with the Egyptians. The strongman, Sidqi Pasha, had resigned the year before because of ill health; and the Wafdists, together with the other parties, did not hide their dislike of the constitution of 1930. In 1935, following the advice of the British, Kind Fuad suspended the 1930 constitution; but against their advice he reinstated the 1923 constitution. Accordingly, elections were held in 1935 and the Wafd won again. Fuad died in April of 1936, and his sixteen-year-old son, Faruq, was proclaimed king. The Egyptians mourned Fuad sincerely and received Faruq very enthusiastically, thereby presenting a paradox to the observers of the Egyptian scene. On the one hand, the Egyptians showed a high regard for the institution of monarchy and the person of the king; but on the other hand, they repeatedly defeated the palace party and elected the antimonarchical Wafd.

By 1936, the Wafd Party was older, mellower, and corruptible. The four years of Sidqi "dictatorship" had taught Nahhas Pasha and the Wafd Party that politics was the art of the possible and not the demand of the absolute. Moreover, Egyptians of all parties were also apprehensive about the Italian threat and did not think that Italian masters could be preferable to British. Events had prepared both the British and the Egyptians to negotiate.

The British entered negotiations with Nahhas Pasha, the new prime minister, and on August 26, 1936, signed a treaty of alliance recognizing Egypt as a sovereign state. After solemnly stating in the first article that "the military occupation of Egypt by the forces of His Majesty the King [of England] and Emperor is terminated," it goes on in sixteen additional articles to define the nature of Egypt's independence. On the positive side, as far as the Egyptians were concerned, were provisions such as the exchange of ambassadors between the two countries, the possibility of Egyptian membership in the League of Nations, the abolition of capitulations, the return of Egyptian troops to the Sudan, and unrestricted Egyptian immigration to the Sudan. On the negative side, however, were articles that limited the sovereignty of Egypt. These articles implied that Britain was responsible for the defense of Egypt, and held Egypt responsible for putting at the disposal of Britain in time of war "all the facilities and assistance . . . including the use of . . . ports, aerodromes, and means of communication." Furthermore, Britain was permitted to station not more than 10,000 troops and 400 pilots in the Suez Canal area for its defense. The agreement was for twenty years.

Britain had not given up much, but the Egyptians had received more than they expected. Consequently, the Wafd Party accepted the treaty and the Egyptian parliament ratified it on December 22, 1936. On May 8, 1937, the capitulations were abolished, and on May 26 of the same year Egypt was admitted to the League of Nations. For a time, Nahhas Pasha, as prime minister and regent for the young king, had absolute control of the country. But Faruq came of age in 1937, and once more the old rivalry between the palace and the Wafd started. The king dismissed Nahhas Pasha and chose the non-Wafdist Mahmud Pasha, who had to cope with a Wafdist parliament. The Wafd Party had lost a good deal of its virility and influence over the years. Nahhas Pasha did not have the charisma of Zaghlul. Among the leaders of the Wafd who had enjoyed positions of leadership, and had developed vested interests, some had become corrupt and others just old and tired. Furthermore, they had lost their anti-British zeal that had made them so popular. Later, young nationalists were to denounce the treaty of 1936 as a "shotgun marriage" and blamed the Wafd for it.

THE SOCIAL AND INTELLECTUAL ATMOSPHERE

Egyptian men of affairs were preoccupied with the British between the two wars and did not pay much attention to social reform. Neither were the British any more interested in social or economic reforms than they had been before the war. Indeed, the British had unilaterally relinquished any responsibility for the development of Egypt in 1920 and by agreement with Egypt in 1936, while continuing to occupy the country. Nevertheless, changes did occur by force of circumstance and without conscious planning on the part of anyone in particular.

During World War I, inflation and shortages of consumer goods hurt the villagers and town people; but in Cairo and Alexandria and other cities where the soldiers were stationed, there was a business boom. The urban population made huge profits; farmers in search of work and food rushed to the cities. Land prices rose in the cities and housing rents rose from 60 percent to 100 percent. Cotton was in great demand and construction went on at a rapid pace. All of this brought a nouveau riche class into being, which joined the old wealthy class and developed a political front made up of landlords, businessmen, and professionals. These groups united to protect their economic gains and, at the same time, to wrest power from Britain.

The war needs brought some industrialization. In 1920, the Misr Bank was established; this bank gradually developed an industrial combine with subsidiaries in cotton, silk, woolens, cigarettes, soap, shipping, insurance, motion pictures, and other enterprises. In 1922, the Egyptian Federation of Industries was established and by 1937 it had some 430 members. A new commercial middle class was created that prospered and allied itself with the less prosperous but more articulate middle class made up of white-collar workers, the intelligentsia, and civil servants. This commercial class did not try to destroy the landed gentry but married into it and formed a governing class that comprised about 20 percent of the population. The remaining 80 percent of the people lived in the rural areas; 90 percent of these were illiterate. Notwithstanding the growth of the Egyptian middle class, it is important to note that ownership of the largest trading companies, manufacturing firms, and public utilities was in the hands of foreigners. In addition, the commercial class as such acted as agents for the landed gentry or for foreign business interests and thus was entirely dependent on the vicissitudes of the world economy.

The new industries created new needs, and the satisfaction of these needs changed the Egyptians' values and life-style. The press, radio, and telephone, as well as the new industries, demanded a new type of education. Between the two wars and up to the revolution of 1952 there were two types of education, each independent of the other and each performing in a closed circuit of its own. There was the venerable Azhar University, which represented the older, religious type of education. Most of the shaykhs of Azhar rejected modernism and did not see any need for fundamental change. Even men like Muhammad Abduh, who believed in the necessity of institutional change to fit new situations, did not intend any basic theological reconstruction. The Azharites did not debate doctrine. The modern schools, on the other hand, were hostile to Azhar and developed a system of values all their own. It is not that they rejected Islam, but they imported both the content and method of education from the West and were insulated from the influences of Azhar and the latter's insistence on the Shari'a. Thus Western ways were not slow in coming to Egypt. Men wore European clothes, women appeared in public without the veil, European laws became popular, and child marriage was abolished. As the nouveaux riches became more westernized, the shaykhs became more rigid and people like Abduh, who were trying to steer a middle course, were forgotten.

At the time Egypt declared its independence in 1936 there were, intellectually and religiously speaking, four distinct groups. With two of these groups—the ultraconservatives of Azhar and the moderate reform school of Abduh—we are already familiar. The third was the militant Muslim groups and the fourth, the proponents of a secular state.

THE MUSLIM BROTHERHOOD

At least three factors were responsible for the rise of the militant Muslim groups that wielded great influence in Egypt until well after World War II. One was the colonial occupation by the British and the humiliation devout

Muslims felt in being ruled by Christians. Another was the rapid seculariza-tion of the Egyptian educated and middle classes, and the corresponding deterioration of Muslim laws and institutions. A third was the threat of Turkey and, as it appeared to Egyptian eyes, the complete de-Islamization of that country. The abolition of the caliphate by the Turks so disturbed the shaykhs of Azhar that they called a conference on the caliphate in May 1926. Of the thirty-eight delegates, one-third were Egyptians. The conference was inconclusive, but it revealed the seriousness of the situation to Egyptians and other Muslims.

The militant Muslims were spiritual heirs of the fundamentalist Wah-habis of Arabia and the militant Jamal al-Din al-Afghani. By far the most important, influential, and largest of the militant groups organized between the two wars in Egypt was the Muslim Brotherhood, *al-Ikhwan al-Muslimin*. It was started in the city of Ismailia on the Canal in 1928 by a twenty-two-year-old school teacher, Hasan al-Banna. Ismailia not only was a town where British military forces were garrisoned but also the center for a large num-ber of displaced peasant families and unemployed Egyptian laborers. Both the British military and the growing poverty of the lower classes were fertile ground for Islamic militancy in the 1920s and 1930s. Al-Banna and six young companions started the movement with nothing but a strong faith in the sufficiency of Islam and complete dedication to the cause. In a relatively short time it had become a very strong force in Egypt and other Muslim countries, and was still a power to be reckoned with in the 1980s. In its missionary zeal and organization it was similar to the medieval Ismai'li group called the Brethren of Sincerity. In its militancy and method it had copied another Ismai'li organization, the Assassins.

The energetic and capable young leader of the Brotherhood was not a Shi'i like the Isma'ilis but a strict Sunni brought up in a family that belonged, like the Wahhabis, to the fundamentalist Hanbali school. He borrowed, how-ever, the Isma'ili table of organization. Hasan al-Banna, as the absolute leader of the Brotherhood, was called "Guide General." A select group of missionaries who worked under him were called devotees, the same name used by the Isma'ilis. The general headquarters of the movement was in Cairo, and from these modern offices the supreme leader administered the varied programs of the Brotherhood.

The Muslim Brotherhood was a militant group that believed in the sufficiency and supremacy of Islam and in the literal interpretation of the Koran and the Sunna. It worked for the revival of the principle of jihad, holy war. Unlike the Wahhabis, however, it believed in reform and in the utilization of certain Western methods in education, industry and technol-ogy. Unlike Abduh, the Brotherhood did not think that a restatement of Islamic doctrine was necessary. It was strongly against the secularization of Muslim life and worked for the reinstatement of the laws of the Koran. It was pan-Islamic and preached military preparedness on the part of all Mus-lims. "A strong army," the Brotherhood proclaimed, "is more important than prayer or fasting." It emphasized government by Allah for Muslims, with Koranic tolerance for the minorities, provided they stay loyal to the government of Islam.

The above objectives and ideas were implemented and taught through diverse means. Branches of the Brotherhood in different cities and towns of Egypt conducted evening schools for adults and lectured on Islam and contemporary Egypt. They also opened day schools for both boys and girls. In contrast to the ultraconservatives, the Brotherhood believed in education for women, though never in coeducation. They did charitable works in towns, had dispensaries for the care of the sick, and distributed free food for the needy. Their missionaries preached in mosques. Each member was enjoined to forswear evil in his own life as well as forbid it in others. This important injunction of the Shari'a covers such things as gambling, dancing, theater and movies, and drinking. The Brotherhood also had a youth organization. Boys up to the age of about sixteen joined the *Kashshaf*, which was something like the Boy Scouts and had some of the same activities. After that, young men joined a paramilitary organization that conducted secret drills and war games.

The membership of the Brotherhood was kept a secret, and no accurate statistics are available. It is estimated that by 1939 the Brotherhood had about 500 branches with a membership of about 500,000. By 1953, the estimate was 2,000 branches and 2,000,000 members. What made the Brotherhood formidable was not so much numbers but the fact that it was full of fervor and was totally commited to its cause. Equally secret was the Brotherhood's source of income. The early members were mostly poor students, but in six years they were able to move their headquarters to Cairo and widen their base of membership. They operated a printing press and other enterprises such as the Islamic Transaction Company, the Ikhwan Spinning and Weaving Company, and the Commercial and Engineering Company.

The slogan of the Muslim Brotherhood was "God is most great, thanks be to God," and their emblem was a Koran between two swords. Between the two wars, the Brotherhood was like an iceberg in that most of its activities were underground. After World War II it became more open and clashed head-on with other militant groups. The consequences of this clash will be discussed in the next chapter.

THE PROPONENTS OF SECULARISM

Those in Egypt who favored the establishment of a secularist state had no organization such as the Muslim Brotherhood. Perhaps they did not feel the need of one because they were in the majority. Furthermore, the proponents of secularism were individualistic enough not to be doctrinaire and would not undergo the discipline of forming an ideological organization. Some were agnostics and did not care about Islam or any other religion. Others were devout Muslims who believed that religion was a personal matter and should be kept separate from government. Whether agnostics or believers, they had two things in common: First, they believed in the separation of religion and state and the freedom of religion within the state. Second, they believed in the importance of Islamic culture in the life of Egypt. Even the Christian Copts adhered to this concept. The identification of Islam with all other aspects of life was so complete that for an atheist to say he was not a Muslim was tantamount to confessing that he was not an Egyptian. The religious and the secularist groups cooperated. Some of the secularists ignored Islam altogether, and some practiced it privately but did not believe in imposing it on the nation.

In the period between the two wars, perhaps the person most influential in articulating the ideas of the secularists was Taha Husayn (b. 1889). This blind genius, educator, and humanitarian was educated at Azhar and in France. In a sense, he rejected both the religious fundamentalism of Azhar and the colonialists' desire to dominate the Middle East as he witnessed it in France. For the culture and the civilization of the West, however, his love and admiration knew no bounds. While in France, he wrote about the North African historian Ibn Khaldun.

In 1919 he returned to Egypt with a French wife and spent his energies in education. He wrote novels, histories, biographies, and treatises on education. His most important books, however, were *Pre-Islamic Poetry*, published in 1926, and *The Future of Culture in Egypt*, published in 1938. The first shocked the Muslim world and branded him as a heretic. The second laid some of the intellectual foundations of the modern Egyptian secularist state.

In his *Pre-Islamic Poetry*, Taha Husayn applied modern critical methods of scholarship to a number of poems known as the *mu'alliqat* and doubted whether they were pre-Islamic at all.[2] This caused a great uproar and opposition. The religious community was afraid that the application of critical methods to any ancient text might encourage the critical study of the Koran and Hadith and cast doubt on the authority of the scriptures. Furthermore, the place of the Arabic language is considered to be so holy and so sacrosanct in the study of the Koran that any tampering with it might destroy the faith. Many books were written in opposition, and Husayn's book had to be withdrawn. But Taha Husayn was perhaps the first Muslim to encourage the application of the critical methods to the study of the Koran.

The Future of Culture in Egypt was written to present a set of goals for the country, which had won its independence in 1936. Taha Husayn idealized the agreement of 1936 as a sign of European trust in Egypt and an Egyptian promise to follow in the footsteps of Europe. Western civilization, according to him, reached a high pinnacle when it set reason free to direct man's actions, and set religion free to inspire man to action. Egypt must use its independence as a means to achieve this high goal. He believed that Egypt was part of Europe by its connection with Greco-Roman civilization. He was very much like the Turkish sociologist, Ziya Gökalp, when he said that Egyptians should take the civilization of Europe, but not its religion, and graft their Egyptian culture to it. It is evident that language is fundamental to nationalism. The Turks, as we have seen, rejected Arabic and Persian; and the Persians rejected Arabic and Turkish. Taha Husayn exalted Arabic not for the sake of religion but for the sake of the nation. He went so far as to volunteer to help improve the poor Arabic that the Christians used in their ritual so that Egyptian Christians might worship in good Arabic.

[2]See p. 26.

Another prominent secularist was Ali Abd al-Raziq (1888–1966). In the early 1920s, the Islamic world was in an uproar because the Turks had exiled the Ottoman sultan and abolished the caliphate. Abd al-Raziq wrote a book in 1925 in which he not only stated that the caliphate had been harmful to Islam, but claimed that Muhammad had not instituted it for his followers. He denied that there was such a thing as an "Islamic government."

According to his view, Muhammad had started a community (*ummah*) and not a government. Muhammad was a prophet and not a political leader. Furthermore, forms of government are of no concern to God. They are worldly affairs and should be judged by human reason. Consequently it was not necessary for all Muslims to be members of one state, or to have the same form of government, or to be ruled by a single caliph.

These ideas created so much controversy that both Abd al-Raziq and Taha Husayn were asked by the Azhar shaykhs to recant their blasphemy. While Taha Husayn did recant some of his ideas under pressure, Abd al-Raziq held his ground. As a result he lost his judgeship and spent the rest of his life in obscurity until his death in 1966.

EGYPT IN WORLD WAR II

The Egyptians went through World War II with a limited political independence and with varied ideologies. The concerned and articulate among them, from the agnostic secularist to the fundamentalist Muslim, thought in terms of loyalty to Egypt or to Islam or to both. They did not consider themselves "Arabs" and therefore many did not involve themselves in the affairs of the Fertile Crescent. The events in the last years of the war, the spectre of Zionism, and the anti-isolationism of the young Egyptian leaders changed the situation considerably and placed Egypt at the center of Arab nationalism.

In 1939, three years after the Anglo-Egyptian treaty, Britain had not evacuated Egypt as it had promised. When the war came in September, the British used the provisions of the treaty and sent more troops into the country. During the war, the Egyptians did nothing to sabotage the British war effort. But neither did the government bow to the British demand to declare war on the Axis powers. They believed that the Axis powers were going to win and did not want to do anything to antagonize the victors. Such passive resistance was not acceptable to the British. It is one of the ironies of history that in 1942 the British surrounded the royal Abdin Palace in Cairo with tanks and told King Faruq either to appoint the Wafdist Nahhas Pasha, an old anti-British protagonist, as prime minister, or leave the country. If Faruq had rejected the British ultimatum he probably would have become the greatest hero in modern Egyptian history. But he submitted and appointed the formerly anti-British Nahhas Pasha. The latter then chose to cooperate with Britain.

Nahhas Pasha held office until 1944, but apparently nothing was done to check the corruption within the government or to ease the tension between the king and his prime minister. When the danger of German victory was lifted by the defeat of General Rommel at al-Alamayn and the landing of Americans in North Africa, Nahhas Pasha had served his usefulness to the British. King Faruq took advantage of the situation and dismissed him. He chose the anti-Wafd leader of the Sa'd Party, Ahmad Maher, to form a government. On February 24, 1945, Maher was assassinated by a young Egyptian. Nukrashi Pasha, who was second in command of the Sa'd Party, succeeded him. Two days later he declared war on Germany and Japan. Egypt also later became a charter member of the United Nations.

SOCIAL AND POLITICAL CONDITIONS

The small but growing middle class in Egypt was increasingly dissatisfied with the rulers of the country during and after World War II. Throughout the century between 1850 and 1950, the main spokesmen for Egyptian nationalism constituted approximately one-half of 1 percent of the population. These people were served by the small landowners and their families who were educated enough to work in the bureaucracy. The peasants, small shopkeepers, and minor officials, who comprised nearly 80 percent of the population, were asked to work and left to shift for themselves.

Egypt, like all victims of imperialism, had to go through two revolutions: one for independence and the other for social reform. It is understandable, therefore, why during the last half of the nineteenth century the cry for national independence became the hallmark of all nationalist groups and the most important plank in the program of every political party. What neither these political parties nor the king, who was engaged in a private struggle against them, perceived was the growing number of educated but landless Egyptians who wanted reform while they were struggling for independence.

The Wafd Party, which had come to power and popularity on the program of national independence, had become middle aged and content without adding any planks for reform to its program. There was corruption, graft, and high living among the privileged who succeeded each other in forming governments. The king's preoccupation was to set one political group against the other and reap the lion's share of power and privilege for himself.

THE FREE OFFICERS' CLUB

In 1936, when Egypt became partially independent, the army, which had been the exclusive preserve of the privileged class, was opened to the sons of the lower middle class. Young men were attracted to it because the army provided a good education and opportunity for advancement. Among the young men who attended the military school was Gamal Abd al-Nasser, the son of a postal clerk, born in 1918. As a student in high school he had taken part in numerous demonstrations for independence. As a young officer, he had regularly gathered a number of his officer friends to discuss Egypt's problems. These young men were the heirs of the ordeals that Egypt had experienced for a century. They had read about Muhammad Ali, had discussed the rise and fall of 'Urabi, Zaghlul, and other nationalists, had studied the ideas of Muhammad Abduh, and had been influenced by the revolution in Russia. Among these officers, at least two were communist-oriented, four or five were members of the Muslim Brotherhood, and the rest were nationalists.

It is quite likely that these young officers would have spent their time in discussion groups had it not been for the war against Israel in 1948. Nasser and his friends were in Palestine during the last stages of the 1948 war against Israel. The weapons they had received were faulty due to corruption and graft in the high echelons of their government. Their discussion was about the predicament of Egypt rather than the war with Israel. It was the defeat in Palestine which convinced the young Egyptian officers that the first order of business was to cleanse Egypt of corruption and graft. When they returned to Egypt, Nasser formed the Secret Free Officers' Society, whose purpose was not merely discussion but action.

THE WAFD PARTY AND THE BRITISH

While the young officers were planning their revolution, the Egyptian government under Nahhas Pasha, the veteran leader of the Wafd, was pressing the British to evacuate the Suez Canal zone and to cede the Sudan to Egypt. The British, as usual, were moving so slowly that to Egyptian eyes they were not moving at all. Britain claimed that the Treaty of 1936, according to one of its articles, could not be revised for twenty years, which meant that they had to wait until 1956. On the question of the Sudan, the British believed that the Sudanese had to be consulted before any decisions could be reached. Negotiations dragged on until 1951, when Nahhas Pasha, perhaps encouraged by the example of Dr. Mosaddeq of Iran, unilaterally cancelled the Treaty of 1936 and proclaimed Faruq "king of the Sudan." He then encouraged Egyptians to harass and kill British soldiers in the canal zone and everywhere else in Egypt. Egyptian laborers in the canal zone went on a general strike and guerrilla attacks against British forces became worse by the day. When the British retaliated in January 1952 by fighting the police and declaring martial law in villages under their control, angry Egyptians in Cairo moved toward the center of the town. The government allowed them to proceed to where the Western businesses and buildings were concentrated. They burned and looted theaters, hotels, restaurants, and shops. By that time, there was indiscriminate destruction and when it was finished some 12,000 Egyptians were homeless. It was reported that the Muslim Brotherhood had a major role in this anti-European program. The Wafd Party's strategy had backfired. Nahhas Pasha resigned and for some months there was a succession of unstable governments.

Chapter Thirty-Two
The New Egypt

THE REVOLUTION OF 1952 AND THE NEW REGIME

A new Egypt came into being as a result of the political revolution of July 23, 1952. For the first time since the conquest of Egypt by Rome, Egyptians— not Peninsula Arabs, Mamluks, Turks, or British—controlled the affairs of the country. After years of struggle for independence, the 1952 revolution initiated far-reaching social and economic reforms. For the first time in modern Egyptian history a revolution was launched not just with antiforeign slogans but with promises to purge corruption and graft. This revolution, carried out by a small band of young officers, sons of lower-middle-class Egyptians, was in the context of Egyptian history and had its roots in events that have been described in previous chapters.

The Coup d'Etat

For some time, the Free Officers were laying plans; and on July 23, 1952, they struck. Because the Free Officers were all young (the average age was 34) and unknown, they had arranged with a respected and popular older officer, General Muhammad Nagib, to act as leader. The general was told of the plans rather late and tentatively accepted the offer. It is said that in the early hours of July 23, Nasser telephoned Nagib and asked him to go to the revolutionary headquarters. "If we fail," Nasser is supposed to have

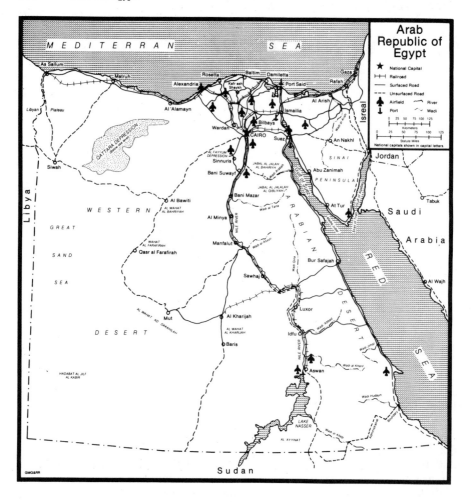

said, "you have suppressed us. If we succeed, you are the leader of the new Egypt." Between one o'clock in the morning and noon, Nasser took the capital without resistance. Faruq hoped for British interference but nothing happened.

It is evident that the young officers did not have a prearranged plan for a social and economic revolution. They wanted to purge corruption and believed that an energetic civilian rule would somehow be established. Foremost among the corrupt leaders, in their view, was the king, who was forced to abdicate in favor of his infant son on July 26. Faruq left Egypt permanently, and a year later Egypt was proclaimed a republic. What disappointed Nasser and his friends was the fact that the Egyptian people did not rise in enthusiasm. "The vanguard performed its task," says Nasser in his *Philosophy of the Revolution,* "it stormed the walls of the fort of tyranny . . . and stood by expecting the mass formations to arrive at their ultimate object." But all they got was chaos, dissension, and idleness. Then it was that they decided to stay in power and improvise policies as they went along.

The Anglo-Egyptian Agreements of 1953 and 1954

The young officers had not come to power and popularity because of anti-British slogans. Perhaps because of this they were able to negotiate with the British in an objective atmosphere. With the able assistance of General Nagib, who was half Sudanese himself, the Egyptian government was able to bring all the Sudanese factions into the Egyptian camp. The Sudanese were willing to cooperate, because the new Egyptian government was flexible and more understanding of Sudanese nationalism. On February 12, 1953, Egypt and Britain agreed to grant self-government to the Sudan and a plebiscite was to be held within three years to determine the Sudan's relationship to Egypt. The agreement was a great accomplishment for the new Egyptian government because it had achieved accommodation with Britain and close cooperation with the Sudanese nationalists.

The next problem was the cooperation of the Suez Canal zone. Here, too, negotiations were carried out in a relaxed atmosphere. The new situation had finally convinced the British that it was no longer worthwhile for them to maintain a base at the Suez Canal zone. In 1954 Britain agreed to evacuate the canal zone. The only condition was that they be allowed to reoccupy the zone in case of an attack on Turkey or on any of the Arab countries.

The amicable solution of the Anglo-Egyptian conflict over the Sudan and the Suez Canal zone made it possible for the young officers to direct their attention to the internal problems of Egypt. It was the intention of the young officers to purge the government and establish an "honest" civilian rule. In good faith they chose a former prime minister, Ali Maher, who had a reputation for honesty and progressivism, to form a government. But this did not prove satisfactory. The older men were too conservative to condone radical change. As most of them had tremendous vested interests in landholdings, they could not be expected to carry out meaningful reforms. So, willy-nilly, the young officers formed the Revolutionary Command Council (RCC) and took over the government, with General Nagib as prime minister. The RCC dismissed some 800 civilians from important posts in the government and retired 100 older military officers. It banned all parties but the Muslim Brotherhood.

Having purged the government of undesirable personnel, the RCC felt its way, rather gingerly at first, in the role of social revolutionaries. The sine qua non of social change in the Middle East was land reform. Except for the landlords themselves, practically everyone was in favor of it. The more conservative Muslim Brotherhood believed that the maximum landholding should be limited to 500 *feddans*, or acres, and everything in excess should be divided among the peasants. Radical groups in Egypt wanted the maximum to be set at 50 to 100 feddans. The RCC settled on 200. In Egypt, where the yield per acre is high, 200 feddans was more than adequate, hence only very large landowners were affected. As the vast landholdings of the king were expropriated and all of the land was not distributed, the government became the largest landlord in Egypt.

The Struggle for Power

The new regime was not without enemies and its decision to become revolutionary gained it some more. The enemies of the regime may be divided into four categories: First, the old politicians, who were denied the right of political activity; second, the Muslim Brotherhood, in whose eyes the RCC was too secular and radical; third, the communists, in whose eyes the RCC was neither radical nor doctrinaire enough; fourth, the rich landlords, who were dispossessed by the land reform law of 1952. These groups had money and the support of many young Egyptians who believed more in the ideals of parliamentary democracy, which the RCC had violated, than they did in social and economic reform. The only thing, however, that prevented these opposition groups from moving against the regime was the lack of a common issue. This issue was provided in February 1954.

General Nagib, it will be recalled, had been brought in to be the figurehead of the new regime. Actual power was in the hands of the RCC, headed by Nasser. But General Nagib had become extremely popular among the Egyptians and was recognized as the real leader of the revolution. He wanted more power as prime minister of the country than the single vote allotted to him in the thirteen-man RCC would allow. In February 1954, the RCC announced the resignation of General Nagib. This created an uproar which the RCC did not expect. The opposition groups rallied around the general and demonstrated on his behalf. The RCC did an unorthodox thing—perhaps the only way open to it—by reinstating General Nagib.

Meanwhile, Nasser was working behind the scenes to isolate Nagib and to reinstate the power of the RCC. By April, a general strike materialized in support of the RCC, the army staged a strike, and demonstrations took place in the streets. The RCC "elevated" General Nagib to the presidency and made Nasser the prime minister of Egypt. In October 1954, a member of the Muslim Brotherhood made an unsuccessful attempt on the life of Nasser. This gave the RCC the necessary excuse to outlaw the Brotherhood, put General Nagib under house arrest, and to purge its own organization of communist and Brotherhood members. By the end of 1954, Nasser was the acknowledged leader of the revolution, and he promised that by 1956 he would present the country with a new constitution.

NASSER AND THE ARAB WORLD

Any nation involved in a serious program of economic, political, and social revolution needs a certain degree of isolation and noninvolvement in external affairs in order to put its house in order and establish the foundations of its revolution. In the Middle East, the Arabic-speaking countries have difficulty focusing their thinking and limiting their activities to a single country. As we have seen, it was relatively easy for Turkey and Iran to limit their nationalism to the Turks and Iranians respectively. It was not so easy for Egypt. While it is true that the Free Officers had planned the revolution to free Egypt, it must be remembered that part of the planning was done while they were fighting in Palestine in defense of the "Arab cause." By language and religion, they were tied to the countries of the Fertile Crescent and North Africa. While it is true that until the beginning of World War II, Egyptian nationalists did not consider themselves to be Arabs, the situation had changed drastically since the war. After all, Britain did use Nahhas Pasha to establish the League of the Arab States, Cairo did become the headquarters of the league, and the Egyptians did fight in Palestine against Israel.

It was not only nationalism, however, which caused Egypt to become involved in the affairs of other Arabic-speaking countries. Economic and historical factors played an important role in shaping Nasser's policy. From the time of the pharaohs, the commercial and cultural route connecting Egypt with the outside world lay through Sinai and the Fertile Crescent. The fate of the Crescent in a large measure determined the fate of Egypt. Israel, established athwart this route, cut this historic link and was considered to be a threat to Egypt. The moderate General Nagib spoke as though he would not have any objection to the existence of Israel provided a link was established between Egypt and the Fertile Crescent through the southern Negev.

In addition to the above considerations, Egypt was drawn into the affairs of the Arabic-speaking countries by Nasser's popularity among the nationalists of these countries. Indeed, Nasser could not remain indifferent even if he so wanted. Egypt was the first Arab country after the defeat in Palestine to purge itself and to stand on its own feet. Nasser was at the center of this revolution and was a hero to the nationalists of the Arabic-speaking countries. Egypt became the model country and Nasser the model leader.

In his *Philosophy of the Revolution,* Nasser saw the role of the Egyptian revolution in three concentric circles. The innermost was the Arab circle, which was "as much a part of us as we are a part of it. . . ." Second was the African circle, "in which fate has placed us. . . ," and the struggle which it was going through "will affect us whether we want or not." The third was the Islamic circle, "with which we are tied by bonds which are not only forged by religious faith but also tightened by the facts of history." Nasser was perhaps the first Egyptian nationalist leader who tried to combine the anticipated concepts of pan-Arabism and pan-Islamism. Pan-Arabism rejected the Islamic faith, or any faith for that matter, as a basis for nationalism, while pan-Islamism refused to identify Islam with Arabism. The enmity between the pan-Islamic Muslim Brotherhood, which is not without strength in the Arab world, and the secular pan-Arabists makes it premature to judge whether such a fusion is workable or not.

Nasser was also the first Egyptian leader to connect the destiny of Egypt with the continent of Africa. This was an uncharted course without much historical precedence. What was important in Nasser's "circle" thesis, however, was the circle that he omitted—the *Egyptian circle.* During the Palestine War in 1948, Nasser and his friends "were fighting in Palestine but [their] dreams were in Egypt." By 1955, Palestine, Egypt, and the other Arab countries had merged into one "Arab Nation" in the thinking of pan-Arabists like Nasser. Nevertheless, *The Philosophy of the Revolution* implied, and Nasser's subsequent actions left no doubt, that the center of all the circles is Cairo. Perhaps the Africans and non-Arab Muslims did not pay too much attention to such an implication, but the point was not lost to the Arabic-speaking peoples in general. The Iraqis and Syrians were particularly incensed, because each group considered its own capital, Baghdad or Damascus, the center of pan-Arabism and/or pan-Islamism.

The Suez Canal Crisis

The events that led to the nationalization of the Suez Canal Company in 1956 were partially forced upon Egypt by the outside. One of the first was the creation of the Baghdad Pact in 1955. The fact that Iraq was a member of it was considered both an affront and a threat to Nasser. Nasser believed that the American-sponsored Baghdad Pact was a new form of Western imperialism. The fact that Iraq was being armed by the United States also alarmed Egypt. Not only was there nationalistic rivalry between the two countries, but Iraq, with its monarchy, landed aristocracy, and conservativism also could become a center of opposition to Nasser. So he directed the full force of his propaganda against the pact.

Furthermore, a number of Israeli raids across the Egyptian border were costly to the Egyptian army and increased Nasser's desire to strengthen his army. He tried to procure arms from the West but was not successful. The United States would not sell him arms partly because of Israel and partly because of Egypt's neutralism and its recognition of the Peoples' Republic of China. Nasser, like other Arab leaders, was apprehensive of Israel's intentions and believed that Egypt should build its defenses. After repeated rebuffs from the Western powers, Egypt arranged with Czechoslovakia in September 1955 for the delivery of arms. Western control over the supply of arms in the Middle East was broken and opened the way for the other countries of the area to purchase arms from the Soviet bloc.

The Aswan Dam and the USSR. Notwithstanding these developments, the major emphasis of the RCC was still on internal reform. The formulation of Egypt's main problem was quite simple, even though its solution was well-nigh impossible. Egypt needed more food for its teeming population, more land to raise the food, and more water to irrigate the additional land. Water could be had by enlarging the high Aswan Dam in upper Egypt, but over a billion dollars was necessary to build the dam. Egypt looked to the United States for this money and the United States arranged to provide the necessary funds with the help of Britain and the World Bank.

Egypt, however, delayed the signing of the agreement, perhaps because it believed it could get a better deal by using the rivalry of the Cold War between the United States and the USSR. Nasser claimed that the Soviet Union was willing to lend him more money "with no strings attached," a claim which the Russians denied. Nasser negotiated trade and cultural agreements with China and engaged in diatribes against "American imperialism," which did not please American congressmen. Furthermore, he began training special commandos (Fedayi'in) to raid Israel. The case dragged on until July 1956. Nasser was then ready to accept the American offer, but Secretary of State John Foster Dulles abruptly cancelled the whole project. Dulles gave Egyptian economic inability as reason for the cancellation, but it seems that he wanted to humiliate Nasser in the process. The move, however, left Egypt without the necessary capital to implement its reforms, including the building of the Aswan Dam. Seizing the Suez Canal revenues was a possible solution, particularly in the charged nationalistic atmosphere of the day. Influenced by Dr. Mosaddeq's actions in nationalizing Iran's oil fields in 1951, and by the popular demands for a confrontation with the British, Nasser retaliated by nationalizing the Suez Canal Company on July 26, 1956.

The Nationalization of the Suez Canal. It will be recalled that the Suez Canal was operated by the Suez Canal Company, founded in 1854. It was registered in Egypt and France and was not involved in political and military negotiations carried on between Egypt and Britain. The company had the concession to operate the canal for 99 years and was to hand it over to the government of Egypt in 1968. In the Anglo-Egyptian agreement of 1936, the canal was recognized as belonging to Egypt and in 1954, Egypt was solely responsible for its defense. That the nationalization of the canal announced by Nasser on July 26, 1956, was a direct reaction to the cancellation of the Aswan loan by the United States, there is no doubt. But it is doubtful whether a nationalist government under Nasser would have allowed the company to operate until 1968.

The reaction of the West to the nationalization of the Suez Canal Company was impulsively negative and revealed an attitude that imperialism had cultivated among the Europeans toward the people of the East. The West showed the same attitude toward Egypt that it had toward the Iranians when they nationalized the Anglo-Iranian Oil Company in 1951. Like a two-pronged spike, this attitude was directed against the Easterners' ability and their honesty. It was said that the Egyptians had neither the mechanical ability nor the knowledge to operate the canal. Furthermore, the Europeans believed that the Egyptians could not be trusted with the control of the canal. With more than half of Europe's oil needs passing through the canal, Egypt would have its "thumb on Europe's windpipe" and could not be trusted, it was pointed out, to act responsibly in the company of nations.

Britain and France tried to use every means in their power to stop Egypt. They froze Egyptian assets, called their reserve forces to arms, ordered their navies into the Mediterranean, and strengthened their army and air bases in Cyprus. They also withdrew their pilots from the service of the Canal Company and encouraged other non-Egyptian pilots to resign. They called a conference of eighteen nations who used the canal and proposed a "users' company" to "cooperate" with Egypt in the operation of the canal. British and French ships refused to pay the regular dues to the nationalized company. The counsels of the United States were divided on this matter. The Americans took part in these meetings and protests but did not join in them wholeheartedly. On October 5, 1956, the case was taken to the Security Council of the United Nations. The Security Council, however, issued a set of six principles governing the affairs of the canal, which were accepted by all parties concerned.

The Anglo-French-Israeli invasion of Egypt.   Apparently, the Anglo-French acceptance of the principles recommended by the United Nations was a ruse. On October 29, 1956, with full cooperation of France and Britain, Israel invaded Sinai. By the next day, Israel had advanced seventy-five miles. On the same day, France and Britain sent an ultimatum to both sides to stop fighting and withdraw their troops a distance of ten miles from either side of the canal. As Nasser refused to comply, Anglo-French air and naval forces attacked Egypt and occupied Port Said. The Anglo-French-Israeli alliance had planned well and expected a quick occupation of the canal and the fall of Nasser from power.

They expected the USSR to object, but what surprised the invading forces was the severe remonstrance from the United States. It is quite likely that the attack was scheduled just one week before the U.S. presidential elections in the expectation that no candidate in his right mind would jeopardize Jewish votes and censure Israel. President Eisenhower, who was a candidate for reelection, severely censured Israel and its allies, perhaps against the advice of his political advisers. A union of the United States and the USSR was too strong to ignore. By December, the Anglo-French forces evacuated Egypt and by March 1957, the Israeli troops evacuated Sinai, the Gaza Strip, and the Strait of Tiran. A United Nations peacekeeping force was dispatched to guard both sides of the Israeli-Egyptian border and the approaches to the Strait of Tiran. Israel refused to allow UN forces on its soil but Egypt offered no objection.

By April 1957, the Suez Canal was cleared of the ships that Egypt had sunk to block passage. The Egyptians operated the canal efficiently and indeed arranged for widening it to permit two-way traffic. Egypt lost greatly by the destruction of Port Said, defeat in Sinai, and loss of revenue from the canal. But these losses were compensated by political gains. The Arabs were impressed that Nasser had challenged both France and Britain, who only a few years before were masters of all Egypt and the Fertile Crescent, and had won. He was looked upon as the leader of true Arab nationalism and the Arab people's savior from foreign encroachment and internal corruption.

Nasser's Egypt and Nasserism were clearly the center of Arab-world attention following the nationalization of the Suez Canal and the successful Egyptian confrontation with the British-French-Israeli forces. By 1958, Egypt was the major concern of Britain and the United States as the latter rushed forces to Lebanon to protect the Chamoun government from the pro-Nasserist nationalist challenges in Beirut's streets. Iraq's July Revolution further frightened the United States into issuing the Eisenhower Doctrine. This was followed by the signing of a mutual defense pact with Iran, and restructuring the 1955 Baghdad Pact into the 1958 Central Treaty Organization (CENTO), which bound Turkey, Iran, Pakistan, and Britain in a collective security pact. For Egypt, the critical event in 1958 was not just the Iraqi Revolution but the establishment of the United Arab Republic.

The Myth of Arab Unity

The Arabic-speaking peoples have been searching for an identity. Ever since World War II, they have talked of unity while remaining as separate as ever; they have spoken of one "Arab Nation," while acting as a dozen different nations. The only things they have in common are language and religion. These entities have not united the English-speaking peoples, nor have they created a desire among the Spanish-speaking peoples to declare themselves as one nation. But the idea of one Arab nation persists.

One of the factors that separates one Arabic-speaking country from another is the form of it's government. There are monarchies, republics, dictatorships, parademocracies, and small shaykhdoms on the Persian Gulf that defy classification. They are also separated by their respective degrees of education and their general attitude toward the modern world. Countries like Lebanon and Egypt, which have numerous universities and attitudes that embrace the virtues and vices of Europe, have more in common with France and Italy than they have with Saudi Arabia and Yaman. Perhaps the most important thing that separates them is economic philosophy. Even though during the last few years the "have" countries such as Saudi Arabia, Kuwait, and Iraq have been helping the "have not" countries such as Egypt, Syria, and others, they are still very far from sharing their wealth. To these factors should be added the intense rivalries between Egypt, Syria, and Iraq for the leadership of the "United Arab Nation," if and when it is established.

It is difficult to determine how deep into the masses this idea of unity has penetrated, but there is no question that the literate population seems to be obsessed with it. Consequently, it is difficult to narrate the history of each Arabic-speaking country separately. They belong together. After World War II, two factors, one negative and the other positive, kept the possibility of unity alive among the Arab countries.

The negative factor was Israel. Its establishment enraged all of the Arabic-speaking countries, its presence frustrated them, its real and imaginary expansionist policies frightened them. But anger, frustration, and fear did not unite the Arabs much beyond the talking stage. Often hatred or fear of a common enemy has united countries even though they believe in antithetical ideologies, forms of government, and policies. The alliance between the USSR and the United States against Hitler is a case in point. The Arabs may fear and hate Israel, but such sentiments are not able to unite them against Israel. One must conclude that their hatred and fear of Israel are not as deep as some of the differences that separate them.

The positive factor for the unity of the Arabs was the appearance of a popular and charismatic leader in the person of Gamal Abd al-Nasser. The Fertile Crescent and Egypt probably had not seen a more popular or potentially powerful leader since Saladin defeated the Crusaders and captured Jerusalem. Photographs of Nasser could be seen in practically every Arab marketplace, home, and tent from Yaman to Morocco. He arranged for British troops to leave Suez, he rid Egypt of a corrupt king, he withstood the combined attacks of the Anglo-French-Israeli alliance, he was courted by the United States and the USSR, and he was the hope of Arab unity. Notwithstanding all this, Nasser failed to unite the Arabs because he could not rise above the differences which separated them.

The United Arab Republic and Arab Socialism

The concept of the United Arab Republic goes back to Nasser's idea of the place of Egypt in the circles described in his *Philosophy of Revolution*, and his experiences at the 1955 Bandung Conference of nonaligned nations. The Indonesian conference had gathered together Nehru of India, Tito of Yugoslavia, Nkrumah of Ghana, and other leaders of developing countries, including Egypt. The conviction that there existed a "Third World" of nations neither aligned completely with the United States nor with the Soviet Union dominated the conference deliberations (the First World was comprised of the capitalist countries and the Second World of the communist). Nasser returned to Egypt determined to utilize Egypt's political and geographical position within the Arab and African nations as a bridge between the African and Middle Eastern regions. Furthermore, riding his tide of popularity in the wake of the Suez Canal episode, Nasser began to argue for "Arab Socialism" as a form specific to the nationalist ideology of the Arab world for social as well as political change. He also argued that Egypt's form of Arab Socialism, or Nasserism, could not only liberate the rest of the Arab world but would be a model for the rising African nations to follow. What was not readily apparent in Nasser's ideology, however, was its profoundly antisocialist and anticommunist positions. Indeed, Nasserism represented the aspirations of Egypt's professional class of managers, middle-level military, teachers, lawyers, doctors, and other white-collar workers, as well as petty tradesmen, shopkeepers, and industrialists. Nasser stood in opposition to the old landed families and land interests as well as to the emerging militant industrial workers. In espousing Arab Socialism, Nasser was articulating the interests of Egypt's middle- and upper-middle-class industrialists on the one hand and the land-hungry and impoverished peasantry on the other. The middle stratum of salaried professionals and self-employed shopkeepers formed the cores of his supporters, and they were the most enthusiastic about the nationalization and confrontation of 1956.

Syria gave Nasser the opportunity to build an Egyptian hegemony in the region within the context of Bandung Third Worldism, and declare the establishment of the United Arab Republic. In 1956, Syrian conservative and moderate politicians had come under the influence of Nasser and hoped that he might save them from leftist domination. There was a split within the leftist camp; the communists favored collaboration with the Soviet Union and the Ba'thists were for independent action. The communists gained increasing influence in the army and brought General Afif Bizri, chief of staff of the Syrian army, to a pro-Soviet position. The more powerful the communists became, the more the Ba'thists thought of union with Egypt, which would save Syria from communism and would be a step toward the ultimate union of all Arabs.

In the beginning, Ba'thists considered Nasser to be a military dictator and looked down upon the Revolutionary Command Council of Egypt as a group without ideology. But after the nationalization of the Suez Company and the Sinai war, Nasser had emerged with new ideas. The slogan of the RCC—"Discipline, Unity, Work"—was changed to "Democracy, Socialism, and Cooperative Society." Nasser "Egyptianized" all foreign industry and property and at the same time nationalized many Egyptian-owned private industries. This endeared him to Ba'th's socialist eyes. They thought they would add an ideological dimension to Nasser's pragmatism and use his popularity and power for the unification and socialization of all the Arab world.

In January 1958, the Ba'thists, who were afraid of a communist coup, went to Cairo and asked for union. The United Arab Republic was established after a remarkably short negotiation. Having been disappointed with the confederation of the League of Arab States, the two countries set up a model of the opposite extreme—that of a totally centralized union. The union was hailed as the first step toward the unity of all Arabs. As the first president of the U.A.R., Nasser was the idol of all Arabs. Not to be outdone, the Hashimite kings of Jordan and Iraq announced a federal union, but it did not impress even the citizens of those countries. The U.A.R. became the Arabs' hope for the future. But this hope was short-lived.

The demise of the U.A.R.   Some groups in Syria, such as the moderates, conservatives, military, and small businessmen, gradually realized that Syria was becoming a province of Egypt rather than an equal partner in a union. Businessmen and shopkeepers suffered under economic restrictions that were based on Egyptian needs. The army was disgruntled because it had come under the control of the U.A.R. vice-president, Hakim Amer, who acted as Nasser's proconsul in Syria. The Ba'thists, as the enthusiastic proponents of union, had suffered the most. They had accepted the disbanding of all political parties, including their own, confident that they would be given a free hand in building the new National Union Party of the U.A.R. But Nasser refused to give them that opportunity. Indeed, in the first election in 1959, the Ba'thists were pushed out of the government altogether. Perhaps the severest blow came when Nasser began to collaborate with such former enemies as Jordan and Saudi Arabia, against which both Nasser and Ba'thists had poured so much invective.

For whatever reason, Nasser did not take into account the existing agricultural, economic, and social differences between Syria and Egypt and forced upon Syria his Arab Socialism, which was devised for Egyptian needs. For their part, the Ba'thist ideologists of Syria did not take into account the pragmatism of Nasser, who introduced and discarded ideological principles as he went along. Consequently in September 1961, the Syrians seceded from the union. The Syrian secession, however, did not prevent Egypt from continuing to use the name and perpetuating the fiction of the U.A.R. for some time and to act as though nothing had happened. Nasser's successor,

Anwar Sadat, changed the name to the "Arab Republic of Egypt" on May 1, 1971.

Nasser was involved anywhere in the Arab world where there was a revolution. He supported Qasim of Iraq; but when it appeared that Qasim would not follow Nasser's lead, the two became enemies. Nasser also involved himself in the civil war in Yaman, supporting the republican south against the royalist north. The civil war lasted six years and caused Egypt enormous losses in men and money.

Arab Socialism in Egypt

Nasser had spent a good deal of his energy in the cause of pan-Arabism, and all he had to show for it was the name "U.A.R.," which he insisted on continuing as a symbol of a goal to be achieved. He had not, however, neglected reforms at home. He and his friends assumed power without a well-defined ideological program. Consequently, he was not bound to a preconceived ideology and was free to try different programs and shift position as he went along. Perhaps because of his meeting with Nehru of India, his friendship with Tito of Yugoslavia, his visit to the Soviet Union, his association with the Ba'thists of Syria, and the general needs of all developing nations, he followed programs that were socialist in nature. Land reform, which he started in 1952, was the beginning. In 1956, when the Suez Canal Company and many other foreign enterprises were nationalized, the government formed the Economic Organization, which was to manage the industries. In a short time, the Economic Organization was the operating industrial, commercial, financial, and agricultural concerns. Indeed, the acquisition of the foreign concerns demanded the formation of the Economic Organization.

Because 50 percent of Egypt's national income was in the hands of 1.5 percent of the population, Nasser ordered the nationalization of all important concerns such as banks, cotton, fertilizer, insurance, iron, pubic utilities, steel, and textiles. Only small industries were left for private enterprise. Salaries were restricted and all income above 10,000 Egyptian pounds was taxed at a rate of 90 percent. The maximum landholding was decreased from 200 to 100 feddans. There were laws for the benefit of laborers. In forbidding persons to hold more than one job, many positions were opened up to the large number of educated unemployed.

Indeed, in the first ten years of the Nasser regime, Egypt could boast of building more houses, schools, hospitals and infirmaries, social service centers, and agricultural cooperatives than it had during the half century before the RCC came to power. In 1959, Egypt and the Sudan reached an agreement on the use of the Nile, and the Soviet Union agreed to extend a $300 million loan to build the high Aswan Dam. The RCC was the first government in Egypt to pay serious attention to the population problem and to establish family planning centers. Given the lack of education, the increase in population, and the difficult odds, perhaps these reforms, even after the completion of the Aswan Dam, did not make too much difference in the standard of living. But their psychological effect was tremendous; and to the Egyptians, Egypt was a country on the move.

Nasser and the Non-Arabs

The building of the Aswan Dam by the Soviet Union brought the two countries together. There were great quantities of arms deliveries, agricultural and industrial equipment, and Soviet technical and military advisers. Frequent visits by the Soviet hierarchy and Soviet bloc leaders, including China, encouraged Nasser to espouse pro-Soviet policies. Notwithstanding this, Nasser outlawed the Communist Party in Egypt and imprisoned many communists, to the embarrassment of the Soviet leaders.

Nasser's relations with Europe and the United States fluctuated from the correct to the strained, depending upon the circumstances. The U.A.R. and Britain resumed diplomatic relations in 1956, only to become strained once more because of Nasser's interest in South Yaman and the problem of Aden. The good relationship with West Germany broke down when Nasser raised the level of the Egyptian office in East Germany to a consulate. Nasser always remained suspicious of the United States, even though the United States had helped Egypt in 1956 in its war with Israel, England, and France. The U.S. request that Nasser cease interfering in the Congo led to a harsh reaction by Nasser and the burning of the American library in Cairo.

The Six-Day War of 1967

After the failure of the U.A.R., Egypt and the Arab countries of the Fertile Crescent returned to their traditional ways. This generally meant coups in Syria and Iraq and Cold War among the Arab leaders. About the only thing these countries could agree on was their opposition to Israel. Syrians as usual were at the forefront, claiming to be more ardent Arabs and better opponents of Israel than anyone else. The Soviet Union was arming Egypt and Syria; France was selling arms and airplanes to Israel; and the United States was providing some military equipment to Israel, Jordan, and Saudi Arabia.

Israel, in the meantime, had developed the port of Eilat on the Gulf of Aqaba. It built an oil pipeline from Eilat to Haifa, through which Iranian oil flowed for the use of Israeli industries. Egypt broke diplomatic relations with Iran for its willingness to sell oil to Israel. Israel also defied UN injunction and diverted Jordan River water for agricultural purposes in the Negev.

These and the unsettled problems between Israel and its Arab neighbors caused periodic clashes. Because the border between Israel and Egypt was guarded by a UN peacekeeping force, there were not many incidents. Jordan's vulnerable position did not allow it to cause too much trouble for Israel. Syria was in a better position to attack both Israeli settlements and the Israeli encroachment on land designated by the United Nations as a neutral, or demilitarized, zone. Israel retaliated periodically, not against Syria but against innocent Jordan villages on the border. Jordan's inability to retaliate against Israel gave Egypt and Syria an excuse to attack Husayn for his "pro-Israeli" policies.

It is difficult to determine why Israel punished Jordan for the sins of Syria. Since there was a mutual aid treaty between Syria and Egypt, perhaps Israel was afraid that attacking Syria might involve Egypt in the conflict.

Furthermore, the Palestinian refugees had formed a government in exile and the Palestine Liberation Army, which had training camps in Syria and the Gaza Strip. Israeli attacks on Jordan might bring this army into Jordan, in which case Israel would have an excuse to wage a "defensive war" and occupy the West Bank, a goal which the Herut Party had been advocating for a long time.

In any case, the situation grew very tense. On May 15, 1967, Israel celebrated its nineteenth anniversary of independence with military parades in "demilitarized" Jerusalem against United Nations objections. Prime Minister Eshkol of Israel reminded the Israelis of the gravity of the situation and said that Israel "will be forced to take suitable retaliatory measures" to counteract increasing Syrian agitation against Israel. The various commando groups that had been training in Syria and the Gaza Strip under the direction of the PLO increased their maneuvering activities. The Syrians taunted President Nasser for hiding behind the United Nations forces. On May 17, the U.A.R. requested that all UN forces evacuate Egyptian soil. Secretary-General U Thant complied with the request, permitting Egyptian troops to replace the UN emergency forces and occupy Sharm al-Shaykh, which controlled the approach to the Gulf of Aqaba and the Straits of Tiran.

On May 22, the U.A.R. closed the Gulf of Aqaba to Israeli ships and all non-Israeli ships carrying strategic material to Israel. Israel considered the closing of an international waterway an act of war and started to mobilize. On May 30, Egypt and Jordan signed a military alliance to repel an attack on either nation. On June 3, Libya joined the Egyptian army, and the next day Iraq joined the Egyptian-Jordanian alliance. The ring around Israel was complete.

The great powers did not want war in the Middle East. But the Soviet Union was sympathetic with the Arabs; the United States and Great Britain agreed with Israel that the Straits of Tiran were international; and France declared its neutrality in the conflict. It is even doubtful whether Egypt wanted war, but Israel could not gamble on that.

On Monday morning June 5, 1967, Israeli air and land forces attacked and fighting began from Sinai to Syria and along the Jordanian border. Within two hours the Israeli planes had destroyed the entire Egyptian, Syrian, and Jordanian air forces. Then, with complete air superiority, the Israeli ground forces advanced on all fronts. In six short days Israeli soldiers stood along the Suez Canal in the south, the Jordan River in the east, and the Syrian Golan Heights overlooking the Sea of Galilee in the northeast. They had captured nine Egyptian generals, over 300 officers, thousands of prisoners, and millions of dollars' worth of Russian-made military equipment, most of it undamaged. The Six-Day War exposed once again the disunity of the Arabs as well as the audacity and the solidarity of the Israelis. Israel had dealt a severe blow to the Arab states with American money, French airplanes, and its own Israeli pilots.

The Death of Nasser

The defeat of the Egyptian military (both armored and infantry divisions) in Gaza and in the Sinai was humiliating and humbling for the proud Nasser. His public address in June 1967, following the Six-Day War, was for the purpose of resigning in the face of the military disaster. The popular outpouring in support of Nasser was both genuine and ardent. With broad-based public support but increasing middle- and upper-middle-class discontent with both nationalization and Nasser, Nasser began to reconstruct the Egyptian armed forces and economy through a series of treaties and internal reforms.

Between 1968 and 1970, Nasser completed a number of commercial and military agreements with the Soviet Union. This brought to Egypt large Soviet missions and trade conferences stitching Egypt's economy more closely to the USSR's than ever before. Nasser was forced to abandon the Bandung Conference's idealistic nonaligned policies in order to heal the ravages of foreign wars, nationalization, and rampant corruption. Unemployment rates and food prices soared, while loans from the World Bank ended. On the other hand, the Aswan Dam was completed and Arab states such as Saudi Arabia, Kuwait, and Libya rallied to his side.

A national referendum was held in 1968, which endorsed Nasser almost unanimously. On the strength of this, new elections were held in 1969. The Egyptians sent a large majority of Nasser's party (the Arab Socialist Union, which was the only party in Egypt) to the new National Assembly. Nasser was elected president and Anwar Sadat, a classmate of Nasser's and an original member of the RCC, was elected vice-president. On September 28, 1970, Nasser died suddenly of a heart attack. Millions filled the streets as Egypt laid its national leader to rest.

SADAT'S POLICIES

Anwar Sadat, like his other colleagues on the RCC, was overshadowed by Nasser's dashing personality. He had been a revolutionary from his student days and had been jailed for his activities. After the revolution, he was editor of *Gumhurriya*, the main organ of the RCC, and for many years served as president of the Egyptian National Assembly, before becoming vice-president. After a vote of the National Assembly and approval by a national referendum, Anwar Sadat was sworn in as Egypt's second president on October 17, 1970.

Within seven years, Sadat's accomplishments were of such a magnitude that he was as well known in the international world as he was to the Egyptians and other Arab peoples. His meteoric rise, particularly following his November 1977 visit to Jerusalem, created an anomaly for many observers. On the one hand, Sadat gained the international reputation and respect that had eluded Nasser. On the other hand, he never began to reach the levels of popular support that Nasser had so carefully cultivated and harvested. When Sadat was assassinated and laid to rest, Cairo's streets were nearly empty—a stark contrast to the tumultuous farewell that had been given by millions of Egyptians on Nasser's death. Part of the reason for the anomaly lay in Sadat's character and Egypt's social structure, while part was clearly due to Sadat's decision to recognize Israel and to sign the Camp David Accords, apparently on his own.

Sadat had religious proclivities; on the whole, he was politically more conservative than Nasser, leaning more toward the right than to the left, and was more Egyptian in his sympathies than pan-Arab. He began a series of internal reforms, some of which were to redo what Nasser and his supporters had constructed over a twenty-year period. He concentrated his attention on four matters: democratizing the political process; decentralizing economic production, which he called *infitah*, or "Open Door"; expanding Egypt's relations with other countries; and reforming the military.

In the field of democratization, he gave more freedom (although it was still limited) to the press; he also did away with Nasser's single-party system and allowed other political parties to function. One of the first acts of his presidency was to appoint a commission to prepare a new constitution. As in all Islamic countries, the question of Islam and its place in the government was paramount. This question was debated publicly in the press and over 6,000 letters were sent in, expressing a broad range of ideas from the most conservative to the most liberal on all aspects of the constitution. The most important question was the place of the Islamic Shari'a, including the position of women and personal status laws dealing with every aspect of life in the constitution. Opinion differed mainly among those who wanted Shari'a to be *the source* of all laws, and those who preferred it to be *a source* among other sources. The constitution was ratified on September 11, 1971, with the following statement about Islam and the Shari'a: "Islam is the religion of the state, Arabic is its official language, and the principles of the Islamic Shari'a *a principal source* of legislation."

In the matter of decentralization, Sadat went counter to Nasser's centralized economy. He inaugurated the Open Door in economic activity for the private sector and encouraged foreign investments. The public sector would no longer be dominant and instead would now cooperate with the private sector. Egypt's Open Door policy followed the October War and renewed the interest of the United States in Egypt's economy and military prowess. Attracting large sums of U.S. aid and drawing on U.S. corporate planning skills, Sadat and his advisors accelerated the construction of commercial industries. In agriculture, Egypt's Aswan Dam, completed in 1970, had begun to expand land cultivation by massive irrigation projects in the Upper Nile region as well as by land reclamation projects in the Delta and along the middle Nile. The Suez Canal, closed since 1967, opened in 1975. The rates were doubled and Japan lent money to widen it. The Open Door regulated the activities of foreign companies. They were required to involve Egyptian capital in every venture. Exemption from this requirement was possible only in "free zones" in Cairo, Alexandria, Port Said, and Suez, where industrial production could be increased for exports to Arab markets. On the whole, the flow of foreign capital and technology did not reach expected levels.

Concerning Egypt's relation with the world, Sadat disliked Nasser's policies, which, in his view, had made Egypt much too dependent on the Soviet Union. Consequently, on July 18, 1972, he ordered the vast majority of Russian technicians and advisors out of Egypt. He opened the door to European and American aid and investments, made friends with Saudi Arabia and other Arab states, and re-established diplomatic relations with Iran. Egypt received loans from all of the above sources, including the Soviet Union and China.

One of Sadat's major aims was to reform the army. A good deal of foreign funds went into arms purchases, training programs, and airfield construction. As early as 1972, he ordered the cabinet to introduce an austerity program and put Egypt on a war economy.

The October War and Its Aftermath

Anwar Sadat, like most Egyptians, was ashamed of Egypt's defeat at the hands of Israel in 1967 and the loss of the Sinai. Apparently, soon after he became president he and Egypt's high-ranking officers planned to rectify this shameful defeat. He arranged for a simultaneous strike with Syria and kept the whole operation secret. Finally on October 10, 1973, he took the Israelis by complete surprise, crossed the Suez Canal, and broke through the Bar Lev Line. This psychological "victory," which showed that the Israelis were not invincible, made Sadat popular with the Arab leaders. Furthermore, according to the final disengagement agreement, Egypt got back the Abu Rudeis oilfields and the strategic Mitla and Gidi passes. Nevertheless, the jubilation in Egypt did not last very long. The Open Door policy, which was started in 1974, did not produce the hoped-for results. Inflation and high food prices along with a lowering of wages, brought students and workers to the streets. Between 1976 and 1977, demonstrations in Alexandria, Cairo, and other Egyptian cities and towns became frequent, despite increased police and paramilitary surveillance and arrests of dissidents. Accompanying the student and worker unrest was the appearance of fundamentalist Islamic groups, collectively known as the Muslim Brotherhood, or *Ikhwan*, and a series of bombings and assassinations. In February 1977, moreover, in response to the International Monetary Fund's insistence that the state stop subsidizing commodities such as wheat and dairy products, demonstrators took to the streets of Cairo and Alexandria in what was known as the "bread riots." Massive demonstrations took place, and attacks on nightclubs, cinemas, and banks accompanied public cries for an end to Sadat's rule and the restoration of subsidies. Once order was restored after a week, Sadat quickly moved to curb further violence by reinstating the commodity programs and carefully distinguishing his open support for the moderate Islamic leaders and opposition to the fundamentalists.

Sadat's Trip to Jerusalem and the Camp David Accords

Sadat knew that Egypt's psychological victory did not spell the defeat of Israel. Most of the Sinai was still occupied by Israel and no solution to the Palestinian problem was in sight. He must have concluded that it was virtually impossible in the foreseeable future for the Arab states to defeat Israel. So far three wars had resulted only in the expansion of Israeli territory. While it was true that the fourth war had shaken Israel to the core, it had bounced back with the help of the United States and was still a power to contend with. Heretofore, the Arab states had generally reacted to Israeli initiatives. Sadat, therefore, decided to put forth a bold initiative himself. In a speech to the Egyptian Assembly he announced that he might go to Jerusalem in search of peace. On October 9, 1977, Sadat made his historic trip to Jerusalem. His trip to Jerusalem, his visit to the Wailing Wall, his prayers in the Aqsa Mosque, and his speech in the Israeli Knesset electrified the people of Israel, Europe, and the United States but horrified many in the Middle East, particularly the Palestinians. Denunciations from Arab capitals came as quickly as congratulations from Israel, Europe, and the United States. The contrast between the two receptions could not have been greater.

On his return Sadat invited the United States, the Soviet Union, Israel, and the Arab states to come to Cairo and set an agenda for peace. With the exception of the United States and Israel, all the others declined. Later, Sadat and Begin met at Ismailia, where Begin outlined his plan of giving local self-government to the Palestinians under Israeli authority. Sadat rejected it, insisting that Israel withdraw from the West Bank and Gaza.

Volumes have been written both for and against Sadat's trip to Jerusalem. There is no question, however, that Sadat had made a bold move for peace and had garnered the support of most of the world. One wonders what would have happened if the Palestinians and the Arab states had not deserted him. One remembers that the same Palestinians and Arab leaders gathered in Fez in September 1982, to consider the Reagan initiative. They formulated an eight-point peace plan that asked for exactly the same things that Sadat had asked for in his speech to the Israeli Knesset. The Fez statement recognized the rights of *all* states in the area—i.e., the Arab states recognized the existence of Israel—which was what Sadat had done by going to Israel. The only difference between the two was that in 1977, the Arabs had made the initiative and had the force of world opinion, including that of a large number of Israelis, behind them; while in Fez, five years later, they were reacting out of weakness again to a vague proposal by President Reagan that Israel had rejected out of hand.

The Camp David Accord.   But that was not to be and Sadat was left alone. In March 1979, following six months of intense negotiations between Sadat and Begin culminating at Camp David, near Washington, D.C., President Carter brought the two leaders together in a historic signing ceremony. The Camp David Accord spelled out the steps that Israel was prepared to take in exchange for Egypt's recognition of Israel. The Israeli armed forces were to withdraw from the Sinai in three stages, relinquishing control over all territory, all oilfields, and all Israeli settlements. Furthermore, Egypt demanded that the question of Palestinian autonomy be linked to the Sinai withdrawal and the recognition of Israel. On the question of linkage, Begin equivocated and left the matter up in the air for later discussion, as McMahon had done with Sharif Husayn in 1916. Sadat did not insist. Palestine once more became the stumbling block, it seemed, to Israel's recognition among Arab leaders. Sadat's agreement to the Accord, furthermore, cast doubt on his future as Syria and other Arab states joined to oust Egypt from the Arab community.

The Arab states suspended economic aid to Egypt and transferred the

Arab League headquarters from Cairo to Tunis. In his anger, Sadat is reported to have said: "Egypt can live without the Arabs but the Arabs cannot live without Egypt." It is too early to determine why Sadat, who had insisted on a comprehensive peace, signed a separate peace at the last moment and relegated the Palestinian question to a later date. Even after the signing, when, contrary to the assurances he had given to Sadat and Carter, Begin approved more settlements on the West Bank, why did Sadat not insist on the linkage between the separate peace and the West Bank settlements?

Muhammad Ibrahim Kamil, the Egyptian prime minister, who had been present at Camp David and who had resigned in protest over the Accords on the last day at Camp David, suggested that Sadat did so in desperation and because he was left alone. The only person Sadat had behind him was Carter, and Carter had hoped to settle the Palestinian question in his second term. The only consistent person at Camp David was Begin, who knew what he did and did not want. Perhaps Sadat felt that gaining the Sinai without warfare would profit Egypt and be a step toward solving the Palestinian problem. Given the many precedents in international relations, there is nothing to prevent Egypt from discarding the peace agreement in the future and joining the rest of the Arab states against Israel.

Furthermore, it must be noted that the Egyptians have never been as conscientiously "Arab" as the Arabic-speaking peoples of the Fertile Crescent and the Persian Gulf. The concept of Arab nationalism had been introduced in Egypt only in the 1950s. Egyptian identity, however, went deeper and farther back in history than the advent of Arab nationalism. Perhaps this was the reason why a separate peace agreement was welcomed by enough Egyptians to make it plausible, and an Israeli delegation and Israeli tourists have been received without incident. Nevertheless, it was a fatal miscalculation for Sadat to have signed a separate peace with Israel. As a practicing Muslim, Sadat must have known, more than anyone else, the close connection of Islam with Arabism and the emotional attachment of all Muslims to Jerusalem, if not to Palestine. It was, in fact, a group of Islamic fundamentalists who killed Anwar Sadat in the midst of the October War celebration in 1981.

Egypt After Sadat

Vice-President Husni Mubarak assumed control and, in due time, was elected president of Egypt. Although he punished Sadat's murderers after a noisy public trial, he released Sadat's political prisoners and invited them to the presidential palace for discussions. He continued Sadat's Open Door policy and stressed the need for greater production. He continued relations with Israel and presided over Egypt's repossession of the last section of the Sinai. Israel did not make things easy for him. While Mubarak was arranging a visit to Israel, Israeli leaders insisted that he visit Jerusalem or not come at all. Of course, Mubarak did not go. Then there was the question of Taba, a one-square-mile section of the Sinai, on which Israel had started to build a hotel two years after signing the peace agreement. In the end Israel evacuated the Sinai, but not without bulldozing buildings and uprooting trees and every other green thing.

Mubarak also tried to cultivate the friendship of the Soviet Union and the Arab states. When Israel invaded Lebanon, Egypt protested and recalled its ambassador from Tel Aviv. The Arab states, for their part, readmitted Egypt into the Arab League. As Egypt eases its way back into the Arab world, it remains to be seen if President Mubarak and his supporters can begin to solve Egypt's problems any better than had Sadat or Nasser.

Chapter Thirty-Three
The Shaping
of Modern Iran

The history of Iran since World War I has been profoundly shaped by the Pahlavis and their policies. From the time Reza Shah appeared on the scene in 1921 as the leader of a coup until the departure of his son, Mohammad Reza Shah, from the throne of Iran in 1979, both father and son guided and shaped Iran's westernization, industrialization, secularism, and intense nationalism. Compulsory education, the opening of universities, land reform, reforestation, hydroelectric dams, the building of roads and introduction of machinery—all had wrought more changes in fifty years than had occurred in the previous five hundred. And yet by 1978 almost every segment of Iranian society that the Pahlavis claimed to have helped turned against them, their supporters, and their policies. A new regime came to power that was diametrically opposed to the westernization, secularism, and nationalism that the Pahlavis had espoused.

THE COUP D'ETAT OF 1921

Iran was in a state of hiatus in 1920. The constitutional monarchy was neither strong nor constitutional. The cabinet changed hands from one member of the landed gentry to another. The failure of the 1919 Anglo-Iranian agreement had left a vacuum, and the establishment of the Soviet

Republic of Gilan had made the Iranian leaders apprehensive of Bolshevism. This hiatus was broken by a coup d'etat in the early hours of February 21, 1921. Some 2,500 Cossacks under the command of Colonel Reza Khan, accompanied by newspaper editor Sayyed Ziya al-Din Tabatabai, moved to Tehran from Qazvin, sixty miles to the west, and took control of the capital. There was practically no opposition. In the morning, a number of well-known individuals from different economic and political groups were arrested. The frightened shah was forced to appoint Sayyed Ziya as prime minister and to give the title of commander of the army to Reza Khan.

Sayyed Ziya was a moderate nationalist and editor of the middle-of-the-road newspaper *Ra'd*, which was known for its pro-British editorials. He was suspect among liberals because of his pro-British attitude and was not prominent enough socially to be a confidant of the landed gentry. His political activity was centered in the Pulad Committee, which had been founded by the British in Esfahan. His only official connection with the government was membership in the Iranian delegation of 1919 to the Caucasus to sign treaties of friendship with some of the states that had hoped to be independent of Bolshevik Russia.

Reza Khan, on the other hand, was a military man, tall, with a commanding personality, and with little education. He had risen to a position of command in the Russian-dominated Cossack force by dint of courage and initiative. When the Bolshevik Revolution left the Russian officers of the Iranian Cossack regiment stranded, Reza Khan led a group of Iranian officers who ousted the Russians and took control of the regiment themselves. Because of his military upbringing, his brand of nationalism envisaged the glory of Iran under a unified military regime. Because of his harsh experience under Russian commanders, he was generally antiforeign—especially anti-Bolshevik and anti-Russian.

So far as can be ascertained, these two men, Reza Khan and Sayyed Ziya, who were opposites in temperament, education, and almost everything else, did not know each other. They had met, probably for the first time, on the night of the coup in Shahabad, a few miles outside Tehran. Furthermore, their plans after the success of the coup were not coordinated. A large number of men were arrested but it was evident that a list had not been prepared in advance. They arrested liberals, moderates, conservatives, rich and poor, seemingly without discrimination. Sometimes Reza would free a person whom Ziya had ordered arrested. Sayyed Ziya did not even have his cabinet picked before the coup. A third group must have made the preliminary arrangements; all evidence seems to point to the British.

To say that Sayyed Ziya and Reza Khan were aided by the British in taking control of the Iranian government is not to say that they had made the interests of Iran subservient to those of Britain. The government of Sayyed Ziya did not last more than three months. He was highhanded with all types of people from the shah down, but he did not have the power to back up his pretensions. The military was loyal to his rival, Reza Khan. On April 25, 1921, Reza Khan was admitted to the cabinet as minister of war.

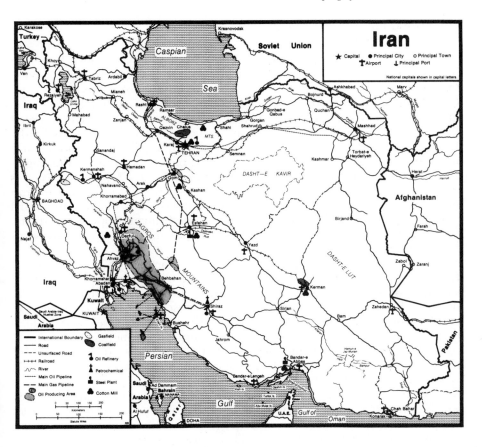

The immediate issue between the two was the fate of the Gendarmerie, a military force under the minister of interior, and also of the British military advisors who were still around. Reza Khan wanted to unify the armed forces and dismiss the British. Sayyed Ziya opposed both moves and was defeated. On May 24, 1921, he was forced to leave Iran. He lived in Palestine and did not return until World War II, when British and Russian forces were once again in Iran and his rival had been removed from the throne.

Reza Khan was different. He believed that nothing could be accomplished without a strong central military government that was free of foreign intervention. He used the British to come to power and then tried more than once to get rid of them. In his career he was forced to employ foreign advisors, though he was not at ease in their presence and never kept them on a project more than a few years. Such xenophobia was not healthy, but one wonders whether, in the second decade of the twentieth century, any other attitude would have convinced the Iranians that they could build an army without a foreign advisor and construct a railroad from the Caspian Sea to the Persian Gulf without floating a foreign loan.

THE RUSSO-IRANIAN TREATY OF 1921

Five days after the coup d'etat, the Russo-Iranian Treaty, which had been negotiated between the previous Iranian cabinet and Moscow, was signed. One immediate result of the treaty was the withdrawal of Soviet troops from Gilan, which caused the eventual destruction of the Soviet Republic of Gilan. Mirza Kuchek Khan became a fugitive in the mountains of Gilan and died from exposure. The text of the treaty, which was published widely by the Russians, was ostensibly a declaration of anti-imperialist and anticolonialist policy of the Bolshevik government and was a pleasant contrast to the Anglo-Iranian Agreement of 1919 that had just been officially repudiated. By this treaty, the Russians gave all their assets, concessions, and properties to Iran provided that Iran promise (Article 13) not to cede any of these to a third power, but to "retain them for the benefit of the Iranian people." The treaty, however, retained some vestiges of tsarist imperialism and some provisions for future Soviet imperialism.

For example, the Caspian fishery concession of 1867 and the tariff regulation of 1902 remained unchanged. Fish were necessary for the food supply of Russia and the tariff was favorable to the Soviet Union. In 1927, the new Irano-Soviet Fisheries Company was set up, with a concession to operate for twenty-five years. But the tariff was not revised and Iranian trade suffered as a result. Iran tried to set up state monopolies in order to compete with Soviet trade monopolies. On the whole, the growing rigidity of the governments of the Soviet Union and Iran, under Stalin and Reza Shah, was not conducive to freedom of trade.

What caused Iran a good deal of trouble in later years was Article 6, which stated that if a third power attempted "to use Iranian territory as a base of operation against Russia . . . Russia shall have the right to advance her troops into the Persian interior.. . ." This article was used by the Soviet Union to invade Iran in September 1941 and at other times to object to Iran's security agreements with noncommunist countries after World War II.

IRANIAN OIL: THE SECOND PHASE

On November 22, 1921, the Iranian government signed a contract allowing the Standard Oil Company to exploit the northern oil for fifty years. The Anglo-Persian Oil Company filed a protest on the ground that the concession for northern oil had been given in 1916 to Khoshtaria.[1] They claimed that the Iranian government had no right to grant concessions for the same territory to two parties. The Russians, on the other hand, who did not want American interests to be in northern Iran, protested that according to Article 13 of the treaty, Iran had promised not to cede to a third party a concession which the Soviet government had given up. Iran's answer to both was that since the Khoshtaria agreement had not been ratified by the Majles,

[1]See p. 211.

as the constitution required, it had become null and void and could not be considered valid.

The wrangling over this matter, especially between the British and Americans, continued for some time. On February 28, 1922, the British and American companies agreed to a partnership in which the Americans would have voting control. The Iranians, however, did not agree that the British company should have a hand in the north and rejected the whole project.

At this time, the Sinclair Oil Company became interested in the project. Sinclair's advantage over Standard was that it had received oil concessions on Sakhalin Island from the Soviet Union and also the rights to market Soviet oil in the world. It was believed that the Soviet Union would permit Sinclair to export the northern oil via its territory.

The Sinclair oil negotiation and the events connected with it have all the ingredients for international intrigue, scandal, arson, and murder. In the summer of 1942, when the Sinclair representative was in Iran, Tehran was rocked by two events. First, a bizarre religious revival occurred, which culminated in the report that a miracle had been wrought at one of the water fountains of the city. Hundreds of the sick and afflicted went to this place to be cured and thousands of others went to watch. Second, Major Imbrie, the United States vice-consul, at the instigation of an American employee of the Anglo-Iranian Oil Company, went to photograph the place of the miracle. He was murdered by the mob, but his companion was not harmed. The official investigation seems to indicate that the police looked the other way and did not try to rescue the American. The summer of 1924 was also the date of the American Teapot Dome scandal, which involved the Sinclair Company. How much each of these events contributed to the failure of the project is conjecture. What is important, however, is that the question of northern oil did not come up again until after World War II.

IRANIAN OIL: THE THIRD PHASE

After the Iranian government failed to involve the Americans in the northern oil, the Anglo-Iranian Oil Company had a virtual monopoly for the exploitation of the country's oil. With the exception of technical experts, most of the administrators of the company in Iran were recruited from members of the British government in India. These individuals brought their paternalistic attitude of superiority with them and dealt with Iranians as they had dealt with the Indians. For a long time, all the accounts of the company were in Indian rupees and the laborers were paid in that currency.

The establishment of a strong nationalistic government in Iran under Reza Shah could not allow the old order to last in the administration of the oil company and its relation with the government. In 1928, when the shah went to Khuzestan to open a new road, he did not accept the invitation of the company to visit the oil installations. Instead he sent them a message saying that he was not satisfied with the "pittance" that Iran was receiving from the large profits of the company and wanted to revise the D'Arcy concession. While prolonged negotiations were going on in 1931, the oil royalties showed a sharp decline and the Iranian government refused to accept payment. On November 27, 1932, Taqizadeh, the minister of finance, in a letter to the company, announced the cancellation of the D'Arcy concession on the grounds that the government could not be bound by a concession granted prior to the establishment of constitutional regime. The letter further stated that the government was willing to negotiate a new concession. The British government objected and the matter went to the League of Nations. In the end, however, it was settled out of court by the untimely intervention of the shah in 1933. He became impatient and personally negotiated a new agreement that, on its surface, was a victory for Iran, but in the long run was worse than the D'Arcy concession. The shah was unaware of the implications of the agreement and no one dared to oppose him.

The concession of 1933 contained two superficial advantages for Iran that no doubt pleased Reza Shah. The area of the concession was reduced considerably, but the company had gathered considerable geological data and saw to it that almost all of the oil was within the 100,000 square miles left to it. Secondly, the royalty on the basis of per ton production guaranteed Iran a fixed income in time of depression, but in times of prosperity all that Iran received was 20 percent of the dividends distributed to ordinary stockholders. The most serious losses to Iran in the new agreement were twofold. In one article the company was exempted from all taxation, and in the other the duration of the concession was set at sixty years from 1933, which extended the time of the concession by thirty years.

REZA SHAH PAHLAVI

The Iranian government's attempt to involve the Americans in northern Iran failed, but it succeeded in employing Dr. Arthur Millspaugh, the economic advisor to the U.S. Department of State, as a financial advisor. Dr. Millspaugh and his party arrived in Iran in 1922 and for five years served Iran well. Thanks to Millspaugh's financial and economic policies, the minister of war, Reza Khan, had enough money to organize and train the army. Reza Khan used it to subdue rebellion, disarm tribes, and bring every corner of the country under the authority of the central government. Ruthless methods were used, but the roads were made safe from brigands; and for the first time in almost a century well-laden caravans could travel in all parts of the country without fear of being robbed. To a people who had been at the mercy of outlaws all their lives, security was more important than the freedom to vote.

In October 1923, Reza Khan became prime minister, the first time since the revolution that a military man had become the head of government. Indeed, at this time most of the governors of the provinces were military men and those who were not were under the power of the military commanders of the areas. Elections for the fifth session of the Majles were held, mostly under the influence of military governors or commanders. In many ways it was one of the most eventful sessions in the modern history of

Iran. It was also the last one, until 1942, in which the deputies dared to speak their minds.

Soon after Reza Khan became prime minister, Ahmad Shah went on one of his frequent trips to Europe. In February 1924, there was talk of establishing a republic; telegrams came in from many parts of the country, instigated by military commanders, asking the Majles to depose the Qajar Dynasty. Criticism against the dynasty was fairly common, but there was sharp disagreement over the establishment of a republic. Both inside and outside the Majles, proponents of a republic were liberals, moderates, military people, and others who had hitched their wagons to Reza Khan's star. The opponents were the clerics and the shopkeepers of the bazaars, who generally followed the clerics. Allied to the clerics was a small number of intensely anticlerical liberals who were ideologically in favor of a republic, but whose devotion to the principles of democracy and civilian rule made them oppose this particular movement because it was led by "a dictator and a cossack."

The masses of Tehran were under the influence of the clergy, so they demonstrated against the republic and Reza Khan. The murder of the young anticlerical poet Eshqi, who had lampooned the dictatorship of Reza Khan and his "synthetic republic," added fuel to the fire. Reza Khan was shrewd enough to see the handwriting on the wall. He hurried to the shrine city of Qom south of Tehran, consulted with the chief religious dignitaries, and issued a proclamation stating that since the defense of Islam was the foundation of the program of the Iranian government, he and the religious dignitaries had decided to ask the people "to stop [mention of] the republic and instead spend their energies helping me to . . . strengthen the foundations of Islam and the independence of the country."

The failure of the republican movement did not save the Qajar Dynasty. From Paris, the shah dismissed Reza Khan as prime minister and asked the Majles to recommend another person. The Majles ignored the wishes of the shah and recommended Reza Khan, who almost immediately took steps to assume complete sovereignty. Deputies were called to his house to sign a resolution asking the Majles to depose Ahmad Shah, make Reza Khan the provisional head of the state, and call a constituent assembly to choose a permanent one. Most of them signed the document. On October 31, 1925, the Majles deposed the unlamented Qajar Dynasty and called for a constituent assembly.

Only four deputies had the courage to oppose the resolution. Of these, Yahya Dowlatabadi left public life, while Dr. Mohammad Mosaddeq went into political exile within Iran for a while and assumed a great power after World War II; Taqizadeh and Ala served the new shah in important posts. It is important to note that in their speeches none of them defended the pleasure loving Ahmad Shah or his brother the crown prince. All of them opposed the resolution because it was "against the constitution." Only Dr. Mosaddeq, a constitutional lawyer, explained that it was to the advantage of the country to have Reza active as prime minister rather than inactive as a constitutional monarch. If Reza Khan were to become an active monarch, he would then become a dictator rather than a constitutional monarch.

The liberal and the socialist factions of the Majles who had signed the resolution agreed with Dr. Mosaddeq, but they thought they had taken care of the problem. In return for their signature, Reza Khan had agreed to make the kingship elective. They thought they had arrived at a republican form of government through the back door and were quite satisfied. In December, however, when the constituent assembly convened, there was no mention of an elected shah; instead, a permanent dynasty was established. On December 12, 1925, Iran had a new king, Reza Shah Pahlavi.

Reza Shah and Reform

Reza Shah was popular among the masses because his military power had brought security to the country. Villagers no longer needed to carry guns to defend themselves against brigands. The ruthlessness of the shah was directed against tribal chiefs and grandees, not against peasants. He was also popular among the educated classes and among liberals because he was a reformer with an open determination to westernize Iran. The reforms began almost as soon as he became prime minister and continued for over fifteen years.

All his life the army remained the object of his special devotion. Oil royalties were spent to supply its needs for weapons, and compulsory military service was enacted to meet its needs for men. It was through the army that most of his reforms were channelled. He built roads, constructed a wireless service, and took over from the British the management of the telegraph company. His crowning glory in the field of communication was the building of a railway from the Caspian Sea to the Persian Gulf. This bold project, which was started in 1927 and completed in 1938, was financed by a special tax on sugar and tea, with no foreign loans. Reza Shah did not abolish private enterprise, but organized foreign trade monopolies and subjected all commerce to strict governmental control. In 1928, he established the National Bank of Iran and withdrew the privilege of issuing banknotes from the British Imperial Bank. In 1927, he had abolished extraterritoriality.

Almost as soon as he became king he curbed the powers of the ulama. Religious endowments were taken out of their hands, Islamic law was partially set aside in favor of Western law, and Islamic education was abandoned in the public schools. The Islamic lunar calendar was abolished and gave place to the old Iranian-Zoroastrian solar calendar with Iranian names for the months of the year. The month-long mourning for the death of Husayn, the grandson of the Prophet, was reduced to three weeks, and carried on without religious processions. Some mosques were "modernized" by the introduction of chairs, and some old shrines were changed into museums. The call to prayer was frowned upon, and making the pilgrimage to Mecca was discouraged.

Reza Shah abolished all titles and asked the people to select family names; he himself chose the name of Pahlavi, honored in pre-Islamic Iranian history. He introduced modern education and established schools, founding the University of Tehran in 1934. He prohibited the use of Iranian attire and hats for men, in favor of European costume. He took away the divorce privileges of men and in 1935 abolished the use of the veil by women. He established the Iranian Academy, whose main task was to rid the Persian language of borrowed Arabic words. In all these and other reforms he used force. In order to silence critics, all criticism was banned, the number of newspapers dwindled to a handful, and the handpicked deputies of the Majles eulogized His Majesty the Shahanshah.

Reza Shah's Reforms: An Evaluation

Many writers compare Reza Shah's reforms with those of Atatürk, and there are those who believe that Reza Shah emulated the Turkish reformer. On the surface it appears that he did, and it may be likely that he was influenced by the Turkish dictator. But this should not obscure the differences between the two individuals and especially the two countries. Reza Shah had practically no education, no knowledge of the world, and no well-defined program. He did not form a party, did not make speeches, and had no ideology to expound. In every one of the above points the opposite was true in the case of Atatürk. Reza Shah's choice of reforms was based on suggestions from his advisors, his concept of nationalism, and his control of the sources of power.

Furthermore, Reza Shah had an insatiable thirst for wealth, especially in real estate. When Reza Shah died, he was not only the largest landowner in the history of the country, but he also owned factories and hotels. No doubt he rationalized that he was developing all this for the good of the country. This was partly true, but for the acquisition and management of these lands he had to depend on others, who in the process acquired land and business monopolies for themselves. Reza Shah's pampering of the army made tyrants of a large number of his officers, who suppressed the masses, especially in the provinces, for their own gains. When war clouds began to gather in the late 1930s, the very army that had been the object of his devotion was the most important single reason the masses had become disaffected. To strengthen himself and to make his dictatorship more efficient he sought help from Hitler, who was glad to send him advisors. Throughout his life, perhaps as a result of his experience in the Cossack Brigade, he was wary of the Russians. He had his quarrels with the British over oil and other subjects, but managed to solve them amicably. Under Reza Shah, Iran and Turkey, which had been old foes, started a friendship which has continued. In 1937, Afghanistan, Iran, Iraq, and Turkey signed the Sa'dabad pact which became a forerunner of CENTO after World War II.

Nevertheless, Reza Shah was a reformer whose lack of education made him susceptible to the glitter of Western civilization instead of its substance. He accepted the suggestion of his advisors by sending scores of students to Europe to study, but did not allow them to express themselves when they returned. The outward facade of democracy was maintained and the handpicked members of the Majles went through the motions of decision making. Reza Shah was a staunch nationalist and a reformer. The merchants and the growing middle class liked him because he established law and order, and the modernists liked all his reforms. What gradually became unbearable was the realization that Iranian nationalism was going the way of fascist Italy and

Nazi Germany. The democracy that they had expected from liberal nationalism was nonexistent. The outward slogan was "God, Shah, Country" and the inner, "The People Be Damned!" There were improvements, however, in communications, commerce, industry, and education. A new group had risen and became the entrepreneurs and contractors of the new era. The old titles were abolished and some of the holders of those titles left public life. Their places were taken by members of the emerging middle class who, because of their education, held the new titles of *doktor* or *mohandes* ("engineer"). These people eventually took the leadership in Iran when Reza Shah was forced to abdicate in 1941.

IRAN IN WORLD WAR II

It will be recalled that Reza Shah in his later years found the efficient dictatorship of Hitler to his liking. He probably thought that he could use the Germans to free himself from British influence. In any case Iran availed itself more and more of the technical services and economic opportunities readily provided by Germany. By 1939 over 41 percent of the foreign trade of Iran was with Germany, and German engineers and technicians came to Iran in great numbers. With these came Nazi propaganda and good-will tours by men like the Nazi youth leader Von Schirach. For the first time, the Iranian army discriminated against conscripts who belonged to minority religious groups, and the Iranian Boy Scout movement began to resemble the Nazi youth movement. At the outbreak of the war, a large number of the Iranian ruling circles, especially army officers, were pro-German, and there was a brisk commerce with Germany through the Soviet Union.

The German invasion of Russia changed the situation of Iran drastically. The Soviet Union needed supplies to fight Germany, and of the three routes available for sending such aid—Iran, Murmansk, and Vladivostok—Iran was the only all-weather route. In the summer of 1941, Britain and the Soviet Union asked Iran, which had declared its neutrality, to permit the transportation of lend-lease material through its territory. Reza Shah's refusal changed the request into an ultimatum. In 1941, Reza Shah and his military subordinates were expecting a Germany victory and were not ready to be persuaded otherwise. When the ultimatum was also refused, Britain and the Soviet Union simultaneously invaded Iran and the army of Reza Shah crumbled like a house of cards. The Russians and the British occupied Iran, and Reza Shah abdicted under pressure in favor of his twenty-year-old son, Mohammad Reza Pahlavi. The ex-shah was taken to the island of Mauritius and later to Johannesburg, where he died on July 26, 1944.

The departure of Reza Shah created a reaction that has had few parallels in the history of the country. The shah had not yet left the country when the members of the Majles, the old handpicked eulogists of his ex-majesty, began abusing him. People in general reverted to their old ways as if twenty years of Reza Shah's rule had not happened. Newspapers that had been suppressed years before started publishing again as though no interruption had occurred. In the same way, here a man raised his voice to call the faithful to prayer, there a woman put on her veil, and the clerics donned their turbans and walked in the streets reciting their prayers.

Even the Allies acted as though nothing had intervened since the days of World War I. Soviet troops occupied the northern provinces and the British occupied the south. Both countries rushed their troops to Tehran. Later, when the United States entered the war, its troops shared the south with the British and established a base in Tehran. From 1941 until 1945, Iran was the only country in which soldiers of the three major allies mingled.

The coming of the Allies in 1941 and the collapse of the dictator ushered in a period of freedom and a new effort on the part of some to establish a constitutional government. But the Allies were more interested in winning the war than in democracy for Iran. They preferred to do business with the known and tried older men rather than the hot-headed and unpredictable younger nationalists. So the older men stayed and carried on their business in the old way. In 1942, Qavam al-Saltaneh once again became prime minister after a lapse of twenty years. He believed in involving a third power to neutralize the Anglo-Russian rivalry. Just as he had done twenty years before, he arranged for the coming of an American financial adviser. Early in 1943, Dr. Arthur Millspaugh, who had had the same position from 1922 to 1927, returned to Iran. Oddly enough, Dr. Millspaugh, now twenty years older, forgot that his Iranian assistants had ideas of their own and would not take orders as their counterparts had done before. He complained that the United States did not help him. His only support came from Seyyed Ziya, the old rival of Reza Shah, who had returned from Palestine and had revived his old newspaper. Since he was known to be pro-British, his support was the kiss of death to Millspaugh's plans, and Millspaugh was forced to resign in 1945.

The younger men, however, would not be denied. The year 1942 produced a bumper crop of political parties, each with permits to publish two or three newspapers, so that if one was suppressed one day, another could be published the next. Most of the parties did not have a national base but represented either personal ambitions or interest groups. About the only exception to the rule was the *Tudeh* ("masses") Party, which had a good organization and a broad base of support. It was Marxist but had enough nationalists in it to make pronouncements that were not entirely to Moscow's liking. At no time did it claim to be communist or ask for the nationalization of property. The party was strongest in the north. It edited six newspapers and organized demonstrations, mass meetings, and strikes. In the election of 1943, about the only significant change in the Majles was the fact that there were eight Tudeh members in it. The rest were old-timers.

To counteract Soviet political activity directly in the north and through the Tudeh Party the British had brought back the 1921 coup d'etat prime minister, Sayyed Ziya. He organized the anticommunist National Will Party with a platform of justice, distribution of public domain lands, and defense of Islam and religious education in public schools.

While these political activities were going on, the presence of foreign troops handling war supplies to Russia and their immense expenditure created a rocketing inflation. Entrepreneurs and contractors supplying the

Allies became wealthy, land prices and house rentals went up, and in general the gap between the rich and poor widened. Poor crops caused near-famine and Iranians, even in Tehran, had to stand in long lines to buy bread.

To appease Iranian sensitivities, the British and the Soviet Union concluded the Tripartite Treaty of Alliance with Iran on January 29, 1942. It claimed that the presence of Allied troops in Iran did not constitute an occupation and provided for the withdrawal of foreign troops within six months after the end of hostilities. Later, American troops came to Iran on the strength of this treaty. At the end of the Tehran Conference in December 1943, President Roosevelt suggested that he, Churchill, and Stalin issue a communiqué honoring the territorial integrity and independence of Iran, acknowledging Iran's services on behalf of the war, promising economic assistance, and invoking the principles of the Atlantic Charter. The Iranians, fearful that the old Anglo-Russian rivalry would start all over again at their expense, pinned their hopes on the presence of a third power, the United States. This new relationship went through many happy and sad vicissitudes in the postwar period.

Chapter Thirty-Four
Iran: The White Revolution and the Islamic Revolution

The White Revolution of Mohammad Reza Shah Pahlavi was an extension of Reza Shah's reforms which, in turn, was a continuation, albeit unfaithful, of the Constitutional Revolution of 1906. The purpose of the Constitutional Revolution was not only to limit the power of the monarch and put legislation in the hands of the elected representatives, but also to usher medieval Iran and its institutions into the modern era. The models for this program were the educational, social, economic, and political institutions of the West. The two Pahlavi monarchs tried to carry out this program by ignoring the Constitution and taking all powers into their own hands. An examination of the reforms of both Pahlavis will show that had they honored the Constitution and had they involved the citizens in decision making, Iran would have experienced a real revolution in most aspects of life.

The Mosaddeq movement in the 1950s tried to check the power of the Shah but failed. The announced purpose of Ayatollah Khomayni and all the different groups with him was to uphold the Constitution of 1906 and to carry out the reforms without the Shah. As soon as he came to power, however, Khomayni denounced the Constitution, the parliamentary system, the flag, Iranian nationalism, and the educational, judicial, social, and economic systems that had been established. Although the present regime has continued some of the Pahlavi industrialization program, in most other matters it has taken the country back to pre-1906 when Islamic laws and institutions prevailed and when the Shi'i clergy had predominant position. In reality, what has happened in Iran is an Islamic Counter-Revolution that has checked and, in some cases, reversed the social, economic, political, judicial, and educational programs envisaged by the revolutionaries of 1906 and later years.

From the time of the Iranian Revolution in 1906 until nearly the end of World War I, tsarist Russia sided with the Iranian reactionaries who preferred the status quo, while Britain appeared to side with the revolutionaries who desired change. During World War II, when the two countries occupied Iran, their positions were reversed. The Soviet Union sided with the revolutionaries who demanded change while Britain sided with reactionaries who were satisfied with the status quo. The British, who supported the revolutionaries of the earlier years, did so for their own ends and not for the sake of democracy or freedom. They did not hesitate to betray the Iranian Revolution by signing the Anglo-Russian Convention of 1907 or by advising the Iranian Majles to accept the Russian ultimatum to dismiss Shuster. Similarly, the Russians, who sided with the Iranian communists and radicals in the 1940s and early 1950s, did so for their own ends and not for the sake of the people or of the revolution. They also betrayed their comrades in 1946 and abandoned them altogether in 1953.

Between 1945 and 1978, Iran underwent a series of internal conflicts between major interest groups and between the monarchy and the general population. It began with the conflict between the nationalist-dominated Majles under Mosaddeq's leadership and the monarchist-dominated government under the shah's leadership. This conflict culminated in the nationalization of the Iranian oil industry and put the control of Iran's oil wealth in the hands of the Majles. The shah and his supporters among the leading landed families, import-export merchant families, military officials, and several religious leaders sided with the interests of British Petroleum and the United States against the nationalist movement between 1951 and 1953. The CIA-assisted coup was directed against the nationalist movement and worked for the benefit of American oil companies. The coup gave a boost to the shah and his supporters and aimed a blow against the British monopoly of the Iranian oilfields.

IRANIAN OIL: THE FOURTH PHASE

It will be recalled that during World War II two important political parties were organized in Iran. One was Tudeh, which was supported by the Soviet Union and was founded by some of the young men whom Reza Shah had sent to Europe and who had been imprisoned after their return on the charge that they were communists. The other party was the National Will, founded by Sayyed Ziya and supported by the British. For a time, the rivalry between these two parties had all the earmarks and the promise of a genuine two-party system that was divided along ideological, social, and economic lines. There is no telling what the outcome would have been had the parties had the opportunity to fight it out. But Iran had oil. The oil in the south was under the control of the British, and it was no secret that the Soviet Union, like tsarist Russia, wanted similar privileges in the north. Toward the end of the war, there were indications that American oil companies wanted to renew their attempt, which had failed in 1924, to gain oil concessions in the north. The Anglo-Iranian Oil Company[1] was no more friendly to the American "intrusion" in 1944 than it had been in 1924. As the Soviet Union was occupying northern Iran, however, it was in a good position to drive its rivals out of the field. There were long and heated debates on this question in the Iranian Majles. Dr. Mohammad Mosaddeq, an independent deputy, was able to persuade the Majles to pass a law forbidding the Iranian government to grant or negotiate oil concessions to any foreign country without approval of the Majles. The Tudeh Party, however, was in favor of giving the northern oil concession to the Soviet Union on the principle of "positive neutrality." This was based on the argument that because Britain had the oil concession in the south, the Soviet Union should be given the oil concession in the north.

On December 12, 1945, the Azerbaijani members of the Tudeh formed a party of their own called "Demokrat," deposed the governor at Tabriz, and proclaimed the Autonomous Republic of Azerbaijan. They had the Soviet army's full protection. When a contingent of the Iranian army was dispatched to Azerbaijan to quell the rebellion, the Soviet army refused to allow them to enter the province. Shortly afterward, the Kurds of Iran under Qadi Mohammad, at the instigation of the Soviet Union, formed a republic of their own with Mahabad as their capital.

According to the Tripartite Agreement of 1942, signed by Britain, Iran, and the Soviet Union and adhered to by the United States, foreign troops were to evacuate Iran within six months after the end of hostilities. By March 2, 1946, American and British troops were out of the country but the Soviet army refused to leave. Iran appealed to the United Nations. Pressure of world opinion and the demands of Britain and the United States were certainly factors in the ultimate Russian decision to evacuate Iran, but it withdrew only after it was assured an oil concession.

Ahmad Qavam, the Iranian prime minister, led a delegation to Moscow in March 1946 for talks with Stalin. Qavam agreed to the formation of the Irano-Soviet Oil Company for the exploitation of oil in northern Iran. Qavam promised Stalin that he would persuade the new Majles, yet to be elected, to ratify the agreement provided the Russians evacuate Iran. Stalin agreed and Qavam proceeded to make good his promise.

The Soviet army evacuated Iran on May 9, 1946. The Iranian army took possession of Azerbaijan and Kurdestan, and severely punished the leaders of those two provinces. The Soviet Union, whose declared policy was helping "national liberation movements" anywhere in the world, betrayed one that it had helped instigate in exchange for oil concession in northern Iran.

The fifteenth Majles was elected during the summer of 1947, with Qavam in power and his party in the majority. He presented the Irano-Soviet oil concession to the Majles; and on October 22, 1947, the Majles

---

[1]Later the name was changed to British Petroleum.

defeated it almost unanimously with only two dissenting votes. Qavam resigned, his party was disbanded, and Tudeh was discredited.

The evaluation of Qavam's role in this episode is a subject of controversy among Iranian historians. There are those who believe that he acted cleverly by deceiving the Russians and saving the province of Azerbaijan for Iran. There are also those who think that Qavam did not see anything wrong in the establishment of the Irano-Soviet Oil Company as the price of saving Azerbaijan. After all, the Irano-Soviet Fisheries Company had been in operation for some time. The pressure that the United States brought to bear on the Soviet Union to evacuate Iran cannot be exaggerated. This was done in special letters to Stalin and protests in the United Nations. The most supportive statement was made by Mr. George Allen, the U.S. ambassador in Iran, a few weeks before the Majles was to vote on Qavam's Irano-Soviet oil proposal. He said that Iran was free to dispose its resources in any way it desired and assured patriotic Iranians "that American people will support fully their freedom to make their own choice." The role of the shah was that of constitutional monarch. He showed determination by refusing to go along with compromise plans in dealing with the republicans. This was not the first nor the last time that attempts would be made to establish autonomous republics in Iran.

THE AFTERMATH OF WORLD WAR II

The physical removal of the Soviet army from the northern provinces and the failure of the republican movements in Azerbaijan removed the danger of the dismemberment of Iran. But it did not open the door for reform so badly needed in the country. The abdication of the dictator, Reza Shah, did not free the country, but freed the hands of the oligarchy to reclaim their lost prestige and property and to continue their paternalistic rule. The oligarchy—sometimes referred to as the "one thousand families"—buttressed by the clergy and supported by the old army officers, paid lip service to the constitution and the democracy it envisaged, and ruled without regard to the changing times.

As the Majles, composed mostly of the members of the oligarchy or their supporters, could not be expected to change the status quo, there were groups clamoring for change outside the halls of parliament. The evacuation of foreign troops had brought in its wake economic depression and unemployment. Bankruptcies became frequent, and, for the first time, Iran had an army of educated unemployed. High school and university graduates and even students who had returned from Europe aimlessly walked the streets. The radical groups of both right and left, who led in the seemingly endless demonstrations and rioting, were recruited mostly from the educated unemployed.

Some radical groups were religiously oriented. After the abdication of Reza Shah, governments and individuals reestablished those religious practices which the ex-shah had tried to destroy. Women were permitted to put on their veils; the clergy donned their religious garb; religious processions came into vogue; the Koran was chanted on the radio; religious education became compulsory in the schools; the old, discontinued seminary was revived as the Faculty of Theology under the University of Tehran; and thousands were given passports to make the pilgrimage to Mecca.

The radical religious activity, however, was in the formation of political activist groups. One of these was the "Devotees of Islam," similar to the Muslim Brotherhood of Egypt. A second group was the "Warriors of Islam," under the leadership of Ayatollah Abul-Qasem Kashani, an important member of the ulama who later became a member of the Majles and eventually its speaker. These two groups separately and sometimes jointly used every means in their power, especially assassination and terrorism, to gain political control. An important nonreligious group on the right was the Pan-Iranist Party, which espoused an extremist racist nationalism of the German National Socialist variety.

On the left, in addition to the well-organized Tudeh Party, which, even after the setback over oil and Azerbaijan, was still strong and active, there were two others. One was the Toilers Party, and the other was the Third Force Party. Both of these were anti-Stalinist but had as members Marxists and socialists of different varieties. At the center was the Iran Party, made up of a group of young intellectuals, businessmen, lawyers, doctors, and teachers.

The position of the young shah in the early postwar period was rather ambivalent. He was close to the old army officers and the nonpolitical but conservative clergy. His youth and the presence of foreign troops in Iran during the war years united the country behind him. His stand on the Azerbaijan republican movement vis-à-vis the Soviet Union and the Iranian appeasers made him popular. Perhaps these experiences gave him confidence and enabled him to be more active after the Azerbaijan incident and he began to take a larger part in the affairs of the country. One of the first things the shah did was to implement, for the first time, a constitutional provision for the organization of a senate. In it the shah was entitled to appoint thirty senators. Although his appointees were mostly older army officers and conservative intellectuals, the shah was beginning to have some influence in the affairs of the country.

The first seven-year plan.   Americans were beginning to be involved in the affairs of Iran at a rapidly increasing pace. As early as 1947, a United States army mission had arrived in Iran. The Morrison Knudson Company was employed by Iran to survey Iran's needs and resources for an all-embracing development plan. Its report was given to another American firm, Overseas Consultants, for implementation. They prepared a seven-year development program. The result was one of the most comprehensive plans ever produced for an underdeveloped country. The plan provided for the expenditure of $650,000,000 and encompassed social, educational, economic, and technical problems. It was expected that the plan would be financed by royalties from the Anglo-Iranian Oil Company and economic aid from the United States. The government was negotiating with the British oil company for a revision of the terms which, added to the aid from the United States, was deemed sufficient to start the development program.

The seven-year development plan needed money, and the negotiations with the officers of the AIOC were not fruitful. The shah decided to come to the United States to make a personal plea for economic aid. He arrived on November 16, 1949, and made a good impression across the country. But the U.S. government was not willing to involve itself so deeply in the military development of Iran. In any case, the disappointed shah went back empty-handed. But he did not give up the idea of reform.

MOSADDEQ AND OIL NATIONALIZATION

The nationalization of Iran's oil industry, which drained the Iranians economically and emotionally, must be understood in the context of its time. The vast expansion of the oil industry after the war made a revision of the Anglo-Iranian Oil Agreement necessary. Furthermore, the success of the seven-year plan depended upon increased oil royalties. Added to these was the emotional involvement of the Iranians in the recent Azerbaijan crisis and the defeat of the Irano-Soviet oil concession. Lack of sensitivity on the part of the British to the changing situation in Iran contributed to the intensity of the crisis. It was hard for Britain to accept its reduced economic and political role in the world scene. The second most important British interest in Iran, the Imperial Bank of Iran, had ended in 1948, and was brought under the jurisdiction of the Iranian government. Also, Britain's predominant political place in Iran was taken over by the United States, which had announced the Point Four Program in 1950, as part of the larger Operations Mission in Iran.

The chairman of the Majles committee for oil was Dr. Mohammad Mosaddeq, who had a reputation for honesty and for being a nationalist. Mosaddeq himself introduced the idea of nationalization. Eight members of the Majles, a number of them from the Iran Party, formed a coalition called the National Front under the leadership of Dr. Mosaddeq and pushed for nationalization. They espoused the principle of "negative neutralism." "Now that we have refused to give the northern oil to the Russians," they argued, "we should take the southern oil away from the British."

By January 1951 it was reported that Aramco (the Arabian-American Oil Company) had revised its arrangement with Saudi Arabia and had agreed on a 50-50 profit-sharing plan. This news advanced the cause of nationalization. By the time the British company brought itself to report to Prime Minister Razmara that it was ready to make a similar arrangement, it was too late. General Razmara had already expressed himself against the practicality of nationalization and was a target of great criticism. On March 7, 1951, he was murdered in the Sepahsalar Mosque by a member of the Devotees of Islam. On March 15, the Majles approved the principle of nationalization. On April 30, the Majles passed a nine-point enabling law that included a provision for compensating the company. The British government protested the nationalization and insisted that under the 1933 agreement Iran should submit to arbitration. Hosayn Ala, who had been appointed a caretaker prime minister, replied that the British government had no right to interfere in a matter between Iran and an oil company. On April 15, the British closed the Abadan oil refinery and on April 27, Ala resigned. On April 28, Mosaddeq was appointed prime minister and on the same day the Majles voted unanimously to seize the company's properties in Iran. On May 2, 1951, the young shah signed the Nationalization Bill, completing the process.

Events occurred swiftly and surprised practically everyone concerned with the crisis. The British were surprised to see that Iran was not intimidated by threats, the freezing of Iranian assets, or even the sending of gunboats to the Persian Gulf. Western observers were surprised that Iran was not brought to its knees when the oil refinery in Abadan closed down and royalties stopped coming in. The Iranians were pleasantly surprised that they could twist the British lion's tail and get away with it. Perhaps the most surprised of all was Dr. Mosaddeq when he realized how popular he was with the people. It has been suggested that Mosaddeq's greatest mistake was not realizing the extent of his own popularity.

In the course of the crisis, which lasted two years, half a dozen alternative proposals were made, most of them accepting the principle of nationalization, but they all failed to bring about a solution. The British complained to the United Nations. In September 1952 Mosaddeq went to New York to defend Iran's case, contending that nationalization was an internal matter and not subject to international jurisdiction. The Security Council referred the question of jurisdiction to the World Court and the court decided in favor of Iran, stating that the problem was an internal question and outside of the competency of the World Court or of the United Nations.

The intervention of two American presidents, Truman and Eisenhower, and the World Bank failed to solve the problem. Mosaddeq took over the oil installations in Abadan and broke diplomatic relations with Britain. But he was in political and financial trouble at home. It will be recalled that the National Front was a coalition of parties, interest groups, and individuals with diverse opinions joined together for the purpose of nationalization. When the failure to find a solution dragged on, disagreement developed. At the opening of the seventeenth Majles in July 1952, Mosaddeq demanded extraordinary powers for six months. When some of the deputies balked, he threatened to resign. Such threats were usually followed by mass demonstrations in which the members of the Tudeh Party and Muslim groups participated.

As the crisis worsened, Mosaddeq demanded more power. The more power he sought, the more friends he lost and, in the end, he had to rely upon Tudeh members. In the summer of 1953, communication between the shah and his prime minister, and between the prime minister, his cabinet, and the Majles had broken down. Even then, Mosaddeq was so popular that it took the combined efforts of the shah, the Iranian army, and the American CIA to oust him. On August 13, 1953, the shah issued an order dismissing Mosaddeq from office and another one appointing General Fazlollah Zahedi as prime minister. Mosaddeq refused to comply and arrested the messenger who had brought him the order. On August 16, the shah and Empress Sorayya left the country in order to "prevent bloodshed." For three days Tehran was in the hands of Mosaddeq's followers, over whom he had no control. One of the curious aspects of these turbulent days was Moscow's attitude. The mobs in the streets, at the initial instigation of the Tudeh Party, were smashing statues of both the shah and his father. The members of the Tudeh Party could probably have taken control of the government, but on strict orders from Moscow they stayed home. They paid heavily for their inaction, because under the new regime soon to come to power, they were hunted all over the country; and those of their leaders who were not executed or imprisoned fled the country and continued to live precarious lives in communist countries.

By August 19, General Zahedi, with CIA assistance, made his move and was able to arouse pro-shah sentiment. His soldiers surrounded and partially demolished Mosaddeq's house. By nightfall, he published the shah's letter appointing him prime minister. On August 22, the shah returned to Tehran in triumph. Mosaddeq was arrested and later tried. He was imprisoned for 3 years and then under house arrest in his home in Ahmadabad near Tehran to the end of his life on March 5, 1967. Even Zahedi's ruthlessness was not able to suppress the followers of Mosaddeq.

Mosaddeq: An Evaluation

There is little doubt that in Dr. Mohammad Mosaddeq the Iranians had found what they had been unconsciously looking for: an honest, charismatic, popular leader they could follow. In the history of modern Iran the popularity of the oil nationalization parallels the strike against the tobacco monopoly in 1890, the granting of the constitution in 1906, the rally in support of Morgan Shuster in 1911, and the demonstrations of 1979. It is doubtful whether the British and other Westerners understood the Iranian point of view. The British at first tried gunboat diplomacy to bring the Iranian government to its knees. Having failed in that and in the World Court, the British froze Iranian assets, and persuaded Europeans to boycott Iranian oil and Americans to withhold economic aid, but to no avail.

The British looked at the Anglo-Iranian Oil Company as a business venture that had to produce a profit. In all the plans that were submitted, the British not only wanted payment for the assets of the company, which the Iranian government acknowledged, but they also wanted to be compensated for all the profits they would have made until 1993. All along, the British company felt that it had done Iran a great service by exploiting the oil and was genuinely surprised when the Iranians were not grateful. In the light of such an attitude the company's huge profits, which in some years reached 150 percent, were not relevant. What was pertinent in their minds was that the oil income of the Iranian government would not exist at all were it not for the effort and industry of the British.

The Iranians, on the other hand, wanted a larger share of the profits; were rebuffed at the constant refusal of the company to open its books to Iranian inspectors; were frustrated at the slowness of the British to replace foreign technicians with Iranians; and were angry when they realized that the company violated the political independence of the country. Because most of the oil royalties had gone to support the Iranian army and had not trickled down to the people, the small merchants, the bureaucrats, and the students who supported Mosaddeq did not care if the whole company was shut down.

Dr. Mosaddeq was responsible for the sense of hope and pride which the Iranians exhibited during most of the crisis. But he was also responsible for the partial failure of the movement, and for letting the Iranians down. Mosaddeq was woefully ignorant about the oil industry. He either did not read all the excellent reports that were prepared for him or if he did, he did not heed their suggestions nor investigate the questions they raised, both of which are severe shortcomings in a leader. For example, he believed that Europe's need for Iranian oil was so great that countries would vie with each other to buy it from him. He should have known that Britain and the United States could tap, as they did, the vast reserves of oil in Aden, Bahrayn, Kuwait, and Saudi Arabia. Furthermore, Iran did not have a single oil tanker to transport oil. He was shown several charts indicating the interrelatedness of the major oil companies of Europe and America and the control they exercised on shipping and the oil market. Even if the British company had not challenged the nationalization, Iran had to depend upon the existing companies to market the oil.

In the second place, Mosaddeq allowed his personal hatred for the British to cloud his judgment. Among the several plans that were offered, perhaps the one presented by the World Bank was the best. It adhered to all the points of the Iranian nationalization law. And yet Mosaddeq rejected it because the bank insisted on the freedom, as a neutral world body, to use British as well as other personnel in its operations.

Perhaps Mosaddeq's greatest shortcoming was that he was not a revolutionary. He was so immersed in nationalization that it had become an end in itself rather than a means toward reform. Nevertheless, Dr. Mosaddeq's name will go down in Iranian history as the leader who stirred the Iranians to their depths.

ECONOMIC RECOVERY AND U.S. AID

The years between 1953 and 1973 saw a consolidation of state power in the monarchy and its supporters. The solution of the oil controversy was an important step toward Iran's economic recovery. An agreement was reached and passed by the Majles on October 21, 1954. In brief, the agreement accepted the principle of nationalization and recognized the National Iranian Oil Company. A consortium of eight companies was formed to operate the oilfields in the southwest and the refinery in Abadan. The Anglo-Iranian Oil Company (now called British Petroleum) held 40 percent of the shares; five major American companies held 35 percent while nine minor American companies held 5 percent; the Dutch Bataafse Petroleum Maatschappij N.V. held 14 percent; and the Compagnie Française des Petroles held the remaining 6 percent. The consortium was incorporated in the Netherlands but its permanent headquarters were in Iran. The president of the consortium was Dutch.

It was arranged that Iran pay the former AIOC the sum of $25 million in ten years without interest. In addition, the other members of the consortium agreed to pay the British company 10 percent per barrel of crude oil and other products exported from Iran until $510 million had been paid. The British company did not lose much, but for the Iranians the agreement was not as good as some of the plans Dr. Mosaddeq had rejected. In later years the National Iranian Oil Company made separate arrangements with other companies. It discovered oil in central Iran; drilled for oil in the Persian Gulf; and became a well-organized economic institution.

Further seven-year plans and the Plan Organization. Another means of economic recovery was planning under the general supervision of the Plan Organization. There were four seven-year plans. The first one, spanning the years 1948–1954, had been a complete failure mostly because of the oil controversy. By the time the second seven-year plan was launched (1955–1961), the Majles had passed a law to attract foreign capital. An American company headed by David Lilienthal was employed to survey Khuzestan for massive hydroelectric dams, petrochemical plants, and large-scale agricultural projects. Despite the fact that political considerations, personal ambitions, and corruption marred the activities of the Plan Organization, it remained one of the better-run programs of the shah's regime.

The U.S. Point Four Program and Military Aid

Another factor in the economic life of Iran was the Point Four Program, which was first mentioned in President Truman's inaugural address on January 20, 1949, and implemented in Iran in 1952. Under it, Iran received more aid than any country in the Middle East or Africa except Turkey. It was also the largest in size. From 1952 to 1962, the United States had between 200 and 300 personnel each year in Iran and the United Nations had an additional 100 to 150. This program has been strongly praised and just as strongly criticized by experts in the field. Considering the vast expenditures of money and manpower, Iran should have benefitted more than it did. Perhaps the most important cause of its shortcoming was the fact that military and strategic considerations usually outweighed economic and social ones.

United States military aid to Iran had always been dovetailed, in purpose and execution, with its economic aid. Indeed, the whole purpose of American aid was ostensibly to enable the monarchy to defend itself against foreign (mainly Soviet) aggression and domestic opposition. In both instances, internal security and a developing economy were paramount, and American aid focused accordingly on these two questions.

The United States military mission began in 1943, with the establishment of the Gendarmerie (state police) for internal security. Later it became quite extensive and was referred to as GENMISH. Then in 1947, another mission with the acronym ARMISH was sent by the United States army to enhance the efficiency of the Iranian army. Both agreements bound the government of Iran to consult with the United States on the employment of any personnel "of other foreign governments for duties of any nature connected with the Iranian army."

The United States-Iran Mutual Defense Assistance Agreement was signed on May 23, 1950, and the Military Assistance Advisory Group (MAAG) was created. The express purpose of the United States was the extension of the Truman Doctrine, the inclusion of Iran in the military assistance program that was being extended to South Korea and the Philippines, and military assistance "aimed at the internal security, not the national defense, of Iran." In return Iran promised to "facilitate the production [and] transport . . . of raw and semiprocessed materials required by the United States. . . ." Thus United States aid began with the sale of arms for oil, a process that accelerated at breakneck speed in the 1960s and 1970s.

The creation of SAVAK.   Both the shah and the United States military mission were interested in internal security, which the state police was unable to guarantee. For this purpose SAVAK (Organization for State Intelligence and Security) was established in 1957, with the help of the American CIA and FBI. Its aim was to uncover and combat "anti-regime activities within the country"; to provide "advice and assistance on military matters to the government of Iran"; and assist Iran in "administering the United States Security Assistance activities." In later years SAVAK became notorious for its cruelty and terrorized Iranians in practically all walks of life.

The question of extraterritoriality.   Discussions began in early 1962 over the possibility of extraterritorial legal status for U.S. advisors in Iran. On October 13, 1964, the Majles granted such immunity to American advisors and, by implication, to their dependents. The last of the American military missions was accepted by the Iranian government in January 1973. This was the Technical Assistance Field Team (TAFT), which had become necessary because of the skyrocketing increase in U.S. arms sales that had resulted from President Nixon's visit to Iran in May 1972.

The American military and economic aid, briefly described here, revealed two changes in Iranian foreign policy. The first had to do with the traditional neutrality of Iran. It will be recalled that successive Iranian governments since the turn of the century had tried to remain neutral between contending great powers. The shah broke this tradition and joined the American bloc. Over the protests of the Soviet Union, an American military mission was established in Iran, and Iran received not only tremendous amounts of economic aid but great quantities of military equipment under a mutual defense agreement. The Irano-American alliance, however, did not prevent the Soviet Union from inviting the shah and the empress to visit Moscow and other parts of the country as its official guests. Iran and Turkey showed that with post-Stalinist Russia, one did not have to be neutral in order to be in its favor.

The second change in Iranian foreign policy had to do with the extraterritorial status of foreign residents of Iran. It was ironic that on May 8, 1928, Reza Shah announced to a jubilant nation an end to foreigners' extraterritorial privileges in Iran. Thirty-six years later, his son reinstated them for a large number of Americans in the country, an action that was to haunt him later. Both events involved Americans in practically every phase of Iranian life. One is reminded of the Anglo-Iranian Agreement of 1919 that would have given the British the same measure of power in Iranian affairs, had it not met with universal popular opposition. The difference was that the Iranians were freer in 1919 to express their ideas than they were in the 1960s, while the nature and scope of the opposition had changed.

THE WHITE REVOLUTION

With the fall of Mosaddeq, his followers were pushed underground but were not subdued. They held demonstrations, published clandestine literature, and carried on strikes in colleges and high schools. It was soon discovered that a large number of young army officers had been influenced by the Tudeh Party. These were symptoms of a basic alienation that the educated youth felt toward the established authority of their country. There was practically no communication between the shah and these people, some of whom belonged to the Tudeh and some to the National Front. Most of them, however, did not belong to any organized group. They had simply lost confidence in their own government.

By 1961, the shah began to court the support of the peasants and had gained the confidence of some former members and followers of the National Front and the Tudeh parties. The army remained entirely loyal and the shah believed he was ready. At his urging, a bill was sent to the Majles limiting the amount of land a person could own. Any excess had to be sold to the government in order to be distributed among the peasants. The Majles, still made up of landlords, attached so many amendments to the bill that it became meaningless. The shah, who had returned from exile determined to rule, dissolved the Majles on May 6, 1961, and, in effect, suspended the constitution by not calling for an election. A new liberal cabinet implemented a royal decree for land reform. All land, in excess of 400 irrigated and 800 unirrigated hectares, had to be sold to the government. The price of the land was to be determined according to income tax statements filed by the landlords themselves. As there was hardly a landlord who had not devalued his land in order to pay less taxes, a cry of "foul" was raised, but there was nothing the landlords could do. The shah, however, did not press the point too strongly.

The shah was the first Iranian monarch to support a peasant movement. In January 1963, on the occasion of the opening of a conference on rural cooperatives, he unfolded a six-point program. In a national referendum, these points—which the shah referred to as the "White Revolution"—were endorsed by a landslide. The six objectives of the revolution were: land redistribution, nationalization of the forests, the sale of shares in government-owned factories to underwrite land reform, the sharing of factory profits with workers, electoral reform and the enfranchisement of women, and the creation of a literacy corps. The literacy corps was primarily carried out by educated young men who agreed to spend their time in these creative services in lieu of two years in the army.

These were far-reaching reforms. The implementation of land reform and the enfrachisement of women aroused the combined wrath of landlords and clerics. Between June 5 and 9, 1963, uprisings by the clerics of Qom's major theological schools and the shopkeepers of Tehran, Tabriz, and Mashhad resulted in bloody street battles. These events were harbingers of the guerrilla movement and the 1977–1979 demonstrations by the national-ist-Islamic coalitions that culminated in the recent revolution.

The shah, however, did not accept the reported advice of several high-ranking military and civilian officials to meet with some of the leaders of the opposition. He remained adamant in his refusal and sent many leaders and important clerics to jail or into exile. Among the exiled was a hitherto unknown cleric in Qom by the name of Ruhollah Khomayni, who proved to be a fiery and determined leader. His attacks on the shah were not so much against land reform and women's suffrage as against the government's use of arbitrary power and the shah's giving extraterritorial status to Americans in Iran. He was sentenced to death but the shah was persuaded to commute the sentence to exile, a decision he had reason to regret fifteen years later.

The elections of 1965 brought an almost entirely new group to the Majles, the majority of whom were committed to a program of moderniza-tion and to the shah's White Revolution. In the new Majles, the shah worked through the recently formed New Iran Party. Even though other parties were in existence and had deputies in the Majles, the New Iran Party be-came the executor of His Majesty's will.

Toward a New Civilization

In 1977 the shah published a book entitled *Toward a New Civilization.* In it he presented his views of what the White Revolution had accomplished in Iran. By 1977, the original six points of the Revolution had increased to nineteen. Land had been distributed to 15 percent of the peasants. A series of dams had been built, the country had been industralized, many universi-ties had been established and the standard of living had risen. Miles of roads had been built connecting different parts of the country; and Iran itself had been connected, by Iran Air, with the capitals of Europe and Asia. Literacy, health, and development corps had been organized when young men and women, after receiving instruction, were sent to all parts of the country in order to take the fruits of the Revolution to the remotest villages. All this and much more had been achieved. The nation, by a vote of the senate, bestowed upon him the title of *Aryamehr,* or "Sun of the Aryans." He himself felt that he was ready to be crowned shah of Iran. He ascended the throne of Iran on October 26, 1967; on that day he also crowned his wife Farah empress, the first woman to be so honored since A.D. 632.

The White Revolution had strengthened the position of Iran in the Middle East and had enhanced its standing among the nations of the world. When it became evident in 1971 that Britain was unwilling to defend the

Persian Gulf any longer and that the United States was unable to do so, Iran seemed the logical country to be made into a fortress protecting U.S. interests in the region. The Nixon Doctrine was a two-pronged strategy proclaimed in Guam in 1969, that was originally formulated for Southeast Asia, but was extended to the Persian Gulf. Iran, as the regional surrogate of the United States, would receive all the weapons it needed for the defense of the Persian Gulf. With this blank check and the enormous amount of petrodollars that was pouring in, the shah went on a weapon-buying spree, the likes of which has not been seen in history. From 1950 to 1970, Iran's military purchases from the United States came to $1.8 billion. Between 1971 and 1978, the shah, who had total control of the country's income, spent an additional $18.1 billion on weapons.

The shah was strong enough to be diplomatic about relinquishing Iran's claim to the island of Bahrayn; to flex his muscles by occupying Abu Musa and the Tunb Islands in the Persian Gulf; to force Iraq to surrender its claim to Iran's section of the Shatt al-Arab; and to send a detachment to help Qabus, the hard-pressed sultan of Oman, against leftist insurgents in the Dhofar region.

The close relationship between Iran and the United States did not prevent other countries from gaining concessions in Iran. The Soviet Union built a steel mill in Esfahan in return for Iranian natural gas. The Japanese, British, French, Germans, Italians, and others contracted to build factories, roads, ships, docks, military bases, and a hundred and one other things. By 1978, all roads led to Tehran.

THE ISLAMIC REVOLUTION

Notwithstanding the shah's accomplishments, real and perceived, there were rumblings of discontent in the country. They began with the June 1963 uprising in Qom and increased in intensity and number until they reached enormous proportions inn 1978 and a full-fledged revolution in 1979. Volumes have been written on the causes of this momentous event. A full discussion is outside the scope of this book but the main points are as follows:

1. There were severe economic and social dislocations caused by the manner in which the government conducted the White Revolution.
2. There was political unrest that sent thousands to prison and hundreds to their deaths. This was the result of the shah's neglect of the constitution and his antiquated interpretation of the institution of monarchy.
3. There was unparalleled corruption at every level of government—from the members of the royal family on down to the lowest functionaries.
4. The only outlet the people had to protest their economic misery, which practically everyone felt, and the political suppression, which the educated felt, was the Shi'i religious organization. The Shi'i clergy had their own sources of dissatisfaction, especially their loss of power and the abandonment of the values they cherished.

Economic and Social Dislocation

The original six points of the White Revolution that the people en-dorsed in 1963 were all necessary and useful. If the shah had allowed more time for the implementation of the original program, he might have had a greater chance of success. Instead, the shah added thirteen more points in rapid succession. The combined nineteen points of the White Revolution raised expectations; but the fact that most of them were either not imple-mented at all or were poorly administered turned the popular disappoint-ment into resentment. The land reform law was very necessary and many benefitted from its first phase. There was, however, only one law for a large country like Iran with its varied climate, lifestyles, and traditions. Time was needed to adapt the law to the needs of each locality; farmers needed to be taught how to work in cooperatives; laws were needed to protect the farmers; and money was needed to help them stand on their feet. However, not enough time was allowed for adaptation or education or laws, because the government functionaries were busy nodding their heads in praise of some new point the shah had added to the White Revolution. Money there was aplenty—but for other projects.

Agriculture was put on the back burner in favor of industralization. Factories were installed for which there were no trained Iranian workers; millions of tons of goods were brought by uncounted ships for which there were no docking facilities; thousands of huge trucks were imported for which there were no drivers; and tens of thousands of cars were imported for which there were no roads or city streets. As if there weren't enough motor vehicles already, contracts were signed with the United States, Britain, France, Germany, and Japan to assemble still more automobiles. The amount of social dislocation and confusion was staggering. On the one hand, thousands of semiskilled and skilled laborers from Korea, Pakistan, the Phil-ippines, and other countries were brought into Iran, which upset the social and cultural patterns of the country. On the other hand, farmers and villagers by the hundreds of thousands, most of them unskilled, were pushed off their lands into urban shantytowns in search of work.

Billions of petrodollars were spent by one man, apparently without consultation with anyone. The shah spent millions to save the tottering Ger-man Krupp Munitions Company, to the surprise of the Germans. He bought two ten-year-old luxury liners that were losing money from Italy for recre-ational facilities for Iranian naval officers in the Persian Gulf. The shah spent billions to purchase his favorite toys—sophisticated armaments—that Iran did not need and could not use, from the United States, Britain, France, Germany, Israel, and even the Soviet Union.

Political Unrest

The shah had the constitution of 1906 amended in order to give him-self more power. Then he turned around and issued an imperial decree that Iranians were free to express their opinions on every subject except three: the constitution, the monarchy, and the White Revolution. Even though he was seemingly defending the constitution, in reality he was attacking it because he placed the constitution and monarchy on the same level and considered them to be two pillars upon which the country rested. Actually, there was no monarchy *outside* of the constitution. Indeed, Iranians in the first decade of this century struggled for the express purpose of limiting the power of monarchy and clearly defined it in the constitution. The intention of the shah to elevate the monarchy as an independent entity separate from the constitution had only one meaning: he did not like the limitations the constitution had placed on the monarchy. Not only did he concentrate all power in his own hands, but a succession of prime ministers and ministers received written and oral orders from the shah, which the constitution explicitly forbade. Were some deputy to ask even the most innocuous question, he would be reminded that it was ordered by His Imperial Majesty—and that was enough to silence anyone.

The most tragic fact in the life of Mohammad Reza Shah Pahlavi is that with all his education and knowledge of the world he did not give hundreds of Iranians who graduated from Iranian universities or returned to Iran with degrees from the best universities in Europe and the United States a chance to express their opinions or the freedom to do a job. Usually those who were chosen accepted everything he said and reported to him what he wanted to hear. Most educated young men and women, however, either left Iran in droves, joined the silent opposition, or became active in underground revolutionary activities. The political unrest was exacerbated when the shah organized the Rastakhiz Party as Iran's sole political party in 1975. He decreed that everyone should join it and those who would not had to keep silent or leave the country.

Corruption

No country in the world is free from corruption. The situation in Iran, however, was different in that the "revolution from the top," as the shah used to call the White Revolution, was also corrupt from the top. Practically no concession was granted and no enterprise launched without giving a share to one or more members of the royal family or to others close to the shah. The flood of billions of petrodollars opened the way to importing goods from abroad. There was more profit to be made in importing items than in educating Iranians to produce them. This was especially true of agricultural products. For example, it was more profitable to import tons of frozen meat from Peru than to help the sheepherders of Iran produce more meat. The same arrangement was made with regard to rice from the United States, eggs from Denmark, butter from Holland, potatoes from Pakistan, oranges from Israel, and onions, beans, wheat, sugar, and vegetable oils from other countries. The Royal Investigation Commission was established in 1976 to act as the shah's "eyes and ears" in order to suppress corruption. Daily arrests were made with great fanfare, mostly of shopkeepers and small bazaar merchants, not of extortioners in high places.

The common people had no recourse against wholesale corruption for fear of SAVAK. To the SAVAK everyone was suspect, and it saw little difference between the criticism of a concerned patriot and the activity of a subversive. With the passage of time, SAVAK widened the scope of its activities and "improved" its means of physical and psychological torture. The popularity of the shah decreased in proportion to the cruelty of the SAVAK. Many simply disappeared, thousands were jailed and tortured without trial, and hundreds of thousands were alienated. Anyone who complained against corruption, injustice, and torture was considered to be subversive and put in jail.

The Shi'i Clergy

The Iranian Shi'i clergy, in their long struggle before 1979, never gained absolute power. Nonetheless, not much was accomplished without their involvement. Their cooperation was essential in the constitutional revolution of 1906, as well as the oil nationalization in 1951. In the 1970s, however, they had a determined and charismatic leader in the person of Ayatollah Khomayni. Khomayni was living in exile in Iraq, out of reach of SAVAK, and electrified the Iranian public with denunciations of the monarchy. The Shi'i organization had a communication network and was in touch with a wide range of people from the smallest villages to the largest cities and was therefore able to coopt other groups that had no national base. Such groups included members of the university community whose freedom had been usurped; the middle class in the private and public sectors who were under heavy economic and psychological pressure; owners of industries who became victims of wrong-headed economic policies; educated young officers who were rendered inactive; farmers who had been uprooted; and youth who had lost their religious and cultural moorings and were on the brink of becoming aimless. All of these and others poured into the streets of Tehran and other cities in orderly demonstrations shouting "Death to the Shah."

The Shah Goes into Exile

All through 1978 there were strikes and demonstrations in which hundreds died. The reaction of the shah to all this was to keep changing prime ministers, but the new ones were either old cronies or army generals with bad reputations. It was not until January 1979, that the shah made a substantive change by asking Dr. Shahpur Bakhtyar, a former Mosaddeq supporter who had gone to jail for his activities, to form a government—but it was too late.

In the meantime, Khomayni was forced out of Iraq in June 1978 and was permitted to go to Nauphle-le-Chateau near Paris. There, he had access to the world press to broadcast his message. The British Broadcasting Company (BBC), which had millions of listeners in Iran, relayed every word Khomayni uttered and every instruction he gave to the demonstrators. He was steadfast in his demand that the shah abdicate, but not quite honest in his repeated assertions that his purpose was to reinstate the constitution of 1906.

The shah, who had one of the best-equipped armies in the area under his command, panicked and did not know what to do. Almost daily he asked the American and British ambassadors what to do. Britain was noncommital; and the United States, which had some 40,000 of its citizens in Iran, was not in any position to offer him more help. Indeed, the United States did not have a clear policy toward Iran. President Carter reasoned that the shah with all his experience knew what was best, and assured him that the United States would back him in whatever he decided. The shah, however, was not able to decide, partly because he did not want too much bloodshed, and partly because he could not be sure whether his soldiers would shoot at the demonstrators, who were placing flowers in the muzzles of their rifles.

Finally, the shah left the country on January 16, 1979, and with his departure an era in the history of modern Iran came to an end. Mohammad Reza Shah was, by far, more educated and enlightened than his father, but was not as strong and ruthless. Nonetheless, he was being compared to his father by the people and reminded by members of his family, especially his mother and twin sister, as to how his father would have handled certain issues. He was more suited by nature to be a constitutional monarch but the circumstances of Iranian life encouraged him to be a dictator. He wanted to be as strong as his father and as popular as Dr. Mosaddeq. Since he could not accomplish both, he opted for the strength of his father and made himself believe that he was as popular as Dr. Mosaddeq. His repeated statements, both written and oral, that he and his people loved each other, were not demagoguery but the statements of a person totally cut off from reality. It is ironic that in the supreme test of power he failed and left the country a weak and unpopular man.

The Islamic Republic of Iran

Ayatollah Ruhollah Khomayni arrived in Iran on February 1, 1979, and was welcomed by millions of deliriously happy people. Shortly after his arrival, some of the army barracks in Tehran were stormed and weapons were widely distributed. In the midst of street clashes, the army commanders ordered the troops to their quarters and announced that the army would remain neutral. In such circumstances, the position of Prime Minister Bakhtyar became completely untenable and he fled the country on February 10. The Islamic Revolutionary Council took over the government. Mehdi Bazargan, a devout Muslim, a Mosaddeq supporter, and a foe of the shah's regime, was appointed prime minister and formed a provisional government. Thousands were released from prison and hundreds returned from exile.

A reign of terror unlike anything in the history of modern Iran was soon launched. Overnight Islamic courts were set up all over the country in which former prime ministers, ministers, high-ranking army officers, and thousands of others were tried summarily and executed. From the very beginning Khomayni left no doubt that to him Islam was more important than Iran. He, who had repeatedly said that it was his aim to reinstate the constitution, denounced it as the instrument of the devil and described the emblem of the lion and sun on the Iranian flag as a "disgrace to Islam." He called a national referendum on March 30–31; the people obeyed Khomayni's injunction and overwhelmingly approved the establishment of an "Islamic," not an "Iranian" republic. The fighting arm of the revolution was made up of thousands of Revolutionary Guards who had been recruited from the lower classes all over the country, and who were devoted to Khomayni and ready to become martyrs. They were armed and, for a time, terrorized the people, especially the rich.

A Council of Experts, mostly clergy, was chosen to draft a new constitution. The drafters approved the principle of the "government of the jurist," which was proposed by Khomayni. This principle, which has its critics among the high Shi'i clergy, states that the supreme head of the government should be a "just Muslim (Shi'i) jurist," because he alone knows the laws of God and the will of the Hidden Imam. Khomayni was proclaimed to be the jurist, and in that position he wields more power than any shah in the history of modern Iran.

As soon as the revolution was a reality, the different groups who had supported it jockeyed for positions of leadership. The period from 1979 to 1981 saw the consolidation of Khomayni's fundamentalist position first against the shah, then against the left (mainly the *Mojahedin*), and finally against the nationalists (mainly Bazargan and a few others, including Bani Sadr). In the midst of this struggle, the seizure of the United States embassy on November 2, 1979, played into the hands of the fundamentalists. Khomayni and his lieutenants used it to discredit the United States, which he called "Satan Number One," but mainly to consolidate his power over individuals as well as over communities, provinces, and the state.

Two days after the seizure of the American hostages, Bazargan was forced to resign. Bani Sadr, who straddled the fence between fundamentalism and nationalism, chose to embrace Khomayni when he was elected the republic's first president in January 1980. He was ignominiously dismissed, however, in June 1981 and soon after was forced to flee for his life to Paris. The bloodiest struggle for supremacy occurred between the fundamentalists and the leftist Mojahedin, who claim to be an Islamic group with socialist undertones. The Mojahedin were mostly men and women students who were devoted to their cause. They fought Khomayni's Guards in the streets and, in suicidal missions, killed a number of the clergy. They are alleged to have bombed the Islamic Republican Party's headquarters in July 1981, killing seventy-two individuals, including the second president of the republic and the head of the Islamic Party. The longest struggle, however, has been between the Kurds and the Islamic Republic. It has lasted for six years, with heavy losses on both sides.

The hardest blow, but also a helpful one, was the attack of Saddam Husayn of Iraq on September 20, 1980. It was a hard blow because it caused an enormous loss of life and property, not to mention billions of dollars in expenditures. It was helpful because it enabled the government to avoid the inevitable decisions regarding fundamental reforms that had been promised and were now being demanded by many segments of the Iranian population. By December 1981, Iran had driven most of the Iraqi troops out of Khuzestan and was in a good position to make peace with reasonable reparations. Khomayni, however, who has stated that the war between "Truth" (Islam) and "Falsehood" (Saddam Husayn), believes that there cannot be peace between the two. He wants Husayn overthrown and an Islamic government set up in Iraq. Consequently the war has continued.

Despite a long and expensive war with Iraq and an equally brutal civil war against the Kurds, and severe shortages and rationing of almost all the necessities of daily life, the republic has lasted for six years; it has also held two elections and has paid all its bills. During this time it has carried on a cultural revolution by purging from the schools and universities all those who do not strictly adhere to Islamic ideology.

The regime has been able to identify itself with the dispossessed. The poor are the first recipients of all rationed goods, while the rich have to pay high prices for the same goods in open black markets. The poor, by the hundreds of thousands, have been given jobs as "guards" of the revolution; and they zealously protect Islam, which is identified with their newly found privileges. The Islamic government has been impartial in its denunciation of all influences from the United States, Europe, and the Soviet Union. The last group to be purged from the inner circle of power was the Tudeh (Communist) Party in February 1983. The leaders were all arrested and publicly tried; and some of them were executed in December of the same year. The general slogan is "America is worse than Britain; Britain is worse than America; and the Soviet Union is worse than either."

Notwithstanding all this, signs of cracks have begun to appear in the foundation of the republic, and there have been more and more reports of dissatisfaction. Whatever the reasons, the Islamic Republic has demonstrated a staying power; and as long as Khomayni is alive, it is not likely to collapse. The future of the republic depends upon whether Khomayni's successor will be accepted peacefully and whether the leading clergy and their followers can settle their political and theological differences and, more importantly, will be able to share their new-found power.

Glossary

Adet "Habit"; the customary law observed by Turks.
Aghani, Kitab al- *The Book of Songs*, depicting the personal and social life of early Arabs.
Akhi The artisan and merchant members of the early Turkish Sufi orders.
Alawi A sect within the Shi'i community; President Asad of Syria is an Alawi.
Amir "Commander" of an army or a people; also "Emir."
Anjoman "Society"; political clubs during the Iranian constitutional revolution.
Ansar "Supporters"; the Medinese followers of Muhammad.
Asabiyyah Clan spirit or group solidarity.
Ashkenazim A name usually applied to European Jews.
Assassins The band of Muslim devotees under the leadership of Hasan Sabbah.
Ayatollah "Sign of God"; a high Shi'i cleric considered worthy of imitation by others.
Babi Follower of the Bab, or "The Gate." He founded a religion that became the precurser of Bahaism.
Badr The first battle between Muhammad and the Meccans.
Bahri The Turkish Mamluk rulers of Egypt.
Bayan The holy book of the Babis written by the Bab.
Bedouin Desert nomads.
Bektashi The Dervish order of which the Ottoman sultans were members.
Berber An ethnic group in North Africa.
Bey An honorific title in the Ottoman Empire.
Burji The Circassian Mamluk rulers of Egypt.
Byzantine The Eastern Roman Empire; Constantinople was its capital.
Caliph A head of state who was a successor of Muhammad.
Client *See* Mawali.
Coptic The indigenous Christians of Egypt.
Dargah The Iranian royal household.

Darvish   Usually applied to Muslim Sufi orders; also *dervish.*
Dhimmi   Followers of the protected religions who had freedom of worship within the Islamic state.
Druze   An offshoot of extreme Shi'ism mixed with other beliefs.
Dunam   A unit of land in Palestine equal to a quarter of an acre, or 1,000 square meters.
Fatwa   The authoritative opinion of a high cleric in matters affecting the community of Islam; *fatva* in Persian and *fetva* in Turkish.
Feddan   A unit of land in Arabic-speaking countries equal to 1.038 acres.
Fellahin   "Farmers"; usually applied to the peasants of Egypt.
Ghazi   The fighting members of the early Turkish Sufi orders in Anatolia.
Hadith   The tradition concerning the words and practices of Muhammad, and (for the Shi'is) of the Imams.
Haganah   The unofficial and irregular fighting force of the Jewish Agency in Palestine.
Hajj   The pilgrimage to Mecca.
Haji   One who has made the pilgrimage to Mecca.
Hanif   A group of people in Arabia who had monotheistic ideas at the time of the Prophet.
Hashim   An ancestor of Muhammad from whom the modern king of Jordan claims descent.
Hectare   A unit of land in the Iraqi-Iranian region equal to 2.471 acres.
Herut   A right-wing party in Israel.
Hidden Imam   The vanished twelfth Shi'i Imam who will reappear on the Day of Judgment.
Hijra   The flight of Muhammad from Mecca to Medina.
Hira   The hill near Mecca where Muhammad received his first revelation.
Hojja   Turkish name for a religious leader.
Histadrut   The Federation of Jewish Labor in Israel.
Iblis   One of the names of the devil.
Ihud   "Union"; the party in Israel that advocated union between the Arabs and Israelis.
Ijtihad   The independent interpretation of Islamic laws.
Ikhwan   The Muslim Brotherhood, a fundamentalist group in Egypt and the Fertile Crescent.
ilkhan   The Mongol dynasty established in Iran.
Imam   A leader in prayer among the Sunnis; one of the twelve successors of Muhammad among the Shi'is.
Irgun   A leading Zionist terrorist group once headed by Menachem Begin.
Islam   The religious system established by Muhammad.
Isma'ili   A Shi'i group whose leader is a descendant of the seventh Imam; also called "Seveners."
Ja'fari   The Shi'i school of jurisprudence.
Jangali   "Junglemen"; a nationalist fighting group in Iran at the turn of the century.
Janissaries   The main Ottoman army that was recruited from Christian communities and trained from childhood.
Jihad   Striving for a religious cause, especially warfare for the protection of Islam.
Jinn   A heavenly being, usually mischievous.
Jizya   A headtax exacted from non-Muslims within Islamic society.
Ka'ba   A cubic structure in Mecca that is the object of pilgrimage for Muslims.
Karbalai   One who has made the pilgrimage to Karbala, the burial place of Husayn, the third Shi'i Imam.
Knesset   The parliament of Israel.
Khadija   The first wife of Muhammad.
Khaqan   The king of kings among the Mongols.
Kharijites   The seceders who disagreed with Ali's acceptance of arbitration with Mu'awiya.
Khedive   The title of the Egyptian head of state.
Kibbutz   An Israeli agricultural collective.
Levant   The eastern Mediterranean region.
Mahdi   "Guide"; the title of the twelfth Shi'i Imam, who will return to inaugurate the reign of justice; similar to *Messiah;* also *Mehdi.*
Majlis   An audience given by the kings, amirs, and shaykhs of Arabic-speaking nations; in Iran it is *Majles,* which means "parliament."
Maronites   The Uniate Christians of Lebanon who have accepted the suzerainty of the pope.
Marwa   A small hill near Mecca that is part of the traditional Muslim pilgrimage route.

Masnavi A book of Sufi poetry by Jalal al-Din Rumi; also a poetic meter that in Arabic is spelled *Mathnawi.*
Mawali "Clients"; non-Arab Muslims.
Millet System A system that protected religious groups within the Islamic state (Arabic *millah;* Persian *mellat*). In modern times the term denotes "nation."
Minaret A tall tower next to a mosque from which the faithful are called to prayer.
Mojahedin "Those who participate in jihad"; in present-day Iran the term refers to a well-organized Islamic group with a Marxist orientation that is opposed to the Islamic Republic.
Mu'alliqat Poetry that was judged to be good in pre-Islamic Arabia; it was hung from the walls of Ka'ba.
Mu'azzin A person who gives the call to prayer.
Mufti A Muslim religious lawyer.
Muhajirun Those who fled with Muhammad from Mecca to Medina.
Mujtahid One who practices Ijtihad.
Mushav A private Israeli cooperative farming unit, as opposed to a collective Kibbutz.
Muslim Anyone who has accepted Islam.
Murj'ite A member of an Islamic sect that believed that men should be judged only by God and not by other men.
Mu'tazila A rationalistic approach in Islamic thought.
Muwahhidun "Unitarian"; a title assumed by the Wahhabis.
Molla A low-level Shi'i cleric; also *mullah.*
Molla Bashi Head Molla in the Safavid regime corresponding to the Shaykh al-Islam in the Ottoman court.
Mosalman The Persian, Pakistan, and Indian term for "Muslim"; also "Musulman."
Nestorian Members of a Christian sect who live in Iran and Iraq; many have migrated to the United States.
Ojak "Hearth"; a political or social club in Turkey.
Osmanli The Turkish word for "Ottoman."
Porte The European designation for the Ottoman Empire; sometimes the "Sublime Porte."
Palmach A Zionist commando organization connected with the Haganah.
Pasha An honorific title in Ottoman Turkey.
Pahalik The region under the jurisdiction of a pasha.
Qadi A Muslim judge; also *qazi.*
Qaf An allegorical mountain in Sufi thought.
Qanat An underground waterway in Iran.
Qanun "Canon"; refers to secular law.
Qawm "People," or "group," as district from "millet."
Qibla The direction of Mecca toward which Muslims pray.
Qizilbash "Red head"; a Shi'i fighting order that supported the Safavids.
Quraysh The tribe to which Muhammad belonged.
Ramadan The month of fasting in Islam; also *Ramazan.*
Rumeli The European region of the Ottoman Empire.
Sabians A religious group mentioned in the Koran; also known as the Christians of St. John.
Safa *See* Marwa.
Salam "Peace"; a Muslim salutation; in Hebrew, *shalom.*
Sayyid A descendent of Muhammad.
Sephardim Originally the term applied only to Spanish Jews, but now also to non-European Jews.
Shari'a The religious law of Islam.
Shaykh "Elder"; a title given to the head of a tribe or group.
Shaykhi A Shi'i sect from which Babi-Bahaism emerged.
Shaykh al-Islam The highest religious dignitary in the Ottoman Empire.
Shi'a Partisans of Ali; the second largest group in Islam.
Shu'ubiyya A group of non-Arab Muslims who sought to establish their superiority over Arabs through literature.
Simorgh "Thirty bird"; an allegorical bird in Sufi thought.
Sufi A member of an Islamic mystic group.
Sunna The practices of the Prophet.

Sunni   The largest branch of Islam; those who follow the sunna of the Prophet.
Stern   A Zionist terrorist group in Palestine.
Tanzimat   A nineteenth-century period of modernization in the Ottoman Empire.
Taqlid   The imitation of the practices and pronouncements of an ayatollah or mujtahid.
Tawhid   Belief in the unity of God.
Tudeh   "Masses"; the name of the Communist Party in Iran.
Uniate   Those Orthodox Christians who accept the suzerainty of the pope but are allowed to follow their own religious rites.
Uhud   The second battle between Muhammad and the Meccans in which Muhammad was defeated.
Ulama   Those learned in religion; the term usually refers to Muslim clergy.
Ummah   The entire community of Muslims; also *ommat*.
Urf   Secular or customary law in Islam.
Urubah   Arab nationalism.
Wahhabi   The fundamentalist Islamic sect that prevails in Saudi Arabia.
Waqf   A religious endowment; also *vaqf*.
Wafd   "Delegation"; a political party in Egypt.
Watan   "Fatherland" or "homeland"; also *vatan*.
Yahweh   One of the names of the Hebrew God.
Yathrib   The original name of Medina.
Yazidi   A heterodox religious sect in Shi'ism.
Yom Kippur   The Day of Atonement in Judaism. Egypt attacked Israel on this day in 1973.
Zaka   A tax levied on Muslim property according to Koranic law.
Zamzam   A well near Mecca from which it is claimed Hagar drew water for her son Isma'il.
Zaydi   A Shi'i community in Oman.

Bibliography

PART I   THE RISE AND FALL OF THE ISLAMIC EMPIRE

ABU-LUGHOD, JANET L. *Cairo: 1001 Years of the City Victorious.* Princeton: Princeton University Press, 1971.
ADAMS, R. *Land Behind Baghdad: A History of Settlement on the Diyala Plains.* Chicago: University of Chicago Press, 1965.
ANDRAE, TOR. *Mohammed: The Man and His Faith.* New York: Harper and Rowe, Pub., 1960.
ARBERRY, ARTHUR J. *The Holy Koran: An Introduction with Selections.* New York: Macmillan, 1953.
ARDALAN, NADER and BAKHTIAR, LALEH. *The Sense of Unity: The Sufi Tradition in Persian Architecture.* Chicago: University of Chicago Press, 1973.
BOSWORTH, CLIFFORD E. *The Ghaznavids: Their Empire, Afghanistan, and Eastern Iran, 944–1040.* Edinburgh: Edinburgh University Press, 1963.
———. *Sistan under the Arabs from the Islamic Conquest to the Rise of the Saffarids (30–250 A.H./651–864 A.D.)* Rome: IsMEO, 1968.
BROCKELMANN, CARL. *History of the Islamic Peoples.* New York: Putnam's, 1947.
BULLIET, RICHARD W. *The Camel and the Wheel.* Cambridge, Mass.: Harvard University Press, 1975.
———. *The Patricians of Nishapur: A Study in Medieval Islamic Social History.* Cambridge, Mass.: Harvard University Press, 1972.
CRESWELL, K. A. C. *Early Muslim Architecture: Umayyads, Early 'Abassids and Tulunids.* 2 vols. Oxford: Oxford University Press, 1932–1940. New York: Hacker Art Books, 1979.
DENNET, DANIEL. *Conversion and the Poll Tax in Early Islam.* Cambridge, Mass.: Harvard University Press, 1950.
DONALDSON, DWIGHT M. *The Shi'ite Religion: A History of Islam in Persia and Irak.* London: Luzac, 1933.

FRYE, RICHARD N. *Bukhara: The Medieval Achievement.* Norman: University of Oklahoma Press, 1965.
———. *The Golden Age of Persia.* London: Weidenfeld and Nicolson, 1975.
GIBB, H. A. R. *Arabic Literature: An Introduction.* London: Oxford University Press, 1926.
———. *Mohammedanism: An Historical Survey.* London: Oxford University Press, 1949.
GOITEIN, SOLOMON D. *A Mediterranean Society: The Jewish Communities of the Arab World as Portrayed in the Documents of the Cairo Geniza.* 5 vols. Berkeley: University of California Press, 1967–1984.
HITTI, PHILIP K. *History of the Arabs.* 9th ed. New York: Macmillan, 1961.
HOURANI, ALBERT B., and STERN, SAMUEL M., eds. *The Islamic City.* Oxford: Bruno Cassirer, 1970. Philadelphia: University of Pennsylvania Press, 1970.
HODGSON, MARSHALL G. S. *The Order of Assassins: The Struggle of the Early Nizari Ismailis against the Islamic World.* The Hague: Mouton, 1955.
———. *The Venture of Islam: Conscience and History in a World Civilization.* 3 vols. Chicago: University of Chicago Press, 1974.
LASSNER, JACOB. *The Topography of Baghdad in the Early Middle Ages.* Detroit: Wayne State University Press, 1970.
LESTRANGE, GUY. *Baghdad during the Abbasid Caliphate.* Oxford: The Clarendon Press, 1924.
———. *The Lands of the Eastern Caliphate: Mesopotamia, Persia, and Central Asia from the Moslem Conquest to the Time of Timur.* London: Frank Cass, 1966.
LEWIS, ARCHIBALD R. *Naval Power and Trade in the Mediterranean, A.D. 500–1100.* Princeton: Princeton University Press, 1951.
LEWIS, BERNARD. *The Arabs in History.* London: Hutchinson's University Library, 1950.
NICHOLSON, REYNOLD A. *A Literary History of the Arabs.* Rev. ed. Cambridge, Eng.: Cambridge University Press, 1962.
———. *The Mystics of Islam.* London: G. Bell & Sons, 1963.
POPE, ARTHUR UPHAM. *An Introduction to Persian Art since the Seventh Century A.D.* Westport, Conn.: Greenwood Press, 1972–1977.
RICHARDS, DONALD S., ed. *Islam and the Trade of Asia.* Philadelphia: University of Pennsylvania Press, 1970.
———, ed. *Islamic Civilization, 950–1150.* Philadelphia: University of Pennyslvania Press, 1973.
RODINSON, MAXIME. *Muhammad.* New York: Pantheon, 1971.
ROSENTHAL, ERWIN I. J. *Political Thought in Medieval Islam.* Cambridge, Eng.: Cambridge University Press, 1958.
RYPKA, JAN. *History of Iranian Literature.* Dordrecht, Neth.: D. Reidel, 1968.
SCHACHT, JOSEPH. *The Origins of Muhammadan Jurisprudence.* Oxford: The Clarendon Press, 1953.
———, and BOSWORTH, C. E., eds. *The Legacy of Islam.* 2nd ed. Oxford: The Clarendon Press, 1974.
SHABAN, M. A. *The Abbasid Revolution.* Cambridge, Eng.: Cambridge University Press, 1970.
———. *Islamic History, A.D. 600–750: A New Interpretation.* Cambridge, Eng.: Cambridge University Press, 1971.
STERN, SAMUEL M., HOURANI, ALBERT, and BROWN, VIVIAN, eds. *Islamic Philosophy and the Classical Tradition.* Columbia: University of South Carolina Press, 1972.
TRIMINGHAM, J. SPENCER, *The Sufi Orders in Islam.* Oxford: The Clarendon Press, 1971.
UDOVITCH, ABRAHAM L. *Partnership and Profits in Medieval Islam.* Princeton: Princeton University Press, 1970.
———, ed. *The Islamic Middle East, 700–1900: Studies in Economic and Social History.* Princeton: Darwin Press, 1981.
VON GRUNEBAUM, GUSTAV E. *Medieval Islam.* Chicago: University of Chicago Press, 1946.
———, ed. *Unity and Variety in Muslim Civilization.* Chicago: University of Chicago Press, 1955.
WATSON, ANDREW M. *Agricultural Innovations in the Early Islamic World.* New York: Cambridge University Press, 1983.
WATT, W. MONTGOMERY. *Muhammad: Prophet and Statesman.* London: Oxford University Press, 1961.
———. *Muhammad at Mecca.* Oxford: The Clarendon Press, 1953.
———. *Muhammad at Medina.* Oxford: The Clarendon Press, 1956.

PART II THE HEIRS AND INNOVATORS
OF THE ISLAMIC EMPIRE

ALDERSON, ANTHONY D. *The Structure of the Ottoman Dynasty.* Oxford: The Clarendon Press, 1956.

ARBERRY, ARTHUR J. *Classical Persian Literature.* London: George Allen & Unwin, 1958.

ASHTOR, ELIYAHU. *A Social and Economic History of the Near East in the Middle Ages.* Berkeley: University of California Press, 1976.

ATKIN, MURIEL. *Russia and Iran, 1780–1828.* Minneapolis: University of Minnesota Press, 1981.

AYALON, D. *Gunpowder and Firearms in the Mamluk Kingdom.* London: Valentine, Mitchell, 1956.

BARTHOLD, VASILI V. *Turkestan down to the Mongol Invasion.* 3rd ed. London: Luzac, 1968.

BAYERLE, GUSTAV. *Ottoman Diplomacy in Hungary.* Bloomington: Indiana University Press, 1972.

BENVENISTI, MERON. *The Crusaders in the Holy Land.* New York: Macmillan, 1972.

BODMAN, HERBERT L. *Political Factions in Aleppo, 1760–1826.* Chapel Hill: University of North Carolina Press, 1963.

BRAUDEL, FERNAND. *The Mediterranean and the Mediterranean World in the Age of Philip II.* 2 vols. New York: Harper and Row, Pub., 1975.

BROWNE, EDWARD G. *A Literary History of Persia.* 4 vols. Cambridge, Eng.: Cambridge University Press, 1964.

CAHEN, C. *Pre-Ottoman Turkey: A General Survey of the Material and Spiritual Culture and History, c. 1071–1330.* Trans. J. Jones Williams. London: Sidgwick & Jackson, 1968.

COOK, M. A. *Population Pressure in Rural Anatolia, 1450–1600.* London: Oxford University Press, 1972.

———, ed. *Studies in the Economic History of the Middle East.* London: Oxford University Press, 1970.

DAVIS, RALPH. *English Overseas Trade in the Seventeenth and Eighteenth Centuries.* London: Historical Association, 1967.

DEREK, H., and GRABAR, O. *Islamic Architecture and Its Decoration.* 2nd ed. London: Faber and Faber, 1967.

DOLS, MICHAEL W. *The Black Death in the Middle East.* Princeton: Princeton University Press, 1977.

FISHER, ALAN W. *The Russian Annexation of the Crimea, 1772–1783.* Cambridge, Eng.: Cambridge University Press, 1970.

FISHER, SIDNEY N. *The Foreign Relations of Turkey, 1481–1512.* Urbana: University of Illinois Press, 1948.

GIBB, ELIAS J. W. *A History of Ottoman Poetry.* 6 vols. London: Luzac, 1900–1909.

GIBB, HAMILTON A. R., and BOWEN, HAROLD. *Islamic Society and the West.* London: Oxford University Press, 1950.

———. *Islamic Society in the Eighteenth Century.* London: Oxford University Press, 1957.

GUILMARTIN, J. F. *Gunpowder and Galleys: Changing Technology and Mediterranean Warfare at Sea in the Sixteenth Century.* London: Cambridge University Press, 1974.

HARIK, I. *Politics and Change: Lebanon, 1711–1845.* Princeton: Princeton University Press, 1968.

HEYD, URIEL. *Ottoman Documents on Palestine, 1552–1615.* Oxford: The Clarendon Press, 1960.

———. *Studies in Old Ottoman Criminal Law.* Oxford: The Clarendon Press, 1973.

HOLT, PETER M. *Egypt and the Fertile Crescent, 1516–1922.* Ithaca, N.Y.: Cornell University Press, 1966.

———. *Political and Social Change in Modern Egypt: Historical Studies from the Ottoman Conquest to the United Arab Republic.* London: Oxford University Press, 1968.

HOURANI, GEORGE F. *Arab Seafaring in the Indian Ocean.* Princeton: Princeton University Press, 1951.

HOWARTH, H. B. *History of the Mongols.* 4 vols. London: Longmans, 1870–1927.

INALCIK, HALIL. *The Ottoman Empire: The Classical Age, 1300–1600.* Trans. Itzkowitz and Imber. New York: Knopf, 1973.

ITZKOWITZ, NORMAN. *The Ottoman Empire and Islamic Tradition.* New York: Knopf, 1972.

JELAVICH, CHARLES and BARBARA, eds. *The Balkans in Transition.* Hamden, Conn.: Archon Books, 1963.

KARPAT, KEMAL H., ed. *The Ottoman State and Its Place in World History.* Leiden, Neth.: Brill, 1974.
KEDDIE, NIKKI R., ed. *Scholars, Saints and Sufis.* Berkeley: University of California Press, 1972.
KEYVANI, MEHDI. *Artisans and Guild Life in the Later Safavid Period.* Berlin: Klaus Schwartz Verlag, 1982.
KRITZECK, JAMES, ed. *An Anthology of Islamic Literature.* New York: Holt, Rinehart & Winston, 1964.
LESTRANGE, GUY. *Mesopotamia and Persia under the Mongols in the Fourteenth Century A.D.* London: Royal Asiatic Society, 1903.
LAMBTON, ANN K. S. *Landlord and Peasant in Persia.* London: Oxford University Press, 1953.
LAPIDUS, IRA M., ed. *Middle Eastern Cities.* Berkeley: University of California Press, 1969.
————. *Muslim Cities in the Later Middle Ages.* Cambridge, Mass.: Harvard University Press, 1967.
LEVY, REUBEN. *The Social Structure of Islam.* Cambridge, Eng.: Cambridge University Press, 1962.
LEWIS, BERNARD. *Istanbul and the Civilization of the Ottoman Empire.* Rev. ed. Norman: University of Oklahoma Press, 1968.
LOCKHART, LAURENCE. *The Fall of the Safavid Dynasty and the Afghan Occupation of Persia.* Cambridge: Cambridge University Press, 1958.
————. *Nadir Shah: A Critical Study Based Mainly upon Contemporary Sources.* London: Luzac, 1938.
LOKKEGAARD, FREDE. *Islamic Taxation in the Classical Period.* New York: Arno Press, 1973.
LONGRIGG, STEPHEN H. *Four Centuries of Modern Iraq.* Oxford: The Clarendon Press, 1925.
MAZZAOUI, MICHEL M. *The Origins of the Safawids: Shi'ism, Sufism, and the Gulat.* Weisbaden, 1972.
MERRIMAN, ROGER B. *Suleiman the Magnificent, 1520–1566.* Cambridge, Mass.: Harvard University Press, 1944.
MEZ, ADAM. *The Renaissance of Islam.* Trans. S. Khuda-Bakhsh and D. S. Margoliouth. London: Luzac, 1937.
NAFF, T., and OWEN, E. R. J., eds. *Studies in Eighteenth-Century Islamic History.* Carbondale: Southern Illinois University Press, 1975.
OKYAR, OSMAN and INALCIK, HALIL, eds. *Social and Economic History of Turkey (1071–1920).* Ankara: Meteksan Ltd. Sirketi, 1980.
OLSON, ROBERT W. *The Siege of Mosul and Ottoman-Persian Relations, 1718–1743.* Bloomington: Indiana University Press, 1975.
PERRY, J. R. *Karim Khan Zand, 1747–1779.* Chicago: University of Chicago Press, 1979.
RABIE, H. *The Financial System of Egypt, 1169–1314.* London, 1972.
RAFEQ, A. K. *The Province of Damascus, 1723–1783.* Beirut: Khayyat's, 1966.
RAMAZANI, ROUHOLLAH K. *The Foreign Policy of Iran, 1500–1941.* Charlottesville: University of Virginia Press, 1966.
RICE, TAMARA T. *The Seljuks in Asia Minor.* New York: Praeger, 1961.
RUNCIMAN, STEVEN. *The Fall of Constantinople, 1453.* Cambridge, Eng.: Cambridge University Press, 1965.
————. *A History of the Crusades.* 4 vols. Cambridge, Eng.: Cambridge University Press, 1951–1958.
SAVORY, ROGER M. *Iran under the Safavids.* Cambridge, Eng.: Cambridge University Press, 1980.
SHAW, STANFORD. *The Budget of Ottoman Egypt, 1596–1597.* The Hague: Mouton, 1968.
————. *The Financial and Administrative Organization and Development of Ottoman Egypt, 1517–1798.* Princeton: Princeton University Press, 1962.
————. *A History of the Ottoman Empire and Modern Turkey.* 2 vols. Cambridge, Eng.: Cambridge University Press, 1976–1977.
SPULER, BERTOLD. *The Muslim World, Part II: The Mongol Period.* Leiden, Neth.: Brill, 1960–1967.
STAVRIANOS, LEFTEN S. *The Balkans since 1453.* New York: Rhinehart, 1958.
STEENSGAARD, NIELS. *The Asian Trade Revolution in the Seventeenth Century.* Chicago: University of Chicago Press, 1974.
SYKES, PERCY. *A History of Persia.* 2 vols. 3rd ed. London: Macmillan, 1951.
WITTEK, PAUL. *The Rise of the Ottoman Empire.* London: Royal Asiatic Society, 1938.
WOOD, ALFRED C. *A History of the Levant Company.* London: Oxford University Press, 1935.
WOODS, J. E. *The Aqquyunlu—Clan, Confederation, Empire: A Study in Fifteenth-Century Turko-Iranian Politics.* Minneapolis-Chicago: Bibliotheca Islamic, 1976.
ZIADEH, NICOLA A. *Damascus under the Mamluks.* Norman: University of Oklahoma Press, 1964.

PART III IMPERIALISM, REFORMS, AND INNOVATIONS

AHMAD, FEROZ. *The Young Turks: The Committee of Union and Progress in Turkish Politics, 1908–1914.* Oxford: The Clarendon Press, 1969.

AHMED, JAMAL M. *The Intellectual Origins of Egyptian Nationalism.* London: Oxford University Press, 1960.

ALGAR, HAMID. *Religion and State in Iran, 1785–1906: The Role of the Ulama in the Qajar Period.* Berkeley: University of California Press, 1980.

ANDERSON, MATHEW S. *The Eastern Question.* New York: St. Martin's, 1966.

ANTONIUS, GEORGE. *The Arab Awakening.* 4th ed. Beirut: Khayyat's, 1961; New York: Capricorn Books, 1965.

BAER, GABRIEL. *Egyptian Guilds in Modern Times.* Jerusalem: Israel Oriental Society, 1964.

———. *A History of Landownership in Modern Egypt, 1800–1950.* London: Oxford University Press, 1962.

———. *Studies in the Social History of Modern Egypt.* Chicago: University of Chicago Press, 1969.

BAKHASH, SHAUL. *Iran: Monarchy, Bureaucracy, and Reform under the Qajars, 1858–1896.* London: Ithaca Press, 1978.

BERKES, NIYAZI. *The Development of Secularism in Turkey.* Montreal: McGill University Press, 1964.

BERQUE, J. *Egypt: Imperialism and Revolution.* Trans. Jean Stewart. New York: Praeger, 1972.

BROWNE, EDWARD G. *The Persian Revolution of 1905–1909.* London: Frank Cass, 1966.

BUSCH, BRITON C. *Britain and the Persian Gulf, 1894–1914.* Berkeley: University of California Press, 1967.

CURZON, GEORGE. *Persia and the Persian Question.* 2 vols. London: Frank Cass, 1968.

DAVIS, RALPH. *Aleppo and Devonshire Square.* London: Macmillan, 1967.

DAVISON, RODERIC H. *Reform in the Ottoman Empire, 1856–1876.* Princeton: Princeton University Press, 1963.

DAWN, C. ERNEST. *From Ottomanism to Arabism.* Urbana: University of Illinois Press, 1973.

ENAYAT, HAMID. *Modern Islamic Political Thought.* Austin: University of Texas Press, 1982.

FASA'I, HASAN. *A History of Persia under Qajar Rule.* Trans. Herbert Busse. New York: Columbia University Press, 1972.

GRABILL, JOSEPH L. *Protestant Diplomacy and the Near East: Missionary Influence on American Policy, 1810–1927.* Minneapolis: University of Minnesota Press, 1971.

GREAVES, ROSE L. *Persia and the Defense of India, 1884–1892.* New York: Oxford University Press, 1959.

HERSHLAG, ZVI Y. *Introduction to the Modern Economic History of the Middle East.* Leiden, Neth.: Brill, 1964.

HOPWOOD, DEREK. *The Russian Presence in Syria and Palestine, 1843–1914.* Oxford: The Clarendon Press, 1969.

HOURANI, ALBERT. *Arabic Thought in the Liberal Age, 1798–1939.* 2nd ed. London: Oxford University Press, 1970.

HUREWITZ, JACOB C. *Diplomacy in the Near and Middle East.* Vol. I, 1535–1914. Princeton: Van Nostrand, 1956.

ISSAWI, CHARLES, ed. *The Economic History of Iran, 1800–1914.* Chicago: University of Chicago Press, 1971.

———, ed. *The Economic History of the Middle East, 1800–1914.* Chicago: University of Chicago Press, 1966.

———, ed. *The Economic History of Turkey, 1800–1914.* Chicago: University of Chicago Press, 1980.

JELAVICH, BARBARA. *The Ottoman Empire: The Great Powers and the Straits Question, 1870–1887.* Bloomington: Indiana University Press, 1973.

KAZEMZADEH, FIRUZ. *Russia and Britain in Persia, 1864–1914: A Study in Imperialism.* New Haven: Yale University Press, 1968.

KEDDIE, NIKKI R. *Religion and Rebellion in Iran: The Iranian Tobacco Protest of 1891–1892.* London: Frank Cass, 1966.

———. *Sayyid Jamal ad-Din "Al-Afghani": A Political Biography.* Berkeley: University of California Press, 1972.

KEDOURIE, ELIE. *Afghani and 'Abduh: An Essay on Religious Unbelief and Political Activism in Modern Islam.* London: Frank Cass, 1966.

KELLY, J. B. *Britain and the Persian Gulf, 1795–1880.* Oxford: The Clarendon Press, 1968.

LANDAU, JACOB M. *The Hejaz Railway and the Muslim Pilgrimage.* Detroit: Wayne State University Press, 1971.

———. *Jews in Nineteenth-Century Egypt.* New York: New York University Press, 1969.

LANDES, DAVID S. *Bankers and Pashas: International Finance and Economic Imperialism in Egypt.* Cambridge, Mass.: Harvard University Press, 1958.

MCDANIEL, ROBERT A. *The Shuster Mission and the Persian Constitutional Revolution.* Minneapolis: Bibliotheca Islamica, 1974.

MARDIN, SERIF. *The Genesis of Young Ottoman Thought: A Study in the Modernization of Turkish Political Ideas.* Princeton: Princeton University Press, 1962.

MARLOW, JOHN. *Arab Nationalism and British Imperialism: A Study in Power Politics.* London: Cresset Press, 1961.

———. *World Ditch: The Making of the Suez Canal.* New York: Macmillan, 1964.

MARTIN, BRADFORD G. *German-Persian Diplomatic Relations, 1873–1912.* The Hague: Mouton, 1959.

MILLER, W. *The Ottoman Empire and Its Successors, 1801–1927.* Cambridge, Eng.: Cambridge University Press, 1936.

OWEN, EDWARD R. J. *Cotton and the Egyptian Economy, 1820–1914.* Oxford: The Clarendon Press, 1969.

———. *The Middle East in the World Economy, 1800–1914.* London and New York: Methuen, 1981.

———, ed. *Studies in the Economic and Social History of Palestine: Nineteenth and Twentieth Centuries.* London, 1983.

POLK, WILLIAM R. *The Opening of South Lebanon, 1788–1840.* Cambridge, Mass.: Harvard University Press, 1963.

———, and CHAMBERS, RICHARD, eds. *The Beginnings of Modernization in the Middle East.* Chicago: University of Chicago Press, 1968.

RAMSAUR, ERNEST E. *The Young Turks: Prelude to the Revolution of 1908.* Princeton: Princeton University Press, 1957.

RIVLIN, HELEN A. B. *The Agricultural Policy of Muhammad Ali in Egypt.* Cambridge, Mass.: Harvard University Press, 1961.

SALIBI, KAMAL S. *The Modern History of Lebanon.* New York: Praeger, 1965.

SANJIAN, AVEDIS K. *The Armenian Communities in Syria under Ottoman Dominion.* Cambridge, Mass.: Harvard University Press, 1965.

SAYYID, AFAF LUTFI, AL-. *Egypt and Cromer: A Study in Anglo-Egyptian Relations.* New York: Praeger, 1968.

SHARABI, HISHAM. *Arab Intellectuals and the West: The Formative Years, 1875–1914.* Baltimore: Johns Hopkins Press, 1970.

SHAW, STANFORD. *Between Old and New: The Ottoman Empire under Sultan Selim III, 1789–1807.* Cambridge, Mass.: Harvard University Press, 1971.

SHUSTER, W. MORGAN. *The Strangling of Persia.* New York: Century, 1912.

SKENDI, STAVRO. *The Albanian National Awakening, 1787–1912.* Princeton: Princeton University Press, 1967.

TIBAWI, ABDUL LATIF. *A Modern History of Syria, Including Lebanon and Palestine.* New York: St. Martin's, 1969.

TIGNOR, ROBERT L. *Modernization and British Colonial Rule in Egypt, 1882–1914.* Princeton: Princeton University Press, 1966.

VON GRUNEBAUM, G. E. *Modern Islam: A Search for Cultural Identity.* Berkeley: University of California Press, 1962.

WINDER, R. B. *Saudi Arabia in the Nineteenth Century.* New York: St. Martin's, 1966.

YOUNG, T. CUYLER, ed. *Near Eastern Culture and Society.* Princeton: Princeton University Press, 1951.

ZEINE, ZEINE N. *Arab-Turkish Relations and the Emergence of Arab Nationalism.* Beirut: Khayyat's, 1958.

———. *The Struggle for Arab Independence: Western Diplomacy and the Rise and Fall of Faisal's Kingdom in Syria.* Beirut: Khayyat's, 1960.

PART IV THE SHAPING OF THE MODERN MIDDLE EAST

ABDEL-FADEL, M. *Development, Income Distribution, and Social Policy in Rural Egypt, 1952–1970: A Study in the Political Economy of Agrarian Transition.* Cambridge, Eng.: Cambridge University Press, 1975.

ABRAHAMIAN, ERVAND. *Iran between Two Revolutions.* Princeton: Princeton University Press, 1982.

ABU-LUGHOD, IBRAHIM, ed. *The Transformation of Palestine.* Evanston, Ill: Northwestern University Press, 1971.

AGWANI, MUHAMMAD, ed. *The Lebanese Crisis, 1958: A Documentary Study.* Bombay: Asia Publishing House, 1965.

AKHAVI, S. *Religion and Politics in Contemporary Iran.* Albany: State University of New York, 1980.

ALON, AMOS. *Israelis: Founders and Sons.* New York: Holt, Rinehart & Winston, 1971.

ANTHONY, JOHN D. *Arab States of the Lower Gulf: People, Politics, Petroleum.* Washington, D.C.: Middle East Institute, 1975.

ANTOUN, R., and HARIK, I., eds. *Rural Politics and Social Change in the Middle East.* Bloomington: Indiana University Press, 1972.

ASMAR, FOUZI EL-. *To Be an Arab in Israel.* Beirut: Institute for Palestine Studies, 1978.

AVERY, PETER. *Modern Iran.* New York: Praeger, 1965.

BAER, G. *Fellah and Townsman in the Middle East: Studies in Social History.* London: Frank Cass, 1982.

BANANI, AMIN. *The Modernization of Iran, 1921–1941.* Stanford: Stanford University Press, 1961.

BARBOUR, NEVILL. *Nisi Dominus: A Survey of the Palestine Controversy.* London: Harrap, 1946.

BASHEAR, SULIMAN. *Communism in the Arab East, 1918–1928.* London: Ithaca Press, 1980.

BASHIRIYEH, HOSSEIN. *The State and Revolution In Iran.* London: Croom Helm Ltd., 1984

BATATU, HANNA. *The Old Social Classes and the Revolutionary Movements of Iraq.* Princeton: Princeton University Press, 1978.

BATES, DANIEL and RASSAM, AMAL. *Peoples and Cultures of the Middle East.* Englewood Cliffs, N.J.: Prentice-Hall, 1983.

BECK, LOIS, and KEDDIE, NIKKI, eds. *Women in the Muslim World.* Cambridge, Mass.: Harvard University Press, 1978.

BEGIN, MENACHEM. *The Revolt.* Rev. ed. New York: Nash, 1977.

BELING, W.A. *Pan-Arabism and Labor.* Cambridge, Mass.: Harvard University Press, 1961.

BEN-GURION, DAVID. *Rebirth and Destiny of Israel.* New York: Philosophical Library, 1954.

BENEDICT, PETER, TUMERTEKIM, EROL, and MANSUR, FATMA. *Turkey: Geographic and Social Perspectives.* Leiden, Neth.: Brill, 1974.

BERBEROGHLU, BERCH. *Turkey in Crisis: From State Capitalism to Neo-Colonialism.* London: Zed Press, 1982.

BERGER, MORROE. *The Arab World Today.* London: Weidenfeld & Nicholson, 1962; New York: Doubleday, 1962.

BHARIER, JULIAN. *Economic Development in Iran, 1900–1970.* London: Oxford University Press, 1971.

BILL, JAMES and LEIDEN, CARL. *The Middle East: Politics and Power.* Boston: Allyn & Bacon, 1974.

BINDER, LEONARD. *The Ideological Revolution in the Middle East.* New York: John Wiley, 1964.

BONINE, MICHAEL, and KEDDIE, NIKKI, eds. *Modern Iran: The Dialectics of Continuity and Change.* Albany: State University of New York, 1981.

BRENNER, L. *The Iron Wall: Zionist Revisionism from Jabotinsky to Shamir.* London: Zed Press, 1984.

BROWN, LEON C., ed. *From Madina to Metropolis.* Princeton: Darwin Press, 1973.

BUDEIRI, MUSA. *The Palestine Communist Party, 1919–1948: Arab and Jew in the Struggle for Internationalism.* London: Ithaca Press, 1979.

BUSCH, BRITON C. *Britain, India and the Arabs, 1914–1921.* Berkeley: University of California Press, 1971.

CAMPBELL, JOHN C. *Defense of the Middle East: Problems of American Policy.* New York: Harper & Row, Pub., 1960.

CHALIAND, GERARD, and TERNON, YVES. *The Armenians: From Genocide to Resistance.* Trans. Tony Berret. London: Zed Press, 1983.

CHALIAND, ET AL., eds. *People without a Country: The Kurds and Kurdistan.* London: Zed Press, 1980.

CHOMSKY, NOAM. *Peace in the Middle East*. New York: Pantheon, 1969.
COHEN, ABNER. *Arab Border Villages in Israel*. Manchester, Eng.: Manchester University Press, 1965.
COOLEY, JOHN K. *Green March, Black September: The Story of the Palestinian Arabs*. London: Frank Cass, 1973.
COTTAM, RICHARD W. *Nationalism in Iran*. Rev. ed. Pittsburgh: University of Pittsburgh Press, 1979.
DANN, URI. *Iraq under Qassem: A Political History, 1958–1963*. New York: Praeger, 1969.
DAVIS, HELEN. compiler. *Constitutions, Electoral Laws, Treaties of States in the Near and Middle East*. Durham, N.C.: Duke University Press, 1947.
DAVIS, URIEL. *Israel: Utopia Incorporated*. London: Zed Press, 1977.
DICKSON, HAROLD R. *Kuwait and Her Neighbours*. London: George Allen & Unwin, 1956.
EICKELMAN, DALE F. *The Middle East: An Anthropological Approach*. Englewood Cliffs, N.J.: Prentice-Hall, 1981.
ELWELL-SUTTON, L. P. *Persian Oil: A Study in Power Politics*. London: Laurence & Wishart, 1955.
ENGLISH, PAUL W. *City and Village in Iran*. Madison: University of Wisconsin Press, 1966.
FISCHER, MICHAEL M. J. *Iran: From Religious Dispute to Revolution*. Cambridge, Mass.: Harvard University Press, 1980.
GABBAY, RONY E. *Communism and Agrarian Reform in Iraq*. London: Croom Helm, 1978.
GHASSEMLOU, ABDUL RAHMAN. *The Kurds and Kurdistan*. Trans. Michael Pattis. London: Zed Press, 1980.
HADDAD, ROBERT. *Syrian Christians in Muslim Societies: An Interpretation*. Princeton: Princeton University Press, 1970.
HAIM, SYLVIA G., ed. *Arab Nationalism*. Berkeley: University of California Press, 1962.
HALLIDAY, FRED. *Arabia Without Sultans: A Political Survey of Instability in the Arab World*. New York: Vintage, 1975.
——. *Iran: Dictatorship and Development*. New York: Penguin, 1979.
HALPERN, BEN. *The Idea of the Jewish State*. Cambridge, Mass.: Harvard University Press, 1961.
HARRIS, CHRISTIAN PHELPS. *Nationalism and Revolution in Egypt*. The Hague: Mouton, 1964.
HAY, SIR RUPERT. *The Persian Gulf States*. Washington, D.C.: Middle East Institute, 1959.
HELMREICH, PAUL C. *From Paris to Sèvres: The Partition of the Ottoman Empire at the Peace Conference of 1919–1920*. Columbus: Ohio State University Press, 1974.
HIRST, DAVID. *The Gun and the Olive Branch: The Roots of Violence in the Middle East*. London: Faber & Faber, 1977.
HITTI, PHILIP K. *History of Syria*. London: Macmillan, 1951.
——. *Lebanon in History*. London: Macmillan, 1962.
HOOGLUND, ERIC. *Land and Revolution in Iran*. Austin: University of Texas Press, 1982.
HOPWOOD, DEREK, ed. *The Arabian Peninsula: Society and Politics*. London: George Allen and Unwin, 1972.
HOURANI, ALBERT H. *Syria and Lebanon: A Political Essay*. London: Oxford University Press, 1946.
HOVANESIAN, RICHARD. *Armenia on the Road to Independence, 1918*. Berkeley: University of California Press, 1967.
——. *The Republic of Armenia, Vol. I: The First Year, 1918–1919*. Berkeley: University of California Press, 1971.
HOWARD, HARRY N. *The King-Crane Commission: An Inquiry in the Middle East*. Beirut: Khayyat's, 1963.
HUDSON, MICHAEL C. *Arab Politics: The Search for Legitimacy*. New Haven: Yale University Press, 1977.
HUREWITZ, JACOB. *Diplomacy in the Near and Middle East*. Vol. II, 1914–1915. Princeton: Van Nostrand, 1956.
HUSSEIN, MAHMOUD. *Class Conflict in Egypt, 1945–1970*. Trans. Michel Chirman and others. New York: Monthly Review Press, 1973.
IBRAHIM, SAAD EDDIN, and HOPKINS, NICHOLAS, eds. *Arab Society in Transition*. Cairo: American University Press, 1977.
ISSAWI, CHARLES. *Egypt in Revolution: An Economic Analysis*. New York: Oxford University Press, 1963.

————. *An Economic History of the Middle East and North Africa.* New York: Columbia University Press, 1982.

JURAYS, SABRI. *The Arabs in Israel: 1948–1966.* New York: Monthly Review Press, 1976.

KAZEMI, FARHAD. *Poverty and Revolution In Iran.* New York: New York University Press, 1980.

KAZZIHA, WALID W. *Revolutionary Transformation in the Arab World.* New York: Barnes and Noble, 1975.

KEDDIE, NIKKI R. and Richard, Yann. *Roots of Revolution.* New Haven, Conn.: Yale University Press, 1981.

KEDOURIE, ELIE. *In the Anglo-Arab Labyrinth: The McMahon-Husayn Correspondence and Its Interpretations, 1914–1939.* Cambridge, Eng.: Cambridge University Press, 1976.

KERR, MALCOM. *The Arab Cold War, 1958–1967: A Study of Ideology in Politics.* New York: Oxford University Press, 1967.

KHADDURI, MAJID. *Independent Iraq: A Study in Iraqi Politics since 1932.* London: Oxford University Press, 1951.

————. *Republican Iraq: A Study in Iraqi Politics since the Revolution of 1958.* New York: Oxford University Press, 1969.

KHALIDI, WALID, ed. *From Haven to Conquest: Readings in Zionism and the Palestine Problem until 1948.* Beirut: Institute of Palestine Studies, 1971.

KHOURI, FRED J. *The Arab-Israeli Dilemma.* Syracuse, N.Y.: Syracuse University Press, 1968.

KINROSS, LORD. *Atatürk.* New York: Morrow, 1965.

LACKNER, HELEN. *A House Built on Sand: A Political Economy of Saudi Arabia.* London: Ithaca Press, 1978.

LAMBTON, ANN K.S. *The Persian Land Reform, 1962–1966.* Oxford: The Clarendon Press, 1969.

LANDAU, JACOB M. *Radical Politics in Modern Turkey.* Leiden, Neth.: Brill, 1974.

LAQUEUR, WALTER Z., ed. *The Israeli-Arab Reader: A Documentary History of the Middle East Conflict.* New York: Citadel Press, 1969.

————. *The Soviet Union and the Middle East.* New York: Praeger, 1969.

————, ed. *Middle East in Transition.* New York: Praeger, 1958.

LENCZOWSKI, GEORGE, ed. *Iran under the Pahlavis.* Stanford, Calif.: Hoover Institute, 1978.

————, ed. *Political Elites in the Middle East.* Washington, D.C.: American Enterprise Institute, 1975.

————. *Russia and the West in Iran, 1914–1948: A Study in Big Power Rivalry.* Ithaca, N.Y.: Cornell University Press, 1949.

LESCH, ANN M. *Arab Politics in Palestine, 1917–1939: The Frustration of a Nationalist Movement.* Ithaca, N.Y.: Cornell University Press, 1979.

LEWIS, BERNARD. *The Emergence of Modern Turkey.* London: Oxford University Press, 1961.

LILIENTHAL, ALFRED. *What Price Israel?* Chicago: Henry Regnery, 1953.

LONGRIGG, STEPHEN H. *Iraq, 1900–1950: A Political, Social, and Economic History.* London: Oxford University Press, 1953.

MABRO, ROBERT, and RADWAN, SAMIR, *The Industrialization of Egypt, 1939–1973.* Oxford: The Clarendon Press, 1976.

MANSFIELD, PETER. *Nasser's Egypt.* Rev. ed. Baltimore: Penguin, 1969.

————. *The Ottoman Empire and Its Successors.* New York: St. Martin's, 1973.

MARLOWE, JOHN. *The Persian Gulf in the Twentieth Century.* London: Cresset Press, 1962.

MAYFIELD, JAMES B. *Rural Politics in Nasser's Egypt.* Austin: University of Texas Press, 1971.

MEEKER, MICHAEL E. *Literature and Violence in North Arabia.* London: Cambridge University Press, 1979.

MITCHELL, RICHARD P. *The Society of the Muslim Brothers.* London: Oxford University Press, 1969.

NALBANDIAN, LOUISE. *Armenian Revolutionary Movement.* Berkeley: University of California Press, 1963.

NASR, SEYYED HOSSEIN. *Ideals and Realities of Islam.* 2nd ed. London: George Allen & Unwin, 1975.

NASSER, GAMAL ABD AL-. *The Philosophy of the Revolution.* Washington, D.C.: Public Affairs Press, 1955.

NEGUIB, MOHAMMED. *Egypt's Destiny.* London: Gollancz, 1955.

NELSON, CYNTHIA, ed. *The Desert and the Sown: Nomads in a Wider Society.* Berkeley: University of California Press, 1973.

NEVAKIVI, JUKKA. *Britain, France, and the Arab Middle East, 1914–1920.* London: Athlone Press, 1969.

PAHLAVI, MOHAMMED REZA SHAH. *Mission for My Country.* New York: McGraw-Hill, 1961.

PATAI, RAPHAEL. *The Kingdom of Jordan.* Princeton: Princeton University Press, 1958.

PETERSON, JOHN E. *Oman in the Twentieth Century: Political Foundations of an Emerging State.* London: Croom Helm, 1978.

PORATH, YEHOSHUA. *The Emergence of the Palestinian-Arab National Movement, 1918–1929.* London: Frank Cass, 1974.

RICHARDS, ALAN. *Egypt's Agricultural Development, 1800–1980: Technical and Social Change.* Boulder, Colo.: Westview Press, 1982.

RODINSON, MAXIME. *The Arabs.* Trans. Arthur Goldhammer. Chicago: University of Chicago Press, 1981.

SADAT, ANWAR AL-. *Revolt on the Nile.* New York: John Day, 1957.

SAADAWI, N. EL-. *The Hidden Face of Eve: Women in the Arab World.* London: Zed Press, 1980.

SAFRAN, NADAV. *Israel: The Embattled Ally.* Cambridge, Mass.: Harvard University Press, 1978.

SAID, EDWARD W. *The Question of Palestine.* New York: Times Books, 1980.

SAYEGH, FAYEZ A., ed. *The Dynamics of Neutralism in the Arab World.* San Francisco: Chandler, 1964.

SAYIGH, ROSEMARY. *Palestinians: From Peasants to Revolutionaries.* London: Zed Press, 1979.

SHIBI, Y. *The Aswan High Dam.* Beirut: Arab Institute for Research and Publishing, 1971.

SHWADRAN, BENJAMIN. *Middle East Oil and the Great Powers.* New York: Praeger, 1955.

SMITH, WILFRED C. *Islam in Modern History.* Princeton: Princeton University Press, 1957.

SPARROW, GERALD. *Modern Jordan.* London: George Allen & Unwin, 1961.

STILLMAN, NORMAN A. *The Jews of Arab Lands: A History and Source Book.* Philadelphia: Jewish Publication Society of America, 1979.

STORK, JOE. *Middle East Oil and the Energy Crisis.* New York: Monthly Review Press, 1975.

SUNAR, ILKAY. *State and Society in the Politics of Turkey's Development.* Ankara: Ankara Universitesi Basimeri, 1974.

SWEET, LOUISE, ed. *Peoples and Cultures of the Middle East.* 2 vols. Garden City, N.Y.: Natural History Press, 1970.

SYKES, CHRISTOPHER. *Crossroads to Israel.* Bloomington: Indiana Unviersity Press, 1973.

TABARI, AZAR, and YEGANEH, NAHID, eds. *In the Shadow of Islam: The Women's Movement in Iran.* London: Zed Press, 1983.

TIBAWI, ABDUL LATIF. *Islamic Education: Its Traditions and Modernization into the Arab National System.* London: Luzac, 1972.

UPTON, JOSEPH M. N. *The History of Modern Iran: An Interpretation.* Cambridge, Mass.: Harvard University Press, 1960.

VATIKIOTIS, P.J. *The Modern History of Egypt.* 2nd. ed. Baltimore: Johns Hopkins University Press, 1980.

WARRINER, DOREEN. *Land and Poverty in the Middle East.* London: Royal Institute of International Affairs, 1957.

WENNER, MANFRED W. *Modern Yemen, 1918–1966.* Baltimore: Johns Hopkins University Press, 1967.

WEIZMANN, CHAIM. *Trial and Error.* New York: Harper & Row, Pub., 1949.

ZABIH, SEPEHR. *The Communist Movement in Iran.* Berkeley: University of California Press, 1966.

ZONIS, MARVIN. *The Political Elite of Iran.* Princeton: Princeton University Press, 1971.

Index

459

462